Texas Family Code

1998 Edition
[Supersedes 1996 Edition]

WITH TABLES
AND INDEX

As Amended through the 1997 Regular Session of the 75th Legislature

WEST GROUP
ST. PAUL, MINNESOTA

ISBN 0–314–21935–8

PRINTED ON 10% POST CONSUMER RECYCLED PAPER

PREFACE

This Pamphlet contains the text of the Family Code, as amended through the 1997 Regular Session of the 75th Legislature. The Family Code constitutes a unit of the Texas Legislative Council's statutory revision program. Title 1 of the Code was originally enacted by Acts 1969, 61st Leg., ch. 888; Titles 2 and 3 were added by Acts 1973, 63rd Leg., chs. 543 and 544, respectively; Title 4 was added by Acts 1979, 66th Leg., ch. 98; and Title 5 was added by Acts 1995, 74th Leg., ch. 20.

Included in this Pamphlet are tax charts promulgated by the Attorney General relating to child support following Section 154.061. Also included in this Pamphlet are Penal Code, §§ 25.03, 25.031, 25.05, and 25.07, relating to certain offenses against the family, and Texas Constitution, Art. 16, § 15, relating to community property.

Disposition and Derivation Tables are included preceding the Code, thus providing a means of tracing repealed subject matter into the Code and of searching out the source of Code sections.

A detailed descriptive word Index at the end of the Code is furnished to facilitate the search for specific textual provisions. A Table of Sections Affected indicates sections of the Family Code affected by the 1997 Regular Session of the 75th Legislature.

Comprehensive coverage of the judicial constructions and interpretations of the Code, together with cross references, references to law review commentaries discussing particular provisions, and other editorial features, is provided in the volumes of Vernon's Texas Statutes and Codes Annotated.

WEST GROUP

November, 1997

*

TABLE OF CONTENTS

FAMILY CODE

Section Analysis, see beginning of each Chapter

TITLE 1. HUSBAND AND WIFE

SUBTITLE A. THE MARRIAGE RELATIONSHIP

SUBTITLE B. PROPERTY RIGHTS AND LIABILITIES

TITLE 1. THE MARRIAGE RELATIONSHIP

SUBTITLE A. MARRIAGE

TABLE OF CONTENTS

SUBTITLE B. PROPERTY RIGHTS AND LIABILITIES

SUBTITLE C. DISSOLUTION OF MARRIAGE

TITLE 2. CHILD IN RELATION TO THE FAMILY

SUBTITLE A. LIMITATIONS OF MINORITY

TABLE OF CONTENTS

TABLE OF CONTENTS

TABLE OF CONTENTS

SUBTITLE B. SUITS AFFECTING THE PARENT–CHILD RELATIONSHIP

TABLE OF CONTENTS

TABLE OF CONTENTS

TABLE OF CONTENTS

PENAL CODE

TITLE 6. OFFENSES AGAINST THE FAMILY

CONSTITUTION

INDEX

EFFECTIVE DATES

The following table shows the date of adjournment and the effective date of ninety day bills enacted at sessions of the legislature beginning with the year 1945:

Year	Leg.	Session	Adjournment Date	Effective Date
1945	49	Regular	June 5, 1945	September 4, 1945
1947	50	Regular	June 6, 1947	September 5, 1947
1949	51	Regular	June 6, 1949	September 5, 1949
1951	52	Regular	June 8, 1951	September 7, 1951
1953	53	Regular	May 27, 1953	August 26, 1953
1954	53	1st C.S.	May 13, 1954	August 12, 1954
1955	54	Regular	June 7, 1955	September 6, 1955
1957	55	Regular	May 23, 1957	August 22, 1957
1957	55	1st C.S.	November 12, 1957	February 11, 1958
1957	55	2nd C.S.	December 3, 1957	March 4, 1958
1959	56	Regular	May 12, 1959	August 11, 1959
1959	56	1st C.S.	June 16, 1959	September 15, 1959
1959	56	2nd C.S.	July 16, 1959	October 15, 1959
1959	56	3rd C.S.	August 6, 1959	November 5, 1959
1961	57	Regular	May 29, 1961	August 28, 1961
1961	57	1st C.S.	August 8, 1961	November 7, 1961
1961	57	2nd C.S.	August 14, 1961	November 13, 1961
1962	57	3rd C.S.	February 1, 1962	May 3, 1962
1963	58	Regular	May 24, 1963	August 23, 1963
1965	59	Regular	May 31, 1965	August 30, 1965
1966	59	1st C.S.	February 23, 1966	*
1967	60	Regular	May 29, 1967	August 28, 1967
1968	60	1st C.S.	July 3, 1968	*
1969	61	Regular	June 2, 1969	September 1, 1969
1969	61	1st C.S.	August 26, 1969	*
1969	61	2nd C.S.	September 9, 1969	December 9, 1969
1971	62	Regular	May 31, 1971	August 30, 1971
1971	62	1st C.S.	June 4, 1971	September 3, 1971
1972	62	2nd C.S.	March 30, 1972	June 29, 1972
1972	62	3rd C.S.	July 7, 1972	*
1972	62	4th C.S.	October 17, 1972	January 16, 1973
1973	63	Regular	May 28, 1973	August 27, 1973
1973	63	1st C.S.	December 20, 1973	*
1975	64	Regular	June 2, 1975	September 1, 1975
1977	65	Regular	May 30, 1977	August 29, 1977
1977	65	1st C.S.	July 21, 1977	*
1978	65	2nd C.S.	August 8, 1978	November 7, 1978
1979	66	Regular	May 28, 1979	August 27, 1979
1981	67	Regular	June 1, 1981	August 31, 1981
1981	67	1st C.S.	August 11, 1981	November 10, 1981
1982	67	2nd C.S.	May 28, 1982	*
1982	67	3rd C.S.	September 9, 1982	*
1983	68	Regular	May 30, 1983	August 29, 1983

EFFECTIVE DATES

Year	Leg.	Session	Adjournment Date	Effective Date
1983	68	1st C.S.	June 25, 1983	September 23, 1983
1984	68	2nd C.S.	July 3, 1984	October 2, 1984
1985	69	Regular	May 27, 1985	August 26, 1985
1985	69	1st C.S.	May 30, 1985	August 29, 1985
1986	69	2nd C.S.	September 4, 1986	December 4, 1986
1986	69	3rd C.S.	September 30, 1986	December 30, 1986
1987	70	Regular	June 1, 1987	August 31, 1987
1987	70	1st C.S.	June 3, 1987	September 2, 1987
1987	70	2nd C.S.	July 21, 1987	October 20, 1987
1989	71	Regular	May 29, 1989	August 28, 1989
1989	71	1st C.S.	July 19, 1989	October 18, 1989
1989	71	2nd C.S.	December 12, 1989	*
1990	71	3rd C.S.	March 28, 1990	*
1990	71	4th C.S.	May 1, 1990	*
1990	71	5th C.S.	May 30, 1990	*
1990	71	6th C.S.	June 7, 1990	September 6, 1990
1991	72	Regular	May 27, 1991	August 26, 1991
1991	72	1st C.S.	August 13, 1991	November 12, 1991
1991	72	2nd C.S.	August 25, 1991	November 24, 1991
1992	72	3rd C.S.	January 8, 1992	April 8, 1992
1992	72	4th C.S.	December 3, 1992	*
1993	73	Regular	May 31, 1993	August 30, 1993
1995	74	Regular	May 29, 1995	August 28, 1995
1997	75	Regular	June 2, 1997	September 1, 1997

* No legislation for which the ninety day effective date is applicable.

DISPOSITION TABLE

Showing where provisions of former articles of Vernon's Annotated Civil Statutes and Penal Code of 1925 are covered in the Texas Family Code as originally enacted.

Vernon's Ann. Civ.St.Article	V.T.C.A. Family Code Section
46a, § 1	11.04(b)
	11.08
	16.01
	to
	16.03
§ 1a	11.08
§ 1b	——
§ 1c	——
§ 1d	11.09
§ 1e	——
§ 2	11.12
§ 3	16.04
§ 4	11.14
§ 5	16.07
§ 6(a)	15.02
§ 6(b)	16.05(c)
§ 6(c)	——
§ 6(d)	16.03(d)
§ 6(e)	16.03(e)
§ 6(f)	15.03
§ 7	——
§ 8	——
§ 9	16.09
§ 10	11.17
§ 10a	——
46b	——
46b–1, § 1	16.51
	16.53
§ 2	16.52
§ 3	16.54
§ 4	——
§ 5	16.55
§ 6	——
201	
to	
223	——
695c–2, § 1	——
§ 2	34.01
§ 3	34.02
§ 4	34.03
§ 5	34.04
§ 6	34.05
§ 7	34.06
§ 8	——
2328b–4, § 1	21.02
§ 2	21.03
§ 3	21.04
§ 4	21.05
§ 5	21.11
§ 6	21.12
§ 7	21.21
§ 8	21.22
§ 9	21.23
§ 10	21.24
§ 11	21.25
§ 12	21.26
§ 13	21.27
§ 14	21.28(b)
§ 15	21.29
§ 16	21.30
§ 17	21.31(1), (2)
§ 18	21.32
§ 19	21.33
§ 20	21.34
§ 21	21.35
§ 22	21.36
§ 23	21.37
§ 24	21.38
§ 25	21.39
§ 26	21.40
§ 27	21.41
§ 28	21.42
§ 29	21.43
§ 30	21.44
§ 31	21.45(a), (c)
§ 32	21.61
§ 33	21.62
§ 34	21.63
§ 35	21.64
§ 36	21.65
§ 37	21.66
§ 38	——
§ 39	——
§ 40	21.06
§ 41	21.01
2330	15.02
2331	11.08
2332	11.09
2332a	11.17
2333	11.14
2334	11.13
2335	
to	
2337	15.05
2338–1, § 1	51.01
§ 2	——

	§ 3	51.02
		51.03(a)
	§ 4	51.04(b), (c), (e), (f)
	§ 5(a)	51.04(a)
		51.05
	§ 5(b)	——
	§ 5(c)	54.05(a), (b)
	§ 5(d)	51.03(c)
	§ 6(a)	51.07(b)
	§ 6(b)	54.02(a)(1), (2)
	§ 6(c)	54.02(c)
	§ 6(d)	54.02(d)
	§ 6(e)	51.10(h), (i)
	§ 6(f)	54.02(e)
	§ 6(g)	54.02(a)(3)
	§ 6(h)	54.02(f)
	§ 6(i)	54.02(g)
	§ 6(j)	54.02(h)
	§ 6(k)	54.02(i)
	§ 7	53.01
		53.04
	§ 7–A	51.06(a)
	§ 7–B(a)	51.10(d), (e)
		54.07
	§ 7–B(b)	51.10(f)
	§ 7–B(c)	51.10(h)
	§ 7–B(d), (e)	51.10(i)
	§ 8	53.06
	§ 9	53.07
	§ 10	53.06
	§ 11	52.01
		52.02
	§ 12	51.08
	§ 13(a)	54.08
	§ 13(b)	54.02(c)
	§ 13(c)	54.04(d)
	§ 13(d)	51.13(a)
	§ 13(e)	51.13(a), (b)
	§ 13(f)	——
	§ 13–A	54.06
		54.07
	§ 13–B	——
	§ 14	54.05
	§ 15	51.14
	§ 15–A	54.08
	§ 16	55.01
		55.02(a)
	§ 17	51.12(a), (b)
	§ 18	51.05
	§ 19	——
	§ 20	54.07
	§ 21	56.01
	§ 21–A	56.02
	§ 22 to § 24–A	——
2338–5,	§ 10	11.12
2338–8,	§ 20	11.12
2338–11,	§ 10	11.12
2338–11a,	§ 10	11.12
2338–11b,	§ 10	11.12
2338–13,	§ 20	11.12
2338–14,	§ 10	11.12
2338–15,	§ 12	11.12
2338–15a,	§ 12	11.12
2338–15b,	§ 12	11.12
2338–15c,	§ 12	11.12
2338–16,	§ 13	11.12
2338–17,	§ 17	11.12
2338–20,	§ 19	11.12
4445b		35.03
4447h,	§ 1	——
	§ 2	35.02
	§ 3	35.01
4602		1.83
4603		1.51(a)
4604		1.01
		1.82
4604c		1.21
4604d,	§ 1	1.31
		1.32
		1.33
	§ 2	1.26
		1.27
	§ 3	1.23
	§ 4	1.24
		1.25
		1.29
		1.30
	§ 5	1.34
	§ 6	1.26
		1.28
	§ 7	1.07(a)
	§ 8	1.22
	§ 9	1.35
	§ 10	1.32
	§ 13	1.36
		1.37
4605		1.02
	subsec. (a)	1.51(b)
		1.52
	subsec. (b)	1.03
		1.04
		1.06
	subsec. (c)	1.05
	subsec. (d)	1.03
4606		1.08
		1.84(a)
		1.85
4607		——
4608		——
4609		——
4610		5.41
4613		5.01(a)(1)
		5.01(a)(2)
		5.01(b)
		5.21
		5.61(a)
4614		4.02
4615		5.01(a)(3)
4617		5.25
4618,	§ 1	5.81

Article	Section	Family Code Section
	§ 2	5.82
		5.83
	§ 3	5.84
		5.85
4619		5.02
4620		5.61(b)
		5.61(c)
		5.61(d)
4621		5.22
		5.23
4622		5.24(a)
		5.24(b)
4624		5.62
4624a		5.42
4625		4.03
4626		4.04
4627		4.01
4628		2.43
4629,	subsec. (1)	3.02
	subsec. (2)	3.05
	subsec. (3)	3.03
	subsec. (4)	3.06
	subsec. (5)	3.04
	subsec. (6)	3.07
4630		3.08
4631		3.21
		3.22
		3.23
4632		3.53
		3.60
		3.61
		3.64
4633		3.62
4634		3.57
4635		3.56
4636		3.58
4637		3.59
4638		3.63
4639		11.11
		14.01
4639a,	§ 1	11.05
		11.13
		14.03
		14.05(a)
		14.08(a)
		14.09
	§ 1a to § 3	——
4639a–1		14.05(b)
4640		3.66
4641		3.65
5143		——
5143a		——
5143e,	§ 1	25.01
	§ 2	25.02
	§ 3	25.03
	§ 4	25.04
	§ 5	25.05
	§ 6	25.06
	§ 7	25.07
	§ 8	25.08
	§ 9	25.09
5921		31.01
5921a		——
5921b		31.01
		31.08
5922		31.02
		31.03
5922a		31.02
		31.03
		31.05
5923		31.04
		31.06
		31.07
5923a		31.04
		31.06
		31.07
		31.08
5923–1,	§ 1	33.01
	§ 2	33.02
		33.03
	§ 3	——
5928		32.21
		32.22
5929		32.01
		32.02
		32.04
5930		32.05
		32.23
5931		32.24
6632		5.03
		5.24(c)
6647		5.03
		5.24(c)

Vernon's Ann. P.C. (1925) Article	**V.T.C.A. Family Code Section**
404	1.09
406	1.81(b)
492	——
493	——
496	2.21
497	2.21

DERIVATION TABLE

Showing where provisions of the Texas Family Code as originally enacted were formerly covered in Vernon's Annotated Civil Statutes and Penal Code of 1925.

V.T.C.A. Family Code Section	Vernon's Ann. Civ.St.Article
1.01	4604
1.02	4605
1.03	4605(b), (d)
1.04	4605(b)
1.05	4605(c)
1.06	4605(b)
1.07	4604d, § 7
1.08	4606
1.09	P.C. 404
1.21	4604c
1.22	4604d, § 8
1.23	4604d, § 3
1.24	4604d, § 4
1.25	4604d, § 4
1.26	4604d, §§ 2, 6
1.27	4604d, § 2
1.28	4604d, § 6
1.29	4604d, § 4
1.30	4604d, § 4
1.31	4604d, § 1
1.32	4604d, §§ 1, 10
1.33	4604d, § 1
1.34	4604d, § 5
1.35	4604d, § 9
1.36	4604d, § 13
1.37	4604d, § 13
1.38	—
1.51	4603 4605(a)
1.52	4605(a)
1.53	—
1.81	P.C. 406
1.82	4604
1.83	4602
1.84	4606
1.85	4606
1.91 to 1.95	—
2.01 to 2.03	—
2.21	P.C. 496 P.C. 497
2.22 to 2.24	—
2.41	—
2.42	—
2.43	4628
2.44 to 2.47	—
3.01	—
3.02	4629(1)
3.03	4629(3)
3.04	4629(5)
3.05	4629(2)
3.06	4629(4)
3.07	4629(6)
3.08	4630
3.21 to 3.23	4631
3.24	—
3.25	—
3.51	—
3.52	—
3.53	4632
3.54	—
3.55	—
3.56	4635
3.57	4634
3.58	4636
3.59	4637
3.60	4632
3.61	4632
3.62	4633
3.63	4638
3.64	4632
3.65	4641
3.66	4640
4.01	4627
4.02	4614
4.03	4625
4.04	4626
5.01	4613 4615
5.02	4619
5.03	6632 6647
5.21	4613
5.22	4621
5.23	4621
5.24	4622 6632

DERIVATION TABLE

	6647
5.25	4617
5.26	—
5.27	—
5.41	4610
5.42	4624a
5.61	4613
	4620
5.62	4624
5.81	4618, § 1
5.82	4618, § 2
5.83	4618, § 2
5.831	—
5.84	4618, § 3
5.85	4618, § 3
5.86	—
5.87	—
11.01 to 11.03	—
11.04(a)	—
11.04(b)	46a, § 1
11.04(c)	—
11.05	4639a, § 1
11.06	—
11.07	—
11.08	46a, §§ 1, 1a
	2331
11.09	46a, § 1d
	2332
11.10	—
11.11	4639
11.12	46a, § 2
	2338—5, § 10
	2338—8, § 20
	2338–11, § 10
	2338–11a, § 10
	2338–11b, § 10
	2338–13, § 20
11.12	2338–14, § 10
	2338–15, § 12
	2338–15a, § 12
	2338–15b, § 12
	2338–15c, § 12
	2338–16, § 13
	2338–17, § 17
	2338—20, § 19
11.13	2334
	4639a, § 1
11.14	46a, § 4
	2333
11.15	—
11.16	—
11.17	46a, § 10
	2332a
11.18	—
11.19	—
12.01 to 12.04	—
13.01 to 13.06	—
14.01	4639
14.02	—
14.03	4639a, § 1
14.04	—
14.05(a)	4639a, § 1
14.05(b)	4639a–1
14.05(c)	—
14.05(d)	—
14.06	—
14.07	—
14.08(a)	4639a, § 1
14.08(b) to 14.08(d)	—
14.09	4639a, § 1
14.10	—
15.01	—
15.02	46a, § 6(a)
	2330
15.03	46a, § 6(f)
15.04	—
15.05	2335 to 2337
15.06	—
15.07	—
16.01	46a, § 1
16.02	46a, § 1
16.03(a)	46a, § 1
16.03(b)	—
16.03(c)	—
16.03(d)	46a, § 6(d)
16.03(e)	46a, § 6(e)
16.04	46a, § 3
16.05(a)	—
16.05(b)	—
16.05(c)	46a, § 6(b)
16.05(d)	—
16.06	—
16.07	46a, § 5
16.08	—
16.09	46a, § 9
16.10 to 16.12	—
16.51	46b–1, § 1
16.52	46b–1, § 2
16.53	46b–1, § 1
16.54	46b–1, § 3
16.55	46b–1, § 5
17.01 to 17.09	—
21.01 to 21.66	2328b—4
25.01 to 25.09	5143e

DERIVATION TABLE

Section	Source
31.01	5921
	5921b
31.02	5922
	5922a
31.03	5922
	5922a
31.04	5923
	5923a
31.05	5922a
31.06	5923
	5923a
31.07	5923
	5923a
31.08	5921b
	5923a
32.01	5929
32.02	5929
32.03	—
32.04	5929
32.05	5930
32.21	5928
32.22	5928
32.23	5930
32.24	5931
33.01	5923–1, § 1
33.02	5923–1, § 2
33.03	5923–1, § 2
34.01	695c—2, § 2
34.02	695c—2, § 3
34.03	695c—2, § 4
34.04	695c—2, § 5
34.05	695c—2, § 6
34.06	695c—2, § 7
35.01	4447h, § 3
35.02	4447h, § 2
35.03	4445b
51.01	2338–1, § 1
51.02	2338–1, § 3
51.03(a)	2338–1, § 3
51.03(b)	—
51.03(c)	2338–1, § 5(d)
51.04(a)	2338–1, § 5(a)
51.04(b)	2338–1, § 4
51.04(c)	2338–1, § 4
51.04(d)	—
51.04(e)	2338–1, § 4
51.04(f)	2338–1, § 4
51.05	2338–1, §§ 5(a), 18
51.06(a)	2338–1, § 7–A
51.06(b)	—
51.07(a)	—
51.07(b)	2338–1, § 6(a)
51.08	2338–1, § 12
51.09	—
51.10(a) to 51.10(c)	—
51.10(d)	2338–1, § 7–B(a)
51.10(e)	2338–1, § 7–B(a)
51.10(f)	2338–1, § 7–B(b)
51.10(g)	—
51.10(h)	2338–1, §§ 6(e), 7–B(c)
51.10(i)	2338–1, §§ 6(e), 7–B(d), (e)
51.11	—
51.12(a)	2338–1, § 17
51.12(b)	2338–1, § 17
51.12(c)	—
51.12(d)	—
51.13(a)	2338–1, § 13(d), (e)
51.13(b)	2338–1, § 13(e)
51.13(c)	—
51.14	2338–1, § 15
51.15 to 51.17	—
52.01	2338–1, § 11
52.02	2338–1, § 11
52.03	—
52.04	—
53.01	2338–1, § 7
53.02	—
53.03	—
53.04	2338–1, § 7
53.05	—
53.06	2338–1, §§ 8, 10
53.07	2338–1, § 9
54.01	—
54.02(a)(1), (2)	2338–1, § 6(b)
54.02(a)(3)	2338–1, § 6(g)
54.02(b)	—
54.02(c)	2338–1, §§ 6(c), 13(b)
54.02(d)	2338–1, § 6(d)
54.02(e)	2338–1, § 6(f)
54.02(f)	2338–1, § 6(h)
54.02(g)	2338–1, § 6(i)
54.02(h)	2338–1, § 6(j)
54.02(i)	2338–1, § 6(k)
54.03	—
54.04(a) to 54.04(c)	—
54.04(d)	2338–1, § 13(c)
54.04(e) to 54.04(h)	—
54.05	2338–1, §§ 5(c), 14
54.06	2338–1, § 13–A
54.07	2338–1, §§ 7–B(a). 13–A, 20
54.08	2338–1, §§ 13(a), 15–A
54.09	—
55.01	2338–1, § 16
55.02(a)	2338–1, § 16
55.02(b) to 55.02(e)	—
55.03 to 55.05	—
56.01	2338–1, § 21
56.02	2338–1, § 21–A

FAMILY CODE
TABLE OF SECTIONS AFFECTED BY THE 75TH LEGISLATURE, REGULAR SESSION

Sec.	Effect	Acts 1997 Regular Session Ch.	Sec.
1.001	Added	7	1
1.001 note	—	7	4
1.002, 1.003	Added	7	1
1.01 to 1.07	Repealed	7	3
1.07(c)	Amended	698	1
1.08, 1.09	Repealed	7	3
1.101 to 1.108	Added	7	1
1.51 to 1.53	Repealed	7	3
1.81 to 1.86	Repealed	7	3
1.91 to 1.95	Repealed	7	3
2.001 to 2.004	Added	7	1
2.004(b)	Amended	776	1
2.005 to 2.009	Added	7	1
2.009(a)	Amended	776	2
2.009(d)	Added	776	2
2.01 to 2.03	Repealed	7	3
2.010 to 2.012	Added	7	1
2.101 to 2.103	Added	7	1
2.201 to 2.209	Added	7	1
2.21 to 2.24	Repealed	7	3
2.301	Added	7	1
2.302	Added	7	1
2.401	Added	7	1
2.401(c)	Added	1362	1
2.401 note	—	1362	5 6
2.402	Added	7	1
2.402(c)	Repealed	1362	4
2.403	Added	7	1
2.404	Added	7	1
2.404(b)	Amended	1362	2
2.405	Added	7	1
2.41 to 2.48	Repealed	7	3
2.501	Added	7	1
3.001 to 3.005	Added	7	1
3.01 to 3.08	Repealed	7	3
3.101 to 3.104	Added	7	1
3.201 to 3.203	Added	7	1
3.21 to 3.26	Repealed	7	3
3.301 to 3.309	Added	7	1
3.51 to 3.521	Repealed	7	3
3.522	Redes. as 3.523	165	31.01 (27)
	Repealed	7	3

Sec.	Effect	Acts 1997 Regular Session Ch.	Sec.
3.523	Redes. from 3.522	165	31.01 (27)
3.53 to 3.55	Repealed	7	3
3.57 to 3.64	Repealed	7	3
3.64(b)	Amended	165	7.08
3.65 to 3.66	Repealed	7	3
3.70 to 3.77	Repealed	7	3
3.90 to 3.93	Repealed	7	3
3.9601 to 3.9611	Repealed	7	3
4.001 to 4.010	Added	7	1
4.01 to 4.06	Repealed	7	3
4.101 to 4.106	Added	7	1
5.001	Added	7	1
5.002	Added	7	1
5.01 to 5.04	Repealed	7	3
5.101 to 5.108	Added	7	1
5.21 to 5.27	Repealed	7	3
5.41 to 5.50	Repealed	7	3
5.51 to 5.56	Repealed	7	3
5.61	Repealed	7	3
5.62	Repealed	7	3
5.81 to 5.87	Repealed	7	3
6.001 to 6.008	Added	7	1
6.101	Added	7	1
6.101(a)	Amended	1362	3
6.102 to 6.111	Added	7	1
6.201 to 6.203	Added	7	1
6.301 to 6.308	Added	7	1
6.401 to 6.403	Added	7	1
6.4035	Added	614	1
6.4035 note	—	614	4(c)
6.404	Added	7	1
6.404(a)	Amended	937	1
6.404 note	—	937	4
6.405 to 6.409	Added	7	1
6.501	Added	7	1
6.502, 6.503	Added	7	1
6.504	Added	7	1
	Amended	1193	1
6.504 note	—	1193	25(c)
6.505	Added	7	1
6.505(e)	Added	1325	1
6.505 note	—	1325	2
6.506, 6.507	Added	7	1
6.601	Added	7	1
6.602	Added	7	1
6.701 to 6.709	Added	7	1
6.710	Added	614	2
6.710 note	—	614	4(d)
6.801	Added	7	1
6.802	Added	7	1
7.001 to 7.006	Added	7	1
8.001 to 8.011	Added	7	1
9.001 to 9.014	Added	7	1
9.101 to 9.105	Added	7	1
9.201 to 9.205	Added	7	1
9.301	Added	7	1
9.302	Added	7	1
32.005(b)	Amended	575	1
32.101(b)	Amended	165	7.09(a)

Sec.	Effect	Acts 1997 Regular Session Ch.	Sec.
32.101(e)	Amended	165	7.09(a)
32.101 note	—	165	7.09(f)
32.102	Redes. from		
32.103	165	7.09(d)	
	Repealed	165	7.09(c)
32.103	Redes. as		
32.102	165	7.09(d)	
	Redes. from		
32.104	165	7.09(e)	
32.103(a)	Amended	165	7.09(b)
32.104	Redes. as		
32.103	165	7.09(e)	
32.105	Repealed	165	7.09(c)
32.24	Repealed	165	7.10(b)
32.241	Repealed	165	7.10(c)
41.002	Amended	783	1
41.002 note	—	783	2
41.0025	Added	40	1
41.0025 note	—	40	2
45.105	Added	165	7.10(a)
45.106	Added	165	7.10(a)
51.02(15)	Amended	165	6.06
		1013	13
		1086	47
51.02(16)	Amended	165	30.182
		822	2
		1086	41
51.03(a)	Amended	1013	14
		1086	1
51.03(b)	Amended	165	6.07
		1013	14
		1015	15
		1086	1
51.031	Amended	1086	2
51.031 note	—	1086	53
51.0411	Added	1086	3
51.0411 note	—	1086	55
51.09	Amended	1086	4
51.095	Added	1086	4
51.12(a)	Amended	1374	1
51.12(c)	Amended	772	1
51.12(d)	Amended	772	1
		1374	1
51.12(g)	Amended	1374	1
51.12(i)	Added	772	1
		1374	1
51.12(j)	Added	1374	1
51.12 note	—	1374	10
51.13(d)	Amended	1086	5
51.16(m)	Repealed	165	10.05 (b)
51.19	Added	1086	6
52.01(a)	Amended	165	6.08
52.02(a)	Amended	1013	15
		1374	2
52.02(c)	Added	1013	15
52.02(d)	Added	1013	15
52.025(b)	Amended	1086	48
52.026(a)	Amended	1374	3
52.026(b)	Amended	1374	3
52.027(b)	Amended	1374	4

TABLE OF SECTIONS AFFECTED

Sec.	Effect	Acts 1997 Regular Session Ch.	Sec.
52.027(d)	Amended	1374	4
52.027(i)	Amended	822	3
52.04(c)	Added	1091	1
52.041(c)	Added	1015	16
52.041(d)	Added	1015	16
52.041(e)	Added	1015	16
53.01(d)	Amended	1374	5
53.013	Amended	1086	7
53.02(a)	Amended	1374	6
53.02(e)	Added	1015	17
53.03(a)	Amended	1013	16
53.03(g)	Added	593	6
		1013	16
53.045(a)	Amended	1086	8
54.01(e)	Amended	1086	9
54.01(f)	Amended	1015	18
54.01(h)	Amended	922	1
54.01 note	—	922	2
54.011(a)	Amended	1374	7
54.021(c)	Amended	865	1
54.021(d)	Amended	865	1
54.021(f)	Amended	865	1
54.021 note	—	865	4(b)
54.022(e)	Amended	713	1
54.022(g)	Amended	713	1
54.022(h)	Added	713	1
54.022 note	—	713	2
54.03(i)	Added	1086	10
54.03(j)	Added	1086	10
54.04(d)	Amended	1086	11
54.04(p)	Added	669	2
54.0405	Added	669	1
54.0405 note	—	669	6
54.041(f)	Amended	165	6.09
54.042	Amended	593	3
54.042(a)	Amended	165	30.183
		1013	17
54.042(c)	Amended	165	30.183
		1013	17
54.042(f)	Added	1013	17
54.044(i)	Added	1358	2
54.046	Added	593	7
		1013	18
54.06(b)	Amended	165	7.11
54.08	Amended	1086	12
54.08 note	—	1086	51
54.10(b)	Amended	1086	13
55.03(a)	Amended	1086	14
56.01(b)	Amended	1086	15
57.001(3)	Amended	368	1
58.001(c)	Amended	1086	16
58.001(d)	Added	1086	16
58.001(e)	Added	1086	16
58.001(f)	Added	1086	16
58.002(c)	Added	1086	17
58.002(d)	Added	1086	17
58.003(m)	Added	165	10.05 (a)
		1086	18
58.004	Repealed	1086	49(a) 49(c)

Sec.	Effect	Acts 1997 Regular Session Ch.	Sec.
58.007(a)	Amended	1086	19
58.007(c)	Amended	1086	20
58.007(g)	Added	1086	20
58.007 note	—	1086	52
58.104(f)	Amended	1086	21
58.106(a)	Amended	380	1
58.106(c)	Added	380	1
58.106 note	—	380	2
59.001 note	—	1394	9
59.003	Amended	1086	22
59.003(a)	Amended	1015	19
59.004(a)	Amended	1086	23
59.005(a)	Amended	1086	24
59.006(a)	Amended	1086	25
59.007(a)	Amended	1086	26
59.008(a)	Amended	1086	27
59.009(a)	Amended	1086	28
59.010(a)	Amended	1086	29
71.001	Added	34	1
71.001 note	—	34	3
71.002	Added	34	1
	Amended	1220	1
71.002 note	—	1220	2
71.003 to 71.007	Added	34	1
71.008	Added	1193	2
71.01	Repealed	34	2
71.01(a)	Amended	165	7.12
71.01(b)(2)	Amended	165	7.13
71.02 to 71.04	Repealed	34	2
71.05	Repealed	34	2
71.05(c)	Amended	165	7.14
71.06 to 71.09	Repealed	34	2
71.09(a)	Amended	752	4
71.10, 71.11	Repealed	34	2
71.11(a)	Amended	165	7.15
71.12 to 71.15	Repealed	34	2
71.15(f)	Amended	165	7.16
71.16 to 71.18	Repealed	34	2
71.18(c)	Redes. as 71.18(e)	165	31.01 (28)
71.18(e)	Added	165	31.01 (28)
	Redes. from 71.18(c)	165	31.01 (28)
71.19	Repealed	34	2
73.01 to 73.05	Repealed	34	2
81.001	Added	34	1
81.002	Added	34	1
	Amended	1193	3
81.002 note	—	1193	25(b)
81.003	Added	34	1
	Amended	1193	4
81.004	Added	34	1
	Amended	1193	5
81.005	Added	34	1
81.005(a)	Amended	1193	6
81.006	Added	34	1
81.007	Added	34	1
81.0075	Added	1193	7

Sec.	Effect	Acts 1997 Regular Session Ch.	Sec.
81.008	Added	34	1
82.001	Added	34	1
82.002	Added	34	1
82.002(a)	Amended	1193	8
82.002(c)	Added	1193	8
82.003, 82.004	Added	34	1
82.005	Added	34	1
	Amended	1193	9
82.006 to 82.009	Added	34	1
82.021	Added	34	1
82.022	Added	34	1
82.041(a)	Amended	1193	10
82.041 to 82.043	Added	34	1
83.001 to 83.004	Added	34	1
83.005	Added	34	1
	Amended	1193	11
83.006, 83.007	Added	34	1
84.001	Added	34	1
84.002	Added	34	1
	Amended	1193	12
84.003, 84.004	Added	34	1
85.001	Added	34	1
85.002	Added	34	1
	Amended	1193	13
85.003 to 85.007	Added	34	1
85.008	Added	34	1
	Repealed	1193	24
85.009	Added	34	1
85.021	Added	34	1
85.022	Added	34	1
85.022(a)	Amended	1193	14
85.023	Added	34	1
85.024	Added	34	1
85.024(a)	Amended	1193	15
85.025, 85.026	Added	34	1
85.041	Added	34	1
85.042	Added	34	1
85.042(a)	Amended	614	3
85.042(c)	Amended	614	3
85.042(d)	Added	614	3
85.042 note	—	614	4(b)
85.061	Added	1193	16
85.062	Added	1193	16
85.063	Added	1193	16
85.064	Added	1193	16
85.065	Added	1193	16
86.001, 86.002	Added	34	1
86.003	Added	34	1
	Amended	852	1
86.003 note	—	852	3
86.004	Added	34	1
	Amended	852	2
86.005	Added	1193	17
87.001 to 87.003	Added	34	1
87.004	Added	1193	18
88.001	Added	1193	19
88.002	Added	1193	19
88.003	Added	1193	19
88.004	Added	1193	19
91.001 to 91.004	Added	34	1
92.001	Added	34	1

Sec.	Effect	Acts 1997 Regular Session Ch.	Sec.
101.0011	Added	911	5
101.011	Amended	911	1
101.011 note	—	911	98(b), (c)
101.012	Amended	911	2
101.0161	Added	911	5
101.020	Amended	911	3
101.0201	Added	911	5
101.0301	Added	911	5
101.034	Amended	911	4
102.003	Amended	575	3
102.0085(a)	Amended	937	2
102.0085(c)	Amended	937	2
102.009(a)	Amended	561	1
		599	1
102.009 note	—	561	32(b)
102.011(b)	Amended	561	2
104.006	Added	575	4
105.001(b)	Amended	575	5
105.001(h)	Added	575	5
105.002(c)	Amended	180	1
105.002(d)	Added	180	1
105.002 note	—	180	2
105.006(b)	Amended	911	6
105.006(c)	Amended	911	6
105.006(e)	Amended	911	6
105.006(f)	Added	786	1
		911	6
105.006(g)	Amended	911	6
105.006 note	—	786	3
105.008	Added	911	7
106.001	Amended	15	1
106.001 note	—	15	4
106.002(a)	Amended	15	2
107.001	Amended	1294	1
107.001 note	—	1294	10
107.002	Amended	1294	2
107.003	Added	1294	3
107.006(a)	Amended	1294	4
107.006(c)	Amended	1294	4
107.013	Amended	561	3
107.0135	Added	1294	5
107.014	Amended	650	1
107.014 note	—	650	2
107.016	Amended	575	6
107.031(d)	Added	1294	6
110.002(a)	Amended	911	8
		976	6
110.004	Amended	911	9
110.006	Added	702	1
110.006 note	—	702	15(b)
152.003(e)	Amended	575	7
152.007(g)	Amended	15	3
153.0071(f)	Repealed	937	3
153.009(b)	Amended	781	1
153.009(d)	Amended	781	1
153.010	Amended	645	1
153.013(c)	Added	786	2
153.131	Amended	1193	20
153.139	Repealed	561	30
153.312(a)	Amended	802	1

Sec.	Effect	Acts 1997 Regular Session Ch.	Sec.
153.312 note	—	802	2
153.316	Amended	9	1
153.316 note	—	9	2
153.317	Amended	9	1
153.433	Amended	1397	1
153.434	Amended	561	4
154.007(a)	Amended	911	10
154.182(b)	Amended	550	2
154.182(c)	Added	550	2
154.182 note	—	550	9, 10
154.184(b)	Amended	911	11
154.186	Amended	911	12
154.187(a)	Amended	911	13
154.187(c)	Amended	911	13
154.187(d)	Amended	911	13
154.189	Amended	911	14
154.193	Added	911	15
154.242(b)	Amended	702	2
		1053	2
154.302	Amended	1173	1
154.303	Amended	1173	2
155.004(a)	Amended	575	8
156.401(a)	Amended	911	16
157.002(b)	Amended	911	17
157.065(a)	Amended	911	18
157.065(d)	Repealed	911	97(a)
157.102	Amended	702	3
157.168	Amended	974	1
157.168 note	—	974	2
157.211	Amended	702	4
157.261	Amended	702	5
157.311	Amended	420	1
		911	19
157.312(d)	Added	420	2
		911	20
157.312(e)	Added	420	2
		911	20
157.312(f)	Added	420	2
		911	20
157.312 note	—	420	31
157.313(a)	Amended	420	3
		911	21
157.313(d)	Added	911	21
157.314	Amended	420	4
		911	22
157.316	Amended	420	5
		911	23
157.317(a)	Amended	420	6
		911	24
157.318	Amended	420	7
		911	25
157.319	Amended	420	8
		911	26
157.320(d)	Added	911	27
157.321	Amended	420	9
		911	28
157.322(a)	Amended	420	10
		911	29
157.322(b)	Amended	420	10
		911	29
157.322(c)	Repealed	911	97(a)

Sec.	Effect	Acts 1997 Regular Session Ch.	Sec.
157.322(d)	Repealed	911	97(a)
157.322(e)	Repealed	911	97(a)
157.323	Amended	420	11
		911	30
157.324	Amended	420	12
		911	31
157.325(b)	Amended	420	13
		911	32
157.326	Amended	420	14
		911	33
158.001	Amended	911	34
158.002	Amended	911	35
158.006	Amended	911	36
158.009	Amended	911	37
158.010	Amended	911	38
158.011(a)	Amended	911	39
158.102	Amended	911	40
158.103	Amended	911	41
158.104	Amended	702	6
158.105(b)	Amended	702	7
158.106(a)	Amended	911	42
158.107	Repealed	911	97(a)
158.201	Amended	911	43
158.202	Amended	911	44
158.203	Amended	702	8
158.205	Amended	911	45
158.206(a)	Amended	911	46
158.207(b)	Amended	911	47
158.209(c)	Amended	911	48
158.209(d)	Amended	911	48
158.210(b)	Amended	420	15
Ch. 158, Subch. D heading	Amended	911	49
158.301	Amended	911	50
158.302	Amended	911	51
158.303(a)	Amended	911	52
158.303(c)	Amended	911	52
158.304	Amended	911	53
158.305	Repealed	911	97(a)
158.306	Amended	911	54
158.307(a)	Amended	911	55
158.308	Amended	911	56
158.309	Amended	911	57
158.310(a)	Amended	911	58
158.310(c)	Amended	911	58
158.311(a)	Amended	911	59
158.312(a)	Amended	911	60
158.314	Amended	911	61
158.315	Amended	911	62
158.317	Amended	911	63
158.319	Amended	911	64
158.401(b)	Amended	911	65
158.402	Amended	911	66
158.501	Added	911	67
158.502	Added	911	67
158.503	Added	911	67
158.504	Added	911	67
158.505	Added	911	67
158.506	Added	911	67
158.507	Added	911	67
158.508	Added	911	67

Sec.	Effect	Acts 1997 Regular Session Ch.	Sec.
159.101(7)	Amended	607	1
159.101(16)	Amended	607	1
159.101(19)	Amended	607	1
159.101 note	—	607	19
159.102	Amended	607	2
159.201	Amended	561	5
159.203	Amended	607	3
159.205(a)	Amended	607	4
159.207	Amended	607	5
159.301	Amended	607	6
159.303	Amended	607	7
159.304	Amended	607	8
159.305(a)	Amended	607	9
159.305(b)	Amended	607	9
159.305(e)	Amended	607	9
159.306	Amended	607	10
159.307(b)	Amended	607	11
159.313(a)	Amended	607	12
159.313(c)	Amended	607	12
159.501	Amended	607	13
159.502	Amended	607	13
159.503	Added	607	13
159.504	Added	607	13
159.505	Added	607	13
159.506	Added	607	13
159.507	Added	607	13
159.604(a)	Amended	607	14
159.605(a)	Amended	607	15
159.605(b)	Amended	607	15
159.606(a)	Amended	607	16
159.606(c)	Amended	607	16
159.611(a)	Amended	607	17
159.611(c)	Amended	607	17
159.613	Added	607	18
159.614	Added	607	18
160.101(a)	Amended	962	1
160.110(g)	Amended	962	2
160.251	Added	561	6
160.252	Added	561	6
160.253	Added	561	6
160.254	Added	561	6
160.255	Added	561	6
160.256	Added	561	6
160.257	Added	561	6
160.258	Added	561	6
160.259	Added	561	6
160.260	Added	561	6
160.261	Added	561	6
160.262	Added	561	6
160.263	Added	561	6
161.001	Amended	575	9
		1022	60
161.001 note	—	1022	105(h)
161.002(b)	Amended	561	7
161.002(c)	Added	561	7
161.002(d)	Added	561	7
161.002(e)	Added	561	7
161.002(f)	Added	561	7
161.007	Added	561	8
161.103	Amended	561	9
161.103 note	—	561	32(c)

Sec.	Effect	Acts 1997 Regular Session Ch.	Sec.
161.1035	Added	561	10
161.106(f)	Added	561	11
161.106(g)	Added	561	11
161.106(h)	Added	561	11
161.106(i)	Added	561	11
161.106(j)	Added	561	11
161.108	Added	561	12
161.109	Added	561	12
161.2011	Added	1022	61
161.211	Added	600	1
		601	2
162.001	Amended	561	14
162.001 note	—	561	32(d)
162.0025	Added	561	13
162.0045	Added	561	15
162.0085(a)	Amended	561	16
162.012(a)	Amended	600	2
		601	1
162.012 note	—	600	22
		601	3
162.018(d)	Added	561	17
162.025	Amended	561	18
162.309	Added	165	7.17(a)
162.402(7)	Amended	561	19
162.402(11)	Amended	561	19
162.402(14)	Added	561	19
162.402 note	—	561	32(f)
162.403(a)	Amended	561	20
162.403(c)	Amended	561	20
162.404	Added	561	21
162.407(b)	Amended	561	22
162.407(c)	Amended	561	22
162.408	Amended	561	23
162.411(d)	Amended	561	24
162.414(c)	Amended	561	25
162.420	Amended	561	26
162.421(a)	Amended	561	27
162.422(a)	Amended	561	28
162.422(b)	Amended	561	28
162.601	Added	1309	1
162.601 note	—	1309	2
201.1085	Added	600	3
		1022	62
201.1085 note	—	1022	116
202.002(b)	Amended	702	9
203.004(c)	Added	702	10
203.006(a)	Amended	702	11
203.007	Amended	165	7.18
231.0011(m)	Added	702	12
231.0011 note	—	420	30
231.0012	Added	420	16
231.0013	Added	420	16
231.002(d)	Amended	874	1
		911	68
231.002(e)	Added	874	1
		911	68
231.002(f)	Added	911	68
231.004	Repealed	911	97(a)
231.007(f)	Amended	165	7.19
231.010	Added	420	17
231.101(b)	Amended	911	69

Sec.	Effect	Acts 1997 Regular Session Ch.	Sec.
231.101(c)	Added	702	13
		911	69
231.101(d)	Added	911	69
231.101 note	—	702	15(d)
231.104(a)	Amended	911	70
231.105	Amended	911	71
231.106	Amended	911	72
231.107	Amended	911	73
231.108(e)	Added	911	74
231.115	Added	165	7.20(a)
		911	75
231.116	Added	420	18
231.202	Amended	165	7.21(a)
231.2025	Added	420	19
231.301	Amended	911	76
231.302(a)	Amended	420	20
		911	77
231.302(b)	Amended	420	20
		911	77
231.302(e)	Amended	420	20
		911	77
231.302(g)	Added	911	77
231.303	Amended	911	78
231.304	Repealed	911	97(b)
231.307	Added	911	79
231.308	Added	420	21
231.309	Added	420	21
231.401	Redes. as 233.001 and amended	911	80
231.402	Redes. as 233.002 and amended	911	80
231.403	Redes. as 233.003 and amended	911	80
231.404	Redes. as 233.004 and amended	911	80
231.405	Redes. as 233.005 and amended	911	80
231.406	Redes. as 233.006 and amended	911	80
231.407	Redes. as 233.007 and amended	911	80
231.408	Redes. as 233.008 and amended	911	80
231.409	Redes. as 233.009 and amended	911	80
231.410	Redes. as 233.010 and amended	911	80
231.411	Redes. as 233.011 and amended	911	80
231.412	Redes. as 233.012 and amended	911	80
231.413	Redes. as 233.013 and amended	911	80
231.414	Redes. as 233.014 and amended	911	80
231.415	Redes. as 233.015 and amended	911	80
231.416	Redes. as 233.016 and amended	911	80
231.417	Redes. as 233.017 and amended	911	80

Sec.	Effect	Acts 1997 Regular Session Ch.	Sec.
231.418	Redes. as 233.018 and amended	911	80
231.419	Redes. as 233.019 and amended	911	80
231.420	Redes. as 233.020 and amended	911	80
231.421	Redes. as 233.021 and amended	911	80
231.422	Redes. as 233.022 and amended	911	80
231.423	Redes. as 233.023 and amended	911	80
231.424	Redes. as 233.024 and amended	911	80
231.425	Redes. as 233.025 and amended	911	80
231.426	Redes. as 233.026 and amended	911	80
231.427	Redes. as 233.027 and amended	911	80
231.428	Redes. as 233.028 and amended	911	80
231.429	Redes. as 233.029 and amended	911	80
231.430	Repealed	911	97(a)
231.431	Repealed	911	97(a)
Ch. 232 heading	Amended	911	81
232.001(4)	Added	911	82
232.002	Amended	165	7.22
		1280	1.02
		1288	2
232.003	Amended	420	22
			23
		911	83
232.004(a)	Amended	420	24
232.004(d)	Amended	911	84
232.005	Amended	911	85
232.006(a)	Amended	911	86
		976	7
232.006(c)	Amended	911	86
232.007(a)	Amended	911	87
232.007(c)	Amended	911	87
232.007(d)	Added	911	87
232.008	Amended	911	88
232.008(c)	Amended	976	8
232.009	Amended	420	25
		911	89
232.011(a)	Amended	911	90
232.011(d)	Amended	911	90
232.011(e)	Amended	911	90
232.011(h)	Amended	165	30.184
232.012	Amended	911	91
232.013(a)	Amended	911	92
232.013(b)	Amended	976	9
232.013(c)	Amended	911	92
232.014	Amended	911	93
232.015	Repealed	165	7.23
233.001	Added	420	26
	Redes. from 231.401 and amended	911	80

Sec.	Effect	Acts 1997 Regular Session Ch.	Sec.
233.002	Added	420	26
	Redes. from 231.402 and amended	911	80
233.003	Added	420	26
	Redes. from 231.403 and amended	911	80
233.004	Added	420	26
	Redes. from 231.404 and amended	911	80
233.005	Added	911	80
	Redes. from 231.405 and amended	911	80
233.006	Added	911	80
	Redes. from 231.406 and amended	911	80
233.007	Added	911	80
	Redes. from 231.407 and amended	911	80
233.008	Added	911	80
	Redes. from 231.408 and amended	911	80
233.009	Added	911	80
	Redes. from 231.409 and amended	911	80
233.010	Added	911	80
	Redes. from 231.410 and amended	911	80
233.011	Added	911	80
	Redes. from 231.411 and amended	911	80
233.012	Added	911	80
	Redes. from 231.412 and amended	911	80
233.013	Added	911	80
	Redes. from 231.413 and amended	911	80
233.014	Added	911	80
	Redes. from 231.414 and amended	911	80
233.015	Added	911	80
	Redes. from 231.415 and amended	911	80
233.016	Added	911	80
	Redes. from 231.416 and amended	911	80
233.017	Added	911	80
	Redes. from 231.417 and amended	911	80
233.018	Added	911	80
	Redes. from 231.418 and amended	911	80
233.019	Added	911	80
	Redes. from 231.419 and amended	911	80
233.020	Added	911	80
	Redes. from 231.420 and amended	911	80
233.021	Added	911	80
	Redes. from 231.421 and amended	911	80

Sec.	Effect	Acts 1997 Regular Session Ch.	Sec.
233.022	Added	911	80
	Redes. from 231.422 and amended	911	80
233.023	Added	911	80
	Redes. from 231.423 and amended	911	80
233.024	Added	911	80
	Redes. from 231.424 and amended	911	80
233.025	Added	911	80
	Redes. from 231.425 and amended	911	80
233.026	Added	911	80
	Redes. from 231.426 and amended	911	80
233.027	Added	911	80
	Redes. from 231.427 and amended	911	80
233.0271	Added	911	80
233.028	Added	911	80
	Redes. from 231.428 and amended	911	80
233.029	Added	911	80
	Redes. from 231.429 and amended	911	80
234.001	Added	420	27
		911	94
234.002	Added	420	27
		911	94
234.003	Added	420	27
		911	94
234.004	Added	911	94
234.005	Added	911	94
234.101	Added	911	94
234.102	Added	911	94
234.102 note	—	911	98(d)
234.103	Added	911	94
234.104	Added	911	94
261.001(1)	Amended	575	10
261.001(7)	Added	575	10
		1022	63
261.004	Added	1022	64
261.101(a)	Amended	1022	65
261.101(b)	Amended	162	1
		1022	65
261.101(c)	Amended	1022	65
261.101(d)	Amended	575	11
261.101 note	—	1022	109
261.105(a)	Amended	1022	66
261.1055	Added	1022	67
261.107	Amended	575	2
		1022	68
261.107 note	—	575	37, 38
261.201(a)	Amended	575	12
		1022	69
261.201(c)	Amended	575	12
261.201(d)	Amended	575	12
261.201(e)	Amended	575	12
261.201(f)	Amended	575	12
261.201(g)	Added	575	12

Sec.	Effect	Acts 1997 Regular Session Ch.	Sec.
261.301(a)	Amended	1022	70
		1137	1
261.3015	Added	1022	71
261.3019	Added	1022	72
261.302(b)	Amended	575	13
261.302(e)	Added	575	14
		1022	73
261.305(a)	Amended	575	15
261.305(b)	Amended	575	15
261.305(c)	Amended	575	15
261.305(d)	Amended	575	15
261.311	Amended	1022	74
261.312(c)	Amended	575	16
261.315	Added	575	17
		1022	75
261.405	Amended	162	2
		1374	8
261.406(a)	Amended	575	18
261.406(b)	Amended	575	18
261.406(d)	Added	575	18
262.008	Added	600	4
262.101	Amended	752	1
262.1015(c)	Amended	575	19
262.1015(d)	Amended	575	19
262.1015(f)	Amended	575	19
262.1015(g)	Amended	575	19
262.1015(h)	Added	575	19
262.102(c)	Added	752	2
262.104	Amended	575	20
262.108	Amended	1374	9
262.109(a)	Amended	1022	76
262.109 note	—	1022	108(a), (b)
262.111	Redes. as 262.112	165	31.01 (29)
262.112	Redes. from 262.111	165	31.01 (29)
262.201(c)	Amended	600	5
		603	1
		752	3
		1022	77
262.201(e)	Added	575	21
		1022	78
262.201 note	—	603	14
262.2015	Added	1022	79
262.203	Amended	575	22
263.006	Added	600	6
		603	2
		1022	80
263.1015	Added	600	7
263.201	Amended	600	8
		603	3
		1022	81
Ch. 263, Subch. D heading	Amended	600	9
		603	4
		1022	82

Sec.	Effect	Acts 1997 Regular Session Ch.	Sec.
263.301(a)	Amended	600	10
		603	5
		1022	83
263.301(b)	Amended	600	10
		603	5
		1022	83
263.301 note	—	1022	108(c)
263.302	Amended	600	11
		603	6
		1022	84
263.3025	Added	600	12
		603	7
		1022	85
263.303	Amended	600	13
		603	8
		1022	86
263.304	Amended	600	14
		603	9
		1022	87
263.305	Amended	600	15
		603	10
		1022	88
263.306	Amended	600	16
		603	11
		1022	89
263.308	Repealed	603	13
		1022	104(a)
263.309	Repealed	603	13
		1022	104(a)
263.401	Added	600	17
		603	12
		1022	90
263.402	Added	600	17
		603	12
		1022	90
263.403	Added	600	17
		603	12
		1022	90
263.404	Added	600	17
263.501	Added	600	17
		603	12
		1022	90
263.502	Added	600	17
		603	12
		1022	90
263.503	Added	600	17
		603	12
		1022	90
264.004(c)	Added	575	23
264.005(f)	Added	575	24
264.005(g)	Added	575	24
264.006	Amended	575	25
264.009	Amended	1022	91
264.011	Added	575	26
264.012	Added	575	26
264.101	Amended	575	27
264.1015	Added	575	28
264.104(b)	Amended	575	29
264.104(c)	Added	575	29
264.105	Amended	575	30
264.106	Amended	1022	92

TABLE OF SECTIONS AFFECTED

Sec.	Effect	Acts 1997 Regular Session Ch.	Sec.
264.106 note	—	1022	103
264.1061	Added	1022	92
264.1075	Added	1022	93
264.109	Redes. as 264.110	165	31.01 (30)
264.110	Redes. from 264.109	165	31.01 (30)
264.111	Added	600	18
264.112	Added	600	18
264.206	Added	600	19
		1022	94
264.207	Added	600	19
		1022	94
264.302(c)	Amended	575	31
264.302(e)	Amended	1086	30
264.406(f)	Added	575	32
264.408	Added	575	33
264.409	Added	575	33
264.410	Added	575	33
264.411	Added	575	33
264.514(a)	Amended	1022	95
		1301	2
264.514(c)	Added	1022	95
264.602(d)	Added	1294	7
264.603(a)	Amended	600	20
264.604(a)	Amended	1294	8
264.607(a)	Amended	1294	9
264.701(b)	Amended	165	6.10

FAMILY CODE

TITLE 1. HUSBAND AND WIFE

SUBTITLE A. THE MARRIAGE RELATIONSHIP

CHAPTER 1. ENTERING THE MARRIAGE RELATIONSHIP [REPEALED]

SUBCHAPTER A. APPLICATION FOR MARRIAGE LICENSE

§§ 1.01 to 1.06. Repealed by Acts 1997, 75th Leg., ch. 7, § 3, eff. April 17, 1997

§ 1.07. Issuance of License

(a), (b) Repealed by Acts 1997, 75th Leg., ch. 7, § 3, eff. April 17, 1997.

(c) On the proper execution of the application, the clerk shall prepare the license. The clerk shall enter on the license the names of the licensees, the date that the license is issued, and the name of the person appointed to act as proxy for an absent applicant, if any.

(d), (e) Repealed by Acts 1997, 75th Leg., ch. 7, § 3, eff. April 17, 1997.

Acts 1969, 61st Leg., p. 2707, ch. 888, § 1, eff. Jan. 1, 1970. Amended by Acts 1973, 63rd Leg., p. 1599, ch. 577, § 6, eff. Jan. 1, 1974; Acts 1975, 64th Leg., p. 620, ch. 254, § 2, eff. Sept. 1, 1975; Acts 1985, 69th Leg., ch. 32, § 2, eff. April 11, 1985; Acts 1985, 69th Leg., ch. 816, § 1, eff. Sept. 1, 1985; Acts 1987, 70th Leg., ch. 221, § 16, eff. Sept. 1, 1987; Acts 1987, 70th Leg., ch. 273, § 1, eff. Jan. 1, 1988; Acts 1989, 71st Leg., ch. 369, § 1, eff. Sept. 1, 1989; Acts 1989, 71st Leg., ch. 1195, § 3(a), eff. Sept. 1, 1989; Acts 1995, 74th Leg., ch. 655, § 5.05, eff. Sept. 1, 1995; Acts 1997, 75th Leg., ch. 698, § 1, eff. Sept. 1, 1997.

Repeal

Without reference to the amendment of this section by Acts 1997, 75th Leg., ch. 698, § 1, Acts 1997, 75th Leg., ch. 7, § 3 repeals this section effective April 17, 1997.

Section 4 of Acts 1987, 70th Leg., ch. 273, provides:

"This Act takes effect January 1, 1988, and applies only to:

"(1) a marriage license issued on or after that date; and

"(2) a marriage ceremony conducted on the basis of a marriage license issued on or after that date."

Section 3(b) of Acts 1989, 71st Leg., ch. 1195, provides:

"The Texas Department of Health shall prepare and distribute to county clerks the informational materials described by this Act as soon as possible after the effective date of this Act, but not later than January 1, 1990. A county clerk is not required to make the notations on marriage licenses described by Subsection (e), Section 1.07, Family Code, as added by this Act, before January 1, 1990."

§§ 1.08, 1.09. Repealed by Acts 1997, 75th Leg., ch. 7, § 3, eff. April 17, 1997

SUBCHAPTER B. MEDICAL EXAMINATION

§§ 1.21 to 1.38. Repealed by Acts 1983, 68th Leg., p. 2899, ch. 493, § 2, eff. Aug. 29, 1983

SUBCHAPTER C. UNDERAGE APPLICANTS

§§ 1.51 to 1.53. Repealed by Acts 1997, 75th Leg., ch. 7, § 3, eff. April 17, 1997

SUBCHAPTER D. CEREMONY AND RETURN OF LICENSE

§§ 1.81 to 1.86. Repealed by Acts 1997, 75th Leg., ch. 7, § 3, eff. April 17, 1997

SUBCHAPTER E. MARRIAGE WITHOUT FORMALITIES

§§ 1.91 to 1.95. Repealed by Acts 1997, 75th Leg., ch. 7, § 3, eff. April 17, 1997

CHAPTER 2. VALIDITY OF MARRIAGE [REPEALED]

SUBCHAPTER A. GENERAL PROVISIONS

§§ 2.01 to 2.03. Repealed by Acts 1997, 75th Leg., ch. 7, § 3, eff. April 17, 1997

SUBCHAPTER B. VOID MARRIAGES

§§ 2.21 to 2.24. Repealed by Acts 1997, 75th Leg., ch. 7, § 3, eff. April 17, 1997

SUBCHAPTER C. VOIDABLE MARRIAGES

§§ 2.41 to 2.48. Repealed by Acts 1997, 75th Leg., ch. 7, § 3, eff. April 17, 1997

CHAPTER 3. DISSOLUTION OF MARRIAGE [REPEALED]

SUBCHAPTER A. GROUNDS FOR DIVORCE; DEFENSES

§§ 3.01 to 3.08. Repealed by Acts 1997, 75th Leg., ch. 7, § 3, eff. April 17, 1997

SUBCHAPTER B. JURISDICTION AND VENUE; RESIDENCE QUALIFICATIONS

§§ 3.21 to 3.26. Repealed by Acts 1997, 75th Leg., ch. 7, § 3, eff. April 17, 1997

SUBCHAPTER C. SUIT

§§ 3.51 to 3.55. Repealed by Acts 1997, 75th Leg., ch. 7, § 3, eff. April 17, 1997

§ 3.56. Repealed by Acts 1981, 67th Leg., p. 2655, ch. 711, § 3, eff. Sept. 1, 1981

Section 4 of the 1981 repealing act provides:

"This Act takes effect September 1, 1981, and applies only to suits for divorce, annulment, or to declare a marriage void filed on or after the effective date of this Act."

§§ 3.57 to 3.581. Repealed by Acts 1997, 75th Leg., ch. 7, § 3, eff. April 17, 1997

§§ 3.582, 3.583. Repealed by Acts 1995, 74th Leg., ch. 1024, § 26, eff. Sept. 1, 1195; Acts 1997, 75th Leg., ch. 7, § 3, eff. April 17, 1997

§§ 3.59 to 3.66. Repealed by Acts 1997, 75th Leg., ch. 7, § 3, eff. April 17, 1997

SUBCHAPTER D. ENFORCEMENT

§§ 3.70 to 3.77. Repealed by Acts 1997, 75th Leg., ch. 7, § 3, eff. April 17, 1997

SUBCHAPTER E. [BLANK]

SUBCHAPTER F. DIVISION OF PROPERTY FOLLOWING A DECREE OF DIVORCE OR ANNULMENT

§§ 3.90 to 3.93. Repealed by Acts 1997, 75th Leg., ch. 7, § 3, eff. April 17, 1997

SUBCHAPTER G. MAINTENANCE

§§ 3.9601 to 3.9611. Repealed by Acts 1997, 75th Leg., ch. 7, § 3, eff. April 17, 1997

CHAPTER 4. RIGHTS, DUTIES, POWERS, AND LIABILITIES OF SPOUSES [REPEALED]

§§ 4.01 to 4.06. Repealed by Acts 1997, 75th Leg., ch. 7, § 3, eff. April 17, 1997

SUBTITLE B. PROPERTY RIGHTS AND LIABILITIES

CHAPTER 5. MARITAL PROPERTY [REPEALED]

SUBCHAPTER A. SEPARATE AND COMMUNITY PROPERTY

§§ 5.01 to 5.04. Repealed by Acts 1997, 75th Leg., ch. 7, § 3, eff. April 17, 1997

[Sections 5.05 to 5.20 reserved for expansion]

SUBCHAPTER B. MANAGEMENT, CONTROL AND DISPOSITION OF MARITAL PROPERTY

§§ 5.21 to 5.27. Repealed by Acts 1997, 75th Leg., ch. 7, § 3, eff. April 17, 1997

[Sections 5.28 to 5.40 reserved for expansion]

SUBCHAPTER C. PROPERTY AGREEMENTS

Subchapter C, formerly consisting of §§ 5.41 to 5.46, was revised by Acts 1987, 70th Leg., ch. 678, § 1.

DISPOSITION TABLE

Showing where the subject matter of former provisions of Subchapter C may be found in the revised subchapter.

Former Section	Revised Section
5.41	5.42, 5.43. 5.56
5.42	5.52, 5.54, 5.56
5.43	5.53
5.44	5.42, 5.54
5.45	5.46, 5.55
5.46	5.56

PART 1. UNIFORM PREMARITAL AGREEMENT ACT

§§ 5.41 to 5.50. Repealed by Acts 1997, 75th Leg., ch. 7, § 3, eff. April 17, 1997

PART 2. OTHER PROPERTY AGREEMENTS

§§ 5.51 to 5.56. Repealed by Acts 1997, 75th Leg., ch. 7, § 3, eff. April 17, 1997

[Sections 5.57 to 5.60 reserved for expansion]

SUBCHAPTER D. MARITAL PROPERTY LIABILITIES

§§ 5.61, 5.62. Repealed by Acts 1997, 75th Leg., ch. 7, § 3, eff. April 17, 1997

[Sections 5.63 to 5.80 reserved for expansion]

SUBCHAPTER E. HOMESTEAD RIGHTS

§§ 5.81 to 5.87. Repealed by Acts 1997, 75th Leg., ch. 7, § 3, eff. April 17, 1997

[Chapters 6 to 10 reserved for expansion]

TITLE 1. THE MARRIAGE RELATIONSHIP

Acts 1997, 75th Leg., ch. 7, § 1 reenacted Title 1

DISPOSITION TABLE

Showing where provisions of former Title 1 of the Family Code are covered in Title 1 as reenacted by Acts 1997, 75th Leg., ch. 7.

Former Section	New Section
1.01	2.001
1.02	2.002
(2)(B)	2.003
1.03	2.004
1.04	2.005
1.045	
1.05(a), (b)	2.006
(c)	2.007
1.06	2.008
1.07	2.009
(e)	2.010
1.08	2.011
1.09	2.012
1.51	2.101
1.52	2.102
1.53	2.103
1.81	2.201 2.207
1.82	2.203 2.204
1.83	2.202 2.205
1.84	2.206
1.85	2.208
1.86	2.209
1.91	2.401
1.92	2.402
1.93	2.403
1.94	2.404
1.95	2.405
2.01	1.101 1.102
2.02	2.301
2.03	2.302
2.21	6.201
2.22	6.202
2.23	6.203
2.24	6.307
2.41(a)	6.101
(b)	6.102
(a), (b)	6.103
(c)	6.104
2.42	6.105
2.43	6.106
2.44	6.107
2.45	6.108
2.46	6.109
2.47	6.111
2.48	6.110
3.01	6.001
3.02	6.002
3.03	6.003
3.04	6.004
3.05	6.005
3.06	6.006
3.07	6.007
3.08	6.008
3.21	6.301
3.22	6.303
3.23	6.304
3.24	6.302
3.25	6.306
(b)	6.307
3.26	6.305
3.51	6.401
3.52	6.402
3.521	6.409
3.53	6.403 6.701
3.54(a) to (c)	6.505
(d)	6.705
(e)	6.708
3.55(a), (b)	6.406
(c), (d)	6.407
3.57	6.707
3.58(a), (b)	6.501
(c)	6.502

Former Section	New Section
(d), (e)	6.503
(f)	6.506
(g)	6.507
(h), (i)	6.709
3.59	6.502
3.60	6.702
3.61	6.703
3.62	6.704
3.63(a)	7.001
(b)	7.002
3.631	7.006
3.632(a)	7.004
(b), (c)	9.301
(d), (e)	7.005
3.633	9.302
(a)	7.003
3.64	6.706
3.65	6.708
3.66(a), (b)	6.801
(c)	6.802
3.70(a), (b)	9.001
(c)	9.002
	9.003
(d)	9.004
(e)	9.005
3.71	9.007
(a)	9.006
3.711	9.101 to 9.105
3.72	9.008
3.73	9,009
3.74	9.010
3.75	9.011
3.76	9.012
3.77	9.013
	9.014
3.90(a), (b)	9,201
(c)	9.202
3.91	9.203
3.92	9.204
3.93	9.205
3.9601	8.001
3.9602	8.002
3.9603	8.003
3.9604	8.004
3.9605	8.005
3.9606	8.006
3.9607	8.007
3.9608	8.008
3.9609	8.009
3.9610	8.010
3.9611	8.011
4.01	1.103
4.02	2.501
4.03	1.104
4.031	3.201
4.04	1.105
4.05	1.106
4.06	1.107
5.01(a)	3.001
(b)	3.002
5.02	3.003
5.03	3.004
5.04	3.005
5.21	3.101

Former Section	New Section
5.22	3.102
5.23	3.103
5.24	3.104
5.25(a), (b)	3.301
(c)	3.303
(d)	3.304
(e)	3.305
(f)	3.306
(h)	3.308
5.26	3.302
(c)	3.303
(d)	3.304
(e)	3.306
(f)	3.307
(g)	3.308
5.27	3.309
5.41	4.001
5.42	4.002
5.43	4.003
5.44	4.004
5.45	4.005
5.46	4.006
5.47	4.007
5.48	4.008
5.49	4.009
5.50	4.010
5.51	4.101
5.52	4.102
5.53	4.103
5.54	4.104
5.55	4.105
5.56	4.106
5.61	3.202
5.62	3.203
5.81	5.001
5.82	5.002
5.83	5.101
5.831	5.107
5.84	5.107
5.85(a)	5.102, 5.103
(b)	5.103 to 5.105
(c)	5.106
5.86	5.108
5.87(a)	5.102
(b)	5.103 to 5.105
(c)	5.106

SUBTITLE A. MARRIAGE

CHAPTER 1. GENERAL PROVISIONS

SUBCHAPTER A. DEFINITIONS

Section

SUBCHAPTER B. PUBLIC POLICY

SUBCHAPTER A. DEFINITIONS

§ 1.001. Applicability of Definitions

(a) The definitions in this subchapter apply to this title.

(b) Except as provided by this subchapter, the definitions in Chapter 101 apply to terms used in this title.

(c) If, in another part of this title, a term defined by this subchapter has a meaning different from the meaning provided by this subchapter, the meaning of that other provision prevails.

Added by Acts 1997, 75th Leg., ch. 7, § 1, eff. April 17, 1997.

Section 4 of Acts 1997, 75th Leg., ch. 7, provides:

"The change in law made by this Act does not affect a proceeding under the Family Code pending on the effective date of this Act. A proceeding pending on the effective date of this Act is governed by the law in effect at the time the proceeding was commenced, and the former law is continued in effect for that purpose."

§ 1.002. Court

"Court" means the district court, juvenile court having the jurisdiction of a district court, or other court expressly given jurisdiction of a suit under this title.

Added by Acts 1997, 75th Leg., ch. 7, § 1, eff. April 17, 1997.

§ 1.003. Suit for Dissolution of Marriage

"Suit for dissolution of a marriage" includes a suit for divorce or annulment or to declare a marriage void.

Added by Acts 1997, 75th Leg., ch. 7, § 1, eff. April 17, 1997.

[Sections 1.004 to 1.100 reserved for expansion]

SUBCHAPTER B. PUBLIC POLICY

§ 1.101. Every Marriage Presumed Valid

In order to promote the public health and welfare and to provide the necessary records, this code specifies detailed rules to be followed in establishing the marriage relationship. However, in order to provide stability for those entering into the marriage relationship in good faith and to provide for an orderly determination of parentage and security for the children of the relationship, it is the policy of this state to preserve and uphold each marriage against claims of invalidity unless a strong reason exists for holding the marriage void or voidable. Therefore, every marriage entered into in this state is presumed to be valid unless expressly made void by Chapter 6 or unless expressly made voidable by Chapter 6 and annulled as provided by that chapter.

Added by Acts 1997, 75th Leg., ch. 7, § 1, eff. April 17, 1997.

§ 1.102. Most Recent Marriage Presumed Valid

When two or more marriages of a person to different spouses are alleged, the most recent marriage is presumed to be valid as against each marriage that precedes the most recent marriage until one who asserts the validity of a prior marriage proves the validity of the prior marriage.

Added by Acts 1997, 75th Leg., ch. 7, § 1, eff. April 17, 1997.

§ 1.103. Persons Married Elsewhere

The law of this state applies to persons married elsewhere who are domiciled in this state.

Added by Acts 1997, 75th Leg., ch. 7, § 1, eff. April 17, 1997.

§ 1.104. Capacity of Spouse

Except as expressly provided by statute or by the constitution, a person, regardless of age, who has been married in accordance with the law of this state has the capacity and power of an adult, including the capacity to contract.

Added by Acts 1997, 75th Leg., ch. 7, § 1, eff. April 17, 1997.

§ 1.105. Joinder in Civil Suits

(a) A spouse may sue and be sued without the joinder of the other spouse.

(b) When claims or liabilities are joint and several, the spouses may be joined under the rules relating to joinder of parties generally.

Added by Acts 1997, 75th Leg., ch. 7, § 1, eff. April 17, 1997.

§ 1.106. Criminal Conversation Not Authorized

A right of action by one spouse against a third party for criminal conversation is not authorized in this state.

Added by Acts 1997, 75th Leg., ch. 7, § 1, eff. April 17, 1997.

§ 1.107. Alienation of Affection Not Authorized

A right of action by one spouse against a third party for alienation of affection is not authorized in this state.

Added by Acts 1997, 75th Leg., ch. 7, § 1, eff. April 17, 1997.

§ 1.108. Promise or Agreement Must be in Writing

A promise or agreement made on consideration of marriage or nonmarital conjugal cohabitation is not enforceable unless the promise or agreement or a memorandum of the promise or agreement is in writing and signed by the person obligated by the promise or agreement.

Added by Acts 1997, 75th Leg., ch. 7, § 1, eff. April 17, 1997.

CHAPTER 2. THE MARRIAGE RELATIONSHIP

SUBCHAPTER A. APPLICATION FOR MARRIAGE LICENSE

SUBCHAPTER A. APPLICATION FOR MARRIAGE LICENSE

§ 2.001. Marriage License

(a) A man and a woman desiring to enter into a ceremonial marriage must obtain a marriage license from the county clerk of any county of this state.

(b) A license may not be issued for the marriage of persons of the same sex.

Added by Acts 1997, 75th Leg., ch. 7, § 1, eff. April 17, 1997.

Section 4 of Acts 1997, 75th Leg., ch. 7, provides:

"The change in law made by this Act does not affect a proceeding under the Family Code pending on the effective date of this Act. A proceeding pending on the effective date of this Act is governed by the law in effect at the time the proceeding was commenced, and the former law is continued in effect for that purpose."

§ 2.002. Application for License

Except as provided by Section 2.006, each person applying for a license must:

(1) appear before the county clerk;

(2) submit the person's proof of identity and age as provided by this subchapter;

(3) provide the information applicable to that person for which spaces are provided in the application for a marriage license;

(4) mark the appropriate boxes provided in the application; and

(5) take the oath printed on the application and sign the application before the county clerk.

Added by Acts 1997, 75th Leg., ch. 7, § 1, eff. April 17, 1997.

§ 2.003. Application for License by Minor

In addition to the other requirements provided by this chapter, a person under 18 years of age applying for a license must provide to the county clerk:

(1) documents establishing, as provided by Section 2.102, parental consent for the person to the marriage;

(2) documents establishing that a prior marriage of the person has been dissolved; or

(3) a court order granted under Section 2.103 authorizing the marriage of the person.

Added by Acts 1997, 75th Leg., ch. 7, § 1, eff. April 17, 1997.

§ 2.004. Application Form

(a) The county clerk shall furnish the application form as prescribed by the bureau of vital statistics.

(b) The application form must contain:

(1) a heading entitled "Application for Marriage License, ____________ County, Texas";

(2) spaces for each applicant's full name, including the woman's maiden surname, address, social security number, if any, date of birth, and place of birth, including city, county, and state;

(3) a space for indicating the document tendered by each applicant as proof of identity and age;

(4) spaces for indicating whether each applicant has been divorced within the last 30 days;

(5) printed boxes for each applicant to check "true" or "false" in response to the following statement: "I am not presently married.";

(6) printed boxes for each applicant to check "true" or "false" in response to the following statement: "The other applicant is not related to me as:

(A) an ancestor or descendant, by blood or adoption;

(B) a brother or sister, of the whole or half blood or by adoption;

(C) a parent's brother or sister, of the whole or half blood or by adoption; or

(D) a son or daughter of a brother or sister, of the whole or half blood or by adoption.";

(7) printed boxes for each applicant to check "true" or "false" in response to the following statement: "I am not presently delinquent in the payment of court-ordered child support.";

(8) a printed oath reading: "I SOLEMNLY SWEAR (OR AFFIRM) THAT THE INFORMATION I HAVE GIVEN IN THIS APPLICATION IS CORRECT.";

(9) spaces immediately below the printed oath for the applicants' signatures;

(10) a certificate of the county clerk that:

(A) each applicant made the oath and the date and place that it was made; or

(B) an applicant did not appear personally but the prerequisites for the license have been fulfilled as provided by this chapter;

(11) spaces for indicating the date of the marriage and the county in which the marriage is performed; and

(12) a space for the address to which the applicants desire the completed license to be mailed.

Added by Acts 1997, 75th Leg., ch. 7, § 1, eff. April 17, 1997. Amended by Acts 1997, 75th Leg., ch. 776, § 1, eff. Sept. 1, 1997.

§ 2.005. Proof of Identity and Age

(a) The county clerk shall require proof of the identity and age of each applicant.

(b) The proof must be established by a certified copy of the applicant's birth certificate or by some certificate, license, or document issued by this state or another state, the United States, or a foreign government.

Added by Acts 1997, 75th Leg., ch. 7, § 1, eff. April 17, 1997.

§ 2.006. Absent Applicant

(a) If an applicant is unable to appear personally before the county clerk to apply for a marriage license, any adult person or the other applicant may apply on behalf of the absent applicant.

(b) The person applying on behalf of an absent applicant shall provide to the clerk:

(1) the affidavit of the absent applicant as provided by this subchapter;

(2) proof of the identity and age of the absent applicant as provided by this subchapter; and

(3) if required because the absent applicant is a person under 18 years of age, the documents establishing parental consent, documents establishing that a prior marriage has been dissolved, or a court order authorizing the marriage of the absent, underage applicant.

Added by Acts 1997, 75th Leg., ch. 7, § 1, eff. April 17, 1997.

§ 2.007. Affidavit of Absent Applicant

The affidavit of an absent applicant must include:

(1) the absent applicant's full name, including the maiden surname of a female applicant, address, date of birth, place of birth, including city, county, and state, citizenship, and social security number, if any;

(2) a declaration that the absent applicant has not been divorced within the last 30 days;

(3) a declaration that the absent applicant is:

(A) not presently married; or

(B) married to the other applicant and they wish to marry again;

(4) a declaration that the other applicant is not related to the absent applicant as:

(A) an ancestor or descendant, by blood or adoption;

(B) a brother or sister, of the whole or half blood or by adoption;

(C) a parent's brother or sister, of the whole or half blood or by adoption; or

(D) a son or daughter of a brother or sister, of the whole or half blood or by adoption;

(5) a declaration that the absent applicant desires to marry and the name, age, and address of the person to whom the absent applicant desires to be married;

(6) the approximate date on which the marriage is to occur;

(7) the reason the absent applicant is unable to appear personally before the county clerk for the issuance of the license; and

(8) if the absent applicant will be unable to attend the ceremony, the appointment of any adult, other than the other applicant, to act as proxy for the purpose of participating in the ceremony.

Added by Acts 1997, 75th Leg., ch. 7, § 1, eff. April 17, 1997.

§ 2.008. Execution of Application by Clerk

(a) The county clerk shall:

(1) determine that all necessary information, other than the date of the marriage ceremony, the county in which the ceremony is conducted, and the name of the person who performs the ceremony, is recorded on the application and that all necessary documents are submitted;

(2) administer the oath to each applicant appearing before the clerk;

(3) have each applicant appearing before the clerk sign the application in the clerk's presence; and

(4) execute the clerk's certificate on the application.

(b) A person appearing before the clerk on behalf of an absent applicant is not required to take the oath on behalf of the absent applicant.

Added by Acts 1997, 75th Leg., ch. 7, § 1, eff. April 17, 1997.

§ 2.009. Issuance of License

(a) Except as provided by Subsections (b) and (d), the county clerk may not issue a license if either applicant:

(1) fails to provide the information required by this subchapter;

(2) fails to submit proof of age and identity;

(3) is under 14 years of age and has not been granted a court order as provided by Section 2.103;

(4) is 14 years of age or older but under 18 years of age and has not presented at least one of the following:

(A) parental consent as provided by Section 2.102;

(B) documents establishing that a prior marriage of the applicant has been dissolved; or

(C) a court order as provided by Section 2.103;

(5) checks "false" in response to a statement in the application, except as provided by Subsection (b) or (d), or fails to make a required declaration in an affidavit required of an absent applicant; or

(6) indicates that the applicant has been divorced by a decree of a court of this state within the last 30 days, unless:

(A) the applicants were divorced from each other; or

(B) the prohibition against remarriage is waived as provided by Section 6.802.

(b) If an applicant checks "false" in response to the statement "I am not presently married," the county clerk shall inquire as to whether the applicant is presently married to the other applicant. If the applicant states that the applicant is currently married to the other applicant, the county clerk shall record that statement on the license before the administration of the oath. The county clerk may not refuse to issue a license on the ground that the applicants are already married to each other.

(c) On the proper execution of the application, the clerk shall:

(1) prepare the license;

(2) record on the reverse side of the license the names of the licensees, the date that the license is issued, and, if applicable, the name of the person appointed to act as proxy for an absent applicant, if any;

(3) record the time at which the license was issued; and

(4) distribute to each applicant printed materials about acquired immune deficiency syndrome (AIDS) and human immunodeficiency virus (HIV) and note on the license that the distribution was made.

(d) The county clerk may not refuse to issue a license to an applicant on the ground that the applicant checked "false" in response to the statement "I am not presently delinquent in the payment of court-ordered child support."

Added by Acts 1997, 75th Leg., ch. 7, § 1, eff. April 17, 1997. Amended by Acts 1997, 75th Leg., ch. 776, § 2, eff. Sept. 1, 1997.

§ 2.010. Aids Information

Materials providing information about acquired immune deficiency syndrome (AIDS) and human immunodeficiency virus (HIV) shall be prepared and provided to the clerk by the Texas Department of Health and shall be designed to inform the applicants about:

(1) the incidence and mode of transmission of AIDS and HIV;

(2) the local availability of medical procedures, including voluntary testing, designed to show or help show whether a person has AIDS or HIV infection, antibodies to HIV, or infection with any other probable causative agent of AIDS; and

(3) available and appropriate counseling services regarding AIDS and HIV infection.

Added by Acts 1997, 75th Leg., ch. 7, § 1, eff. April 17, 1997.

§ 2.011. Recording

The county clerk shall record all licenses issued by the clerk and all documents submitted with an application for a license or note a summary of the documents on the application.

Added by Acts 1997, 75th Leg., ch. 7, § 1, eff. April 17, 1997.

§ 2.012. Violation by County Clerk; Penalty

A county clerk or deputy county clerk who violates or fails to comply with this subchapter commits an offense. An offense under this section is a misdemeanor punishable by a fine of not less than $200 and not more than $500.

Added by Acts 1997, 75th Leg., ch. 7, § 1, eff. April 17, 1997.

[Sections 2.013 to 2.100 reserved for expansion]

SUBCHAPTER B. UNDERAGE APPLICANTS

§ 2.101. General Age Requirement

Except as otherwise provided by this subchapter or on a showing that a prior marriage has been dissolved, a county clerk may not issue a marriage license if either applicant is under 18 years of age.

Added by Acts 1997, 75th Leg., ch. 7, § 1, eff. April 17, 1997.

§ 2.102. Parental Consent for Underage Applicant

(a) If an applicant is 14 years of age or older but under 18 years of age, the county clerk shall issue the license if parental consent is given as provided by this section.

(b) Parental consent must be evidenced by a written declaration on a form supplied by the county clerk in which the person consents to the marriage and swears that the person is a parent (if there is no judicially designated managing conservator or guardian of the applicant's person) or a judicially designated managing conservator or guardian (whether an individual, authorized agency, or court) of the applicant's person.

(c) Except as otherwise provided by this section, consent must be acknowledged before a county clerk.

(d) If the person giving parental consent resides in another state, the consent may be acknowledged before an officer authorized to issue marriage licenses in that state.

(e) If the person giving parental consent is unable because of illness or incapacity to comply with the provisions of Subsection (c) or (d), the consent may be acknowledged before any officer authorized to take acknowledgments. A consent under this subsection must be accompanied by a physician's affidavit stating that the person giving parental consent is unable to comply because of illness or incapacity.

(f) Parental consent must be given at the time the application for the marriage license is made or not earlier than the 30th day preceding the date the application is made.

Added by Acts 1997, 75th Leg., ch. 7, § 1, eff. April 17, 1997.

§ 2.103. Court Order for Underage Applicant

(a) A minor may petition the court in the minor's own name for an order granting permission to marry. In a suit under this section, the trial judge may advance the suit if the best interest of the applicant would be served by an early hearing.

(b) The petition must be filed in the county where a parent resides if a managing conservator or a guardian of the person has not been appointed. If a managing conservator or a guardian of the person has been appointed, the petition must be filed in the county where the managing conservator or the guardian of the person resides. If no person authorized to consent to marriage for the minor resides in this state, the petition must be filed in the county where the minor lives.

(c) The petition must include:

(1) a statement of the reasons the minor desires to marry;

(2) a statement of whether each parent is living or is dead;

(3) the name and residence address of each living parent; and

(4) a statement of whether a managing conservator or a guardian of the person has been appointed for the minor.

(d) Process shall be served as in other civil cases on each living parent of the minor or, if a managing conservator or a guardian of the person has been appointed, on the managing conservator or guardian of the person. Citation may be given by publication as in other civil cases, except that notice shall be published one time only.

(e) The court shall appoint a guardian ad litem to represent the minor in the proceeding and to speak for or against the petition in the manner the guardian ad litem believes to be in the best interest of the minor. The court shall specify a fee to be paid by the minor for the services of the guardian ad litem. The fee shall be collected in the same manner as other costs of the proceeding.

(f) If after a hearing the court, sitting without a jury, believes marriage to be in the best interest of the minor, the court, by order, shall grant the minor permission to marry.

Added by Acts 1997, 75th Leg., ch. 7, § 1, eff. April 17, 1997.

[Sections 2.104 to 2.200 reserved for expansion]

SUBCHAPTER C. CEREMONY AND RETURN OF LICENSE

§ 2.201. Expiration of License

If a marriage ceremony has not been conducted before the 31st day after the date the license is issued, the marriage license expires.

Added by Acts 1997, 75th Leg., ch. 7, § 1, eff. April 17, 1997.

§ 2.202. Persons Authorized to Conduct Ceremony

(a) The following persons are authorized to conduct a marriage ceremony:

(1) a licensed or ordained Christian minister or priest;

(2) a Jewish rabbi;

(3) a person who is an officer of a religious organization and who is authorized by the organization to conduct a marriage ceremony; and

(4) a justice of the supreme court, judge of the court of criminal appeals, justice of the courts of appeals, judge of the district, county, and probate courts, judge of the county courts at law, judge of the courts of domestic relations, judge of the juvenile courts, retired justice or judge of those courts, justice of the peace, retired justice of the peace, or judge or magistrate of a federal court of this state.

(b) For the purposes of this section, a retired judge or justice is a former judge or justice who is vested in the Judicial Retirement System of Texas Plan One or the Judicial Retirement System of Texas Plan Two or who has an aggregate of at least 12 years of service as judge or justice of any type listed in Subsection (a)(4).

Added by Acts 1997, 75th Leg., ch. 7, § 1, eff. April 17, 1997.

§ 2.203. Ceremony

(a) On receiving an unexpired marriage license, an authorized person may conduct the marriage ceremony as provided by this subchapter.

(b) A person unable to appear for the ceremony may assent to marriage by the appearance of a proxy appointed in the affidavit authorized by Subchapter A.

Added by Acts 1997, 75th Leg., ch. 7, § 1, eff. April 17, 1997.

§ 2.204. 72-Hour Waiting Period; Exceptions

(a) Except as provided by this section, a marriage ceremony may not take place during the 72-hour period immediately following the issuance of the marriage license.

(b) The 72-hour waiting period after issuance of a marriage license does not apply to an applicant who:

(1) is a member of the armed forces of the United States and on active duty; or

(2) obtains a written waiver under Subsection (c).

(c) An applicant may request a judge of a court with jurisdiction in family law cases, a justice of the supreme court, a judge of the court of criminal appeals, or a judge of a court of appeals for a written waiver permitting the marriage ceremony to take place during the 72-hour period immediately following the issuance of the marriage license. If the judge finds that there is good cause for the marriage to take place during the period, the judge shall sign the waiver.

Added by Acts 1997, 75th Leg., ch. 7, § 1, eff. April 17, 1997.

§ 2.205. Discrimination in Conducting Marriage Prohibited

(a) A person authorized to conduct a marriage ceremony by this subchapter is prohibited from discriminating on the basis of race, religion, or national origin against an applicant who is otherwise competent to be married.

(b) On a finding by the State Commission on Judicial Conduct that a person has intentionally violated Subsection (a), the commission may recommend to the supreme court that the person be removed from office.

Added by Acts 1997, 75th Leg., ch. 7, § 1, eff. April 17, 1997.

§ 2.206. Return of License; Penalty

(a) The person who conducts a marriage ceremony shall record on the license the date on which and the county in which the ceremony is performed and the person's name, subscribe the license, and return the license to the county clerk who issued it not later than the 30th day after the date the ceremony is conducted.

(b) A person who fails to comply with this section commits an offense. An offense under this section is a misdemeanor punishable by a fine of not less than $200 and not more than $500.

Added by Acts 1997, 75th Leg., ch. 7, § 1, eff. April 17, 1997.

§ 2.207. Marriage Conducted After License Expired; Penalty

(a) A person who is to conduct a marriage ceremony shall determine whether the license has expired from the county clerk's endorsement on the license.

(b) A person who conducts a marriage ceremony after the marriage license has expired commits an offense. An offense under this section is a misdemeanor punishable by a fine of not less than $200 and not more than $500.

Added by Acts 1997, 75th Leg., ch. 7, § 1, eff. April 17, 1997.

§ 2.208. Recording and Delivery of License

(a) The county clerk shall record a returned marriage license and mail the license to the address indicated on the application.

(b) On the application form the county clerk shall record:

(1) the date of the marriage ceremony;

(2) the county in which the ceremony was conducted; and

(3) the name of the person who conducted the ceremony.

Added by Acts 1997, 75th Leg., ch. 7, § 1, eff. April 17, 1997.

§ 2.209. Duplicate License

(a) On the application and proof of identity of a person whose marriage is recorded in the records of the county clerk, the county clerk shall issue a duplicate marriage license completed with information as contained in the records.

(b) On the application and proof of identity of both persons to whom a marriage license was issued but not recorded as required by Section 2.208, the county clerk shall issue a duplicate license if each person applying submits to the clerk an affidavit stating:

(1) that the persons to whom the original license was issued were married to each other before the expiration date of the original license by a person authorized to conduct a marriage ceremony;

(2) the name of the person who conducted the ceremony; and

(3) the date of the ceremony.

Added by Acts 1997, 75th Leg., ch. 7, § 1, eff. April 17, 1997.

[Sections 2.210 to 2.300 reserved for expansion]

SUBCHAPTER D. VALIDITY OF MARRIAGE

§ 2.301. Fraud, Mistake, or Illegality in Obtaining License

Except as otherwise provided by this chapter, the validity of a marriage is not affected by any fraud, mistake, or illegality that occurred in obtaining the marriage license.

Added by Acts 1997, 75th Leg., ch. 7, § 1, eff. April 17, 1997.

§ 2.302. Ceremony Conducted by Unauthorized Person

The validity of a marriage is not affected by the lack of authority of the person conducting the marriage ceremony if:

(1) there was a reasonable appearance of authority by that person; and

(2) at least one party to the marriage participated in the ceremony in good faith and that party treats the marriage as valid.

Added by Acts 1997, 75th Leg., ch. 7, § 1, eff. April 17, 1997.

[Sections 2.303 to 2.400 reserved for expansion]

SUBCHAPTER E. MARRIAGE WITHOUT FORMALITIES

§ 2.401. Proof of Informal Marriage

(a) In a judicial, administrative, or other proceeding, the marriage of a man and woman may be proved by evidence that:

(1) a declaration of their marriage has been signed as provided by this subchapter; or

(2) the man and woman agreed to be married and after the agreement they lived together in this state

as husband and wife and there represented to others that they were married.

(b) If a proceeding in which a marriage is to be proved as provided by Subsection (a)(2) is not commenced before the second anniversary of the date on which the parties separated and ceased living together, it is rebuttably presumed that the parties did not enter into an agreement to be married.

(c) A person under 18 years of age may not:

(1) be a party to an informal marriage; or

(2) execute a declaration of informal marriage under Section 2.402.

Added by Acts 1997, 75th Leg., ch. 7, § 1, eff. April 17, 1997. Amended by Acts 1997, 75th Leg., ch. 1362, § 1, eff. Sept. 1, 1997.

Section 5 of Acts 1997, 75th Leg., ch. 1362 provides:

"This Act takes effect only if S.B. 334, 75th Legislature, Regular Session, becomes law. If that legislation does not become law, this Act has no effect."

S.B. No. 334 was enacted as Acts 1997, 75th Leg., ch. 7.

§ 2.402. Declaration and Registration of Informal Marriage

(a) A declaration of informal marriage must be signed on a form prescribed by the bureau of vital statistics and provided by the county clerk. Each party to the declaration shall provide the information required in the form.

(b) The declaration form must contain:

(1) a heading entitled "Declaration and Registration of Informal Marriage, __________ County, Texas";

(2) spaces for each party's full name, including the woman's maiden surname, address, date of birth, place of birth, including city, county, and state, and social security number, if any;

(3) a space for indicating the type of document tendered by each party as proof of age and identity;

(4) printed boxes for each party to check "true" or "false" in response to the following statement: "The other party is not related to me as:

(A) an ancestor or descendant, by blood or adoption;

(B) a brother or sister, of the whole or half blood or by adoption;

(C) a parent's brother or sister, of the whole or half blood or by adoption; or

(D) a son or daughter of a brother or sister, of the whole or half blood or by adoption.";

(5) a printed declaration and oath reading: "I SOLEMNLY SWEAR (OR AFFIRM) THAT WE, THE UNDERSIGNED, ARE MARRIED TO EACH OTHER BY VIRTUE OF THE FOLLOWING FACTS: ON OR ABOUT (DATE) WE AGREED TO BE MARRIED, AND AFTER THAT DATE WE LIVED TOGETHER AS HUSBAND AND WIFE AND IN THIS STATE WE REPRESENTED TO OTHERS THAT WE WERE MARRIED. SINCE THE DATE OF MARRIAGE TO THE OTHER PARTY I HAVE NOT BEEN MARRIED TO ANY OTHER PERSON. THIS DECLARATION IS TRUE AND THE INFORMATION IN IT WHICH I HAVE GIVEN IS CORRECT.";

(6) spaces immediately below the printed declaration and oath for the parties' signatures; and

(7) a certificate of the county clerk that the parties made the declaration and oath and the place and date it was made.

(c) Repealed by Acts 1997, 75th Leg., ch. 1362, § 4, eff. Sept. 1, 1997.

Added by Acts 1997, 75th Leg., ch. 7, § 1, eff. April 17, 1997. Amended by Acts 1997, 75th Leg., ch. 1362, § 4, eff. Sept. 1, 1997.

Section 5 of Acts 1997, 75th Leg., ch. 1362 provides:

"This Act takes effect only if S.B. 334, 75th Legislature, Regular Session, becomes law. If that legislation does not become law, this Act has no effect."

Senate Bill No. 334, Acts of the 75th Legislature, Regular Session, was enacted as chapter 7.

§ 2.403. Proof of Identity and Age

The county clerk shall require proof of the identity and age of each party to the declaration of informal marriage to be established by a certified copy of the party's birth certificate or by some certificate, license, or document issued by this state or another state, the United States, or a foreign government.

Added by Acts 1997, 75th Leg., ch. 7, § 1, eff. April 17, 1997.

§ 2.404. Recording of Declaration of Informal Marriage

(a) The county clerk shall:

(1) determine that all necessary information is recorded on the declaration of informal marriage form and that all necessary documents are submitted to the clerk;

(2) administer the oath to each party to the declaration;

(3) have each party sign the declaration in the clerk's presence; and

(4) execute the clerk's certificate to the declaration.

(b) The county clerk may not certify or record the declaration if:

(1) either party fails to supply any information or provide any document required by this subchapter;

(2) either party is under 18 years of age; or

(3) either party checks "false" in response to the statement of relationship to the other party.

(c) On execution of the declaration, the county clerk shall record the declaration and all documents submitted with the declaration or note a summary of them on the declaration form, deliver the original of the declaration to the parties, and send a copy to the bureau of vital statistics.

(d) A declaration recorded as provided in this section is prima facie evidence of the marriage of the parties.

(e) At the time the parties sign the declaration, the clerk shall distribute to each party printed materials about acquired immune deficiency syndrome (AIDS) and human immunodeficiency virus (HIV). The clerk shall note on the declaration that the distribution was made. The materials shall be prepared and provided to the clerk by the Texas Department of Health and shall be designed to inform the parties about:

(1) the incidence and mode of transmission of AIDS and HIV;

(2) the local availability of medical procedures, including voluntary testing, designed to show or help show whether a person has AIDS or HIV infection, antibodies to HIV, or infection with any other probable causative agent of AIDS; and

(3) available and appropriate counseling services regarding AIDS and HIV infection.

Added by Acts 1997, 75th Leg., ch. 7, § 1, eff. April 17, 1997. Amended by Acts 1997, 75th Leg., ch. 1362, § 2, eff. Sept. 1, 1997.

Section 5 of Acts 1997, 75th Leg., ch. 1362 provides:

"This Act takes effect only if S.B. 334, 75th Legislature, Regular Session, becomes law. If that legislation does not become law, this Act has no effect."

Senate Bill No. 334, Acts of the 75th Legislature, Regular Session, was enacted as chapter 7.

§ 2.405. Violation by County Clerk; Penalty

A county clerk or deputy county clerk who violates this subchapter commits an offense. An offense under this section is a misdemeanor punishable by a fine of not less than $200 and not more than $500.

Added by Acts 1997, 75th Leg., ch. 7, § 1, eff. April 17, 1997.

[Sections 2.406 to 2.500 reserved for expansion]

SUBCHAPTER F. RIGHTS AND DUTIES OF SPOUSES

§ 2.501. Duty to Support

(a) Each spouse has the duty to support the other spouse.

(b) A spouse who fails to discharge the duty of support is liable to any person who provides necessaries to the spouse to whom support is owed.

Added by Acts 1997, 75th Leg., ch. 7, § 1, eff. April 17, 1997.

SUBTITLE B. PROPERTY RIGHTS AND LIABILITIES

CHAPTER 3. MARITAL PROPERTY RIGHTS AND LIABILITIES

SUBCHAPTER A. GENERAL RULES FOR SEPARATE AND COMMUNITY PROPERTY

SUBCHAPTER B. MANAGEMENT, CONTROL, AND DISPOSITION OF MARITAL PROPERTY

SUBCHAPTER C. MARITAL PROPERTY LIABILITIES

SUBCHAPTER D. MANAGEMENT, CONTROL, AND DISPOSITION OF MARITAL PROPERTY UNDER UNUSUAL CIRCUMSTANCES

SUBCHAPTER A. GENERAL RULES FOR SEPARATE AND COMMUNITY PROPERTY

§ 3.001. Separate Property

A spouse's separate property consists of:

(1) the property owned or claimed by the spouse before marriage;

(2) the property acquired by the spouse during marriage by gift, devise, or descent; and

(3) the recovery for personal injuries sustained by the spouse during marriage, except any recovery for loss of earning capacity during marriage.

Added by Acts 1997, 75th Leg., ch. 7, § 1, eff. April 17, 1997.

Section 4 of Acts 1997, 75th Leg., ch. 7, provides:

"The change in law made by this Act does not affect a proceeding under the Family Code pending on the effective date of this Act. A proceeding pending on the effective date of this Act is governed by the law in effect at the time the proceeding was commenced, and the former law is continued in effect for that purpose."

§ 3.002. Community Property

Community property consists of the property, other than separate property, acquired by either spouse during marriage.

Added by Acts 1997, 75th Leg., ch. 7, § 1, eff. April 17, 1997.

§ 3.003. Presumption of Community Property

(a) Property possessed by either spouse during or on dissolution of marriage is presumed to be community property.

(b) The degree of proof necessary to establish that property is separate property is clear and convincing evidence.

Added by Acts 1997, 75th Leg., ch. 7, § 1, eff. April 17, 1997.

§ 3.004. Recordation of Separate Property

(a) A subscribed and acknowledged schedule of a spouse's separate property may be recorded in the deed records of the county in which the parties, or one of them, reside and in the county or counties in which the real property is located.

(b) A schedule of a spouse's separate real property is not constructive notice to a good faith purchaser for value or a creditor without actual notice unless the instrument is acknowledged and recorded in the deed records of the county in which the real property is located.

Added by Acts 1997, 75th Leg., ch. 7, § 1, eff. April 17, 1997.

§ 3.005. Gifts Between Spouses

If one spouse makes a gift of property to the other spouse, the gift is presumed to include all the income and property that may arise from that property.

Added by Acts 1997, 75th Leg., ch. 7, § 1, eff. April 17, 1997.

[Sections 3.006 to 3.100 reserved for expansion]

SUBCHAPTER B. MANAGEMENT, CONTROL, AND DISPOSITION OF MARITAL PROPERTY

§ 3.101. Managing Separate Property

Each spouse has the sole management, control, and disposition of that spouse's separate property.

Added by Acts 1997, 75th Leg., ch. 7, § 1, eff. April 17, 1997.

§ 3.102. Managing Community Property

(a) During marriage, each spouse has the sole management, control, and disposition of the community property that the spouse would have owned if single, including:

(1) personal earnings;

(2) revenue from separate property;

(3) recoveries for personal injuries; and

(4) the increase and mutations of, and the revenue from, all property subject to the spouse's sole management, control, and disposition.

(b) If community property subject to the sole management, control, and disposition of one spouse is mixed or combined with community property subject to the sole management, control, and disposition of the other spouse, then the mixed or combined community property is subject to the joint management, control, and disposition of the spouses, unless the spouses provide otherwise by power of attorney in writing or other agreement.

(c) Except as provided by Subsection (a), community property is subject to the joint management, control, and disposition of the spouses unless the spouses provide otherwise by power of attorney in writing or other agreement.

Added by Acts 1997, 75th Leg., ch. 7, § 1, eff. April 17, 1997.

§ 3.103. Managing Earnings of Minor

During the marriage of the parents of an unemancipated minor for whom a managing conservator has not been appointed, the earnings of the minor are subject to the joint management, control, and disposition of the parents of the minor, unless otherwise provided by agreement of the parents or by judicial order.

Added by Acts 1997, 75th Leg., ch. 7, § 1, eff. April 17, 1997.

§ 3.104. Protection of Third Persons

(a) During marriage, property is presumed to be subject to the sole management, control, and disposition of a spouse if it is held in that spouse's name, as shown by muniment, contract, deposit of funds, or other evidence of ownership, or if it is in that spouse's possession and is not subject to such evidence of ownership.

(b) A third person dealing with a spouse is entitled to rely, as against the other spouse or anyone claiming from that spouse, on that spouse's authority to deal with the property if:

(1) the property is presumed to be subject to the sole management, control, and disposition of the spouse; and

(2) the person dealing with the spouse:

(A) is not a party to a fraud on the other spouse or another person; and

(B) does not have actual or constructive notice of the spouse's lack of authority.

Added by Acts 1997, 75th Leg., ch. 7, § 1, eff. April 17, 1997.

[Sections 3.105 to 3.200 reserved for expansion]

SUBCHAPTER C. MARITAL PROPERTY LIABILITIES

§ 3.201. Spousal Liability

(a) A person is personally liable for the acts of the person's spouse only if:

(1) the spouse acts as an agent for the person; or

(2) the spouse incurs a debt for necessaries as provided by Subchapter F, Chapter 2.

(b) Except as provided by this subchapter, community property is not subject to a liability that arises from an act of a spouse.

(c) A spouse does not act as an agent for the other spouse solely because of the marriage relationship.

Added by Acts 1997, 75th Leg., ch. 7, § 1, eff. April 17, 1997.

§ 3.202. Rules of Marital Property Liability

(a) A spouse's separate property is not subject to liabilities of the other spouse unless both spouses are liable by other rules of law.

(b) Unless both spouses are personally liable as provided by this subchapter, the community property subject to a spouse's sole management, control, and disposition is not subject to:

(1) any liabilities that the other spouse incurred before marriage; or

(2) any nontortious liabilities that the other spouse incurs during marriage.

(c) The community property subject to a spouse's sole or joint management, control, and disposition is subject to the liabilities incurred by the spouse before or during marriage.

(d) All community property is subject to tortious liability of either spouse incurred during marriage.

Added by Acts 1997, 75th Leg., ch. 7, § 1, eff. April 17, 1997.

§ 3.203. Order in Which Property is Subject to Execution

(a) A judge may determine, as deemed just and equitable, the order in which particular separate or community property is subject to execution and sale to satisfy a judgment, if the property subject to liability for a judgment includes any combination of:

(1) a spouse's separate property;

(2) community property subject to a spouse's sole management, control, and disposition;

(3) community property subject to the other spouse's sole management, control, and disposition; and

(4) community property subject to the spouses' joint management, control, and disposition.

(b) In determining the order in which particular property is subject to execution and sale, the judge shall consider the facts surrounding the transaction or occurrence on which the suit is based.

Added by Acts 1997, 75th Leg., ch. 7, § 1, eff. April 17, 1997.

[Sections 3.204 to 3.300 reserved for expansion]

SUBCHAPTER D. MANAGEMENT, CONTROL, AND DISPOSITION OF MARITAL PROPERTY UNDER UNUSUAL CIRCUMSTANCES

§ 3.301. Incapacitated, Missing, Abandoned, or Separated Spouse

(a) A spouse may file a sworn petition stating the facts that make it desirable for the petitioning spouse to manage, control, and dispose of community property described or defined in the petition that would otherwise be subject to the sole or joint management, control, and disposition of the other spouse if:

(1) because of physical or mental incapacity, the other spouse is unable to manage, control, or dis-

pose of the community property subject to that spouse's sole or joint management, control, and disposition;

(2) the other spouse has disappeared and that spouse's location remains unknown to the petitioning spouse, unless the spouse is reported to be a prisoner of war or missing on public service;

(3) the other spouse has permanently abandoned the petitioning spouse; or

(4) the spouses are permanently separated.

(b) The petition may be filed in a court in the county in which the petitioner resided at the time the incapacity or separation began, or the abandonment or disappearance occurred, not earlier than the 60th day after the date of the occurrence of the event. If both spouses are nonresidents of this state at the time the petition is filed, the petition may be filed in a court in a county in which any part of the described or defined community property is located.

Added by Acts 1997, 75th Leg., ch. 7, § 1, eff. April 17, 1997.

§ 3.302. Spouse Missing on Public Service

(a) If a spouse is reported by an executive department of the United States to be a prisoner of war or missing on the public service of the United States, the spouse of the prisoner of war or missing person may file a sworn petition stating the facts that make it desirable for the petitioner to manage, control, and dispose of the community property described or defined in the petition that would otherwise be subject to the sole or joint management, control, and disposition of the imprisoned or missing spouse.

(b) The petition may be filed in a court in the county in which the petitioner resided at the time the report was made not earlier than six months after the date of the notice that a spouse is reported to be a prisoner of war or missing on public service. If both spouses were nonresidents of this state at the time the report was made, the petition shall be filed in a court in a county in which any part of the described or defined property is located.

Added by Acts 1997, 75th Leg., ch. 7, § 1, eff. April 17, 1997.

§ 3.303. Appointment of Attorney

(a) Except as provided by Subsection (b), the court may appoint an attorney in a suit filed under this subchapter for the respondent.

(b) The court shall appoint an attorney in a suit filed under this subchapter for a respondent reported to be a prisoner of war or missing on public service.

(c) The court shall allow a reasonable fee for an appointed attorney's services as a part of the costs of the suit.

Added by Acts 1997, 75th Leg., ch. 7, § 1, eff. April 17, 1997.

§ 3.304. Notice of Hearing; Citation

(a) Notice of the hearing, accompanied by a copy of the petition, shall be issued and served on the attorney representing the respondent, if an attorney has been appointed.

(b) If an attorney has not been appointed for the respondent, citation shall be issued and served on the respondent as in other civil cases.

Added by Acts 1997, 75th Leg., ch. 7, § 1, eff. April 17, 1997.

§ 3.305. Citation by Publication

(a) If the residence of the respondent, other than a respondent reported to be a prisoner of war or missing on public service, is unknown, citation shall be published in a newspaper of general circulation published in the county in which the petition was filed. If that county has no newspaper of general circulation, citation shall be published in a newspaper of general circulation in an adjacent county or in the nearest county in which a newspaper of general circulation is published.

(b) The notice shall be published once a week for two consecutive weeks before the hearing, but the first notice may not be published after the 20th day before the date set for the hearing.

Added by Acts 1997, 75th Leg., ch. 7, § 1, eff. April 17, 1997.

§ 3.306. Court Order for Management, Control, and Disposition of Community Property

(a) After hearing the evidence in a suit under this subchapter, the court, on terms the court considers just and equitable, shall render an order describing or defining the community property at issue that will be subject to the management, control, and disposition of each spouse during marriage.

(b) The court may:

(1) impose any condition and restriction the court deems necessary to protect the rights of the respondent;

(2) require a bond conditioned on the faithful administration of the property; and

(3) require payment to the registry of the court of all or a portion of the proceeds of the sale of the

property, to be disbursed in accordance with the court's further directions.

Added by Acts 1997, 75th Leg., ch. 7, § 1, eff. April 17, 1997.

§ 3.307. Continuing Jurisdiction of Court; Vacating Original Order

(a) The court has continuing jurisdiction over the court's order rendered under this subchapter.

(b) On the motion of either spouse, the court shall amend or vacate the original order after notice and hearing if:

(1) the incapacitated spouse's capacity is restored;

(2) the spouse who disappeared reappears;

(3) the abandonment or permanent separation ends; or

(4) the spouse who was reported to be a prisoner of war or missing on public service returns.

Added by Acts 1997, 75th Leg., ch. 7, § 1, eff. April 17, 1997.

§ 3.308. Recording Order to Affect Real Property

An order authorized by this subchapter affecting real property is not constructive notice to a good faith purchaser for value or to a creditor without actual notice unless the order is recorded in the deed records of the county in which the real property is located.

Added by Acts 1997, 75th Leg., ch. 7, § 1, eff. April 17, 1997.

§ 3.309. Remedies Cumulative

The remedies provided in this subchapter are cumulative of other rights, powers, and remedies afforded spouses by law.

Added by Acts 1997, 75th Leg., ch. 7, § 1, eff. April 17, 1997.

CHAPTER 4. PREMARITAL AND MARITAL PROPERTY AGREEMENTS

SUBCHAPTER A. UNIFORM PREMARITAL AGREEMENT ACT

Section

Section

SUBCHAPTER B. MARITAL PROPERTY AGREEMENT

SUBCHAPTER A. UNIFORM PREMARITAL AGREEMENT ACT

§ 4.001. Definitions

In this subchapter:

(1) "Premarital agreement" means an agreement between prospective spouses made in contemplation of marriage and to be effective on marriage.

(2) "Property" means an interest, present or future, legal or equitable, vested or contingent, in real or personal property, including income and earnings.

Added by Acts 1997, 75th Leg., ch. 7, § 1, eff. April 17, 1997.

Section 4 of Acts 1997, 75th Leg., ch. 7, provides:

"The change in law made by this Act does not affect a proceeding under the Family Code pending on the effective date of this Act. A proceeding pending on the effective date of this Act is governed by the law in effect at the time the proceeding was commenced, and the former law is continued in effect for that purpose."

§ 4.002. Formalities

A premarital agreement must be in writing and signed by both parties. The agreement is enforceable without consideration.

Added by Acts 1997, 75th Leg., ch. 7, § 1, eff. April 17, 1997.

§ 4.003. Content

(a) The parties to a premarital agreement may contract with respect to:

(1) the rights and obligations of each of the parties in any of the property of either or both of them whenever and wherever acquired or located;

(2) the right to buy, sell, use, transfer, exchange, abandon, lease, consume, expend, assign, create a security interest in, mortgage, encumber, dispose of, or otherwise manage and control property;

(3) the disposition of property on separation, marital dissolution, death, or the occurrence or nonoccurrence of any other event;

(4) the modification or elimination of spousal support;

(5) the making of a will, trust, or other arrangement to carry out the provisions of the agreement;

(6) the ownership rights in and disposition of the death benefit from a life insurance policy;

(7) the choice of law governing the construction of the agreement; and

(8) any other matter, including their personal rights and obligations, not in violation of public policy or a statute imposing a criminal penalty.

(b) The right of a child to support may not be adversely affected by a premarital agreement.

Added by Acts 1997, 75th Leg., ch. 7, § 1, eff. April 17, 1997.

§ 4.004. Effect of Marriage

A premarital agreement becomes effective on marriage.

Added by Acts 1997, 75th Leg., ch. 7, § 1, eff. April 17, 1997.

§ 4.005. Amendment or Revocation

After marriage, a premarital agreement may be amended or revoked only by a written agreement signed by the parties. The amended agreement or the revocation is enforceable without consideration.

Added by Acts 1997, 75th Leg., ch. 7, § 1, eff. April 17, 1997.

§ 4.006. Enforcement

(a) A premarital agreement is not enforceable if the party against whom enforcement is requested proves that:

(1) the party did not sign the agreement voluntarily; or

(2) the agreement was unconscionable when it was signed and, before signing the agreement, that party:

(A) was not provided a fair and reasonable disclosure of the property or financial obligations of the other party;

(B) did not voluntarily and expressly waive, in writing, any right to disclosure of the property or financial obligations of the other party beyond the disclosure provided; and

(C) did not have, or reasonably could not have had, adequate knowledge of the property or financial obligations of the other party.

(b) An issue of unconscionability of a premarital agreement shall be decided by the court as a matter of law.

(c) The remedies and defenses in this section are the exclusive remedies or defenses, including common law remedies or defenses.

Added by Acts 1997, 75th Leg., ch. 7, § 1, eff. April 17, 1997.

§ 4.007. Enforcement: Void Marriage

If a marriage is determined to be void, an agreement that would otherwise have been a premarital agreement is enforceable only to the extent necessary to avoid an inequitable result.

Added by Acts 1997, 75th Leg., ch. 7, § 1, eff. April 17, 1997.

§ 4.008. Limitation of Actions

A statute of limitations applicable to an action asserting a claim for relief under a premarital agreement is tolled during the marriage of the parties to the agreement. However, equitable defenses limiting the time for enforcement, including laches and estoppel, are available to either party.

Added by Acts 1997, 75th Leg., ch. 7, § 1, eff. April 17, 1997.

§ 4.009. Application and Construction

This subchapter shall be applied and construed to effect its general purpose to make uniform the law with respect to the subject of this subchapter among states enacting these provisions.

Added by Acts 1997, 75th Leg., ch. 7, § 1, eff. April 17, 1997.

§ 4.010. Short Title

This subchapter may be cited as the Uniform Premarital Agreement Act.

Added by Acts 1997, 75th Leg., ch. 7, § 1, eff. April 17, 1997.

[Sections 4.011 to 4.100 reserved for expansion]

SUBCHAPTER B. MARITAL PROPERTY AGREEMENT

§ 4.101. Definition

In this subchapter, "property" has the meaning assigned by Section 4.001.

Added by Acts 1997, 75th Leg., ch. 7, § 1, eff. April 17, 1997.

§ 4.102. Partition or Exchange of Community Property

At any time, the spouses may partition or exchange between themselves any part of their community property, then existing or to be acquired, as the spouses may desire. Property or a property interest transferred to a spouse by a partition or exchange agreement becomes that spouse's separate property.

Added by Acts 1997, 75th Leg., ch. 7, § 1, eff. April 17, 1997.

§ 4.103. Agreement Between Spouses Concerning Income or Property From Separate Property

At any time, the spouses may agree that the income or property arising from the separate property that is then owned by one of them, or that may thereafter be acquired, shall be the separate property of the owner.

Added by Acts 1997, 75th Leg., ch. 7, § 1, eff. April 17, 1997.

§ 4.104. Formalities

A partition or exchange agreement must be in writing and signed by both parties.

Added by Acts 1997, 75th Leg., ch. 7, § 1, eff. April 17, 1997.

§ 4.105. Enforcement

(a) A partition or exchange agreement is not enforceable if the party against whom enforcement is requested proves that:

(1) the party did not sign the agreement voluntarily; or

(2) the agreement was unconscionable when it was signed and, before execution of the agreement, that party:

(A) was not provided a fair and reasonable disclosure of the property or financial obligations of the other party;

(B) did not voluntarily and expressly waive, in writing, any right to disclosure of the property or financial obligations of the other party beyond the disclosure provided; and

(C) did not have, or reasonably could not have had, adequate knowledge of the property or financial obligations of the other party.

(b) An issue of unconscionability of a partition or exchange agreement shall be decided by the court as a matter of law.

(c) The remedies and defenses in this section are the exclusive remedies or defenses, including common law remedies or defenses.

Added by Acts 1997, 75th Leg., ch. 7, § 1, eff. April 17, 1997.

§ 4.106. Rights of Creditors and Recordation Under Partition or Exchange Agreement

(a) A provision of a partition or exchange agreement made under this subchapter is void with respect to the rights of a preexisting creditor whose rights are intended to be defrauded by it.

(b) A partition or exchange agreement made under this subchapter may be recorded in the deed records of the county in which a party resides and in the county in which the real property affected is located. An agreement made under this subchapter is constructive notice to a good faith purchaser for value or a creditor without actual notice only if the instrument is acknowledged and recorded in the county in which the real property is located.

Added by Acts 1997, 75th Leg., ch. 7, § 1, eff. April 17, 1997.

CHAPTER 5. HOMESTEAD RIGHTS

SUBCHAPTER A. SALE OF HOMESTEAD; GENERAL RULE

SUBCHAPTER B. SALE OF HOMESTEAD UNDER UNUSUAL CIRCUMSTANCES

SUBCHAPTER A. SALE OF HOMESTEAD; GENERAL RULE

§ 5.001. Sale, Conveyance, or Encumbrance of Homestead

Whether the homestead is the separate property of either spouse or community property, neither spouse may sell, convey, or encumber the homestead without the joinder of the other spouse except as provided in this chapter or by other rules of law.

Added by Acts 1997, 75th Leg., ch. 7, § 1, eff. April 17, 1997.

Section 4 of Acts 1997, 75th Leg., ch. 7, provides:

"The change in law made by this Act does not affect a proceeding under the Family Code pending on the effective date of this Act. A proceeding pending on the effective date of this Act is governed by the law in effect at the time the proceeding was commenced, and the former law is continued in effect for that purpose."

§ 5.002. Sale of Homestead for Incapacitated Spouse

If the homestead is the separate property of a spouse and the other spouse has been judicially declared incapacitated, the owner may sell, convey, or encumber the homestead without the joinder of the other spouse.

Added by Acts 1997, 75th Leg., ch. 7, § 1, eff. April 17, 1997.

[Sections 5.003 to 5.100 reserved for expansion]

SUBCHAPTER B. SALE OF HOMESTEAD UNDER UNUSUAL CIRCUMSTANCES

§ 5.101. Sale of Separate Homestead Under Unusual Circumstances

If the homestead is the separate property of a spouse, that spouse may file a sworn petition that gives a description of the property, states the facts that make it desirable for the spouse to sell, convey, or encumber the homestead without the joinder of the other spouse, and alleges that the other spouse:

(1) is incapacitated, whether judicially declared incapacitated or not;

(2) has disappeared and that the location of the spouse remains unknown to the petitioning spouse;

(3) has permanently abandoned the homestead and the petitioning spouse;

(4) has permanently abandoned the homestead and the spouses are permanently separated; or

(5) has been reported by an executive department of the United States to be a prisoner of war or missing on public service of the United States.

Added by Acts 1997, 75th Leg., ch. 7, § 1, eff. April 17, 1997.

§ 5.102. Sale of Community Homestead Under Unusual Circumstances

If the homestead is the community property of the spouses, one spouse may file a sworn petition that gives a description of the property, states the facts that make it desirable for the petitioning spouse to sell, convey, or encumber the homestead without the joinder of the other spouse, and alleges that the other spouse:

(1) is incapacitated, whether judicially declared incapacitated or not;

(2) has disappeared and that the location of the spouse remains unknown to the petitioning spouse;

(3) has permanently abandoned the homestead and the petitioning spouse;

(4) has permanently abandoned the homestead and the spouses are permanently separated; or

(5) has been reported by an executive department of the United States to be a prisoner of war or missing on public service of the United States.

Added by Acts 1997, 75th Leg., ch. 7, § 1, eff. April 17, 1997.

§ 5.103. Time for Filing Petition

The petitioning spouse may file the petition in a court of the county in which any portion of the property is located not earlier than the 60th day after the date of the occurrence of an event described by Sections 5.101(1)–(4) and 5.102(1)–(4) or not less than six months after the date the other spouse has been reported to be a prisoner of war or missing on public service.

Added by Acts 1997, 75th Leg., ch. 7, § 1, eff. April 17, 1997.

§ 5.104. Appointment of Attorney

(a) Except as provided by Subsection (b), the court may appoint an attorney in a suit filed under this subchapter for the respondent.

(b) The court shall appoint an attorney in a suit filed under this subchapter for a respondent reported to be a prisoner of war or missing on public service.

(c) The court shall allow a reasonable fee for the appointed attorney's services as a part of the costs of the suit.

Added by Acts 1997, 75th Leg., ch. 7, § 1, eff. April 17, 1997.

§ 5.105. Citation; Notice of Hearing

Citation and notice of hearing for a suit filed as provided by this subchapter shall be issued and served in the manner provided in Subchapter D, Chapter 3.

Added by Acts 1997, 75th Leg., ch. 7, § 1, eff. April 17, 1997.

§ 5.106. Court Order

(a) After notice and hearing, the court shall render an order the court deems just and equitable with respect to the sale, conveyance, or encumbrance of a separate property homestead.

(b) After hearing the evidence, the court, on terms the court deems just and equitable, shall render an order describing or defining the community property at issue that will be subject to the management, control, and disposition of each spouse during marriage.

(c) The court may:

(1) impose any conditions and restrictions the court deems necessary to protect the rights of the respondent;

(2) require a bond conditioned on the faithful administration of the property; and

(3) require payment to the registry of the court of all or a portion of the proceeds of the sale of the

property to be disbursed in accordance with the court's further directions.

Added by Acts 1997, 75th Leg., ch. 7, § 1, eff. April 17, 1997.

§ 5.107. Sale of Community Homestead for Spouse Judicially Declared Incapacitated

If the homestead is the community property of the spouses and one spouse has been judicially declared incapacitated, the competent spouse may sell, convey, or encumber the homestead without the joinder of the other spouse.

Added by Acts 1997, 75th Leg., ch. 7, § 1, eff. April 17, 1997.

§ 5.108. Remedies and Powers Cumulative

The remedies and the powers of a spouse provided by this subchapter are cumulative of the other rights, powers, and remedies afforded the spouses by law.

Added by Acts 1997, 75th Leg., ch. 7, § 1, eff. April 17, 1997.

SUBTITLE C. DISSOLUTION OF MARRIAGE

CHAPTER 6. SUIT FOR DISSOLUTION OF MARRIAGE

SUBCHAPTER A. GROUNDS FOR DIVORCE AND DEFENSES

§ 6.001. Insupportability

On the petition of either party to a marriage, the court may grant a divorce without regard to fault if the marriage has become insupportable because of discord or conflict of personalities that destroys the legitimate ends of the marital relationship and prevents any reasonable expectation of reconciliation.

Added by Acts 1997, 75th Leg., ch. 7, § 1, eff. April 17, 1997.

Section 4 of Acts 1997, 75th Leg., ch. 7, provides:

"The change in law made by this Act does not affect a proceeding under the Family Code pending on the effective date of this Act. A proceeding pending on the effective date of this Act is governed by the law in effect at the time the proceeding was commenced, and the former law is continued in effect for that purpose."

§ 6.002. Cruelty

The court may grant a divorce in favor of one spouse if the other spouse is guilty of cruel treatment toward the complaining spouse of a nature that renders further living together insupportable.

Added by Acts 1997, 75th Leg., ch. 7, § 1, eff. April 17, 1997.

§ 6.003. Adultery

The court may grant a divorce in favor of one spouse if the other spouse has committed adultery.

Added by Acts 1997, 75th Leg., ch. 7, § 1, eff. April 17, 1997.

§ 6.004. Conviction of Felony

(a) The court may grant a divorce in favor of one spouse if during the marriage the other spouse:

(1) has been convicted of a felony;

(2) has been imprisoned for at least one year in the state penitentiary, a federal penitentiary, or the penitentiary of another state; and

(3) has not been pardoned.

(b) The court may not grant a divorce under this section against a spouse who was convicted on the testimony of the other spouse.

Added by Acts 1997, 75th Leg., ch. 7, § 1, eff. April 17, 1997.

§ 6.005. Abandonment

The court may grant a divorce in favor of one spouse if the other spouse:

(1) left the complaining spouse with the intention of abandonment; and

(2) remained away for at least one year.

Added by Acts 1997, 75th Leg., ch. 7, § 1, eff. April 17, 1997.

§ 6.006. Living Apart

The court may grant a divorce in favor of either spouse if the spouses have lived apart without cohabitation for at least three years.

Added by Acts 1997, 75th Leg., ch. 7, § 1, eff. April 17, 1997.

§ 6.007. Confinement in Mental Hospital

The court may grant a divorce in favor of one spouse if at the time the suit is filed:

(1) the other spouse has been confined in a state mental hospital or private mental hospital, as defined in Section 571.003, Health and Safety Code, in this state or another state for at least three years; and

(2) it appears that the hospitalized spouse's mental disorder is of such a degree and nature that adjustment is unlikely or that, if adjustment occurs, a relapse is probable.

Added by Acts 1997, 75th Leg., ch. 7, § 1, eff. April 17, 1997.

§ 6.008. Defenses

(a) The defenses to a suit for divorce of recrimination and adultery are abolished.

(b) Condonation is a defense to a suit for divorce only if the court finds that there is a reasonable expectation of reconciliation.

Added by Acts 1997, 75th Leg., ch. 7, § 1, eff. April 17, 1997.

[Sections 6.009 to 6.100 reserved for expansion]

SUBCHAPTER B. GROUNDS FOR ANNULMENT

§ 6.101. Annulment of Marriage of Person Under Age 14

(a) The court may grant an annulment of a licensed marriage of a person under 14 years of age unless a court order has been obtained as provided in Subchapter B, Chapter 2.

(b) A petition for annulment under this section may be filed by a next friend for the benefit of a person under 14 years of age or on the petition of the parent or the judicially designated managing conservator or guardian, whether an individual, authorized agency, or court, of the person.

(c) A suit by a parent, managing conservator, or guardian of the person may be brought at any time before the person is 14 years of age.

(d) A suit under this section to annul the marriage of a person 14 years of age or older that was entered into before the person was 14 years of age is barred unless the suit is filed within the later of:

(1) 90 days after the date the petitioner knew or should have known of the marriage; or

(2) 90 days after the date of the 14th birthday of the underage party.

Added by Acts 1997, 75th Leg., ch. 7, § 1, eff. April 17, 1997. Amended by Acts 1997, 75th Leg., ch. 1362, § 3, eff. Sept. 1, 1997.

Section 5 of Acts 1997, 75th Leg., ch. 1362 provides:

"This Act takes effect only if S.B. 334, 75th Legislature, Regular Session, becomes law. If that legislation does not become law, this Act has no effect."

Senate Bill No. 334, Acts of the 75th Legislature, Regular Session, was enacted as chapter 7.

§ 6.102. Annulment of Marriage of Person Under Age 18

(a) The court may grant an annulment of a licensed or informal marriage of a person 14 years of age or older but under 18 years of age that occurred without parental consent or without a court order as provided by Subchapters B and E, Chapter 2.

(b) A petition for annulment under this section may be filed by:

(1) a next friend for the benefit of the underage party;

(2) a parent; or

(3) the judicially designated managing conservator or guardian of the person of the underage party, whether an individual, authorized agency, or court.

(c) A suit filed under this subsection by a next friend is barred unless it is filed within 90 days after the date of the marriage.

Added by Acts 1997, 75th Leg., ch. 7, § 1, eff. April 17, 1997.

§ 6.103. Underage Annulment Barred by Adulthood

A suit to annul a marriage may not be filed under Section 6.101 or 6.102 by a parent, managing conservator, or guardian of a person after the 18th birthday of the person.

Added by Acts 1997, 75th Leg., ch. 7, § 1, eff. April 17, 1997.

§ 6.104. Discretionary Annulment of Underage Marriage

(a) An annulment under Section 6.101 or 6.102 of a marriage may be granted at the discretion of the court sitting without a jury.

(b) In exercising its discretion, the court shall consider the pertinent facts concerning the welfare of the parties to the marriage, including whether the female is pregnant.

Added by Acts 1997, 75th Leg., ch. 7, § 1, eff. April 17, 1997.

§ 6.105. Under Influence of Alcohol or Narcotics

The court may grant an annulment of a marriage to a party to the marriage if:

(1) at the time of the marriage the petitioner was under the influence of alcoholic beverages or narcotics and as a result did not have the capacity to consent to the marriage; and

(2) the petitioner has not voluntarily cohabited with the other party to the marriage since the effects of the alcoholic beverages or narcotics ended.

Added by Acts 1997, 75th Leg., ch. 7, § 1, eff. April 17, 1997.

§ 6.106. Impotency

The court may grant an annulment of a marriage to a party to the marriage if:

(1) either party, for physical or mental reasons, was permanently impotent at the time of the marriage;

(2) the petitioner did not know of the impotency at the time of the marriage; and

(3) the petitioner has not voluntarily cohabited with the other party since learning of the impotency.

Added by Acts 1997, 75th Leg., ch. 7, § 1, eff. April 17, 1997.

§ 6.107. Fraud, Duress, or Force

The court may grant an annulment of a marriage to a party to the marriage if:

(1) the other party used fraud, duress, or force to induce the petitioner to enter into the marriage; and

(2) the petitioner has not voluntarily cohabited with the other party since learning of the fraud or since being released from the duress or force.

Added by Acts 1997, 75th Leg., ch. 7, § 1, eff. April 17, 1997.

§ 6.108. Mental Incapacity

(a) The court may grant an annulment of a marriage to a party to the marriage on the suit of the party or the party's guardian or next friend, if the court finds it to be in the party's best interest to be represented by a guardian or next friend, if:

(1) at the time of the marriage the petitioner did not have the mental capacity to consent to marriage or to understand the nature of the marriage ceremony because of a mental disease or defect; and

(2) since the marriage ceremony, the petitioner has not voluntarily cohabited with the other party during a period when the petitioner possessed the mental capacity to recognize the marriage relationship.

(b) The court may grant an annulment of a marriage to a party to the marriage if:

(1) at the time of the marriage the other party did not have the mental capacity to consent to marriage or to understand the nature of the marriage ceremony because of a mental disease or defect;

(2) at the time of the marriage the petitioner neither knew nor reasonably should have known of the mental disease or defect; and

(3) since the date the petitioner discovered or reasonably should have discovered the mental disease or defect, the petitioner has not voluntarily cohabited with the other party.

Added by Acts 1997, 75th Leg., ch. 7, § 1, eff. April 17, 1997.

§ 6.109. Concealed Divorce

(a) The court may grant an annulment of a marriage to a party to the marriage if:

(1) the other party was divorced from a third party within the 30-day period preceding the date of the marriage ceremony;

(2) at the time of the marriage ceremony the petitioner did not know, and a reasonably prudent person would not have known, of the divorce; and

(3) since the petitioner discovered or a reasonably prudent person would have discovered the fact of the divorce, the petitioner has not voluntarily cohabited with the other party.

(b) A suit may not be brought under this section after the first anniversary of the date of the marriage.

Added by Acts 1997, 75th Leg., ch. 7, § 1, eff. April 17, 1997.

§ 6.110. Marriage Less Than 72 Hours After Issuance of License

(a) The court may grant an annulment of a marriage to a party to the marriage if the marriage ceremony took place in violation of Section 2.204 during the 72-hour period immediately following the issuance of the marriage license.

(b) A suit may not be brought under this section after the 30th day after the date of the marriage.

Added by Acts 1997, 75th Leg., ch. 7, § 1, eff. April 17, 1997.

§ 6.111. Death of Party to Voidable Marriage

A marriage subject to annulment may not be challenged in a proceeding instituted after the death of either party to the marriage.

Added by Acts 1997, 75th Leg., ch. 7, § 1, eff. April 17, 1997.

[Sections 6.112 to 6.200 reserved for expansion]

SUBCHAPTER C. DECLARING A MARRIAGE VOID

§ 6.201. Consanguinity

A marriage is void if one party to the marriage is related to the other as:

(1) an ancestor or descendant, by blood or adoption;

(2) a brother or sister, of the whole or half blood or by adoption;

(3) a parent's brother or sister, of the whole or half blood or by adoption; or

(4) a son or daughter of a brother or sister, of the whole or half blood or by adoption.

Added by Acts 1997, 75th Leg., ch. 7, § 1, eff. April 17, 1997.

§ 6.202. Marriage During Existence of Prior Marriage

(a) A marriage is void if entered into when either party has an existing marriage to another person that has not been dissolved by legal action or terminated by the death of the other spouse.

(b) The later marriage that is void under this section becomes valid when the prior marriage is dissolved if, after the date of the dissolution, the parties have lived together as husband and wife and represented themselves to others as being married.

Added by Acts 1997, 75th Leg., ch. 7, § 1, eff. April 17, 1997.

§ 6.203. Certain Void Marriages Validated

Except for a marriage that would have been void under Section 6.201, a marriage that was entered into before January 1, 1970, in violation of the prohibitions of Article 496, Penal Code of Texas, 1925, is validated from the date the marriage commenced if the parties continued until January 1, 1970, to live together as husband and wife and to represent themselves to others as being married.

Added by Acts 1997, 75th Leg., ch. 7, § 1, eff. April 17, 1997.

[Sections 6.204 to 6.300 reserved for expansion]

SUBCHAPTER D. JURISDICTION, VENUE, AND RESIDENCE QUALIFICATIONS

§ 6.301. General Residency Rule for Divorce Suit

A suit for divorce may not be maintained in this state unless at the time the suit is filed either the petitioner or the respondent has been:

(1) a domiciliary of this state for the preceding six-month period; and

(2) a resident of the county in which the suit is filed for the preceding 90-day period.

Added by Acts 1997, 75th Leg., ch. 7, § 1, eff. April 17, 1997.

§ 6.302. Suit for Divorce by Nonresident Spouse

If one spouse has been a domiciliary of this state for at least the last six months, a spouse domiciled in another state or nation may file a suit for divorce in the county in which the domiciliary spouse resides at the time the petition is filed.

Added by Acts 1997, 75th Leg., ch. 7, § 1, eff. April 17, 1997.

§ 6.303. Absence on Public Service

Time spent by a Texas domiciliary outside this state or outside the county of residence of the domiciliary while in the service of the armed forces or other service of the United States or of this state is considered residence in this state and in that county.

Added by Acts 1997, 75th Leg., ch. 7, § 1, eff. April 17, 1997.

§ 6.304. Armed Forces Personnel Not Previously Residents

A person not previously a resident of this state who is serving in the armed forces of the United States and has been stationed at one or more military installations in this state for at least the last six months and at a military installation in a county of this state for at least the last 90 days is considered to be a Texas domiciliary and a resident of that county for those periods for the purpose of filing suit for dissolution of a marriage.

Added by Acts 1997, 75th Leg., ch. 7, § 1, eff. April 17, 1997.

§ 6.305. Acquiring Jurisdiction Over Nonresident Respondent

(a) If the petitioner in a suit for dissolution of a marriage is a resident or a domiciliary of this state at the time the suit for dissolution is filed, the court may exercise personal jurisdiction over the respondent or over the respondent's personal representative although the respondent is not a resident of this state if:

(1) this state is the last marital residence of the petitioner and the respondent and the suit is filed before the second anniversary of the date on which marital residence ended; or

(2) there is any basis consistent with the constitutions of this state and the United States for the exercise of the personal jurisdiction.

(b) A court acquiring jurisdiction under this section also acquires jurisdiction over the respondent in a suit affecting the parent-child relationship.

Added by Acts 1997, 75th Leg., ch. 7, § 1, eff. April 17, 1997.

§ 6.306. Jurisdiction to Annul Marriage

(a) A suit for annulment of a marriage may be maintained in this state only if the parties were married in this state or if either party is domiciled in this state.

(b) A suit for annulment is a suit in rem, affecting the status of the parties to the marriage.

Added by Acts 1997, 75th Leg., ch. 7, § 1, eff. April 17, 1997.

§ 6.307. Jurisdiction to Declare Marriage Void

(a) Either party to a marriage made void by this chapter may sue to have the marriage declared void, or the court may declare the marriage void in a collateral proceeding.

(b) The court may declare a marriage void only if:

(1) the purported marriage was contracted in this state; or

(2) either party is domiciled in this state.

(c) A suit to have a marriage declared void is a suit in rem, affecting the status of the parties to the purported marriage.

Added by Acts 1997, 75th Leg., ch. 7, § 1, eff. April 17, 1997.

§ 6.308. Exercising Partial Jurisdiction

(a) A court in which a suit for dissolution of a marriage is filed may exercise its jurisdiction over those portions of the suit for which it has authority.

(b) The court's authority to resolve the issues in controversy between the parties may be restricted because the court lacks:

(1) the required personal jurisdiction over a nonresident party in a suit for dissolution of the marriage;

(2) the required jurisdiction under Chapter 152; or

(3) the required jurisdiction under Chapter 159.

Added by Acts 1997, 75th Leg., ch. 7, § 1, eff. April 17, 1997.

[Sections 6.309 to 6.400 reserved for expansion]

SUBCHAPTER E. FILING SUIT

§ 6.401. Caption

(a) Pleadings in a suit for divorce or annulment shall be styled "In the Matter of the Marriage of ________ and ________."

(b) Pleadings in a suit to declare a marriage void shall be styled "A Suit To Declare Void the Marriage of ________ and ________."

Added by Acts 1997, 75th Leg., ch. 7, § 1, eff. April 17, 1997.

§ 6.402. Pleadings

(a) A petition in a suit for dissolution of a marriage is sufficient without the necessity of specifying the underlying evidentiary facts if the petition alleges the grounds relied on substantially in the language of the statute.

(b) Allegations of grounds for relief, matters of defense, or facts relied on for a temporary order that are stated in short and plain terms are not subject to special exceptions because of form or sufficiency.

(c) The court shall strike an allegation of evidentiary fact from the pleadings on the motion of a party or on the court's own motion.

Added by Acts 1997, 75th Leg., ch. 7, § 1, eff. April 17, 1997.

§ 6.403. Answer

The respondent in a suit for dissolution of a marriage is not required to answer on oath or affirmation.

Added by Acts 1997, 75th Leg., ch. 7, § 1, eff. April 17, 1997.

§ 6.4035. Waiver of Service

(a) A party to a suit for the dissolution of a marriage may waive the issuance or service of process after the suit is filed by filing with the clerk of the court in which the suit is filed the waiver of the party acknowledging receipt of a copy of the filed petition.

(b) The waiver must contain the mailing address of the party who executed the waiver.

(c) The waiver must be sworn but may not be sworn before an attorney in the suit.

(d) The Texas Rules of Civil Procedure do not apply to a waiver executed under this section.

Added by Acts 1997, 75th Leg., ch. 614, § 1, eff. Sept. 1, 1997.

Section 4(c) of Acts 1997, 75th Leg., ch. 614 provides:

"The change in law made by this Act regarding waiver of service of process in a suit for dissolution of a marriage applies only to a suit filed on or after the effective date of this Act. A suit filed before the effective date of this Act is governed by the law in effect on the date the suit was filed, and the former law is continued in effect for that purpose."

§ 6.404. Statement on Alternate Dispute Resolution

(a) A party to a proceeding under this title shall include in the first pleading filed by the party in the proceeding the following statement:

"I AM AWARE THAT IT IS THE POLICY OF THE STATE OF TEXAS TO PROMOTE THE AMICABLE AND NONJUDICIAL SETTLEMENT OF DISPUTES INVOLVING CHILDREN AND FAMILIES. I AM AWARE OF ALTERNATIVE DISPUTE RESOLUTION METHODS, INCLUDING MEDIATION. WHILE I RECOGNIZE THAT ALTERNATIVE DISPUTE RESOLUTION IS AN ALTERNATIVE TO AND NOT A SUBSTITUTE FOR A TRIAL AND THAT THIS CASE MAY BE TRIED IF IT IS NOT SETTLED, I REPRESENT TO THE COURT THAT I WILL ATTEMPT IN GOOD FAITH TO RESOLVE BEFORE FINAL TRIAL CONTESTED ISSUES IN THIS CASE BY ALTERNATIVE DISPUTE RESOLUTION WITHOUT THE NECESSITY OF COURT INTERVENTION."

(b) The statement prescribed by Subsection (a) must be printed in boldfaced type or capital letters and signed by the party.

(c) The statement prescribed by Subsection (a) is not required for:

(1) a pleading in which citation on all respondents entitled to service of citation is requested, issued, and given by publication;

(2) a motion or pleading that seeks a protective order as provided by Chapter 71; or

(3) a special appearance under Rule 120a, Texas Rules of Civil Procedure.

Added by Acts 1997, 75th Leg., ch. 7, § 1, eff. April 17, 1997. Amended by Acts 1997, 75th Leg., ch. 937, § 1, eff. Sept. 1, 1997.

Section 4 of Acts 1997, 75th Leg., ch. 937 provides:

"This Act takes effect September 1, 1997, and applies only to a suit filed under Title 1, Family Code, or Chapter 151, 153, 154, 156, 157, 160, 161, or 262, Family Code, on or after that date."

§ 6.405. Protective Order

(a) The petition in a suit for dissolution of a marriage must state whether a protective order under Chapter 71 is in effect or if an application for a protective order is pending with regard to the parties to the suit.

(b) The petitioner shall attach to the petition a copy of each protective order issued under Chapter 71 in which one of the parties to the suit was the applicant and the other party was the respondent without regard to the date of the order. If a copy of the protective order is not available at the time of filing, the petition must state that a copy of the order will be filed with the court before any hearing.

Added by Acts 1997, 75th Leg., ch. 7, § 1, eff. April 17, 1997.

§ 6.406. Mandatory Joinder of Suit Affecting Parent-Child Relationship

(a) The petition in a suit for dissolution of a marriage shall state whether there are children born or adopted of the marriage who are under 18 years of age or who are otherwise entitled to support as provided by Chapter 154.

(b) If the parties are parents of a child, as defined by Section 101.003, and the child is not under the continuing jurisdiction of another court as provided by Chapter 155, the suit for dissolution of a marriage must include a suit affecting the parent-child relationship under Title 5.

Added by Acts 1997, 75th Leg., ch. 7, § 1, eff. April 17, 1997.

§ 6.407. Transfer of Suit Affecting Parent-Child Relationship to Divorce Court

(a) If a suit affecting the parent-child relationship is pending at the time the suit for dissolution of a marriage is filed, the suit affecting the parent-child relationship shall be transferred as provided by Section 103.002 to the court in which the suit for dissolution is filed.

(b) If the parties are parents of a child, as defined by Section 101.003, and the child is under the continuing jurisdiction of another court under Chapter 155, either party to the suit for dissolution of a marriage may move that court for transfer of the suit affecting the parent-child relationship to the court having jurisdiction of the suit for dissolution. The court with continuing jurisdiction shall transfer the proceeding as provided by Chapter 155. On the transfer of the proceedings, the court with jurisdiction of the suit for dissolution of a marriage shall consolidate the two causes of action.

(c) After transfer of a suit affecting the parent-child relationship as provided in Chapter 155, the court with jurisdiction of the suit for dissolution of a marriage has jurisdiction to render an order in the suit affecting the parent-child relationship as provided by Title 5.

Added by Acts 1997, 75th Leg., ch. 7, § 1, eff. April 17, 1997.

§ 6.408. Service of Citation

Citation on the filing of an original petition in a suit for dissolution of a marriage shall be issued and served as in other civil cases. Citation may also be served on any other person who has or who may assert an interest in the suit for dissolution of the marriage.

Added by Acts 1997, 75th Leg., ch. 7, § 1, eff. April 17, 1997.

§ 6.409. Citation by Publication

(a) Citation in a suit for dissolution of a marriage may be by publication as in other civil cases, except that notice shall be published one time only.

(b) The notice shall be sufficient if given in substantially the following form:

"STATE OF TEXAS

To (name of person to be served with citation), and to all whom it may concern (if the name of any person to be served with citation is unknown), Respondent(s),

"You have been sued. You may employ an attorney. If you or your attorney do not file a written answer with the clerk who issued this citation by 10 a.m. on the Monday next following the expiration of 20 days after you were served this citation and petition, a default judgment may be taken against you. The petition of ________, Petitioner, was filed in the Court of ________ County, Texas, on the _____ day of ________, against ________, Respondent(s), numbered _____, and entitled 'In the Matter of Marriage of ________ and ________. The suit requests ________ (statement of relief sought).'

"The Court has authority in this suit to enter any judgment or decree dissolving the marriage and providing for the division of property that will be binding on you.

"Issued and given under my hand and seal of said Court at ________, Texas, this the _____ day of ________, _____.

" . . . .

Clerk of the _____ Court of

__________ County, Texas

By ______, Deputy."

(c) The form authorized in this section and the form authorized by Section 102.010 may be combined in appropriate situations.

(d) If the citation is for a suit in which a parent-child relationship does not exist, service by publication may be completed by posting the citation at the courthouse door for seven days in the county in which the suit is filed.

(e) If the petitioner or the petitioner's attorney of record makes an oath that no child presently under 18 years of age was born or adopted by the spouses and that no appreciable amount of property was accumulated by the spouses during the marriage, the court may dispense with the appointment of an attorney ad litem. In a case in which citation was by publication, a statement of the evidence, approved and signed by the judge, shall be filed with the papers of the suit as a part of the record.

Added by Acts 1997, 75th Leg., ch. 7, § 1, eff. April 17, 1997.

[Sections 6.410 to 6.500 reserved for expansion]

SUBCHAPTER F. TEMPORARY ORDERS

§ 6.501. Temporary Restraining Order

(a) After the filing of a suit for dissolution of a marriage, on the motion of a party or on the court's own motion, the court may grant a temporary restraining order without notice to the adverse party for the preservation of the property and for the protection of the parties as necessary, including an order prohibiting one or both parties from:

(1) intentionally communicating by telephone or in writing with the other party by use of vulgar, profane, obscene, or indecent language or in a coarse or offensive manner, with intent to annoy or alarm the other;

(2) threatening the other, by telephone or in writing, to take unlawful action against any person, intending by this action to annoy or alarm the other;

(3) placing a telephone call, anonymously, at an unreasonable hour, in an offensive and repetitious manner, or without a legitimate purpose of communication with the intent to annoy or alarm the other;

(4) intentionally, knowingly, or recklessly causing bodily injury to the other or to a child of either party;

(5) threatening the other or a child of either party with imminent bodily injury;

(6) intentionally, knowingly, or recklessly destroying, removing, concealing, encumbering, transferring, or otherwise harming or reducing the value of the property of the parties or either party with intent to obstruct the authority of the court to order a division of the estate of the parties in a manner that the court deems just and right, having due regard for the rights of each party and any children of the marriage;

(7) intentionally falsifying a writing or record relating to the property of either party;

(8) intentionally misrepresenting or refusing to disclose to the other party or to the court, on proper request, the existence, amount, or location of any property of the parties or either party;

(9) intentionally or knowingly damaging or destroying the tangible property of the parties or either party; or

(10) intentionally or knowingly tampering with the tangible property of the parties or either party and causing pecuniary loss or substantial inconvenience to the other.

(b) A temporary restraining order under this subchapter may not include a provision:

(1) the subject of which is a requirement, appointment, award, or other order listed in Section 886A, Texas Probate Code; or

(2) that:

(A) excludes a spouse from occupancy of the residence where that spouse is living except as provided in a protective order made in accordance with Title 4;

(B) prohibits a party from spending funds for reasonable and necessary living expenses; or

(C) prohibits a party from engaging in acts reasonable and necessary to conduct that party's usual business and occupation.

Added by Acts 1997, 75th Leg., ch. 7, § 1, eff. April 17, 1997.

§ 6.502. Temporary Injunction and Other Temporary Orders

While a suit for dissolution of a marriage is pending and on the motion of a party or on the court's own motion after notice and hearing, the court may render an appropriate order, including the granting of a temporary injunction for the preservation of the property and protection of the parties as deemed necessary and equitable and including an order directed to one or both parties:

(1) requiring a sworn inventory and appraisement of the real and personal property owned or claimed by the parties and specifying the form,

manner, and substance of the inventory and appraisal and list of debts and liabilities;

(2) requiring payments to be made for the support of either spouse;

(3) requiring the production of books, papers, documents, and tangible things by a party;

(4) ordering payment of reasonable attorney's fees and expenses;

(5) appointing a receiver for the preservation and protection of the property of the parties;

(6) awarding one spouse exclusive occupancy of the residence during the pendency of the case;

(7) prohibiting the parties, or either party, from spending funds beyond an amount the court determines to be for reasonable and necessary living expenses;

(8) awarding one spouse exclusive control of a party's usual business or occupation; or

(9) prohibiting an act described by Section 6.501(a).

Added by Acts 1997, 75th Leg., ch. 7, § 1, eff. April 17, 1997.

§ 6.503. Affidavit, Verified Pleading, and Bond Not Required

(a) A temporary restraining order or temporary injunction under this subchapter:

(1) may be granted without an affidavit or a verified pleading stating specific facts showing that immediate and irreparable injury, loss, or damage will result before notice can be served and a hearing can be held; and

(2) need not:

(A) define the injury or state why it is irreparable;

(B) state why the order was granted without notice; or

(C) include an order setting the suit for trial on the merits with respect to the ultimate relief sought.

(b) In a suit for dissolution of a marriage, the court may dispense with the issuance of a bond between the spouses in connection with temporary orders for the protection of the parties and their property.

Added by Acts 1997, 75th Leg., ch. 7, § 1, eff. April 17, 1997.

§ 6.504. Protective Orders

On the motion of a party to a suit for dissolution of a marriage, the court may render a protective order as provided by Subtitle B, Title 4.

Added by Acts 1997, 75th Leg., ch. 7, § 1, eff. April 17, 1997. Amended by Acts 1997, 75th Leg., ch. 1193, § 1, eff. Sept. 1, 1997.

Section 25(b), (c) of Acts 1997, 75th Leg., ch. 1193 provides:

"(b) The changes in law made by Sections 3 through 6 and Section 13 of this Act apply to a pending application for a protective order regardless of whether the application is filed before, on, or after the effective date of this Act.

"(c) Except as provided by Subsection (b) of this section, the change in law made by this Act applies only to an application for a protective order made on or after the effective date of this Act. An application for a protective order made before the effective date of this Act is governed by the law in effect on the date the application was made, and the former law is continued in effect for that purpose."

§ 6.505. Counseling

(a) While a divorce suit is pending, the court may direct the parties to counsel with a person named by the court.

(b) The person named by the court to counsel the parties shall submit a written report to the court and to the parties before the final hearing. In the report, the counselor shall give only an opinion as to whether there exists a reasonable expectation of reconciliation of the parties and, if so, whether further counseling would be beneficial. The sole purpose of the report is to aid the court in determining whether the suit for divorce should be continued pending further counseling.

(c) A copy of the report shall be furnished to each party.

(d) If the court believes that there is a reasonable expectation of the parties' reconciliation, the court may by written order continue the proceedings and direct the parties to a person named by the court for further counseling for a period fixed by the court not to exceed 60 days, subject to any terms, conditions, and limitations the court considers desirable. In ordering counseling, the court shall consider the circumstances of the parties, including the needs of the parties' family and the availability of counseling services. At the expiration of the period specified by the court, the counselor to whom the parties were directed shall report to the court whether the parties have complied with the court's order. Thereafter, the court shall proceed as in a divorce suit generally.

(e) If the court orders counseling under this section and the parties to the marriage are the parents of a child under 18 years of age born or adopted during the marriage, the counseling shall include counseling on issues that confront children who are the subject of a suit affecting the parent-child relationship.

Added by Acts 1997, 75th Leg., ch. 7, § 1, eff. April 17, 1997. Amended by Acts 1997, 75th Leg., ch. 1325, § 1, eff. Sept. 1, 1997.

Section 2 of Acts 1997, 75th Leg., ch. 1325 provides:

"This Act takes effect September 1, 1997, and applies only to a suit filed on or after that date. A suit filed before the effective date of this Act is governed by the law in effect at the time the suit was filed, and the former law is continued in effect for that purpose."

§ 6.506. Contempt

The violation of a temporary restraining order, temporary injunction, or other temporary order issued under this subchapter is punishable as contempt.

Added by Acts 1997, 75th Leg., ch. 7, § 1, eff. April 17, 1997.

§ 6.507. Interlocutory Appeal

An order under this subchapter, except an order appointing a receiver, is not subject to interlocutory appeal.

Added by Acts 1997, 75th Leg., ch. 7, § 1, eff. April 17, 1997.

[Sections 6.508 to 6.600 reserved for expansion]

SUBCHAPTER G. ALTERNATIVE DISPUTE RESOLUTION

§ 6.601. Arbitration Procedures

(a) On written agreement of the parties, the court may refer a suit for dissolution of a marriage to arbitration. The agreement must state whether the arbitration is binding or nonbinding.

(b) If the parties agree to binding arbitration, the court shall render an order reflecting the arbitrator's award.

Added by Acts 1997, 75th Leg., ch. 7, § 1, eff. April 17, 1997.

§ 6.602. Mediation Procedures

(a) On the written agreement of the parties or on the court's own motion, the court may refer a suit for dissolution of a marriage to mediation.

(b) A mediated settlement agreement is binding on the parties if the agreement:

(1) provides in a separate paragraph that the agreement is not subject to revocation;

(2) is signed by each party to the agreement; and

(3) is signed by the party's attorney, if any, who is present at the time the agreement is signed.

(c) If a mediated settlement agreement meets the requirements of this section, a party is entitled to judgment on the mediated settlement agreement notwithstanding Rule 11, Texas Rules of Civil Procedure, or another rule of law.

Added by Acts 1997, 75th Leg., ch. 7, § 1, eff. April 17, 1997.

[Sections 6.603 to 6.700 reserved for expansion]

SUBCHAPTER H. TRIAL AND APPEAL

§ 6.701. Failure to Answer

In a suit for divorce, the petition may not be taken as confessed if the respondent does not file an answer.

Added by Acts 1997, 75th Leg., ch. 7, § 1, eff. April 17, 1997.

§ 6.702. Waiting Period

(a) The court may not grant a divorce before the 60th day after the date the suit was filed. A decree rendered in violation of this subsection is not subject to collateral attack.

(b) A waiting period is not required before a court may grant an annulment or declare a marriage void other than as required in civil cases generally.

Added by Acts 1997, 75th Leg., ch. 7, § 1, eff. April 17, 1997.

§ 6.703. Jury

In a suit for dissolution of a marriage, either party may demand a jury trial unless the action is a suit to annul an underage marriage under Section 6.101 or 6.102.

Added by Acts 1997, 75th Leg., ch. 7, § 1, eff. April 17, 1997.

§ 6.704. Testimony of Husband or Wife

(a) In a suit for dissolution of a marriage, the husband and wife are competent witnesses for and against each other. A spouse may not be compelled to testify as to a matter that will incriminate the spouse.

(b) If the husband or wife testifies, the court or jury trying the case shall determine the credibility of the witness and the weight to be given the witness's testimony.

Added by Acts 1997, 75th Leg., ch. 7, § 1, eff. April 17, 1997.

§ 6.705. Testimony by Marriage Counselor

(a) The report by the person named by the court to counsel the parties to a suit for divorce may not be admitted as evidence in the suit.

(b) The person named by the court to counsel the parties is not competent to testify in any suit involving the parties or their children.

(c) The files, records, and other work products of the counselor are privileged and confidential for all purposes and may not be admitted as evidence in any suit involving the parties or their children.

Added by Acts 1997, 75th Leg., ch. 7, § 1, eff. April 17, 1997.

§ 6.706. Change of Name

(a) In a decree of divorce or annulment, the court shall change the name of a party specifically requesting the change to a name previously used by the party unless the court states in the decree a reason for denying the change of name.

(b) The court may not deny a change of name solely to keep the last name of family members the same.

(c) A change of name does not release a person from liability incurred by the person under a previous name or defeat a right the person held under a previous name.

(d) A person whose name is changed under this section may apply for a change of name certificate from the clerk of the court as provided by Section 45.106.

Added by Acts 1997, 75th Leg., ch. 7, § 1, eff. April 17, 1997.

§ 6.707. Transfers and Debts Pending Decree

(a) A transfer of real or personal community property or a debt incurred by a spouse while a suit for divorce or annulment is pending that subjects the other spouse or the community property to liability is void with respect to the other spouse if the transfer was made or the debt incurred with the intent to injure the rights of the other spouse.

(b) A transfer or debt is not void if the person dealing with the transferor or debtor spouse did not have notice of the intent to injure the rights of the other spouse.

(c) The spouse seeking to void a transfer or debt incurred while a suit for divorce or annulment is pending has the burden of proving that the person dealing with the transferor or debtor spouse had notice of the intent to injure the rights of the spouse seeking to void the transaction.

Added by Acts 1997, 75th Leg., ch. 7, § 1, eff. April 17, 1997.

§ 6.708. Costs

(a) In a suit for dissolution of a marriage, the court as it considers reasonable may award costs to a party. Costs may not be adjudged against a party against whom a divorce is granted for confinement in a mental hospital under Section 6.007.

(b) The expenses of counseling may be taxed as costs against either or both parties.

Added by Acts 1997, 75th Leg., ch. 7, § 1, eff. April 17, 1997.

§ 6.709. Temporary Orders During Appeal

(a) Not later than the 30th day after the date an appeal is perfected, on the motion of a party or on the court's own motion, after notice and hearing, the trial court may render a temporary order necessary for the preservation of the property and for the protection of the parties during the appeal, including an order to:

(1) require the support of either spouse;

(2) require the payment of reasonable attorney's fees and expenses;

(3) appoint a receiver for the preservation and protection of the property of the parties; or

(4) award one spouse exclusive occupancy of the parties' residence pending the appeal.

(b) The trial court retains jurisdiction to enforce a temporary order under this section unless the appellate court, on a proper showing, supersedes the trial court's order.

Added by Acts 1997, 75th Leg., ch. 7, § 1, eff. April 17, 1997.

§ 6.710. Copy of Decree

The clerk of the court shall mail a copy of the final decree of dissolution of a marriage to the party who waived service of process under Section 6.4035 by mailing the copy of the decree to the party at the mailing address contained in the waiver or to the office of the party's attorney of record.

Added by Acts 1997, 75th Leg., ch. 614, § 2, eff. Sept. 1, 1997.

Section 4(d) of Acts 1997, 75th Leg., ch. 614 provides:

"The change in law made by this Act regarding information that must be provided after issuance of a protective order applies only to a protective order rendered on or after the effective date of this Act. A protective order rendered before the effective date of this Act is governed by the law in effect on the date the order was rendered, and the former law is continued in effect for that purpose."

[Sections 6.711 to 6.800 reserved for expansion]

SUBCHAPTER I. REMARRIAGE

§ 6.801. Remarriage

(a) Except as otherwise provided by this subchapter, neither party to a divorce may marry a third party before the 31st day after the date the divorce is decreed.

(b) The former spouses may marry each other at any time.

Added by Acts 1997, 75th Leg., ch. 7, § 1, eff. April 17, 1997.

§ 6.802. Waiver of Prohibition Against Remarriage

For good cause shown the court may waive the prohibition against remarriage provided by this subchapter as to either or both spouses if a record of the proceedings is made and preserved or if findings of fact and conclusions of law are filed by the court.

Added by Acts 1997, 75th Leg., ch. 7, § 1, eff. April 17, 1997.

CHAPTER 7. AWARD OF MARITAL PROPERTY

Section

§ 7.001. General Rule of Property Division

In a decree of divorce or annulment, the court shall order a division of the estate of the parties in a manner that the court deems just and right, having due regard for the rights of each party and any children of the marriage.

Added by Acts 1997, 75th Leg., ch. 7, § 1, eff. April 17, 1997.

Section 4 of Acts 1997, 75th Leg., ch. 7, provides:

"The change in law made by this Act does not affect a proceeding under the Family Code pending on the effective date of this Act. A proceeding pending on the effective date of this Act is governed by the law in effect at the time the proceeding was commenced, and the former law is continued in effect for that purpose."

§ 7.002. Division of Property Under Special Circumstances

In addition to the division of the estate of the parties required by Section 7.001, in a decree of divorce or annulment the court shall order a division of the following real and personal property, wherever situated, in a manner that the court deems just and right, having due regard for the rights of each party and any children of the marriage:

(1) property that was acquired by either spouse while domiciled in another state and that would have been community property if the spouse who acquired the property had been domiciled in this state at the time of the acquisition; or

(2) property that was acquired by either spouse in exchange for real or personal property and that would have been community property if the spouse who acquired the property so exchanged had been domiciled in this state at the time of its acquisition.

Added by Acts 1997, 75th Leg., ch. 7, § 1, eff. April 17, 1997.

§ 7.003. Disposition of Retirement and Employment Benefits and Other Plans

In a decree of divorce or annulment, the court shall determine the rights of both spouses in a pension, retirement plan, annuity, individual retirement account, employee stock option plan, stock option, or other form of savings, bonus, profit-sharing, or other employer plan or financial plan of an employee or a participant, regardless of whether the person is self-employed, in the nature of compensation or savings.

Added by Acts 1997, 75th Leg., ch. 7, § 1, eff. April 17, 1997.

§ 7.004. Disposition of Rights in Insurance

In a decree of divorce or annulment, the court shall specifically divide or award the rights of each spouse in an insurance policy.

Added by Acts 1997, 75th Leg., ch. 7, § 1, eff. April 17, 1997.

§ 7.005. Insurance Coverage Not Specifically Awarded

(a) If in a decree of divorce or annulment the court does not specifically award all of the rights of the spouses in an insurance policy other than life insurance in effect at the time the decree is rendered, the policy remains in effect until the policy expires according to the policy's own terms.

(b) The proceeds of a valid claim under the policy are payable as follows:

(1) if the interest in the property insured was awarded solely to one former spouse by the decree, to that former spouse;

(2) if an interest in the property insured was awarded to each former spouse, to those former spouses in proportion to the interests awarded; or

(3) if the insurance coverage is directly related to the person of one of the former spouses, to that former spouse.

(c) The failure of either former spouse to change the endorsement on the policy to reflect the distribution of proceeds established by this section does not relieve the insurer of liability to pay the proceeds or any other obligation on the policy.

(d) This section does not affect the right of a former spouse to assert an ownership interest in an undivided life insurance policy, as provided by Subchapter D, Chapter 9.

Added by Acts 1997, 75th Leg., ch. 7, § 1, eff. April 17, 1997.

§ 7.006. Agreement Incident to Divorce or Annulment

(a) To promote amicable settlement of disputes in a suit for divorce or annulment, the spouses may enter into a written agreement concerning the division of the property and the liabilities of the spouses and maintenance of either spouse. The agreement may be revised or repudiated before rendition of the divorce or annulment unless the agreement is binding under another rule of law.

(b) If the court finds that the terms of the written agreement in a divorce or annulment are just and right, those terms are binding on the court. If the court approves the agreement, the court may set forth the agreement in full or incorporate the agreement by reference in the final decree.

(c) If the court finds that the terms of the written agreement in a divorce or annulment are not just and right, the court may request the spouses to submit a revised agreement or may set the case for a contested hearing.

Added by Acts 1997, 75th Leg., ch. 7, § 1, eff. April 17, 1997.

CHAPTER 8. MAINTENANCE

Section

§ 8.001. Definition

In this chapter, "maintenance" means an award in a suit for dissolution of a marriage of periodic payments from the future income of one spouse for the support of the other spouse.

Added by Acts 1997, 75th Leg., ch. 7, § 1, eff. April 17, 1997.

Section 4 of Acts 1997, 75th Leg., ch. 7, provides:

"The change in law made by this Act does not affect a proceeding under the Family Code pending on the effective date of this Act. A proceeding pending on the effective date of this Act is governed by the law in effect at the time the proceeding was commenced, and the former law is continued in effect for that purpose."

§ 8.002. Eligibility for Maintenance

In a suit for dissolution of a marriage or in a proceeding for maintenance in a court with personal jurisdiction over both former spouses following the dissolution of their marriage by a court that lacked personal jurisdiction over an absent spouse, the court may order maintenance for either spouse only if:

(1) the spouse from whom maintenance is requested was convicted of or received deferred adjudication for a criminal offense that also constitutes an act of family violence under Chapter 71 and the offense occurred:

(A) within two years before the date on which a suit for dissolution of the marriage is filed; or

(B) while the suit is pending; or

(2) the duration of the marriage was 10 years or longer, the spouse seeking maintenance lacks sufficient property, including property distributed to the spouse under this code, to provide for the spouse's minimum reasonable needs, as limited by Section 8.005, and the spouse seeking maintenance:

(A) is unable to support himself or herself through appropriate employment because of an incapacitating physical or mental disability;

(B) is the custodian of a child who requires substantial care and personal supervision because a physical or mental disability makes it necessary, taking into consideration the needs of the child, that the spouse not be employed outside the home; or

(C) clearly lacks earning ability in the labor market adequate to provide support for the spouse's minimum reasonable needs, as limited by Section 8.005.

Added by Acts 1997, 75th Leg., ch. 7, § 1, eff. April 17, 1997.

§ 8.003. Factors in Determining Maintenance

A court that determines that a spouse is eligible to receive maintenance under this chapter shall determine the nature, amount, duration, and manner of periodic payments by considering all relevant factors, including:

(1) the financial resources of the spouse seeking maintenance, including the community and separate property and liabilities apportioned to that spouse in the dissolution proceeding, and that spouse's ability to meet the spouse's needs independently;

(2) the education and employment skills of the spouses, the time necessary to acquire sufficient education or training to enable the spouse seeking maintenance to find appropriate employment, the availability of that education or training, and the feasibility of that education or training;

(3) the duration of the marriage;

(4) the age, employment history, earning ability, and physical and emotional condition of the spouse seeking maintenance;

(5) the ability of the spouse from whom maintenance is requested to meet that spouse's personal needs and to provide periodic child support payments, if applicable, while meeting the personal needs of the spouse seeking maintenance;

(6) acts by either spouse resulting in excessive or abnormal expenditures or destruction, concealment, or fraudulent disposition of community property, joint tenancy, or other property held in common;

(7) the comparative financial resources of the spouses, including medical, retirement, insurance, or other benefits, and the separate property of each spouse;

(8) the contribution by one spouse to the education, training, or increased earning power of the other spouse;

(9) the property brought to the marriage by either spouse;

(10) the contribution of a spouse as homemaker;

(11) marital misconduct of the spouse seeking maintenance; and

(12) the efforts of the spouse seeking maintenance to pursue available employment counseling as provided by Chapter 304, Labor Code.

Added by Acts 1997, 75th Leg., ch. 7, § 1, eff. April 17, 1997.

§ 8.004. Presumption

(a) Except as provided by Subsection (b), it is presumed that maintenance is not warranted unless the spouse seeking maintenance has exercised diligence in:

(1) seeking suitable employment; or

(2) developing the necessary skills to become self-supporting during a period of separation and during the time the suit for dissolution of the marriage is pending.

(b) This section does not apply to a spouse who is not able to satisfy the presumption in Subsection (a) because of an incapacitating physical or mental disability.

Added by Acts 1997, 75th Leg., ch. 7, § 1, eff. April 17, 1997.

§ 8.005. Duration of Maintenance Order

(a) Except as provided by Subsection (b), a court:

(1) may not order maintenance that remains in effect for more than three years after the date of the order; and

(2) shall limit the duration of a maintenance order to the shortest reasonable period that allows the spouse seeking maintenance to meet the spouse's minimum reasonable needs by obtaining appropriate employment or developing an appropriate skill, unless the ability of the spouse to provide for the spouse's minimum reasonable needs through employment is substantially or totally diminished because of:

(A) physical or mental disability;

(B) duties as the custodian of an infant or young child; or

(C) another compelling impediment to gainful employment.

(b) If a spouse seeking maintenance is unable to support himself or herself through appropriate employment because of an incapacitating physical or mental disability, the court may order maintenance for an indefinite period for as long as the disability continues. The court may order periodic review of its order, on the request of either party or on its own motion, to determine whether the disability is continuing. The continuation of spousal maintenance under these circumstances is subject to a motion to modify as provided by Section 8.008.

Added by Acts 1997, 75th Leg., ch. 7, § 1, eff. April 17, 1997.

§ 8.006. Amount of Maintenance

(a) A court may not order maintenance that requires a spouse to pay monthly more than the lesser of:

(1) $2,500; or

(2) 20 percent of the spouse's average monthly gross income.

(b) The court shall set the amount that a spouse is required to pay in a maintenance order to provide for the minimum reasonable needs of the spouse receiving the maintenance under the order, considering employment or property received in the dissolution of the marriage or otherwise owned by the spouse receiving the maintenance that contributes to the minimum reasonable needs of that spouse.

(c) Department of Veterans Affairs service-connected disability compensation, social security benefits and disability benefits, and workers' compensation benefits are excluded from maintenance.

Added by Acts 1997, 75th Leg., ch. 7, § 1, eff. April 17, 1997.

§ 8.007. Termination

(a) The obligation to pay future maintenance terminates on the death of either party or on the remarriage of the party receiving maintenance.

(b) After a hearing, the court shall terminate the maintenance order if the party receiving maintenance cohabits with another person in a permanent place of abode on a continuing, conjugal basis.

Added by Acts 1997, 75th Leg., ch. 7, § 1, eff. April 17, 1997.

§ 8.008. Modification of Maintenance Order

(a) The amount of maintenance specified in a court order or the portion of a decree that provides for the support of a former spouse may be reduced by the filing of a motion in the court that originally rendered the order. A party affected by the order or the portion of the decree to be modified may file the motion.

(b) Notice of a motion to modify maintenance and the response, if any, are governed by the Texas Rules of Civil Procedure applicable to the filing of an original lawsuit. Notice must be given by service of citation, and a response must be in the form of an answer due on or before 10 a.m. of the first Monday after 20 days after the date of service. A court shall set a hearing on the motion in the manner provided by Rule 245, Texas Rules of Civil Procedure.

(c) After a hearing, the court may modify an original or modified order or portion of a decree providing for maintenance on a proper showing of a material and substantial change in circumstances of either party. The court shall apply the modification only to payment accruing after the filing of the motion to modify.

(d) A loss of employment or circumstances that render a former spouse unable to support himself or herself through appropriate employment by reason of incapacitating physical or mental disability that occur after the divorce or annulment are not grounds for the institution of spousal maintenance for the benefit of the former spouse.

Added by Acts 1997, 75th Leg., ch. 7, § 1, eff. April 17, 1997.

§ 8.009. Enforcement of Maintenance Order

(a) The court may enforce by contempt the court's maintenance order or an agreement for the payment of maintenance voluntarily entered into between the parties and approved by the court.

(b) On the suit to enforce of a party entitled to receive maintenance payments, the court may render judgment against a defaulting party for an amount unpaid and owing after notice by service of citation, answer, if any, and a hearing finding that the defaulting party has failed or refused to carry out the terms of the order. The judgment may be enforced by any means available for the enforcement of judgment for debts.

(c) It is an affirmative defense to an allegation of contempt of court or the violation of a condition of probation requiring payment of court-ordered maintenance that the obligor:

(1) lacked the ability to provide maintenance in the amount ordered;

(2) lacked property that could be sold, mortgaged, or otherwise pledged to raise the funds needed;

(3) attempted unsuccessfully to borrow the needed funds; and

(4) did not know of a source from which the money could have been borrowed or otherwise legally obtained.

(d) The issue of the existence of an affirmative defense does not arise unless evidence is admitted supporting the defense. If the issue of the existence of an affirmative defense arises, an obligor must prove the affirmative defense by a preponderance of the evidence.

Added by Acts 1997, 75th Leg., ch. 7, § 1, eff. April 17, 1997.

§ 8.010. Putative Spouse

In a suit to declare a marriage void, a putative spouse who did not have knowledge of an existing impediment to a valid marriage may be awarded maintenance if otherwise qualified to receive maintenance under this chapter.

Added by Acts 1997, 75th Leg., ch. 7, § 1, eff. April 17, 1997.

§ 8.011. Unmarried Cohabitants

An order for maintenance is not authorized between unmarried cohabitants under any circumstances.

Added by Acts 1997, 75th Leg., ch. 7, § 1, eff. April 17, 1997.

CHAPTER 9. POST-DECREE PROCEEDINGS

SUBCHAPTER A. SUIT TO ENFORCE DECREE

Section

SUBCHAPTER A. SUIT TO ENFORCE DECREE

§ 9.001. Enforcement of Decree

(a) A party affected by a decree of divorce or annulment providing for a division of property as provided by Chapter 7 may request enforcement of that decree by filing a suit to enforce as provided by this chapter in the court that rendered the decree.

(b) Except as otherwise provided in this chapter, a suit to enforce shall be governed by the Texas Rules of Civil Procedure applicable to the filing of an original lawsuit.

(c) A party whose rights, duties, powers, or liabilities may be affected by the suit to enforce is entitled to receive notice by citation and shall be commanded to appear by filing a written answer. Thereafter, the proceedings shall be as in civil cases generally.

Added by Acts 1997, 75th Leg., ch. 7, § 1, eff. April 17, 1997.

Section 4 of the Acts 1997, 75th Leg., ch. 7, provides:

"The change in law made by this Act does not affect a proceeding under the Family Code pending on the effective date of this Act. A proceeding pending on the effective date of this Act is governed by the law in effect at the time the proceeding was commenced, and the former law is continued in effect for that purpose."

§ 9.002. Continuing Authority to Enforce Decree

The court that rendered the decree of divorce or annulment retains the power to enforce the property division as provided by Chapter 7.

Added by Acts 1997, 75th Leg., ch. 7, § 1, eff. April 17, 1997.

§ 9.003. Filing Deadlines

(a) A suit to enforce the division of tangible personal property in existence at the time of the decree of divorce or annulment must be filed before the second anniversary of the date the decree was signed or becomes final after appeal, whichever date is later, or the suit is barred.

(b) A suit to enforce the division of future property not in existence at the time of the original decree must be filed before the second anniversary of the date the right to the property matures or accrues or the decree becomes final, whichever date is later, or the suit is barred.

Added by Acts 1997, 75th Leg., ch. 7, § 1, eff. April 17, 1997.

§ 9.004. Applicability to Undivided Property

The procedures and limitations of this subchapter do not apply to existing property not divided on divorce, which are governed by Subchapter C and by the rules applicable to civil cases generally.

Added by Acts 1997, 75th Leg., ch. 7, § 1, eff. April 17, 1997.

§ 9.005. No Jury

A party may not demand a jury trial if the procedures to enforce a decree of divorce or annulment provided by this subchapter are invoked.

Added by Acts 1997, 75th Leg., ch. 7, § 1, eff. April 17, 1997.

§ 9.006. Enforcement of Division of Property

(a) Except as provided by this subchapter and by the Texas Rules of Civil Procedure, the court may render further orders to enforce the division of property made in the decree of divorce or annulment to assist in the implementation of or to clarify the prior order.

(b) The court may specify more precisely the manner of effecting the property division previously made if the substantive division of property is not altered or changed.

(c) An order of enforcement does not alter or affect the finality of the decree of divorce or annulment being enforced.

Added by Acts 1997, 75th Leg., ch. 7, § 1, eff. April 17, 1997.

§ 9.007. Limitation on Power of Court to Enforce

(a) A court may not amend, modify, alter, or change the division of property made or approved in the decree of divorce or annulment. An order to enforce the division is limited to an order to assist in the implementation of or to clarify the prior order and may not alter or change the substantive division of property.

(b) An order under this section that amends, modifies, alters, or changes the actual, substantive division of property made or approved in a final decree of divorce or annulment is beyond the power of the divorce court and is unenforceable.

(c) The power of the court to render further orders to assist in the implementation of or to clarify the property division is abated while an appellate proceeding is pending.

Added by Acts 1997, 75th Leg., ch. 7, § 1, eff. April 17, 1997.

§ 9.008. Clarification Order

(a) On the request of a party or on the court's own motion, the court may render a clarifying order before a motion for contempt is made or heard, in conjunction with a motion for contempt or on denial of a motion for contempt.

(b) On a finding by the court that the original form of the division of property is not specific enough to be enforceable by contempt, the court may render a clarifying order setting forth specific terms to enforce compliance with the original division of property.

(c) The court may not give retroactive effect to a clarifying order.

(d) The court shall provide a reasonable time for compliance before enforcing a clarifying order by contempt or in another manner.

Added by Acts 1997, 75th Leg., ch. 7, § 1, eff. April 17, 1997.

§ 9.009. Delivery of Property

To enforce the division of property made in a decree of divorce or annulment, the court may make an order to deliver the specific existing property awarded, without regard to whether the property is of especial value, including an award of an existing sum of money or its equivalent.

Added by Acts 1997, 75th Leg., ch. 7, § 1, eff. April 17, 1997.

§ 9.010. Reduction to Money Judgment

(a) If a party fails to comply with a decree of divorce or annulment and delivery of property awarded in the decree is no longer an adequate remedy, the court may render a money judgment for the damages caused by that failure to comply.

(b) If a party did not receive payments of money as awarded in the decree of divorce or annulment, the court may render judgment against a defaulting party for the amount of unpaid payments to which the party is entitled.

(c) The remedy of a reduction to money judgment is in addition to the other remedies provided by law.

(d) A money judgment rendered under this section may be enforced by any means available for the enforcement of judgment for debt.

Added by Acts 1997, 75th Leg., ch. 7, § 1, eff. April 17, 1997.

§ 9.011. Right to Future Property

(a) The court may, by any remedy provided by this chapter, enforce an award of the right to receive installment payments or a lump-sum payment due on the maturation of an existing vested or nonvested right to be paid in the future.

(b) The subsequent actual receipt by the non-owning party of property awarded to the owner in a decree of divorce or annulment creates a fiduciary obligation in favor of the owner and imposes a constructive trust on the property for the benefit of the owner.

Added by Acts 1997, 75th Leg., ch. 7, § 1, eff. April 17, 1997.

§ 9.012. Contempt

(a) The court may enforce by contempt an order requiring delivery of specific property or an award of a right to future property.

(b) The court may not enforce by contempt an award in a decree of divorce or annulment of a sum of money payable in a lump sum or in future installment payments in the nature of debt, except for:

(1) a sum of money in existence at the time the decree was rendered; or

(2) a matured right to future payments as provided by Section 9.011.

(c) This subchapter does not detract from or limit the general power of a court to enforce an order of the court by appropriate means.

Added by Acts 1997, 75th Leg., ch. 7, § 1, eff. April 17, 1997.

§ 9.013. Costs

The court may award costs in a proceeding to enforce a property division under this subchapter as in other civil cases.

Added by Acts 1997, 75th Leg., ch. 7, § 1, eff. April 17, 1997.

§ 9.014. Attorney's Fees

The court may award reasonable attorney's fees as costs in a proceeding under this subchapter. The court may order the attorney's fees to be paid directly to the attorney, who may enforce the order for fees in the attorney's own name by any means available for the enforcement of a judgment for debt.

Added by Acts 1997, 75th Leg., ch. 7, § 1, eff. April 17, 1997.

[Sections 9.015 to 9.100 reserved for expansion]

SUBCHAPTER B. POST-DECREE QUALIFIED DOMESTIC RELATIONS ORDER

§ 9.101. Jurisdiction for Qualified Domestic Relations Order

(a) Notwithstanding any other provision of this chapter, the court that rendered a final decree of divorce or annulment or another final order dividing property under this title retains continuing, exclusive jurisdiction to render an enforceable qualified domestic relations order or similar order permitting payment of pension, retirement plan, or other employee benefits divisible under the law of this state or of the United States to an alternate payee or other lawful payee.

(b) Unless prohibited by federal law, a suit seeking a qualified domestic relations order or similar order under this section applies to a previously divided pension, retirement plan, or other employee benefit divisible under the law of this state or of the United States, whether the plan or benefit is private, state, or federal.

Added by Acts 1997, 75th Leg., ch. 7, § 1, eff. April 17, 1997.

§ 9.102. Procedure

(a) A party to a decree of divorce or annulment may petition the court for a qualified domestic relations order or similar order.

(b) Except as otherwise provided by this code, a petition under this subchapter is governed by the Texas Rules of Civil Procedure that apply to the filing of an original lawsuit.

(c) Each party whose rights may be affected by the petition is entitled to receive notice by citation and shall be commanded to appear by filing a written answer.

(d) The proceedings shall be conducted in the same manner as civil cases generally.

Added by Acts 1997, 75th Leg., ch. 7, § 1, eff. April 17, 1997.

§ 9.103. Prior Failure to Render Qualified Domestic Relations Order

A party may petition a court to render a qualified domestic relations order or similar order if the court that rendered a final decree of divorce or annulment or another final order dividing property under this chapter did not provide a qualified domestic relations order or similar order permitting payment of benefits to an alternate payee or other lawful payee.

Added by Acts 1997, 75th Leg., ch. 7, § 1, eff. April 17, 1997.

§ 9.104. Defective Prior Domestic Relations Order

If a plan administrator or other person acting in an equivalent capacity determines that a domestic relations order does not satisfy the requirements of a qualified domestic relations order or similar order, the court retains continuing, exclusive jurisdiction over the parties and their property to the extent necessary to render a qualified domestic relations order.

Added by Acts 1997, 75th Leg., ch. 7, § 1, eff. April 17, 1997.

§ 9.105. Liberal Construction

The court shall liberally construe this subchapter to effect payment of retirement benefits that were divided by a previous decree that failed to contain a qualified domestic relations order or similar order or that contained an order that failed to meet the requirements of a qualified domestic relations order or similar order.

Added by Acts 1997, 75th Leg., ch. 7, § 1, eff. April 17, 1997.

[Sections 9.106 to 9.200 reserved for expansion]

SUBCHAPTER C. POST-DECREE DIVISION OF PROPERTY

§ 9.201. Procedure for Division of Certain Property Not Divided on Divorce or Annulment

(a) Either former spouse may file a suit as provided by this subchapter to divide property not divided or awarded to a spouse in a final decree of divorce or annulment.

(b) Except as otherwise provided by this subchapter, the suit is governed by the Texas Rules of Civil

Procedure applicable to the filing of an original lawsuit.

Added by Acts 1997, 75th Leg., ch. 7, § 1, eff. April 17, 1997.

§ 9.202. Limitations

(a) A suit under this subchapter must be filed before the second anniversary of the date a former spouse unequivocally repudiates the existence of the ownership interest of the other former spouse and communicates that repudiation to the other former spouse.

(b) The two-year limitations period is tolled for the period that a court of this state does not have jurisdiction over the former spouses or over the property.

Added by Acts 1997, 75th Leg., ch. 7, § 1, eff. April 17, 1997.

§ 9.203. Division of Undivided Assets When Prior Court Had Jurisdiction

(a) If a court of this state failed to dispose of property subject to division in a final decree of divorce or annulment even though the court had jurisdiction over the spouses or over the property, the court shall divide the property in a manner that the court deems just and right, having due regard for the rights of each party and any children of the marriage.

(b) If a final decree of divorce or annulment rendered by a court in another state failed to dispose of property subject to division under the law of that state even though the court had jurisdiction to do so, a court of this state shall apply the law of the other state regarding undivided property as required by Section 1, Article IV, United States Constitution (the full faith and credit clause), and enabling federal statutes.

Added by Acts 1997, 75th Leg., ch. 7, § 1, eff. April 17, 1997.

§ 9.204. Division of Undivided Assets When Prior Court Lacked Jurisdiction

(a) If a court of this state failed to dispose of property subject to division in a final decree of divorce or annulment because the court lacked jurisdiction over a spouse or the property, and if that court subsequently acquires the requisite jurisdiction, that court may divide the property in a manner that the court deems just and right, having due regard for the rights of each party and any children of the marriage.

(b) If a final decree of divorce or annulment rendered by a court in another state failed to dispose of property subject to division under the law of that state because the court lacked jurisdiction over a spouse or the property, and if a court of this state subsequently acquires the requisite jurisdiction over the former spouses or over the property, the court in this state may divide the property in a manner that the court deems just and right, having due regard for the rights of each party and any children of the marriage.

Added by Acts 1997, 75th Leg., ch. 7, § 1, eff. April 17, 1997.

§ 9.205. Attorney's Fees

In a proceeding to divide property previously undivided in a decree of divorce or annulment as provided by this subchapter, the court may award reasonable attorney's fees as costs. The court may order the attorney's fees to be paid directly to the attorney, who may enforce the order in the attorney's own name by any means available for the enforcement of a judgment for debt.

Added by Acts 1997, 75th Leg., ch. 7, § 1, eff. April 17, 1997.

[Sections 9.206 to 9.300 reserved for expansion]

SUBCHAPTER D. DISPOSITION OF UNDIVIDED BENEFICIAL INTEREST

§ 9.301. Pre-Decree Designation of Ex-Spouse as Beneficiary of Life Insurance

(a) If a decree of divorce or annulment is rendered after an insured has designated the insured's spouse as a beneficiary under a life insurance policy in force at the time of rendition, a provision in the policy in favor of the insured's former spouse is not effective unless:

(1) the decree designates the insured's former spouse as the beneficiary;

(2) the insured redesignates the former spouse as the beneficiary after rendition of the decree; or

(3) the former spouse is designated to receive the proceeds in trust for, on behalf of, or for the benefit of a child or a dependent of either former spouse.

(b) If a designation is not effective under Subsection (a), the proceeds of the policy are payable to the named alternative beneficiary or, if there is not a named alternative beneficiary, to the estate of the insured.

(c) An insurer who pays the proceeds of a life insurance policy issued by the insurer to the beneficiary under a designation that is not effective under Subsection (a) is liable for payment of the proceeds to the person or estate provided by Subsection (b) only if:

(1) before payment of the proceeds to the designated beneficiary, the insurer receives written notice at the home office of the insurer from an

interested person that the designation is not effective under Subsection (a); and

(2) the insurer has not interpleaded the proceeds into the registry of a court of competent jurisdiction in accordance with the Texas Rules of Civil Procedure.

Added by Acts 1997, 75th Leg., ch. 7, § 1, eff. April 17, 1997.

§ 9.302. Pre-Decree Designation of Ex-Spouse as Beneficiary in Retirement Benefits and Other Financial Plans

(a) If a decree of divorce or annulment is rendered after a spouse, acting in the capacity of a participant, annuitant, or account holder, has designated the other spouse as a beneficiary under an individual retirement account, employee stock option plan, stock option, or other form of savings, bonus, profit-sharing, or other employer plan or financial plan of an employee or a participant in force at the time of rendition, the designating provision in the plan in favor of the other former spouse is not effective unless:

(1) the decree designates the other former spouse as the beneficiary;

(2) the designating former spouse redesignates the other former spouse as the beneficiary after rendition of the decree; or

(3) the other former spouse is designated to receive the proceeds or benefits in trust for, on behalf of, or for the benefit of a child or dependent of either former spouse.

(b) If a designation is not effective under Subsection (a), the benefits or proceeds are payable to the named alternative beneficiary or, if there is not a named alternative beneficiary, to the designating former spouse.

(c) A business entity, employer, pension trust, insurer, financial institution, or other person obligated to pay retirement benefits or proceeds of a financial plan covered by this section who pays the benefits or proceeds to the beneficiary under a designation of the other former spouse that is not effective under Subsection (a) is liable for payment of the benefits or proceeds to the person provided by Subsection (b) only if:

(1) before payment of the benefits or proceeds to the designated beneficiary, the payor receives written notice at the home office or principal office of the payor from an interested person that the designation of the beneficiary or fiduciary is not effective under Subsection (a); and

(2) the payor has not interpleaded the benefits or proceeds into the registry of a court of competent jurisdiction in accordance with the Texas Rules of Civil Procedure.

(d) This section does not affect the right of a former spouse to assert an ownership interest in an undivided pension, retirement, annuity, or other financial plan described by this section as provided by this subchapter.

(e) This section does not apply to the disposition of a beneficial interest in a retirement benefit or other financial plan of a public retirement system as defined by Section 802.001, Government Code.

Added by Acts 1997, 75th Leg., ch. 7, § 1, eff. April 17, 1997.

TITLE 2. CHILD IN RELATION TO THE FAMILY

DISPOSITION TABLE

Showing where provisions of former Title 2 of the Family Code are covered in Titles 2 and 5 following amendment by Acts 1995, 74th Leg., ch. 20.

Former Section	New Section
11.01	101.001
(1)	101.003
(2)	101.008
(3)	101.024
(4)	101.025
(5)	101.032
(6)	101.019
(7)	101.002
(8)	101.014
(9)	101.022
(10)	101.021
(11)	101.018
11.02	102.001
11.03(a)	102.003
(b), (c)	102.004
(d)	102.005
(g), (h)	102.006
(i)	102.007
11.04	103.001
11.05(a)	155.001
	155.002
(b)	155.001
	155.004
(c)	155.103
	155.004
(d), (e)	155.001
(f)	155.004
(g)	155.003
	155.004
	156.001
(h)	155.005
	155.205
11.051	102.011
11.06(a)	103.002

Former Section	New Section
(b)	155.201
	to
	155.204
(c)	103.002
	155.201
(d)	155.202
(f) to (i)	155.204
(j)	155.205
	155.207
(k)	155.206
(*l*)	110.005
(m)	155.207
11.061	155.301
(a), (b)	103.003
11.07(c)	102.013
11.071(a), (b)	155.101
(c)	155.104
(d)	155.102
11.08(a), (b)	102.008
(d)	162.002
(e)	161.101
11.09(a), (b), (c)	102.009
(d), (e)	102.010
(f)	102.009
11.10(a), (b)(1)	107.001
(b)(2)	107.002
(c), (d)	107.002
(e)	107.003
11.101	107.004
11.11(a)	156.006
	105.001
(b) to (d)	105.001
(e), (f)	109.001
(g)	105.001
	109.001
11.12	107.005
11.13	105.002
11.14(a), (b)	105.003
(c)	107.005
(d)	105.003
(e)	104.001
(f), (g)	105.003
(h)	105.004
	161.202
(j)	160.108
11.15(a)	105.005
(c)	101.007
11.155	105.006
11.16	161.209
	162.019
11.17(a)	108.001
(b)	108.002
	108.003
	108.004
	108.005
	162.023
	162.024
(c)	108.006
(d)	162.022
	108.001
(e)	108.007
(f)	161.210
	162.021
11.171	108.006
11.18(a)	106.001
	106.002
(b)	110.003
(c)	107.005
11.181	231.211
11.19	109.002
11.191	109.003
11.20	264.009
11.21(a), (b)	104.002
(c)	104.004
(d)	104.003
(e)	104.005
11.22(a), (b)	157.421
(c)	157.423
(d)	157.424
(e)	157.425
(f)	157.426
(g)	157.421
(h), (i)	157.422
(j)	110.001
11.51	152.001
11.52	152.002
11.53	152.003
11.54	152.004
11.55	152.005
11.56	152.006
11.57	152.007
11.58	152.008
11.59	152.009
11.60	152.010
11.61	152.011
11.62	152.012
11.63	152.013
11.64	152.014
11.65	152.015
11.66	152.016
11.67	152.017
11.68	152.018
11.69	152.019
11.70	152.020
11.71	152.021
11.72	152.022
11.73	152.023
11.74	152.024
11.75	152.025
12.01	151.001
12.02	151.002
12.03	151.101
12.03A	151.102
12.03B	151.103
12.04	151.003
12.05	151.004
12.06(a), (b)	160.101
(c)	160.110
13.01	160.002
13.015	231.112
13.02(a)	160.102
	160.103
(b)	160.107
(d)	160.102
13.03	160.104
13.04(a) to (e)	160.105
(f)	160.004
(g)	160.105

CHILD IN RELATION TO THE FAMILY

Former Section	New Section
13.05	160.106
13.06(a), (b)	160.109
(c)	160.110
	160.109
(d)	160.110
(e) to (g)	160.109
13.07	160.003
13.08, 13.09	160.006
13.21(a), (b)	160.201
(c)	160.205
(d)	160.201
13.22	160.202
(c)	160.204
13.23	160.203
13.24	160.206
13.42(a)	160.005
13.43(b), (c)	108.008
(e), (f)	108.009
13.44	160.007
14.01(a)	153.005
	153.372
(b)(1)	153.131
(b)(2)	153.373
(c)(1)	153.003
(c)(2)	153.004
(d)	153.374
(e)	153.375
14.02(a)	153.071
	153.073
(b)	153.072
(b)(1)(A) to (C)	153.074
(b)(1)(D)	153.073
(b)(2)	153.073
(b)(3)	153.132
(c)	153.371
(d)	161.104
14.021(a)	153.001
(b)	101.016
	153.135
	153.136
(c), (d)	153.133
(e), (f)	153.134
(g)	153.138
	156.401
	156.104
(h)	153.138
	153.004
(i)	153.139
(j)	153.372
14.03(a)	153.006
(b)	153.192
(c)	153.006
	153.192
(d)	153.004
	153.075
	153.191
	153.193
(e)	153.432
	153.433
(e)(3)	153.004
(f)	153.432
(g)	153.434
(h)	153.010
(i)	153.011

Former Section	New Section
(j)	111.001
14.032(a)	153.251
(b)	153.254
(c)	153.256
(d)	153.003
(e), (f)	111.002
14.033(a)(1)	101.028
(a)(2)	101.029
(b)	153.311
(c)	153.312
(d)	153.315
(e)(1) to (3)	153.314
(4) to (7)	153.312
(8) to (10)	153.314
(f)(1)	153.313
(f)(2)	153.314
(3) to (6)	153.313
(g)	153.316
(h)	153.257
(i)	153.317
(k)	153.252
	153.258
(*l*)	105.001
(m)	153.253
(n)	153.255
(*o*)	156.302
(p)	111.003
14.034	153.137
14.04(a), (b)	153.376
(c)	153.012
	153.377
14.045	105.007
14.05(a)	154.001
	154.002
	154.003
(b)	154.001
(c)	154.005
(d)	154.001
	154.006
(e)	154.007
	158.001
(h), (i)	111.001
(j)	154.122
14.0501	154.241
14.0502	154.242
14.0503	154.004
14.0504	154.243
14.051(a)	154.301
(b)	154.302
(c)	154.303
(d) to (f)	154.305
(g)	154.306
(i)	154.304
14.052(a)	154.121
(c), (d)	111.002
14.053(a)	154.061
(b)	154.062
(c)	154.065
(d)	154.064
	154.183
(e)	154.067
(f)	154.066
(g)	154.063
(h)	154.061

Former Section	New Section
(i)	154.010
(k)	154.068
(*l*)	154.131
14.054	154.123
14.055(a)	154.122
	154.125
(b)	154.125
(c)	154.126
(d)	154.127
(e)	105.001
(f) to (h)	154.128
(i)	154.070
(j)	154.129
14.056(a)	156.402
(b)	156.402
	156.403
(c)	156.404
	156.405
(d)	156.406
14.057	154.130
14.058	111.003
14.06	153.007
	154.124
14.061(a)	154.008
	154.181
	154.182
(b)	154.182
(c)	154.183
(d)	101.015
(e), (f)	154.185
(g)	154.186
(h) to (k)	154.187
(*l*)	154.188
(m)	154.189
	154.190
(n), (*o*)	154.191
(p)	154.187
(q)	154.192
(r)	154.184
14.062	154.009
14.07(a)	153.002
	153.008
(b)	153.431
(c)	153.009
14.08(a)	156.002
(b)	156.003
	156.004
(c)(1)	156.101
(c)(2)	156.401
(c)(3)	156.301
(c)(3)(C)	156.303
(c)(4)	156.103
(c)(5)	156.104
(d), (e)	156.102
(g)	156.006
(h)	156.407
(i)	156.105
14.081(b)	156.201
(c)	156.202
(d)	156.203
14.082	156.005
14.10(a), (b)	157.372
(c)	157.373
(d)	157.374

Former Section	New Section
(e)	157.375
(f)	157.376
14.13	110.002
14.30(a)(1)	101.011
(a)(2)	101.010
(a)(3)	101.012
(b)	157.001
(d)	157.003
14.31	157.001
14.311(a)	157.002
(b), (c)	157.162
	157.002
(d), (e)	157.002
(f)	157.064
14.312	157.002
14.313(a)	157.003
14.314(a)	157.061
	157.062
(b)	157.062
(c)	157.063
	157.065
(d)	157.065
(e)	157.066
14.315	157.062
14.316	158.201
14.317(a)	157.114
	157.115
(b)	157.066
(d)	157.102
(e)	110.001
	157.103
14.318(a)	157.101
(b)	157.104
(c)	157.105
(d)	157.106
(e)	157.107
(f)	157.108
14.32(b)	157.161
(d)	157.061
(f)	157.163
14.33(a)	157.166
(b)	157.164
(c)	157.167
(d)	157.162
14.34(a)	157.265
(b)	157.266
(c)	157.267
	157.268
14.40(a)	157.001
(b)	157.005
(c)	157.008
(e)(1)	157.165
	157.211
(e)(2)	157.212
(e)(3)	157.213
(e)(4)	157.214
(e)(5)	157.215
(e)(6)	157.216
(f)	157.113
(g)	157.008
(h)	157.006
14.41(a)	157.261
	157.263
	157.264

Former Section	New Section
	158.005
	158.311
(b)	157.005
(c)	157.008
(d)	157.262
(e)	157.263
14.42(a)	157.109
(b), (c)	157.110
(d)	157.112
(e)	157.111
(f)	157.110
14.43(a)	158.001
	158.311
(a)(2), (3)	158.002
(b)	158.006
(d)	158.003
	to
	158.005
	158.007
(e)	158.103
(f)	158.009
(g)	158.104
	158.105
(h)	158.105
	158.010
	158.202
	158.203
(i)	158.204
(j)	158.205
(k)	158.008
(*l*)	158.206
	to
	158.208
(m)	158.209
(n)	158.210
(*o*)	158.211
(p)	158.106
(q)	158.401
	to
	158.403
(r)	158.102
14.44(a)	158.301
	158.306
	158.311
(b)	158.302
(c)	158.307
	158.308
(d)	158.304
	158.309
	158.310
(e)	158.317
(g)	158.305
(h)	158.303
14.45(a)	158.312
	158.313
	158.316
(b)	158.314
(c)	158.315
(f)	158.401
(g)	158.106
(h)	110.004
14.50(a)	157.001
(b)	157.004
(c)	157.007

Former Section	New Section
(d)(1)	157.211
(d)(2)	157.212
(d)(3)	157.213
(d)(4)	157.214
(d)(5)	157.215
(d)(6)	157.216
(d)(7)	157.217
14.51(a)	157.109
(b), (c)	157.110
(d)	157.112
(e)	157.111
(f)	157.110
14.52	231.006
14.80(2)	101.034
(3)	101.004
(4)	101.006
(5)	101.020
(7)	101.005
14.801	231.429
14.802(a)	231.401
	231.402
(b)	231.405
(c)	231.408
(d)	231.413
(e), (f)	231.407
(g)	231.403
	231.404
14.803(a)	231.405
(b), (c)	231.406
14.804(a)	231.409
(b), (c)	231.410
(d)	231.411
(e)	231.412
(f)	231.414
(g)	231.418
(h) to (j)	231.415
(k)	231.416
14.805	231.417
14.806(a)	231.419
(b)	231.420
(c), (d)	231.421
	231.422
(e)	231.422
14.807(b), (c)	231.424
(d), (e)	231.423
(f)	231.425
(g)	231.426
(h), (i)	231.427
14.808	231.428
14.809	231.430
14.81	201.110
14.82(a), (b)	201.101
(c)	201.102
(d)	201.103
(e)	201.102
(f), (g)	201.104
(h)	201.111
14.83(a), (b)	201.105
(c)	201.106
(d), (e)	201.107
14.84	201.108
14.85	201.109
14.86	231.003
14.87	231.004

FAMILY CODE

Former Section	New Section
14.91	202.001
14.92	202.002
14.93	202.003
14.94	202.004
14.95	202.005
14.971(a), (b)	157.311
(c), (d)	157.312
14.972(a)	157.316
(b)	157.317
(e)	157.318
14.973	157.313
14.974	157.314
14.975	157.315
14.976(a), (b)	157.319
(c)	157.320
14.977	157.320
14.978	157.322
14.979	157.323
14.980	157.321
14.981	157.324
14.982	157.325
14.983	157.326
15.01	161.005
15.02(a)	161.001
15.021(a)	161.102
(b)	161.201
(c)	161.102
15.022	161.006
15.023	161.002
15.024	161.003
15.025(a), (b)	161.004
15.03	161.103
15.04	161.105
15.041(a) to (d)	161.106
(e)	161.204
15.05(a)	161.206
(b)	161.207
(c)	161.205
15.051(a)(1)	101.027
(2), (3)	161.107
(b)	161.208
(c)	161.107
15.06	161.203
15.07	161.206
16.01, 16.02	162.001
16.03(a)	162.002
(b) to (d)	162.001
16.031(a)	162.003
(b)	162.004
16.032(a)	162.005
(b) to (e)	162.007
(f)	162.005
(g)	162.006
(h)	162.008
(i) to (k)	162.006
(*l*)	162.005
(n)	162.006
16.04	162.009
16.05	162.010
16.06	162.011
16.07	162.014
16.08	162.016
16.081	162.015
16.09(a)	162.017
(b), (c)	162.018
(d) to (f)	162.017
16.10	162.020
16.11	162.013
16.12	162.012
16.51	162.501
	162.502
16.52	162.504
16.53	162.503
16.54	162.505
16.55	162.507
17.001	101.009
17.01	262.001
17.011	262.006
17.02(a)	262.102
(b)	262.101
(c)	262.103
(d)	262.102
17.03(a)(1)	262.110
(a)(2)	262.004
(a)(3) to (6)	262.104
(b)	262.105
(c)	262.106
(d), (e)	262.107
(g)	262.005
(h)	262.108
(i)	262.107
17.031	262.109
17.04	262.201
17.05(a)	262.002
(b)	262.202
17.06(a)	262.203
(b), (c)	262.204
18.01	263.001
18.02	263.002
18.03(a)	263.101
(b) to (d)	263.102
18.04	263.103
18.05	263.104
18.06	263.105
18.07(a)	263.201
(b) to (d)	263.202
18.08(a)	263.304
(b), (c)	263.301
18.09(a), (b)	263.306
(c)	263.308
18.10(a)	263.305
(b), (c)	263.303
18.11	263.003
18.12	263.301
18.13	263.004
18.14	263.302
18.15	263.307
18.16	263.309
21.01	159.101
(19)	101.030
(22)	101.035
21.02	159.102
21.03	159.103
21.04	159.201
21.05	159.202
21.06	159.203
21.07	159.204
21.08	159.205

CHILD IN RELATION TO THE FAMILY

Former Section	New Section
21.09	159.206
21.10	159.207
21.11	159.208
21.12	159.209
21.13	159.301
21.14	159.302
21.15	159.303
21.16	159.304
21.17	159.305
21.18	159.306
21.19	159.307
21.20	159.308
21.21	159.309
21.22	159.310
21.23	159.311
21.24	159.312
21.25	159.313
21.26	159.314
21.27	159.315
21.28	159.316
21.29	159.317
21.30	159.318
21.31	159.319
21.32	159.401
21.33	159.501
21.34	159.502
21.35	159.601
21.36	159.602
21.37	159.603
21.38	159.604
21.39	159.605
21.40	159.606
21.41	159.607
21.42	159.608
21.43	159.609
21.44	159.610
21.45	159.611
21.46	159.612
21.47	159.701
21.48	159.801
21.49	159.802
21.50	159.901
21.51	159.902
31.01	31.001
31.02	31.002
31.03(a)	31.003
31.04	31.004
31.06	31.005
31.07	31.006
31.08	31.007
32.01	45.001
32.02	45.002
32.03	45.003
32.04	45.004
32.05	45.005
32.21(a)	45.101
(b)	45.102
32.22	45.103
32.23	45.104
33.01	41.001
33.02	41.002
33.03	41.003
34.01	261.101
34.012	261.001

Former Section	New Section
34.013	261.003
34.02(a)	261.102
	261.103
(b)	261.104
(c)	261.105
(d)	261.101
34.03	261.106
34.031	261.107
34.032	261.108
34.04	261.202
34.05(a), (b)	261.301
(c)	261.302
	261.303
	261.305
(e)	261.308
(g)	261.306
34.051	261.307
34.052	261.309
34.053	261.304
34.054	261.310
34.055	261.311
34.06	261.002
34.07	261.109
34.08	261.201
34.22	261.401
34.23	261.402
34.24	261.403
34.51	264.201
34.52	264.202
34.53	264.203
34.54	264.204
34.601	264.601
34.602	264.602
34.603	264.603
34.604	264.604
34.605	264.605
34.606	264.606
34.607	264.607
34.608	264.608
34.609	264.609
34.610	264.610
34.611	264.611
34.612	264.612
35.01	32.001
35.011	32.101
35.012	32.102
35.013	32.103
35.014	32.104
35.015	32.105
35.02	32.002
35.03(a) to (f)	32.003
(g)	32.004
35.04	32.005
35.05	32.201
36.01	42.001
36.02(a), (b)	42.002
(c), (d)	42.003
36.03	42.006
36.04	42.007
36.05	42.005
36.06	42.008
36.07	42.004
36.08	42.009

FAMILY CODE

Government Code Former Section	Family Code New Section
54.001	201.001
54.002	201.002
54.003	201.003
54.004	201.004
54.005	201.005
54.006	201.006
54.007	201.007
54.008	201.008
54.009	201.010
54.010(a), (b)	201.011
(c)	201.012
54.011	201.014
54.012(a) to (i)	201.015
(j)	201.016
54.013	201.013
54.014	201.005
54.017	201.017
54.018	201.009

Human Resources Code Former Section	Family Code New Section
41.001	264.002
41.0011	264.003
41.0012	264.004
41.002	264.005
41.003	264.006
41.004	264.007
41.006	264.008
41.021	264.101
41.022	264.102
41.023	264.103
41.024	264.104
41.025	264.105
41.026	264.106
41.028	264.108
42.002(12)	101.017
45.001	162.101
45.002(a) to (c), (e)	162.102
45.003(a) to (d)	162.103
45.004	162.104
45.005	162.105
45.006	162.106
45.007	162.107
45.021	162.108
45.022	162.101
45.023	162.109
45.024	162.110
45.025	162.111
45.026	162.112
45.027	162.113
45.028	162.114
47.001	162.301
47.002	162.302
47.003	162.303
47.004	162.304
47.005	162.305
47.031	162.306
47.032	162.307
47.041	162.308
49.001	162.401
49.002	162.402
49.003(a) to (c)	162.403
49.004	162.404
49.005	162.405
(b)	108.003

Human Resources Code Former Section	Family Code New Section
49.006	162.406
49.007	162.407
49.008	162.408
49.009	162.409
49.010	162.410
49.011	162.411
49.012	162.412
49.013	162.413
49.014	162.414
49.015	162.415
49.016	162.416
49.017, 49.018	162.417
49.019	162.418
49.020	162.419
49.021	162.420
49.022	162.421
49.023	162.422
76.001	231.001
76.002(a), (d)	231.002
(e)	231.101
(f)	231.002
(g)	231.210
(i)	231.005
76.003(a)	231.104
(b)	231.105
(e)	231.106
(f)	231.107
76.004	231.101
(a)	231.103
(b)	231.002
76.0041	231.007
76.005	231.008
76.006	231.108
76.007(a) to (e)	231.109
(f)	231.110
(g)	231.111
76.008	231.009
76.009(a)	231.202
(b)	231.204
(c)	231.207
(d)	231.208
(e), (f)	231.205
(g)	231.201
(h)	231.203
(i)	231.206
	231.209
76.011	231.304
77.001(a)	231.301
(b)	231.302
(c)	231.303
(d)	231.302
151.001	203.003
151.002	203.004
151.003(a)	203.001
(b)	203.002
151.004	203.005
151.005	203.006
151.006	203.007
151.007	203.008
151.008	203.009
151.009	203.010
151.010	203.011
151.011	203.012

SUBTITLE A. LIMITATIONS OF MINORITY

CHAPTER 31. REMOVAL OF DISABILITIES OF MINORITY

A former Chapter 31, consisting of §§ 31.01 to 31.08, was repealed by Acts 1995, 74th Leg., ch. 20, § 2(1).

§ 31.001. Requirements

(a) A minor may petition to have the disabilities of minority removed for limited or general purposes if the minor is:

(1) a resident of this state;

(2) 17 years of age, or at least 16 years of age and living separate and apart from the minor's parents, managing conservator, or guardian; and

(3) self-supporting and managing the minor's own financial affairs.

(b) A minor may file suit under this chapter in the minor's own name. The minor need not be represented by next friend.

Amended by Acts 1995, 74th Leg., ch. 20, § 1, eff. April 20, 1995.

Section 3 of the 1995 amendatory act provides:

"(a) The change in law made by this Act does not affect a proceeding under the Family Code pending on the effective date of this Act. A proceeding pending on the effective date of this Act is governed by the law in effect at the time the proceeding was commenced, and the former law is continued in effect for that purpose.

"(b) The enactment of this Act does not by itself constitute a material and substantial change of circumstances sufficient to warrant modification of a court order or portion of a decree that provides for the support of or possession of and access to a child entered before the effective date of this Act."

§ 31.002. Requisites of Petition; Verification

(a) The petition for removal of disabilities of minority must state:

(1) the name, age, and place of residence of the petitioner;

(2) the name and place of residence of each living parent;

(3) the name and place of residence of the guardian of the person and the guardian of the estate, if any;

(4) the name and place of residence of the managing conservator, if any;

(5) the reasons why removal would be in the best interest of the minor; and

(6) the purposes for which removal is requested.

(b) A parent of the petitioner must verify the petition, except that if a managing conservator or guardian of the person has been appointed, the petition must be verified by that person. If the person who is to verify the petition is unavailable or that person's whereabouts are unknown, the guardian ad litem shall verify the petition.

Amended by Acts 1995, 74th Leg., ch. 20, § 1, eff. April 20, 1995.

§ 31.003. Venue

The petitioner shall file the petition in the county in which the petitioner resides.

Amended by Acts 1995, 74th Leg., ch. 20, § 1, eff. April 20, 1995.

§ 31.004. Guardian Ad Litem

The court shall appoint a guardian ad litem to represent the interest of the petitioner at the hearing.

Amended by Acts 1995, 74th Leg., ch. 20, § 1, eff. April 20, 1995.

§ 31.005. Order

The court may remove the disabilities of minority of a minor if the court finds the removal to be in the best interest of the petitioner. The order must state the limited or general purposes for which disabilities are removed.

Amended by Acts 1995, 74th Leg., ch. 20, § 1, eff. April 20, 1995.

§ 31.006. Effect of General Removal

Except for specific constitutional and statutory age requirements, a minor whose disabilities are removed for general purposes has the capacity of an adult, including the capacity to contract.

Amended by Acts 1995, 74th Leg., ch. 20, § 1, eff. April 20, 1995.

§ 31.007. Registration of Order of Another State or Nation

(a) A nonresident minor who has had the disabilities of minority removed in the state of the minor's residence may file a certified copy of the order removing disabilities in the deed records of any county in this state.

(b) When a certified copy of the order of a court of another state or nation is filed, the minor has the capacity of an adult, except as provided by Section 31.006 and by the terms of the order.

Amended by Acts 1995, 74th Leg., ch. 20, § 1, eff. April 20, 1995.

CHAPTER 32. CONSENT TO TREATMENT OF CHILD BY NON—PARENT OR CHILD

SUBCHAPTER A. CONSENT TO MEDICAL, DENTAL, PSYCHOLOGICAL, AND SURGICAL TREATMENT

Section

SUBCHAPTER B. IMMUNIZATION

SUBCHAPTER C. MISCELLANEOUS PROVISIONS

A former Chapter 32, consisting of §§ 32.01 to 32.25, was repealed by Acts 1995, 74th Leg., ch. 20, § 2(1).

SUBCHAPTER A. CONSENT TO MEDICAL, DENTAL, PSYCHOLOGICAL, AND SURGICAL TREATMENT

§ 32.001. Consent by Non-Parent

(a) The following persons may consent to medical, dental, psychological, and surgical treatment of a child when the person having the right to consent as otherwise provided by law cannot be contacted and that person has not given actual notice to the contrary:

(1) a grandparent of the child;

(2) an adult brother or sister of the child;

(3) an adult aunt or uncle of the child;

(4) an educational institution in which the child is enrolled that has received written authorization to consent from a person having the right to consent;

(5) an adult who has actual care, control, and possession of the child and has written authorization to consent from a person having the right to consent;

(6) a court having jurisdiction over a suit affecting the parent-child relationship of which the child is the subject;

(7) an adult responsible for the actual care, control, and possession of a child under the jurisdiction of a juvenile court or committed by a juvenile court to the care of an agency of the state or county; or

(8) a peace officer who has lawfully taken custody of a minor, if the peace officer has reasonable grounds to believe the minor is in need of immediate medical treatment.

(b) The Texas Youth Commission may consent to the medical, dental, psychological, and surgical treatment of a child committed to it under Title 3 when the person having the right to consent has been contacted and that person has not given actual notice to the contrary.

(c) This section does not apply to consent for the immunization of a child.

(d) A person who consents to the medical treatment of a minor under Subsection (a)(7) or (8) is immune from liability for damages resulting from the examination or treatment of the minor, except to the extent of the person's own acts of negligence. A physician or dentist licensed to practice in this state, or a hospital or medical facility at which a minor is treated is immune from liability for damages resulting from the examination or treatment of a minor under this section, except to the extent of the person's own acts of negligence.

Amended by Acts 1995, 74th Leg., ch. 20, § 1, eff. April 20, 1995; Acts 1995, 74th Leg., ch. 751, § 5, eff. Sept. 1, 1995.

§ 32.002. Consent Form

(a) Consent to medical treatment under this subchapter must be in writing, signed by the person giving consent, and given to the doctor, hospital, or other medical facility that administers the treatment.

(b) The consent must include:

(1) the name of the child;

(2) the name of one or both parents, if known, and the name of any managing conservator or guardian of the child;

(3) the name of the person giving consent and the person's relationship to the child;

(4) a statement of the nature of the medical treatment to be given; and

(5) the date the treatment is to begin.

Amended by Acts 1995, 74th Leg., ch. 20, § 1, eff. April 20, 1995.

Amendment by Acts 1995, 74th Leg., ch. 123, § 4

Section 4 of Acts 1995, 74th Leg., ch. 123, eff. Sept. 1, 1995, amends subsec. (a) of V.T.C.A., Family Code § 35.02 [now this section] without reference to the repeal of said section by Acts 1995, 74th Leg., ch. 20, § 2(1). As so amended, subsec. (a) reads:

"Consent to medical treatment under Sections 35.01 and 35.011 of this code shall be in writing, signed by the person giving consent, and given to the doctor, hospital, or other medical facility that administers the treatment."

§ 32.003. Consent to Treatment by Child

(a) A child may consent to medical, dental, psychological, and surgical treatment for the child by a licensed physician or dentist if the child:

(1) is on active duty with the armed services of the United States of America;

(2) is:

(A) 16 years of age or older and resides separate and apart from the child's parents, managing conservator, or guardian, with or without the consent of the parents, managing conservator, or guardian and regardless of the duration of the residence; and

(B) managing the child's own financial affairs, regardless of the source of the income;

(3) consents to the diagnosis and treatment of an infectious, contagious, or communicable disease that is required by law or a rule to be reported by the licensed physician or dentist to a local health officer or the Texas Department of Health, including all diseases within the scope of Section 81.041, Health and Safety Code;

(4) is unmarried and pregnant and consents to hospital, medical, or surgical treatment, other than abortion, related to the pregnancy;

(5) consents to examination and treatment for drug or chemical addiction, drug or chemical dependency, or any other condition directly related to drug or chemical use; or

(6) is unmarried and has actual custody of the child's biological child and consents to medical, dental, psychological, or surgical treatment for the child.

(b) Consent by a child to medical, dental, psychological, and surgical treatment under this section is not subject to disaffirmance because of minority.

(c) Consent of the parents, managing conservator, or guardian of a child is not necessary in order to authorize hospital, medical, surgical, or dental care under this section.

(d) A licensed physician, dentist, or psychologist may, with or without the consent of a child who is a patient, advise the parents, managing conservator, or guardian of the child of the treatment given to or needed by the child.

(e) A physician, dentist, psychologist, hospital, or medical facility is not liable for the examination and treatment of a child under this section except for the provider's or the facility's own acts of negligence.

(f) A physician, dentist, psychologist, hospital, or medical facility may rely on the written statement of the child containing the grounds on which the child has capacity to consent to the child's medical treatment.

Amended by Acts 1995, 74th Leg., ch. 20, § 1, eff. April 20, 1995; Acts 1995, 74th Leg., ch. 751, § 6, eff. Sept. 1, 1995.

§ 32.004. Consent to Counseling

(a) A child may consent to counseling for:

(1) suicide prevention;

(2) chemical addiction or dependency; or

(3) sexual, physical, or emotional abuse.

(b) A licensed or certified physician, psychologist, counselor, or social worker having reasonable grounds to believe that a child has been sexually, physically, or emotionally abused, is contemplating suicide, or is suffering from a chemical or drug addiction or dependency may:

(1) counsel the child without the consent of the child's parents or, if applicable, managing conservator or guardian;

(2) with or without the consent of the child who is a client, advise the child's parents or, if applicable, managing conservator or guardian of the treatment given to or needed by the child; and

(3) rely on the written statement of the child containing the grounds on which the child has capacity to consent to the child's own treatment under this section.

(c) Unless consent is obtained as otherwise allowed by law, a physician, psychologist, counselor, or social worker may not counsel a child if consent is prohibited by a court order.

(d) A physician, psychologist, counselor, or social worker counseling a child under this section is not liable for damages except for damages resulting from the person's negligence or wilful misconduct.

(e) A parent, or, if applicable, managing conservator or guardian, who has not consented to counseling treatment of the child is not obligated to compensate a physician, psychologist, counselor, or social worker for counseling services rendered under this section.

Amended by Acts 1995, 74th Leg., ch. 20, § 1, eff. April 20, 1995.

§ 32.005. Examination Without Consent of Abuse or Neglect of Child

(a) Except as provided by Subsection (c), a physician, dentist, or psychologist having reasonable grounds to believe that a child's physical or mental condition has been adversely affected by abuse or neglect may examine the child without the consent of the child, the child's parents, or other person authorized to consent to treatment under this subchapter.

(b) An examination under this section may include X-rays, blood tests, photographs, and penetration of tissue necessary to accomplish those tests.

(c) Unless consent is obtained as otherwise allowed by law, a physician, dentist, or psychologist may not examine a child:

(1) 16 years of age or older who refuses to consent; or

(2) for whom consent is prohibited by a court order.

(d) A physician, dentist, or psychologist examining a child under this section is not liable for damages except for damages resulting from the physician's or dentist's negligence.

Amended by Acts 1995, 74th Leg., ch. 20, § 1, eff. April 20, 1995; Acts 1997, 75th Leg., ch. 575, § 1, eff. Sept. 1, 1997.

[Sections 32.006 to 32.100 reserved for expansion]

SUBCHAPTER B. IMMUNIZATION

§ 32.101. Who May Consent to Immunization of Child

(a) In addition to persons authorized to consent to immunization under Chapter 151 and Chapter 153, the following persons may consent to the immunization of a child:

(1) a guardian of the child; and

(2) a person authorized under the law of another state or a court order to consent for the child.

(b) If the persons listed in Subsection (a) are not available and the authority to consent is not denied under Subsection (c), consent to the immunization of a child may be given by:

(1) a grandparent of the child;

(2) an adult brother or sister of the child;

(3) an adult aunt or uncle of the child;

(4) a stepparent of the child;

(5) an educational institution in which the child is enrolled that has written authorization to consent for the child from a parent, managing conservator, guardian, or other person who under the law of another state or a court order may consent for the child;

(6) another adult who has actual care, control, and possession of the child and has written authorization to consent for the child from a parent, managing conservator, guardian, or other person who, under the law of another state or a court order, may consent for the child;

(7) a court having jurisdiction of a suit affecting the parent-child relationship of which the minor is the subject;

(8) an adult having actual care, control, and possession of the child under an order of a juvenile court or by commitment by a juvenile court to the care of an agency of the state or county; or

(9) an adult having actual care, control, and possession of the child as the child's primary caregiver.

(c) A person otherwise authorized to consent under Subsection (a) may not consent for the child if the person has actual knowledge that a parent, managing conservator, guardian of the child, or other person who under the law of another state or a court order may consent for the child:

(1) has expressly refused to give consent to the immunization;

(2) has been told not to consent for the child; or

(3) has withdrawn a prior written authorization for the person to consent.

(d) The Texas Youth Commission may consent to the immunization of a child committed to it if a parent, managing conservator, or guardian of the minor or other person who, under the law of another state or court order, may consent for the minor has been contacted and:

(1) refuses to consent; and

(2) does not expressly deny to the Texas Youth Commission the authority to consent for the child.

(e) A person who consents under this section shall provide the health care provider with sufficient and accurate health history and other information about the minor for whom the consent is given and, if necessary, sufficient and accurate health history and information about the minor's family to enable the person who may consent to the minor's immunization and the health care provider to determine adequately the risks and benefits inherent in the proposed immunization and to determine whether immunization is advisable.

Amended by Acts 1995, 74th Leg., ch. 20, § 1, eff. April 20, 1995; Acts 1997, 75th Leg., ch. 165, § 7.09(a), eff. Sept. 1, 1997.

§ 32.102. Informed Consent to Immunization

(a) A person authorized to consent to the immunization of a child has the responsibility to ensure that the consent, if given, is an informed consent. The person authorized to consent is not required to be present when the immunization of the child is requested if a consent form that meets the requirements of Section 32.002 has been given to the health care provider.

(b) The responsibility of a health care provider to provide information to a person consenting to immunization is the same as the provider's responsibility to a parent.

(c) As part of the information given in the counseling for informed consent, the health care provider shall provide information to inform the person authorized to consent to immunization of the procedures available under the National Childhood Vaccine Injury Act of 1986 (42 U.S.C. Section 300aa–1 et seq.) to seek possible recovery for unreimbursed expenses for certain injuries arising out of the administration of certain vaccines.

Amended by Acts 1995, 74th Leg., ch. 20, § 1, eff. April 20, 1995. Renumbered from § 32.103 and amended by Acts 1997, 75th Leg., ch. 165, § 7.09(b), (d), eff. Sept. 1, 1997.

§ 32.103. Limited Liability for Immunization

(a) In the absence of wilful misconduct or gross negligence, a health care provider who accepts the health history and other information given by a person who is delegated the authority to consent to the immunization of a child during the informed consent counseling is not liable for an adverse reaction to an immunization or for other injuries to the child resulting from factual errors in the health history or information given by the person to the health care provider.

(b) A person consenting to immunization of a child, a physician, nurse, or other health care provider, or a public health clinic, hospital, or other medical facility is not liable for damages arising from an immunization administered to a child authorized under this subchapter except for injuries resulting from the person's or facility's own acts of negligence.

Amended by Acts 1995, 74th Leg., ch. 20, § 1, eff. April 20, 1995. Renumbered from § 32.104 by Acts 1997, 75th Leg., ch. 165, § 7.09(e), eff. Sept. 1, 1997.

§ 32.104. Renumbered as V.T.C.A., Family Code § 32.103 by Acts 1997, 75th Leg., ch. 165, § 7.09(e), eff. Sept. 1, 1997

§ 32.105. Repealed by Acts 1997, 75th Leg., ch. 165, § 7.09(c), eff. Sept. 1, 1997

[Sections 32.106 to 32.200 reserved for expansion]

SUBCHAPTER C. MISCELLANEOUS PROVISIONS

§ 32.201. Emergency Shelter for Minor Mothers

(a) An emergency shelter facility may provide shelter and care to a minor mother who is the sole financial support of her child or children.

(b) An emergency shelter facility may provide shelter or care only during an emergency constituting an immediate danger to the physical health or safety of the minor mother or her child or children.

(c) Shelter or care provided under this section may not be provided after the 15th day after the date the shelter or care is commenced unless:

(1) the facility receives consent to continue services from a parent or guardian of the minor mother; or

(2) the minor mother has qualified for Aid to Families with Dependent Children under Chapter 31, Human Resources Code, and is on the waiting list for housing assistance.

Amended by Acts 1995, 74th Leg., ch. 20, § 1, eff. April 20, 1995.

[Chapters 33 to 40 reserved for expansion]

SUBTITLE B. PARENTAL LIABILITY

CHAPTER 41. LIABILITY OF PARENTS FOR CONDUCT OF CHILD

Section

§ 41.001. Liability

A parent or other person who has the duty of control and reasonable discipline of a child is liable for any property damage proximately caused by:

(1) the negligent conduct of the child if the conduct is reasonably attributable to the negligent failure of the parent or other persons to exercise that duty; or

(2) the wilful and malicious conduct of a child who is at least 12 years of age but under 18 years of age.

Amended by Acts 1995, 74th Leg., ch. 20, § 1, eff. April 20, 1995.

§ 41.002. Limit of Damages

Recovery for damage caused by wilful and malicious conduct is limited to actual damages, not to exceed $25,000 per occurrence, plus court costs and reasonable attorney's fees.

Amended by Acts 1995, 74th Leg., ch. 20, § 1, eff. April 20, 1995; Acts 1997, 75th Leg., ch. 783, § 1, eff. Sept. 1, 1997.

Section 2 of Acts 1997, 75th Leg., ch. 783 provides:

"This Act takes effect September 1, 1997, and applies only to a cause of action that accrues on or after that date. A cause of action that accrued before the effective date of this Act is governed by the law in effect at the time the cause of action accrued, and that law is continued in effect for that purpose."

§ 41.0025. Liability for Property Damage to an Inn or Hotel

(a) Notwithstanding Section 41.002, recovery of damages by an inn or hotel for wilful and malicious conduct is limited to actual damages, not to exceed $25,000 per occurrence, plus court costs and reasonable attorney's fees.

(b) In this section "occurrence" means one incident on a single day in one hotel room. The term does not include incidents in separate rooms or incidents that occur on different days.

Added by Acts 1997, 75th Leg., ch. 40, § 1, eff. Sept. 1, 1997.

Section 2 of Acts 1997, 75th Leg., ch. 40 provides:

"This Act takes effect September 1, 1997, and applies only to property damage that occurs on or after that date. Damage that occurs before the effective date of this Act is governed by the law in effect on the date the damage occurred, and the former law is continued in effect for that purpose."

§ 41.003. Venue

A suit as provided by this chapter may be filed in the county in which the conduct of the child occurred or in the county in which the defendant resides.

Amended by Acts 1995, 74th Leg., ch. 20, § 1, eff. April 20, 1995.

CHAPTER 42. CIVIL LIABILITY FOR INTERFERENCE WITH POSSESSORY INTEREST IN CHILD

Section

§ 42.001. Definitions

In this chapter:

(1) "Order" means a temporary or final order of a court of this state or another state or nation.

(2) "Possessory right" means a court-ordered right of possession of or access to a child, including conservatorship, custody, and visitation.

Amended by Acts 1995, 74th Leg., ch. 20, § 1, eff. April 20, 1995.

§ 42.002. Liability for Interference with Possessory Right

(a) A person who takes or retains possession of a child or who conceals the whereabouts of a child in violation of a possessory right of another person may be liable for damages to that person.

(b) A possessory right is violated by the taking, retention, or concealment of a child at a time when another person is entitled to possession of or access to the child.

Amended by Acts 1995, 74th Leg., ch. 20, § 1, eff. April 20, 1995.

§ 42.003. Aiding or Assisting Interference with Possessory Right

(a) A person who aids or assists in conduct for which a cause of action is authorized by this chapter is jointly and severally liable for damages.

(b) A person who was not a party to the suit in which an order was rendered providing for a possessory right is not liable unless the person at the time of the violation:

(1) had actual notice of the existence and contents of the order; or

(2) had reasonable cause to believe that the child was the subject of an order and that the person's actions were likely to violate the order.

Amended by Acts 1995, 74th Leg., ch. 20, § 1, eff. April 20, 1995.

§ 42.004. Notice

(a) As a prerequisite to the filing of suit, a person who has been denied a possessory right shall give written notice of the specific violation alleged to the person alleged to be in violation of the order.

(b) The notice shall be by certified or registered mail, return receipt requested, to the last known address of the person alleged to be in violation of the order.

(c) The person giving notice shall include a statement of intention to file suit unless the person alleged to have violated the order promptly and fully complies with the order.

(d) A suit may not be filed until the 31st day after the date on which the notice is mailed.

(e) Notice need not be given to a person aiding or assisting conduct denying a possessory right.

(f) A party may introduce evidence that notice has been given as provided by this section.

Amended by Acts 1995, 74th Leg., ch. 20, § 1, eff. April 20, 1995.

§ 42.005. Venue

A suit may be filed in a county in which:

(1) the plaintiff resides;

(2) the defendant resides;

(3) a suit affecting the parent-child relationship as provided by Chapter 102 may be brought, concerning the child who is the subject of the court order; or

(4) a court has continuing, exclusive jurisdiction as provided by Chapter 155.

Amended by Acts 1995, 74th Leg., ch. 20, § 1, eff. April 20, 1995.

§ 42.006. Damages

(a) Damages may include:

(1) the actual costs and expenses incurred, including attorney's fees, in:

(A) locating a child who is the subject of the order;

(B) recovering possession of the child if the petitioner is entitled to possession; and

(C) enforcing the order and prosecuting the suit; and

(2) mental suffering and anguish incurred by the plaintiff because of a violation of the order.

(b) A person liable for damages who acted with malice or with an intent to cause harm to the plaintiff may be liable for exemplary damages.

Amended by Acts 1995, 74th Leg., ch. 20, § 1, eff. April 20, 1995; Acts 1995, 74th Leg., ch. 751, § 7, eff. Sept. 1, 1995.

§ 42.007. Affirmative Defense

The defendant may plead as an affirmative defense that:

(1) the defendant acted in violation of the order with the express consent of the plaintiff; or

(2) after receiving notice of an alleged violation, the defendant promptly and fully complied with the order.

Amended by Acts 1995, 74th Leg., ch. 20, § 1, eff. April 20, 1995.

§ 42.008. Remedies Not Affected

This chapter does not affect any other civil or criminal remedy available to any person, including the child, for interference with a possessory right, nor does it affect the power of a parent to represent the interest of a child in a suit filed on behalf of the child.

Amended by Acts 1995, 74th Leg., ch. 20, § 1, eff. April 20, 1995.

§ 42.009. Frivolous Suit

A person sued for damages as provided by this chapter is entitled to recover attorney's fees and court costs if:

(1) the claim for damages is dismissed or judgment is awarded to the defendant; and

(2) the court or jury finds that the claim for damages is frivolous, unreasonable, or without foundation.

Amended by Acts 1995, 74th Leg., ch. 20, § 1, eff. April 20, 1995.

[Chapters 43 to 44 reserved for expansion]

SUBTITLE C. CHANGE OF NAME

CHAPTER 45. CHANGE OF NAME

SUBCHAPTER A. CHANGE OF NAME OF CHILD

Section

SUBCHAPTER A. CHANGE OF NAME OF CHILD

§ 45.001. Who May File; Venue

A parent, managing conservator, or guardian of a child may file a petition requesting a change of name of the child in the county where the child resides.

Amended by Acts 1995, 74th Leg., ch. 20, § 1, eff. April 20, 1995.

§ 45.002. Requirements of Petition

(a) A petition to change the name of a child must be verified and include:

(1) the present name and place of residence of the child;

(2) the reason a change of name is requested;

(3) the full name requested for the child; and

(4) whether the child is subject to the continuing exclusive jurisdiction of a court under Chapter 155.

(b) If the child is 12 years of age or older, the child's written consent to the change of name must be attached to the petition.

Amended by Acts 1995, 74th Leg., ch. 20, § 1, eff. April 20, 1995.

§ 45.003. Citation

(a) The following persons are entitled to citation in a suit under this subchapter:

(1) a parent of the child whose parental rights have not been terminated;

(2) any managing conservator of the child; and

(3) any guardian of the child.

(b) Citation must be issued and served in the same manner as under Chapter 102.

Amended by Acts 1995, 74th Leg., ch. 20, § 1, eff. April 20, 1995.

§ 45.004. Order

(a) The court may order the name of a child changed if the change is in the best interest of the child.

(b) If the child is subject to the continuing jurisdiction of a court under Chapter 155, the court shall send a copy of the order to the central record file as provided in Chapter 108.

Amended by Acts 1995, 74th Leg., ch. 20, § 1, eff. April 20, 1995.

§ 45.005. Liabilities and Rights Unaffected

A change of name does not:

(1) release a child from any liability incurred in the child's previous name; or

(2) defeat any right the child had in the child's previous name.

Amended by Acts 1995, 74th Leg., ch. 20, § 1, eff. April 20, 1995.

[Sections 45.006 to 45.100 reserved for expansion]

SUBCHAPTER B. CHANGE OF NAME OF ADULT

§ 45.101. Who May File; Venue

An adult may file a petition requesting a change of name in the county of the adult's place of residence.

Amended by Acts 1995, 74th Leg., ch. 20, § 1, eff. April 20, 1995.

§ 45.102. Requirements of Petition

(a) A petition to change the name of an adult must be verified and include:

(1) the present name and place of residence of the petitioner;

(2) the full name requested for the petitioner;

(3) the reason the change in name is requested; and

(4) whether the petitioner has been the subject of a final felony conviction.

(b) The petition must include each of the following or a reasonable explanation why the required information is not included:

(1) the petitioner's:

(A) full name;

(B) sex;

(C) race;

(D) date of birth;

(E) driver's license number for any driver's license issued in the 10 years preceding the date of the petition;

(F) social security number; and

(G) assigned FBI number, state identification number, if known, or any other reference number in a criminal history record system that identifies the petitioner;

(2) any offense above the grade of Class C misdemeanor for which the petitioner has been charged; and

(3) the case number and the court if a warrant was issued or a charging instrument was filed or presented for an offense listed in Subsection (b)(2).

Amended by Acts 1995, 74th Leg., ch. 20, § 1, eff. April 20, 1995.

§ 45.103. Order

(a) The court shall order a change of name under this subchapter for a person other than a person with a final felony conviction if the change is in the interest or to the benefit of the petitioner and in the interest of the public.

(b) A court may order a change of name under this subchapter for a person with a final felony conviction if, in addition to the requirements of Subsection (a), the person has:

(1) received a certificate of discharge by the pardons and paroles division of the Texas Department of Criminal Justice or completed a period of probation ordered by a court and not less than two years have passed from the date of the receipt of discharge or completion of probation; or

(2) been pardoned.

Amended by Acts 1995, 74th Leg., ch. 20, § 1, eff. April 20, 1995.

§ 45.104. Liabilities and Rights Unaffected

A change of name under this subchapter does not release a person from liability incurred in that person's previous name or defeat any right the person had in the person's previous name.

Amended by Acts 1995, 74th Leg., ch. 20, § 1, eff. April 20, 1995.

§ 45.105. Change of Name in Divorce Suit

(a) On the final disposition of a suit for divorce, for annulment, or to declare a marriage void, the court shall enter a decree changing the name of a party specially praying for the change to a prior used name unless the court states in the decree a reason for denying the change of name. The court may not deny a change of name solely to keep last names of family members the same.

(b) A person whose name is changed under this section may apply for a change of name certificate from the clerk of the court as provided by Section 45.106.

Added by Acts 1997, 75th Leg., ch. 165, § 7.10(a), eff. Sept. 1, 1997.

§ 45.106. Change of Name Certificate

(a) A person whose name is changed under Section 3.64 or 45.105 may apply to the clerk of the court ordering the name change for a change of name certificate.

(b) A certificate under this section is a one-page document that includes:

(1) the name of the person before the change of name was ordered;

(2) the name to which the person's name was changed by the court;

(3) the date on which the name change was made;

(4) the person's social security number and driver's license number, if any;

(5) the name of the court in which the name change was ordered; and

(6) the signature of the clerk of the court that issued the certificate.

(c) An applicant for a certificate under this section shall pay a $10 fee to the clerk of the court for issuance of the certificate.

(d) A certificate under this section constitutes proof of the change of name of the person named in the certificate.

Added by Acts 1997, 75th Leg., ch. 165, § 7.10(a), eff. Sept. 1, 1997.

TITLE 3. JUVENILE JUSTICE CODE

Acts 1995, ch. 262, § 1 amended the Title 3 heading from "Delinquent Children and Children in Need of Supervision".

Enactment

Title 3 of the Texas Family Code was added by Acts 1973, 63rd Leg., p. 1460, ch. 544, § 1, effective September 1, 1973. Sections 4 and 5 thereof provide:

"Sec. 4. This Act takes effect on September 1, 1973, and governs all proceedings, orders, and judgments brought after it takes effect, and also further proceedings in actions then pending, except to the extent that

in the opinion of the court its application in an action pending when this Act takes effect would not be feasible or would work injustice. All things properly done under any previously existing rule or statute prior to the taking effect of this Act shall be treated as valid.

"Sec. 5. If any provision of this Act or the application thereof to any person or circumstance is held invalid, such invalidity shall not affect other provisions or applications of this Act which can be given effect without the invalid provision or application, and to this end the provisions of this Act are declared to be severable."

CHAPTER 51. GENERAL PROVISIONS

§ 51.01. Purpose and Interpretation

This title shall be construed to effectuate the following public purposes:

(1) to provide for the protection of the public and public safety;

(2) consistent with the protection of the public and public safety:

(A) to promote the concept of punishment for criminal acts;

(B) to remove, where appropriate, the taint of criminality from children committing certain unlawful acts; and

(C) to provide treatment, training, and rehabilitation that emphasizes the accountability and responsibility of both the parent and the child for the child's conduct;

(3) to provide for the care, the protection, and the wholesome moral, mental, and physical development of children coming within its provisions;

(4) to protect the welfare of the community and to control the commission of unlawful acts by children;

(5) to achieve the foregoing purposes in a family environment whenever possible, separating the child from the child's parents only when necessary for the child's welfare or in the interest of public safety and when a child is removed from the child's family, to give the child the care that should be provided by parents; and

(6) to provide a simple judicial procedure through which the provisions of this title are executed and enforced and in which the parties are assured a fair hearing and their constitutional and other legal rights recognized and enforced.

Acts 1973, 63rd Leg., p. 1460, ch. 544, § 1, eff. Sept. 1, 1973. Amended by Acts 1995, 74th Leg., ch. 262, § 2, eff. Jan. 1, 1996.

Sections 104 and 106(a) of the 1995 amendatory act provide:

"Sec. 104. (a) An amendment to any provision of Title 3, Family Code, made by another Act of the 74th Legislature, Regular Session, 1995, applies only to conduct that occurs on or after the effective date of the other Act and before January 1, 1996. The amendment made by the other Act continues in effect only for the limited purpose of the prosecution of the conduct committed before January 1, 1996.

"(b) For purposes of Subsection (a) of this section, conduct violating the penal law of this state occurs before January 1, 1996, only if every element of the violation occurs before that date."

"Sec. 106. (a) Except as provided by Subsection (b) of this section, this Act applies only to conduct that occurs on or after January 1, 1996. Conduct violating a penal law of this state occurs on or after January 1, 1996, if every element of the violation occurs on or after that date. Conduct that occurs before January 1, 1996, is governed by the law in effect at the time the conduct occurred, and that law is continued in effect for that purpose."

§ 51.02. Definitions

In this title:

(1) "Aggravated controlled substance felony" means an offense under Subchapter D, Chapter 481, Health and Safety Code,[1] that is punishable by:

(A) a minimum term of confinement that is longer than the minimum term of confinement for a felony of the first degree; or

(B) a maximum fine that is greater than the maximum fine for a felony of the first degree.

(2) "Child" means a person who is:

(A) ten years of age or older and under 17 years of age; or

(B) seventeen years of age or older and under 18 years of age who is alleged or found to have engaged in delinquent conduct or conduct indicating a need for supervision as a result of acts committed before becoming 17 years of age.

(3) "Custodian" means the adult with whom the child resides.

(4) "Guardian" means the person who, under court order, is the guardian of the person of the child or the public or private agency with whom the child has been placed by a court.

(5) "Judge" or "juvenile court judge" means the judge of a juvenile court.

(6) "Juvenile court" means a court designated under Section 51.04 of this code to exercise jurisdiction over proceedings under this title.

(7) "Law-enforcement officer" means a peace officer as defined by Article 2.12, Code of Criminal Procedure.

(8) "Nonoffender" means a child who:

(A) is subject to jurisdiction of a court under abuse, dependency, or neglect statutes under Title 5[2] for reasons other than legally prohibited conduct of the child; or

(B) has been taken into custody and is being held solely for deportation out of the United States.

(9) "Parent" means the mother, the father whether or not the child is legitimate, or an adoptive parent, but does not include a parent whose parental rights have been terminated.

(10) "Party" means the state, a child who is the subject of proceedings under this subtitle, or the child's parent, spouse, guardian, or guardian ad litem.

(11) "Prosecuting attorney" means the county attorney, district attorney, or other attorney who regularly serves in a prosecutory capacity in a juvenile court.

(12) "Referral to juvenile court" means the referral of a child or a child's case to the office or official, including an intake officer or probation officer, designated by the juvenile court to process children within the juvenile justice system.

(13) "Secure correctional facility" means any public or private residential facility, including an alcohol or other drug treatment facility, that:

(A) includes construction fixtures designed to physically restrict the movements and activities of juveniles or other individuals held in lawful custody in the facility; and

(B) is used for the placement of any juvenile who has been adjudicated as having committed an offense, any nonoffender, or any other individual convicted of a criminal offense.

(14) "Secure detention facility" means any public or private residential facility that:

(A) includes construction fixtures designed to physically restrict the movements and activities of juveniles or other individuals held in lawful custody in the facility; and

(B) is used for the temporary placement of any juvenile who is accused of having committed an offense, any nonoffender, or any other individual accused of having committed a criminal offense.

(15) "Status offender" means a child who is accused, adjudicated, or convicted for conduct that would not, under state law, be a crime if committed by an adult, including:

(A) truancy under Section 51.03(b)(2);

(B) running away from home under Section 51.03(b)(3);

(C) a fineable only offense under Section 51.03(b)(1) transferred to the juvenile court under Section 51.08(b), but only if the conduct constituting the offense would not have been criminal if engaged in by an adult;

(D) failure to attend school under Section 25.094, Education Code;

(E) a violation of standards of student conduct as described by Section 51.03(b)(5);

(F) a violation of a juvenile curfew ordinance or order;

(G) a violation of a provision of the Alcoholic Beverage Code applicable to minors only; or

(H) a violation of any other fineable only offense under Section 8.07(a)(4) or (5), Penal Code, but only if the conduct constituting the offense would not have been criminal if engaged in by an adult.

(16) "Traffic offense" means:

(A) a violation of a penal statute cognizable under Chapter 729, Transportation Code, except for:

(i) conduct constituting an offense under Section 550.021, Transportation Code;

(ii) conduct constituting an offense punishable as a Class B misdemeanor under Section 550.022, Transportation Code; or

(iii) conduct constituting an offense punishable as a Class B misdemeanor under Section 550.024, Transportation Code; or

(B) a violation of a motor vehicle traffic ordinance of an incorporated city or town in this state.

(17) "Valid court order" means a court order entered under Section 54.04 concerning a child adjudicated to have engaged in conduct indicating a need for supervision as a status offender.

Acts 1973, 63rd Leg., p. 1460, ch. 544, § 1, eff. Sept. 1, 1973. Amended by Acts 1975, 64th Leg., p. 2152, ch. 693, § 1, eff. Sept. 1, 1975; Acts 1995, 74th Leg., ch. 262, § 3, eff. Jan. 1, 1996; Acts 1997, 75th Leg., ch. 165, §§ 6.06, 30.182, eff. Sept. 1, 1997; Acts 1997, 75th Leg., ch. 822, § 2, eff. Sept. 1, 1997; Acts 1997, 75th Leg., ch. 1013, § 13, eff. Sept. 1, 1997; Acts 1997, 75th Leg., ch. 1086, §§ 41, 47, eff. Sept. 1, 1997.

[1] V.T.C.A., Health & Safety Code § 481.101 et seq.

[2] V.T.C.A., Family Code § 101.001 et seq.

Section 5 of Acts 1997, 75th Leg., ch. 822, provides:

"(a) The change in law made by this Act applies only to conduct violating a penal law of this state that occurs on or after the effective date of this Act. For purposes of this section, conduct occurs before the effective date of this Act if any element of the conduct occurs before the effective date.

"(b) Conduct that occurs before the effective date of this Act is covered by the law in effect when the conduct occurred, and the former law is continued in effect for that purpose."

For application provisions of Acts 1997, 75th Leg., ch. 1013, see notes following V.T.C.A., Family Code § 51.03.

§ 51.03. Delinquent Conduct; Conduct Indicating a Need for Supervision

(a) Delinquent conduct is:

(1) conduct, other than a traffic offense, that violates a penal law of this state or of the United States punishable by imprisonment or by confinement in jail;

(2) conduct that violates a reasonable and lawful order of a juvenile court entered under Section 54.04 or 54.05 of this code, except an order prohibiting the following conduct:

(A) a violation of the penal laws of this state of the grade of misdemeanor that is punishable by fine only or a violation of the penal ordinances of any political subdivision of this state;

(B) the unexcused voluntary absence of a child from school; or

(C) the voluntary absence of a child from his home without the consent of his parent or guardian for a substantial length of time or without intent to return;

(3) conduct that violates a lawful order of a municipal court or justice court under circumstances that would constitute contempt of that court;

(4) conduct that violates Section 49.04, 49.05, 49.06, 49.07, or 49.08, Penal Code; or

(5) conduct that violates Section 106.041, Alcoholic Beverage Code, relating to driving under the influence of alcohol by a minor (third or subsequent offense).

(b) Conduct indicating a need for supervision is:

(1) subject to Subsection (f) of this section, conduct, other than a traffic offense, that violates:

(A) the penal laws of this state of the grade of misdemeanor that are punishable by fine only; or

(B) the penal ordinances of any political subdivision of this state;

(2) the unexcused voluntary absence of a child on 10 or more days or parts of days within a six-month period or three or more days or parts of days within a four-week period from school without the consent of his parents;

(3) the voluntary absence of a child from his home without the consent of his parent or guardian for a substantial length of time or without intent to return;

(4) conduct prohibited by city ordinance or by state law involving the inhalation of the fumes or vapors of paint and other protective coatings or glue and other adhesives and the volatile chemicals itemized in Section 484.002, Health and Safety Code;

(5) an act that violates a school district's previously communicated written standards of student conduct for which the child has been expelled under Section 37.007, Education Code; or

(6) conduct that violates a reasonable and lawful order of a court entered under Section 264.305.

(c) Nothing in this title prevents criminal proceedings against a child for perjury.

(d) For the purpose of Subsection (b)(2) of this section an absence is excused when the absence results from:

(1) illness of the child;

(2) illness or death in the family of the child;

(3) quarantine of the child and family;

(4) weather or road conditions making travel dangerous;

(5) an absence approved by a teacher, principal, or superintendent of the school in which the child is enrolled; or

(6) circumstances found reasonable and proper.

(e) For the purposes of Subdivisions (2) and (3) of Subsection (b) of this section, "child" does not include a person who is married, divorced, or widowed.

(f) Conduct described under Subsection (b)(1) of this section, other than conduct that violates Section 49.02, Penal Code, prohibiting public intoxication, does not constitute conduct indicating a need for supervision unless the child has been referred to the juvenile court under Section 51.08(b) of this code.

Acts 1973, 63rd Leg., p. 1460, ch. 544, § 1, eff. Sept. 1, 1973. Amended by Acts 1975, 64th Leg., p. 2153, ch. 693, §§ 2 to 4, eff. Sept. 1, 1975; Acts 1977, 65th Leg., p. 906, ch. 340, § 1, eff. June 6, 1977; Acts 1987, 70th Leg., ch. 511, § 1, eff. Sept. 1, 1987; Acts 1987, 70th Leg., ch. 924, § 1, eff. Sept. 1, 1987; Acts 1987, 70th Leg., ch. 955, § 1, eff. June 19, 1987; Acts 1987, 70th Leg., ch. 1040, § 20, eff. Sept. 1, 1987; Acts 1987, 70th Leg., ch. 1099, § 48, eff. Sept. 1, 1987; Acts 1989, 71st Leg., ch. 1100, § 3.02, eff. Aug. 28, 1989; Acts 1989, 71st Leg., ch. 1245, §§ 1, 4, eff. Sept. 1, 1989; Acts 1991, 72nd Leg., ch. 14, § 284(35), eff. Sept. 1, 1991; Acts 1991, 72nd Leg., ch. 16, § 7.02, eff. Aug. 26, 1991; Acts 1991, 72nd Leg., ch. 169, § 1, eff. Sept. 1, 1991; Acts 1993, 73rd Leg., ch. 46, § 1, eff. Sept. 1, 1993; Acts 1995, 74th Leg., ch. 76, § 14.30, eff. Sept. 1, 1995; Acts 1995, 74th Leg., ch. 262, § 4, eff. Jan. 1, 1996; Acts 1997, 75th Leg., ch. 165, § 6.07, eff. Sept. 1, 1997; Acts 1997, 75th Leg., ch. 1013, § 14, eff. Sept. 1, 1997; Acts 1997, 75th Leg., ch. 1015, § 15, eff. June 19, 1997; Acts 1997, 75th Leg., ch. 1086, § 1, eff. Sept. 1, 1997.

Section 2 of Acts 1987, 70th Leg., ch. 511 provides:

"(a) This Act takes effect September 1, 1987, and applies only to conduct occurring on or after that date. Conduct violating the penal law of this state occurs on or after the effective date of this Act if every element of the violation occurs on or after that date.

"(b) A juvenile proceeding for conduct occurring before the effective date is governed by the law existing at the time the conduct occurred and that law is continued in effect for that purpose only."

Section 2 of Acts 1987, 70th Leg., ch. 924, provides:

"This Act takes effect September 1, 1987, and applies to conduct that occurs on or after that date. Conduct that occurs before that date is governed by the law in effect when the conduct occurred, and that law is continued in effect for that purpose."

Section 35 of Acts 1987, 70th Leg., ch. 1040 provides:

"(a) This Act applies only to offenses and conduct occurring on or after its effective date. For the purposes of this section, an offense or delinquent conduct based on an offense occurs on or after the effective date if all the elements of the offense occur on or after the effective date.

"(b) An offense or conduct that occurs before the effective date of this Act shall be prosecuted under the law in effect immediately before the effective date of this Act, and that law is continued in effect for that purpose only."

Section 52(b) of Acts 1987, 70th Leg., ch. 1099 provides:

"Until the child's 21st birthday, the Texas Youth Commission may offer care, treatment, education, and training, if needed, to a child who was:

"(1) accepted for admission at the Corsicana State Home, the West Texas Children's Home at Pyote, or the Waco State Home under Section 61.061, Human Resources Code, as amended, before the effective date of this Act;

"(2) the subject of a suit affecting the parent-child relationship under Subtitle A, Title 2, Family Code, at the time of admission; and

"(3) placed in the commission's managing or possessory conservatorship."

This section formerly contained two subsecs. (e). Acts 1989, 71st Leg., ch. 1100, § 3.02, redesignated the current subsec. (e) as (f), and Acts 1989, 71st Leg., ch. 1245, § 4, repealed the other subsec. (e). Due to one repeal of the subsec. (e), the redesignation of the remaining subsec. (e) was not executed.

Section 1.02(b) of Acts 1989, 71st Leg., ch. 1100, provides:

"If any provision of this Act conflicts with a statute enacted by the 71st Legislature, Regular Session, 1989, the statute controls."

Section 5 of Acts 1989, 71st Leg., ch. 1245, provides:

"(a) This Act takes effect September 1, 1989, and applies only to conduct that occurs on or after that date. Conduct violating the penal law of this state occurs on or after the effective date of this Act if every element of the violation occurs on or after that date.

"(b) Conduct that occurs before the effective date of this Act is governed by the law in effect at the time the conduct occurred and that law is continued in effect for that purpose."

Section 5 of Acts 1991, 72nd Leg., ch. 169 provides:

"(a) This Act applies only to an offense or conduct that occurs on or after the effective date of this Act. For the purposes of this section, the offense or conduct occurs on or after the effective date of this Act if every element of the offense or of conduct that violates a penal law of this state or of a penal ordinance of a political subdivision of this state occurs on or after that date.

"(b) An offense or conduct that occurs before the effective date of this Act is governed by the law in effect at the time the offense or conduct occurred, and that law is continued in effect for that purpose."

Section 2 of Acts 1993, 73rd Leg., ch. 46, provides:

"(a) The substantive change in law made by this Act relating to conduct that violates a penal law of the United States applies only to conduct that occurs on or after the effective date of this Act. Conduct violating a penal law of the United States occurs on or after the effective date of this Act if every element of the violation occurs on or after that date.

"(b) Conduct that occurs before the effective date of this Act is covered by the law in effect at the time the conduct occurred, and the former law is continued in effect for that purpose."

Section 7 of Acts 1993, 73rd Leg., ch. 358, provides:

"(a) The change in law made by this Act applies only if the final absence that makes Section 51.03(b)(2), Family Code, applicable to a child's conduct occurs on or after the effective date of this Act.

"(b) The change in law made by this Act applies only to an offense committed on or after the effective date of this Act. For the purposes of this section, an offense is committed before the effective date of this Act if any element of the offense occurs before the effective date.

"(c) An offense committed before the effective date of this Act is covered by the law in effect at the time the offense was committed, and the former law is continued in effect for that purpose."

Section 104 of Acts 1995, 74th Leg., ch. 262 provides:

"(a) An amendment to any provision of Title 3, Family Code, made by another Act of the 74th Legislature, Regular Session, 1995, applies only to conduct that occurs on or after the effective date of the other Act and before January 1, 1996. The amendment made by the other Act continues in effect only for the limited purpose of the prosecution of the conduct committed before January 1, 1996.

"(b) For purposes of Subsection (a) of this section, conduct violating the penal law of this state occurs before January 1, 1996, only if every element of the violation occurs before that date."

Section 42 of Acts 1997, 75th Leg., ch. 1013 provides:

"(a) The changes in law made by this Act apply only to an offense committed on or after the effective date of this Act. For the purposes of this section, an offense is committed before the effective date of this Act if any element of the offense occurs before that date.

"(b) An offense committed before the effective date of this Act is covered by the law in effect when the offense was committed, and the former law is continued in effect for that purpose."

Section 20 of Acts 1997, 75th Leg., ch. 1015 provides:

"This Act takes effect beginning with the 1997–1998 school year."

For application provisions of Acts 1997, 75th Leg., ch. 1086, see notes following V.T.C.A., Family Code § 51.031.

§ 51.031. Habitual Felony Conduct

(a) Habitual felony conduct is conduct violating a penal law of the grade of felony, other than a state jail felony, if:

(1) the child who engaged in the conduct has at least two previous final adjudications as having engaged in delinquent conduct violating a penal law of the grade of felony;

(2) the second previous final adjudication is for conduct that occurred after the date the first previous adjudication became final; and

(3) all appeals relating to the previous adjudications considered under Subdivisions (1) and (2) have been exhausted.

(b) For purposes of this section, an adjudication is final if the child is placed on probation or committed to the Texas Youth Commission.

(c) An adjudication based on conduct that occurred before January 1, 1996, may not be considered in a disposition made under this section.

Added by Acts 1995, 74th Leg., ch. 262, § 5, eff. Jan. 1, 1996. Amended by Acts 1997, 75th Leg., ch. 1086, § 2, eff. Sept. 1, 1997.

Section 53 of Acts 1997, 75th Leg., ch. 1086 provides:

"(a) The change in law made by this Act applies only to conduct that occurs on or after the effective date of this Act. Conduct violating a penal law of the state occurs on or after the effective date of this Act if every element of the violation occurs on or after that date."

"(b) Conduct that occurs before the effective date of this Act is covered by the law in effect at the time the conduct occurred, and the former law is continued in effect for that purpose."

§ 51.04. Jurisdiction

(a) This title covers the proceedings in all cases involving the delinquent conduct or conduct indicating a need for supervision engaged in by a person who was a child within the meaning of this title at the time he engaged in the conduct, and the juvenile court has exclusive original jurisdiction over proceedings under this title.

(b) In each county, the county's juvenile board shall designate one or more district, criminal district, domestic relations, juvenile, or county courts or county courts at law as the juvenile court, subject to Subsections (c) and (d) of this section.

(c) If the county court is designated as a juvenile court, at least one other court shall be designated as the juvenile court. A county court does not have jurisdiction of a proceeding involving a petition approved by a grand jury under Section 53.045 of this code.

(d) If the judge of a court designated in Subsection (b) or (c) of this section is not an attorney licensed in this state, there shall also be designated an alternate court, the judge of which is an attorney licensed in this state.

(e) A designation made under Subsection (b) or (c) of this section may be changed from time to time by the authorized boards or judges for the convenience of the people and the welfare of children. However, there must be at all times a juvenile court designated for each county. It is the intent of the legislature that in selecting a court to be the juvenile court of each county, the selection shall be made as far as practicable so that the court designated as the juvenile court will be one which is presided over by a judge who has a sympathetic understanding of the problems of child welfare and that changes in the designation of juvenile courts be made only when the best interest of the public requires it.

(f) If the judge of the juvenile court or any alternate judge named under Subsection (b) or (c) of this section is not in the county or is otherwise unavailable, any magistrate may conduct the detention hearing provided for in Section 54.01 of this code.

(g) The juvenile board, or if there is no juvenile board, the juvenile court, may appoint a referee to conduct hearings under this title and in accordance with Section 54.10 of this code. The referee shall be an attorney licensed to practice law in this state. Payment of any referee services shall be provided from county funds.

Acts 1973, 63rd Leg., p. 1460, ch. 544, § 1, eff. Sept. 1, 1973. Amended by Acts 1975, 64th Leg., p. 1357, ch. 514, § 1, eff. June 19, 1975; Acts 1975, 64th Leg., p. 2153, ch. 693, §§ 5 to 7, eff. Sept. 1, 1975; Acts 1977, 65th Leg., p. 1112, ch. 411, § 1, eff. June 15, 1977; Acts 1987, 70th Leg., ch. 385, § 1, eff. Sept. 1, 1987; Acts 1993, 73rd Leg., ch. 168, § 4, eff. Aug. 30, 1993.

Section 20 of the 1987 amendatory act provides:

"(a) This Act applies only to offenses and conduct occurring on or after its effective date. For the purposes of this section, an offense or delinquent conduct based on an offense occurs on or after the effective date if all the elements of the offense occur on or after the effective date.

"(b) An offense or conduct that occurs before the effective date of this Act shall be prosecuted under the law in effect immediately before the effective date of this Act, and that law is continued in effect for that purpose only."

Section 7 of the 1993 amendatory act provides:

"Sections 3, 4, and 5 of this Act apply only to a trial that began on or after the effective date of this Act. A trial that began before the effective date of this Act is governed by the law in effect at the time the trial began and that law is continued in effect for that purpose."

§ 51.041. Jurisdiction After Appeal

The court retains jurisdiction over a person, without regard to the age of the person, for conduct engaged in by the person before becoming 17 years of age if, as a result of an appeal by the person under Chapter 56 of an order of the court, the order is reversed or modified and the case remanded to the court by the appellate court.

Added by Acts 1995, 74th Leg., ch. 262, § 6, eff. Jan. 1, 1996.

§ 51.0411. Jurisdiction for Transfer or Release Hearing

The court retains jurisdiction over a person, without regard to the age of the person, who is referred to the court under Section 54.11 for transfer to the Texas Department of Criminal Justice or release under supervision.

Added by Acts 1997, 75th Leg., ch. 1086, § 3, eff. June 19, 1997.

Section 55 of Acts 1997, 75th Leg., ch. 1086 provides:

"(a) Except as provided by Subsection (b) of this section, this Act takes effect September 1, 1997.

"(b) The following sections of this Act take effect immediately and apply to a person in the custody of the Texas Youth Commission or committed to the custody of the Texas Youth Commission on or after the effective date of the section:

"(1) Section 51.0411, Family Code, as added by this Act;

"(2) Sections 574.001 and 593.041, Health and Safety Code, as amended by this Act;

"(3) Sections 61.077 and 61.093, Human Resources Code, as amended by this Act; and

"(4) Section 61.0772, Human Resources Code, as added by this Act."

§ 51.042. Objection to Jurisdiction Because of Age of the Child

(a) A child who objects to the jurisdiction of the court over the child because of the age of the child must raise the objection at the adjudication hearing or discretionary transfer hearing, if any.

(b) A child who does not object as provided by Subsection (a) waives any right to object to the jurisdiction of the court because of the age of the child at a later hearing or on appeal.

Added by Acts 1995, 74th Leg., ch. 262, § 6, eff. Jan. 1, 1996.

§ 51.045. Juries in County Courts at Law

If a provision of this title requires a jury of 12 persons, that provision prevails over any other law that limits the number of members of a jury in a particular county court at law. The state and the defense are entitled to the same number of peremptory challenges allowed in a district court.

Added by Acts 1987, 70th Leg., ch. 385, § 2, eff. Sept. 1, 1987.

Section 20 of the 1987 Act provides:

"(a) This Act applies only to offenses and conduct occurring on or after its effective date. For the purposes of this section, an offense or delinquent conduct based on an offense occurs on or after the effective date if all the elements of the offense occur on or after the effective date.

"(b) An offense or conduct that occurs before the effective date of this Act shall be prosecuted under the law in effect immediately before the effective date of this Act, and that law is continued in effect for that purpose only."

§ 51.05. Court Sessions and Facilities

(a) The juvenile court shall be deemed in session at all times. Suitable quarters shall be provided by the commissioners court of each county for the hearing of cases and for the use of the judge, the probation officer, and other employees of the court.

(b) The juvenile court and the juvenile board shall report annually to the commissioners court on the suitability of the quarters and facilities of the juvenile court and may make recommendations for their improvement.

Acts 1973, 63rd Leg., p. 1460, ch. 544, § 1, eff. Sept. 1, 1973. Amended by Acts 1975, 64th Leg., p. 2154, ch. 693, § 8, eff. Sept. 1, 1975.

§ 51.06. Venue

(a) A proceeding under this title shall be commenced in:

(1) the county in which the child resides; or

(2) the county in which the alleged delinquent conduct or conduct indicating a need for supervision occurred.

(b) An application for a writ of habeas corpus brought by or on behalf of a person who has been committed to an institution under the jurisdiction of the Texas Youth Commission and which attacks the validity of the judgment of commitment shall be brought in the county in which the court that entered the judgment of commitment is located.

Acts 1973, 63rd Leg., p. 1460, ch. 544, § 1, eff. Sept. 1, 1973. Amended by Acts 1983, 68th Leg., p. 161, ch. 44, art. 1, § 1, eff. April 26, 1983; Acts 1995, 74th Leg., ch. 262, § 7, eff. Jan. 1, 1996.

§ 51.07. Transfer to Another County

(a) When a child has been found to have engaged in delinquent conduct or conduct indicating a need for supervision under Section 54.03 of this code, the juvenile court, with the consent of the child and appropriate adult given in accordance with Section 51.09 of this code, may transfer the case and transcripts of records and documents to the juvenile court of the county where the child resides for disposition of the case under Section 54.04 of this code.

(b) When a child who is on probation moves with his family from one county to another, the juvenile court may transfer the case to the juvenile court in the county of the child's new residence if the transfer is in the best interest of the child. In all other cases of transfer, consent of the receiving court is required. The transferring court shall forward transcripts of records and documents in the case to the judge of the receiving court.

Acts 1973, 63rd Leg., p. 1460, ch. 544, § 1, eff. Sept. 1, 1973.

§ 51.08. Transfer from Criminal Court

(a) If the defendant in a criminal proceeding is a child who is charged with an offense other than perjury, a traffic offense, a misdemeanor punishable by fine only other than public intoxication, or a violation of a penal ordinance of a political subdivision, unless he has been transferred to criminal court under Section 54.02 of this code, the court exercising criminal jurisdiction shall transfer the case to the juvenile court, together with a copy of the accusatory pleading and other papers, documents, and transcripts of testimony relating to the case, and shall order that the child be taken to the place of detention designated by the juvenile court, or shall release him to the custody of his parent, guardian, or custodian, to be brought before the juvenile court at a time designated by that court.

(b) A court in which there is pending a complaint against a child alleging a violation of a misdemeanor offense punishable by fine only other than a traffic offense or public intoxication or a violation of a penal ordinance of a political subdivision other than a traffic offense:

(1) shall waive its original jurisdiction and refer a child to juvenile court if the child has previously been convicted of:

(A) two or more misdemeanors punishable by fine only other than a traffic offense or public intoxication;

(B) two or more violations of a penal ordinance of a political subdivision other than a traffic offense; or

(C) one or more of each of the types of misdemeanors described in Paragraph (A) or (B) of this subdivision; and

(2) may waive its original jurisdiction and refer a child to juvenile court if the child:

(A) has not previously been convicted of a misdemeanor punishable by fine only other than a traffic offense or public intoxication or a violation of a penal ordinance of a political subdivision other than a traffic offense; or

(B) has previously been convicted of fewer than two misdemeanors punishable by fine only other than a traffic offense or public intoxication or two violations of a penal ordinance of a political subdivision other than a traffic offense.

(c) A court in which there is pending a complaint against a child alleging a violation of a misdemeanor offense punishable by fine only other than a traffic offense or public intoxication or a violation of a penal ordinance of a political subdivision other than a traffic offense shall notify the juvenile court of the county in which the court is located of the pending complaint and shall furnish to the juvenile court a copy of the final disposition of any matter for which the court does not waive its original jurisdiction under Subsection (b) of this section.

Acts 1973, 63rd Leg., p. 1460, ch. 544, § 1, eff. Sept. 1, 1973. Amended by Acts 1987, 70th Leg., ch. 1040, § 21, eff. Sept. 1, 1987; Acts 1989, 71st Leg., ch. 1245, § 2, eff. Sept. 1, 1989; Acts 1991, 72nd Leg., ch. 169, § 2, eff. Sept. 1, 1991.

Section 35 of the 1987 amendatory act provides:

"(a) This Act applies only to offenses and conduct occurring on or after its effective date. For the purposes of this section, an offense or delinquent conduct based on an offense occurs on or after the effective date if all the elements of the offense occur on or after the effective date.

"(b) An offense or conduct that occurs before the effective date of this Act shall be prosecuted under the law in effect immediately before the effective date of this Act, and that law is continued in effect for that purpose only."

Section 5 of the 1991 amendatory act provides:

"(a) This Act applies only to an offense or conduct that occurs on or after the effective date of this Act. For the purposes of this section, the offense or conduct occurs on or after the effective date of this Act if every element of the offense or of conduct that violates a penal law of this state or of a penal ordinance of a political subdivision of this state occurs on or after that date.

"(b) An offense or conduct that occurs before the effective date of this Act is governed by the law in effect at the time the offense or conduct occurred, and that law is continued in effect for that purpose."

§ 51.09. Waiver of Rights

Unless a contrary intent clearly appears elsewhere in this title, any right granted to a child by this title or by the constitution or laws of this state or the United States may be waived in proceedings under this title if:

(1) the waiver is made by the child and the attorney for the child;

(2) the child and the attorney waiving the right are informed of and understand the right and the possible consequences of waiving it;

(3) the waiver is voluntary; and

(4) the waiver is made in writing or in court proceedings that are recorded.

Acts 1973, 63rd Leg., p. 1460, ch. 544, § 1, eff. Sept. 1, 1973. Amended by Acts 1975, 64th Leg., p. 2154, ch. 693, § 9, eff. Sept. 1, 1975; Acts 1989, 71st Leg., ch. 84, § 1, eff. Sept. 1, 1989; Acts 1991, 72nd Leg., ch. 64, § 1, eff. Sept. 1, 1991; Acts 1991, 72nd Leg., ch. 429, § 1, eff. Sept. 1, 1991; Acts 1991, 72nd Leg., ch. 557, § 1, eff. Sept. 1, 1991; Acts 1991, 72nd Leg., ch. 593, § 1, eff. Aug. 26, 1991; Acts 1995, 74th Leg., ch. 262, §§ 8, 9, eff. Jan. 1, 1996; Acts 1997, 75th Leg., ch. 1086, § 4, eff. Sept. 1, 1997.

Section 2 of the 1989 amendatory act provides:

"This Act takes effect September 1, 1989, and applies only to the admissibility of a statement made on or after that date. The admissibility of a statement made before the effective date of this Act is governed by the law in effect at the time the statement was made, and that law is continued in effect for that purpose."

Section 2 of Acts 1991, 72nd Leg., ch. 64 provides:

"This Act takes effect September 1, 1991, and applies only to a child who appears before a magistrate on or after the effective date of this Act."

Section 2 of Acts 1991, 72nd Leg., ch. 429 provides:

"(a) The change in law made by this Act applies only to conduct that occurs on or after the effective date of this Act. Conduct violating a penal law of this state occurs on or after the effective date of this Act if every element of the violation occurs on or after that date.

"(b) Conduct that occurs before the effective date of this Act is covered by the law in effect at the time the conduct occurred, and the former law is continued in effect for that purpose."

Section 4 of Acts 1991, 72nd Leg., ch. 557 provides:

"(a) The change in law made by this Act applies only to conduct that occurs on or after the effective date of this Act. Conduct violating a penal law of this state occurs on or after the effective date of this Act if every element of the violation occurs on or after that date.

"(b) Conduct that occurs before the effective date of this Act is governed by the law in effect at the time the conduct occurred, and the former law is continued in effect for that purpose."

§ 51.095. Admissibility of a Statement of a Child

(a) Notwithstanding Section 51.09, the statement of a child is admissible in evidence in any future proceeding concerning the matter about which the statement was given if:

(1) the statement is made in writing when the child is in a detention facility or other place of confinement or in the custody of an officer and:

(A) the statement shows that the child has at some time before the making of the statement received from a magistrate a warning that:

(i) the child may remain silent and not make any statement at all and that any statement that the child makes may be used in evidence against the child;

(ii) the child has the right to have an attorney present to advise the child either prior to any questioning or during the questioning;

(iii) if the child is unable to employ an attorney, the child has the right to have an attorney appointed to counsel with the child before or during any interviews with peace officers or attorneys representing the state; and

(iv) the child has the right to terminate the interview at any time;

(B) and:

(i) the statement must be signed in the presence of a magistrate by the child with no law enforcement officer or prosecuting attorney present, except that a magistrate may require a bailiff or a law enforcement officer if a bailiff is not available to be present if the magistrate determines that the presence of the bailiff or law enforcement officer is necessary for the personal safety of the magistrate or other court personnel, provided that the bailiff or law enforcement officer may not carry a weapon in the presence of the child; and

(ii) the magistrate must be fully convinced that the child understands the nature and contents of the statement and that the child is signing the same voluntarily, and if a statement is taken, the magistrate must sign a written statement verifying the foregoing requisites have been met;

(C) the child knowingly, intelligently, and voluntarily waives these rights before and during the making of the statement and signs the statement in the presence of a magistrate; and

(D) the magistrate certifies that the magistrate has examined the child independent of any law enforcement officer or prosecuting attorney, except as required to ensure the personal safety of the magistrate or other court personnel, and has determined that the child understands the nature and contents of the statement and has knowingly, intelligently, and voluntarily waived these rights;

(2) the statement is made orally and the child makes a statement of facts or circumstances that are found to be true, which conduct tends to establish his guilt, such as the finding of secreted or stolen property, or the instrument with which he states the offense was committed;

(3) the statement was res gestae of the delinquent conduct or the conduct indicating a need for supervision or of the arrest;

(4) the statement is made:

(A) in open court at the child's adjudication hearing;

(B) before a grand jury considering a petition, under Section 53.045, that the child engaged in delinquent conduct; or

(C) at a preliminary hearing concerning the child held in compliance with this code, other than at a detention hearing under Section 54.01; or

(5) the statement is made orally when the child is in a detention facility or other place of confinement or in the custody of an officer and the statement is recorded by an electronic recording device, including a device that records images, and:

(A) before making the statement, the child is given the warning described by Subdivision (1)(A) by a magistrate, the warning is a part of the recording, and the child knowingly, intelligently, and voluntarily waives each right stated in the warning;

(B) the recording device is capable of making an accurate recording, the operator of the device is competent to use the device, the recording is accurate, and the recording has not been altered;

(C) each voice on the recording is identified; and

(D) not later than the 20th day before the date of the proceeding, the attorney representing the child is given a complete and accurate copy of each recording of the child made under this subdivision.

(b) This section and Section 51.09 do not preclude the admission of a statement made by the child if:

(1) the statement does not stem from custodial interrogation; or

(2) without regard to whether the statement stems from custodial interrogation, the statement is voluntary and has a bearing on the credibility of the child as a witness.

(c) An electronic recording of a child's statement made under Subsection (a)(5) shall be preserved until all juvenile or criminal matters relating to any conduct referred to in the statement are final, including the exhaustion of all appeals, or barred from prosecution.

Added by Acts 1997, 75th Leg., ch. 1086, § 4, eff. Sept. 1, 1997.

§ 51.10. Right to Assistance of Attorney; Compensation

(a) A child may be represented by an attorney at every stage of proceedings under this title, including:

(1) the detention hearing required by Section 54.01 of this code;

(2) the hearing to consider transfer to criminal court required by Section 54.02 of this code;

(3) the adjudication hearing required by Section 54.03 of this code;

(4) the disposition hearing required by Section 54.04 of this code;

(5) the hearing to modify disposition required by Section 54.05 of this code;

(6) hearings required by Chapter 55 of this code;

(7) habeas corpus proceedings challenging the legality of detention resulting from action under this title; and

(8) proceedings in a court of civil appeals or the Texas Supreme Court reviewing proceedings under this title.

(b) The child's right to representation by an attorney shall not be waived in:

(1) a hearing to consider transfer to criminal court as required by Section 54.02 of this code;

(2) an adjudication hearing as required by Section 54.03 of this code;

(3) a disposition hearing as required by Section 54.04 of this code;

(4) a hearing prior to commitment to the Texas Youth Commission as a modified disposition in accordance with Section 54.05(f) of this code; or

(5) hearings required by Chapter 55 of this code.

(c) If the child was not represented by an attorney at the detention hearing required by Section 54.01 of this code and a determination was made to detain the child, the child shall immediately be entitled to representation by an attorney. The court shall order the retention of an attorney according to Subsection (d) or appoint an attorney according to Subsection (f).

(d) The court shall order a child's parent or other person responsible for support of the child to employ an attorney to represent the child, if:

(1) the child is not represented by an attorney;

(2) after giving the appropriate parties an opportunity to be heard, the court determines that the parent or other person responsible for support of the child is financially able to employ an attorney to represent the child; and

(3) the child's right to representation by an attorney:

(A) has not been waived under Section 51.09 of this code; or

(B) may not be waived under Subsection (b) of this section.

(e) The court may enforce orders under Subsection (c) of this section by proceedings under Section 54.07 of this code or by appointing counsel and ordering the parent or other person responsible for support of the child to pay a reasonable attorney's fee set by the court. The order may be enforced under Section 54.07 of this code.

(f) The court shall appoint an attorney to represent the interest of a child entitled to representation by an attorney, if:

(1) the child is not represented by an attorney;

(2) the court determines that the child's parent or other person responsible for support of the child is

financially unable to employ an attorney to represent the child; and

(3) the child's right to representation by an attorney:

(A) has not been waived under Section 51.09 of this code; or

(B) may not be waived under Subsection (b) of this section.

(g) The juvenile court may appoint an attorney in any case in which it deems representation necessary to protect the interests of the child.

(h) Any attorney representing a child in proceedings under this title is entitled to 10 days to prepare for any adjudication or transfer hearing under this title.

(i) Except as provided in Subsection (d) of this section, an attorney appointed under this section to represent the interests of a child shall be paid from the general fund of the county in which the proceedings were instituted according to the schedule in Article 26.05 of the Texas Code of Criminal Procedure, 1965. For this purpose, a bona fide appeal to a court of civil appeals or proceedings on the merits in the Texas Supreme Court are considered the equivalent of a bona fide appeal to the Texas Court of Criminal Appeals.

Acts 1973, 63rd Leg., p. 1460, ch. 544, § 1, eff. Sept. 1, 1973. Amended by Acts 1983, 68th Leg., p. 161, ch. 44, art. 1, § 2, eff. April 26, 1983; Acts 1995, 74th Leg., ch. 262, § 11, eff. Jan. 1, 1996.

§ 51.11. Guardian Ad Litem

(a) If a child appears before the juvenile court without a parent or guardian, the court shall appoint a guardian ad litem to protect the interests of the child. The juvenile court need not appoint a guardian ad litem if a parent or guardian appears with the child.

(b) In any case in which it appears to the juvenile court that the child's parent or guardian is incapable or unwilling to make decisions in the best interest of the child with respect to proceedings under this title, the court may appoint a guardian ad litem to protect the interests of the child in the proceedings.

(c) An attorney for a child may also be his guardian ad litem. A law-enforcement officer, probation officer, or other employee of the juvenile court may not be appointed guardian ad litem.

Acts 1973, 63rd Leg., p. 1460, ch. 544, § 1, eff. Sept. 1, 1973.

§ 51.115. Attendance at Hearing: Parent or Other Guardian

(a) Each parent of a child, each managing and possessory conservator of a child, each court-appointed custodian of a child, and a guardian of the person of the child shall attend each hearing affecting the child held under:

(1) Section 54.02 (waiver of jurisdiction and discretionary transfer to criminal court);

(2) Section 54.03 (adjudication hearing);

(3) Section 54.04 (disposition hearing);

(4) Section 54.05 (hearing to modify disposition); and

(5) Section 54.11 (release or transfer hearing).

(b) Subsection (a) does not apply to:

(1) a person for whom, for good cause shown, the court waives attendance;

(2) a person who is not a resident of this state; or

(3) a parent of a child for whom a managing conservator has been appointed and the parent is not a conservator of the child.

(c) A person required under this section to attend a hearing is entitled to reasonable written or oral notice that includes a statement of the place, date, and time of the hearing and that the attendance of the person is required. The notice may be included with or attached to any other notice required by this chapter to be given the person. Separate notice is not required for a disposition hearing that convenes on the adjournment of an adjudication hearing. If a person required under this section fails to attend a hearing, the juvenile court may proceed with the hearing.

(d) A person who is required by Subsection (a) to attend a hearing, who receives the notice of the hearing, and who fails to attend the hearing may be punished by the court for contempt by a fine of not less than $100 and not more than $1,000. In addition to or in lieu of contempt, the court may order the person to receive counseling or to attend an educational course on the duties and responsibilities of parents and skills and techniques in raising children.

Added by Acts 1995, 74th Leg., ch. 262, § 10, eff. Jan. 1, 1996.

§ 51.116. Right to Reemployment

(a) An employer may not terminate the employment of a permanent employee because the employee is required under Section 51.115 to attend a hearing.

(b) An employee whose employment is terminated in violation of this section is entitled to return to the same employment that the employee held when notified of the hearing if the employee, as soon as practical after the hearing, gives the employer actual notice that the employee intends to return.

(c) A person who is injured because of a violation of this section is entitled to reinstatement to the person's former position and to damages, but the damages may not exceed an amount equal to six months' compensation at the rate at which the person was compensated when required to attend the hearing.

(d) The injured person is also entitled to reasonable attorney's fees in an amount approved by the court.

(e) It is a defense to an action brought under this section that the employer's circumstances changed while the employee attended the hearing so that reemployment was impossible or unreasonable. To establish a defense under this subsection, an employer must prove that the termination of employment was because of circumstances other than the employee's attendance at the hearing.

Added by Acts 1995, 74th Leg., ch. 262, § 10, eff. Jan. 1, 1996.

§ 51.12. Place and Conditions of Detention

(a) Except as provided by Subsection (h), a child may be detained only in a:

(1) juvenile processing office in compliance with Section 52.025;

(2) place of nonsecure custody in compliance with Section 52.027;

(3) certified juvenile detention facility that complies with the requirements of Subsection (f); or

(4) secure detention facility as provided by Subsection (i).

(b) The proper authorities in each county shall provide a suitable place of detention for children who are parties to proceedings under this title, but the juvenile court shall control the conditions and terms of detention and detention supervision and shall permit visitation with the child at all reasonable times.

(c) In each county, each judge of the juvenile court and the members of the juvenile board shall personally inspect the juvenile pre-adjudication secure detention facilities and any public or private juvenile secure correctional facilities used for post-adjudication confinement that are located in the county and operated under authority of the juvenile board at least annually and shall certify in writing to the authorities responsible for operating and giving financial support to the facilities and to the Texas Juvenile Probation Commission that they are suitable or unsuitable for the detention of children in accordance with:

(1) the requirements of Subsections (a), (f), and (g); and

(2) minimum professional standards for the detention of children in pre-adjudication or post-adjudication secure confinement promulgated by the Texas Juvenile Probation Commission or, at the election of the juvenile board, the current standards promulgated by the American Correctional Association.

Text of subsec. (d) as amended by Acts 1997, 75th Leg., ch. 772, § 1

(d) No child shall be placed in a facility that has not been certified under Subsection (c) of this section as suitable for the detention of children and registered under Subsection (i) of this section. A child detained in a facility that has not been certified under Subsection (c) of this section as suitable for the detention of children or that has not been registered under Subsection (i) of this section shall be entitled to immediate release from custody in that facility.

Text of subsec. (d) as amended by Acts 1997, 75th Leg., ch. 1374, § 1

(d) Except as provided by Subsection (i), a child may not be placed in a facility that has not been certified under Subsection (c) as suitable for the detention of children. Except as provided by Subsection (i), a child detained in a facility that has not been certified under Subsection (c) as suitable for the detention of children shall be entitled to immediate release from custody in that facility.

(e) If there is no certified place of detention in the county in which the petition is filed, the designated place of detention may be in another county.

(f) A child detained in a building that contains a jail, lockup, or other place of secure confinement, including an alcohol or other drug treatment facility, shall be separated by sight and sound from adults detained in the same building. Children and adults are separated by sight and sound only if they are unable to see each other and conversation between them is not possible. The separation must extend to all areas of the facility, including sally ports and passageways, and those areas used for admission, counseling, sleeping, toileting, showering, dining, recreational, educational, or vocational activities, and health care. The separation may be accomplished through architectural design.

(g) Except for a child detained in a juvenile processing office, a place of nonsecure custody, or a secure detention facility as provided by Subsection (i), a child detained in a building that contains a jail or lockup may not have any contact with:

(1) part-time or full-time security staff, including management, who have contact with adults detained in the same building; or

(2) direct-care staff who have contact with adults detained in the same building.

(h) This section does not apply to a person:

(1) after transfer to criminal court for prosecution under Section 54.02; or

(2) who is at least 18 years of age and who has been taken into custody after having:

(A) escaped from a juvenile facility; or

(B) violated a condition of probation or of release under supervision of the Texas Youth Commission.

Text of subsection (i) as added by Acts 1997, 75th Leg., ch. 772, § 1

(i) Except for a facility operated or certified by the Texas Youth Commission, a governmental unit or private entity that operates or contracts for the operation of a juvenile pre-adjudication secure detention facility or a juvenile post-adjudication secure correctional facility in this state shall:

(1) register the facility annually with the Texas Juvenile Probation Commission; and

(2) adhere to all applicable minimum standards for the facility.

Text of subsection (i) as added by Acts 1997, 75th., ch. 1374, § 1

(i) After being taken into custody, a child may be detained in a secure detention facility until the child is released under Section 53.01, 53.012, or 53.02 or until a detention hearing is held under Section 54.01(a), regardless of whether the facility has been certified under Subsection (c), if:

(1) a certified juvenile detention facility is not available in the county in which the child is taken into custody;

(2) the detention facility complies with:

(A) the short-term detention standards adopted by the Texas Juvenile Probation Commission; and

(B) the requirements of Subsection (f); and

(3) the detention facility has been designated by the county juvenile board for the county in which the facility is located.

(j) If a child who is detained under Subsection (i) is not released from detention at the conclusion of the detention hearing for a reason stated in Section 54.01(e), the child may be detained after the hearing only in a certified juvenile detention facility.

Acts 1973, 63rd Leg., p. 1460, ch. 544, § 1, eff. Sept. 1, 1973. Amended by Acts 1975, 64th Leg., p. 2155, ch. 693, §§ 10, 11, eff. Sept. 1, 1975; Acts 1985, 69th Leg., ch. 293, § 1, eff. Aug. 26, 1985; Acts 1987, 70th Leg., ch. 149, § 31, eff. Sept. 1, 1987; Acts 1995, 74th Leg., ch. 262, § 12, eff. Jan. 1, 1996; Acts 1997, 75th Leg., ch. 772, § 1, eff. Sept. 1, 1997; Acts 1997, 75th Leg., ch. 1374, § 1, eff. Sept. 1, 1997.

Section 10 of Acts 1997, 75th Leg., ch. 1374 provides:

"The change in law made by this Act applies only to a child taken into custody on or after the effective date of this Act."

§ 51.13. Effect of Adjudication or Disposition

(a) Except as provided by Subsection (d), an order of adjudication or disposition in a proceeding under this title is not a conviction of crime, and does not impose any civil disability ordinarily resulting from a conviction or operate to disqualify the child in any civil service application or appointment.

(b) The adjudication or disposition of a child or evidence adduced in a hearing under this title may be used only in subsequent proceedings under this title in which the child is a party or in subsequent sentencing proceedings in criminal court against the child to the extent permitted by the Texas Code of Criminal Procedure, 1965.

(c) A child may not be committed or transferred to a penal institution or other facility used primarily for the execution of sentences of persons convicted of crime, except:

(1) for temporary detention in a jail or lockup pending juvenile court hearing or disposition under conditions meeting the requirements of Section 51.12 of this code;

(2) after transfer for prosecution in criminal court under Section 54.02 of this code; or

(3) after transfer from the Texas Youth Commission under Section 61.084, Human Resources Code.

(d) An adjudication under Section 54.03 that a child engaged in conduct that occurred on or after January 1, 1996, and that constitutes a felony offense resulting in commitment to the Texas Youth Commission under Section 54.04(d)(2), (d)(3), or (m) or 54.05(f) is a final felony conviction only for the purposes of Sections 12.42(a)–(c) and (e), Penal Code.

Acts 1973, 63rd Leg., p. 1460, ch. 544, § 1, eff. Sept. 1, 1973. Amended by Acts 1987, 70th Leg., ch. 385, § 3, eff. Sept. 1, 1987; Acts 1993, 73rd Leg., ch. 799, § 1, eff. June 18, 1993; Acts 1995, 74th Leg., ch. 262, § 13, eff. Jan. 1, 1996; Acts 1997, 75th Leg., ch. 1086, § 5, eff. Sept. 1, 1997.

Section 20 of the 1987 amendatory act provides:

"(a) This Act applies only to offenses and conduct occurring on or after its effective date. For the purposes of this section, an offense or delinquent conduct based on an offense occurs on or after the effective date if all the elements of the offense occur on or after the effective date.

"(b) An offense or conduct that occurs before the effective date of this Act shall be prosecuted under the law in effect immediately before the effective date of this Act, and that law is continued in effect for that purpose only."

§ 51.14. Repealed by Acts 1995, 74th Leg., ch. 262, § 100(a), eff. Jan. 1, 1996

§ 51.15. Repealed by Acts 1995, 74th Leg., ch. 262, § 100(a), eff. Jan. 1, 1996

Acts 1995, 74th Leg., ch. 669 added subsec. (j) effective Aug. 28, 1995. However, subsec. (j) continued in effect only for purposes of prosecutions of conduct committed before Jan. 1, 1996, pursuant to Acts 1995, 74th Leg., ch. 262, § 104, which provides:

"(a) An amendment to any provision of Title 3, Family Code, made by another Act of the 74th Legislature, Regular Session, 1995, applies only to conduct that occurs on or after the effective date of the other Act and before January 1, 1996. The amendment made by the other Act continues in effect only for the limited purpose of the prosecution of the conduct committed before January 1, 1996.

"(b) For purposes of Subsection (a) of this section, conduct violating the penal law of this state occurs before January 1, 1996, only if every element of the violation occurs before that date."

§ 51.151. Polygraph Examination

If a child is taken into custody under Section 52.01 of this code, a person may not administer a polygraph examination to the child without the consent of the child's attorney or the juvenile court unless the child is transferred to criminal court for prosecution under Section 54.02 of this code.

Added by Acts 1987, 70th Leg., ch. 708, § 1, eff. Sept. 1, 1987.

Section 3 of the 1987 Act provides:

"This Act takes effect September 1, 1987, and applies to a polygraph examination conducted on or after that date. An examination conducted before that date is subject to the law in effect before the effective date of this Act, and that law is continued in effect for that purpose."

§ 51.16. Repealed by Acts 1995, 74th Leg., ch. 262, § 100(a), eff. Jan. 1, 1996

§ 51.17. Procedure and Evidence

(a) Except for the burden of proof to be borne by the state in adjudicating a child to be delinquent or in need of supervision under Section 54.03(f) or otherwise when in conflict with a provision of this title, the Texas Rules of Civil Procedure govern proceedings under this title.

(b) Discovery in a proceeding under this title is governed by the Code of Criminal Procedure and by case decisions in criminal cases.

(c) Except as otherwise provided by this title, the Texas Rules of Criminal Evidence and Chapter 38, Code of Criminal Procedure, apply in a judicial proceeding under this title.

Acts 1973, 63rd Leg., p. 1460, ch. 544, § 1, eff. Sept. 1, 1973. Amended by Acts 1995, 74th Leg., ch. 262, § 14, eff. Jan. 1, 1996.

§ 51.18. Election Between Juvenile Court and Alternate Juvenile Court

(a) This section applies only to a child who has a right to a trial before a juvenile court the judge of which is not an attorney licensed in this state.

(b) On any matter that may lead to an order appealable under Section 56.01 of this code, a child may be tried before either the juvenile court or the alternate juvenile court.

(c) The child may elect to be tried before the alternate juvenile court only if the child files a written notice with that court not later than 10 days before the date of the trial. After the notice is filed, the child may be tried only in the alternate juvenile court. If the child does not file a notice as provided by this subsection, the child may be tried only in the juvenile court.

(d) If the child is tried before the juvenile court, the child is not entitled to a trial de novo before the alternate juvenile court.

(e) The child may appeal any order of the juvenile court or alternate juvenile court only as provided by Section 56.01 of this code.

Added by Acts 1977, 65th Leg., p. 1112, ch. 411, § 2, eff. June 15, 1977. Amended by Acts 1993, 73rd Leg., ch. 168, § 3, eff. Aug. 30, 1993.

Section 7 of the 1993 amendatory act provides:

"Sections 3, 4, and 5 of this Act apply only to a trial that began on or after the effective date of this Act. A trial that began before the effective date of this Act is governed by the law in effect at the time the trial began and that law is continued in effect for that purpose."

§ 51.19. Limitation Periods

(a) The limitation periods and the procedures for applying the limitation periods under Chapter 12, Code of Criminal Procedure, and other statutory law apply to proceedings under this title.

(b) For purposes of computing a limitation period, a petition filed in juvenile court for a transfer or an adjudication hearing is equivalent to an indictment or information and is treated as presented when the petition is filed in the proper court.

(c) The limitation period is two years for an offense or conduct that is not given a specific limitation period under Chapter 12, Code of Criminal Procedure, or other statutory law.

Added by Acts 1997, 75th Leg., ch. 1086, § 6, eff. Sept. 1, 1997.

CHAPTER 52. PROCEEDINGS BEFORE AND INCLUDING REFERRAL TO JUVENILE COURT

Section

§ 52.01. Taking into Custody; Issuance of Warning Notice

(a) A child may be taken into custody:

(1) pursuant to an order of the juvenile court under the provisions of this subtitle;[1]

(2) pursuant to the laws of arrest;

(3) by a law-enforcement officer, including a school district peace officer commissioned under Section 37.081, Education Code, if there is probable cause to believe that the child has engaged in:

(A) conduct that violates a penal law of this state or a penal ordinance of any political subdivision of this state; or

(B) delinquent conduct or conduct indicating a need for supervision;

(4) by a probation officer if there is probable cause to believe that the child has violated a condition of probation imposed by the juvenile court; or

(5) pursuant to a directive to apprehend issued as provided by Section 52.015.

(b) The taking of a child into custody is not an arrest except for the purpose of determining the validity of taking him into custody or the validity of a search under the laws and constitution of this state or of the United States.

(c) A law-enforcement officer authorized to take a child into custody under Subdivisions (2) and (3) of Subsection (a) of this section may issue a warning notice to the child in lieu of taking him into custody if:

(1) guidelines for warning disposition have been issued by the law-enforcement agency in which the officer works;

(2) the guidelines have been approved by the juvenile court of the county in which the disposition is made;

(3) the disposition is authorized by the guidelines;

(4) the warning notice identifies the child and describes his alleged conduct;

(5) a copy of the warning notice is sent to the child's parent, guardian, or custodian as soon as practicable after disposition; and

(6) a copy of the warning notice is filed with the law-enforcement agency and the office or official designated by the juvenile court.

(d) A warning notice filed with the office or official designated by the juvenile court may be used as the basis of further action if necessary.

Acts 1973, 63rd Leg., p. 1460, ch. 544, § 1, eff. Sept. 1, 1973. Amended by Acts 1993, 73rd Leg., ch. 115, § 2, eff. May 11, 1993; Acts 1995, 74th Leg., ch. 262, § 15, eff. Jan. 1, 1996; Acts 1997, 75th Leg., ch. 165, § 6.08, eff. Sept. 1, 1997.

[1] So in enrolled bill; probably should read "this title;".

§ 52.015. Directive to Apprehend

(a) On the request of a law-enforcement or probation officer, a juvenile court may issue a directive to apprehend a child if the court finds there is probable cause to take the child into custody under the provisions of this title.

(b) On the issuance of a directive to apprehend, any law-enforcement or probation officer shall take the child into custody.

(c) An order under this section is not subject to appeal.

Added by Acts 1995, 74th Leg., ch. 262, § 16, eff. Jan. 1, 1996.

§ 52.02. Release or Delivery to Court

(a) Except as provided by Subsection (c), a person taking a child into custody, without unnecessary delay and without first taking the child to any place other than a juvenile processing office designated under Section 52.025, shall do one of the following:

(1) release the child to a parent, guardian, custodian of the child, or other responsible adult upon

that person's promise to bring the child before the juvenile court as requested by the court;

(2) bring the child before the office or official designated by the juvenile court if there is probable cause to believe that the child engaged in delinquent conduct or conduct indicating a need for supervision;

(3) bring the child to a detention facility designated by the juvenile court;

(4) bring the child to a secure detention facility as provided by Section 51.12(i);

(5) bring the child to a medical facility if the child is believed to suffer from a serious physical condition or illness that requires prompt treatment; or

(6) dispose of the case under Section 52.03.

(b) A person taking a child into custody shall promptly give notice of his action and a statement of the reason for taking the child into custody, to:

(1) the child's parent, guardian, or custodian; and

(2) the office or official designated by the juvenile court.

(c) A person who takes a child into custody and who has reasonable grounds to believe that the child has been operating a motor vehicle in a public place while having any detectable amount of alcohol in the child's system may, before complying with Subsection (a):

(1) take the child to a place to obtain a specimen of the child's breath or blood as provided by Chapter 724, Transportation Code; and

(2) perform intoxilyzer processing and videotaping of the child in an adult processing office of a police department.

(d) Notwithstanding Section 51.09(a), a child taken into custody as provided by Subsection (c) may submit to the taking of a breath specimen or refuse to submit to the taking of a breath specimen without the concurrence of an attorney, but only if the request made of the child to give the specimen and the child's response to that request is videotaped. A videotape made under this subsection must be maintained until the disposition of any proceeding against the child relating to the arrest is final and be made available to an attorney representing the child during that period.

Acts 1973, 63rd Leg., p. 1460, ch. 544, § 1, eff. Sept. 1, 1973. Amended by Acts 1991, 72nd Leg., ch. 495, § 1, eff. Sept. 1, 1991; Acts 1997, 75th Leg., ch. 1013, § 15, eff. Sept. 1, 1997; Acts 1997, 75th Leg., ch. 1374, § 2, eff. Sept. 1, 1997.

Section 3 of the 1991 amendatory act provides:

"(a) The change in law made by this Act applies only to conduct that occurs on or after the effective date of this Act. Conduct violating a penal law of this state occurs on or after the effective date of this Act if every element of the violation occurs on or after that date.

"(b) Conduct that occurs before the effective date of this Act is covered by the law in effect at the time the conduct occurred, and the former law is continued in effect for that purpose."

For application provisions of Acts 1997, 75th Leg., ch. 1013, see notes following V.T.C.A., Family Code § 51.03.

§ 52.025. Designation of Juvenile Processing Office

(a) The juvenile court may designate an office or a room, which may be located in a police facility or sheriff's offices, as the juvenile processing office for the temporary detention of a child taken into custody under Section 52.01 of this code. The office may not be a cell or holding facility used for detentions other than detentions under this section. The juvenile court by written order may prescribe the conditions of the designation and limit the activities that may occur in the office during the temporary detention.

(b) A child may be detained in a juvenile processing office only for:

(1) the return of the child to the custody of a person under Section 52.02(a)(1);

(2) the completion of essential forms and records required by the juvenile court or this title;

(3) the photographing and fingerprinting of the child if otherwise authorized at the time of temporary detention by this title;

(4) the issuance of warnings to the child as required or permitted by this title; or

(5) the receipt of a statement by the child under Section 51.095(a)(1), (2), (3), or (5).

(c) A child may not be left unattended in a juvenile processing office and is entitled to be accompanied by the child's parent, guardian, or other custodian or by the child's attorney.

(d) A child may not be detained in a juvenile processing office for longer than six hours.

Added by Acts 1991, 72nd Leg., ch. 495, § 2, eff. Sept. 1, 1991. Amended by Acts 1997, 75th Leg., ch. 1086, § 48, eff. Sept. 1, 1997.

Section 3 of the 1991 Act provides:

"(a) The change in law made by this Act applies only to conduct that occurs on or after the effective date of this Act. Conduct violating a penal law of this state occurs on or after the effective date of this Act if every element of the violation occurs on or after that date.

"(b) Conduct that occurs before the effective date of this Act is covered by the law in effect at the time the conduct occurred, and the former law is continued in effect for that purpose."

§ 52.026. Responsibility for Transporting Juvenile Offenders

(a) It shall be the duty of the law enforcement officer who has taken a child into custody to transport the child to the appropriate detention facility if the child is not released to the parent, guardian, or custodian of the child.

(b) If the juvenile detention facility is located outside the county in which the child is taken into custody, it shall be the duty of the sheriff of that county to transport the child to the appropriate juvenile detention facility unless the child is:

(1) detained in a secure detention facility under Section 51.12(i); or

(2) released to the parent, guardian, or custodian of the child.

(c) On adoption of an order by the juvenile board and approval of the juvenile board's order by record vote of the commissioners court, it shall be the duty of the sheriff of the county in which the child is taken into custody to transport the child to and from all scheduled juvenile court proceedings and appearances and other activities ordered by the juvenile court.

Added by Acts 1993, 73rd Leg., ch. 411, § 1, eff. Aug. 30, 1993. Amended by Acts 1997, 75th Leg., ch. 1374, § 3, eff. Sept. 1, 1997.

§ 52.027. Children Taken into Custody for Traffic Offenses, Other Fineable Only Offenses, or as a Status Offender

(a) A child may be released to the child's parent, guardian, custodian, or other responsible adult as provided in Section 52.02(a)(1) if the child is taken into custody:

(1) for a traffic offense;

(2) for an offense other than public intoxication punishable by fine only; or

(3) as a status offender or nonoffender.

(b) A child described by Subsection (a) must be taken only to a place previously designated by the head of the law enforcement agency with custody of the child as an appropriate place of nonsecure custody for children unless the child:

(1) is released under Section 52.02(a)(1);

(2) is taken before a municipal court or justice court; or

(3) for truancy or running away, is taken to a juvenile detention facility, or a secure detention facility, as authorized by Sections 51.12(a)(3) and (4), respectively, for the detention of the child as provided by Section 54.011.

(c) A place of nonsecure custody for children must be an unlocked, multipurpose area. A lobby, office, or interrogation room is suitable if the area is not designated, set aside, or used as a secure detention area and is not part of a secure detention area. A place of nonsecure custody may be a juvenile processing office designated under Section 52.025 if the area is not locked when it is used as a place of nonsecure custody.

(d) The following procedures shall be followed in a place of nonsecure custody for children:

(1) a child may not be secured physically to a cuffing rail, chair, desk, or other stationary object;

(2) the child may be held in the nonsecure facility only long enough to accomplish the purpose of identification, investigation, processing, release to parents, or the arranging of transportation to the appropriate juvenile court, juvenile detention facility, secure detention facility, municipal court, or justice court;

(3) residential use of the area is prohibited; and

(4) the child shall be under continuous visual supervision by a law enforcement officer or facility staff person during the time the child is in nonsecure custody.

(e) Notwithstanding any other provision of this section, a child may not, under any circumstances, be detained in a place of nonsecure custody for more than six hours.

(f) A child taken into custody for a traffic offense or an offense, other than public intoxication, punishable by fine only may be presented or detained in a detention facility designated by the juvenile court under Section 52.02(a)(3) only if:

(1) the child's non-traffic case is transferred to the juvenile court by a municipal court or justice court under Section 51.08(b); or

(2) the child is referred to the juvenile court by a municipal court or justice court for contempt of court under Subsection (h).

(g) A law enforcement officer may issue a field release citation, as provided by Article 14.06, Code of Criminal Procedure, in place of taking a child into custody for a traffic offense or an offense, other than public intoxication, punishable by fine only.

(h) A municipal court or justice court may not hold a child in contempt for intentionally refusing to obey a lawful order of disposition after an adjudication of guilt of a traffic offense or other offense punishable by fine only. The municipal court or justice court shall instead refer the child to the appropriate juvenile court for delinquent conduct for contempt of the municipal court or justice court order.

(i) In this section, "child" means a person who:

(1) is at least 10 years of age and younger than 17 years of age and who is charged with or convicted of a traffic offense; or

(2) is at least 10 years of age and younger than 18 years of age and who:

(A) is charged with or convicted of an offense, other than public intoxication, punishable by fine only as a result of an act committed before becoming 17 years of age;

(B) is a status offender and was taken into custody as a status offender for conduct engaged in before becoming 17 years of age; or

(C) is a nonoffender and became a nonoffender before becoming 17 years of age.

Added by Acts 1995, 74th Leg., ch. 262, § 17, eff. Jan. 1, 1996. Amended by Acts 1997, 75th Leg., ch. 822, § 3, eff. Sept. 1, 1997; Acts 1997, 75th Leg., ch. 1374, § 4, eff. Sept. 1, 1997.

For application provision of Acts 1997, 75th Leg., ch. 822, see notes following V.T.C.A., Family Code § 51.02.

§ 52.028. Children Taken into Custody for Violation of Juvenile Curfew Ordinance or Order

(a) A peace officer taking into custody a person under 17 years of age for violation of a juvenile curfew ordinance of a municipality or order of the commissioners court of a county shall, without unnecessary delay:

(1) release the person to the person's parent, guardian, or custodian;

(2) take the person before a municipal or justice court to answer the charge; or

(3) take the person to a place designated as a juvenile curfew processing office by the head of the law enforcement agency having custody of the person.

(b) A juvenile curfew processing office must observe the following procedures:

(1) the office must be an unlocked, multipurpose area that is not designated, set aside, or used as a secure detention area or part of a secure detention area;

(2) the person may not be secured physically to a cuffing rail, chair, desk, or stationary object;

(3) the person may not be held longer than necessary to accomplish the purposes of identification, investigation, processing, release to parents, guardians, or custodians, and arrangement of transportation to school or court;

(4) a juvenile curfew processing office may not be designated or intended for residential purposes;

(5) the person must be under continuous visual supervision by a peace officer or other person during the time the person is in the juvenile curfew processing office; and

(6) a person may not be held in a juvenile curfew processing office for more than six hours.

(c) A place designated under this section as a juvenile curfew processing office is not subject to the approval of the juvenile board having jurisdiction where the governmental entity is located.

Added by Acts 1995, 74th Leg., ch. 262, § 17, eff. May 31, 1995.

Section 107 of the 1995 Act provides:

"A designation by a municipality or a county of a juvenile curfew processing office for the detention of a person who is alleged to have violated a curfew ordinance or order made before Section 52.028, Family Code, as added by this Act, takes effect is validated if the processing office otherwise meets the requirements of that section."

§ 52.03. Disposition Without Referral to Court

(a) A law-enforcement officer authorized by this title to take a child into custody may dispose of the case of a child taken into custody without referral to juvenile court, if:

(1) guidelines for such disposition have been issued by the law-enforcement agency in which the officer works;

(2) the guidelines have been approved by the juvenile board of the county in which the disposition is made;

(3) the disposition is authorized by the guidelines; and

(4) the officer makes a written report of his disposition to the law-enforcement agency, identifying the child and specifying the grounds for believing that the taking into custody was authorized.

(b) No disposition authorized by this section may involve:

(1) keeping the child in law-enforcement custody; or

(2) requiring periodic reporting of the child to a law-enforcement officer, law-enforcement agency, or other agency.

(c) A disposition authorized by this section may involve:

(1) referral of the child to an agency other than the juvenile court;

(2) a brief conference with the child and his parent, guardian, or custodian; or

(3) referral of the child and the child's parent, guardian, or custodian for services under Section 264.302.

(d) Statistics indicating the number and kind of dispositions made by a law-enforcement agency under the authority of this section shall be reported at least annually to the office or official designated by the juvenile court, as ordered by the court.

Acts 1973, 63rd Leg., p. 1460, ch. 544, § 1, eff. Sept. 1, 1973. Amended by Acts 1995, 74th Leg., ch. 262, § 18, eff. Jan. 1, 1996.

§ 52.031. First Offender Program

(a) A juvenile board may establish a first offender program under this section for the referral and disposition of children taken into custody for:

(1) conduct indicating a need for supervision; or

(2) delinquent conduct other than conduct that constitutes:

(A) a felony of the first, second, or third degree, an aggravated controlled substance felony, or a capital felony; or

(B) a state jail felony or misdemeanor involving violence to a person or the use or possession of a firearm, illegal knife, or club, as those terms are defined by Section 46.01, Penal Code, or a prohibited weapon, as described by Section 46.05, Penal Code.

(b) Each juvenile board in the county in which a first offender program is established shall designate one or more law enforcement officers and agencies, which may be law enforcement agencies, to process a child under the first offender program.

(c) The disposition of a child under the first offender program may not take place until:

(1) guidelines for the disposition have been issued by the agency designated under Subsection (b); and

(2) the juvenile board has approved the guidelines.

(d) A law enforcement officer taking a child into custody may refer the child to the law enforcement officer or agency designated under Subsection (b) for disposition under the first offender program and not refer the child to juvenile court only if:

(1) the child has not previously been adjudicated as having engaged in delinquent conduct;

(2) the referral complies with guidelines for disposition under Subsection (c); and

(3) the officer reports in writing the referral to the agency, identifying the child and specifying the grounds for taking the child into custody.

(e) A child referred for disposition under the first offender program may not be detained in law enforcement custody.

(f) The parent, guardian, or other custodian of the child must receive notice that the child has been referred for disposition under the first offender program. The notice must:

(1) state the grounds for taking the child into custody;

(2) identify the law enforcement officer or agency to which the child was referred;

(3) briefly describe the nature of the program; and

(4) state that the child's failure to complete the program will result in the child being referred to the juvenile court.

(g) The child and the parent, guardian, or other custodian of the child must consent to participation by the child in the first offender program.

(h) Disposition under a first offender program may include:

(1) voluntary restitution by the child or the parent, guardian, or other custodian of the child to the victim of the conduct of the child;

(2) voluntary community service restitution by the child;

(3) educational, vocational training, counseling, or other rehabilitative services; and

(4) periodic reporting by the child to the law enforcement officer or agency to which the child has been referred.

(i) The case of a child who successfully completes the first offender program is closed and may not be referred to juvenile court, unless the child is taken into custody under circumstances described by Subsection (j)(3).

(j) The case of a child referred for disposition under the first offender program shall be referred to juvenile court if:

(1) the child fails to complete the program;

(2) the child or the parent, guardian, or other custodian of the child terminates the child's participation in the program before the child completes it; or

(3) the child completes the program but is taken into custody under Section 52.01 before the 90th

day after the date the child completes the program for conduct other than the conduct for which the child was referred to the first offender program.

(k) A statement made by a child to a person giving advice or supervision or participating in the first offender program may not be used against the child in any proceeding under this title or any criminal proceeding.

(*l*) The law enforcement agency must report to the juvenile board in December of each year the following:

(1) the last known address of the child, including the census tract;

(2) the gender and ethnicity of the child referred to the program; and

(3) the offense committed by the child.

Added by Acts 1995, 74th Leg., ch. 262, § 19, eff. Jan. 1, 1996.

§ 52.04. Referral to Juvenile Court

(a) The following shall accompany referral of a child or a child's case to the office or official designated by the juvenile court or be provided as quickly as possible after referral:

(1) all information in the possession of the person or agency making the referral pertaining to the identity of the child and his address, the name and address of the child's parent, guardian, or custodian, the names and addresses of any witnesses, and the child's present whereabouts;

(2) a complete statement of the circumstances of the alleged delinquent conduct or conduct indicating a need for supervision;

(3) when applicable, a complete statement of the circumstances of taking the child into custody; and

(4) when referral is by an officer of a law-enforcement agency, a complete statement of all prior contacts with the child by officers of that law-enforcement agency.

(b) The office or official designated by the juvenile court may refer the case to a law-enforcement agency for the purpose of conducting an investigation to obtain necessary information.

(c) If the office of the prosecuting attorney is designated by the juvenile court to conduct the preliminary investigation under Section 53.01, the referring entity shall first transfer the child's case to the juvenile probation department for statistical reporting purposes only. On the creation of a statistical record or file for the case, the probation department shall within three business days forward the case to the prosecuting attorney for review under Section 53.01.

Acts 1973, 63rd Leg., p. 1460, ch. 544, § 1, eff. Sept. 1, 1973. Amended by Acts 1997, 75th Leg., ch. 1091, § 1, eff. June 19, 1997.

§ 52.041. Referral of Child to Juvenile Court After Expulsion

(a) A school district that expels a child shall refer the child to juvenile court in the county in which the child resides.

(b) The board of the school district or a person designated by the board shall deliver a copy of the order expelling the student and any other information required by Section 52.04 on or before the second working day after the date of the expulsion hearing to the authorized officer of the juvenile court.

(c) Within five working days of receipt of an expulsion notice under this section by the office or official designated by the juvenile court, a preliminary investigation and determination shall be conducted as required by Section 53.01.

(d) The office or official designated by the juvenile court shall within two working days notify the school district that expelled the child if:

(1) a determination was made under Section 53.01 that the person referred to juvenile court was not a child within the meaning of this title;

(2) a determination was made that no probable cause existed to believe the child engaged in delinquent conduct or conduct indicating a need for supervision;

(3) no deferred prosecution or formal court proceedings have been or will be initiated involving the child;

(4) the court or jury finds that the child did not engage in delinquent conduct or conduct indicating a need for supervision and the case has been dismissed with prejudice; or

(5) the child was adjudicated but no disposition was or will be ordered by the court.

(e) In any county where a juvenile justice alternative education program is operated, no student shall be expelled without written notification by the board of the school district or its designated agent to the juvenile board's designated representative. The notification shall be made not later than two business days following the board's determination that the student is to be expelled. Failure to timely notify the designated representative of the juvenile board shall result in the child's duty to continue attending the school district's educational program, which shall be provided to that child until such time as the notification to the juvenile board's designated representative is properly made.

Added by Acts 1995, 74th Leg., ch. 262, § 20, eff. Jan. 1, 1996. Amended by Acts 1997, 75th Leg., ch. 1015, § 16, eff. June 19, 1997.

Section 20 of Acts 1997, 75th Leg., ch. 1015 provides:

"This Act takes effect beginning with the 1997–1998 school year."

CHAPTER 53. PROCEEDINGS PRIOR TO JUDICIAL PROCEEDINGS

Section

§ 53.01. Preliminary Investigation and Determinations; Notice to Parents

(a) On referral of a person believed to be a child or on referral of the person's case to the office or official designated by the juvenile court, the intake officer, probation officer, or other person authorized by the court shall conduct a preliminary investigation to determine whether:

(1) the person referred to juvenile court is a child within the meaning of this title; and

(2) there is probable cause to believe the person engaged in delinquent conduct or conduct indicating a need for supervision.

(b) If it is determined that the person is not a child or there is no probable cause, the person shall immediately be released.

(c) When custody of a child is given to the office or official designated by the juvenile court, the intake officer, probation officer, or other person authorized by the court shall promptly give notice of the whereabouts of the child and a statement of the reason he was taken into custody to the child's parent, guardian, or custodian unless the notice given under Section 52.02(b) of this code provided fair notice of the child's present whereabouts.

(d) Unless the juvenile board approves a written procedure proposed by the office of prosecuting attorney and chief juvenile probation officer which provides otherwise, if it is determined that the person is a child and, regardless of a finding of probable cause, or a lack thereof, there is an allegation that the child engaged in delinquent conduct of the grade of felony, or conduct constituting a misdemeanor offense involving violence to a person or the use or possession of a firearm, illegal knife, or club, as those terms are defined by Section 46.01, Penal Code, or prohibited weapon, as described by Section 46.05, Penal Code, the case shall be promptly forwarded to the office of the prosecuting attorney, accompanied by:

(1) all documents that accompanied the current referral; and

(2) a summary of all prior referrals of the child to the juvenile court, juvenile probation department, or a detention facility.

(e) If a juvenile board adopts an alternative referral plan under Subsection (d), the board shall register the plan with the Texas Juvenile Probation Commission.

(f) A juvenile board may not adopt an alternate referral plan that does not require the forwarding of a child's case to the prosecuting attorney as provided by Subsection (d) if probable cause exists to believe that the child engaged in delinquent conduct that violates Section 19.03, Penal Code (capital murder), or Section 19.02, Penal Code (murder).

Acts 1973, 63rd Leg., p. 1460, ch. 544, § 1, eff. Sept. 1, 1973. Amended by Acts 1995, 74th Leg., ch. 262, § 21, eff. Jan. 1, 1996; Acts 1997, 75th Leg., ch. 1374, § 5, eff. Sept. 1, 1997.

§ 53.012. Review by Prosecutor

(a) The prosecuting attorney shall promptly review the circumstances and allegations of a referral made under Section 53.01 for legal sufficiency and the desirability of prosecution and may file a petition without regard to whether probable cause was found under Section 53.01.

(b) If the prosecuting attorney does not file a petition requesting the adjudication of the child referred to the prosecuting attorney, the prosecuting attorney shall:

(1) terminate all proceedings, if the reason is for lack of probable cause; or

(2) return the referral to the juvenile probation department for further proceedings.

(c) The juvenile probation department shall promptly refer a child who has been returned to the department under Subsection (b)(2) and who fails or refuses to participate in a program of the department to the prosecuting attorney for review of the child's case and determination of whether to file a petition.

Added by Acts 1995, 74th Leg., ch. 262, § 22, eff. Jan. 1, 1996.

§ 53.013. Progressive Sanctions Program

(a) Each juvenile board may adopt a progressive sanctions program using the guidelines for progressive sanctions in Chapter 59.

(b) A juvenile court or probation department that deviates from the guidelines under Section 59.003 shall state in writing the reasons for the deviation and submit the statement to the juvenile board regardless of whether the juvenile board has adopted a progressive sanctions program.

Added by Acts 1995, 74th Leg., ch. 262, § 22, eff. Jan. 1, 1996. Amended by Acts 1997, 75th Leg., ch. 1086, § 7, eff. Sept. 1, 1997.

§ 53.02. Release from Detention

(a) If a child is brought before the court or delivered to a detention facility as authorized by Sections 51.12(a)(3) and (4), the intake or other authorized officer of the court shall immediately make an investigation and shall release the child unless it appears that his detention is warranted under Subsection (b). The release may be conditioned upon requirements reasonably necessary to insure the child's appearance at later proceedings, but the conditions of the release must be in writing and filed with the office or official designated by the court and a copy furnished to the child.

(b) A child taken into custody may be detained prior to hearing on the petition only if:

(1) he is likely to abscond or be removed from the jurisdiction of the court;

(2) suitable supervision, care, or protection for him is not being provided by a parent, guardian, custodian, or other person;

(3) he has no parent, guardian, custodian, or other person able to return him to the court when required;

(4) he may be dangerous to himself or he may threaten the safety of the public if released; or

(5) he has previously been found to be a delinquent child or has previously been convicted of a penal offense punishable by a term in jail or prison and is likely to commit an offense if released.

(c) If the child is not released, a request for detention hearing shall be made and promptly presented to the court, and an informal detention hearing as provided in Section 54.01 of this code shall be held promptly, but not later than the time required by Section 54.01 of this code.

(d) A release of a child to an adult under Subsection (a) must be conditioned on the agreement of the adult to be subject to the jurisdiction of the juvenile court and to an order of contempt by the court if the adult, after notification, is unable to produce the child at later proceedings.

(e) Unless otherwise agreed in the memorandum of understanding under Section 37.011, Education Code, in a county with a population greater than 125,000, if a child being released under this section is expelled under Section 37.007, Education Code, the release shall be conditioned on the child's attending a juvenile justice alternative education program pending a deferred prosecution or formal court disposition of the child's case.

Acts 1973, 63rd Leg., p. 1460, ch. 544, § 1, eff. Sept. 1, 1973. Amended by Acts 1979, 66th Leg., p. 1102, ch. 518, § 1, eff. June 11, 1979; Acts 1981, 67th Leg., p. 291, ch. 115, § 1, eff. Aug. 31, 1981; Acts 1995, 74th Leg., ch. 262, § 23, eff. Jan. 1, 1996; Acts 1997, 75th Leg., ch. 1015, § 17, eff. June 19, 1997; Acts 1997, 75th Leg., ch. 1374, § 6, eff. Sept. 1, 1997.

Section 20 of Acts 1997, 75th Leg., ch. 1015 provides:

"This Act takes effect beginning with the 1997–1998 school year."

§ 53.03. Deferred Prosecution

(a) Subject to Subsections (e) and (g), if the preliminary investigation required by Section 53.01 of this code results in a determination that further proceedings in the case are authorized, the probation officer or other designated officer of the court, subject to the direction of the juvenile court, may advise the parties for a reasonable period of time not to exceed six months concerning deferred prosecution and rehabilitation of a child if:

(1) deferred prosecution would be in the interest of the public and the child;

(2) the child and his parent, guardian, or custodian consent with knowledge that consent is not obligatory; and

(3) the child and his parent, guardian, or custodian are informed that they may terminate the deferred prosecution at any point and petition the court for a court hearing in the case.

(b) Except as otherwise permitted by this title, the child may not be detained during or as a result of the deferred prosecution process.

(c) An incriminating statement made by a participant to the person giving advice and in the discussions or conferences incident thereto may not be used against the declarant in any court hearing.

(d) The court may adopt a fee schedule for deferred prosecution services and rules for the waiver of a fee for financial hardship in accordance with guidelines that the Texas Juvenile Probation Commission shall provide. The maximum fee is $15 a month. If the court adopts a schedule and rules for waiver, the probation officer or other designated officer of the court shall collect the fee authorized by the schedule from the parent, guardian, or custodian of a child for whom a deferred prosecution is authorized under this section or waive the fee in accordance with the rules adopted by the court. The officer shall deposit the fees received under this section in the county treasury to the credit of a special fund that may be used only for juvenile probation or community-based juvenile corrections services or facilities in which a juvenile may be required to live while under court supervision. If the court does not adopt a schedule and rules for waiver, a fee for deferred prosecution services may not be imposed.

(e) A prosecuting attorney may defer prosecution for any child. A probation officer or other designated officer of the court:

(1) may not defer prosecution for a child for a case that is required to be forwarded to the prosecuting attorney under Section 53.01(d); and

(2) may defer prosecution for a child who has previously been adjudicated for conduct that constitutes a felony only if the prosecuting attorney consents in writing.

(f) The probation officer or other officer designated by the court supervising a program of deferred prosecution for a child under this section shall report to the juvenile court any violation by the child of the program.

Text of subsec. (g) as added by Acts 1997, 75th Leg., ch. 593, § 6

(g) If the child is alleged to have engaged in delinquent conduct or conduct indicating a need for supervision that violates Section 28.08, Penal Code, deferred prosecution under this section may include:

(1) voluntary attendance in a class with instruction in self-responsibility and empathy for a victim of an offense conducted by a local juvenile probation department, if the class is available; and

(2) voluntary restoration of the property damaged by the child by removing or painting over any markings made by the child, if the owner of the property consents to the restoration.

Text of subsec. (g) as added by Acts 1997, 75th Leg., ch. 1013, § 16

(g) Prosecution may not be deferred for a child alleged to have engaged in conduct that:

(1) is an offense under Section 49.04, 49.05, 49.06, 49.07, or 49.08, Penal Code; or

(2) is a third or subsequent offense under Section 106.04 or 106.041, Alcoholic Beverage Code.

Acts 1973, 63rd Leg., p. 1460, ch. 544, § 1, eff. Sept. 1, 1973. Amended by Acts 1983, 68th Leg., p. 3261, ch. 565, § 1, eff. Sept. 1, 1983; Acts 1987, 70th Leg., ch. 1040, § 22, eff. Sept. 1, 1987; Acts 1995, 74th Leg., ch. 262, § 24, eff. Jan. 1, 1996; Acts 1997, 75th Leg., ch. 593, § 6, eff. Sept. 1, 1997; Acts 1997, 75th Leg., ch. 1013, § 16, eff. Sept. 1, 1997.

Section 5 of the 1983 amendatory act provides:

"This Act applies only to a child's conduct that occurs and civil liability for a cause of action that arises on or after the effective date of this Act."

Section 8 of Acts 1997, 75th Leg., ch. 593 provides:

"(a) The change in law made by this Act applies only to an offense committed or, for the purposes of Title 3, Family Code, to conduct that occurs on or after the effective date of this Act. For purposes of this section, an offense is committed on or after the effective date of this Act if every element of the offense occurs on or after the effective date and conduct violating a penal law of this state occurs on or after the effective date of this Act if every element of the violation occurs on or after that date.

"(b) An offense committed before the effective date of this Act is covered by the law in effect when the offense was committed, and the former law is continued in effect for that purpose. Conduct that occurs before the effective date of this Act is covered by the law in effect at the time the conduct occurred, and the former law is continued in effect for that purpose."

For application provisions of Acts 1997, 75th Leg., ch. 1013, see notes following V.T.C.A., Family Code § 51.03.

§ 53.04. Court Petition; Answer

(a) If the preliminary investigation, required by Section 53.01 of this code results in a determination that further proceedings are authorized and warranted, a petition for an adjudication or transfer hearing of a child alleged to have engaged in delinquent conduct or conduct indicating a need for supervision may be made as promptly as practicable by a prosecuting attorney who has knowledge of the facts alleged or is informed and believes that they are true.

(b) The proceedings shall be styled "In the matter of ______________."

(c) The petition may be on information and belief.

(d) The petition must state:

(1) with reasonable particularity the time, place, and manner of the acts alleged and the penal law or standard of conduct allegedly violated by the acts;

(2) the name, age, and residence address, if known, of the child who is the subject of the petition;

(3) the names and residence addresses, if known, of the parent, guardian, or custodian of the child and of the child's spouse, if any;

(4) if the child's parent, guardian, or custodian does not reside or cannot be found in the state, or if their places of residence are unknown, the name and residence address of any known adult relative residing in the county or, if there is none, the name and residence address of the known adult relative residing nearest to the location of the court; and

(5) if the child is alleged to have engaged in habitual felony conduct, the previous adjudications in which the child was found to have engaged in conduct violating penal laws of the grade of felony.

(e) An oral or written answer to the petition may be made at or before the commencement of the hearing. If there is no answer, a general denial of the alleged conduct is assumed.

Acts 1973, 63rd Leg., p. 1460, ch. 544, § 1, eff. Sept. 1, 1973. Amended by Acts 1995, 74th Leg., ch. 262, § 25, eff. Jan. 1, 1996.

§ 53.045. Violent or Habitual Offenders

(a) Except as provided by Subsection (e), the prosecuting attorney may refer the petition to the grand jury of the county in which the court in which the petition is filed presides if the petition alleges that the child engaged in delinquent conduct that constitutes habitual felony conduct as described by Section 51.031 or that included the violation of any of the following provisions:

(1) Section 19.02, Penal Code (murder);

(2) Section 19.03, Penal Code (capital murder);

(3) Section 20.04, Penal Code (aggravated kidnapping);

(4) Section 22.011, Penal Code (sexual assault) or Section 22.021, Penal Code (aggravated sexual assault);

(5) Section 22.02, Penal Code (aggravated assault);

(6) Section 29.03, Penal Code (aggravated robbery);

(7) Section 22.04, Penal Code (injury to a child, elderly individual, or disabled individual), if the offense is punishable as a felony, other than a state jail felony;

(8) Section 22.05(b), Penal Code (felony deadly conduct involving discharging a firearm);

(9) Subchapter D, Chapter 481, Health and Safety Code,[1] if the conduct constitutes a felony of the first degree or an aggravated controlled substance felony (certain offenses involving controlled substances);

(10) Section 15.03, Penal Code (criminal solicitation);

(11) Section 21.11(a)(1), Penal Code (indecency with a child);

(12) Section 15.031, Penal Code (criminal solicitation of a minor);

(13) Section 15.01, Penal Code (criminal attempt), if the offense attempted was an offense under Section 19.02, Penal Code (murder) or Section 19.03, Penal Code (capital murder), or an offense listed by Section 3g(a)(1), Article 42.12, Code of Criminal Procedure; or

(14) Section 28.02, Penal Code (arson), if bodily injury or death is suffered by any person by reason of the commission of the conduct.

(b) A grand jury may approve a petition submitted to it under this section by a vote of nine members of the grand jury in the same manner that the grand jury votes on the presentment of an indictment.

(c) The grand jury has all the powers to investigate the facts and circumstances relating to a petition submitted under this section as it has to investigate other criminal activity but may not issue an indictment unless the child is transferred to a criminal court as provided by Section 54.02 of this code.

(d) If the grand jury approves of the petition, the fact of approval shall be certified to the juvenile court, and the certification shall be entered in the record of the case. For the purpose of the transfer of a child to the Texas Department of Corrections as provided by Section 61.084(c), Human Resources Code, a juvenile court petition approved by a grand jury under this section is an indictment presented by the grand jury.

(e) The prosecuting attorney may not refer a petition that alleges the child engaged in conduct that violated Section 22.011(a)(2), Penal Code, or Sections 22.021(a)(1)(B) and (2)(B), Penal Code, unless the child is more than three years older than the victim of the conduct.

Added by Acts 1987, 70th Leg., ch. 385, § 7, eff. Sept. 1, 1987. Amended by Acts 1991, 72nd Leg., ch. 574, § 1, eff. Sept. 1, 1991; Acts 1995, 74th Leg., ch. 262, §§ 26, 27, eff. Jan. 1, 1996; Acts 1997, 75th Leg., ch. 1086, § 8, eff. Sept. 1, 1997.

[1] V.T.C.A., Health & Safety Code § 481.101 et seq.

Section 20 of the 1987 Act provides:

"(a) This Act applies only to offenses and conduct occurring on or after its effective date. For the purposes of this section, an offense or delinquent conduct based on an offense occurs on or after the effective date if all the elements of the offense occur on or after the effective date.

"(b) An offense or conduct that occurs before the effective date of this Act shall be prosecuted under the law in effect immediately before the effective date of this Act, and that law is continued in effect for that purpose only."

Section 5 of the 1991 amendatory act provides:

"(a) This Act takes effect September 1, 1991, and applies only to conduct that occurs on or after that date. Conduct violating the penal laws of this state occurs on or after the effective date of this Act if every element of the violation occurs on or after that date.

"(b) Conduct that occurs before the effective date of this Act is governed by the law in effect at the time the conduct occurred and that law is continued in effect for that purpose."

§ 53.05. Time Set for Hearing

(a) After the petition has been filed, the juvenile court shall set a time for the hearing.

(b) The time set for the hearing shall not be later than 10 working days after the day the petition was filed if:

(1) the child is in detention; or

(2) the child will be taken into custody under Section 53.06(d) of this code.

Acts 1973, 63rd Leg., p. 1460, ch. 544, § 1, eff. Sept. 1, 1973. Amended by Acts 1995, 74th Leg., ch. 262, § 28, eff. Jan. 1, 1996.

§ 53.06. Summons

(a) The juvenile court shall direct issuance of a summons to:

(1) the child named in the petition;

(2) the child's parent, guardian, or custodian;

(3) the child's guardian ad litem; and

(4) any other person who appears to the court to be a proper or necessary party to the proceeding.

(b) The summons must require the persons served to appear before the court at the time set to answer the allegations of the petition. A copy of the petition must accompany the summons.

(c) The court may endorse on the summons an order directing the person having the physical custody or control of the child to bring the child to the hearing. A person who violates an order entered under this subsection may be proceeded against under Section 53.08 or 54.07 of this code.

(d) If it appears from an affidavit filed or from sworn testimony before the court that immediate detention of the child is warranted under Section 53.02(b) of this code, the court may endorse on the summons an order that a law-enforcement officer shall serve the summons and shall immediately take the child into custody and bring him before the court.

(e) A party, other than the child, may waive service of summons by written stipulation or by voluntary appearance at the hearing.

Acts 1973, 63rd Leg., p. 1460, ch. 544, § 1, eff. Sept. 1, 1973. Amended by Acts 1995, 74th Leg., ch. 262, § 29, eff. Jan. 1, 1996.

§ 53.07. Service of Summons

(a) If a person to be served with a summons is in this state and can be found, the summons shall be served upon him personally at least two days before the day of the adjudication hearing. If he is in this state and cannot be found, but his address is known or can with reasonable diligence be ascertained, the summons may be served on him by mailing a copy by registered or certified mail, return receipt requested, at least five days before the day of the hearing. If he is outside this state but he can be found or his address is known, or his whereabouts or address can with reasonable diligence be ascertained, service of the summons may be made either by delivering a copy to him personally or mailing a copy to him by registered or certified mail, return receipt requested, at least five days before the day of the hearing.

(b) The juvenile court has jurisdiction of the case if after reasonable effort a person other than the child cannot be found nor his post-office address ascertained, whether he is in or outside this state.

(c) Service of the summons may be made by any suitable person under the direction of the court.

(d) The court may authorize payment from the general funds of the county of the costs of service and of necessary travel expenses incurred by persons summoned or otherwise required to appear at the hearing.

(e) Witnesses may be subpoenaed in accordance with the Texas Code of Criminal Procedure, 1965.

Acts 1973, 63rd Leg., p. 1460, ch. 544, § 1, eff. Sept. 1, 1973.

§ 53.08. Writ of Attachment

(a) The juvenile court may issue a writ of attachment for a person who violates an order entered under Section 53.06(c).

(b) A writ of attachment issued under this section is executed in the same manner as in a criminal proceeding as provided by Chapter 24, Code of Criminal Procedure.

Added by Acts 1995, 74th Leg., ch. 262, § 30, eff. Jan. 1, 1996.

CHAPTER 54. JUDICIAL PROCEEDINGS

§ 54.01. Detention Hearing

(a) If the child is not released under Section 53.02 of this code, a detention hearing without a jury shall be held promptly, but not later than the second working day after he is taken into custody; provided, however, that when a child is detained on a Friday or Saturday, then such detention hearing shall be held on the first working day after the child is taken into custody.

(b) Reasonable notice of the detention hearing, either oral or written, shall be given, stating the time, place, and purpose of the hearing. Notice shall be given to the child and, if they can be found, to his parents, guardian, or custodian. Prior to the commencement of the hearing, the court shall inform the parties of the child's right to counsel and to appointed counsel if they are indigent and of the child's right to remain silent with respect to any allegations of delinquent conduct or conduct indicating a need for supervision.

(c) At the detention hearing, the court may consider written reports from probation officers, professional court employees, or professional consultants in addition to the testimony of witnesses. Prior to the detention hearing, the court shall provide the attorney for the child with access to all written matter to be considered by the court in making the detention decision. The court may order counsel not to reveal items to the child or his parent, guardian, or guardian ad litem if such disclosure would materially harm the treatment and rehabilitation of the child or would substantially decrease the likelihood of receiving information from the same or similar sources in the future.

(d) A detention hearing may be held without the presence of the child's parents if the court has been unable to locate them. If no parent or guardian is present, the court shall appoint counsel or a guardian ad litem for the child.

(e) At the conclusion of the hearing, the court shall order the child released from detention unless it finds that:

(1) he is likely to abscond or be removed from the jurisdiction of the court;

(2) suitable supervision, care, or protection for him is not being provided by a parent, guardian, custodian, or other person;

(3) he has no parent, guardian, custodian, or other person able to return him to the court when required;

(4) he may be dangerous to himself or may threaten the safety of the public if released; or

(5) he has previously been found to be a delinquent child or has previously been convicted of a penal offense punishable by a term in jail or prison and is likely to commit an offense if released.

(f) Unless otherwise agreed in the memorandum of understanding under Section 37.011, Education Code, a release may be conditioned on requirements reasonably necessary to insure the child's appearance at later proceedings, but the conditions of the release must be in writing and a copy furnished to the child. In a county with a population greater than 125,000, if a child being released under this section is expelled under Section 37.007, Education Code, the release shall be conditioned on the child's attending a juvenile justice alternative education program pending a deferred prosecution or formal court disposition of the child's case.

(g) No statement made by the child at the detention hearing shall be admissible against the child at any other hearing.

(h) A detention order extends to the conclusion of the disposition hearing, if there is one, but in no event for more than 10 working days. Further detention orders may be made following subsequent detention hearings. The initial detention hearing may not be waived but subsequent detention hearings may be waived in accordance with the requirements of Section 51.09. Each subsequent detention order shall extend for no more than 10 working days, except that in a county that does not have a certified juvenile detention facility, as described by Section 51.12(a)(3), each subsequent detention order shall extend for no more than 15 working days.

(i) A child in custody may be detained for as long as 10 days without the hearing described in Subsection (a) of this section if:

(1) a written request for shelter in detention facilities pending arrangement of transportation to his place of residence in another state or country or another county of this state is voluntarily executed by the child not later than the next working day after he was taken into custody;

(2) the request for shelter contains:

(A) a statement by the child that he voluntarily agrees to submit himself to custody and detention for a period of not longer than 10 days without a detention hearing;

(B) an allegation by the person detaining the child that the child has left his place of residence in another state or country or another county of this state, that he is in need of shelter, and that an effort is being made to arrange transportation to his place of residence; and

(C) a statement by the person detaining the child that he has advised the child of his right to demand a detention hearing under Subsection (a) of this section; and

(3) the request is signed by the juvenile court judge to evidence his knowledge of the fact that the child is being held in detention.

(j) The request for shelter may be revoked by the child at any time, and on such revocation, if further detention is necessary, a detention hearing shall be held not later than the next working day in accordance with Subsections (a) through (g) of this section.

(k) Notwithstanding anything in this title to the contrary, the child may sign a request for shelter without the concurrence of an adult specified in Section 51.09 of this code.

(*l*) The juvenile board or, if there is none, the juvenile court, may appoint a referee to conduct the detention hearing. The referee shall be an attorney licensed to practice law in this state. Such payment or additional payment as may be warranted for referee services shall be provided from county funds. Before commencing the detention hearing, the referee shall inform the parties who have appeared that they are entitled to have the hearing before the juvenile court judge or a substitute judge authorized by Section 51.04(f) of this code. If a party objects to the referee conducting the detention hearing, an authorized judge shall conduct the hearing within 24 hours. At the conclusion of the hearing, the referee shall transmit written findings and recommendations to the juvenile court judge or substitute judge. The juvenile court judge or substitute judge shall adopt, modify, or reject the referee's recommendations not later than the next working day after the day that the judge receives the recommendations. Failure to act within that time results in release of the child by operation of law. A recommendation that the child be released operates to secure his immediate release, subject to the power of the juvenile court judge or substitute judge to reject or modify that recommendation. The effect of an order detaining a child shall be computed from the time of the hearing before the referee.

(m) The detention hearing required in this section may be held in the county of the designated place of detention where the child is being held even though the designated place of detention is outside the county of residence of the child or the county in which the alleged delinquent conduct or conduct indicating a need for supervision occurred.

(n) An attorney appointed by the court under Section 51.10(c) because a determination was made under this section to detain a child who was not represented by an attorney may request on behalf of the child and is entitled to a de novo detention hearing under this section. The attorney must make the request not later than the 10th working day after the date the attorney is appointed. The hearing must take place not later than the second working day after the date the attorney filed a formal request with the court for a hearing.

(*o*) The court or referee shall find whether there is probable cause to believe that a child taken into custody without an arrest warrant or a directive to apprehend has engaged in delinquent conduct or conduct indicating a need for supervision. The court or referee must make the finding within 48 hours, including weekends and holidays, of the time the child was taken into custody. The court or referee may make the finding on any reasonably reliable information without regard to admissibility of that information under the Texas Rules of Criminal Evidence. A finding of probable cause is required to detain a child after the 48th hour after the time the child was taken into custody. If a court or referee finds probable cause, additional findings of probable cause are not required in the same cause to authorize further detention.

Acts 1973, 63rd Leg., p. 1460, ch. 544, § 1, eff. Sept. 1, 1973. Amended by Acts 1975, 64th Leg., p. 2156, ch. 693, §§ 14, 15, eff. Sept. 1, 1975; Acts 1979, 66th Leg., p. 1102, ch. 518, § 2, eff. June 11, 1979; Acts 1995, 74th Leg., ch. 262, § 31, eff. Jan. 1, 1996; Acts 1997, 75th Leg., ch. 922, § 1, eff. Sept. 1, 1997; Acts 1997, 75th Leg., ch. 1015, § 18, eff. June 19, 1997; Acts 1997, 75th Leg., ch. 1086, § 9, eff. Sept. 1, 1997.

Section 2 of Acts 1997, 75th Leg., ch. 922 provides:

"(a) The change in law made by this Act applies only to a child who is taken into custody for conduct that occurs on or after the effective date of this Act. Conduct violating a penal law of this state occurs on or after the effective date of this Act if every element of the violation occurs on or after that date.

"(b) Conduct that occurs before the effective date of this Act is covered by the law in effect at the time the conduct occurred, and the former law is continued in effect for that purpose."

Section 20 of Acts 1997, 75th Leg., ch. 1015 provides:

"This Act takes effect beginning with the 1997–1998 school year."

§ 54.011. Detention Hearings for Status Offenders and Nonoffenders

(a) The detention hearing for a status offender or nonoffender who has not been released administratively under Section 53.02 shall be held before the 24th hour after the time the child arrived at a detention facility, excluding hours of a weekend or a holiday. Except as otherwise provided by this section, the judge or referee conducting the detention hearing shall release the status offender or nonoffender from secure detention.

(b) The judge or referee may order a child in detention accused of the violation of a valid court order as defined by Section 51.02 detained not longer than 72 hours after the time the detention order was entered, excluding weekends and holidays, if:

(1) the judge or referee finds at the detention hearing that there is probable cause to believe the child violated the valid court order; and

(2) the detention of the child is justified under Section 54.01(e)(1), (2), or (3).

(c) Except as provided by Subsection (d), a detention order entered under Subsection (b) may be extended for one additional 72-hour period, excluding weekends and holidays, only on a finding of good cause by the juvenile court.

(d) A detention order for a child under this section may be extended on the demand of the child's attorney only to allow the time that is necessary to comply with the requirements of Section 51.10(h), entitling the attorney to 10 days to prepare for an adjudication hearing.

(e) A status offender may be detained for a necessary period, not to exceed five days, to enable the child's return to the child's home in another state under Chapter 60.

Added by Acts 1995, 74th Leg., ch. 262, § 32, eff. Jan. 1, 1996. Amended by Acts 1997, 75th Leg., ch. 1374, § 7, eff. Sept. 1, 1997.

§ 54.012. Interactive Video Recording of Detention Hearing

(a) A detention hearing under Section 54.01, other than the first detention hearing, may be held using interactive video equipment if:

(1) the child and the child's attorney agree to the video hearing; and

(2) the parties to the proceeding have the opportunity to cross-examine witnesses.

(b) A detention hearing may not be held using video equipment unless the video equipment for the hearing provides for a two-way communication of image and sound among the child, the court, and other parties at the hearing.

(c) A recording of the communications shall be made. The recording shall be preserved until the earlier of:

(1) the 91st day after the date on which the recording is made if the child is alleged to have engaged in conduct constituting a misdemeanor;

(2) the 120th day after the date on which the recording is made if the child is alleged to have engaged in conduct constituting a felony; or

(3) the date on which the adjudication hearing ends.

(d) An attorney for the child may obtain a copy of the recording on payment of the reasonable costs of reproducing the copy.

Added by Acts 1995, 74th Leg., ch. 262, § 33, eff. Jan. 1, 1996.

§ 54.02. Waiver of Jurisdiction and Discretionary Transfer to Criminal Court

(a) The juvenile court may waive its exclusive original jurisdiction and transfer a child to the appropriate district court or criminal district court for criminal proceedings if:

(1) the child is alleged to have violated a penal law of the grade of felony;

(2) the child was:

(A) 14 years of age or older at the time he is alleged to have committed the offense, if the offense is a capital felony, an aggravated controlled substance felony, or a felony of the first degree, and no adjudication hearing has been conducted concerning that offense; or

(B) 15 years of age or older at the time the child is alleged to have committed the offense, if the offense is a felony of the second or third degree or a state jail felony, and no adjudication hearing has been conducted concerning that offense; and

(3) after a full investigation and a hearing, the juvenile court determines that there is probable cause to believe that the child before the court committed the offense alleged and that because of the seriousness of the offense alleged or the background of the child the welfare of the community requires criminal proceedings.

(b) The petition and notice requirements of Sections 53.04, 53.05, 53.06, and 53.07 of this code must be satisfied, and the summons must state that the hearing is for the purpose of considering discretionary transfer to criminal court.

(c) The juvenile court shall conduct a hearing without a jury to consider transfer of the child for criminal proceedings.

(d) Prior to the hearing, the juvenile court shall order and obtain a complete diagnostic study, social evaluation, and full investigation of the child, his circumstances, and the circumstances of the alleged offense.

(e) At the transfer hearing the court may consider written reports from probation officers, professional court employees, or professional consultants in addition to the testimony of witnesses. At least one day prior to the transfer hearing, the court shall provide the attorney for the child with access to all written matter to be considered by the court in making the transfer decision. The court may order counsel not to reveal items to the child or his parent, guardian, or guardian ad litem if such disclosure would materially harm the treatment and rehabilitation of the child or would substantially decrease the likelihood of receiving information from the same or similar sources in the future.

(f) In making the determination required by Subsection (a) of this section, the court shall consider, among other matters:

(1) whether the alleged offense was against person or property, with greater weight in favor of transfer given to offenses against the person;

(2) the sophistication and maturity of the child;

(3) the record and previous history of the child; and

(4) the prospects of adequate protection of the public and the likelihood of the rehabilitation of the child by use of procedures, services, and facilities currently available to the juvenile court.

(g) If the petition alleges multiple offenses that constitute more than one criminal transaction, the juvenile court shall either retain or transfer all offenses relating to a single transaction. A child is not subject to criminal prosecution at any time for any offense arising out of a criminal transaction for which the juvenile court retains jurisdiction.

(h) If the juvenile court waives jurisdiction, it shall state specifically in the order its reasons for waiver and certify its action, including the written order and findings of the court, and shall transfer the person to the appropriate court for criminal proceedings. On transfer of the person for criminal proceedings, the person shall be dealt with as an adult and in accordance with the Code of Criminal Procedure. The transfer of custody is an arrest.

(i) A waiver under this section is a waiver of jurisdiction over the child and the criminal court may not remand the child to the jurisdiction of the juvenile court.

(j) The juvenile court may waive its exclusive original jurisdiction and transfer a person to the appropriate district court or criminal district court for criminal proceedings if:

(1) the person is 18 years of age or older;

(2) the person was:

(A) 14 years of age or older and under 17 years of age at the time he is alleged to have committed a capital felony, an aggravated controlled substance felony, or a felony of the first degree; or

(B) 15 years of age or older and under 17 years of age at the time the person is alleged to have committed a felony of the second or third degree or a state jail felony;

(3) no adjudication concerning the alleged offense has been made or no adjudication hearing concerning the offense has been conducted;

(4) the juvenile court finds from a preponderance of the evidence that:

(A) for a reason beyond the control of the state it was not practicable to proceed in juvenile court before the 18th birthday of the person; or

(B) after due diligence of the state it was not practicable to proceed in juvenile court before the 18th birthday of the person because:

(i) the state did not have probable cause to proceed in juvenile court and new evidence has been found since the 18th birthday of the person;

(ii) the person could not be found; or

(iii) a previous transfer order was reversed by an appellate court or set aside by a district court; and

(5) the juvenile court determines that there is probable cause to believe that the child before the court committed the offense alleged.

(k) The petition and notice requirements of Sections 53.04, 53.05, 53.06, and 53.07 of this code must be satisfied, and the summons must state that the hearing is for the purpose of considering waiver of jurisdiction under Subsection (j) of this section.

(*l*) The juvenile court shall conduct a hearing without a jury to consider waiver of jurisdiction under Subsection (j) of this section.

(m) Notwithstanding any other provision of this section, the juvenile court shall waive its exclusive original jurisdiction and transfer a child to the appropriate district court or criminal court for criminal proceedings if:

(1) the child has previously been transferred to a district court or criminal district court for criminal proceedings under this section, unless:

(A) the child was not indicted in the matter transferred by the grand jury;

(B) the child was found not guilty in the matter transferred;

(C) the matter transferred was dismissed with prejudice; or

(D) the child was convicted in the matter transferred, the conviction was reversed on appeal, and the appeal is final; and

(2) the child is alleged to have violated a penal law of the grade of felony.

(n) A mandatory transfer under Subsection (m) may be made without conducting the study required in discretionary transfer proceedings by Subsection (d). The requirements of Subsection (b) that the summons state that the purpose of the hearing is to consider discretionary transfer to criminal court does not apply to a transfer proceeding under Subsection (m). In a proceeding under Subsection (m), it is sufficient that the summons provide fair notice that the purpose of the hearing is to consider mandatory transfer to criminal court.

Acts 1973, 63rd Leg., p. 1460, ch. 544, § 1, eff. Sept. 1, 1973. Amended by Acts 1975, 64th Leg., p. 2156, ch. 693, § 16, eff. Sept. 1, 1975; Acts 1987, 70th Leg., ch. 140, §§ 1 to 3, eff. Sept. 1, 1987; Acts 1995, 74th Leg., ch. 262, § 34, eff. Jan. 1, 1996.

Section 5 of the 1987 amendatory act provides:

"This Act applies to a transfer to a district court under Section 54.02, Family Code, that occurs on or after the effective date of this Act. If a transfer to a district court occurred before the effective date of this Act, the provisions of Title 3, Family Code, and of Article 16.01, Code of Criminal Procedure, as they existed on the date of the transfer apply to the transfer and to the examining trial of the child transferred, and that law is continued in effect for that purpose."

§ 54.021. Justice or Municipal Court: Truancy

(a) The juvenile court may waive its exclusive original jurisdiction and transfer a child to an appropriate justice or municipal court, with the permission of the justice or municipal court, for disposition in the manner provided by Subsection (b) of this section if the child is alleged to have engaged in conduct described in Section 51.03(b)(2) of this code. A waiver of jurisdiction under this subsection may be for an individual case or for all cases in which a child is alleged to have engaged in conduct described in Section 51.03(b)(2) of this code. The waiver of a juvenile court's exclusive original jurisdiction for all cases in which a child is alleged to have engaged in conduct described in Section 51.03(b)(2) of this code is effective for a period of one year.

(b) A justice or municipal court may exercise jurisdiction over a person alleged to have engaged in conduct indicating a need for supervision by engaging in conduct described in Section 51.03(b)(2) in a case where the juvenile court has waived its original jurisdiction under this section. A justice or municipal court may exercise jurisdiction under this section without regard to whether the justice of the peace or municipal judge for the court is a licensed attorney or the hearing for a case is before a jury consisting of six persons.

(c) On a finding that a person has engaged in conduct described by Section 51.03(b)(2) or conduct that violates Section 25.094, Education Code, the justice or municipal court shall enter an order appropriate to the nature of the conduct.

(d) On a finding by the justice or municipal court that the person has engaged in truant conduct described in Section 51.03(b)(2) or conduct that violates Section 25.094, Education Code, the court has jurisdiction to enter an order that includes one or more of the following provisions requiring that:

(1) the person attend a preparatory class for the high school equivalency examination provided under Section 7.111, Education Code, if the court determines that the person is too old to do well in a formal classroom environment;

(2) the person attend a special program that the court determines to be in the best interests of the person, including:

(A) an alcohol and drug abuse program;

(B) rehabilitation;

(C) counseling, including self-improvement counseling;

(D) training in self-esteem and leadership;

(E) work and job skills training;

(F) training in parenting, including parental responsibility;

(G) training in manners;

(H) training in violence avoidance;

(I) sensitivity training; and

(J) training in advocacy and mentoring;

(3) the person and the person's parents, managing conservator, or guardian attend a class for students at risk of dropping out of school designed for both the person and the person's parents, managing conservator, or guardian;

(4) the person complete reasonable community service requirements;

(5) the person's driver's license be suspended in the manner provided by Section 54.042 of this code;

(6) the person attend school without unexcused absences; or

(7) the person participate in a tutorial program provided by the school attended by the person in the academic subjects in which the person is enrolled for a total number of hours ordered by the court.

(e) An order under Subsection (d)(3) that requires the parent, managing conservator, or guardian of a person to attend a class for students at risk of dropping out of school is enforceable in the justice court by contempt.

(f) A school attendance officer may refer a person alleged to have engaged in conduct described in Section 51.03(b)(2) of this code to a justice court in the county where the person resides or where the person's school is located or to a municipal court of the municipality where the person resides or where the person's school is located if the juvenile court having exclusive original jurisdiction has waived its jurisdiction as provided by Subsection (a) of this section for all cases involving conduct described by Section 51.03(b)(2) of this code.

(g) A court having jurisdiction under this section shall endorse on the summons issued to the parent, guardian, or custodian of the person who is the subject of the hearing an order directing the parent, guardian, or custodian to appear personally at the hearing and directing the person having custody of the person to bring the person to the hearing.

(h) A person commits an offense if the person is a parent, guardian, or custodian who fails to attend a hearing under this section after receiving notice under Subsection (g) of this section that the person's attendance was required. An offense under this subsection is a Class C misdemeanor.

Added by Acts 1991, 72nd Leg., ch. 741, § 1, eff. Sept. 1, 1991. Amended by Acts 1993, 73rd Leg., ch. 358, § 1, eff. Sept. 1, 1993; Acts 1995, 74th Leg., ch. 260, § 24, eff. May 30, 1995; Acts 1995, 74th Leg., ch. 262, § 35, eff. Jan. 1, 1996; Acts 1997, 75th Leg., ch. 865, § 1, eff. Sept. 1, 1997.

Section 2 of the 1991 Act provides:

"The change in law made by this Act applies only if the final absence that makes Subdivision (2), Subsection (b), Section 51.03, Family Code, applicable to a child's conduct occurs on or after the effective date of this Act."

For applicability provisions of the 1993 amendatory act, see notes following V.T.C.A., Family Code § 51.03.

Section 104 of Acts 1995, 74th Leg., ch. 262 provides:

"(a) An amendment to any provision of Title 3, Family Code, made by another Act of the 74th Legislature, Regular Session, 1995, applies only to conduct that occurs on or after the effective date of the other Act and before January 1, 1996. The amendment made by the other Act continues in effect only for the limited purpose of the prosecution of the conduct committed before January 1, 1996.

"(b) For purposes of Subsection (a) of this section, conduct violating the penal law of this state occurs before January 1, 1996, only if every element of the violation occurs before that date."

Section 4(b) and (c) of Acts 1997, 75th Leg., ch. 865 provides:

"(b) Except as provided by Subsection (c) of this section, the changes in law made by this Act apply to truancy cases or cases of failure to attend school without regard to whether the conduct involved in those cases occurred before, on, or after the effective date of this Act.

"(c) The change in law made by this Act applies only to conduct that occurs on or after the effective date of this Act. Conduct violating the penal law of this state occurs on or after the effective date of this Act if any element of the violation occurs on or after that date. Conduct that occurs before the effective date of this Act is governed by the law in effect at the time the conduct occurred, and that law is continued in effect for that purpose."

§ 54.022. Justice or Municipal Court: Certain Misdemeanors

(a) On a finding by a justice or municipal court that a child committed a misdemeanor offense punishable by fine only other than a traffic offense or public intoxication or committed a violation of a penal ordinance of a political subdivision other than a traffic offense, the court has jurisdiction to enter an order:

(1) referring the child or the child's parents, managing conservators, or guardians for services under Section 264.302; or

(2) requiring that the child attend a special program that the court determines to be in the best interest of the child and that is approved by the county commissioners court, including a rehabilitation, counseling, self-esteem and leadership, work and job skills training, job interviewing and work preparation, self-improvement, parenting, manners, violence avoidance, tutoring, sensitivity training, parental responsibility, community service, restitution, advocacy, or mentoring program.

(b) On a finding by a justice or municipal court that a child committed an offense described by Subsection (a) and that the child has previously been convicted of an offense described by Subsection (a), the court has the jurisdiction to enter an order that includes one or more of the following provisions, in addition to the provisions under Subsection (a), requiring that:

(1) the child attend a special program that the court determines to be in the best interest of the child and that is approved by the county commissioners court;

(2) the child's parents, managing conservator, or guardian attend a parenting class or parental responsibility program if the court finds the parent, managing conservator, or guardian, by wilful act or omission, contributed to, caused, or encouraged the child's conduct; or

(3) the child and the child's parents, managing conservator, or guardian attend the child's school classes or functions if the court finds the parent, managing conservator, or guardian, by wilful act or omission, contributed to, caused, or encouraged the child's conduct.

(c) The justice or municipal court may order the parents, managing conservator, or guardian of a child required to attend a program under Subsection (a) or (b) to pay an amount not greater than $100 to pay for the costs of the program.

(d) A justice or municipal court may require a child, parent, managing conservator, or guardian required to attend a program, class, or function under this section to submit proof of attendance to the court.

(e) A justice or municipal court shall endorse on the summons issued to a parent, managing conservator, or a guardian an order to appear personally at the hearing with the child. The summons must include a warning that the failure of the parent, managing conservator, or guardian to appear may be punishable as a Class C misdemeanor.

(f) An order under this section involving a child is enforceable under Section 51.03(a)(3) by referral to the juvenile court.

(g) A person commits an offense if the person is a parent, managing conservator, or guardian who fails to attend a hearing under this section after receiving an order under Subsection (e). An offense under this subsection is a Class C misdemeanor.

(h) Any other order under this section is enforceable by the justice or municipal court by contempt.

Added by Acts 1995, 74th Leg., ch. 262, § 36, eff. Jan. 1, 1996. Amended by Acts 1997, 75th Leg., ch. 713, § 1, eff. Sept. 1, 1997.

Section 2 of Acts 1997, 75th Leg., ch. 713 provides:

"The change in law made by this Act applies only to a court order issued on or after the effective date of this Act. An order issued before the effective date of this Act is covered by the law in effect when the order was issued, and the former law is continued in effect for that purpose."

§ 54.03. Adjudication Hearing

(a) A child may be found to have engaged in delinquent conduct or conduct indicating a need for supervision only after an adjudication hearing conducted in accordance with the provisions of this section.

(b) At the beginning of the adjudication hearing, the juvenile court judge shall explain to the child and his parent, guardian, or guardian ad litem:

(1) the allegations made against the child;

(2) the nature and possible consequences of the proceedings, including the law relating to the admissibility of the record of a juvenile court adjudication in a criminal proceeding;

(3) the child's privilege against self-incrimination;

(4) the child's right to trial and to confrontation of witnesses;

(5) the child's right to representation by an attorney if he is not already represented; and

(6) the child's right to trial by jury.

(c) Trial shall be by jury unless jury is waived in accordance with Section 51.09 of this code. If the hearing is on a petition that has been approved by the grand jury under Section 53.045 of this code, the jury must consist of 12 persons. Jury verdicts under this title must be unanimous.

(d) Except as provided by Section 54.031 of this chapter, only material, relevant, and competent evidence in accordance with the Texas Rules of Criminal Evidence and Chapter 38, Code of Criminal Procedure, may be considered in the adjudication hearing. Except in a detention or discretionary transfer hearing, a social history report or social service file shall not be viewed by the court before the adjudication decision and shall not be viewed by the jury at any time.

(e) A child alleged to have engaged in delinquent conduct or conduct indicating a need for supervision need not be a witness against nor otherwise incriminate himself. An extrajudicial statement which was obtained without fulfilling the requirements of this title or of the constitution of this state or the United States, may not be used in an adjudication hearing. A statement made by the child out of court is insufficient to support a finding of delinquent conduct or conduct indicating a need for supervision unless it is corroborated in whole or in part by other evidence. An adjudication of delinquent conduct or conduct indicating a need for supervision cannot be had upon the testimony of an accomplice unless corroborated by other evidence tending to connect the child with the alleged delinquent conduct or conduct indicating a need for supervision; and the corroboration is not sufficient if it merely shows the commission of the alleged conduct. Evidence illegally seized or obtained is inadmissible in an adjudication hearing.

(f) At the conclusion of the adjudication hearing, the court or jury shall find whether or not the child has engaged in delinquent conduct or conduct indicating a need for supervision. The finding must be based on competent evidence admitted at the hearing. The child shall be presumed to be innocent of the charges against him and no finding that a child has engaged in delinquent conduct or conduct indicating a need for supervision may be returned unless the state has proved such beyond a reasonable doubt. In all jury cases the jury will be instructed that the burden is on the state to prove that a child has engaged in delinquent conduct or is in need of supervision beyond a reasonable doubt.

(g) If the court or jury finds that the child did not engage in delinquent conduct or conduct indicating a need for supervision, the court shall dismiss the case with prejudice.

(h) If the finding is that the child did engage in delinquent conduct or conduct indicating a need for supervision, the court or jury shall state which of the allegations in the petition were found to be established by the evidence. The court shall also set a date and time for the disposition hearing.

(i) In order to preserve for appellate or collateral review the failure of the court to provide the child the explanation required by Subsection (b), the attorney for the child must comply with Rule 52(a), Texas Rules of Appellate Procedure, before testimony begins or, if the adjudication is uncontested, before the child pleads to the petition or agrees to a stipulation of evidence.

(j) When the state and the child agree to the disposition of the case, in whole or in part, the prosecuting attorney shall inform the court of the agreement between the state and the child. The court shall inform the child that the court is not required to accept the agreement. The court may delay a decision on whether to accept the agreement until after reviewing a report filed under Section 54.04(b). If the court decides not to accept the agreement, the court shall inform the child of the court's decision and give the child an opportunity to withdraw the plea or stipulation of evidence. If the court rejects the agreement, no document, testimony, or other evidence placed before the court that relates to the rejected agreement may be considered by the court in a subsequent hearing in the case. A statement made by the child before the court's rejection of the agreement to a person writing a report to be filed under Section 54.04(b) may not be admitted into evidence in a subsequent hearing in the case. If the court accepts the agreement, the court shall make a disposition in accordance with the terms of the agreement between the state and the child.

Acts 1973, 63rd Leg., p. 1460, ch. 544, § 1, eff. Sept. 1, 1973. Amended by Acts 1975, 64th Leg., p. 2157, ch. 693, § 17, eff. Sept. 1, 1975; Acts 1979, 66th Leg., p. 1098, ch. 514, § 1, eff. Aug. 27, 1979; Acts 1985, 69th Leg., ch. 590, § 2, eff. Sept. 1, 1985; Acts 1987, 70th Leg., ch. 385, § 8, eff. Sept. 1, 1987; Acts 1987, 70th Leg., ch. 386, § 3, eff. Sept. 1, 1987; Acts 1995, 74th Leg., ch. 262, § 37, eff. Jan. 1, 1996; Acts 1997, 75th Leg., ch. 1086, § 10, eff. Sept. 1, 1997.

Section 20 of Acts 1987, 70th Leg., ch. 385 provides:

"(a) This Act applies only to offenses and conduct occurring on or after its effective date. For the purposes of this section, an offense or delinquent conduct based on an offense occurs on or after the effective date if all the elements of the offense occur on or after the effective date.

"(b) An offense or conduct that occurs before the effective date of this Act shall be prosecuted under the law in effect immediately before the effective date of this Act, and that law is continued in effect for that purpose only."

§ 54.031. Hearsay Statement of Child Abuse Victim

(a) This section applies to a hearing under this title in which a child is alleged to be a delinquent child on the basis of a violation of any of the following provisions of the Penal Code, if a child 12 years of age or younger is the alleged victim of the violation:

(1) Chapter 21 (Sexual Offenses) or 22 (Assaultive Offenses);

(2) Section 25.02 (Prohibited Sexual Conduct); or

(3) Section 43.25 (Sexual Performance by a Child).

(b) This section applies only to statements that describe the alleged violation that:

(1) were made by the child who is the alleged victim of the violation; and

(2) were made to the first person, 18 years of age or older, to whom the child made a statement about the violation.

(c) A statement that meets the requirements of Subsection (b) of this section is not inadmissible because of the hearsay rule if:

(1) on or before the 14th day before the date the hearing begins, the party intending to offer the statement:

(A) notifies each other party of its intention to do so;

(B) provides each other party with the name of the witness through whom it intends to offer the statement; and

(C) provides each other party with a written summary of the statement;

(2) the juvenile court finds, in a hearing conducted outside the presence of the jury, that the statement is reliable based on the time, content, and circumstances of the statement; and

(3) the child who is the alleged victim testifies or is available to testify at the hearing in court or in any other manner provided by law.

Added by Acts 1985, 69th Leg., ch. 590, § 3, eff. Sept. 1, 1985. Amended by Acts 1995, 74th Leg., ch. 76, § 14.31, eff. Sept. 1, 1995.

Section 104 of Acts 1995, 74th Leg., ch. 262 provides:

"(a) An amendment to any provision of Title 3, Family Code, made by another Act of the 74th Legislature, Regular Session, 1995, applies only to conduct that occurs on or after the effective date of the other Act and before January 1, 1996. The amendment made by the other Act continues in effect only for the limited purpose of the prosecution of the conduct committed before January 1, 1996.

"(b) For purposes of Subsection (a) of this section, conduct violating the penal law of this state occurs before January 1, 1996, only if every element of the violation occurs before that date."

§ 54.032. Deferral of Adjudication and Dismissal of Certain Cases on Completion of Teen Court Program

(a) A juvenile court may defer adjudication proceedings under Section 54.03 of this code for 90 days if the child:

(1) is alleged to have engaged in conduct indicating a need for supervision that violated a penal law of this state of the grade of misdemeanor that is punishable by fine only or a penal ordinance of a political subdivision of this state;

(2) waives, under Section 51.09 of this code, the privilege against self-incrimination and testifies under oath that the allegations are true;

(3) presents to the court an oral or written request to attend a teen court program; and

(4) has not successfully completed a teen court program for the violation of the same penal law or ordinance in the two years preceding the date that the alleged conduct occurred.

(b) The teen court program must be approved by the court.

(c) The court shall dismiss the case with prejudice at the conclusion of the deferral period if the child presents satisfactory evidence that the child has successfully completed the teen court program.

(d) A case dismissed under this section may not be part of the child's records for any purpose.

(e) The court may require a child who requests a teen court program to pay a fee not to exceed $10 that is set by the court to cover the costs of administering this section. The court shall deposit the fee in the county treasury of the county in which the court is located. A child who requests a teen court program and does not complete the program is not entitled to a refund of the fee.

(f) A court may transfer a case in which proceedings have been deferred as provided by this section to a court in a contiguous county if the court to which the case is transferred consents. A case may not be transferred unless it is within the jurisdiction of the court to which it is transferred.

(g) In addition to the fee authorized by Subsection (e), the court may require a child who requests a teen court program to pay a $10 fee to cover the cost to the teen court for performing its duties under this section. The court shall pay the fee to the teen court program, and the teen court program must account to the court for the receipt and disbursal of the fee. A child who pays a fee under this subsection is not entitled to a refund of the fee, regardless of whether the child successfully completes the teen court program.

Added by Acts 1989, 71st Leg., ch. 1031, § 2, eff. Sept. 1, 1989. Amended by Acts 1995, 74th Leg., ch. 748, § 1, eff. Sept. 1, 1995.

Section 4 of the 1989 Act provides:

"(a) This Act takes effect September 1, 1989, and applies only to conduct violating the penal laws of this state that occurs or an offense that is committed on or after that date. Conduct violating the penal laws of this state occurs, or an offense is committed, on or after the effective date of this Act if every element of the violation or offense occurs on or after that date.

"(b) Conduct that occurs or an offense committed before the effective date of this Act is governed by the law in effect at the time the conduct occurred or the offense was committed and that law is continued in effect for that purpose."

Section 104 of Acts 1995, 74th Leg., ch. 262 provides:

"(a) An amendment to any provision of Title 3, Family Code, made by another Act of the 74th Legislature, Regular Session, 1995, applies only to conduct that occurs on or after the effective date of the other Act and before January 1, 1996. The amendment made by the other Act continues in effect only for the limited purpose of the prosecution of the conduct committed before January 1, 1996.

"(b) For purposes of Subsection (a) of this section, conduct violating the penal law of this state occurs before January 1, 1996, only if every element of the violation occurs before that date."

Section 3 of Acts 1995, 74th Leg., ch. 748 provides:

"(a) The change in law made by this Act applies only to a child charged with an offense committed on or after the effective date of this Act. For purposes of this section, an offense is committed before the effective date of this Act if any element of the offense occurs before the effective date.

"(b) A child charged with an offense committed before the effective date of this Act is covered by the law in effect when the offense was committed, and the former law is continued in effect for this purpose."

§ 54.033. Sexually Transmitted Disease, AIDS, and HIV Testing

(a) A child found at the conclusion of an adjudication hearing under Section 54.03 of this code to have engaged in delinquent conduct that included a violation of Sections 21.11(a)(1), 22.011, or 22.021, Penal Code, shall undergo a medical procedure or test at the direction of the juvenile court designed to show or help show whether the child has a sexually transmitted disease, acquired immune deficiency syndrome (AIDS), human immunodeficiency virus (HIV) infection, antibodies to HIV, or infection with any other probable causative agent of AIDS. The court may direct the child to undergo the procedure or test on the court's own motion or on the request of the victim of the delinquent conduct.

(b) If the child or another person who has the power to consent to medical treatment for the child refuses to submit voluntarily or consent to the procedure or test, the court shall require the child to submit to the procedure or test.

(c) The person performing the procedure or test shall make the test results available to the local health authority. The local health authority shall be required to notify the victim of the delinquent conduct and the person found to have engaged in the delinquent conduct of the test result.

(d) The state may not use the fact that a medical procedure or test was performed on a child under this section or use the results of the procedure or test in any proceeding arising out of the delinquent conduct.

(e) Testing under this section shall be conducted in accordance with written infectious disease control protocols adopted by the Texas Board of Health that clearly establish procedural guidelines that provide criteria for testing and that respect the rights of the child and the victim of the delinquent conduct.

(f) Nothing in this section allows a court to release a test result to anyone other than a person specifically authorized under this section. Section 81.103(d), Health and Safety Code, may not be construed to allow the disclosure of test results under this section except as provided by this section.

Added by Acts 1993, 73rd Leg., ch. 811, § 2, eff. Sept. 1, 1993.

Section 4(c) and (d) of the 1993 Act provide:

"(c) The change in law made by Section 2 of this Act to the Family Code, adding Section 54.033 to the code and requiring that children found at the conclusion of an adjudication hearing to have engaged in juvenile conduct that included violations of certain sections of the Penal Code undergo certain medical procedures and tests, applies only to a child who engages in the delinquent conduct on or after the effective date of this Act.

"(d) For the purposes of this section, an offense is committed or delinquent conduct that includes a violation of an offense is engaged in before the effective date of this Act if any element of the offense occurs before the effective date."

§ 54.04. Disposition Hearing

(a) The disposition hearing shall be separate, distinct, and subsequent to the adjudication hearing. There is no right to a jury at the disposition hearing unless the child is in jeopardy of a determinate sentence under Subsection (d)(3) or (m) of this section, in which case, the child is entitled to a jury of 12 persons to determine the sentence.

(b) At the disposition hearing, the juvenile court may consider written reports from probation officers, professional court employees, or professional consultants in addition to the testimony of witnesses. Prior to the disposition hearing, the court shall provide the attorney for the child with access to all written matter to be considered in disposition. The court may order counsel not to reveal items to the child or his parent, guardian, or guardian ad litem if such disclosure would materially harm the treatment and rehabilitation of the child or would substantially decrease the likelihood of receiving information from the same or similar sources in the future.

(c) No disposition may be made under this section unless the child is in need of rehabilitation or the protection of the public or the child requires that disposition be made. If the court or jury does not so find, the court shall dismiss the child and enter a final judgment without any disposition. No disposition placing the child on probation outside the child's home may be made under this section unless the court or jury finds that the child, in the child's home, cannot be provided the quality of care and level of support and supervision that the child needs to meet the conditions of the probation.

(d) If the court or jury makes the finding specified in Subsection (c) allowing the court to make a disposition in the case:

(1) the court or jury may, in addition to any order required or authorized under Section 54.041 or 54.042, place the child on probation on such reasonable and lawful terms as the court may determine:

(A) in his own home or in the custody of a relative or other fit person; or

(B) subject to the finding under Subsection (c) on the placement of the child outside the child's home, in:

(i) a suitable foster home; or

(ii) a suitable public or private institution or agency, except the Texas Youth Commission;

(2) if the court or jury found at the conclusion of the adjudication hearing that the child engaged in delinquent conduct and if the petition was not approved by the grand jury under Section 53.045, the court may commit the child to the Texas Youth Commission without a determinate sentence;

(3) if the court or jury found at the conclusion of the adjudication hearing that the child engaged in delinquent conduct that included a violation of a penal law listed in Section 53.045(a) and if the petition was approved by the grand jury under Section 53.045, the court or jury may sentence the child to commitment in the Texas Youth Commission with a possible transfer to the institutional division or the pardons and paroles division of the Texas Department of Criminal Justice for a term of:

(A) not more than 40 years if the conduct constitutes:

(i) a capital felony;

(ii) a felony of the first degree; or

(iii) an aggravated controlled substance felony;

(B) not more than 20 years if the conduct constitutes a felony of the second degree; or

(C) not more than 10 years if the conduct constitutes a felony of the third degree;

(4) the court may assign the child an appropriate sanction level and sanctions as provided by the assignment guidelines in Section 59.003; or

(5) if applicable, the court or jury may make a disposition under Subsection (m).

(e) The Texas Youth Commission shall accept a person properly committed to it by a juvenile court even though the person may be 17 years of age or older at the time of commitment.

(f) The court shall state specifically in the order its reasons for the disposition and shall furnish a copy of the order to the child. If the child is placed on probation, the terms of probation shall be written in the order.

(g) If the court orders a disposition under Subsection (d)(3) or (m) of this section and there is an affirmative finding that the defendant used or exhibited a deadly weapon during the commission of the conduct or during immediate flight from commission of the conduct, the court shall enter the finding in the order. If there is an affirmative finding that the deadly weapon was a firearm, the court shall enter that finding in the order.

(h) At the conclusion of the dispositional hearing, the court shall inform the child of:

(1) the child's right to appeal, as required by Section 56.01 of this code; and

(2) the procedures for the sealing of the child's records under Section 58.003 of this code.

(i) If the court places the child on probation outside the child's home or commits the child to the Texas Youth Commission, the court shall include in its order its determination that:

(1) it is in the child's best interests to be placed outside the child's home;

(2) reasonable efforts were made to prevent or eliminate the need for the child's removal from the home and to make it possible for the child to return to the child's home; and

(3) the child, in the child's home, cannot be provided the quality of care and level of support and supervision that the child needs to meet the conditions of probation.

(j) If the court or jury found that the child engaged in delinquent conduct that included a violation of a penal law of the grade of felony, the court:

(1) shall require that the child's thumbprint be affixed to the order; and

(2) may require that a photograph of the child be attached to the order.

(k) Except as provided by Subsection (m), the period to which a court or jury may sentence a person to commitment to the Texas Youth Commission with a transfer to the Texas Department of Criminal Justice under Subsection (d)(3) of this section applies without regard to whether the person has previously been adjudicated as having engaged in delinquent conduct.

(*l*) A court or jury may place a child on probation under Subsection (d)(1) of this section for any period, except that probation may not continue on or after the child's 18th birthday. The court may, before the period of probation ends, extend the probation for any period, except that the probation may not extend to or after the child's 18th birthday.

(m) The court or jury may sentence a child adjudicated for habitual felony conduct as described by Section 51.031 to a term prescribed by Subsection (d)(3) and applicable to the conduct adjudicated in the pending case if:

(1) a petition was filed and approved by a grand jury under Section 53.045 alleging that the child engaged in habitual felony conduct; and

(2) the court or jury finds beyond a reasonable doubt that the allegation described by Subdivision (1) in the grand jury petition is true.

(n) A court may order a disposition of secure confinement of a status offender adjudicated for violating a valid court order only if:

(1) before the order is issued, the child received the full due process rights guaranteed by the Constitution of the United States or the Texas Constitution; and

(2) the juvenile probation department in a report authorized by Subsection (b):

(A) reviewed the behavior of the child and the circumstances under which the child was brought before the court;

(B) determined the reasons for the behavior that caused the child to be brought before the court; and

(C) determined that all dispositions, including treatment, other than placement in a secure detention facility or secure correctional facility, have been exhausted or are clearly inappropriate.

(*o*) A status offender may not, under any circumstances, be committed to the Texas Youth Commission for engaging in conduct that would not, under state or local law, be a crime if committed by an adult.

(p) Except as provided by Subsection (*l*), a court that places a child on probation under Subsection (d)(1) for conduct described by Section 54.0405(b) and punishable as a felony shall specify a minimum probation period of two years.

Acts 1973, 63rd Leg., p. 1460, ch. 544, § 1, eff. Sept. 1, 1973. Amended by Acts 1975, 64th Leg., p. 2158, ch. 693, § 23, eff. Sept. 1, 1975; Acts 1981, 67th Leg., p. 1802, ch. 394, § 1, eff. Aug. 31, 1981; Acts 1983, 68th Leg., p. 161, ch. 44, art. 1, § 3, eff. April 26, 1983; Acts 1983, 68th Leg., p. 3261, ch. 565, § 2, eff. Sept. 1, 1983; Acts 1987, 70th Leg., ch. 385, § 9, eff. Sept. 1, 1987; Acts 1987, 70th Leg., ch. 1052, § 6.11, eff. Sept. 1, 1987; Acts 1989, 71st Leg., ch. 2, § 16.01(17), eff. Aug. 28, 1989; Acts 1989, 71st Leg., ch. 80, § 1, eff. Sept. 1, 1989; Acts 1991, 72nd Leg., ch. 557, § 2, eff. Sept. 1, 1991; Acts 1991, 72nd Leg., ch. 574, § 2, eff. Sept. 1, 1991; Acts 1991, 72nd Leg., ch. 784, § 8, eff. Sept. 1, 1991; Acts 1993, 73rd Leg., ch. 1048, § 1, eff. Sept. 1, 1993; Acts 1995, 74th Leg., ch. 262, § 38, eff. Jan. 1, 1996; Acts 1997, 75th Leg., ch. 669, § 2, eff. Sept. 1, 1997; Acts 1997, 75th Leg., ch. 1086, § 11, eff. Sept. 1, 1997.

Section 5 of Acts 1983, 68th Leg., p. 3265, ch. 565, provides:

"This Act applies only to a child's conduct that occurs and civil liability for a cause of action that arises on or after the effective date of this Act."

Section 20 of Acts 1987, 70th Leg., ch. 385, provides:

"(a) This Act applies only to offenses and conduct occurring on or after its effective date. For the purposes of this section, an offense or delinquent conduct based on an offense occurs on or after the effective date if all the elements of the offense occur on or after the effective date.

"(b) An offense or conduct that occurs before the effective date of this Act shall be prosecuted under the law in effect immediately before the effective date of this Act, and that law is continued in effect for that purpose only."

Section 4 of Acts 1991, 72nd Leg., ch. 557 provides:

"(a) The change in law made by this Act applies only to conduct that occurs on or after the effective date of this Act. Conduct violating a penal law of this state occurs on or after the effective date of this Act if every element of the violation occurs on or after that date.

"(b) Conduct that occurs before the effective date of this Act is governed by the law in effect at the time the conduct occurred, and the former law is continued in effect for that purpose."

Section 5 of Acts 1991, 72nd Leg., ch. 574 provides:

"(a) This Act takes effect September 1, 1991, and applies only to conduct that occurs on or after that date. Conduct violating the penal laws of this state occurs on or after the effective date of this Act if every element of the violation occurs on or after that date.

"(b) Conduct that occurs before the effective date of this Act is governed by the law in effect at the time the conduct occurred and that law is continued in effect for that purpose."

For application provision of Acts 1997, 75th Leg., ch. 696, see notes following V.T.C.A., Family Code § 54.0405.

§ 54.0405. Child Placed on Probation for Conduct Constituting Sexual Offense

(a) If a court or jury makes a disposition under Section 54.04 in which a child described by Subsection (b) is placed on probation and the court determines that the victim of the offense was a child as defined by Section 22.011(c), Penal Code, the court may require as a condition of probation that the child:

(1) attend psychological counseling sessions for sex offenders as provided by Subsection (e); and

(2) submit to a polygraph examination as provided by Subsection (f) for purposes of evaluating the child's treatment progress.

(b) This section applies to a child placed on probation for conduct constituting an offense:

(1) under Section 21.08, 21.11, 22.011, 22.021, or 25.02, Penal Code;

(2) under Section 20.04(a)(4), Penal Code, if the child engaged in the conduct with the intent to violate or abuse the victim sexually; or

(3) under Section 30.02, Penal Code, punishable under Subsection (d) of that section, if the child engaged in the conduct with the intent to commit a felony listed in Subdivision (1) or (2) of this subsection.

(c) Psychological counseling required as a condition of probation under Subsection (a) must be with an individual or organization that:

(1) provides sex offender treatment or counseling;

(2) is specified by the local juvenile probation department supervising the child; and

(3) meets minimum standards of counseling established by the local juvenile probation department.

(d) A polygraph examination required as a condition of probation under Subsection (a) must be administered by an individual who is:

(1) specified by the local juvenile probation department supervising the child; and

(2) licensed as a polygraph examiner under the Polygraph Examiners Act (Article 4413(29cc), Vernon's Texas Civil Statutes).

(e) A local juvenile probation department that specifies a sex offender treatment provider under Subsection (c) to provide counseling to a child shall:

(1) establish with the cooperation of the treatment provider the date, time, and place of the first counseling session between the child and the treatment provider;

(2) notify the child and the treatment provider, not later than the 21st day after the date the order making the disposition placing the child on probation under Section 54.04 becomes final, of the date, time, and place of the first counseling session between the child and the treatment provider; and

(3) require the treatment provider to notify the department immediately if the child fails to attend any scheduled counseling session.

(f) A local juvenile probation department that specifies a polygraph examiner under Subsection (d) to administer a polygraph examination to a child shall arrange for a polygraph examination to be administered to the child:

(1) not later than the 60th day after the date the child attends the first counseling session established under Subsection (e); and

(2) after the initial polygraph examination, as required by Subdivision (1), on the request of the treatment provider specified under Subsection (c).

(g) A court that requires as a condition of probation that a child attend psychological counseling under Subsection (a) may order the parent or guardian of the child to:

(1) attend four sessions of instruction with an individual or organization specified by the court relating to:

(A) sexual offenses;

(B) family communication skills;

(C) sex offender treatment;

(D) victims' rights;

(E) parental supervision; and

(F) appropriate sexual behavior; and

(2) during the period the child attends psychological counseling, participate in monthly treatment groups conducted by the child's treatment provider relating to the child's psychological counseling.

(h) A court that orders a parent or guardian of a child to attend instructional sessions and participate in treatment groups under Subsection (g) shall require:

(1) the individual or organization specified by the court under Subsection (g) to notify the court immediately if the parent or guardian fails to attend any scheduled instructional session; and

(2) the child's treatment provider specified under Subsection (c) to notify the court immediately if the parent or guardian fails to attend a session in which the parent or guardian is required to participate in a scheduled treatment group.

(i) A court that requires as a condition of probation that a child attend psychological counseling under Subsection (a) may, before the date the probation period ends, extend the probation for any additional period necessary to complete the required counseling as determined by the treatment provider, except that the probation may not be extended to a date after the date of the child's 18th birthday.

Added by Acts 1997, 75th Leg., ch. 669, § 1, eff. Sept. 1, 1997.

Section 6 of Acts 1997, 75th Leg., ch. 669 provides:

"(a) The change in law made by this Act applies only to conduct that occurs on or after the effective date of this Act. Conduct violating a penal law of the state occurs on or after the effective date of this Act if every element of the violation occurs on or after that date.

"(b) Conduct that occurs before the effective date of this Act is covered by the law in effect at the time the conduct occurred, and the former law is continued in effect for that purpose."

§ 54.041. Orders Affecting Parents and Others

(a) When a child has been found to have engaged in delinquent conduct or conduct indicating a need for supervision and the juvenile court has made a finding that the child is in need of rehabilitation or that the protection of the public or the child requires that disposition be made, the juvenile court, on notice by any reasonable method to all persons affected, may:

(1) order any person found by the juvenile court to have, by a wilful act or omission, contributed to, caused, or encouraged the child's delinquent conduct or conduct indicating a need for supervision to do any act that the juvenile court determines to be reasonable and necessary for the welfare of the child or to refrain from doing any act that the juvenile court determines to be injurious to the welfare of the child;

(2) enjoin all contact between the child and a person who is found to be a contributing cause of the child's delinquent conduct or conduct indicating a need for supervision; or

(3) after notice and a hearing of all persons affected order any person living in the same household with the child to participate in social or psychological counseling to assist in the rehabilitation of the child and to strengthen the child's family environment.

(b) If a child is found to have engaged in delinquent conduct or conduct indicating a need for supervision arising from the commission of an offense in which property damage or loss or personal injury occurred, the juvenile court, on notice to all persons affected and on hearing, may order the child or a parent to make full or partial restitution to the victim of the offense. The program of restitution must promote the rehabilitation of the child, be appropriate to the age and physical, emotional, and mental abilities of the child, and not conflict with the child's schooling. When practicable and subject to court supervision, the court may approve a restitution program based on a settlement between the child and the victim of the offense. An order under this subsection may provide for periodic payments by the child or a parent of the child for the period specified in the order but that period may not extend past the date of the 18th birthday of the child or past the date the child is no longer enrolled in an accredited secondary school in a program leading toward a high school diploma, whichever date is later.

(c) Restitution under this section is cumulative of any other remedy allowed by law and may be used in addition to other remedies; except that a victim of an offense is not entitled to receive more than actual damages under a juvenile court order.

(d) A person subject to an order proposed under Subsection (a) of this section is entitled to a hearing on the order before the order is entered by the court.

(e) An order made under this section may be enforced as provided by Section 54.07 of this code.

(f) If a child is found to have engaged in conduct indicating a need for supervision described under Section 51.03(b)(2) of this code, the court may order the child's parents or guardians to attend a class described by Section 25.093(h), Education Code, if the school district in which the child's parents or guardians reside offers a class under that section.

(g) On a finding by the court that a child's parents or guardians have made a reasonable good faith effort to prevent the child from engaging in delinquent conduct or engaging in conduct indicating a need for supervision and that, despite the parents' or guardians' efforts, the child continues to engage in such conduct, the court shall waive any requirement for restitution that may be imposed on a parent under this section.

Added by Acts 1975, 64th Leg., p. 2157, ch. 693, § 18, eff. Sept. 1, 1975. Amended by Acts 1979, 66th Leg., p. 338, ch. 154, § 2, eff. Sept. 1, 1979; Acts 1983, 68th Leg., p. 528, ch. 110, § 1, eff. Aug. 29, 1983; Acts 1983, 68th Leg., p. 3262, ch. 565, § 3, eff. Sept. 1, 1983; Acts 1989, 71st Leg., ch. 1170, § 3, eff. June 16, 1989; Acts 1995, 74th Leg., ch. 262, § 39, eff. Jan. 1, 1996; Acts 1997, 75th Leg., ch. 165, § 6.09, eff. Sept. 1, 1997.

Section 2 of Acts 1983, 68th Leg., p. 529, ch. 110, provides:

"This Act applies to suits in which a finding of delinquency or that a child is a child in need of supervision is made on or after the effective date of this Act."

Section 5 of Acts 1983, 68th Leg., p. 3265, ch. 565, provides:

"This Act applies only to a child's conduct that occurs and civil liability for a cause of action that arises on or after the effective date of this Act."

§ 54.0411. Juvenile Probation Diversion Fund

(a) If a disposition hearing is held under Section 54.04 of this code, the juvenile court, after giving the child, parent, or other person responsible for the child's support a reasonable opportunity to be heard, shall order the child, parent, or other person, if financially able to do so, to pay a fee as costs of court of $20.

(b) Orders for the payment of fees under this section may be enforced as provided by Section 54.07 of this code.

(c) An officer collecting costs under this section shall keep separate records of the funds collected as costs under this section and shall deposit the funds in the county treasury.

(d) Each officer collecting court costs under this section shall file the reports required under Article 103.005, Code of Criminal Procedure. If no funds due as costs under this section have been collected in any quarter, the report required for each quarter shall be filed in the regular manner, and the report must state that no funds due under this section were collected.

(e) The custodian of the county treasury may deposit the funds collected under this section in interest-bearing accounts. The custodian shall keep records of the amount of funds on deposit collected under this section and not later than the last day of the month following each calendar quarter shall send to the comptroller of public accounts the funds collected under this section during the preceding quarter. A county may retain 10 percent of the funds as a service fee and may retain the interest accrued on the funds if the custodian of a county treasury keeps records of the amount of funds on deposit collected under this section and remits the funds to the comptroller within the period prescribed under this subsection.

(f) Funds collected are subject to audit by the comptroller and funds expended are subject to audit by the State Auditor.

(g) The comptroller shall deposit the funds in a special fund to be known as the juvenile probation diversion fund.

(h) The legislature shall determine and appropriate the necessary amount from the juvenile probation diversion fund to the Texas Juvenile Probation Commission for the purchase of services the commission considers necessary for the diversion of any juvenile who is at risk of commitment to the Texas Youth Commission. The Texas Juvenile Probation Commission shall develop guidelines for the use of the fund. The commission may not purchase the services if a person responsible for the child's support or a local juvenile probation department is financially able to provide the services.

Added by Acts 1987, 70th Leg., ch. 1040, § 23, eff. Sept. 1, 1987. Amended by Acts 1989, 71st Leg., ch. 347, § 8, eff. Oct. 1, 1989.

§ 54.042. License Suspension

(a) A juvenile court, in a disposition hearing under Section 54.04, shall:

(1) order the Department of Public Safety to suspend a child's driver's license or permit, or if the child does not have a license or permit, to deny the issuance of a license or permit to the child if the court finds that the child has engaged in conduct that violates a law of this state enumerated in Section 521.342(a), Transportation Code; or

(2) notify the Department of Public Safety of the adjudication, if the court finds that the child has engaged in conduct that violates a law of this state enumerated in Section 521.372(a), Transportation Code.

(b) A juvenile court, in a disposition hearing under Section 54.04, may order the Department of Public Safety to suspend a child's driver's license or permit or, if the child does not have a license or permit, to deny the issuance of a license or permit to the child, if the court finds that the child has engaged in conduct that violates Section 28.08, Penal Code.

(c) The order under Subsection (a)(1) shall specify a period of suspension or denial that is until the child reaches the age of 19 or for a period of 365 days, whichever is longer.

(d) The order under Subsection (b) shall specify a period of suspension or denial that is:

(1) for a period not to exceed 365 days; or

(2) if the court finds the child has been previously adjudicated as having engaged in conduct violating Section 28.08, Penal Code, until the child reaches the age of 19 or for a period not to exceed 365 days, whichever is longer.

(e) A child whose driver's license or permit has been suspended or denied pursuant to this section may, if the child is otherwise eligible for, and fulfils the requirements for issuance of, a provisional driver's license or permit under Chapter 521, Transportation Code , apply for and receive an occupational license in accordance with the provisions of Subchapter L of that chapter.[1]

Text of subsec. (f) as redesignated from subsec. (d) and amended by Acts 1997, 75th Leg., ch. 593, § 3

(f) A juvenile court, in a disposition hearing under Section 54.04, may order the Department of Public Safety to suspend a child's driver's license or permit or, if the child does not have a license or permit, to deny the issuance of a license or permit to the child for a period not to exceed 12 months if the court finds that the child has engaged in conduct in need of supervision or delinquent conduct other than the conduct described by Subsection (a).

Text of subsec. (f) as added by Acts 1997, 75th Leg., ch. 1013, § 17

(f) If a child is adjudicated for conduct that violates Section 49.04, 49.07, or 49.08, Penal Code, and if any conduct on which that adjudication is based is a ground for a driver's license suspension under Chapter 524 or 724, Transportation Code, each of the suspensions shall be imposed. The court imposing a driver's license suspension under this section shall credit a period of suspension imposed under Chapter 524 or 724, Transportation Code, toward the period of suspension required under this section, except that if the child was previously adjudicated for conduct that violates Section 49.04, 49.07, or 49.08, Penal Code, credit may not be given.

(g) A juvenile court that places a child on probation under Section 54.04 may require as a reasonable condition of the probation that if the child violates the probation, the court may order the Department of Public Safety to suspend the child's driver's license or permit or, if the child does not have a license or permit, to deny the issuance of a license or permit to the child for a period not to exceed 12 months. The court may make this order if a child that is on probation under this condition violates the probation. A suspension under this subsection is cumulative of any other suspension under this section.

Added by Acts 1983, 68th Leg., p. 1605, ch. 303, § 25, eff. Jan. 1, 1984. Amended by Acts 1985, 69th Leg., ch. 629, § 1, eff. Sept. 1, 1985; Acts 1991, 72nd Leg., ch. 14, § 284(42), eff. Sept. 1, 1991; Acts 1991, 72nd Leg., ch. 784, § 7, eff. Sept. 1, 1991; Acts 1993, 73rd Leg., ch. 491, § 3, eff. June 15, 1993; Acts 1995, 74th Leg., ch. 76, § 14.32, eff. Sept. 1, 1995; Acts 1995, 74th Leg., ch. 262, § 40, eff. Jan. 1, 1996; Acts 1997, 75th Leg., ch. 165, § 30.183, eff. Sept. 1, 1997; Acts 1997, 75th Leg., ch. 593, § 3, eff. Sept. 1, 1997; Acts 1997, 75th Leg., ch. 1013, § 17, eff. Sept. 1, 1997.

[1] V.T.C.A., Transportation Code § 521.241 et seq.

Section 28(c) of the 1983 Act provides:

"An offense committed before the effective date of this Act is covered by the law in effect when the offense was committed, and the former law is continued in effect for this purpose."

Section 2 of the 1985 amendatory act provides:

"This Act takes effect September 1, 1985, and applies only to findings of a juvenile court based on conduct that occurred on or after that date. Conduct that occurred before the effective date of this Act is covered by the law in effect when the conduct occurred, and the former law is continued in effect for that purpose."

Section 11 of Acts 1991, 72nd Leg., ch. 784 provides:

"(a) The change in law made by this Act applies only to conduct engaged in or to an offense committed on or after the effective date of this Act. For purposes of this section, an offense is committed before the effective date of this Act if any element of the offense occurs before the effective date.

"(b) Conduct engaged in or an offense committed before the effective date of this Act is covered by the law in effect when the conduct occurred or the offense was committed, and the former law is continued in effect for that purpose."

Section 5 of the 1993 amendatory act provides:

"This Act takes effect June 15, 1993, and applies only to a person convicted of an offense committed, or adjudicated under juvenile proceedings for conduct engaged in, on or after the effective date of this Act. For purposes of this section, an offense was committed or conduct was engaged in before the effective date of this Act if any element of the offense or conduct occurred before the effective date. An offense committed or conduct engaged in before the effective date of this Act is covered by the law in effect when the offense was committed or the conduct was engaged in, and the former law is continued in effect for this purpose."

Section 1.02(b) of Acts 1995, 74th Leg., ch. 76 provides:

"If any provision of this Act conflicts with a statute enacted by the 74th Legislature, Regular Session, 1995, the statute controls."

Section 1.02(b) of Acts 1997, 75th Leg., ch. 165 provides:

"If any provision of this Act conflicts with a statute enacted by the 75th Legislature, Regular Session, 1997, the statute controls."

For application provisions of Acts 1997, 75th Leg., ch. 593, see notes following V.T.C.A., Family Code § 53.03.

For application provisions of Acts 1997, 75th Leg., ch. 1013, see notes following V.T.C.A., Family Code § 51.03.

§ 54.043. Monitoring School Attendance

If the court places a child on probation under Section 54.04(d) and requires as a condition of probation that the child attend school, the probation officer charged with supervising the child shall monitor the child's school attendance and report to the court if the child is voluntarily absent from school.

Added by Acts 1993, 73rd Leg., ch. 347, § 6.02, eff. Sept. 1, 1993.

Section 6.03 of the 1993 Act provides:

"(a) The change in law made by this article applies only to an offense committed on or after the effective date of this article. For the purposes of this section, an offense is committed before the effective date of this article if any element of the offense occurs before the effective date.

"(b) An offense committed before the effective date of this article is covered by the law in effect when the offense was committed, and the former law is continued in effect for that purpose."

§ 54.044. Community Service

(a) If the court places a child on probation under Section 54.04(d), the court shall require as a condition of probation that the child work a specified number of hours at a community service project approved by the court and designated by the juvenile board as provided by Subsection (e), unless the court determines and enters a finding on the order placing the child on probation that:

(1) the child is physically or mentally incapable of participating in the project;

(2) participating in the project will be a hardship on the child or the family of the child; or

(3) the child has shown good cause that community service should not be required.

(b) The court may also order under this section that the child's parent perform community service with the child.

(c) The court shall order that the child and the child's parent perform a total of not more than 500 hours of community service under this section.

(d) A municipality or county that establishes a program to assist children and their parents in rendering community service under this section may purchase insurance policies protecting the municipality or county against claims brought by a person other than the child or the child's parent for a cause of action that arises from an act of the child or parent while rendering community service. The municipality or county is not liable under this section to the extent that damages are recoverable under a contract of insurance or under a plan of self-insurance authorized by statute. The liability of the municipality or county for a cause of action that arises from an action of the child or the child's parent while rendering community service may not exceed $100,000 to a single person and $300,000 for a single occurrence in the case of personal injury or death, and $10,000 for a single occurrence of property damage. Liability may not extend to punitive or exemplary damages. This subsection does not waive a defense, immunity, or jurisdictional bar available to the municipality or county or its officers or employees, nor shall this section be construed to waive, repeal, or modify any provision of Chapter 101, Civil Practice and Remedies Code.

(e) For the purposes of this section, a court may submit to the juvenile probation department a list of organizations or projects approved by the court for community service. The juvenile probation department may:

(1) designate an organization or project for community service only from the list submitted by the court; and

(2) reassign or transfer a child to a different organization or project on the list submitted by the court under this subsection without court approval.

(f) A person subject to an order proposed under Subsection (a) or (b) is entitled to a hearing on the order before the order is entered by the court.

(g) On a finding by the court that a child's parents or guardians have made a reasonable good faith effort to prevent the child from engaging in delinquent conduct or engaging in conduct indicating a need for supervision and that, despite the parents' or guardians' efforts, the child continues to engage in such conduct, the court shall waive any requirement for community service that may be imposed on a parent under this section.

(h) An order made under this section may be enforced as provided by Section 54.07.

(i) In a disposition hearing under Section 54.04 in which the court finds that a child engaged in conduct violating Section 521.453, Transportation Code, the court, in addition to any other order authorized under this title and if the court is located in a municipality or county that has established a community service program, may order the child to perform eight hours of community service as a condition of probation under Section 54.04(d) unless the child is shown to have previously engaged in conduct violating Section 521.453, Transportation Code, in which case the court may order the child to perform 12 hours of community service.

Added by Acts 1995, 74th Leg., ch. 262, § 41, eff. Jan. 1, 1996. Amended by Acts 1997, 75th Leg., ch. 1358, § 2, eff. Sept. 1, 1997.

Section 3 of Acts 1997, 75th Leg., ch. 1358 provides:

"(a) The change in law made by this Act applies only to an offense committed or, for purposes of Title 3, Family Code, to conduct that occurs on or after the effective date of this Act. For purposes of this section, an offense is committed on or after the effective date of this Act if every element of the offense occurs on or after that date and conduct violating a penal law of the state occurs on or after the effective date of this Act if every element of the violation occurs on or after that date.

"(b) An offense committed before the effective date of this Act is covered by the law in effect when the offense was committed, and the former law is continued in effect for that purpose. Conduct that occurs before the effective date of this Act is covered by the law in effect at the time the conduct occurred, and the former law is continued in effect for that purpose."

§ 54.045. Admission of Unadjudicated Conduct

(a) During a disposition hearing under Section 54.04, a child may:

(1) admit having engaged in delinquent conduct or conduct indicating a need for supervision for which the child has not been adjudicated; and

(2) request the court to take the admitted conduct into account in the disposition of the child.

(b) If the prosecuting attorney agrees in writing, the court may take the admitted conduct into account in the disposition of the child.

(c) A court may take into account admitted conduct over which exclusive venue lies in another county only if the court obtains the written permission of the prosecuting attorney for that county.

(d) A child may not be adjudicated by any court for having engaged in conduct taken into account under this section, except that, if the conduct taken into account included conduct over which exclusive venue lies in another county and the written permission of the prosecuting attorney of that county was not obtained, the child may be adjudicated for that conduct, but the child's admission under this section may not be used against the child in the adjudication.

Added by Acts 1995, 74th Leg., ch. 262, § 41, eff. Jan. 1, 1996.

§ 54.046. Conditions of Probation for Damaging Property With Graffiti

Text of section as added by Acts 1997, 75th Leg., ch. 593, § 7

(a) If a juvenile court places on probation under Section 54.04(d) a child adjudicated as having engaged in conduct in violation of Section 28.08, Penal Code, in addition to other conditions of probation, the court may, with consent of the owner of the property, order the child as a condition of probation to restore the property by removing or painting over any markings made by the child on the property.

(b) In addition to a condition imposed under Subsection (a), the court may require the child as a condition of probation to attend a class with instruction in self-responsibility and empathy for a victim of an offense conducted by a local juvenile probation department.

Added by Acts 1997, 75th Leg., ch. 593, § 7, eff. Sept. 1, 1997.

For text of section as added by Acts 1997, 75th Leg., ch. 1013, § 18, see § 54.046, post.

For application provisions of Acts 1997, 75th Leg., ch. 593, see notes following V.T.C.A., Family Code § 53.03.

§ 54.046. Alcohol-Related Offense

Text of section as added by Acts 1997, 75th Leg., ch. 1013, § 18

If the court or jury finds at an adjudication hearing for a child that the child engaged in conduct indicating a need for supervision or delinquent conduct that violates the alcohol-related offenses in Section 106.02, 106.025, 106.04, 106.05, or 106.07, Alcoholic Beverage Code, or Section 49.02, Penal Code, the court shall, subject to a finding under Section 54.04(c), order, in addition to any other order authorized by this title, that, in the manner provided by Section 106.071(d), Alcoholic Beverage Code:

(1) the child perform community service; and

(2) the child's driver's license or permit be suspended or that the child be denied issuance of a driver's license or permit.

Added by Acts 1997, 75th Leg., ch. 1013, § 18, eff. Sept. 1, 1997.

For text of section as added by Acts 1997, 75th Leg., ch. 593, § 7, see § 54.046, ante.

For application provisions of Acts 1997, 75th Leg., ch. 1013, see notes following V.T.C.A., Family Code § 51.03.

§ 54.05. Hearing to Modify Disposition

(a) Any disposition, except a commitment to the Texas Youth Commission, may be modified by the juvenile court as provided in this section until:

(1) the child reaches his 18th birthday; or

(2) the child is earlier discharged by the court or operation of law.

(b) Except for a commitment to the Texas Youth Commission, all dispositions automatically terminate when the child reaches his 18th birthday.

(c) There is no right to a jury at a hearing to modify disposition.

(d) A hearing to modify disposition shall be held on the petition of the child and his parent, guardian, guardian ad litem, or attorney, or on the petition of the state, a probation officer, or the court itself. Reasonable notice of a hearing to modify disposition shall be given to all parties. When the petition to modify is filed under Section 51.03(a)(2) of this code, the court must hold an adjudication hearing and make an affirmative finding prior to considering any written reports under Subsection (e) of this section.

(e) After the hearing on the merits or facts, the court may consider written reports from probation officers, professional court employees, or professional consultants in addition to the testimony of other witnesses. Prior to the hearing to modify disposition, the court shall provide the attorney for the child with access to all written matter to be considered by the court in deciding whether to modify disposition. The court may order counsel not to reveal items to the child or his parent, guardian, or guardian ad litem if such disclosure would materially harm the treatment and rehabilitation of the child or would substantially decrease the likelihood of receiving information from the same or similar sources in the future.

(f) A disposition based on a finding that the child engaged in delinquent conduct may be modified so as to commit the child to the Texas Youth Commission if the court after a hearing to modify disposition finds by a preponderance of the evidence that the child violated a reasonable and lawful order of the court. A disposition based on a finding that the child engaged in habitual felony conduct as described by Section 51.031 of this code or in delinquent conduct that included a violation of a penal law listed in Section 53.045(a) of this code may be modified to commit the child to the Texas Youth Commission with a possible transfer to the institutional division or the pardons and paroles division of the Texas Department of Criminal Justice for a definite term prescribed by Section 54.04(d)(3) of this code if the original petition was approved by the grand jury under Section 53.045 of this code and if after a hearing to modify the disposition the court or jury finds that the child violated a reasonable and lawful order of the court.

(g) A disposition based solely on a finding that the child engaged in conduct indicating a need for supervision may not be modified to commit the child to the

Texas Youth Commission. A new finding in compliance with Section 54.03 of this code must be made that the child engaged in delinquent conduct as defined in Section 51.03(a) of this code.

(h) A hearing shall be held prior to commitment to the Texas Youth Commission as a modified disposition. In other disposition modifications, the child and his parent, guardian, guardian ad litem, or attorney may waive hearing in accordance with Section 51.09 of this code. A child in jeopardy of a sentence for a determinate term is entitled to a jury of 12 persons on the issues of the violation of the court's orders and the sentence.

(i) The court shall specifically state in the order its reasons for modifying the disposition and shall furnish a copy of the order to the child.

Acts 1973, 63rd Leg., p. 1460, ch. 544, § 1, eff. Sept. 1, 1973. Amended by Acts 1979, 66th Leg., p. 1829, ch. 743, § 1, eff. Aug. 27, 1979; Acts 1983, 68th Leg., p. 162, ch. 44, art. 1, § 4, eff. April 26, 1983; Acts 1985, 69th Leg., ch. 45, § 3, eff. Sept. 1, 1985; Acts 1987, 70th Leg., ch. 385, § 10, eff. Sept. 1, 1987; Acts 1991, 72nd Leg., ch. 557, § 3, eff. Sept. 1, 1991; Acts 1995, 74th Leg., ch. 262, § 42, eff. Jan. 1, 1996.

Section 4 of the 1985 amendatory act provides:

"This Act takes effect September 1, 1985, and does not apply to delinquent conduct committed before the effective date of this Act. Delinquent conduct committed before the effective date of this Act is governed by the law as it existed on the date the conduct was committed, and that law is continued in effect for that purpose."

Section 20 of the 1987 amendatory act provides:

"(a) This Act applies only to offenses and conduct occurring on or after its effective date. For the purposes of this section, an offense or delinquent conduct based on an offense occurs on or after the effective date if all the elements of the offense occur on or after the effective date.

"(b) An offense or conduct that occurs before the effective date of this Act shall be prosecuted under the law in effect immediately before the effective date of this Act, and that law is continued in effect for that purpose only."

Section 4 of the 1991 amendatory act provides:

"(a) The change in law made by this Act applies only to conduct that occurs on or after the effective date of this Act. Conduct violating a penal law of this state occurs on or after the effective date of this Act if every element of the violation occurs on or after that date.

"(b) Conduct that occurs before the effective date of this Act is governed by the law in effect at the time the conduct occurred, and the former law is continued in effect for that purpose."

§ 54.06. Judgments for Support

(a) At any stage of the proceeding, when a child has been placed outside the child's home, the juvenile court, after giving the parent or other person responsible for the child's support a reasonable opportunity to be heard, shall order the parent or other person to pay in a manner directed by the court a reasonable sum for the support in whole or in part of the child or the court shall waive the payment by order. The court shall order that the payment for support be made to the local juvenile probation department to be used only for residential care and other support for the child unless the child has been committed to the Texas Youth Commission, in which case the court shall order that the payment be made to the Texas Youth Commission for deposit in a special account in the general revenue fund that may be appropriated only for the care of children committed to the commission.

(b) At any stage of the proceeding, when a child has been placed outside the child's home and the parent of the child is obligated to pay support for the child under a court order under Title 5, the juvenile court shall order that the person entitled to receive the support assign the person's right to support for the child placed outside the child's home to the local juvenile probation department to be used for residential care and other support for the child unless the child has been committed to the Texas Youth Commission, in which event the court shall order that the assignment be made to the Texas Youth Commission.

(c) A court may enforce an order for support under this section by ordering garnishment of the wages of the person ordered to pay support or by any other means available to enforce a child support order under Title 5.

(d) An order for support may be enforced as provided in Section 54.07 of this code.

(e) The court shall apply the child support guidelines under Subchapter C, Chapter 154,[1] in an order requiring the payment of child support under this section. The court shall also require in an order to pay child support under this section that health insurance be provided for the child. Subchapter D, Chapter 154, applies to an order requiring health insurance for a child under this section.

(f) An order under this section prevails over any previous child support order issued with regard to the child to the extent of any conflict between the orders.

Acts 1973, 63rd Leg., p. 1460, ch. 544, § 1, eff. Sept. 1, 1973. Amended by Acts 1983, 68th Leg., p. 163, ch. 44, art. 1, § 5, eff. April 26, 1983; Acts 1987, 70th Leg., ch. 1040, § 24, eff. Sept. 1, 1987; Acts 1993, 73rd Leg., ch. 798, § 23, eff. Sept. 1, 1993; Acts 1993, 73rd Leg., ch. 1048, § 2, eff. Sept. 1, 1993; Acts 1995, 74th Leg., ch. 262, § 43, eff. Jan. 1, 1996; Acts 1997, 75th Leg., ch. 165, § 7.11, eff. Sept. 1, 1997.

[1] V.T.C.A., Family Code § 154.181 et seq.

Section 35 of the 1987 amendatory act provides:

"(a) This Act applies only to offenses and conduct occurring on or after its effective date. For the purposes of this section, an offense or delinquent conduct based on an offense occurs on or after the effective date if all the elements of the offense occur on or after the effective date.

"(b) An offense or conduct that occurs before the effective date of this Act shall be prosecuted under the law in effect immediately before the effective date of this Act, and that law is continued in effect for that purpose only."

Section 8(c) of Acts 1993, 73rd Leg., ch. 1048 provides:

"Section 2 of this Act applies to the placement of a child outside the child's home under Title 3, Family Code, without regard to whether the proceedings relating to the child under that title began before, on, or after the effective date of this Act."

§ 54.061. Payment of Probation Fees

(a) If a child is placed on probation under Section 54.04(d)(1) of this code, the juvenile court, after giving the child, parent, or other person responsible for the child's support a reasonable opportunity to be heard, shall order the child, parent, or other person, if financially able to do so, to pay to the court a fee of not more than $15 a month during the period that the child continues on probation.

(b) Orders for the payment of fees under this section may be enforced as provided by Section 54.07 of this code.

(c) The court shall deposit the fees received under this section in the county treasury to the credit of a special fund that may be used only for juvenile probation or community-based juvenile corrections services or facilities in which a juvenile may be required to live while under court supervision.

(d) If the court finds that a child, parent, or other person responsible for the child's support is financially unable to pay the probation fee required under Subsection (a), the court shall enter into the records of the child's case a statement of that finding. The court may waive a fee under this section only if the court makes the finding under this subsection.

Added by Acts 1979, 66th Leg., p. 338, ch. 154, § 1, eff. Sept. 1, 1979. Amended by Acts 1981, 67th Leg., p. 2425, ch. 617, § 4, eff. Sept. 1, 1981; Acts 1987, 70th Leg., ch. 1040, § 25, eff. Sept. 1, 1987; Acts 1995, 74th Leg., ch. 262, § 44, eff. Jan. 1, 1996.

Section 35 of the 1987 amendatory act provides:

"(a) This Act applies only to offenses and conduct occurring on or after its effective date. For the purposes of this section, an offense or delinquent conduct based on an offense occurs on or after the effective date if all the elements of the offense occur on or after the effective date.

"(b) An offense or conduct that occurs before the effective date of this Act shall be prosecuted under the law in effect immediately before the effective date of this Act, and that law is continued in effect for that purpose only."

§ 54.07. Enforcement of Order

(a) Any order of the juvenile court may be enforced by contempt.

(b) The juvenile court may enforce its order for support or for the payment of restitution or probation fees by civil contempt proceedings after 10 days' notice to the defaulting person of his failure or refusal to carry out the terms of the order.

(c) On the motion of the juvenile court or any person or agency entitled to receive restitution or probation payments or payments for the benefit of a child, the juvenile court may render judgment against a defaulting person for any amount unpaid and owing after 10 days' notice to the defaulting person of his failure or refusal to carry out the terms of the order. The judgment may be enforced by any means available for the enforcement of judgments for other debts.

Acts 1973, 63rd Leg., p. 1460, ch. 544, § 1, eff. Sept. 1, 1973. Amended by Acts 1979, 66th Leg., p. 339, ch. 154, § 3, eff. Sept. 1, 1979.

§ 54.08. Public Access to Court Hearings

(a) Except as provided by this section, the court shall open hearings under this title to the public unless the court, for good cause shown, determines that the public should be excluded.

(b) The court may not prohibit a person who is a victim of the conduct of a child, or the person's family, from personally attending a hearing under this title relating to the conduct by the child unless the victim or member of the victim's family is to testify in the hearing or any subsequent hearing relating to the conduct and the court determines that the victim's or family member's testimony would be materially affected if the victim or member of the victim's family hears other testimony at trial.

(c) If a child is under the age of 14 at the time of the hearing, the court shall close the hearing to the public unless the court finds that the interests of the child or the interests of the public would be better served by opening the hearing to the public.

(d) In this section, "family" has the meaning assigned by Section 71.003.

Acts 1973, 63rd Leg., p. 1460, ch. 544, § 1, eff. Sept. 1, 1973. Amended by Acts 1987, 70th Leg., ch. 385, § 11, eff. Sept. 1, 1987; Acts 1995, 74th Leg., ch. 262, § 45, eff. Jan. 1, 1996; Acts 1997, 75th Leg., ch. 1086, § 12, eff. Sept. 1, 1997.

Section 20 of the 1987 amendatory act provides:

"(a) This Act applies only to offenses and conduct occurring on or after its effective date. For the purposes of this section, an offense or delinquent conduct based on an offense occurs on or after the effective date if all the elements of the offense occur on or after the effective date.

"(b) An offense or conduct that occurs before the effective date of this Act shall be prosecuted under the law in effect immediately before the effective date of this Act, and that law is continued in effect for that purpose only."

Section 51 of Acts 1997, 75th Leg., ch. 1086 provides:

"The change in law made by this Act to Section 54.08, Family Code, applies only to a hearing under Title 3, Family Code, commenced on or after the effective date of this Act. A hearing commenced before the effective date of this Act is governed by the law in effect on the date the hearing was commenced, and the former law is continued in effect for that purpose."

§ 54.09. Recording of Proceedings

All judicial proceedings under this chapter except detention hearings shall be recorded by stenographic notes or by electronic, mechanical, or other appropriate means. Upon request of any party, a detention hearing shall be recorded.

Acts 1973, 63rd Leg., p. 1460, ch. 544, § 1, eff. Sept. 1, 1973.

§ 54.10. Hearings Before Referee

(a) Except as provided by Subsection (c) of this section, the hearing provided in Sections 54.01, 54.03, 54.04, and 54.05 of this code and the hearing provided in Article IV, Article V, and Article VI of the Uniform Interstate Compact on Juveniles (Chapter 25 of this code) may be held by a referee appointed in accordance with Section 51.04(g) of this code provided:

(1) the parties have been informed by the referee that they are entitled to have the hearing before the juvenile court judge or in the case of a detention hearing provided for in Section 54.01 of this code, a substitute judge as authorized by Section 51.04(f) of this code; or

(2) the child and the attorney for the child have in accordance with the requirements of Section 51.09 of this code waived the right to have the hearing before the juvenile court judge or substitute judge.

(b) At the conclusion of the hearing, the referee shall transmit written findings and recommendations to the juvenile court judge. The juvenile court judge shall adopt, modify, or reject the referee's recommendations not later than the next working day after the day that the judge receives the recommendations. Failure to act within that time results in release of the child by operation of law and a recommendation that the child be released operates to secure his immediate release subject to the power of the juvenile court judge to modify or reject that recommendation.

(c) The hearings provided by Sections 54.03, 54.04, and 54.05 of this code may not be held before a referee if the grand jury has approved of the petition and the child is subject to a determinate sentence.

Added by Acts 1975, 64th Leg., p. 2157, ch. 693, § 19, eff. Sept. 1, 1975. Amended by Acts 1979, 66th Leg., p. 1830, ch. 743, § 2, eff. Aug. 27, 1979; Acts 1987, 70th Leg., ch. 385, § 12, eff. Sept. 1, 1987; Acts 1991, 72nd Leg., ch. 74, § 1, eff. Sept. 1, 1991; Acts 1997, 75th Leg., ch. 1086, § 13, eff. Sept. 1, 1997.

Section 20 of the 1987 amendatory act provides:

"(a) This Act applies only to offenses and conduct occurring on or after its effective date. For the purposes of this section, an offense or delinquent conduct based on an offense occurs on or after the effective date if all the elements of the offense occur on or after the effective date.

"(b) An offense or conduct that occurs before the effective date of this Act shall be prosecuted under the law in effect immediately before the effective date of this Act, and that law is continued in effect for that purpose only."

Section 2 of the 1991 amendatory act provides:

"This Act takes effect September 1, 1991, and applies to a hearing held on or after the effective date of this Act."

§ 54.11. Release or Transfer Hearing

(a) On receipt of a referral under Section 61.079(a), Human Resources Code, for the transfer to the institutional division of the Texas Department of Criminal Justice of a person committed to the Texas Youth Commission under Section 54.04(d)(3), 54.04(m), or 54.05(f), or on receipt of a request by the commission under Section 61.081(g), Human Resources Code, for approval of the release under supervision of a person committed to the commission under Section 54.04(d)(3), 54.04(m), or 54.05(f), the court shall set a time and place for a hearing on the release of the person.

(b) The court shall notify the following of the time and place of the hearing:

(1) the person to be transferred or released under supervision;

(2) the parents of the person;

(3) any legal custodian of the person, including the Texas Youth Commission;

(4) the office of the prosecuting attorney that represented the state in the juvenile delinquency proceedings;

(5) the victim of the offense that was included in the delinquent conduct that was a ground for the disposition, or a member of the victim's family; and

(6) any other person who has filed a written request with the court to be notified of a release hearing with respect to the person to be transferred or released under supervision.

(c) Except for the person to be transferred or released under supervision and the prosecuting attorney, the failure to notify a person listed in Subsection (b) of this section does not affect the validity of a hearing conducted or determination made under this section if the record in the case reflects that the whereabouts of the persons who did not receive notice were unknown to the court and a reasonable effort was made by the court to locate those persons.

(d) At a hearing under this section the court may consider written reports from probation officers, professional court employees, or professional consultants, in addition to the testimony of witnesses. At least one day before the hearing, the court shall provide the attorney for the person to be transferred or released under supervision with access to all written matter to be considered by the court.

(e) At the hearing, the person to be transferred or released under supervision is entitled to an attorney, to examine all witnesses against him, to present evidence and oral argument, and to previous examination of all reports on and evaluations and examinations of or relating to him that may be used in the hearing.

(f) A hearing under this section is open to the public unless the person to be transferred or released under supervision waives a public hearing with the consent of his attorney and the court.

(g) A hearing under this section must be recorded by a court reporter or by audio or video tape recording, and the record of the hearing must be retained by the court for at least two years after the date of the final determination on the transfer or release of the person by the court.

(h) The hearing on a person who is referred for transfer under Section 61.079(a), Human Resources Code, shall be held not later than the 60th day after the date the court receives the referral.

(i) On conclusion of the hearing on a person who is referred for transfer under Section 61.079(a), Human Resources Code, the court may order:

(1) the return of the person to the Texas Youth Commission; or

(2) the transfer of the person to the custody of the institutional division of the Texas Department of Criminal Justice for the completion of the person's sentence.

(j) On conclusion of the hearing on a person who is referred for release under supervision under Section 61.081(f), Human Resources Code, the court may order the return of the person to the Texas Youth Commission:

(1) with approval for the release of the person under supervision; or

(2) without approval for the release of the person under supervision.

(k) In making a determination under this section, the court may consider the experiences and character of the person before and after commitment to the youth commission, the nature of the penal offense that the person was found to have committed and the manner in which the offense was committed, the abilities of the person to contribute to society, the protection of the victim of the offense or any member of the victim's family, the recommendations of the youth commission and prosecuting attorney, the best interests of the person, and any other factor relevant to the issue to be decided.

Added by Acts 1987, 70th Leg., ch. 385, § 13, eff. Sept. 1, 1987. Amended by Acts 1991, 72nd Leg., ch. 574, § 3, eff. Sept. 1, 1991; Acts 1995, 74th Leg., ch. 262, § 46, eff. Jan. 1, 1996.

Section 20 of the 1987 Act provides:

"(a) This Act applies only to offenses and conduct occurring on or after its effective date. For the purposes of this section, an offense or delinquent conduct based on an offense occurs on or after the effective date if all the elements of the offense occur on or after the effective date.

"(b) An offense or conduct that occurs before the effective date of this Act shall be prosecuted under the law in effect immediately before the effective date of this Act, and that law is continued in effect for that purpose only."

Section 5 of the 1991 amendatory act provides:

"(a) This Act takes effect September 1, 1991, and applies only to conduct that occurs on or after that date. Conduct violating the penal laws of this state occurs on or after the effective date of this Act if every element of the violation occurs on or after that date.

"(b) Conduct that occurs before the effective date of this Act is governed by the law in effect at the time the conduct occurred and that law is continued in effect for that purpose."

CHAPTER 55. PROCEEDINGS CONCERNING CHILDREN WITH MENTAL ILLNESS OR MENTAL RETARDATION

Section

§ 55.01. Physical or Mental Examination

(a) At any stage of the proceedings under this title, the juvenile court may order a child alleged by petition or found to have engaged in delinquent conduct or conduct indicating a need for supervision to be examined by appropriate experts, including a physician, psychiatrist, or psychologist.

(b) If an examination ordered under Subsection (a) of this section is to determine whether the child is mentally retarded, the examination must consist of a determination of mental retardation and an interdisciplinary team recommendation, as provided by Chapter 593, Health and Safety Code, and shall be conducted at a facility approved or operated by the Texas Department of Mental Health and Mental Retardation or at a community center established in accordance with Chapter 534, Health and Safety Code.

Acts 1973, 63rd Leg., p. 1460, ch. 544, § 1, eff. Sept. 1, 1973. Amended by Acts 1977, 65th Leg., p. 1453, ch. 591, § 1, eff. Jan. 1, 1978; Acts 1991, 72nd Leg., ch. 76, § 8, eff. Sept. 1, 1991; Acts 1995, 74th Leg., ch. 262, § 47, eff. May 31, 1995.

Sections 99 and 106(b) of the 1995 amendatory act provide:

"Sec. 99. The Texas Juvenile Probation Commission, in collaboration with the Texas Department of Mental Health and Mental Retardation, shall develop a model protocol by which juvenile probation departments shall refer children with mental impairments to local community management teams of the Children's Mental Health Plan. The protocol is to be distributed to all juvenile boards, chief probation officers, and community management teams no later than January 1, 1996."

"[Sec. 106] (b) Chapter 55, Family Code, as amended by this Act, applies only to conduct that occurs on or after the effective date of that chapter. Conduct violating a penal law of this state occurs on or after that date if every element of the violation occurs on or after that date. Conduct that occurs before the effective date of that chapter is governed by the law in effect at the time the conduct occurred, and that law is continued in effect for that purpose."

§ 55.02. Child With Mental Illness

(a) The court shall initiate proceedings to order temporary or extended mental health services, as provided in Subchapter C, Chapter 574, Health and Safety Code,[1] for a child alleged or found to have engaged in delinquent conduct or conduct indicating a need for supervision, if:

(1) on motion by a party or the court it is alleged that the child is mentally ill; or

(2) a child is found or alleged to be unfit to proceed as a result of mental illness under Section 55.04 of this chapter or is found not responsible for the child's conduct as a result of mental illness under Section 55.05 of this chapter.

(b) Subtitle C, Title 7, Health and Safety Code,[2] governs proceedings for court-ordered mental health services except that the juvenile court shall conduct the proceedings whether or not the juvenile court is also a county court.

(c) If the juvenile court orders mental health services for the child, the child shall be cared for, treated, and released in conformity to Subtitle C, Title 7, Health and Safety Code, except:

(1) a juvenile court order for mental health services of a child automatically expires on the 120th day after the date the child becomes 18 years of age; and

(2) the administrator of a mental health facility shall notify, in writing, the juvenile court that ordered mental health services of the intent to discharge the child at least 10 days prior to discharge.

(d) If the juvenile court orders mental health services for the child, the proceedings under this title then pending in juvenile court shall be stayed.

(e) If the child is discharged from the mental health facility before reaching 18 years of age, the juvenile court may:

(1) dismiss the juvenile court proceedings with prejudice; or

(2) continue with proceedings under this title as though no order of mental health services had been made.

(f) The juvenile court shall transfer all pending proceedings from the juvenile court to a criminal court on the 18th birthday of a child for whom the court has ordered mental health services under this section if:

(1) the child is not discharged or furloughed from the residential care facility before reaching 18 years of age; and

(2) the child is alleged to have engaged in delinquent conduct that included a violation of a penal law listed in Section 53.045.

(g) The juvenile court shall send notification of the transfer of a child under Subsection (f) to the residential care facility. The criminal court shall, within 90 days of the transfer, institute proceedings under Article 46.02, Code of Criminal Procedure. If those or any subsequent proceedings result in a determination that the defendant is competent to stand trial, the defendant may not receive a punishment for the delinquent conduct described by Subsection (f)(2) that results in confinement for a period longer than the maximum period of confinement the defendant could have received if the defendant had been adjudicated for the delinquent conduct while still a child and within the jurisdiction of the juvenile court.

Acts 1973, 63rd Leg., p. 1460, ch. 544, § 1, eff. Sept. 1, 1973. Amended by Acts 1975, 64th Leg., p. 2157, ch. 693, §§ 20 and 21, eff. Sept. 1, 1975; Acts 1991, 72nd Leg., ch. 76, § 9, eff. Sept. 1, 1991; Acts 1995, 74th Leg., ch. 262, § 47, eff. May 31, 1995.

[1] V.T.C.A., Health and Safety Code § 574.031 et seq.

[2] V.T.C.A., Health and Safety Code § 571.001 et seq.

For applicability provisions of the 1995 amendatory act, see note following V.T.C.A., Family Code § 55.01.

§ 55.03. Child With Mental Retardation

(a) If a child is found or alleged to be unfit to proceed as a result of mental retardation under Section 55.04 or is found not responsible for the child's conduct as a result of mental retardation under Section 55.05, the court shall order a determination of mental retardation and an interdisciplinary team recommendation of the child, as provided by Chapter 593, Health and Safety Code, to be performed at a facility approved or operated by the Texas Department of Mental Health and Mental Retardation or at a community center established in accordance with Chapter 534, Health and Safety Code.

(b) A child alleged or found to have engaged in delinquent conduct or conduct indicating a need for supervision may be committed to a residential care facility if:

(1) the child is found unfit to proceed as a result of mental retardation under Section 55.04 of this chapter or is found not responsible for the child's conduct as a result of mental retardation under Section 55.05 of this chapter; and

(2) the child meets the criteria for commitment as provided in Subchapter C, Chapter 593, Health and Safety Code.[1]

(c) Subtitle D, Title 7, Health and Safety Code,[2] governs proceedings for commitment of a child under this section except that:

(1) the juvenile court shall conduct the proceedings whether or not the juvenile court is also a county court; and

(2) on receipt of the court's order entering the findings required by Subtitle D, Title 7, Health and Safety Code, and Subsection (b)(1) of this section, the Texas Department of Mental Health and Mental Retardation or the appropriate community center shall admit the child to a residential care facility.

(d) If the juvenile court enters an order committing the child to a residential care facility, the child shall be cared for, treated, and released in conformity to Subtitle D, Title 7, Health and Safety Code, except that the administrator of the residential care facility shall notify, in writing, the juvenile court that ordered commitment of the child of the intent to discharge the child from the residential care facility or to furlough the child to an alternative placement at least 20 days prior to the date of the discharge or furlough.

(e) If the juvenile court orders commitment of a child to a residential care facility, the proceedings under this title then pending in juvenile court shall be stayed.

(f) If the child committed to a residential care facility is discharged or furloughed from the residential care facility as provided by Subsection (d) of this section and in accordance with Subtitle D, Title 7, Health and Safety Code, before reaching 18 years of age, the juvenile court may:

(1) dismiss the juvenile court proceedings with prejudice; or

(2) continue with proceedings under this title as though no order of commitment had been made.

(g) The juvenile court shall transfer all pending proceedings from the juvenile court to a criminal court on the 18th birthday of a child committed to a residential care facility if:

(1) the child is not discharged or furloughed from the residential care facility before reaching 18 years of age; and

(2) the child is alleged to have engaged in delinquent conduct that included a violation of a penal law listed in Section 53.045.

(h) The juvenile court shall send notification of the transfer of a child under Subsection (g) to the residential care facility. The criminal court shall, within 90 days of the transfer, institute proceedings under Article 46.02, Code of Criminal Procedure. If those or any subsequent proceedings result in a determination that the defendant is competent to stand trial, the defendant may not receive a punishment for the delinquent conduct described by Subsection (g)(2) that results in confinement for a period longer than the maximum period of confinement the defendant could have received if the defendant had been adjudicated for the delinquent conduct while still a child and within the jurisdiction of the juvenile court.

Acts 1973, 63rd Leg., p. 1460, ch. 544, § 1, eff. Sept. 1, 1973. Amended by Acts 1975, 64th Leg., p. 2158, ch. 693, § 22, eff. Sept. 1, 1975; Acts 1977, 65th Leg., p. 1453, ch. 591, § 2, eff. Jan. 1, 1978; Acts 1991, 72nd Leg., ch. 76, § 10, eff. Sept. 1, 1991; Acts 1995, 74th Leg., ch. 262, § 47, eff. May 31, 1995; Acts 1997, 75th Leg., ch. 1086, § 14, eff. Sept. 1, 1997.

[1] V.T.C.A., Health and Safety Code § 593.041 et seq.

[2] V.T.C.A., Health and Safety Code § 591.001 et seq.

For applicability provisions of the 1995 amendatory act, see note following V.T.C.A., Family Code § 55.01.

§ 55.04. Unfitness to Proceed

(a) A child alleged by petition or found to have engaged in delinquent conduct or conduct indicating a need for supervision who as a result of mental illness or mental retardation lacks capacity to understand the proceedings in juvenile court or to assist in his own defense is unfit to proceed and shall not be subjected to discretionary transfer to criminal court, adjudication, disposition, or modification of disposition as long as such incapacity endures.

(b) If on motion by a party or the court it is alleged that a child may be unfit to proceed as a result of mental illness or mental retardation, the court shall order appropriate examinations as provided by Section 55.01 of this chapter. The information obtained from the examinations must include expert opinion as to whether the child is unfit to proceed as a result of mental illness or mental retardation.

(c) The court or jury shall determine whether the child is unfit to proceed as a result of mental illness or mental retardation at a hearing separate from the adjudication hearing.

(d) Unfitness to proceed as a result of mental illness or mental retardation must be proved by a preponderance of the evidence.

(e) If the court or jury determines that the child is fit to proceed, the juvenile court shall continue with proceedings under this title as though no question of fitness to proceed had been raised.

(f) If the court or jury determines that the child is unfit to proceed as a result of mental illness or mental retardation, the court shall initiate proceedings under Section 55.02 or Section 55.03 of this chapter.

(g) A proceeding to determine fitness to proceed may be joined with proceedings under Sections 55.02 and 55.03 of this chapter.

(h) The fact that the child is unfit to proceed as a result of mental illness or mental retardation does not preclude any legal objection to the juvenile court proceedings which is susceptible of fair determination prior to the adjudication hearing and without the personal participation of the child.

Acts 1973, 63rd Leg., p. 1460, ch. 544, § 1, eff. Sept. 1, 1973. Amended by Acts 1995, 74th Leg., ch. 262, § 47, eff. May 31, 1995.

For applicability provisions of the 1995 amendatory act, see note following V.T.C.A., Family Code § 55.01.

§ 55.05. Lack of Responsibility for Conduct

(a) A child alleged by petition to have engaged in delinquent conduct or conduct indicating a need for supervision is not responsible for the conduct if at the time of the conduct, as a result of mental illness or mental retardation, he lacks substantial capacity either to appreciate the wrongfulness of his conduct or to conform his conduct to the requirements of law.

(b) If on motion of a party or the court it is alleged that the child may not be responsible as a result of mental illness or mental retardation for the child's conduct, the court shall order appropriate examinations as provided by Section 55.01 of this chapter. The information obtained from the examinations must include expert opinion as to whether the child is not responsible for the child's conduct as a result of mental illness or mental retardation.

(c) The issue of whether the child is not responsible for his conduct as a result of mental illness or mental retardation shall be tried to the court or jury in the adjudication hearing.

(d) Lack of responsibility for conduct as a result of mental illness or mental retardation must be proved by a preponderance of the evidence.

(e) In its findings or verdict the court or jury must state whether the child is not responsible for his conduct as a result of mental illness or mental retardation.

(f) If the court or jury finds the child is not responsible for his conduct as a result of mental illness or mental retardation, the court shall initiate proceedings under Section 55.02 or 55.03 of this chapter.

(g) A child found not responsible for his conduct as a result of mental illness or mental retardation shall not be subject to proceedings under this title with respect to such conduct, other than proceedings under Section 55.02 or 55.03 of this chapter.

Acts 1973, 63rd Leg., p. 1460, ch. 544, § 1, eff. Sept. 1, 1973. Amended by Acts 1995, 74th Leg., ch. 262, § 47, eff. May 31, 1995.

For applicability provisions of the 1995 amendatory act, see note following V.T.C.A., Family Code § 55.01.

CHAPTER 56. APPEAL

Section

§ 56.01. Right to Appeal

(a) An appeal from an order of a juvenile court is to a court of appeals and the case may be carried to the Texas Supreme Court by writ of error or upon certificate, as in civil cases generally.

(b) The requirements governing an appeal are as in civil cases generally. When an appeal is sought by filing a notice of appeal, security for costs of appeal, or an affidavit of inability to pay the costs of appeal, and the filing is made in a timely fashion after the date the disposition order is signed, the appeal must include the juvenile court adjudication and all rulings contributing to that adjudication. An appeal of the adjudication may be sought notwithstanding that the adjudication order was signed more than 30 days before the date the notice of appeal, security for costs of appeal, or affidavit of inability to pay the costs of appeal was filed. A motion for new trial seeking to vacate an adjudication is timely if the motion is filed not later than the 30th day after the date on which the disposition order is signed.

(c) An appeal may be taken:

(1) by or on behalf of a child from an order entered under:

(A) Section 54.03 of this code with regard to delinquent conduct or conduct indicating a need for supervision;

(B) Section 54.04 of this code disposing of the case;

(C) Section 54.05 of this code respecting modification of a previous juvenile court disposition; or

(D) Chapter 55 of this code committing a child to a facility for the mentally ill or mentally retarded; or

(2) by a person from an order entered under Section 54.11(i)(2) of this code transferring the person to the custody of the institutional division of the Texas Department of Criminal Justice.

(d) A child has the right to:

(1) appeal;

(2) representation by counsel on appeal; and

(3) appointment of an attorney for the appeal if an attorney cannot be obtained because of indigency.

(e) On entering an order that is appealable under this section, the court shall advise the child and the child's parent, guardian, or guardian ad litem of the child's rights listed under Subsection (d) of this section.

(f) If the child and his parent, guardian, or guardian ad litem express a desire to appeal, the attorney who represented the child before the juvenile court shall file a notice of appeal with the juvenile court and inform the court whether that attorney will handle the appeal. Counsel shall be appointed under the standards provided in Section 51.10 of this code unless the right to appeal is waived in accordance with Section 51.09 of this code.

(g) An appeal does not suspend the order of the juvenile court, nor does it release the child from the custody of that court or of the person, institution, or agency to whose care the child is committed, unless the juvenile court so orders. However, the appellate court may provide for a personal bond.

(h) If the order appealed from takes custody of the child from his parent, guardian, or custodian, the appeal has precedence over all other cases.

(i) The appellate court may affirm, reverse, or modify the judgment or order, including an order of disposition or modified disposition, from which appeal was taken. It may reverse or modify an order of disposition or modified order of disposition while affirming the juvenile court adjudication that the child engaged in delinquent conduct or conduct indicating a need for supervision. It may remand an order that it reverses or modifies for further proceedings by the juvenile court.

(j) Neither the child nor his family shall be identified in an appellate opinion rendered in an appeal or habeas corpus proceedings related to juvenile court proceedings under this title. The appellate opinion shall be styled, "In the matter of . . . .," identifying the child by his initials only.

(k) The appellate court shall dismiss an appeal on the state's motion, supported by affidavit showing that the appellant has escaped from custody pending the appeal and, to the affiant's knowledge, has not voluntarily returned to the state's custody on or before the 10th day after the date of the escape. The court may not dismiss an appeal, or if the appeal has been dismissed, shall reinstate the appeal, on the filing of an affidavit of an officer or other credible person showing that the appellant voluntarily returned to custody on or before the 10th day after the date of the escape.

(*l*) The court may order the child, the child's parent, or other person responsible for support of the child to pay the child's costs of appeal, including the costs of representation by an attorney, unless the court determines the person to be ordered to pay the costs is indigent.

(m) For purposes of determining indigency of the child under this section, the court shall consider the assets and income of the child, the child's parent, and any other person responsible for the support of the child.

Acts 1973, 63rd Leg., p. 1460, ch. 544, § 1, eff. Sept. 1, 1973. Amended by Acts 1987, 70th Leg., ch. 385, § 14, eff. Sept. 1, 1987; Acts 1991, 72nd Leg., ch. 680, § 1, eff. Sept. 1, 1991; Acts 1995, 74th Leg., ch. 262, § 48, eff. Jan. 1, 1996; Acts 1997, 75th Leg., ch. 1086, § 15, eff. Sept. 1, 1997.

Section 20 of the 1987 amendatory act provides:

"(a) This Act applies only to offenses and conduct occurring on or after its effective date. For the purposes of this section, an offense or delinquent conduct based on an offense occurs on or after the effective date if all the elements of the offense occur on or after the effective date.

"(b) An offense or conduct that occurs before the effective date of this Act shall be prosecuted under the law in effect immediately before the effective date of this Act, and that law is continued in effect for that purpose only."

Section 2 of the 1991 amendatory act provides:

"This Act takes effect September 1, 1991, and applies only to an appeal from an order entered by a juvenile court on or after that date. An order entered by a juvenile court before the effective date of this Act is governed by the law in effect on the date the order was entered, and the former law is continued in effect for that purpose."

§ 56.02. Transcript on Appeal

(a) An attorney retained to represent a child on appeal who desires to have included in the record on appeal a transcription of notes of the reporter has the responsibility of obtaining and paying for the transcription and furnishing it to the clerk in duplicate in time for inclusion in the record.

(b) The juvenile court shall order the reporter to furnish a transcription without charge to the attorney if the court finds, after hearing or on an affidavit filed by the child's parent or other person responsible for support of the child that the parent or other responsible person is unable to pay or to give security therefor.

(c) On certificate of the court that a transcription has been provided without charge, payment therefor shall be made from the general funds of the county in which the proceedings appealed from occurred.

(d) The court reporter shall report any portion of the proceedings requested by either party or directed by the court and shall report the proceedings in question and answer form unless a narrative transcript is requested.

Acts 1973, 63rd Leg., p. 1460, ch. 544, § 1, eff. Sept. 1, 1973. Amended by Acts 1991, 72nd Leg., ch. 674, § 1, eff. Sept. 1, 1991.

CHAPTER 57. RIGHTS OF VICTIMS

§ 57.001. Definitions

In this chapter:

(1) "Close relative of a deceased victim" means a person who was the spouse of a deceased victim at the time of the victim's death or who is a parent or adult brother, sister, or child of the deceased victim.

(2) "Guardian of a victim" means a person who is the legal guardian of the victim, whether or not the legal relationship between the guardian and victim exists because of the age of the victim or the physical or mental incompetency of the victim.

(3) "Victim" means a person who as the result of the delinquent conduct of a child suffers a pecuniary loss or personal injury or harm.

Added by Acts 1989, 71st Leg., ch. 633, § 1, eff. June 14, 1989. Amended by Acts 1995, 74th Leg., ch. 262, § 49, eff. Jan. 1, 1996; Acts 1997, 75th Leg., ch. 368, § 1, eff. Sept. 1, 1997.

§ 57.002. Victim's Rights

A victim, guardian of a victim, or close relative of a deceased victim is entitled to the following rights within the juvenile justice system:

(1) the right to receive from law enforcement agencies adequate protection from harm and threats of harm arising from cooperation with prosecution efforts;

(2) the right to have the court or person appointed by the court take the safety of the victim or the victim's family into consideration as an element in determining whether the child should be detained before the child's conduct is adjudicated;

(3) the right, if requested, to be informed of relevant court proceedings, including appellate proceedings, and to be informed in a timely manner if those court proceedings have been canceled or rescheduled;

(4) the right to be informed, when requested, by the court or a person appointed by the court concerning the procedures in the juvenile justice system, including general procedures relating to:

(A) the preliminary investigation and deferred prosecution of a case; and

(B) the appeal of the case;

(5) the right to provide pertinent information to a juvenile court conducting a disposition hearing concerning the impact of the offense on the victim and the victim's family by testimony, written statement, or any other manner before the court renders its disposition;

(6) the right to receive information regarding compensation to victims as provided by Subchapter B, Chapter 56, Code of Criminal Procedure,[1] including information related to the costs that may be compensated under that Act and the amount of compensation, eligibility for compensation, and procedures for application for compensation under that Act, the payment of medical expenses under Section 56.06, Code of Criminal Procedure, for a victim of a sexual assault, and when requested, to referral to available social service agencies that may offer additional assistance;

(7) the right to be informed, upon request, of procedures for release under supervision or transfer of the person to the custody of the pardons and paroles division of the Texas Department of Criminal Justice for parole, to participate in the release or transfer for parole process, to be notified, if requested, of release or transfer for parole proceedings concerning the person, to provide to the Texas Youth Commission for inclusion in the person's file information to be considered by the commission before the release under supervision or transfer for parole of the person, and to be notified, if requested, of the person's release or transfer for parole;

(8) the right to be provided with a waiting area, separate or secure from other witnesses, including the child alleged to have committed the conduct and relatives of the child, before testifying in any proceeding concerning the child, or, if a separate waiting area is not available, other safeguards should be taken to minimize the victim's contact with the child and the child's relatives and witnesses, before and during court proceedings;

(9) the right to prompt return of any property of the victim that is held by a law enforcement agency or the attorney for the state as evidence when the property is no longer required for that purpose;

(10) the right to have the attorney for the state notify the employer of the victim, if requested, of the necessity of the victim's cooperation and testimony in a proceeding that may necessitate the absence of the victim from work for good cause;

(11) the right to be present at all public court proceedings related to the conduct of the child as provided by Section 54.08, subject to that section; and

(12) any other right appropriate to the victim that a victim of criminal conduct has under Article 56.02, Code of Criminal Procedure.

Added by Acts 1989, 71st Leg., ch. 633, § 1, eff. June 14, 1989. Amended by Acts 1995, 74th Leg., ch. 76, § 5.95(110), eff. Sept. 1, 1995; Acts 1995, 74th Leg., ch. 262, § 50, eff. Jan. 1, 1996.

[1] Vernon's Ann.C.C.P. art. 56.31 et seq.

Section 1.02(b) of Acts 1995, 74th Leg., ch. 76 provides:

"If any provision of this Act conflicts with a statute enacted by the 74th Legislature, Regular Session, 1995, the statute controls."

§ 57.003. Duty of Juvenile Board

(a) The juvenile board shall ensure to the extent practicable that a victim, guardian of a victim, or close relative of a deceased victim is afforded the rights granted by Section 57.002 and, on request, an explanation of those rights.

(b) The juvenile board may designate a person to serve as victim assistance coordinator in the juvenile board's jurisdiction for victims of juvenile offenders.

(c) The victim assistance coordinator shall ensure that a victim, or close relative of a deceased victim, is afforded the rights granted victims, guardians, and relatives by Section 57.002 and, on request, an explanation of those rights. The victim assistance coordinator shall work closely with appropriate law enforcement agencies, prosecuting attorneys, the Texas Juvenile Probation Commission, and the Texas Youth Commission in carrying out that duty.

(d) The victim assistance coordinator shall ensure that at a minimum, a victim, guardian of a victim, or close relative of a deceased victim receives:

(1) a written notice of the rights outlined in Section 57.002;

(2) an application for compensation under the Crime Victims' Compensation Act (Subchapter B, Chapter 56, Code of Criminal Procedure);[1] and

(3) a victim impact statement with information explaining the possible use and consideration of the victim impact statement at detention, adjudication, and release proceedings involving the juvenile.

(e) The victim assistance coordinator shall, on request, offer to assist a person receiving a form under Subsection (d) to complete the form.

(f) The victim assistance coordinator shall send a copy of the victim impact statement to the court conducting a disposition hearing involving the juvenile.

Added by Acts 1989, 71st Leg., ch. 633, § 1, eff. June 14, 1989. Amended by Acts 1995, 74th Leg., ch. 262, § 51, eff. Jan. 1, 1996.

[1] Vernon's Ann.C.C.P. art. 56.31 et seq.

§ 57.0031. Notification of Rights of Victims of Juveniles

At the initial contact or at the earliest possible time after the initial contact between the victim of a reported crime and the juvenile probation office having the responsibility for the disposition of the juvenile, the office shall provide the victim a written notice:

(1) containing information about the availability of emergency and medical services, if applicable;

(2) stating that the victim has the right to receive information regarding compensation to victims of crime as provided by the Crime Victims' Compensation Act (Subchapter B, Chapter 56, Code of Criminal Procedure),[1] including information about:

(A) the costs that may be compensated and the amount of compensation, eligibility for compensation, and procedures for application for compensation;

(B) the payment for a medical examination for a victim of a sexual assault; and

(C) referral to available social service agencies that may offer additional assistance;

(3) stating the name, address, and phone number of the victim assistance coordinator for victims of juveniles;

(4) containing the following statement: "You may call the crime victim assistance coordinator for the status of the case and information about victims' rights.";

(5) stating the rights of victims of crime under Section 57.002;

(6) summarizing each procedural stage in the processing of a juvenile case, including preliminary investigation, detention, informal adjustment of a case, disposition hearings, release proceedings, restitution, and appeals;

(7) suggesting steps the victim may take if the victim is subjected to threats or intimidation;

(8) stating the case number and assigned court for the case; and

(9) stating that the victim has the right to file a victim impact statement and to have it considered in juvenile proceedings.

Added by Acts 1995, 74th Leg., ch. 262, § 51, eff. Jan. 1, 1996.

[1] Vernon's Ann.C.C.P. art. 56.31 et seq.

§ 57.004. Notification

A court, a person appointed by the court, or the Texas Youth Commission is responsible for notifying a victim, guardian of a victim, or close relative of a deceased victim of a proceeding under this chapter only if the victim, guardian of a victim, or close relative of a deceased victim requests the notification in writing and provides a current address to which the notification is to be sent.

Added by Acts 1989, 71st Leg., ch. 633, § 1, eff. June 14, 1989.

§ 57.005. Liability

The Texas Youth Commission, a juvenile board, a court, a person appointed by a court, an attorney for the state, a peace officer, or a law enforcement agency is not liable for a failure or inability to provide a right listed under Section 57.002 of this code.

Added by Acts 1989, 71st Leg., ch. 633, § 1, eff. June 14, 1989.

§ 57.006. Appeal

The failure or inability of any person to provide a right or service listed under Section 57.002 of this code may not be used by a child as a ground for appeal or for a post conviction writ of habeas corpus.

Added by Acts 1989, 71st Leg., ch. 633, § 1, eff. June 14, 1989.

§ 57.007. Standing

A victim, guardian of a victim, or close relative of a victim does not have standing to participate as a party in a juvenile proceeding or to contest the disposition of any case.

Added by Acts 1989, 71st Leg., ch. 633, § 1, eff. June 14, 1989.

§ 57.008. Court Order for Protection From Juveniles

(a) A court may issue an order for protection from juveniles directed against a child to protect a victim of the child's conduct who, because of the victim's participation in the juvenile justice system, risks further harm by the child.

(b) In the order, the court may prohibit the child from doing specified acts or require the child to do specified acts necessary or appropriate to prevent or reduce the likelihood of further harm to the victim by the child.

Added by Acts 1995, 74th Leg., ch. 262, § 52, eff. Jan. 1, 1996.

CHAPTER 58. RECORDS; JUVENILE JUSTICE INFORMATION SYSTEM

SUBCHAPTER A. RECORDS

SUBCHAPTER B. JUVENILE JUSTICE INFORMATION SYSTEM

SUBCHAPTER A. RECORDS

§ 58.001. Collection of Records of Children

(a) Law enforcement officers and other juvenile justice personnel shall collect information described by Section 58.104 as a part of the juvenile justice information system created under Subchapter B.[1]

(b) The information is available as provided by Subchapter B.

(c) A law enforcement agency may forward information, including photographs and fingerprints, relating to a child who has been detained or taken into custody by the agency to the Department of Public Safety for inclusion in the juvenile justice information system created under Subchapter B only if the child is referred to juvenile court on or before the 10th day after the date the child is detained or taken into custody. If the child is not referred to juvenile court within that time, the law enforcement agency shall destroy all information, including photographs and fingerprints, relating to the child unless the child is placed in a first offender program under Section 52.031 or on informal disposition under Section 52.03. The law enforcement agency may not forward any information to the Department of Public Safety relating to the child while the child is in a first offender program under Section 52.031, or during the 90 days following successful completion of the program or while the child is on informal disposition under Section 52.03. Except as provided by Subsection (f), after the date the child completes an informal disposition under Section 52.03 or after the 90th day after the date the child successfully completes a first offender program under Section 52.031, the law enforcement agency shall destroy all information, including photographs and fingerprints, relating to the child.

(d) If information relating to a child is contained in a document that also contains information relating to an adult and a law enforcement agency is required to destroy all information relating to the child under this section, the agency shall alter the document so that the information relating to the child is destroyed and the information relating to the adult is preserved.

(e) The deletion of a computer entry constitutes destruction of the information contained in the entry.

(f) A law enforcement agency may maintain information relating to a child after the 90th day after the date the child successfully completes a first offender program under Section 52.031 only to determine the child's eligibility to participate in a first offender program.

Added by Acts 1995, 74th Leg., ch. 262, § 53, eff. Jan. 1, 1996. Amended by Acts 1997, 75th Leg., ch. 1086, § 16, eff. Sept. 1, 1997.

[1] V.T.C.A., Family Code § 58.101 et seq.

§ 58.002. Photographs and Fingerprints of Children

(a) Except as provided by Chapter 79, Human Resources Code, a child may not be photographed or fingerprinted without the consent of the juvenile court unless the child is taken into custody for conduct that constitutes a felony or a misdemeanor punishable by confinement in jail.

(b) On or before December 31 of each year, the head of each municipal or county law enforcement agency located in a county shall certify to the juvenile board for that county that the photographs and fingerprints required to be destroyed under Section 58.001 have been destroyed. The juvenile board shall conduct an audit of the records of the law enforcement agency to verify the destruction of the photographs and fingerprints and the law enforcement agency shall make its records available for this purpose. If the audit shows that the certification provided by the head of the law enforcement agency is false, that person is subject to prosecution for perjury under Chapter 37, Penal Code.

(c) This section does not prohibit a law enforcement officer from photographing or fingerprinting a child who is not in custody if the child's parent or guardian voluntarily consents in writing to the photographing or fingerprinting of the child.

(d) This section does not apply to fingerprints that are required or authorized to be submitted or obtained for an application for a driver's license or personal identification card.

Added by Acts 1995, 74th Leg., ch. 262, § 53, eff. Jan. 1, 1996. Amended by Acts 1997, 75th Leg., ch. 1086, § 17, eff. Sept. 1, 1997.

§ 58.003. Sealing of Records

(a) Except as provided by Subsections (b) and (c), on the application of a person who has been found to have engaged in delinquent conduct or conduct indicating a need for supervision, or a person taken into custody to determine whether the person engaged in delinquent conduct or conduct indicating a need for supervision, on the juvenile court's own motion or on receipt of a certification from the Department of

Public Safety of the State of Texas that the records of a person are eligible for sealing under this section, the court shall order the sealing of the records in the case if the court finds that:

(1) two years have elapsed since final discharge of the person or since the last official action in the person's case if there was no adjudication; and

(2) since the time specified in Subdivision (1), the person has not been convicted of a felony or a misdemeanor involving moral turpitude or found to have engaged in delinquent conduct or conduct indicating a need for supervision and no proceeding is pending seeking conviction or adjudication.

(b) A court may not order the sealing of the records of a person who has received a determinate sentence for engaging in delinquent conduct that violated a penal law listed in Section 53.045 or engaging in habitual felony conduct as described by Section 51.031.

(c) Subject to Subsection (b), a court may order the sealing of records concerning a person adjudicated as having engaged in delinquent conduct that violated a penal law of the grade of felony only if:

(1) the person is 21 years of age or older;

(2) the person was not transferred by a juvenile court under Section 54.02 to a criminal court for prosecution;

(3) the records have not been used as evidence in the punishment phase of a criminal proceeding under Section 3(a), Article 37.07, Code of Criminal Procedure; and

(4) the person has not been convicted of a penal law of the grade of felony after becoming age 17.

(d) The court may grant the relief authorized in Subsection (a) at any time after final discharge of the person or after the last official action in the case if there was no adjudication. If the child is referred to the juvenile court for conduct constituting any offense and at the adjudication hearing the child is found to be not guilty of each offense alleged, the court shall immediately order the sealing of all files and records relating to the case.

(e) Reasonable notice of the hearing shall be given to:

(1) the person who made the application or who is the subject of the records named in the motion;

(2) the prosecuting attorney for the juvenile court;

(3) the authority granting the discharge if the final discharge was from an institution or from parole;

(4) the public or private agency or institution having custody of records named in the application or motion; and

(5) the law enforcement agency having custody of files or records named in the application or motion.

(f) A copy of the sealing order shall be sent to each agency or official named in the order.

(g) On entry of the order:

(1) all law enforcement, prosecuting attorney, clerk of court, and juvenile court records ordered sealed shall be sent to the court issuing the order;

(2) all records of a public or private agency or institution ordered sealed shall be sent to the court issuing the order;

(3) all index references to the records ordered sealed shall be deleted;

(4) the juvenile court, clerk of court, prosecuting attorney, public or private agency or institution, and law enforcement officers and agencies shall properly reply that no record exists with respect to the person on inquiry in any matter; and

(5) the adjudication shall be vacated and the proceeding dismissed and treated for all purposes other than a subsequent capital prosecution, including the purpose of showing a prior finding of delinquent conduct, as if it had never occurred.

(h) Inspection of the sealed records may be permitted by an order of the juvenile court on the petition of the person who is the subject of the records and only by those persons named in the order.

(i) On the final discharge of a child or on the last official action in the case if there is no adjudication, the child shall be given a written explanation of the child's rights under this section and a copy of the provisions of this section.

(j) A person whose records have been sealed under this section is not required in any proceeding or in any application for employment, information, or licensing to state that the person has been the subject of a proceeding under this title and any statement that the person has never been found to be a delinquent child shall never be held against the person in any criminal or civil proceeding.

(k) A prosecuting attorney may, on application to the juvenile court, reopen at any time the files and records of a person adjudicated as having engaged in delinquent conduct that violated a penal law of the grade of felony sealed by the court under this section for the purposes of Sections 12.42(a)–(c) and (e), Penal Code.

(*l*) On the motion of a person in whose name records are kept or on the court's own motion, the court may order the destruction of records that have been sealed under this section if:

(1) the records relate to conduct that did not violate a penal law of the grade of felony or a misdemeanor punishable by confinement in jail;

(2) five years have elapsed since the person's 16th birthday; and

(3) the person has not been convicted of a felony.

Text of subsec. (m) as added by Acts 1997, 75th Leg., ch. 165, § 10.05(a)

(m) On request of the Department of Public Safety, a juvenile court shall reopen and allow the department to inspect the files and records of the juvenile court relating to an applicant for a license to carry a concealed handgun under Subchapter H, Chapter 411, Government Code.

Text of subsec. (m) as added by Acts 1997, 75th Leg., ch. 1086, § 18

(m) A record created or maintained under Article 6252–13c.1, Revised Statutes, may not be sealed under this section if the person who is the subject of the record has a continuing obligation to register under that article.

Added by Acts 1995, 74th Leg., ch. 262, § 53, eff. Jan. 1, 1996. Amended by Acts 1997, 75th Leg., ch. 165, § 10.05(a), eff. Sept. 1, 1997; Acts 1997, 75th Leg., ch. 1086, § 18, eff. Sept. 1, 1997.

§ 58.004. Repealed by Acts 1997, 75th Leg., ch. 1086, § 49(a), eff. Sept. 1, 1997

§ 58.005. Confidentiality of Records

(a) Information obtained for the purpose of diagnosis, examination, evaluation, or treatment or for making a referral for treatment of a child by a public or private agency or institution providing supervision of a child by arrangement of the juvenile court or having custody of the child under order of the juvenile court may be disclosed only to:

(1) the professional staff or consultants of the agency or institution;

(2) the judge, probation officers, and professional staff or consultants of the juvenile court;

(3) an attorney for the child;

(4) a governmental agency if the disclosure is required or authorized by law;

(5) a person or entity to whom the child is referred for treatment or services if the agency or institution disclosing the information has entered into a written confidentiality agreement with the person or entity regarding the protection of the disclosed information;

(6) the Texas Department of Criminal Justice and the Texas Juvenile Probation Commission for the purpose of maintaining statistical records of recidivism and for diagnosis and classification; or

(7) with leave of the juvenile court, any other person, agency, or institution having a legitimate interest in the proceeding or in the work of the court.

(b) This section does not apply to information collected under Section 58.104.

Added by Acts 1995, 74th Leg., ch. 262, § 53, eff. Jan. 1, 1996.

§ 58.006. Destruction of Certain Records

The court shall order the destruction of the records relating to the conduct for which a child is taken into custody, including records contained in the juvenile justice information system, if:

(1) a determination that no probable cause exists to believe the child engaged in the conduct is made under Section 53.01 and the case is not referred to a prosecutor for review under Section 53.012; or

(2) a determination that no probable cause exists to believe the child engaged in the conduct is made by a prosecutor under Section 53.012.

Added by Acts 1995, 74th Leg., ch. 262, § 53, eff. Jan. 1, 1996.

§ 58.007. Physical Records or Files

(a) This section applies only to the inspection and maintenance of a physical record or file concerning a child and does not affect the collection, dissemination, or maintenance of information as provided by Subchapter B.[1] This section does not apply to a record or file relating to a child that is required or authorized to be maintained under the laws regulating the operation of motor vehicles in this state or to a record or file relating to a child that is maintained by a municipal or justice court.

(b) Except as provided by Article 15.27, Code of Criminal Procedure, the records and files of a juvenile court, a clerk of court, a juvenile probation department, or a prosecuting attorney relating to a child who is a party to a proceeding under this title are open to inspection only by:

(1) the judge, probation officers, and professional staff or consultants of the juvenile court;

(2) a juvenile justice agency as that term is defined by Section 58.101;

(3) an attorney for a party to the proceeding;

(4) a public or private agency or institution providing supervision of the child by arrangement of the juvenile court, or having custody of the child under juvenile court order; or

(5) with leave of the juvenile court, any other person, agency, or institution having a legitimate interest in the proceeding or in the work of the court.

(c) Except as provided by Subsection (d), law enforcement records and files concerning a child may not be disclosed to the public and shall be:

(1) kept separate from adult files and records; and

(2) maintained on a local basis only and not sent to a central state or federal depository, except as provided by Subchapter B.

(d) The law enforcement files and records of a person who is transferred from the Texas Youth Commission to the institutional division or the pardons and paroles division of the Texas Department of Criminal Justice may be transferred to a central state or federal depository for adult records on or after the date of transfer.

(e) Law enforcement records and files concerning a child may be inspected by a juvenile justice agency as that term is defined by Section 58.101 and a criminal justice agency as that term is defined by Section 411.082, Government Code.

(f) If a child has been reported missing by a parent, guardian, or conservator of that child, information about the child may be forwarded to and disseminated by the Texas Crime Information Center and the National Crime Information Center.

(g) For the purpose of offering a record as evidence in the punishment phase of a criminal proceeding, a prosecuting attorney may obtain the record of a defendant's adjudication that is admissible under Section 3(a), Article 37.07, Code of Criminal Procedure, by submitting a request for the record to the juvenile court that made the adjudication. If a court receives a request from a prosecuting attorney under this subsection, the court shall, if the court possesses the requested record of adjudication, certify and provide the prosecuting attorney with a copy of the record.

Added by Acts 1995, 74th Leg., ch. 262, § 53, eff. Jan. 1, 1996. Amended by Acts 1997, 75th Leg., ch. 1086, §§ 19, 20, eff. Sept. 1, 1997.

[1] V.T.C.A., Family Code § 58.101 et seq.

Section 52 of Acts 1997, 75th Leg., ch. 1086 provides:

"The change in law made by this Act to Section 58.007(a), Family Code, applies to law enforcement files and records maintained by a municipal or justice court before, on, or after September 1, 1997."

[Sections 58.008 to 58.100 reserved for expansion]

SUBCHAPTER B. JUVENILE JUSTICE INFORMATION SYSTEM

§ 58.101. Definitions

In this subchapter:

(1) "Criminal justice agency" has the meaning assigned by Section 411.082, Government Code.

(2) "Department" means the Department of Public Safety of the State of Texas.

(3) "Disposition" means an action that results in the termination, transfer of jurisdiction, or indeterminate suspension of the prosecution of a juvenile offender.

(4) "Incident number" means a unique number assigned to a child during a specific custodial or detention period or for a specific referral to the office or official designated by the juvenile court, if the juvenile offender was not taken into custody before the referral.

(5) "Juvenile justice agency" means an agency that has custody or control over juvenile offenders.

(6) "Juvenile offender" means a child who has been assigned an incident number.

(7) "State identification number" means a unique number assigned by the department to a child in the juvenile justice information system.

(8) "Uniform incident fingerprint card" means a multiple-part form containing a unique incident number with space for information relating to the conduct for which a child has been taken into custody, detained, or referred, the child's fingerprints, and other relevant information.

Added by Acts 1995, 74th Leg., ch. 262, § 53, eff. Jan. 1, 1996.

§ 58.102. Juvenile Justice Information System

(a) The department is responsible for recording data and maintaining a database for a computerized juvenile justice information system that serves:

(1) as the record creation point for the juvenile justice information system maintained by the state; and

(2) as the control terminal for entry of records, in accordance with federal law, rule, and policy, into the federal records system maintained by the Federal Bureau of Investigation.

(b) The department shall develop and maintain the system with the cooperation and advice of the:

(1) Texas Youth Commission;

(2) Texas Juvenile Probation Commission;

(3) Criminal Justice Policy Council; and

(4) juvenile courts and clerks of juvenile courts.

(c) The department may not collect or retain information relating to a juvenile if this chapter prohibits or restricts the collection or retention of the information.

(d) The database must contain the information required by this subchapter.

(e) The department shall designate the offense codes and has the sole responsibility for designating the state identification number for each juvenile whose name appears in the juvenile justice system.

Added by Acts 1995, 74th Leg., ch. 262, § 53, eff. Jan. 1, 1996.

§ 58.103. Purpose of System

The purpose of the juvenile justice information system is to:

(1) provide agencies and personnel within the juvenile justice system accurate information relating to children who come into contact with the juvenile justice system of this state;

(2) provide, where allowed by law, adult criminal justice agencies accurate and easily accessible information relating to children who come into contact with the juvenile justice system;

(3) provide an efficient conversion, where appropriate, of juvenile records to adult criminal records;

(4) improve the quality of data used to conduct impact analyses of proposed legislative changes in the juvenile justice system; and

(5) improve the ability of interested parties to analyze the functioning of the juvenile justice system.

Added by Acts 1995, 74th Leg., ch. 262, § 53, eff. Jan. 1, 1996.

§ 58.104. Types of Information Collected

(a) Subject to Subsection (f), the juvenile justice information system shall consist of information relating to delinquent conduct committed by a juvenile offender that, if the conduct had been committed by an adult, would constitute a criminal offense other than an offense punishable by a fine only, including information relating to:

(1) the juvenile offender;

(2) the intake or referral of the juvenile offender into the juvenile justice system;

(3) the detention of the juvenile offender;

(4) the prosecution of the juvenile offender;

(5) the disposition of the juvenile offender's case, including the name and description of any program to which the juvenile offender is referred; and

(6) the probation or commitment of the juvenile offender.

(b) To the extent possible and subject to Subsection (a), the department shall include in the juvenile justice information system the following information for each juvenile offender taken into custody, detained, or referred under this title for delinquent conduct:

(1) the juvenile offender's name, including other names by which the juvenile offender is known;

(2) the juvenile offender's date and place of birth;

(3) the juvenile offender's physical description, including sex, weight, height, race, ethnicity, eye color, hair color, scars, marks, and tattoos;

(4) the juvenile offender's state identification number, and other identifying information, as determined by the department;

(5) the juvenile offender's fingerprints;

(6) the juvenile offender's last known residential address, including the census tract number designation for the address;

(7) the name and identifying number of the agency that took into custody or detained the juvenile offender;

(8) the date of detention or custody;

(9) the conduct for which the juvenile offender was taken into custody, detained, or referred, including level and degree of the alleged offense;

(10) the name and identifying number of the juvenile intake agency or juvenile probation office;

(11) each disposition by the juvenile intake agency or juvenile probation office;

(12) the date of disposition by the juvenile intake agency or juvenile probation office;

(13) the name and identifying number of the prosecutor's office;

(14) each disposition by the prosecutor;

(15) the date of disposition by the prosecutor;

(16) the name and identifying number of the court;

(17) each disposition by the court, including information concerning custody of a juvenile offender by a juvenile justice agency or probation;

(18) the date of disposition by the court;

(19) any commitment or release under supervision by the Texas Youth Commission;

(20) the date of any commitment or release under supervision by the Texas Youth Commission; and

(21) a description of each appellate proceeding.

(c) The department may designate codes relating to the information described by Subsection (b).

(d) The department shall designate a state identification number for each juvenile offender.

(e) This subchapter does not apply to a disposition that represents an administrative status notice of an agency described by Section 58.102(b).

(f) Records maintained by the department in the depository are subject to being sealed under Section 58.003. The department shall send to the appropriate juvenile court its certification of records that the department determines, according to the department's records, are eligible for sealing under Section 58.003(a).

Added by Acts 1995, 74th Leg., ch. 262, § 53, eff. Jan. 1, 1996. Amended by Acts 1997, 75th Leg., ch. 1086, § 21, eff. Sept. 1, 1997.

§ 58.105. Duties of Juvenile Board

Each juvenile board shall provide for:

(1) the compilation and maintenance of records and information needed for reporting information to the department under this subchapter;

(2) the transmittal to the department, in the manner provided by the department, of all records and information required by the department under this subchapter; and

(3) access by the department to inspect records and information to determine the completeness and accuracy of information reported.

Added by Acts 1995, 74th Leg., ch. 262, § 53, eff. Jan. 1, 1996.

§ 58.106. Confidentiality

(a) Except as otherwise provided by this section, information contained in the juvenile justice information system is confidential information for the use of the department and may not be disseminated by the department except:

(1) with the permission of the juvenile offender, to military personnel of this state or the United States;

(2) to a person or entity to which the department may grant access to adult criminal history records as provided by Section 411.083, Government Code;

(3) to a juvenile justice agency; and

(4) to the Criminal Justice Policy Council, the Texas Youth Commission, and the Texas Juvenile Probation Commission for analytical purposes.

(b) Subsection (a) does not apply to a document maintained by a juvenile justice agency that is the source of information collected by the department.

(c) The department may, if necessary to protect the welfare of the community, disseminate to the public the following information relating to a juvenile offender who has escaped from the custody of the Texas Youth Commission:

(1) the juvenile offender's name, including other names by which the juvenile offender is known;

(2) the juvenile offender's physical description, including sex, weight, height, race, ethnicity, eye color, hair color, scars, marks, and tattoos;

(3) a photograph of the juvenile offender; and

(4) the conduct for which the juvenile offender was committed to the Texas Youth Commission, including the level and degree of the alleged offense.

Added by Acts 1995, 74th Leg., ch. 262, § 53, eff. Jan. 1, 1996. Amended by Acts 1997, 75th Leg., ch. 380, § 1, eff. Sept. 1, 1997.

Section 2 of Acts 1997, 75th Leg., ch. 380 provides:

"The change in law made by this Act applies to information contained in the juvenile justice information system and collected by the Department of Public Safety of the State of Texas before, on, or after the effective date of this Act."

§ 58.107. Compatibility of Data

Data supplied to the juvenile justice information system must be compatible with the system and must contain both incident numbers and state identification numbers.

Added by Acts 1995, 74th Leg., ch. 262, § 53, eff. Jan. 1, 1996.

§ 58.108. Duties of Agencies and Courts

(a) A juvenile justice agency and a clerk of a juvenile court shall:

(1) compile and maintain records needed for reporting data required by the department;

(2) transmit to the department in the manner provided by the department data required by the department;

(3) give the department or its accredited agents access to the agency or court for the purpose of

inspection to determine the completeness and accuracy of data reported; and

(4) cooperate with the department to enable the department to perform its duties under this chapter.

(b) A juvenile justice agency and clerk of a court shall retain documents described by this section.

Added by Acts 1995, 74th Leg., ch. 262, § 53, eff. Jan. 1, 1996.

§ 58.109. Uniform Incident Fingerprint Card

(a) The department may provide for the use of a uniform incident fingerprint card in the maintenance of the juvenile justice information system.

(b) The department shall design, print, and distribute to each law enforcement agency and juvenile intake agency uniform incident fingerprint cards.

(c) The incident cards must:

(1) be serially numbered with an incident number in a manner that allows each incident of referral of a juvenile offender who is the subject of the incident fingerprint card to be readily ascertained; and

(2) be multiple-part forms that can be transmitted with the juvenile offender through the juvenile justice process and that allow each agency to report required data to the department.

(d) Subject to available telecommunications capacity, the department shall develop the capability to receive by electronic means from a law enforcement agency the information on the uniform incident fingerprint card. The information must be in a form that is compatible to the form required of data supplied to the juvenile justice information system.

Added by Acts 1995, 74th Leg., ch. 262, § 53, eff. Jan. 1, 1996.

§ 58.110. Reporting

(a) The department by rule shall develop reporting procedures that ensure that the juvenile offender processing data is reported from the time a juvenile offender is initially taken into custody, detained, or referred until the time a juvenile offender is released from the jurisdiction of the juvenile justice system.

(b) The law enforcement agency or the juvenile intake agency that initiates the entry of the juvenile offender into the juvenile justice information system for a specific incident shall prepare a uniform incident fingerprint card and initiate the reporting process for each incident reportable under this subchapter.

(c) The clerk of the court exercising jurisdiction over a juvenile offender's case shall report the disposition of the case to the department. A clerk of the court who violates this subsection commits an offense. An offense under this subsection is a Class C misdemeanor.

(d) In each county, the reporting agencies may make alternative arrangements for reporting the required information, including combined reporting or electronic reporting, if the alternative reporting is approved by the juvenile board and the department.

(e) Except as otherwise required by applicable state laws or regulations, information required by this chapter to be reported to the department shall be reported promptly. The information shall be reported not later than the 30th day after the date the information is received by the agency responsible for reporting the information, except that a juvenile offender's custody, detention, or referral without previous custody shall be reported to the department not later than the seventh day after the date of the custody, detention, or referral.

(f) Subject to available telecommunications capacity, the department shall develop the capability to receive by electronic means the information required under this section to be reported to the department. The information must be in a form that is compatible to the form required of data to be reported under this section.

Added by Acts 1995, 74th Leg., ch. 262, § 53, eff. Jan. 1, 1996.

§ 58.111. Local Data Advisory Boards

The commissioners court of each county may create a local data advisory board to perform the same duties relating to the juvenile justice information system as the duties performed by a local data advisory board in relation to the criminal history record system under Article 60.09, Code of Criminal Procedure.

Added by Acts 1995, 74th Leg., ch. 262, § 53, eff. Jan. 1, 1996.

§ 58.112. Report to Legislature

Not later than January 15 of each year, the Criminal Justice Policy Council shall submit to the lieutenant governor, the speaker of the house of representatives, and the governor a report that contains the following statistical information relating to children referred to a juvenile court during the preceding year:

(1) the ages, races, and counties of residence of the children transferred to a district court or criminal district court for criminal proceedings; and

(2) the ages, races, and counties of residence of the children committed to the Texas Youth Commis-

sion, placed on probation, or discharged without any disposition.

Added by Acts 1995, 74th Leg., ch. 262, § 53, eff. Jan. 1, 1996.

§ 58.113. Warrants

The department shall maintain in a computerized database that is accessible by the same entities that may access the juvenile justice information system information relating to a warrant of arrest, as that term is defined by Article 15.01, Code of Criminal Procedure, or a directive to apprehend under Section 52.015 for any child, without regard to whether the child has been taken into custody.

Added by Acts 1995, 74th Leg., ch. 262, § 53, eff. Jan. 1, 1996.

CHAPTER 59. PROGRESSIVE SANCTIONS GUIDELINES

Section

§ 59.001. Purposes

The purposes of the progressive sanctions guidelines are to:

(1) ensure that juvenile offenders face uniform and consistent consequences and punishments that correspond to the seriousness of each offender's current offense, prior delinquent history, special treatment or training needs, and effectiveness of prior interventions;

(2) balance public protection and rehabilitation while holding juvenile offenders accountable;

(3) permit flexibility in the decisions made in relation to the juvenile offender to the extent allowed by law;

(4) consider the juvenile offender's circumstances; and

(5) improve juvenile justice planning and resource allocation by ensuring uniform and consistent reporting of disposition decisions at all levels.

Added by Acts 1995, 74th Leg., ch. 262, § 53, eff. Jan. 1, 1996.

§ 59.002. Sanction Level Assignment by Probation Department

(a) The probation department may assign a sanction level of one to a child referred to the probation department under Section 53.012.

(b) The probation department may assign a sanction level of two to a child for whom deferred prosecution is authorized under Section 53.03.

Added by Acts 1995, 74th Leg., ch. 262, § 53, eff. Jan. 1, 1996.

§ 59.003. Sanction Level Assignment Guidelines

(a) Subject to Subsection (e), after a child's first commission of delinquent conduct or conduct indicating a need for supervision, the probation department or prosecuting attorney may, or the juvenile court may, in a disposition hearing under Section 54.04 or a modification hearing under Section 54.05, assign a child one of the following sanction levels according to the child's conduct:

(1) for conduct indicating a need for supervision, other than conduct described in Section 51.03(b)(6) or a Class A or B misdemeanor, the sanction level is one;

(2) for conduct indicating a need for supervision under Section 51.03(b)(6) or a Class A or B misdemeanor, other than a misdemeanor involving the use or possession of a firearm, or for delinquent conduct under Section 51.03(a)(2) or (3), the sanction level is two;

(3) for a misdemeanor involving the use or possession of a firearm or for a state jail felony or a felony of the third degree, the sanction level is three;

(4) for a felony of the second degree, the sanction level is four;

(5) for a felony of the first degree, other than a felony involving the use of a deadly weapon or causing serious bodily injury, the sanction level is five;

(6) for a felony of the first degree involving the use of a deadly weapon or causing serious bodily injury, for an aggravated controlled substance felony, or for a capital felony, the sanction level is six; or

(7) for a felony of the first degree involving the use of a deadly weapon or causing serious bodily injury, for an aggravated controlled substance felony, or for a capital felony, if the petition has been approved by a grand jury under Section 53.045, or if a petition to transfer the child to criminal court has been filed under Section 54.02, the sanction level is seven.

(b) Subject to Subsection (e), if the child subsequently is found to have engaged in delinquent conduct in an adjudication hearing under Section 54.03 or a hearing to modify a disposition under Section 54.05 on two separate occasions and each involves a violation of a penal law of a classification that is less than the classification of the child's previous conduct, the juvenile court may assign the child a sanction level that is one level higher than the previously assigned sanction level, unless the child's previously assigned sanction level is six.

(c) Subject to Subsection (e), if the child's subsequent commission of delinquent conduct or conduct indicating a need for supervision involves a violation of a penal law of a classification that is the same as or greater than the classification of the child's previous conduct, the juvenile court may assign the child a sanction level that is one level higher than the previously assigned sanction level, unless:

(1) the child's previously assigned sanction level is five and the child has not been adjudicated for delinquent conduct;

(2) the child's previously assigned sanction level is six, unless the subsequent violation is of a provision listed under Section 53.045(a) and the petition has been approved by a grand jury under Section 53.045; or

(3) the child's previously assigned sanction level is seven.

(d) Subject to Subsection (e), if the child's previously assigned sanction level is four or five and the child's subsequent commission of delinquent conduct is of the grade of felony, the juvenile court may assign the child a sanction level that is one level higher than the previously assigned sanction level.

(e) A juvenile court or probation department that deviates from the guidelines under this section shall state in writing its reasons for the deviation and submit the statement to the juvenile board regardless of whether a progressive sanctions program has been adopted by the juvenile board. Nothing in this chapter prohibits the imposition of appropriate sanctions that are different from those provided at any sanction level.

(f) The probation department may, in accordance with Section 54.05, request the extension of a period of probation specified under sanction levels one through five if the circumstances of the child warrant the extension.

(g) Before the court assigns the child a sanction level that involves the revocation of the child's probation and the commitment of the child to the Texas Youth Commission, the court shall hold a hearing to modify the disposition as required by Section 54.05.

Added by Acts 1995, 74th Leg., ch. 262, § 53, eff. Jan. 1, 1996. Amended by Acts 1997, 75th Leg., ch. 1015, § 19, eff. June 19, 1997; Acts 1997, 75th Leg., ch. 1086, § 22, eff. Sept. 1, 1997.

Section 20 of Acts 1997, 75th Leg., ch. 1015 provides:

"This Act takes effect beginning with the 1997–1998 school year."

§ 59.004. Sanction Level One

(a) For a child at sanction level one, the juvenile court or probation department may:

(1) require counseling for the child regarding the child's conduct;

(2) inform the child of the progressive sanctions that may be imposed on the child if the child continues to engage in delinquent conduct or conduct indicating a need for supervision;

(3) inform the child's parents or guardians of the parents' or guardians' responsibility to impose reasonable restrictions on the child to prevent the conduct from recurring;

(4) provide information or other assistance to the child or the child's parents or guardians in securing needed social services;

(5) require the child or the child's parents or guardians to participate in a program for services under Section 264.302, if a program under Section 264.302 is available to the child or the child's parents or guardians;

(6) refer the child to a community-based citizen intervention program approved by the juvenile court; and

(7) release the child to the child's parents or guardians.

(b) The probation department shall discharge the child from the custody of the probation department after the provisions of this section are met.

Added by Acts 1995, 74th Leg., ch. 262, § 53, eff. Jan. 1, 1996. Amended by Acts 1997, 75th Leg., ch. 1086, § 23, eff. Sept. 1, 1997.

§ 59.005. Sanction Level Two

(a) For a child at sanction level two, the juvenile court, the prosecuting attorney, or the probation department may, as provided by Section 53.03:

(1) place the child on deferred prosecution or court-ordered probation for not less than three months or more than six months;

(2) require the child to make restitution to the victim of the child's conduct or perform community service restitution appropriate to the nature and degree of harm caused and according to the child's ability;

(3) require the child's parents or guardians to identify restrictions the parents or guardians will impose on the child's activities and requirements the parents or guardians will set for the child's behavior;

(4) provide the information required under Sections 59.004(a)(2) and (4);

(5) require the child or the child's parents or guardians to participate in a program for services under Section 264.302, if a program under Section 264.302 is available to the child or the child's parents or guardians;

(6) refer the child to a community-based citizen intervention program approved by the juvenile court; and

(7) if appropriate, impose additional conditions of probation.

(b) The juvenile court or the probation department shall discharge the child from the custody of the probation department on the date the provisions of this section are met or on the child's 18th birthday, whichever is earlier.

Added by Acts 1995, 74th Leg., ch. 262, § 53, eff. Jan. 1, 1996. Amended by Acts 1997, 75th Leg., ch. 1086, § 24, eff. Sept. 1, 1997.

§ 59.006. Sanction Level Three

(a) For a child at sanction level three, the juvenile court may:

(1) place the child on probation for not less than six months or more than 12 months;

(2) require the child to make restitution to the victim of the child's conduct or perform community service restitution appropriate to the nature and degree of harm caused and according to the child's ability;

(3) impose specific restrictions on the child's activities and requirements for the child's behavior as conditions of probation;

(4) require a probation officer to closely monitor the child's activities and behavior;

(5) require the child or the child's parents or guardians to participate in programs or services designated by the court or probation officer; and

(6) if appropriate, impose additional conditions of probation.

(b) The juvenile court shall discharge the child from the custody of the probation department on the date the provisions of this section are met or on the child's 18th birthday, whichever is earlier.

Added by Acts 1995, 74th Leg., ch. 262, § 53, eff. Jan. 1, 1996. Amended by Acts 1997, 75th Leg., ch. 1086, § 25, eff. Sept. 1, 1997.

§ 59.007. Sanction Level Four

(a) For a child at sanction level four, the juvenile court may:

(1) require the child to participate as a condition of probation for not less than three months or more than 12 months in a highly intensive and regimented program that emphasizes discipline, physical fitness, social responsibility, and productive work;

(2) after release from the program described by Subdivision (1), continue the child on probation supervision for not less than six months or more than 12 months;

(3) require the child to make restitution to the victim of the child's conduct or perform community service restitution appropriate to the nature and degree of harm caused and according to the child's ability;

(4) impose highly structured restrictions on the child's activities and requirements for behavior of the child as conditions of probation;

(5) require a probation officer to closely monitor the child;

(6) require the child or the child's parents or guardians to participate in programs or services designed to address their particular needs and circumstances; and

(7) if appropriate, impose additional sanctions.

(b) The juvenile court shall discharge the child from the custody of the probation department on the date the provisions of this section are met or on the child's 18th birthday, whichever is earlier.

Added by Acts 1995, 74th Leg., ch. 262, § 53, eff. Jan. 1, 1996. Amended by Acts 1997, 75th Leg., ch. 1086, § 26, eff. Sept. 1, 1997.

§ 59.008. Sanction Level Five

(a) For a child at sanction level five, the juvenile court may:

(1) as a condition of probation, place the child for not less than six months or more than 12 months in a post-adjudication secure correctional facility;

(2) after release from the program described by Subdivision (1), continue the child on probation supervision for not less than six months or more than 12 months;

(3) require the child to make restitution to the victim of the child's conduct or perform community service restitution appropriate to the nature and degree of harm caused and according to the child's ability;

(4) impose highly structured restrictions on the child's activities and requirements for behavior of the child as conditions of probation;

(5) require a probation officer to closely monitor the child;

(6) require the child or the child's parents or guardians to participate in programs or services designed to address their particular needs and circumstances; and

(7) if appropriate, impose additional sanctions.

(b) The juvenile court shall discharge the child from the custody of the probation department on the date the provisions of this section are met or on the child's 18th birthday, whichever is earlier.

Added by Acts 1995, 74th Leg., ch. 262, § 53, eff. Jan. 1, 1996. Amended by Acts 1997, 75th Leg., ch. 1086, § 27, eff. Sept. 1, 1997.

§ 59.009. Sanction Level Six

(a) For a child at sanction level six, the juvenile court may commit the child to the custody of the Texas Youth Commission. The commission may:

(1) require the child to participate in a highly structured residential program that emphasizes discipline, accountability, fitness, training, and productive work for not less than nine months or more than 24 months unless the commission extends the period and the reason for an extension is documented;

(2) require the child to make restitution to the victim of the child's conduct or perform community service restitution appropriate to the nature and degree of the harm caused and according to the child's ability, if there is a victim of the child's conduct;

(3) require the child and the child's parents or guardians to participate in programs and services for their particular needs and circumstances; and

(4) if appropriate, impose additional sanctions.

(b) On release of the child under supervision, the Texas Youth Commission parole programs may:

(1) impose highly structured restrictions on the child's activities and requirements for behavior of the child as conditions of release under supervision;

(2) require a parole officer to closely monitor the child for not less than six months; and

(3) if appropriate, impose any other conditions of supervision.

(c) The Texas Youth Commission may discharge the child from the commission's custody on the date the provisions of this section are met or on the child's 19th birthday, whichever is earlier.

Added by Acts 1995, 74th Leg., ch. 262, § 53, eff. Jan. 1, 1996. Amended by Acts 1997, 75th Leg., ch. 1086, § 28, eff. Sept. 1, 1997.

§ 59.010. Sanction Level Seven

(a) For a child at sanction level seven, the juvenile court may certify and transfer the child under Section 54.02 or sentence the child to commitment to the Texas Youth Commission under Section 54.04(d)(3), 54.04(m), or 54.05(f). The commission may:

(1) require the child to participate in a highly structured residential program that emphasizes discipline, accountability, fitness, training, and productive work for not less than 12 months or more than 10 years unless the commission extends the period and the reason for the extension is documented;

(2) require the child to make restitution to the victim of the child's conduct or perform community service restitution appropriate to the nature and degree of harm caused and according to the child's ability, if there is a victim of the child's conduct;

(3) require the child and the child's parents or guardians to participate in programs and services for their particular needs and circumstances; and

(4) impose any other appropriate sanction.

(b) On release of the child under supervision, the Texas Youth Commission parole programs may:

(1) impose highly structured restrictions on the child's activities and requirements for behavior of the child as conditions of release under supervision;

(2) require a parole officer to monitor the child closely for not less than 12 months; and

(3) impose any other appropriate condition of supervision.

Added by Acts 1995, 74th Leg., ch. 262, § 53, eff. Jan. 1, 1996. Amended by Acts 1997, 75th Leg., ch. 1086, § 29, eff. Sept. 1, 1997.

§ 59.011. Duty of Juvenile Board

A juvenile board shall prepare a report to the Texas Juvenile Probation Commission, at least quarterly on forms provided by the commission, showing the referrals, probation or progressive sanctions violations, and commitments to the Texas Youth Commission administered under this chapter according to the progressive sanctions guidelines and the reasons for any deviations from the guidelines.

Added by Acts 1995, 74th Leg., ch. 262, § 53, eff. Jan. 1, 1996.

§ 59.012. Reports by Criminal Justice Policy Council

(a) The Texas Youth Commission shall compile information, at least quarterly, showing the commitments, placements, parole releases, and revocations administered under this chapter according to the progressive sanctions guidelines and the reasons for any deviation from the guidelines.

(b) The Texas Juvenile Probation Commission and the Texas Youth Commission shall compile the information obtained under this section and Section 59.011 and submit this information to the Criminal Justice Policy Council.

(c) The Criminal Justice Policy Council shall analyze the information compiled by the Texas Juvenile Probation Commission and the Texas Youth Commission under this section and submit the council's findings and recommendations at least annually to the governor and both houses of the legislature showing the primary reasons for any deviation and the effect of the implementation of the sanctions guidelines on recidivism rates.

Added by Acts 1995, 74th Leg., ch. 262, § 53, eff. Jan. 1, 1996.

§ 59.013. Liability

The Texas Youth Commission, a juvenile board, a court, a person appointed by a court, an attorney for the state, a peace officer, or a law enforcement agency is not liable for a failure or inability to provide a service listed under Sections 59.004–59.010.

Added by Acts 1995, 74th Leg., ch. 262, § 53, eff. Jan. 1, 1996.

§ 59.014. Appeal

The failure or inability of any person to provide a service listed under Sections 59.004–59.010 or the failure of a court or of any person to make a sanction level assignment as provided in Section 59.002 or 59.003 may not be used by a child as a ground for appeal or for a postconviction writ of habeas corpus.

Added by Acts 1995, 74th Leg., ch. 262, § 53, eff. Jan. 1, 1996.

§ 59.015. Waiver of Sanctions on Parents or Guardians

On a finding by the juvenile court or probation department that a child's parents or guardians have made a reasonable good faith effort to prevent the child from engaging in delinquent conduct or engaging in conduct indicating a need for supervision and that, despite the parents' or guardians' efforts, the child continues to engage in such conduct, the court or probation department shall waive any sanction that may be imposed on the parents or guardians at any sanction level.

Added by Acts 1995, 74th Leg., ch. 262, § 53, eff. Jan. 1, 1996.

CHAPTER 60. UNIFORM INTERSTATE COMPACT ON JUVENILES

Section

§ 60.001. Short Title

This chapter may be cited as the Uniform Interstate Compact on Juveniles.

Added by Acts 1995, 74th Leg., ch. 262, § 53, eff. Jan. 1, 1996.

§ 60.002. Execution of Interstate Compact

The governor shall execute a compact on behalf of the state with any other state or states legally joining in it in substantially the following form:

INTERSTATE COMPACT ON JUVENILES

The contracting states solemnly agree:

Article I

FINDINGS AND PURPOSE

That juveniles who are not under proper supervision and control, or who have absconded, escaped, or run away are likely to endanger their own health, morals, and welfare, and the health, morals, and welfare of others. The cooperation of the states party to this compact is therefore necessary to provide for the welfare and protection of juveniles and of the public with respect to (1) cooperative supervision of delinquent juveniles on probation or parole; (2) the return, from one state to another, of delinquent juveniles who have escaped or absconded; (3) the return, from one state to another, of nondelinquent juveniles who have run away from home; and (4) additional measures for the protection of juveniles and of the public, which any two or more of the party states may find desirable to undertake cooperatively. In carrying out the provisions of this compact the party states shall be guided by the noncriminal, reformative, and protective policies which guide their laws concerning delinquent, neglected, or dependent juveniles generally. It shall be the policy of the states party to this compact to cooperate and observe their respective responsibilities for the prompt return and acceptance of juveniles and delinquent juveniles who become subject to the provisions of this compact. The provisions of this compact shall be reasonably and liberally construed to accomplish the foregoing purposes.

Article II

EXISTING RIGHTS AND REMEDIES

That all remedies and procedures provided by this compact shall be in addition to and not in substitution for other rights, remedies, and procedures, and shall not be in derogation of parental rights and responsibilities.

Article III

DEFINITIONS

That, for the purpose of this compact, "delinquent juvenile" means any juvenile who has been adjudged delinquent and who, at the time the provisions of this compact are invoked, is still subject to the jurisdiction of the court that has made such adjudication or to the jurisdiction or supervision of an agency or institution pursuant to an order of such court; "probation or parole" means any kind of conditional release of juveniles authorized under the laws of the states party hereto; "court" means any court having jurisdiction over delinquent, neglected, or dependent children; "state" means any state, territory, or possessions of the United States, the District of Columbia, and the Commonwealth of Puerto Rico; and "residence" or any variant thereof means a place at which a home or regular place of abode is maintained.

Article IV

RETURN OF RUNAWAYS

(a) That the parent, guardian, person, or agency entitled to legal custody of a juvenile who has not been adjudged delinquent but who has run away without the consent of such parent, guardian, person, or agency may petition the appropriate court in the demanding state for the issuance of a requisition for his return. The petition shall state the name and age of the juvenile, the name of the petitioner, and the basis of entitlement to the juvenile's custody, the circumstances of his running away, his location if known at the time application is made, and such other facts as may tend to show that the juvenile who has run away is endangering his own welfare or the welfare of others and is not an emancipated minor. The petition shall be verified by affidavit, shall be executed in duplicate, and shall be accompanied by two certified copies of the document or documents on which the petitioner's entitlement to the juvenile's custody is based, such as birth certificates, letters of guardianship, or custody decrees. Such further affidavits and other documents as may be deemed proper may be submitted with such petition. The judge of the court to which this application is made may hold a hearing thereon to determine whether for the purposes of this compact the petitioner is entitled to the legal custody of the juvenile, whether or not it appears that the juvenile has in fact run away without consent, whether or not he is an emancipated minor, and whether or not it is in the best interest of the juvenile to compel his return to the state. If the judge determines, either with or without a hearing, that the juvenile should be returned, he shall present to the appropriate court or to the executive authority of the state where the juvenile is alleged to be located a written requisition for the return of such juvenile. Such requisition shall set forth the name and age of the juvenile, the determination of the court that the juvenile has run away without the consent of a parent, guardian, person, or agency entitled to his legal custody, and that it is in the best interest and for the protection of such juvenile that he be returned. In the event that a proceeding for the adjudication of the juvenile as a delinquent, neglected, or dependent juvenile is pending in the court at the time when such juvenile runs away, the court may issue a requisition for the return of such juvenile upon its own motion, regardless of the consent of the parent, guardian, person, or agency entitled to legal custody, reciting therein the nature and circumstances of the pending proceeding. The requisition shall in every case be executed in duplicate and shall be signed by the judge. One copy of the requisition shall be filed with the compact administrator of the demanding state, there to remain on file subject to the provisions of law governing records of such court. Upon the receipt of a requisition demanding the return of a juvenile who has run away, the court or the executive authority to whom the requisition is addressed shall issue an order to any peace officer or other appropriate person directing him to take into custody and detain such juvenile. Such detention order must substantially recite the facts necessary to the validity of its issuance hereunder. No juvenile detained upon such order shall be delivered over to the officer whom the court demanding him shall have appointed to receive him unless he shall first be taken forthwith before a judge of a court in the state, who shall inform him of the demand made for his return, and who may appoint counsel or guardian ad litem for him. If the judge of such court shall find that the requisition is in order, he shall deliver such juvenile over to the officer whom the court demanding him shall have appointed to receive him. The judge, however, may fix a reasonable time to be allowed for the purpose of testing the legality of the proceeding.

Upon reasonable information that a person is a juvenile who has run away from another state party to this compact without the consent of a parent, guardian, person, or agency entitled to his legal custody, such juvenile may be taken into custody without a requisition and brought forthwith before a judge of the appropriate court who may appoint counsel or guardian ad litem for such juvenile and who shall determine after a hearing whether sufficient cause exists to hold the person, subject to the order of the court, for his own protection and welfare, for such a time not exceeding 90 days as will enable his return to another state party to this compact pursuant to a requisition for his return from a court of that state. If, at the time when a state seeks the return of a juvenile who has run away, there is pending in the state wherein he is found any criminal charge, or any proceeding to have him adjudicated a delinquent juvenile for an act committed in such state, or if he is suspected of having committed within such state a criminal offense or an act of juvenile delinquency, he shall not be returned without the consent of such state until discharged from prosecution or other form of proceeding, imprisonment, detention, or supervision for such offense of juvenile delinquency. The duly accredited officers of any state party to this compact, upon the establishment of their authority and the identity of the juvenile being returned, shall be permitted to transport such juvenile through any and all states party to this compact, without interference. Upon his return to the state from which he ran away, the juvenile shall be subject to such further proceedings as may be appropriate under the laws of that state.

(b) That the state to which a juvenile is returned under this article shall be responsible for payment of the transportation costs of such return.

(c) That "juvenile" as used in this article means any person who is a minor under the law of the state of residence of the parent, guardian, person, or agency entitled to the legal custody of such minor.

Article V
RETURN OF ESCAPEES AND ABSCONDERS

(a) That the appropriate person or authority from whose probation or parole supervision a delinquent juvenile has absconded or from whose institutional custody he has escaped shall present to the appropriate court or to the executive authority of the state where the delinquent juvenile is alleged to be located a written requisition for the return of such delinquent juvenile. Such requisition shall state the name and age of the delinquent juvenile, the particulars of his adjudication as a delinquent juvenile, the circumstances of the breach of the terms of his probation or parole or of his escape from an institution or agency vested with his legal custody or supervision, and the location of such delinquent juvenile, if known, at the time the requisition is made. The requisition shall be verified by affidavit, shall be executed in duplicate, and shall be accompanied by two certified copies of the judgment, formal adjudication, or order of commitment which subjects such delinquent juvenile to probation or parole or to the legal custody of the institution or agency concerned. Such further affidavits and other documents as may be deemed proper may be submitted with such requisition. One copy of the requisition shall be filed with the compact administrator of the demanding state, there to remain on file subject to the provisions of law governing records of the appropriate court. Upon the receipt of a requisition demanding the return of a delinquent juvenile who has absconded or escaped, the court or the executive authority to whom the requisition is addressed shall issue an order to any peace officer or other appropriate person directing him to take into custody and detain such delinquent juvenile. Such detention order must substantially recite the facts necessary to the validity of its issuance hereunder. No delinquent juvenile detained upon such order shall be delivered over to the officer whom the appropriate person or authority demanding him shall have appointed to receive him unless he shall first be taken forthwith before a judge of an appropriate court in the state, who shall inform him of the demand made for his return and who may appoint counsel or guardian ad litem for him. If the judge of such court shall find that the requisition is in order, he shall deliver such delinquent juvenile over to the officer whom the appropriate person or authority demanding him shall have appointed to receive him. The judge, however, may fix a reasonable time to be allowed for the purpose of testing the legality of the proceeding.

Upon reasonable information that a person is a delinquent juvenile who has absconded while on probation or parole, or escaped from an institution or agency vested with this legal custody or supervision in any state party to this compact, such person may be taken into custody in any other state party to this compact without a requisition. But in such event, he must be taken forthwith before a judge of the appropriate court, who may appoint counsel or guardian ad litem for such person and who shall determine, after a hearing, whether sufficient cause exists to hold the person subject to the order of the court for such a time, not exceeding 90 days, as will enable his detention under a detention order issued on a requisition pursuant to this article. If, at the time when a state seeks the return of a delinquent juvenile who has either absconded while on probation or parole or escaped from an institution or agency vested with his legal custody or supervision, there is pending in the state wherein he is detained any criminal charge or any proceeding to have him adjudicated a delinquent juvenile for an act committed in such state, or if he is suspected of having committed within such state a criminal offense or an act of juvenile delinquency, he shall not be returned without the consent of such state until discharged from prosecution or other form of proceeding, imprisonment, detention, or supervision for such offense of juvenile delinquency. The duly accredited officers of any state party to this compact, upon the establishment of their authority and the identity of the delinquent juvenile being returned, shall be permitted to transport such delinquent juvenile through any and all states party to this compact, without interference. Upon his return to the state from which he escaped or absconded, the delinquent juvenile shall be subject to such further proceedings as may be appropriate under the laws of that state.

(b) That the state to which a delinquent juvenile is returned under this article shall be responsible for the payment of the transportation costs of such return.

Article VI
VOLUNTARY RETURN PROCEDURE

That any delinquent juvenile who has absconded while on probation or parole, or escaped from an institution or agency vested with his legal custody or supervision in any state party to this compact, and any juvenile who has run away from any state party to this compact, who is taken into custody without a requisition in another state party to this compact under the provisions of Article IV(a) or of Article V(a), may consent to his immediate return to the state from which he absconded, escaped, or ran away. Such consent shall be given by the juvenile or delinquent juvenile and his counsel or guardian ad litem, if any, by executing or subscribing in writing, in the presence of a judge of the appropriate court, which states that the juvenile or delinquent juvenile and his counsel or guardian ad litem, if any, consent to his return to the demanding state. Before such consent shall be executed or subscribed, however, the judge, in the presence of counsel or guardian ad litem, if any, shall inform the juvenile or delinquent juvenile of his rights under this compact. When the consent has been duly executed, it shall be forwarded to and filed with the compact administrator of the state in which the court is located and the judge shall direct the officer having the juvenile or delinquent juvenile in custody to deliver him to the duly accredited officer or officers of the state demanding his return, and shall cause to be delivered to such officer or officers a copy of the consent. The court may, however, upon the request of the state to which the juvenile or delinquent juvenile is being returned, order him to return unaccompanied to such state and shall provide him with a copy of such court order; in such event a copy of the consent shall be forwarded to the compact administrator of the state to which said juvenile or delinquent juvenile is ordered to return.

Article VII
COOPERATIVE SUPERVISION OF PROBATIONERS AND PAROLEES

(a) That the duly constituted judicial and administrative authorities of a state party to this compact (herein called "sending state") may permit any delinquent juvenile within such state, placed on probation or parole, to reside in any other state party to this compact (herein called "receiving state") while on probation or parole, and the receiving state shall accept such delinquent juvenile, if the parent, guardian, or person entitled to the legal custody of such delinquent juvenile is residing or undertakes to reside within the receiving state. Before granting such permission, opportunity shall be given to the receiving state to make such investigations as it deems necessary. The authorities of the sending state shall send to the authorities of the receiving state copies of pertinent court orders, social case studies, and all other available information which may be of value to and assist the receiving state in supervising a probationer or parolee under this compact. A receiving state, in its discretion, may agree to accept supervision of a probationer or parolee in cases where the parent, guardian, or person entitled to the legal custody of the delinquent juvenile is not a resident of the receiving state, and if so accepted the sending state may transfer supervision accordingly.

(b) That each receiving state will assume the duties of visitation and of supervision over any such delinquent juvenile and in the exercise of those duties will be governed by the same standards of visitation and supervision that prevail for its own delinquent juveniles released on probation or parole.

(c) That, after consultation between the appropriate authorities of the sending state and of the receiving state as to the desirability and necessity of returning such a delinquent juvenile, the duly accredited officers of a sending state may enter a receiving state and there apprehend and retake any such delinquent juvenile on probation or parole. For that purpose, no formalities will be required, other than establishing the authority of the officer and the identity of the delinquent juvenile to be retaken and returned. The decision of the sending state to retake a delinquent juvenile on probation or parole shall be conclusive upon and not reviewable within the receiving state, but if, at the time the sending state seeks to retake a delinquent juvenile on probation or parole, there is pending against him within the receiving state any criminal charge or any proceedings to have him adjudicated a delinquent juvenile for any act committed in such state or if he is suspected of having committed within such state a criminal offense or an act of juvenile delinquency, he shall not be returned without the consent of the receiving state until discharged from prosecution or other form of proceeding, imprisonment, detention, or supervision for such offense of juvenile delinquency. The duly accredited officers of the sending state shall be permitted to transport delinquent juveniles being so returned through any and all states party to this compact, without interference.

(d) That the sending state shall be responsible under this article for paying the costs of transporting any delinquent juvenile to the receiving state or of returning any delinquent juvenile to the sending state.

Article VIII
RESPONSIBILITY FOR COSTS

(a) That the provisions of Articles IV(b), V(b), and VII(d) of this compact shall not be construed to alter or affect any internal relationship among the departments, agencies, and officers of and in the government of a party state, or between a party state and its subdivisions, as to the payment of costs, or responsibilities therefor.

(b) That nothing in this compact shall be construed to prevent any party state or subdivision thereof from asserting any right against any person, agency, or other entity in regard to costs for which such party state or subdivision thereof may be responsible pursuant to Articles IV(b), V(b), or VII(d) of this compact.

Article IX
DETENTION PRACTICES

That, to every extent possible, it shall be the policy of states party to this compact that no juvenile or delinquent juvenile shall be placed or detained in any prison, jail, or lockup nor be detained or transported in association with criminal, vicious, or dissolute persons.

Article X
SUPPLEMENTARY AGREEMENTS

That the duly constituted administrative authorities of a state party to this compact may enter into supplementary agreements with any other state or states party hereto for the cooperative care, treatment, and rehabilitation of delinquent juveniles whenever they shall find that such agreements will improve the facilities or programs available for such care, treatment, and rehabilitation. Such care, treatment, and rehabilitation may be provided in an institution located within any state entering into such supplementary agreement. Such supplementary agreements shall (1) provide the rates to be paid for the care, treatment, and custody of such delinquent juveniles, taking into consideration the character of facilities, services, and subsistence furnished; (2) provide that the delinquent juvenile shall be given a court hearing prior to his being sent to another state for care, treatment, and custody; (3) provide that the state receiving such a delinquent juvenile in one of its institutions shall act solely as agent for the state sending such delinquent juvenile; (4) provide that the sending state shall at all times retain jurisdiction over delinquent juveniles sent to an institution in another state; (5) provide for reasonable inspection of such institutions by the sending state; (6) provide that the consent of the parent, guardian, person, or agency entitled to the legal custody of said delinquent juvenile shall be secured prior to his being sent to another state; and (7) make provision for such other matters and details as shall be necessary to protect the rights and equities of such delinquent juveniles and of the cooperating states.

Article XI

ACCEPTANCE OF FEDERAL AND OTHER AID

That any state party to this compact may accept any and all donations, gifts, and grants of money, equipment, and services from the federal or any local government, or any agency thereof and from any person, firm, or corporation, for any of the purposes and functions of this compact, and may receive and utilize the same, subject to the terms, conditions, and regulations governing such donations, gifts, and grants.

Article XII

COMPACT ADMINISTRATORS

That the governor of each state party to this compact shall designate an officer who, acting jointly with like officers of other party states, shall promulgate rules and regulations to carry out more effectively the terms and provisions of this compact.

Article XIII

EXECUTION OF COMPACT

That this compact shall become operative immediately upon its execution by any state as between it and any other state or states so executing. When executed it shall have the full force and effect of law within such state, the form or execution to be in accordance with the laws of the executing state.

Article XIV

RENUNCIATION

That this compact shall continue in force and remain binding upon each executing state until renounced by it. Renunciation of this compact shall be by the same authority which executed it, by sending six months notice in writing of its intention to withdraw from the compact to the other states party hereto. The duties and obligations of a renouncing state under Article VII hereof shall continue as to parolees and probationers residing therein at the time of withdrawal until retaken or finally discharged. Supplementary agreements entered into under Article X hereof shall be subject to renunciation as provided by such supplementary agreements, and shall not be subject to the six months renunciation notice of the present article.

Article XV

SEVERABILITY

That the provisions of this compact shall be severable and if any phrase, clause, sentence, or provision of this compact is declared to be contrary to the constitution of any participating state or of the United States or the applicability thereof to any government, agency, person, or circumstance is held invalid, the validity of the remainder of this compact and the applicability thereof to any government, agency, person, or circumstances shall not be affected thereby. If this compact shall be held contrary to the constitution of any state participating therein, the compact shall remain in full force and effect as to the remaining states and in full force and effect as to the state affected as to all severable matters.

Added by Acts 1995, 74th Leg., ch. 262, § 53, eff. Jan. 1, 1996.

§ 60.003. Execution of Additional Article

The governor shall also execute on the behalf of the state with any other state or states legally joining in it, an additional article to the Interstate Compact on Juveniles in substantially the following form:

Article XVI

ADDITIONAL ARTICLE

That this article shall provide additional remedies, and shall be binding only as among and between those party states which specifically execute the same.

For the purposes of this article, "child," as used herein, means any minor within the jurisdictional age limits of any court in the home state.

When any child is brought before a court of a state of which such child is not a resident, and such state is willing to permit such child's return to the home state of such child, such home state, upon being so advised by the state in which such proceeding is pending, shall immediately institute proceedings to determine the residence and jurisdictional facts as to such child in such home state, and upon finding that such child is in fact a resident of said state and subject to the jurisdiction of the court thereof shall within five days authorize the return of such child to the home state, and to the parent or custodial agency legally authorized to accept such custody in such home state, and at the expense of such home state, to be paid from such funds as such home state may procure, designate, or provide, prompt action being of the essence.

Added by Acts 1995, 74th Leg., ch. 262, § 53, eff. Jan. 1, 1996.

§ 60.004. Execution of Amendment

The governor shall also execute on the behalf of the state with any other state or states legally joining in it, an amendment to the Interstate Compact on Juveniles in substantially the following form:

RENDITION AMENDMENT

(a) This amendment shall provide additional remedies, and shall be binding only as among and between those party states which specifically execute the same.

(b) All provisions and procedures of Articles V and VI of the Interstate Compact on Juveniles shall be construed to apply to any juvenile charged with being a delinquent by reason of a violation of any criminal law. Any juvenile charged with being a delinquent by reason of violating any criminal law shall be returned to the requesting state upon a requisition to the state where the juvenile may be found. A petition in such case shall be filed in a court of competent jurisdiction in the requesting state where the violation of criminal law is alleged to have been committed. The petition may be filed regardless of whether the juvenile has left the state before or after the filing of the petition. The requisition described in Article V of the compact shall be forwarded by the judge of the court in which the petition has been filed.

Added by Acts 1995, 74th Leg., ch. 262, § 53, eff. Jan. 1, 1996.

§ 60.005. Juvenile Compact Administrator

Under the compact, the governor may designate an officer as the compact administrator. The administrator, acting jointly with like officers of other party states, shall adopt regulations to carry out more effectively the terms of the compact. The compact administrator serves at the pleasure of the governor. The compact administrator shall cooperate with all departments, agencies, and officers of and in the government of this state and its subdivisions in facilitating the proper administration of the compact or of a supplementary agreement entered into by this state.

Added by Acts 1995, 74th Leg., ch. 262, § 53, eff. Jan. 1, 1996.

§ 60.006. Supplementary Agreements

A compact administrator may make supplementary agreements with appropriate officials of other states pursuant to the compact. If a supplementary agreement requires or contemplates the use of an institution or facility of this state or requires or contemplates the provision of a service of this state, the supplementary agreement has no force or effect until approved by the head of the department or agency under whose jurisdiction the institution is operated, or whose department or agency is charged with performing the service.

Added by Acts 1995, 74th Leg., ch. 262, § 53, eff. Jan. 1, 1996.

§ 60.007. Financial Arrangements

The compact administrator may make or arrange for the payments necessary to discharge the financial obligations imposed upon this state by the compact or by a supplementary agreement made under the compact, subject to legislative appropriations.

Added by Acts 1995, 74th Leg., ch. 262, § 53, eff. Jan. 1, 1996.

§ 60.008. Enforcement

The courts, departments, agencies, and officers of this state and its subdivisions shall enforce this compact and shall do all things appropriate to effectuate its purposes and intent which are within their respective jurisdictions.

Added by Acts 1995, 74th Leg., ch. 262, § 53, eff. Jan. 1, 1996.

§ 60.009. Additional Procedures Not Precluded

In addition to the procedures provided in Articles IV and VI of the compact for the return of a runaway juvenile, the particular states, the juvenile, or his parents, the courts, or other legal custodian involved may agree upon and adopt any plan or procedure legally authorized under the laws of this state and the other respective party states for the return of the runaway juvenile.

Added by Acts 1995, 74th Leg., ch. 262, § 53, eff. Jan. 1, 1996.

TITLE 4. PROTECTION OF THE FAMILY

CHAPTER 71. PROTECTIVE ORDERS

§§ 71.01 to 71.08. Repealed by Acts 1997, 75th Leg., ch. 34, § 2, eff. May 5, 1997

§ 71.09. Hearing

(a) Unless a later date is requested by the applicant, the court, on the filing of an application, shall set a date and time for the hearing on the application. Except as provided by Subsection (d) of this section, the date must not be later than 14 days after the date the application is filed. If a proceeding for which a legislative continuance is sought under Section 30.003, Civil Practice and Remedies Code, includes an application for a protective order authorized by this code, the continuance is discretionary with the court.

(b) to (e) Repealed by Acts 1997, 75th Leg., ch. 34, § 2, eff. May 5, 1997.

Added by Acts 1979, 66th Leg., p. 185, ch. 98, § 11, eff. Sept. 1, 1979. Amended by Acts 1989, 71st Leg., ch. 614, § 6, eff. Sept. 1, 1989; Acts 1989, 71st Leg., ch. 739, § 16, eff. Sept. 1, 1989; Acts 1991, 72nd Leg., ch. 542, § 5, eff. Sept. 1, 1991; Acts 1991, 72nd Leg., ch. 597, § 67, eff. Sept. 1, 1991; Acts 1995, 74th Leg., ch. 1024, § 9, eff. Sept. 1, 1995; Acts 1997, 75th Leg., ch. 752, § 4, eff. June 17, 1997.

Repeal

Without reference to the amendment of this section by Acts 1997, 75th Leg., ch. 752, § 4, Acts 1997, 75th Leg., ch. 34, § 2 repeals this section effective May 5, 1997.

§§ 71.10 to 71.19. Repealed by Acts 1997, 75th Leg., ch. 34, § 2, eff. May 5, 1997

CHAPTER 72. CONTRIBUTING TO DELINQUENCY OR DEPENDENCY OF A CHILD [REPEALED]

§§ 72.001 to 72.004. Repealed by Acts 1995, 74th Leg., ch. 1024, § 26, eff. Sept. 1, 1995

CHAPTER 73. REPORTING FAMILY VIOLENCE [REPEALED]

§§ 73.01 to 73.05. Repealed by Acts 1997, 75th Leg., ch. 34, § 2, eff. May 5, 1997

TITLE 4. PROTECTIVE ORDERS AND FAMILY VIOLENCE

Acts 1997, 75th Leg., ch. 34, § 1 reenacted Title 4.

DISPOSITION TABLE

Showing where provisions of former Title 4 of the Family Code are covered in Title 4 as reenacted by Acts 1997, 75th Leg., ch. 34

Former Section	New Section
71.01(a)	71.001
(b)(1)	71.002
(2)	71.004
(3)	71.003
(4)	71.005
(5)	71.006
71.02	82.001
71.03	82.003
71.04(a)	82.001
(b)	82.002
(c)	81.007
71.041(a)	81.006
(b)	81.002
(c)	81.004
(d)	81.006
71.05(a)	82.004
(b)	82.006
(c)	82.007
(d)	82.009
71.06(a)	82.005
(b)	85.008
(c)	85.009
(d)	82.005
(e)	82.043
(f)	85.004
71.07(a)	82.043
(b), (c)	82.042
(d), (e)	82.041
(f) to (h)	82.021
71.08	82.021
71.09(a)	84.001
(b)	84.004
(c)	84.003
(d)	84.002
(e)	85.006
71.10(a)	85.001
(b)	81.001, 85.001
(c)	85.002
(d)	85.005
71.11(a)(1) to (4)	85.021
(5)	85.022
(6)	85.021
(b), (c)	85.022
(d)	85.023
(e)	85.024
71.111	85.007
71.12	85.005
71.121(a)	82.022
(b)	84.001
(d)	85.001
(e), (f)	85.003
71.13	85.025
71.14(a)	83.001
(b), (c)	83.002
(d)	83.003
(e)	83.004
(f)	83.005
(g), (h)	83.006

Former Section	New Section
(i)	83.007
71.16	85.026
71.17(a) to (d)	85.041
(e) to (g)	85.042
71.18(a), (b)	86.001
(c)	86.002, 86.003
(d)	86.004
71.19	81.008
73.01	91.001
73.02	91.002
73.03	91.003
73.04	92.001
73.05	91.004

SUBTITLE A. GENERAL PROVISIONS

CHAPTER 71. DEFINITIONS

Section

§ 71.001. Applicability of Definitions

(a) Definitions in this chapter apply to this title.

(b) If, in another part of this title, a term defined by this chapter has a meaning different from the meaning provided by this chapter, the meaning of that other provision prevails.

(c) Except as provided by this chapter, the definitions in Chapter 101 apply to terms used in this title.

Added by Acts 1997, 75th Leg., ch. 34, § 1, eff. May 5, 1997.

Section 3 of Acts 1997, 75th Leg., ch. 34 provides:

"The change in law made by this Act does not affect a proceeding under the Family Code pending on the effective date of this Act. A proceeding pending on the effective date of this Act is governed by the law in effect at the time the proceeding was commenced, and the former law is continued in effect for that purpose."

§ 71.002. Court

"Court" means the district court, court of domestic relations, juvenile court having the jurisdiction of a district court, statutory county court, constitutional county court, or other court expressly given jurisdiction under this title.

Added by Acts 1997, 75th Leg., ch. 34, § 1, eff. May 5, 1997. Amended by Acts 1997, 75th Leg., ch. 1220, § 1, eff. Sept. 1, 1997.

Section 2 of Acts 1997, 75th Leg., ch. 1220 provides:

"(a) Except as provided by Subsection (b) of this section, this Act takes effect on September 1, 1997, and applies only to an application for a protective order made on or after that date.

"(b) This Act takes effect only if the 75th Legislature, at its regular session, enacts H.B. 1441 or S.B. 797 and either bill becomes law. If the legislation does not become law, this Act has no effect."

Senate Bill 797 was enacted as Acts 1997, 75th Leg., ch. 34.

§ 71.003. Family

"Family" includes individuals related by consanguinity or affinity, as determined under Sections 573.022 and 573.024, Government Code, individuals who are former spouses of each other, individuals who are the biological parents of the same child, without regard to marriage, and a foster child and foster parent, without regard to whether those individuals reside together.

Added by Acts 1997, 75th Leg., ch. 34, § 1, eff. May 5, 1997.

§ 71.004. Family Violence

"Family violence" means:

(1) an act by a member of a family or household against another member of the family or household that is intended to result in physical harm, bodily injury, assault, or sexual assault or that is a threat that reasonably places the member in fear of imminent physical harm, bodily injury, assault, or sexual assault, but does not include defensive measures to protect oneself; or

(2) abuse, as that term is defined by Sections 261.001(1)(C), (E), and (G) by a member of a family or household toward a child of the family or household.

Added by Acts 1997, 75th Leg., ch. 34, § 1, eff. May 5, 1997.

§ 71.005. Household

"Household" means a unit composed of persons living together in the same dwelling, without regard to whether they are related to each other.

Added by Acts 1997, 75th Leg., ch. 34, § 1, eff. May 5, 1997.

§ 71.006. Member of a Household

"Member of a household" includes a person who previously lived in a household.

Added by Acts 1997, 75th Leg., ch. 34, § 1, eff. May 5, 1997.

§ 71.007. Prosecuting Attorney

"Prosecuting attorney" means the attorney, determined as provided in this title, who represents the state in a district or statutory county court in the county in which venue of the application for a protective order is proper.

Added by Acts 1997, 75th Leg., ch. 34, § 1, eff. May 5, 1997.

§ 71.008. Protective Order From Another Jurisdiction

"Protective order from another jurisdiction" means a protective order rendered by a military court or a court of another state, tribe, or territory related to protecting an individual from domestic or family violence and that meets the following requirements:

(1) the order is rendered by a court that has jurisdiction over the parties and the matter under the law of the military, state, tribe, or territory; and

(2) the respondent is given notice and an opportunity to be heard consistent with due process either:

(A) before the date the order was rendered; or

(B) in the case of an ex parte order, within the time required by the jurisdiction rendering the order after the date the order is rendered, but not later than a reasonable time.

Added by Acts 1997, 75th Leg., ch. 1193, § 2, eff. Sept. 1, 1997.

Section 25(b), (c) of Acts 1997, 75th Leg., ch. 1193 provides:

"(b) The changes in law made by Sections 3 through 6 and Section 13 of this Act apply to a pending application for a protective order regardless of whether the application is filed before, on, or after the effective date of this Act.

"(c) Except as provided by Subsection (b) of this section, the change in law made by this Act applies only to an application for a protective order made on or after the effective date of this Act. An application for a protective order made before the effective date of this Act is governed by the law in effect on the date the application was made, and the former law is continued in effect for that purpose."

SUBTITLE B. PROTECTIVE ORDERS

CHAPTER 81. GENERAL PROVISIONS

§ 81.001. Entitlement to Protective Order

A court shall render a protective order as provided by Section 85.001(b) if the court finds that family violence has occurred and is likely to occur in the future.

Added by Acts 1997, 75th Leg., ch. 34, § 1, eff. May 5, 1997.

§ 81.002. No Fee for Applicant

An applicant for a protective order or an attorney representing an applicant may not be assessed a fee, cost, charge, or expense by a district or county clerk of the court or a sheriff, constable, or other public official or employee in connection with the filing, serving, or entering of a protective order or for any other service described by this subsection, including:

(1) a fee to dismiss, modify, or withdraw a protective order;

(2) a fee for certifying copies;

(3) a fee for comparing copies to originals;

(4) a court reporter fee;

(5) a judicial fund fee;

(6) a fee for any other service related to a protective order; or

(7) a fee to transfer a protective order.

Added by Acts 1997, 75th Leg., ch. 34, § 1, eff. May 5, 1997. Amended by Acts 1997, 75th Leg., ch. 1193, § 3, eff. Sept. 1, 1997.

Section 25(b), (c) of Acts 1997, 75th Leg., ch. 1193 provides:

"(b) The changes in law made by Sections 3 through 6 and Section 13 of this Act apply to a pending application for a protective order regardless of whether the application is filed before, on, or after the effective date of this Act.

"(c) Except as provided by Subsection (b) of this section, the change in law made by this Act applies only to an application for a protective order made on or after the effective date of this Act. An application for a protective order made before the effective date of this Act is governed by the law in effect on the date the application was made, and the former law is continued in effect for that purpose."

§ 81.003. Fees and Costs Paid by Party Found to Have Committed Family Violence

(a) Except on a showing of good cause or of the indigence of a party found to have committed family violence, the court shall require in a protective order that the party against whom the order is rendered pay the $16 protective order fee, the standard fees charged by the clerk of the court in a general civil proceeding for the cost of serving the order, the costs of court, and all other fees, charges, or expenses incurred in connection with the protective order.

(b) The court may order a party against whom an agreed protective order is rendered under Section 85.005 to pay the fees required in Subsection (a).

Added by Acts 1997, 75th Leg., ch. 34, § 1, eff. May 5, 1997. Amended by Acts 1997, 75th Leg., ch. 1193, § 4, eff. Sept. 1, 1997.

For application provisions of Acts 1997, 75th Leg., ch. 1193, see notes following V.T.C.A., Family Code § 81.002.

§ 81.004. Contempt for Nonpayment of Fee

(a) A party who is ordered to pay fees and costs and who does not pay before the date specified by the order may be punished for contempt of court as provided by Section 21.002, Government Code.

(b) If a date is not specified by the court under Subsection (a), payment of costs is required before the 60th day after the date the order was rendered.

Added by Acts 1997, 75th Leg., ch. 34, § 1, eff. May 5, 1997. Amended by Acts 1997, 75th Leg., ch. 1193, § 5, eff. Sept. 1, 1997.

For application provisions of Acts 1997, 75th Leg., ch. 1193, see notes following V.T.C.A., Family Code § 81.002.

§ 81.005. Attorney's Fees

(a) The court may assess reasonable attorney's fees against the party found to have committed family violence or a party against whom an agreed protective order is rendered under Section 85.005 as compensation for the services of a private or prosecuting attorney or an attorney employed by the Department of Protective and Regulatory Services.

(b) In setting the amount of attorney's fees, the court shall consider the income and ability to pay of the person against whom the fee is assessed.

Added by Acts 1997, 75th Leg., ch. 34, § 1, eff. May 5, 1997. Amended by Acts 1997, 75th Leg., ch. 1193, § 6, eff. Sept. 1, 1997.

For application provisions of Acts 1997, 75th Leg., ch. 1193, see notes following V.T.C.A., Family Code § 81.002.

§ 81.006. Payment of Attorney's Fees

The amount of fees collected under this chapter as compensation for the fees:

(1) of a private attorney shall be paid to the private attorney who may enforce the order for fees in the attorney's own name;

(2) of a prosecuting attorney shall be paid to the credit of the county fund from which the salaries of the employees of the prosecuting attorney are paid or supplemented; and

(3) of an attorney employed by the Department of Protective and Regulatory Services shall be deposited in the general revenue fund to the credit of the Department of Protective and Regulatory Services.

Added by Acts 1997, 75th Leg., ch. 34, § 1, eff. May 5, 1997.

§ 81.007. Prosecuting Attorney

(a) The county attorney or the criminal district attorney is the prosecuting attorney responsible for filing applications under this subtitle unless the district attorney assumes the responsibility by giving notice of that assumption to the county attorney.

(b) The prosecuting attorney responsible for filing an application under this subtitle shall provide notice of that responsibility to all law enforcement agencies in the jurisdiction of the prosecuting attorney.

(c) The prosecuting attorney shall comply with Article 5.06, Code of Criminal Procedure, in filing an application under this subtitle.

Added by Acts 1997, 75th Leg., ch. 34, § 1, eff. May 5, 1997.

§ 81.0075. Representation by Prosecuting Attorney in Certain Subsequent Actions

A prosecuting attorney who represents a party in a proceeding under this subtitle is not precluded from representing the Department of Protective and Regulatory Services in a subsequent action involving the party.

Added by Acts 1997, 75th Leg., ch. 1193, § 7, eff. Sept. 1, 1997.

§ 81.008. Relief Cumulative

Except as provided by this subtitle, the relief and remedies provided by this subtitle are cumulative of other relief and remedies provided by law.

Added by Acts 1997, 75th Leg., ch. 34, § 1, eff. May 5, 1997.

CHAPTER 82. APPLYING FOR PROTECTIVE ORDER

SUBCHAPTER A. APPLICATION FOR PROTECTIVE ORDER

SUBCHAPTER B. PLEADINGS BY RESPONDENT

SUBCHAPTER C. NOTICE OF APPLICATION FOR PROTECTIVE ORDER

SUBCHAPTER A. APPLICATION FOR PROTECTIVE ORDER

§ 82.001. Application

A proceeding under this subtitle is begun by filing "An Application for a Protective Order" with the clerk of the court.

Added by Acts 1997, 75th Leg., ch. 34, § 1, eff. May 5, 1997.

§ 82.002. Who May File Application

(a) An application for a protective order to protect the applicant or any other member of the applicant's family or household may be filed by:

(1) an adult member of the family or household; or

(2) any adult for the protection of a child.

(b) In addition, an application may be filed for the protection of any person alleged to be a victim of family violence by:

(1) a prosecuting attorney; or

(2) the Department of Protective and Regulatory Services.

(c) The person alleged to be the victim of family violence in an application filed under Subsection (b) is considered to be the applicant for a protective order under this subtitle.

Added by Acts 1997, 75th Leg., ch. 34, § 1, eff. May 5, 1997. Amended by Acts 1997, 75th Leg., ch. 1193, § 8, eff. Sept. 1, 1997.

§ 82.003. Venue

An application may be filed in:

(1) the county in which the applicant resides; or

(2) the county in which the respondent resides.

Added by Acts 1997, 75th Leg., ch. 34, § 1, eff. May 5, 1997.

§ 82.004. Contents of Application

An application must state:

(1) the name and county of residence of each applicant;

(2) the name, address, and county of residence of each individual alleged to have committed family violence;

(3) the relationships between the applicants and the individual alleged to have committed family violence; and

(4) a request for one or more protective orders.

Added by Acts 1997, 75th Leg., ch. 34, § 1, eff. May 5, 1997.

§ 82.005. Application Filed During Suit for Dissolution of Marriage or Suit Affecting Parent-Child Relationship

A person who wishes to apply for a protective order with respect to the person's spouse and who is a party to a suit for the dissolution of a marriage or a suit affecting the parent-child relationship that is pending in a court must file the application as required by Subchapter D, Chapter 85.

Added by Acts 1997, 75th Leg., ch. 34, § 1, eff. May 5, 1997. Amended by Acts 1997, 75th Leg., ch. 1193, § 9, eff. Sept. 1, 1997.

For application provisions of Acts 1997, 75th Leg., ch. 1193, see notes following V.T.C.A., Family Code § 81.002.

§ 82.006. Application Filed After Dissolution of Marriage

If an applicant for a protective order is a former spouse of the individual alleged to have committed family violence, the application must include:

(1) a copy of the decree dissolving the marriage; or

(2) a statement that the decree is unavailable to the applicant and that a copy of the decree will be filed with the court before the hearing on the application.

Added by Acts 1997, 75th Leg., ch. 34, § 1, eff. May 5, 1997.

§ 82.007. Application Filed for Child Subject to Continuing Jurisdiction

An application that requests a protective order for a child who is subject to the continuing exclusive jurisdiction of a court under Title 5 or alleges that a child who is subject to the continuing exclusive jurisdiction of a court under Title 5 has committed family violence must include:

(1) a copy of each court order affecting the conservatorship, support, and possession of or access to the child; or

(2) a statement that the orders affecting the child are unavailable to the applicant and that a copy of the orders will be filed with the court before the hearing on the application.

Added by Acts 1997, 75th Leg., ch. 34, § 1, eff. May 5, 1997.

§ 82.008. Application Filed After Expiration of Former Protective Order

(a) If an application for a protective order alleges that the respondent has violated a previously rendered protective order by committing an act prohibited by the order and that the protective order has expired after the date that the violation occurred, the application for the new protective order must include:

(1) a copy of the expired protective order attached to the application or, if a copy of the expired protective order is unavailable, a statement that the order is unavailable to the applicant and that a copy of the order will be filed with the court before the hearing on the application;

(2) a description of the violation of the expired protective order; and

(3) a statement that the violation of the expired order has not been grounds for any other order protecting the applicant that has been issued or requested under this subtitle.

(b) The procedural requirements for an original application for a protective order apply to a protective order requested under this section.

Added by Acts 1997, 75th Leg., ch. 34, § 1, eff. May 5, 1997.

§ 82.009. Application for Temporary ex Parte Order

An application that requests the issuance of a temporary ex parte order under Chapter 83 must:

(1) contain a detailed description of the facts and circumstances concerning the alleged family violence and the need for the immediate protective order; and

(2) be signed by each applicant under an oath that the facts and circumstances contained in the application are true to the best knowledge and belief of each applicant.

Added by Acts 1997, 75th Leg., ch. 34, § 1, eff. May 5, 1997.

[Sections 82.010 to 82.020 reserved for expansion]

SUBCHAPTER B. PLEADINGS BY RESPONDENT

§ 82.021. Answer

A respondent to an application for a protective order who is served with notice of an application for a protective order may file an answer at any time before the hearing. A respondent is not required to file an answer to the application.

Added by Acts 1997, 75th Leg., ch. 34, § 1, eff. May 5, 1997.

§ 82.022. Request by Respondent for Protective Order

To apply for a protective order, a respondent to an application for a protective order must file a separate application.

Added by Acts 1997, 75th Leg., ch. 34, § 1, eff. May 5, 1997.

[Sections 82.023 to 82.040 reserved for expansion]

SUBCHAPTER C. NOTICE OF APPLICATION FOR PROTECTIVE ORDER

§ 82.041. Contents of Notice of Application

(a) A notice of an application for a protective order must:

(1) be styled "The State of Texas";

(2) be signed by the clerk of the court under the court's seal;

(3) contain the name and location of the court;

(4) show the date the application was filed;

(5) show the date notice of the application for a protective order was issued;

(6) show the date, time, and place of the hearing;

(7) show the file number;

(8) show the name of each applicant and each person alleged to have committed family violence;

(9) be directed to each person alleged to have committed family violence;

(10) show the name and address of the attorney for the applicant or the mailing address of the applicant, if the applicant is not represented by an attorney; and

(11) contain the address of the clerk of the court.

(b) The notice of an application for a protective order must state: "An application for a protective order has been filed in the court stated in this notice alleging that you have committed family violence. You may employ an attorney to defend you against this allegation. You or your attorney may, but are not required to, file a written answer to the application. Any answer must be filed before the hearing on the application. If you receive this notice within 48 hours before the time set for the hearing, you may request the court to reschedule the hearing not later than 14 days after the date set for the hearing. If you do not attend the hearing, a default judgment may be taken and a protective order may be issued against you."

Added by Acts 1997, 75th Leg., ch. 34, § 1, eff. May 5, 1997. Amended by Acts 1997, 75th Leg., ch. 1193, § 10, eff. Sept. 1, 1997.

§ 82.042. Issuance of Notice of Application

(a) On the filing of an application, the clerk of the court shall issue a notice of an application for a protective order and deliver the notice as directed by the applicant.

(b) On request by the applicant, the clerk of the court shall issue a separate or additional notice of an application for a protective order.

Added by Acts 1997, 75th Leg., ch. 34, § 1, eff. May 5, 1997.

§ 82.043. Service of Notice of Application

(a) Each respondent to an application for a protective order is entitled to service of notice of an application for a protective order.

(b) An applicant for a protective order shall furnish the clerk with a sufficient number of copies of the application for service on each respondent.

(c) Notice of an application for a protective order must be served in the same manner as citation under the Texas Rules of Civil Procedure, except that service by publication is not authorized.

(d) Service of notice of an application for a protective order is not required before the issuance of a temporary ex parte order under Chapter 83.

(e) The requirements of service of notice under this subchapter do not apply if the application is filed as a motion in a suit for dissolution of a marriage. Notice for the motion is given in the same manner as any other motion in a suit for dissolution of a marriage.

Added by Acts 1997, 75th Leg., ch. 34, § 1, eff. May 5, 1997.

CHAPTER 83. TEMPORARY EX PARTE ORDERS

Section

§ 83.001. Requirements for Temporary ex Parte Order

(a) If the court finds from the information contained in an application for a protective order that there is a clear and present danger of family violence, the court, without further notice to any other member of the family or household and without a hearing, may enter a temporary ex parte order for the protection of the applicant or any other member of the family or household of the applicant.

(b) In a temporary ex parte order, the court may direct a respondent to do or refrain from doing specified acts.

Added by Acts 1997, 75th Leg., ch. 34, § 1, eff. May 5, 1997.

§ 83.002. Duration of Order; Extension

(a) A temporary ex parte order is valid for the period specified in the order, not to exceed 20 days.

(b) On the request of an applicant or on the court's own motion, a temporary ex parte order may be extended for additional 20-day periods.

Added by Acts 1997, 75th Leg., ch. 34, § 1, eff. May 5, 1997.

§ 83.003. Bond Not Required

The court, at the court's discretion, may dispense with the necessity of a bond for a temporary ex parte order.

Added by Acts 1997, 75th Leg., ch. 34, § 1, eff. May 5, 1997.

§ 83.004. Motion to Vacate

Any member of the family or household affected by a temporary ex parte order may file a motion at any time to vacate the order. On the filing of the motion to vacate, the court shall set a date for hearing the motion as soon as possible.

Added by Acts 1997, 75th Leg., ch. 34, § 1, eff. May 5, 1997.

§ 83.005. Conflicting Orders

During the time the order is valid, a temporary ex parte order prevails over any other court order made under Title 5 to the extent of any conflict between the orders.

Added by Acts 1997, 75th Leg., ch. 34, § 1, eff. May 5, 1997. Amended by Acts 1997, 75th Leg., ch. 1193, § 11, eff. Sept. 1, 1997.

§ 83.006. Exclusion of Party From Residence

(a) Subject to the limitations of Section 85.021(2), a person may only be excluded from the occupancy of the person's residence by a temporary ex parte order under this chapter if the applicant:

(1) files a sworn affidavit that provides a detailed description of the facts and circumstances requiring the exclusion of the person from the residence; and

(2) appears in person to testify at a temporary ex parte hearing to justify the issuance of the order without notice.

(b) Before the court may render a temporary ex parte order excluding a person from the person's residence, the court must find from the required affidavit and testimony that:

(1) the applicant requesting the excluding order either resides on the premises or has resided there within 30 days before the date the application was filed;

(2) the person to be excluded has within the 30 days before the date the application was filed committed family violence against a member of the household; and

(3) there is a clear and present danger that the person to be excluded is likely to commit family violence against a member of the household.

Added by Acts 1997, 75th Leg., ch. 34, § 1, eff. May 5, 1997.

§ 83.007. Recess of Hearing to Contact Respondent

The court may recess the hearing on a temporary ex parte order to contact the respondent by telephone and provide the respondent the opportunity to be present when the court resumes the hearing. Without regard to whether the respondent is able to be present at the hearing, the court shall resume the hearing before the end of the working day.

Added by Acts 1997, 75th Leg., ch. 34, § 1, eff. May 5, 1997.

CHAPTER 84. HEARING

Section

§ 84.001. Time Set for Hearing

(a) On the filing of an application for a protective order, the court shall set a date and time for the hearing unless a later date is requested by the applicant. Except as provided by Section 84.002, the court may not set a date later than the 14th day after the date the application is filed.

(b) The court may not delay a hearing on an application in order to consolidate it with a hearing on a subsequently filed application.

Added by Acts 1997, 75th Leg., ch. 34, § 1, eff. May 5, 1997.

§ 84.002. Extended Time for Hearing in District Court In Certain Counties

(a) On the request of the prosecuting attorney in a county with a population of more than 1.5 million or in a county in a judicial district that is composed of more than one county, the district court shall set the hearing on a date and time not later than 20 days after the date the application is filed or 20 days after the date a request is made to reschedule a hearing under Section 84.003.

(b) The district court shall grant the request of the prosecuting attorney for an extended time in which to hold a hearing on a protective order either on a case-by-case basis or for all cases filed under this subtitle.

Added by Acts 1997, 75th Leg., ch. 34, § 1, eff. May 5, 1997. Amended by Acts 1997, 75th Leg., ch. 1193, § 12, eff. Sept. 1, 1997.

§ 84.003. Hearing Rescheduled for Failure of Service

(a) If a hearing set under this chapter is not held because of the failure of a respondent to receive service of notice of an application for a protective order, the applicant may request the court to reschedule the hearing.

(b) Except as provided by Section 84.002, the date for a rescheduled hearing shall be not later than 14 days after the date the request is made.

Added by Acts 1997, 75th Leg., ch. 34, § 1, eff. May 5, 1997.

§ 84.004. Hearing Rescheduled for Insufficient Notice

(a) If a respondent receives service of notice of an application for a protective order within 48 hours before the time set for the hearing, on request by the respondent, the court shall reschedule the hearing for a date not later than 14 days after the date set for the hearing.

(b) The respondent is not entitled to additional service for a hearing rescheduled under this section.

Added by Acts 1997, 75th Leg., ch. 34, § 1, eff. May 5, 1997.

CHAPTER 85. ISSUANCE OF PROTECTIVE ORDER

SUBCHAPTER A. FINDINGS AND ORDERS

Section

SUBCHAPTER A. FINDINGS AND ORDERS

§ 85.001. Required Findings and Orders

(a) At the close of a hearing on an application for a protective order, the court shall find whether:

(1) family violence has occurred; and

(2) family violence is likely to occur in the future.

(b) If the court finds that family violence has occurred and that family violence is likely to occur in the future, the court:

(1) shall render a protective order as provided by Section 85.022 applying only to a person found to have committed family violence; and

(2) may render a protective order as provided by Section 85.021 applying to both parties that is in the best interest of the family or household or member of the family or household.

(c) A protective order that requires the first applicant to do or refrain from doing an act under Section 85.022 shall include a finding that the first applicant has committed family violence and is likely to commit family violence in the future.

Added by Acts 1997, 75th Leg., ch. 34, § 1, eff. May 5, 1997.

§ 85.002. Exception for Violation of Expired Protective Order

If the court finds that a respondent violated a protective order by committing an act prohibited by the order as provided by Section 85.022, that the order was in effect at the time of the violation, and that the order has expired after the date that the violation occurred, the court, without the necessity of making the findings described by Section 85.001(a), shall render a protective order as provided by Section 85.022 applying only to the respondent and may render a protective order as provided by Section 85.021.

Added by Acts 1997, 75th Leg., ch. 34, § 1, eff. May 5, 1997. Amended by Acts 1997, 75th Leg., ch. 1193, § 13, eff. Sept. 1, 1997.

Section 25(b), (c) of Acts 1997, 75th Leg., ch. 1193 provides:

"(b) The changes in law made by Sections 3 through 6 and Section 13 of this Act apply to a pending application for a protective order regardless of whether the application is filed before, on, or after the effective date of this Act.

"(c) Except as provided by Subsection (b) of this section, the change in law made by this Act applies only to an application for a protective order made on or after the effective date of this Act. An application for a protective order made before the effective date of this Act is governed by the law in effect on the date the application was made, and the former law is continued in effect for that purpose."

§ 85.003. Separate Protective Orders Required

(a) A court that renders separate protective orders that apply to both parties and require both parties to do or refrain from doing acts under Section 85.022 shall render two distinct and separate protective orders in two separate documents that reflect the appropriate conditions for each party.

(b) A court that renders protective orders that apply to both parties and require both parties to do or refrain from doing acts under Section 85.022 shall render the protective orders in two separate documents. The court shall provide one of the documents to the applicant and the other document to the respondent.

(c) A court may not render one protective order under Section 85.022 that applies to both parties.

Added by Acts 1997, 75th Leg., ch. 34, § 1, eff. May 5, 1997.

§ 85.004. Protective Order in Suit for Dissolution of Marriage

A protective order in a suit for dissolution of a marriage must be in a separate document entitled "PROTECTIVE ORDER."

Added by Acts 1997, 75th Leg., ch. 34, § 1, eff. May 5, 1997.

§ 85.005. Agreed Order

(a) To facilitate settlement, the parties to a proceeding may agree in writing to the terms of a protective order as provided by Section 85.021. An agreement under this subsection is subject to the approval of the court.

(b) To facilitate settlement, a respondent may agree in writing to the terms of a protective order as provided by Section 85.022, subject to the approval of the court. The court may not approve an agreement that requires the applicant to do or refrain from doing an act under Section 85.022.

(c) If the court approves an agreement between the parties, the court shall render an agreed protective order that is in the best interest of the applicant, the family or household, or a member of the family or household.

(d) An agreed protective order is not enforceable as a contract.

(e) An agreed protective order expires on the date the court order expires.

Added by Acts 1997, 75th Leg., ch. 34, § 1, eff. May 5, 1997.

§ 85.006. Default Order

(a) A court may render a protective order that is binding on a respondent who does not attend a hearing if the respondent received service of the application and notice of the hearing.

(b) If the court reschedules the hearing under Chapter 84, a protective order may be rendered if the respondent does not attend the rescheduled hearing.

Added by Acts 1997, 75th Leg., ch. 34, § 1, eff. May 5, 1997.

§ 85.007. Confidentiality of Certain Information

(a) On request by a member of a family or household, the court may exclude from a protective order the address and telephone number of:

(1) a person protected by the order, in which case the order shall state the county in which the person resides;

(2) the place of employment or business of a person protected by the order; or

(3) the child-care facility or school a child protected by the order attends or in which the child resides.

(b) On granting a request for confidentiality under this section, the court shall order the clerk to:

(1) strike the information described by Subsection (a) from the public records of the court; and

(2) maintain a confidential record of the information for use only by the court.

Added by Acts 1997, 75th Leg., ch. 34, § 1, eff. May 5, 1997.

§ 85.008. Repealed by Acts 1997, 75th Leg., ch. 1193, § 24, eff. Sept. 1, 1997

§ 85.009. Order Valid Until Superseded

A protective order rendered under this chapter is valid and enforceable pending further action by the court that rendered the order until the order is properly superseded by another court with jurisdiction over the order.

Added by Acts 1997, 75th Leg., ch. 34, § 1, eff. May 5, 1997.

[Sections 85.010 to 85.020 reserved for expansion]

SUBCHAPTER B. CONTENTS OF PROTECTIVE ORDER

§ 85.021. Requirements of Order Applying to Any Party

In a protective order, the court may:

(1) prohibit a party from:

(A) removing a child who is a member of the family or household from:

(i) the possession of a person named in the order; or

(ii) the jurisdiction of the court; or

(B) transferring, encumbering, or otherwise disposing of property, other than in the ordinary course of business, that is mutually owned or leased by the parties;

(2) grant exclusive possession of a residence to a party and, if appropriate, direct one or more parties to vacate the residence if the residence:

(A) is jointly owned or leased by the party receiving exclusive possession and a party being denied possession;

(B) is owned or leased by the party retaining possession; or

(C) is owned or leased by the party being denied possession and that party has an obligation to support the party or a child of the party granted possession of the residence;

(3) provide for the possession of and access to a child of a party if the person receiving possession of or access to the child is a parent of the child;

(4) require the payment of support for a party or for a child of a party if the person required to make the payment has an obligation to support the other party or the child; or

(5) award to a party the use and possession of specified property that is community property or jointly owned or leased property.

Added by Acts 1997, 75th Leg., ch. 34, § 1, eff. May 5, 1997.

§ 85.022. Requirements of Order Applying to Person Who Committed Family Violence

(a) In a protective order, the court may order the person found to have committed family violence to:

(1) complete a battering intervention and prevention program as provided by Article 42.141, Code of Criminal Procedure, and that meets the guidelines adopted by the community justice assistance division of the Texas Department of Criminal Justice if a program is available;

(2) counsel with a social worker, family service agency, physician, psychologist, licensed therapist, or licensed professional counselor if a program under Subdivision (1) is not available; or

(3) perform acts specified by the court that the court determines are necessary or appropriate to prevent or reduce the likelihood of family violence.

(b) In a protective order, the court may prohibit the person found to have committed family violence from:

(1) committing family violence;

(2) communicating:

(A) directly with a member of the family or household in a threatening or harassing manner;

(B) a threat through any person to a member of the family or household; and

(C) if the court finds good cause, in any manner with a member of the family or household except through the party's attorney or a person appointed by the court;

(3) going to or near the residence or place of employment or business of a member of the family or household;

(4) going to or near the residence, child-care facility, or school a child protected under the order normally attends or in which the child normally resides; and

(5) engaging in conduct directed specifically toward a person who is a member of the family or household, including following the person, that is reasonably likely to harass, annoy, alarm, abuse, torment, or embarrass the person.

(c) In an order under Subsection (b)(3) or (4), the court shall specifically describe each prohibited location and the minimum distances from the location, if any, that the party must maintain. This subsection does not apply to an order in which Section 85.007 applies.

Added by Acts 1997, 75th Leg., ch. 34, § 1, eff. May 5, 1997. Amended by Acts 1997, 75th Leg., ch. 1193, § 14, eff. Sept. 1, 1997.

§ 85.023. Effect on Property Rights

A protective order or an agreement approved by the court under this subtitle does not affect the title to real property.

Added by Acts 1997, 75th Leg., ch. 34, § 1, eff. May 5, 1997.

§ 85.024. Enforcement of Counseling Requirement

(a) A person found to have engaged in family violence who is ordered to attend a program or counseling under Section 85.022(a)(1) or (2) shall file with the court an affidavit before the 60th day after the date the order was rendered stating either that the person has begun the program or counseling or that a program or counseling is not available within a reasonable distance from the person's residence. A person who files an affidavit that the person has begun the program or counseling shall file with the court before the date the protective order expires a statement that the person completed the program or counseling not later than the 30th day before the expiration date of the protective order. An affidavit under this subsection must be accompanied by a letter, notice, or certificate from the program or counselor that verifies the person's completion of the program or counseling. A person who fails to comply with this subsection may be punished for contempt of court under Section 21.002, Government Code.

(b) A protective order under Section 85.022 must specifically advise the person subject to the order of the requirement of this section and the possible punishment if the person fails to comply with the requirement.

Added by Acts 1997, 75th Leg., ch. 34, § 1, eff. May 5, 1997. Amended by Acts 1997, 75th Leg., ch. 1193, § 15, eff. Sept. 1, 1997.

§ 85.025. Duration of Protective Order

An order under this subtitle is effective for the period stated in the order, not to exceed one year. An order that does not specify the period for which the order is effective expires on the first anniversary of the date the order was issued.

Added by Acts 1997, 75th Leg., ch. 34, § 1, eff. May 5, 1997.

§ 85.026. Warning on Protective Order

(a) Each protective order issued under this subtitle, including a temporary ex parte order, must contain the following printed statement in bold-faced type or capital letters:

"A PERSON WHO VIOLATES THIS ORDER MAY BE PUNISHED FOR CONTEMPT OF

COURT BY A FINE OF AS MUCH AS $500 OR BY CONFINEMENT IN JAIL FOR AS LONG AS SIX MONTHS, OR BOTH."

(b) Each protective order issued under this subtitle, except for a temporary ex parte order, must contain the following printed statement in bold-faced type or capital letters:

"A VIOLATION OF THIS ORDER BY COMMISSION OF AN ACT PROHIBITED BY THE ORDER MAY BE PUNISHABLE BY A FINE OF AS MUCH AS $4,000 OR BY CONFINEMENT IN JAIL FOR AS LONG AS ONE YEAR, OR BOTH. AN ACT THAT RESULTS IN FAMILY VIOLENCE MAY BE PROSECUTED AS A SEPARATE MISDEMEANOR OR FELONY OFFENSE. IF THE ACT IS PROSECUTED AS A SEPARATE FELONY OFFENSE, IT IS PUNISHABLE BY CONFINEMENT IN PRISON FOR AT LEAST TWO YEARS."

(c) Each protective order issued under this subtitle, including a temporary ex parte order, must contain the following printed statement in bold-faced type or capital letters:

"NO PERSON, INCLUDING A PERSON WHO IS PROTECTED BY THIS ORDER, MAY GIVE PERMISSION TO ANYONE TO IGNORE OR VIOLATE ANY PROVISION OF THIS ORDER. DURING THE TIME IN WHICH THIS ORDER IS VALID, EVERY PROVISION OF THIS ORDER IS IN FULL FORCE AND EFFECT UNLESS A COURT CHANGES THE ORDER."

Added by Acts 1997, 75th Leg., ch. 34, § 1, eff. May 5, 1997.

[Sections 85.027 to 85.040 reserved for expansion]

SUBCHAPTER C. DELIVERY OF PROTECTIVE ORDER

§ 85.041. Delivery to Respondent

(a) A protective order rendered under this subtitle shall be:

(1) delivered to the respondent as provided by Rule 21a, Texas Rules of Civil Procedure;

(2) served in the same manner as a writ of injunction; or

(3) served in open court at the close of the hearing as provided by this section.

(b) The court shall serve an order in open court to a respondent who is present at the hearing by giving to the respondent a copy of the order, reduced to writing and signed by the judge or master. A certified copy of the signed order shall be given to the applicant at the time the order is given to the respondent. If the applicant is not in court at the conclusion of the hearing, the clerk of the court shall mail a certified copy of the order to the applicant not later than the third business day after the date the hearing is concluded.

(c) If the order has not been reduced to writing, the court shall give notice orally to a respondent who is present at the hearing of the part of the order that contains prohibitions under Section 85.022 or any other part of the order that contains provisions necessary to prevent further family violence. The clerk of the court shall mail a copy of the order to the respondent and a certified copy of the order to the applicant not later than the third business day after the date the hearing is concluded.

(d) If the respondent is not present at the hearing and the order has been reduced to writing at the conclusion of the hearing, the clerk of the court shall immediately provide a certified copy of the order to the applicant and mail a copy of the order to the respondent not later than the third business day after the date the hearing is concluded.

Added by Acts 1997, 75th Leg., ch. 34, § 1, eff. May 5, 1997.

§ 85.042. Delivery of Order to Other Persons

(a) The clerk of the court issuing an original or modified protective order under this subtitle shall send a copy of the order, along with the information provided by the applicant or the applicant's attorney that is required under Section 411.042(b)(5), Government Code, to the chief of police of the municipality in which the member of the family or household protected by the order resides, if the person resides in a municipality, or to the appropriate constable and the sheriff of the county in which the person resides, if the person does not reside in a municipality. The chief of police or constable and sheriff shall enter the information into the statewide law enforcement information system.

(b) If a protective order made under this chapter prohibits a respondent from going to or near a child-care facility or school, the clerk of the court shall send a copy of the order to the child-care facility or school.

(c) The clerk of a court that vacates an original or modified protective order under this subtitle shall notify the chief of police or constable and sheriff who received a copy of the original or modified order that the order is vacated.

(d) The applicant or the applicant's attorney shall provide to the clerk of the court:

(1) the name and address of each law enforcement agency, child-care facility, and school to which the clerk is required to mail a copy of the order under this section; and

(2) any other information required under Section 411.042(b)(5), Government Code.

Added by Acts 1997, 75th Leg., ch. 34, § 1, eff. May 5, 1997. Amended by Acts 1997, 75th Leg., ch. 614, § 3, eff. Sept. 1, 1997.

Section 4(b) of Acts 1997, 75th Leg., ch. 614 provides:

"Section 3 of this Act takes effect only if the 75th Legislature, at its regular session, enacts S.B. No. 797 and that bill becomes law. If that legislation does not become law, Section 3 of this Act has no effect."

S.B. 797 was enacted as Acts 1997, 75th Leg., ch. 34.

SUBCHAPTER D. RELATIONSHIP BETWEEN PROTECTIVE ORDER AND SUIT FOR DISSOLUTION OF MARRIAGE AND SUIT AFFECTING PARENT-CHILD RELATIONSHIP

§ 85.061. Dismissal of Application Prohibited; Subsequently Filed Suit for Dissolution of Marriage or Suit Affecting Parent-Child Relationship

If an application for a protective order is pending, a court may not dismiss the application or delay a hearing on the application on the grounds that a suit for dissolution of marriage or suit affecting the parent-child relationship is filed after the date the application was filed.

Added by Acts 1997, 75th Leg., ch. 1193, § 16, eff. Sept. 1, 1997.

§ 85.062. Application Filed While Suit for Dissolution of Marriage or Suit Affecting Parent-Child Relationship Pending

(a) If a suit for dissolution of a marriage or suit affecting the parent-child relationship is pending, a party to the suit may apply for a protective order against another party to the suit by filing an application:

(1) in the court in which the suit is pending; or

(2) in a court in the county in which the applicant resides if the applicant resides outside the jurisdiction of the court in which the suit is pending.

(b) An applicant subject to this section shall inform the clerk of the court that renders a protective order that a suit for dissolution of a marriage or a suit affecting the parent-child relationship is pending in which the applicant is party.

(c) If a final protective order is rendered by a court other than the court in which a suit for dissolution of a marriage or a suit affecting the parent-child relationship is pending, the clerk of the court that rendered the protective order shall:

(1) inform the clerk of the court in which the suit is pending that a final protective order has been rendered; and

(2) forward a copy of the final protective order to the court in which the suit is pending.

(d) A protective order rendered by a court in which an application is filed under Subsection (a)(2) is subject to transfer under Section 85.064.

Added by Acts 1997, 75th Leg., ch. 1193, § 16, eff. Sept. 1, 1997.

§ 85.063. Application Filed After Final Order Rendered in Suit for Dissolution of Marriage or Suit Affecting Parent-Child Relationship

(a) If a final order has been rendered in a suit for dissolution of marriage or suit affecting the parent-child relationship, an application for a protective order by a party to the suit against another party to the suit filed after the date the final order was rendered, and that is:

(1) filed in the county in which the final order was rendered, shall be filed in the court that rendered the final order; and

(2) filed in another county, shall be filed in a court having jurisdiction to render a protective order under this subtitle.

(b) A protective order rendered by a court in which an application is filed under Subsection (a)(2) is subject to transfer under Section 85.064.

Added by Acts 1997, 75th Leg., ch. 1193, § 16, eff. Sept. 1, 1997.

§ 85.064. Transfer of Protective Order

(a) If a protective order was rendered before the filing of a suit for dissolution of marriage or suit affecting the parent-child relationship or while the suit is pending as provided by Section 85.062, the court that rendered the order may, on the motion of a party or on the court's own motion, transfer the protective order to the court having jurisdiction of the suit if the court makes the finding prescribed by Subsection (c).

(b) If a protective order that affects a party's right to possession of or access to a child is rendered after the date a final order was rendered in a suit affecting the parent-child relationship, on the motion of a party or on the court's own motion, the court may transfer the protective order to the court of continuing, exclusive jurisdiction if the court makes the finding prescribed by Subsection (c).

(c) A court may transfer a protective order under this section if the court finds that the transfer is:

(1) in the interest of justice; or

(2) for the safety or convenience of a party or a witness.

(d) The transfer of a protective order under this section shall be conducted according to the procedures provided by Section 155.207.

(e) Except as provided by Section 81.002, the fees or costs associated with the transfer of a protective order shall be paid by the movant.

Added by Acts 1997, 75th Leg., ch. 1193, § 16, eff. Sept. 1, 1997.

§ 85.065. Effect of Transfer

(a) A protective order transferred under Section 85.064 has the same effect as if the order remained in the court that rendered the order. The protective order may be enforced by the court that receives the order in the same manner as if the court originally rendered the order.

(b) A protective order that is transferred is enforceable by contempt or by any other means by which the court that rendered the order could enforce the order. The court that receives the protective order may punish a violation of the order regardless of whether the violation occurred before or after the date of the transfer.

(c) A protective order that is transferred is subject to modification by the court that receives the order to the same extent modification is permitted under Chapter 87 by a court that rendered the order.

Added by Acts 1997, 75th Leg., ch. 1193, § 16, eff. Sept. 1, 1997.

CHAPTER 86. LAW ENFORCEMENT DUTIES RELATING TO PROTECTIVE ORDERS

Section

§ 86.001. Adoption of Procedures by Law Enforcement Agency

(a) To ensure that law enforcement officers responding to calls are aware of the existence and terms of protective orders issued under this subtitle, each law enforcement agency shall establish procedures in the agency to provide adequate information or access to information for law enforcement officers of the names of each person protected by an order issued under this subtitle and of each person against whom protective orders are directed.

(b) A law enforcement agency may enter a protective order in the agency's computer records of outstanding warrants as notice that the order has been issued and is currently in effect. On receipt of notification by a clerk of court that the court has vacated or dismissed an order, the law enforcement agency shall remove the order from the agency's computer record of outstanding warrants.

Added by Acts 1997, 75th Leg., ch. 34, § 1, eff. May 5, 1997.

§ 86.002. Duty to Provide Information to Firearms Dealers

(a) On receipt of a request for a law enforcement information system record check of a prospective transferee by a licensed firearms dealer under the Brady Handgun Violence Prevention Act, 18 U.S.C. Section 922, the chief law enforcement officer shall determine whether the Department of Public Safety has in the department's law enforcement information system a record indicating the existence of an active protective order directed to the prospective transferee.

(b) If the department's law enforcement information system indicates the existence of an active protective order directed to the prospective transferee, the chief law enforcement officer shall immediately advise the dealer that the transfer is prohibited.

Added by Acts 1997, 75th Leg., ch. 34, § 1, eff. May 5, 1997.

§ 86.003. Court Order for Law Enforcement Assistance Under Temporary Order

On request by an applicant obtaining a temporary ex parte protective order that excludes the respondent from the respondent's residence, the court granting the temporary order shall render a written order to the sheriff, constable, or chief of police to provide a law enforcement officer from the department of the chief of police, constable, or sheriff to:

(1) accompany the applicant to the residence covered by the order;

(2) inform the respondent that the court has ordered that the respondent be excluded from the residence;

(3) protect the applicant while the applicant takes possession of the residence; and

(4) protect the applicant if the respondent refuses to vacate the residence while the applicant takes possession of the applicant's necessary personal property.

Added by Acts 1997, 75th Leg., ch. 34, § 1, eff. May 5, 1997. Amended by Acts 1997, 75th Leg., ch. 852, § 1, eff. June 18. 1997.

Section 3 of Acts 1997, 75th Leg., ch. 852 provides:

"This Act takes effect only if the 75th Legislature, at its regular session, enacts H.B. 1441 or S.B. 797 and either bill becomes law. If the legislation does not become law, this Act has no effect."

Senate Bill 797 was enacted as Acts 1997, 75th Leg., ch. 34.

§ 86.004. Court Order for Law Enforcement Assistance Under Final Order

On request by an applicant obtaining a final protective order that excludes the respondent from the respondent's residence, the court granting the final order shall render a written order to the sheriff, constable, or chief of police to provide a law enforcement officer from the department of the chief of police, constable, or sheriff to:

(1) accompany the applicant to the residence covered by the order;

(2) inform the respondent that the court has ordered that the respondent be excluded from the residence;

(3) protect the applicant while the applicant takes possession of the residence and the respondent takes possession of the respondent's necessary personal property; and

(4) if the respondent refuses to vacate the residence:

(A) remove the respondent from the residence; and

(B) arrest the respondent for violating the court order.

Added by Acts 1997, 75th Leg., ch. 34, § 1, eff. May 5, 1997. Amended by Acts 1997, 75th Leg., ch. 852, § 2, eff. June 18, 1997.

For effectiveness provisions of Acts 1997, 75th Leg., ch. 852, see note following V.T.C.A., Family Code § 86.003.

§ 86.005. Protective Order From Another Jurisdiction

(a) To ensure that law enforcement officers responding to calls are aware of the existence and terms of a protective order from another jurisdiction, each law enforcement agency shall establish procedures in the agency to provide adequate information or access to information for law enforcement officers regarding the name of each person protected by an order rendered in another jurisdiction and of each person against whom the protective order is directed.

(b) Unless a law enforcement officer knows that the protective order has expired, the officer shall rely on:

(1) a copy of a protective order from another jurisdiction that has been provided to the officer by any source; and

(2) the statement by a person protected by the order that the order remains in effect.

(c) A law enforcement officer acting in good faith is not subject to civil or criminal liability for any action arising in connection with the enforcement of a protective order issued in another jurisdiction that a court later determines was not entitled to full faith and credit under Chapter 88.

Added by Acts 1997, 75th Leg., ch. 1193, § 17, eff. Sept. 1, 1997.

CHAPTER 87. MODIFICATION OF PROTECTIVE ORDERS

Section

§ 87.001. Modification of Protective Order

On the motion of any party, the court, after notice and hearing, may modify an existing protective order to:

(1) exclude any item included in the order; or

(2) include any item that could have been included in the order.

Added by Acts 1997, 75th Leg., ch. 34, § 1, eff. May 5, 1997.

§ 87.002. Modification May Not Extend Duration of Order

A protective order may not be modified to extend the period of the order's validity beyond the first anniversary of the date the original order was rendered.

Added by Acts 1997, 75th Leg., ch. 34, § 1, eff. May 5, 1997.

§ 87.003. Notification of Motion to Modify

Notice of a motion to modify a protective order is sufficient if delivery of the motion is attempted on the respondent at the respondent's last known address by registered or certified mail as provided by Rule 21a, Texas Rules of Civil Procedure.

Added by Acts 1997, 75th Leg., ch. 34, § 1, eff. May 5, 1997.

§ 87.004. Change of Address or Telephone Number

(a) If a protective order contains the address or telephone number of a person protected by the order, of the place of employment or business of the person, or of the child-care facility or school of a child protected by the order and that information is not confidential under Section 85.007, the person protected by the order may file a notification of change of address or telephone number with the court that rendered the order to modify the information contained in the order.

(b) The clerk of the court shall attach the notification of change to the protective order and shall deliver a copy of the notification to the respondent by registered or certified mail as provided by Rule 21a, Texas Rules of Civil Procedure.

(c) The filing of a notification of change of address or telephone number and the attachment of the notification to a protective order does not affect the validity of the order.

Added by Acts 1997, 75th Leg., ch. 1193, § 18, eff. Sept. 1, 1997.

CHAPTER 88. PROTECTIVE ORDER FROM ANOTHER JURISDICTION

§ 88.001. Full Faith and Credit of Protective Order From Another Jurisdiction

(a) Except as provided by Subsection (b), a protective order from another jurisdiction shall be accorded full faith and credit by the courts of this state and enforced as if the order were rendered by a court in this state.

(b) A protective order from another jurisdiction rendered against both the applicant and respondent is not enforceable against the applicant in this state unless:

(1) the respondent filed a cross or counter petition, complaint, or other written pleading seeking a protective order against the applicant; and

(2) the issuing court determined that each party was entitled to a protective order.

Added by Acts 1997, 75th Leg., ch. 1193, § 19, eff. Sept. 1, 1997.

§ 88.002. Presumption of Validity

A protective order from another jurisdiction is presumed to be valid if the order appears authentic on the order's face.

Added by Acts 1997, 75th Leg., ch. 1193, § 19, eff. Sept. 1, 1997.

§ 88.003. Affirmative Defense

It is an affirmative defense in any action seeking enforcement of a protective order rendered in another jurisdiction that the respondent was not given reasonable notice and an opportunity to be heard consistent with due process either:

(1) before the date the order was rendered; or

(2) in the case of an ex parte order, within the time required by the jurisdiction rendering the order after the date the order was rendered, but not later than a reasonable time.

Added by Acts 1997, 75th Leg., ch. 1193, § 19, eff. Sept. 1, 1997.

§ 88.004. Enforcement of an Order

A protective order from another jurisdiction may be enforced even if the order is not entered into the state law enforcement information system maintained by the Department of Public Safety.

Added by Acts 1997, 75th Leg., ch. 1193, § 19, eff. Sept. 1, 1997.

SUBTITLE C. REPORTING FAMILY VIOLENCE

CHAPTER 91. REPORTING FAMILY VIOLENCE

§ 91.001. Definitions

In this subtitle:

(1) "Family violence" has the meaning assigned by Section 71.004.

(2) "Medical professional" means a licensed doctor, nurse, physician assistant, or emergency medical technician.

Added by Acts 1997, 75th Leg., ch. 34, § 1, eff. May 5, 1997.

§ 91.002. Reporting by Witnesses Encouraged

A person who witnesses family violence is encouraged to report the family violence to a local law enforcement agency.

Added by Acts 1997, 75th Leg., ch. 34, § 1, eff. May 5, 1997.

§ 91.003. Information Provided by Medical Professionals

A medical professional who treats a person for injuries that the medical professional has reason to believe were caused by family violence shall:

(1) immediately provide the person with information regarding the nearest family violence shelter center;

(2) document in the person's medical file:

(A) the fact that the person has received the information provided under Subdivision (1); and

(B) the reasons for the medical professional's belief that the person's injuries were caused by family violence; and

(3) give the person a written notice in substantially the following form, completed with the required information, in both English and Spanish:

"NOTICE TO ADULT VICTIMS
OF FAMILY VIOLENCE

"It is a crime for any person to cause you any physical injury or harm even if that person is a member or former member of your family or household.

"You may report family violence to a law enforcement officer by calling the following telephone numbers: ______________________________.

"If you, your child, or any other household resident has been injured or if you feel you are going to be in danger after a law enforcement officer investigating family violence leaves your residence or at a later time, you have the right to:

"Ask the local prosecutor to file a criminal complaint against the person committing family violence; and

"Apply to a court for an order to protect you. You may want to consult with a legal aid office, a prosecuting attorney, or a private attorney. A court can enter an order that:

"(1) prohibits the abuser from committing further acts of violence;

"(2) prohibits the abuser from threatening, harassing, or contacting you at home;

"(3) directs the abuser to leave your household; and

"(4) establishes temporary custody of the children or any property.

"A VIOLATION OF CERTAIN PROVISIONS OF COURT-ORDERED PROTECTION MAY BE A FELONY.

"CALL THE FOLLOWING VIOLENCE SHELTERS OR SOCIAL ORGANIZATIONS IF YOU NEED PROTECTION: ______________________________."

Added by Acts 1997, 75th Leg., ch. 34, § 1, eff. May 5, 1997.

§ 91.004. Application of Subtitle

This subtitle does not affect a duty to report child abuse under Chapter 261.

Added by Acts 1997, 75th Leg., ch. 34, § 1, eff. May 5, 1997.

CHAPTER 92. IMMUNITY

§ 92.001. Immunity

(a) Except as provided by Subsection (b), a person who reports family violence under Section 91.002 or provides information under Section 91.003 is immune from civil liability that might otherwise be incurred or imposed.

(b) A person who reports the person's own conduct or who otherwise reports family violence in bad faith is not protected from liability under this section.

Added by Acts 1997, 75th Leg., ch. 34, § 1, eff. May 5, 1997.

TITLE 5. THE PARENT–CHILD RELATIONSHIP AND THE SUIT AFFECTING THE PARENT–CHILD RELATIONSHIP

DERIVATION TABLE—Title 5

Showing where sections of Title 5 of the Family Code were formerly covered in former Title 2 of the Family Code and provisions of the Government Code and Human Resources Code.

New Family Code Section	Former Family Code Section
101.001	11.01
101.002	11.01(7)
101.003	11.01(1)
101.004	14.80(3)
101.005	14.80(7)
101.006	14.80(4)

FAMILY CODE

New Family Code Section	Former Family Code Section
101.007	11.15(c)
101.008	11.01(2)
101.009	17.001
101.010	14.30(a)(2)
101.011	14.30(a)(1)
101.012	14.30(a)(3)
101.013	—
101.014	11.01(8)
101.015	14.061(d)
101.016	14.021(b)
101.017	Hum Res 42.002(12)
101.018	11.01(11)
101.019	11.01(6)
101.020	14.80(5)
101.021	11.01(10)
101.022	11.01(9)
101.023	—
101.024	11.01(3)
101.025	11.01(4)
101.026	—
101.027	15.051(a)(1)
101.028	14.033(a)(1)
101.029	14.033(a)(2)
101.030	21.01(19)
101.031	—
101.032	11.01(5)
101.033	—
101.034	14.80(2)
101.035	21.01(22)
102.001	11.02
102.002	—
102.003	11.03(a)
102.004	11.03(b), (c)
102.005	11.03(d)
102.006	11.03(g), (h)
102.007	11.03(i)
102.008	11.08(a), (b)
102.009	11.09(a), (b), (c), (f)
102.010	11.09(d), (e)
102.011	11.051
102.012	—
102.013	11.07(c)
103.001	11.04
103.002	11.06(a), (c)
103.003	11.061(a), (b)
104.001	11.14(e)
104.002	11.21(a), (b)
104.003	11.21(d)
104.004	11.21(c)
104.005	11.21(e)
	11.11(a) to (d), (g), 14.033(*l*),
105.001	14.055(e)
105.002	11.13
105.003	11.14(a), (b), (d), (f), (g)
105.004	11.14(h)
105.005	11.15(a)
105.006	11.155
105.007	14.045
106.001	11.18(a)
106.002	11.18(a)
107.001	11.10(a), (b)(1)
107.002	11.10(b)(2), (c), (d)
107.003	11.10(e)
107.004	11.101

New Family Code Section	Former Family Code Section
107.005	11.12, 11.14(c), 11.18(c)
108.001	11.17(a), (d)
108.002	11.17(b)
108.003	11.17(b)
	Hum Res 49.005(b)
108.004	11.17(b)
108.005	11.17(b)
108.006	11.17(c), 11.171
108.007	11.17(e)
108.008	13.43(b), (c)
108.009	13.43(e), (f)
109.001	11.11(e), (f), (g)
109.002	11.19
109.003	11.191
110.001	11.22(j), 14.317(e)
110.002	14.13
110.003	11.18(b)
110.004	14.45(h)
110.005	11.06(*l*)
111.001	14.03(j), 14.05(h)(i)
111.002	14.032(e), (f), 14.052(c), (d)
111.003	14.033(p), 14.058
151.001	12.01
151.002	12.02
151.003	4.02, 12.04
151.004	12.05
151.101	12.03
151.102	12.03A
151.103	12.03B
152.001	11.51
152.002	11.52
152.003	11.53
152.004	11.54
152.005	11.55
152.006	11.56
152.007	11.57
152.008	11.58
152.009	11.59
152.010	11.60
152.011	11.61
152.012	11.62
152.013	11.63
152.014	11.64
152.015	11.65
152.016	11.66
152.017	11.67
152.018	11.68
152.019	11.69
152.020	11.70
152.021	11.71
152.022	11.72
152.023	11.73
152.024	11.74
152.025	11.75
153.001	14.021(a)
153.002	14.07(a)
153.003	14.01(c)(1), 14.032(d)
	14.01(c)(2), 14.03(d), (e)(3),
153.004	14.021(h)
153.005	14.01(a)
153.006	14.03(a), (c)
153.007	14.06
153.008	14.07(a)
153.009	14.07(c)

PARENT–CHILD RELATIONSHIP

New Family Code Section	Former Family Code Section
153.010	14.03(h)
153.011	14.03(i)
153.012	14.04(c)
153.071	14.02(a)
153.072	14.02(b)
153.073	14.02(a), (b)(1)(D), (2)
153.074	14.02(b)(1)(A) to (C)
153.075	14.03(d)
153.131	14.01(b)(1)
153.132	14.02(b)(3)
153.133	14.021(c), (d)
153.134	14.021(e), (f)
153.135	14.021(b)
153.136	14.021(b)
153.137	14.034
153.138	14.021(g), (h)
153.139	14.021(i)
153.191	14.03(d)
153.192	14.03(b), (c)
153.193	14.03(d)
153.251	14.032(a)
153.252	14.033(k)
153.253	14.033(m)
153.254	14.032(b)
153.255	14.033(n)
153.256	14.032(c)
153.257	14.033(h)
153.258	14.033(k)
153.311	14.033(b)
153.312	14.033(c), (e)(4) to (7)
153.313	14.033(f)(1), (3) to (6)
153.314	14.033(e)(1) to (3), (8) to (10), (f)(2)
153.315	14.033(d)
153.316	14.033(g)
153.317	14.033(i)
153.371	14.02(c)
153.372	14.01(a), 14.021(j)
153.373	14.01(b)(2)
153.374	14.01(d)
153.375	14.01(e)
153.376	14.04(a), (b)
153.377	14.04(c)
153.431	14.07(b)
153.432	14.03(e), (f)
153.433	14.03(e)
153.434	14.03(g)
154.001	14.05(a), (b), (d)
154.002	14.05(a)
154.003	14.05(a)
154.004	14.0503
154.005	14.05(c)
154.006	14.05(d)
154.007	14.05(e)
154.008	14.061(a)
154.009	14.062
154.010	14.053(i)
154.061	14.053(a), (h)
154.062	14.053(b)
154.063	14.053(g)
154.064	14.053(d)
154.065	14.053(c)
154.066	14.053(f)
154.067	14.053(e)
154.068	14.053(k)
154.069	—
154.070	14.055(i)
154.121	14.052(a)
154.122	14.05(j), 14.055(a)
154.123	14.054
154.124	14.06
154.125	14.055(a), (b)
154.126	14.055(c)
154.127	14.055(d)
154.128	14.055(f) to (h)
154.129	14.055(j)
154.130	14.057
154.131	14.053(*l*)
154.181	14.061(a)
154.182	14.061(a), (b)
154.183	14.053(d), 14.061(c)
154.184	14.061(r)
154.185	14.061(e), (f)
154.186	14.061(g)
154.187	14.061(h) to (k), (p)
154.188	14.061(*l*)
154.189	14.061(m)
154.190	14.061(m)
154.191	14.061(n), (*o*)
154.192	14.061(q)
154.241	14.0501
154.242	14.0502
154.243	14.0504
154.301	14.051(a)
154.302	14.051(b)
154.303	14.051(c)
154.304	14.051(i)
154.305	14.051(d) to (f)
154.306	14.051(g)
155.001	11.05(a), (b), (d), (e)
155.002	11.05(a)
155.003	11.05(g)
155.004	11.05(b), (c), (f), (g)
155.005	11.05(h)
155.101	11.071(a), (b)
155.102	11.071(d)
155.103	11.05(c)
155.104	11.071(c)
155.201	11.06(b), (c)
155.202	11.06(b), (d)
155.203	11.06(b)
155.204	11.06(b), (f) to (i)
155.205	11.05(h), 11.06(j)
155.206	11.06(k)
155.207	11.06(j), (m)
155.301	11.061
156.001	11.05(g)
156.002	14.08(a)
156.003	14.08(b)
156.004	14.08(b)
156.005	14.082
156.006	11.11(a), 14.08(g)
156.101	14.08(c)(1)
156.102	14.08(d), (e)
156.103	14.08(c)(4)
156.104	14.021(g), 14.08(c)(5)
156.105	14.08(i)
156.201	14.081(b)

New Family Code Section	Former Family Code Section
156.202	14.081(c)
156.203	14.081(d)
156.301	14.08(c)(3)
156.302	14.033(*o*)
156.303	14.08(c)(3)(C)
156.401	14.021(g), 14.08(c)(2)
156.402	14.056(a), (b)
156.403	14.056(b)
156.404	14.056(c)
156.405	14.056(c)
156.406	14.056(d)
156.407	14.08(h)
156.408	—
157.001	14.30(b), 14.31, 14.40(a), 14.50(a)
157.002	14.311(a) to (e), 14.312
157.003	14.30(d), 14.313(a)
157.004	14.50(b)
157.005	14.40(b), 14.41(b)
157.006	14.40(h)
157.007	14.50(c)
157.008	14.40(c), (g), 14.41(c)
157.061	14.314(a), 14.32(d)
157.062	14.314(a), (b), 14.315
157.063	14.314(c)
157.064	14.311(f)
157.065	14.314(c), (d)
157.066	14.314(e), 14.317(b)
157.101	14.318(a)
157.102	14.317(d)
157.103	14.317(e)
157.104	14.318(b)
157.105	14.318(c)
157.106	14.318(d)
157.107	14.318(e)
157.108	14.318(f)
157.109	14.42(a), 14.51(a)
157.110	14.42(b), (c), (f), 14.51(b), (c), (f)
157.111	14.42(e), 14.51(e)
157.112	14.42(d), 14.51(d)
157.113	14.40(f)
157.114	14.317((a)
157.115	14.317(a)
157.161	14.32(b)
157.162	14.311(b), (c), 14.33(d)
157.163	14.32(f)
157.164	14.33(b)
157.165	14.40(e)(1)
157.166	14.33(a)
157.167	14.33(c)
157.211	14.40(e)(1), 14.50(d)(1)
157.212	14.40(e)(2), 14.50(d)(2)
157.213	14.40(e)(3), 14.50(d)(3)
157.214	14.40(e)(4), 14.50(d)(4)
157.215	14.40(e)(5), 14.50(d)(5)
157.216	14.40(e)(6), 14.50(d)(6)
157.217	14.40(e)(7), 14.50(d)(7)
157.261	14.41(a)
157.262	14.41(d)
157.263	14.41(a), (e)
157.264	14.41(a)
157.265	14.34(a)
157.266	14.34(b)
157.267	14.34(c)
157.268	14.34(c)
157.311	14.971(a), (b)
157.312	14.971(c), (d)
157.313	14.973
157.314	14.974
157.315	14.975
157.316	14.972(a)
157.317	14.972(b)
157.318	14.972(e)
157.319	14.976(a), (b)
157.320	14.976(c), 14.977
157.321	14.980
157.322	14.978
157.323	14.979
157.324	14.981
157.325	14.982
157.326	14.983
157.371	—
157.372	14.10(a), (b)
157.373	14.10(c)
157.374	14.10(d)
157.375	14.10(e)
157.376	14.10(f)
157.421	11.22(a), (b), (g)
157.422	11.22(h), (i)
157.423	11.22(c)
157.424	11.22(d)
157.425	11.22(e)
157.426	11.22(f)
158.001	14.05(e), 14.43(a)
158.002	14.43(a)(2), (3)
158.003	14.43(d)
158.004	14.43(d)
158.005	14.41(a), 14.43(d)
158.006	14.43(b)
158.007	14.43(d)
158.008	14.43(k)
158.009	14.43(f)
158.010	14.43(h)
158.101	—
158.102	14.43(r)
158.103	14.43(e)
158.104	14.43(g)
158.105	14.43(g), (h)
158.106	14.43(p), 14.45(g)
158.201	14.316
158.202	14.43(h)
158.203	14.43(h)
158.204	14.43(i)
158.205	14.43(j)
158.206	14.43(*l*)
158.207	14.43(*l*)
158.208	14.43(*l*)
158.209	14.43(m)
158.210	14.43(n)
158.211	14.43(*o*)
158.301	14.44(a)
158.302	14.44(b)
158.303	14.44(h)
158.304	14.44(d)
158.305	14.44(g)
158.306	14.44(a)
158.307	14.44(c)

PARENT–CHILD RELATIONSHIP

New Family Code Section	Former Family Code Section
158.308	14.44(c)
158.309	14.44(d)
158.310	14.44(d)
158.311	14.41(a), 14.43(a), 14.44(a)
158.312	14.45(a)
158.313	14.45(a)
158.314	14.45(b)
158.315	14.45(c)
158.316	14.45(a)
158.317	14.44(e)
158.401	14.43(q), 14.45(f)
158.402	14.43(q)
158.403	14.43(q)
159.001	—
159.101	21.01
159.102	21.02
159.103	21.03
159.201	21.04
159.202	21.05
159.203	21.06
159.204	21.07
159.205	21.08
159.206	21.09
159.207	21.10
159.208	21.11
159.209	21.12
159.301	21.13
159.302	21.14
159.303	21.15
159.304	21.16
159.305	21.17
159.306	21.18
159.307	21.19
159.308	21.20
159.309	21.21
159.310	21.22
159.311	21.23
159.312	21.24
159.313	21.25
159.314	21.26
159.315	21.27
159.316	21.28
159.317	21.29
159.318	21.30
159.319	21.31
159.401	21.32
159.501	21.33
159.502	21.34
159.601	21.35
159.602	21.36
159.603	21.37
159.604	21.38
159.605	21.39
159.606	21.40
159.607	21.41
159.608	21.42
159.609	21.43
159.610	21.44
159.611	21.45
159.612	21.46
159.701	21.47
159.801	21.48
159.802	21.49
159.901	21.50
159.902	21.51
160.001	—
160.002	13.01
160.003	13.07
160.004	13.04(f)
160.005	13.42(a)
160.006	13.08, 13.09
160.007	13.44
160.101	12.06(a), (b)
160.102	13.02(a), (d)
160.103	13.02(a)
160.104	13.03
160.105	13.04(a) to (e), (g)
160.106	13.05
160.107	13.02(b)
160.108	11.14(j)
160.109	13.06(a) to (c), (e) to (g)
160.110	12.06(c), 13.06(c), (d)
160.201	13.21(a), (b), (d)
160.202	13.22
160.203	13.23
160.204	13.22(c)
160.205	13.21(c)
160.206	13.24
161.001	15.02(a)
161.002	15.023
161.003	15.024
161.004	15.025(a), (b)
161.005	15.01
161.006	15.022
161.101	11.08(e)
161.102	15.021(a), (c)
161.103	15.03
161.104	14.02(d)
161.105	15.04
161.106	15.041(a) to (d)
161.107	15.051(a), (c)
161.201	15.021(b)
161.202	11.14(h)
161.203	15.06
161.204	15.041(e)
161.205	15.05(c)
161.206	15.05(a), 15.07
161.207	15.05(b)
161.208	15.051(b)
161.209	11.16
161.210	11.17(f)
162.001	16.01, 16.02, 16.03(b) to (d)
162.002	11.08(d), 16.03(a)
162.003	16.031(a)
162.004	16.031(b)
162.005	16.032(a), (f), (*l*)
162.006	16.032(g), (i) to (k), (n)
162.007	16.032(b) to (e)
162.008	16.032(h)
162.009	16.04
162.010	16.05
162.011	16.06
162.012	16.12
162.013	16.11
162.014	16.07
162.015	16.081
162.016	16.08
162.017	16.09(a), (d) to (f)

New Family Code Section	Former Family Code Section
162.018	16.09(b), (c)
162.019	11.16
162.020	16.10
162.021	11.17(f)
162.022	11.17(d)
162.023	11.17(b)
162.024	11.17(b)

New Family Code Section	Former Human Resources Code Section
162.101	45.001, 45.022
162.102	45.002(a) to (c), (e)
162.103	45.003(a) to (d)
162.104	45.004
162.105	45.005
162.106	45.006
162.107	45.007
162.108	45.021
162.109	45.023
162.110	45.024
162.111	45.025
162.112	45.026
162.113	45.027
162.114	45.028
162.301	47.001
162.302	47.002
162.303	47.003
162.304	47.004
162.305	47.005
162.306	47.031
162.307	47.032
162.308	47.041
162.401	49.001
162.402	49.002
162.403	49.003(a) to (c)
162.404	49.004
162.405	49.005
162.406	49.006
162.407	49.007
162.408	49.008
162.409	49.009
162.410	49.010
162.411	49.011
162.412	49.012
162.413	49.013
162.414	49.014
162.415	49.015
162.416	49.016
162.417	49.017, 49.018
162.418	49.019
162.419	49.020
162.420	49.021
162.421	49.022
162.422	49.023

New Family Code Section	Former Family Code Section
162.501	16.51
162.502	16.51
162.503	16.53
162.504	16.52
162.505	16.54
162.506	new
162.507	16.55

New Family Code Section	Former Government Code Section
201.001	54.001
201.002	54.002
201.003	54.003
201.004	54.004
201.005	54.005, 54.014
201.006	54.006
201.007	54.007
201.008	54.008
201.009	54.018
201.010	54.009
201.011	54.010(a), (b)
201.012	54.010(c)
201.013	54.013
201.014	54.011
201.015	54.012(a) to (i)
201.016	54.012(j)
201.017	54.017

New Family Code Section	Former Family Code Section
201.101	14.82(a), (b)
201.102	14.82(c), (e)
201.103	14.82(d)
201.104	14.82(f), (g)
201.105	14.83(a), (b)
201.106	14.83(c)
201.107	14.83(d), (e)
201.108	14.84
201.109	14.85
201.110	14.81
201.111	14.82(h)
202.001	14.91
202.002	14.92
202.003	14.93
202.004	14.94
202.005	14.95

New Family Code Section	Former Human Resources Code Section
203.002	151.003(b)
203.003	151.001
203.004	151.002
203.005	151.004
203.006	151.005
203.007	151.006
203.008	151.007
203.009	151.008
203.010	151.009
203.011	151.010
203.012	151.011
231.001	76.001
231.002	76.002(a), (d), (f), 76.004(b)
231.003	Fam 14.86
231.004	Fam 14.87
231.005	76.002(i)
231.006	Fam 14.52
231.007	76.0041
231.008	76.005
231.009	76.008
231.101	76.002(e), 76.004
231.102	new
231.103	76.004(a)
231.104	76.003(a)
231.105	76.003(b)
231.106	76.003(e)

PARENT–CHILD RELATIONSHIP

New Family Code Section	Former Human Resources Code Section
231.107	76.003(f)
231.108	76.006
231.109	76.007(a) to (e)
231.110	76.007(f)
231.111	76.007(g)
231.112	Fam 13.015
231.201	76.009(g)
231.202	76.009(a)
231.203	76.009(h)
231.204	76.009(b)
231.205	76.009(e), (f)
231.206	76.009(i)
231.207	76.009(c)
231.208	76.009(d)
231.209	76.009(i)
231.210	76.002(g)
231.211	Fam 11.181
231.301	77.001(a)
231.302	77.001(b), (d)
231.303	77.001(c)
231.304	76.011

New Family Code Section	Former Family Code Section
231.401	14.802(a)
231.402	14.802(a)
231.403	14.802(g)
231.404	14.802(g)
231.405	14.802(b), 14.803(a)
231.406	14.803(b), (c)
231.407	14.802(e), (f)
231.408	14.802(c)
231.409	14.804(a)
231.410	14.804(b), (c)
231.411	14.804(d)
231.412	14.804(e)
231.413	14.802(d)
231.414	14.804(f)
231.415	14.804(h) to (j)
231.416	14.804(k)
231.417	14.805
231.418	14.804(g)
231.419	14.806(a)
231.420	14.806(b)
231.421	14.806(c), (d)
231.422	14.806(c) to (e)
231.423	14.807(d), (e)
231.424	14.807(b), (c)
231.425	14.807(f)
231.426	14.807(g)
231.427	14.807(h), (i)
231.428	14.808
231.429	14.801
231.430	14.809
261.001	34.012
261.002	34.06
261.003	34.013
261.101	34.01, 34.02(d)
261.102	34.02(a)
261.103	34.02(a)
261.104	34.02(b)
261.105	34.02(c)
261.106	34.03
261.107	34.031

New Family Code Section	Former Family Code Section
261.108	34.032
261.109	34.07
261.201	34.08
261.202	34.04
261.301	34.05(a), (b)
261.302	34.05(c)
261.303	34.05(c)
261.304	34.053
261.305	34.05(c)
261.306	34.05(g)
261.307	34.051
261.308	34.05(e)
261.309	34.052
261.310	34.054
261.311	34.055
261.401	34.22
261.402	34.23
261.403	34.24
262.001	17.01
262.002	17.05(a)
262.004	17.03(a)(2)
262.005	17.03(g)
262.006	17.011
262.101	17.02(b)
262.102	17.02(a), (d)
262.103	17.02(c)
262.104	17.03(a)(3) to (6)
262.105	17.03(b)
262.106	17.03(c)
262.107	17.03(d), (e), (i)
262.108	17.03(h)
262.109	17.031
262.110	17.03(a)(1)
262.201	17.04
262.202	17.05(b)
262.203	17.06(a)
262.204	17.06(b), (c)
263.001	18.01
263.002	18.02
263.003	18.11
263.004	18.13
263.101	18.03(a)
263.102	18.03(b) to (d)
263.103	18.04
263.104	18.05
263.105	18.06
263.106	(new)
263.201	18.07(a)
263.202	18.07(b) to (d)
263.301	18.08(b), (c), 18.12
263.302	18.14
263.303	18.10(b), (c)
263.304	18.08(a)
263.305	18.10(a)
263.306	18.09(a), (b)
263.307	18.15
263.308	18.09(c)
263.309	18.16

New Family Code Section	Former Human Resources Code Section
264.001	(new)
264.002	41.001
264.003	41.0011

New Family Code Section	Former Human Resources Code Section
264.004	41.0012
264.005	41.002
264.006	41.003
264.007	41.004
264.008	41.006
264.009	Fam 11.20
264.101	41.021
264.102	41.022
264.103	41.023
264.104	41.024
264.105	41.025
264.106	41.026
264.108	41.028

New Family Code Section	Former Family Code Section
264.201	34.51
264.202	34.52
264.203	34.53
264.204	34.54
264.301	new
264.601	34.601
264.602	34.602
264.603	34.603
264.604	34.604
264.605	34.605
264.606	34.606
264.607	34.607
264.608	34.608
264.609	34.609
264.610	34.610
264.611	34.611
264.612	34.612

Reenactment of Title 2 and Addition of Title 5

Section 1 of Acts 1995, 74th Leg., ch. 20 reenacted Title 2 and added Title 5 of the Family Code, effective April 20, 1995. Section 2(1) of said Act repealed Title 2 of the Family Code, as that title existed before the effective date of the Act. For disposition of provisions of former Title 2 in reenacted Title 2 and added Title 5, see Disposition Table under former Title 2.

SUBTITLE A. GENERAL PROVISIONS

CHAPTER 101. DEFINITIONS

§ 101.001. Applicability of Definitions

(a) Definitions in this subchapter apply to this title.

(b) If, in another part of this title, a term defined by this chapter has a meaning different from the meaning provided by this chapter, the meaning of that other provision prevails.

Added by Acts 1995, 74th Leg., ch. 20, § 1, eff. April 20, 1995.

Section 3 of the 1995 Act provides:

"(a) The change in law made by this Act does not affect a proceeding under the Family Code pending on the effective date of this Act. A proceeding pending on the effective date of this Act is governed by the law in effect at the time the proceeding was commenced, and the former law is continued in effect for that purpose.

"(b) The enactment of this Act does not by itself constitute a material and substantial change of circumstances sufficient to warrant modification of a court order or portion of a decree that provides for the support of or possession of and access to a child entered before the effective date of this Act."

§ 101.0011. Administrative Writ of Withholding

"Administrative writ of withholding" means the document issued by the Title IV-D agency and delivered to an employer directing that earnings be withheld for payment of child support as provided by Chapter 158.

Added by Acts 1997, 75th Leg., ch. 911, § 5, eff. Sept. 1, 1997.

§ 101.002. Authorized Agency

"Authorized agency" means a public social agency authorized to care for children, including the Texas Department of Protective and Regulatory Services.

Added by Acts 1995, 74th Leg., ch. 20, § 1, eff. April 20, 1995.

§ 101.003. Child or Minor; Adult

(a) "Child" or "minor" means a person under 18 years of age who is not and has not been married or who has not had the disabilities of minority removed for general purposes.

(b) In the context of child support, "child" includes a person over 18 years of age for whom a person may be obligated to pay child support.

(c) "Adult" means a person who is not a child.

Added by Acts 1995, 74th Leg., ch. 20, § 1, eff. April 20, 1995.

§ 101.004. Child Support Agency

"Child support agency" means:

(1) the Title IV–D agency;

(2) a county or district attorney or any other county officer or county agency that executes a cooperative agreement with the Title IV–D agency to provide child support services under Part D of Title IV of the federal Social Security Act (42 U.S.C. Section 651 et seq.) and Chapter 231; or

(3) a domestic relations office.

Added by Acts 1995, 74th Leg., ch. 20, § 1, eff. April 20, 1995.

§ 101.005. Child Support Review Officer

"Child support review officer" means an individual designated and trained by a child support agency to conduct reviews under this title.

Added by Acts 1995, 74th Leg., ch. 20, § 1, eff. April 20, 1995. Amended by Acts 1995, 74th Leg., ch. 341, § 2.01, eff. Sept. 1, 1995.

§ 101.006. Child Support Services

"Child support services" means administrative or court actions to:

(1) establish paternity;

(2) establish, modify, or enforce child support or medical support obligations;

(3) locate absent parents; or

(4) cooperate with other states in these actions and any other action authorized or required under Part D of Title IV of the federal Social Security Act (42 U.S.C. Section 651 et seq.) or Chapter 231.

Added by Acts 1995, 74th Leg., ch. 20, § 1, eff. April 20, 1995.

§ 101.007. Clear and Convincing Evidence

"Clear and convincing evidence" means the measure or degree of proof that will produce in the mind of the trier of fact a firm belief or conviction as to the truth of the allegations sought to be established.

Added by Acts 1995, 74th Leg., ch. 20, § 1, eff. April 20, 1995.

§ 101.008. Court

"Court" means the district court, juvenile court having the same jurisdiction as a district court, or other court expressly given jurisdiction of a suit affecting the parent-child relationship.

Added by Acts 1995, 74th Leg., ch. 20, § 1, eff. April 20, 1995.

§ 101.009. Danger to Physical Health or Safety of Child

"Danger to the physical health or safety of a child" includes exposure of the child to loss or injury that jeopardizes the physical health or safety of the child without regard to whether there has been an actual prior injury to the child.

Added by Acts 1995, 74th Leg., ch. 20, § 1, eff. April 20, 1995.

§ 101.010. Disposable Earnings

"Disposable earnings" means the part of the earnings of an individual remaining after the deduction from those earnings of any amount required by law to be withheld, union dues, nondiscretionary retirement contributions, and medical, hospitalization, and disability insurance coverage for the obligor and the obligor's children.

Added by Acts 1995, 74th Leg., ch. 20, § 1, eff. April 20, 1995.

§ 101.011. Earnings

"Earnings" means a payment to or due an individual, regardless of source and how denominated. The term includes a periodic or lump-sum payment for:

(1) wages, salary, compensation received as an independent contractor, overtime pay, severance pay, commission, bonus, and interest income;

(2) payments made under a pension, an annuity, workers' compensation, and a disability or retirement program; and

(3) unemployment benefits.

Added by Acts 1995, 74th Leg., ch. 20, § 1, eff. April 20, 1995. Amended by Acts 1997, 75th Leg., ch. 911, § 1, eff. Sept. 1, 1997.

Section 98(b) and (c) of Acts 1997, 75th Leg., ch. 911 provides:

"(b) The change in law made by this Act does not affect a proceeding under the Family Code pending on the effective date of this Act. A proceeding pending on the effective date of this Act is governed by the law in effect at the time the proceeding was commenced, and the former law is continued in effect for that purpose.

"(c) The enactment of this Act does not by itself constitute a material and substantial change of circumstances sufficient to warrant modification of a court order or portion of a decree that provides for the support of or possession of or access to a child entered before the effective date of this Act."

§ 101.012. Employer

"Employer" means a person, corporation, partnership, workers' compensation insurance carrier, governmental entity, the United States, or any other entity that pays or owes earnings to an individual. The term includes, for the purposes of enrolling dependents in a group health insurance plan, a union, trade association, or other similar organization.

Added by Acts 1995, 74th Leg., ch. 20, § 1, eff. April 20, 1995. Amended by Acts 1995, 74th Leg., ch. 341, § 4.02, eff. Sept. 1, 1995; Acts 1997, 75th Leg., ch. 911, § 2, eff. Sept. 1, 1997.

For application and effectiveness provisions of Acts 1997, 75th Leg., ch. 911, see note following V.T.C.A., Family Code § 101.011.

§ 101.013. Filed

"Filed" means officially filed with the clerk of the court.

Added by Acts 1995, 74th Leg., ch. 20, § 1, eff. April 20, 1995.

§ 101.014. Governmental Entity

"Governmental entity" means the state, a political subdivision of the state, or an agency of the state.

Added by Acts 1995, 74th Leg., ch. 20, § 1, eff. April 20, 1995.

§ 101.015. Health Insurance

"Health insurance" means insurance coverage that provides basic health care services, including usual physician services, office visits, hospitalization, and laboratory, X–ray, and emergency services, that may be provided through a health maintenance organization or other private or public organization.

Added by Acts 1995, 74th Leg., ch. 20, § 1, eff. April 20, 1995.

§ 101.016. Joint Managing Conservatorship

"Joint managing conservatorship" means the sharing of the rights and duties of a parent by two parties, ordinarily the parents, even if the exclusive right to make certain decisions may be awarded to one party.

Added by Acts 1995, 74th Leg., ch. 20, § 1, eff. April 20, 1995.

§ 101.0161. Judicial Writ of Withholding

"Judicial writ of withholding" means the document issued by the clerk of a court and delivered to an employer directing that earnings be withheld for payment of child support as provided by Chapter 158.

Added by Acts 1997, 75th Leg., ch. 911, § 5, eff. Sept. 1, 1997.

§ 101.017. Licensed Child Placing Agency

"Licensed child placing agency" means a person, private association, or corporation approved by the Department of Protective and Regulatory Services to place children for adoption through a license, certification, or other means.

Added by Acts 1995, 74th Leg., ch. 20, § 1, eff. April 20, 1995.

§ 101.018. Local Registry

"Local registry" means an agency or entity operated under the authority of a district clerk, county government, juvenile board, juvenile probation office, domestic relations office, or other county agency or entity that serves a county or a court that has jurisdiction under this title and that:

(1) receives child support payments;

(2) maintains records of child support payments;

(3) distributes child support payments as required by law; and

(4) maintains custody of official child support payment records.

Added by Acts 1995, 74th Leg., ch. 20, § 1, eff. April 20, 1995.

§ 101.019. Managing Conservatorship

"Managing conservatorship" means the relationship between a child and a managing conservator appointed by court order.

Added by Acts 1995, 74th Leg., ch. 20, § 1, eff. April 20, 1995.

§ 101.020. Medical Support

"Medical support" means periodic payments or a lump-sum payment made under an order to cover medical expenses, including health insurance coverage, incurred for the benefit of a child.

Added by Acts 1995, 74th Leg., ch. 20, § 1, eff. April 20, 1995. Amended by Acts 1997, 75th Leg., ch. 911, § 3, eff. Sept. 1, 1997.

For application and effectiveness provisions of Acts 1997, 75th Leg., ch. 911, see note following V.T.C.A., Family Code § 101.011.

§ 101.0201. Notice of Application for Judicial Writ of Withholding

"Notice of application for judicial writ of withholding" means the document delivered to an obligor and filed with the court as required by Chapter 158 for the nonjudicial determination of arrears and initiation of withholding.

Added by Acts 1997, 75th Leg., ch. 911, § 5, eff. Sept. 1, 1997.

§ 101.021. Obligee

"Obligee" means a person or entity entitled to receive payments under an order of child support, including an agency of this state or of another jurisdiction to which a person has assigned the person's right to support.

Added by Acts 1995, 74th Leg., ch. 20, § 1, eff. April 20, 1995.

§ 101.022. Obligor

"Obligor" means a person required to make payments under the terms of a support order for a child.

Added by Acts 1995, 74th Leg., ch. 20, § 1, eff. April 20, 1995.

§ 101.023. Order

"Order" means a final order unless identified as a temporary order or the context clearly requires a different meaning. The term includes a decree and a judgment.

Added by Acts 1995, 74th Leg., ch. 20, § 1, eff. April 20, 1995.

§ 101.024. Parent

"Parent" means the mother, a man presumed to be the biological father or who has been adjudicated to be the biological father by a court of competent jurisdiction, or an adoptive mother or father. The term does not include a parent as to whom the parent-child relationship has been terminated.

Added by Acts 1995, 74th Leg., ch. 20, § 1, eff. April 20, 1995.

§ 101.025. Parent-Child Relationship

"Parent-child relationship" means the legal relationship between a child and the child's biological or adoptive parents as provided by Chapter 151. The term includes the mother and child relationship and the father and child relationship.

Added by Acts 1995, 74th Leg., ch. 20, § 1, eff. April 20, 1995.

§ 101.026. Render

"Render" means the pronouncement by a judge of the court's ruling on a matter. The pronouncement may be made orally in the presence of the court reporter or in writing, including on the court's docket sheet or by a separate written instrument.

Added by Acts 1995, 74th Leg., ch. 20, § 1, eff. April 20, 1995.

§ 101.027. Parent Locator Service

"Parent locator service" means the service established under 42 U.S.C. Section 653.

Added by Acts 1995, 74th Leg., ch. 20, § 1, eff. April 20, 1995.

§ 101.028. School

"School" means a primary or secondary school in which a child is enrolled or, if the child is not enrolled in a primary or secondary school, the public school district in which the child primarily resides.

Added by Acts 1995, 74th Leg., ch. 20, § 1, eff. April 20, 1995.

§ 101.029. Standard Possession Order

"Standard possession order" means an order that provides a parent with rights of possession of a child in accordance with the terms and conditions of Subchapter F, Chapter 153.[1]

Added by Acts 1995, 74th Leg., ch. 20, § 1, eff. April 20, 1995.

[1] V.T.C.A., Family Code § 153.311 et seq.

§ 101.030. State

"State" means a state of the United States, the District of Columbia, the Commonwealth of Puerto Rico, or a territory or insular possession subject to the jurisdiction of the United States. The term includes an Indian tribe and a foreign jurisdiction that has established procedures for rendition and enforcement of an order that are substantially similar to the procedures of this title.

Added by Acts 1995, 74th Leg., ch. 20, § 1, eff. April 20, 1995.

§ 101.0301. State Case Registry

"State case registry" means the registry established and operated by the Title IV-D agency under 42

U.S.C. Section 654a that has responsibility for maintaining records with respect to child support orders in all Title IV-D cases and in all other cases in which a support order is rendered or modified under this title on or after October 1, 1998.

Added by Acts 1997, 75th Leg., ch. 911, § 5, eff. Sept. 1, 1997.

§ 101.031. Suit

"Suit" means a suit affecting the parent-child relationship.

Added by Acts 1995, 74th Leg., ch. 20, § 1, eff. April 20, 1995.

§ 101.032. Suit Affecting the Parent-Child Relationship

(a) "Suit affecting the parent-child relationship" means a suit filed as provided by this title in which the appointment of a managing conservator or a possessory conservator, access to or support of a child, or establishment or termination of the parent-child relationship is requested.

(b) The following are not suits affecting the parent-child relationship:

(1) a habeas corpus proceeding under Chapter 157;

(2) a proceeding filed under Chapter 159 to determine parentage or to establish, enforce, or modify child support, whether this state is acting as the initiating or responding state; and

(3) a proceeding under Title 2.

Added by Acts 1995, 74th Leg., ch. 20, § 1, eff. April 20, 1995.

§ 101.033. Title IV–D Agency

"Title IV–D agency" means the state agency designated under Chapter 231 to provide services under Part D of Title IV of the federal Social Security Act (42 U.S.C. Section 651 et seq.).

Added by Acts 1995, 74th Leg., ch. 20, § 1, eff. April 20, 1995.

§ 101.034. Title IV-D Case

"Title IV-D case" means an action in which services are provided by the Title IV-D agency under Part D, Title IV, of the federal Social Security Act (42 U.S.C. Section 651 et seq.), relating to the location of an absent parent, determination of parentage, or establishment, modification, or enforcement of a child support or medical support obligation.

Added by Acts 1995, 74th Leg., ch. 20, § 1, eff. April 20, 1995. Amended by Acts 1997, 75th Leg., ch. 911, § 4, eff. Sept. 1, 1997.

For application and effectiveness provisions of Acts 1997, 75th Leg., ch. 911, see note following V.T.C.A., Family Code § 101.011.

§ 101.035. Tribunal

"Tribunal" means a court, administrative agency, or quasi-judicial entity of a state authorized to establish, enforce, or modify support orders or to determine parentage.

Added by Acts 1995, 74th Leg., ch. 20, § 1, eff. April 20, 1995.

CHAPTER 102. FILING SUIT

Section

§ 102.001. Suit Authorized; Scope of Suit

(a) A suit may be filed as provided in this title.

(b) One or more matters covered by this title may be determined in the suit. The court, on its own motion, may require the parties to replead in order that any issue affecting the parent-child relationship may be determined in the suit.

Added by Acts 1995, 74th Leg., ch. 20, § 1, eff. April 20, 1995.

§ 102.002. Commencement of Suit

An original suit begins by the filing of a petition as provided by this chapter.

Added by Acts 1995, 74th Leg., ch. 20, § 1, eff. April 20, 1995.

§ 102.003. General Standing to File Suit

An original suit may be filed at any time by:

(1) a parent of the child;

(2) the child through a representative authorized by the court;

(3) a custodian or person having the right of visitation with or access to the child appointed by an order of a court of another state or country;

(4) a guardian of the person or of the estate of the child;

(5) a governmental entity;

(6) an authorized agency;

(7) a licensed child placing agency;

(8) a man alleging himself to be the biological father of a child filing in accordance with Chapter 160, subject to the limitations of Section 160.101, but not otherwise;

(9) a person who has had actual care, control, and possession of the child for not less than six months preceding the filing of the petition;

(10) a person designated as the managing conservator in a revoked or unrevoked affidavit of relinquishment under Chapter 161 or to whom consent to adoption has been given in writing under Chapter 162;

(11) a person with whom the child and the child's guardian, managing conservator, or parent have resided for not less than six months preceding the filing of the petition if the child's guardian, managing conservator, or parent is deceased at the time of the filing of the petition; or

(12) a person who is the foster parent of a child placed by the Department of Protective and Regulatory Services in the person's home for a period of not less than 18 months preceding the date of the filing of the petition.

Added by Acts 1995, 74th Leg., ch. 20, § 1, eff. April 20, 1995. Amended by Acts 1995, 74th Leg., ch. 751, § 8, eff. Sept. 1, 1995; Acts 1997, 75th Leg., ch. 575, § 3, eff. Sept. 1, 1997.

Section 38 of Acts 1997, 75th Leg., ch. 575 provides:

"This Act takes effect September 1, 1997, and applies to a suit affecting the parent-child relationship filed on or after that date. A suit filed before the effective date of this Act is governed by the law in effect on the date the suit was filed, and the former law is continued in effect for that purpose."

§ 102.004. Standing for Grandparent

(a) An original suit requesting managing conservatorship may be filed by a grandparent if there is satisfactory proof to the court that:

(1) the order requested is necessary because the child's present environment presents a serious question concerning the child's physical health or welfare; or

(2) both parents, the surviving parent, or the managing conservator or custodian either filed the petition or consented to the suit.

(b) An original suit requesting possessory conservatorship may not be filed by a grandparent or other person. However, the court may grant a grandparent or other person deemed by the court to have had substantial past contact with the child leave to intervene in a pending suit filed by a person authorized to do so under this subchapter.

(c) Access to a child by a grandparent is governed by the standards established by Chapter 153.

Added by Acts 1995, 74th Leg., ch. 20, § 1, eff. April 20, 1995.

§ 102.005. Standing to Request Termination and Adoption

An original suit requesting only an adoption or for termination of the parent-child relationship joined with a petition for adoption may be filed by:

(1) a stepparent of the child;

(2) an adult who, as the result of a placement for adoption, has had actual possession and control of the child at any time during the 30–day period preceding the filing of the petition;

(3) an adult who has had actual possession and control of the child for not less than two months during the three-month period preceding the filing of the petition; or

(4) another adult whom the court determines to have had substantial past contact with the child sufficient to warrant standing to do so.

Added by Acts 1995, 74th Leg., ch. 20, § 1, eff. April 20, 1995.

§ 102.006. Limitations on Standing

(a) Except as provided by Subsection (b), if the parent-child relationship between the child and every living parent of the child has been terminated, an original suit may not be filed by:

(1) a former parent whose parent-child relationship with the child has been terminated by court order;

(2) the biological father of the child; or

(3) a family member or relative by blood, adoption, or marriage of either a former parent whose parent-child relationship has been terminated or of the biological father of the child.

(b) The limitations on filing suit imposed by this section do not apply to a person who:

(1) has a continuing right to possession of or access to the child under an existing court order; or

(2) has the consent of the child's managing conservator, guardian, or legal custodian to bring the suit.

Added by Acts 1995, 74th Leg., ch. 20, § 1, eff. April 20, 1995.

§ 102.007. Standing of Title IV–D Agency

In providing services authorized by Chapter 231, the Title IV–D agency or a political subdivision contracting with the attorney general to provide Title IV–D services under this title may file a child support action authorized under this title, including a suit for modification or a motion for enforcement.

Added by Acts 1995, 74th Leg., ch. 20, § 1, eff. April 20, 1995. Amended by Acts 1995, 74th Leg., ch. 341, § 2.02, eff. Sept. 1, 1995.

§ 102.008. Contents of Petition

(a) The petition and all other documents in a proceeding filed under this title, except a suit for adoption of an adult, shall be entitled "In the interest of __________, a child." In a suit in which adoption of a child is requested, the style shall be "In the interest of a child."

(b) The petition must include:

(1) a statement that the court in which the petition is filed has continuing, exclusive jurisdiction or that no court has continuing jurisdiction of the suit;

(2) the name, sex, place and date of birth, and place of residence of the child, except that if adoption of a child is requested, the name of the child may be omitted;

(3) the full name, age, and place of residence of the petitioner and the petitioner's relationship to the child or the fact that no relationship exists;

(4) the names, ages, and place of residence of the parents, except in a suit in which adoption is requested;

(5) the name and place of residence of the managing conservator, if any, or the child's custodian, if any, appointed by order of a court of another state or country;

(6) the names and places of residence of the guardians of the person and estate of the child, if any;

(7) the names and places of residence of possessory conservators or other persons, if any, having possession of or access to the child under an order of the court;

(8) the name and place of residence of an alleged father of the child or a statement that the identity of the father of the child is unknown;

(9) a full description and statement of value of all property owned or possessed by the child;

(10) a statement describing what action the court is requested to take concerning the child and the statutory grounds on which the request is made; and

(11) any other information required by this title.

Added by Acts 1995, 74th Leg., ch. 20, § 1, eff. April 20, 1995.

§ 102.0085. Statement on Alternative Dispute Resolution

(a) A party to a proceeding brought under this chapter and Chapters 151, 153, 154, 156, 160, and 161 shall include in the first pleading filed by the party in the proceeding the following statement:

"I AM AWARE THAT IT IS THE POLICY OF THE STATE OF TEXAS TO PROMOTE THE AMICABLE AND NONJUDICIAL SETTLEMENT OF DISPUTES INVOLVING CHILDREN AND FAMILIES. I AM AWARE OF ALTERNATIVE DISPUTE RESOLUTION METHODS, INCLUDING MEDIATION. WHILE I RECOGNIZE THAT ALTERNATIVE DISPUTE RESOLUTION IS AN ALTERNATIVE TO AND NOT A SUBSTITUTE FOR A TRIAL AND THAT THIS CASE MAY BE TRIED IF IT IS NOT SETTLED, I REPRESENT TO THE COURT THAT I WILL ATTEMPT IN GOOD FAITH TO RESOLVE BEFORE FINAL TRIAL CONTESTED ISSUES IN THIS CASE BY ALTERNATIVE DISPUTE RESOLUTION WITHOUT THE NECESSITY OF COURT INTERVENTION."

(b) The statement required by Subsection (a) must be printed in boldfaced type or capital letters and signed by the party.

(c) The statement in Subsection (a) is not required for:

(1) a pleading in which citation on all respondents entitled to service of citation is requested, issued, and given by publication;

(2) a motion or pleading that seeks relief under Section 105.001(c), Subchapter H, Chapter 157 [1], or Chapter 262; or

(3) a special appearance under Rule 120A, Texas Rules of Civil Procedure.

Added by Acts 1995, 74th Leg., ch. 751, § 9, eff. Sept. 1, 1995. Amended by Acts 1997, 75th Leg., ch. 937, § 2, eff. Sept. 1, 1997.

[1] V.T.C.A., Family Code § 157.371 et seq.

Section 4 of Acts 1997, 75th Leg., ch. 937 provides:

"This Act takes effect September 1, 1997, and applies only to a suit filed under Title 1, Family Code, or Chapter 151, 153, 154, 156, 157, 160, 161, or 262, Family Code, on or after that date."

§ 102.009. Service of Citation

(a) Except as provided by Subsection (b), the following are entitled to service of citation on the filing of a petition in an original suit:

(1) a managing conservator;

(2) a possessory conservator;

(3) a person having possession of or access to the child under an order;

(4) a person required by law or by order to provide for the support of the child;

(5) a guardian of the person of the child;

(6) a guardian of the estate of the child;

(7) each parent as to whom the parent-child relationship has not been terminated or process has not been waived under Chapter 161;

(8) an alleged father, unless there is attached to the petition an affidavit of waiver of interest in a child executed by the alleged father as provided by Chapter 161 or unless the petitioner has complied with the provisions of Section 161.002(b)(2) or (b)(3);

(9) a man who has filed a notice of intent to claim paternity as provided by Subchapter D, Chapter 160; [1] and

Text of Subd. (10) as added by Acts 1997, 75th Leg., ch. 561, § 1

(10) the Department of Protective and Regulatory Services, if the petition requests that the department be appointed as managing conservator of the child.

Text of subd. (10) as added by Acts 1997, 75th Leg., ch. 599, § 1

(10) the attorney general, if the petition requests the termination of the parent-child relationship and the Title IV-D agency has filed with the court a notice of assignment under Chapter 231 with respect to the support rights of the child.

(b) Citation may be served on any other person who has or who may assert an interest in the child.

(c) Citation on the filing of an original petition in a suit shall be issued and served as in other civil cases.

(d) If the petition requests the establishment, modification, or enforcement of a support right assigned to the Title IV–D agency under Chapter 231, notice shall be given to the attorney general in a manner provided by Rule 21a, Texas Rules of Civil Procedure.

Added by Acts 1995, 74th Leg., ch. 20, § 1, eff. April 20, 1995. Amended by Acts 1995, 74th Leg., ch. 751, § 10, eff. Sept. 1, 1995; Acts 1997, 75th Leg., ch. 561, § 1, eff. Sept. 1, 1997; Acts 1997, 75th Leg., ch. 599, § 1, eff. Sept. 1, 1997.

[1] V.T.C.A., Family Code § 160.251 et seq.

Section 32(b) to (d) of Acts 1997, 75th Leg., ch. 561 provides:

"(b) Except as otherwise provided by this section, the change in law made by this Act applies only to a suit affecting the parent-child relationship commenced on or after the effective date of this Act. A suit affecting the parent-child relationship commenced before the effective date of this Act is governed by the law in effect on the date it was commenced, and the former law is continued in effect for that purpose.

"(c) The change in law made by this Act pertaining to the termination of the parent-child relationship applies only to an affidavit to relinquish parental rights or an affidavit of waiver of interest in a child executed on or after the effective date of this Act. An affidavit executed before the effective date of this Act is governed by the law in effect on the date the affidavit was executed, and the former law is continued in effect for that purpose.

"(d) The change in law made by this Act pertaining to adoptions applies only to petitions for adoptions filed on or after the effective date of this Act. A petition for adoption filed before the effective date of this Act is governed by the law in effect on the date the petition was filed, and the former law is continued in effect for that purpose; except that for these purposes a petition for adoption shall be considered to be filed at the time that the original petition was filed or at the time that an amended petition seeking the adoption was filed if the amended petition is filed in a cause that has previously been filed and where the court has continuing jurisdiction over the child."

§ 102.010. Service of Citation by Publication

(a) Citation may be served by publication as in other civil cases to persons entitled to service of citation who cannot be notified by personal service or registered or certified mail and to persons whose names are unknown.

(b) Citation by publication shall be published one time. If the name of a person entitled to service of citation is unknown, the notice to be published shall be addressed to "All Whom It May Concern." One or more causes to be heard on a certain day may be included in one notice and hearings may be continued from time to time without further notice.

(c) Citation by publication shall be sufficient if given in substantially the following form:

"STATE OF TEXAS

To (names of persons to be served with citation) and to all whom it may concern (if the name of any person to be served with citation is unknown), Respondent(s),

"You have been sued. You may employ an attorney. If you or your attorney do (does) not file a written answer with the clerk who issued this citation by 10 a.m. on the Monday next following the expiration of 20 days after you were served this citation and petition, a default judgment may be taken against you. The petition of ______________, Petitioner, was filed in the Court of ______________ County, Texas, on the ___ day of _________, _____, against __________, Respondent(s), numbered _____, and entitled 'In the interest of __________, a child (or children).' The suit requests (statement of relief requested, e.g., 'terminate the parent-child relationship'). The date and place of birth of the child (children) who is (are) the subject of the suit: _____________.

"The court has authority in this suit to render an order in the child's (children's) interest that will be binding on you, including the termination of the parent-child relationship, the determination of paternity, and the appointment of a conservator with authority to consent to the child's (children's) adoption.

"Issued and given under my hand and seal of the Court at _________, Texas, this the ___ day of ________, ____.

". . . . .

Clerk of the District Court of

______________ County, Texas.

By ______________, Deputy."

Added by Acts 1995, 74th Leg., ch. 20, § 1, eff. April 20, 1995.

§ 102.011. Acquiring Jurisdiction over Nonresident

(a) The court may exercise status or subject matter jurisdiction over the suit as provided by Chapter 152.

(b) The court may also exercise personal jurisdiction over a person on whom service of citation is required or over the person's personal representative, although the person is not a resident or domiciliary of this state, if:

(1) the person is personally served with citation in this state;

(2) the person submits to the jurisdiction of this state by consent, by entering a general appearance, or by filing a responsive document having the effect of waiving any contest to personal jurisdiction;

(3) the child resides in this state as a result of the acts or directives of the person;

(4) the person resided with the child in this state;

(5) the person resided in this state and provided prenatal expenses or support for the child;

(6) the person engaged in sexual intercourse in this state and the child may have been conceived by that act of intercourse;

(7) the person registered with the paternity registry maintained by the bureau of vital statistics as provided by Chapter 160; or

(8) there is any basis consistent with the constitutions of this state and the United States for the exercise of the personal jurisdiction.

Added by Acts 1995, 74th Leg., ch. 20, § 1, eff. April 20, 1995. Amended by Acts 1997, 75th Leg., ch. 561, § 2, eff. Sept. 1, 1997.

For application provisions of Acts 1997, 75th Leg., ch. 561, see notes following V.T.C.A., Family Code § 102.009.

§ 102.012. Exercising Partial Jurisdiction

(a) A court in which a suit is filed may exercise its jurisdiction over those portions of the suit for which it has authority.

(b) The court's authority to resolve all issues in controversy between the parties may be restricted because the court lacks:

(1) the required personal jurisdiction over a nonresident party;

(2) the required jurisdiction under Chapter 152; or

(3) the required jurisdiction under Chapter 157.

(c) If a provision of Chapter 152 or Chapter 159 expressly conflicts with another provision of this title and the conflict cannot be reconciled, the provision of Chapter 152 or Chapter 159 prevails.

(d) In exercising jurisdiction, the court shall seek to harmonize the provisions of this code, the federal Parental Kidnapping Prevention Act (28 U.S.C. Section 1738A), and the federal Full Faith and Credit for Child Support Order Act (28 U.S.C. Section 1738B).

Added by Acts 1995, 74th Leg., ch. 20, § 1, eff. April 20, 1995.

§ 102.013. Docketing Requirements

(a) In a suit for modification or a motion for enforcement, the clerk shall file the petition or motion and all related papers under the same docket number as the prior proceeding without additional letters, digits, or special designations.

(b) If a suit requests the adoption of a child, the clerk shall file the suit and all other papers relating to the suit in a new file having a new docket number.

Added by Acts 1995, 74th Leg., ch. 20, § 1, eff. April 20, 1995.

CHAPTER 103. VENUE AND TRANSFER OF ORIGINAL PROCEEDINGS

§ 103.001. Venue for Original Suit

(a) Except as otherwise provided by this title, an original suit shall be filed in the county where the child resides, unless:

(1) another court has continuing exclusive jurisdiction under Chapter 155; or

(2) venue is fixed in a suit for dissolution of a marriage under Chapter 3.

(b) A suit in which adoption is requested may be filed in the county where the child resides or in the county where the petitioners reside.

(c) A child resides in the county where the child's parents reside or the child's parent resides, if only one parent is living, except that:

(1) if a guardian of the person has been appointed by order of a county or probate court and a managing conservator has not been appointed, the child resides in the county where the guardian of the person resides;

(2) if the parents of the child do not reside in the same county and if a managing conservator, custodian, or guardian of the person has not been appointed, the child resides in the county where the parent having actual care, control, and possession of the child resides;

(3) if the child is in the care and control of an adult other than a parent and a managing conservator, custodian, or guardian of the person has not been appointed, the child resides where the adult having actual care, control, and possession of the child resides;

(4) if the child is in the actual care, control, and possession of an adult other than a parent and the whereabouts of the parent and the guardian of the person is unknown, the child resides where the adult having actual possession, care, and control of the child resides;

(5) if the person whose residence would otherwise determine venue has left the child in the care and control of the adult, the child resides where that adult resides;

(6) if a guardian or custodian of the child has been appointed by order of a court of another state or country, the child resides in the county where the guardian or custodian resides if that person resides in this state; or

(7) if it appears that the child is not under the actual care, control, and possession of an adult, the child resides where the child is found.

Added by Acts 1995, 74th Leg., ch. 20, § 1, eff. April 20, 1995.

§ 103.002. Transfer of Original Proceedings Within State

(a) If venue of a suit is improper in the court in which an original suit is filed and no other court has continuing, exclusive jurisdiction of the suit, on the timely motion of a party other than the petitioner, the court shall transfer the proceeding to the county where venue is proper.

(b) On a showing that a suit for dissolution of the marriage of the child's parents has been filed in another court, a court in which a suit is pending shall transfer the proceedings to the court where the dissolution of the marriage is pending.

(c) The procedures in Chapter 155 apply to a transfer of:

(1) an original suit under this section; or

(2) a suit for modification or a motion for enforcement under this title.

Added by Acts 1995, 74th Leg., ch. 20, § 1, eff. April 20, 1995.

§ 103.003. Transfer of Original Suit Within State when Party or Child Resides Outside State

(a) A court of this state in which an original suit is filed or in which a suit for child support is filed under Chapter 159 shall transfer the suit to the county of residence of the party who is a resident of this state if all other parties and children affected by the proceedings reside outside this state.

(b) If one or more of the parties affected by the suit reside outside this state and if more than one party or one or more children affected by the proceeding reside in this state in different counties, the court shall transfer the suit according to the following priorities:

(1) to the court of continuing, exclusive jurisdiction, if any;

(2) to the county of residence of the child, if applicable, provided that:

(A) there is no court of continuing, exclusive jurisdiction; or

(B) the court of continuing, exclusive jurisdiction finds that neither a party nor a child affected by the proceeding resides in the county of the court of continuing jurisdiction; or

(3) if Subdivisions (1) and (2) are inapplicable, to the county most appropriate to serve the convenience of the resident parties, the witnesses, and the interest of justice.

(c) If a transfer of an original suit or suit for child support under Chapter 159 is sought under this section, Chapter 155 applies to the procedures for transfer of the suit.

Added by Acts 1995, 74th Leg., ch. 20, § 1, eff. April 20, 1995.

CHAPTER 104. EVIDENCE

§ 104.001. Rules of Evidence

Except as otherwise provided, the Texas Rules of Civil Evidence apply as in other civil cases.

Added by Acts 1995, 74th Leg., ch. 20, § 1, eff. April 20, 1995.

§ 104.002. Prerecorded Statement of Child

If a child 12 years of age or younger is alleged in a suit under this title to have been abused, the recording of an oral statement of the child recorded prior to the proceeding is admissible into evidence if:

(1) no attorney for a party was present when the statement was made;

(2) the recording is both visual and aural and is recorded on film or videotape or by other electronic means;

(3) the recording equipment was capable of making an accurate recording, the operator was competent, and the recording is accurate and has not been altered;

(4) the statement was not made in response to questioning calculated to lead the child to make a particular statement;

(5) each voice on the recording is identified;

(6) the person conducting the interview of the child in the recording is present at the proceeding and available to testify or be cross-examined by either party; and

(7) each party is afforded an opportunity to view the recording before it is offered into evidence.

Added by Acts 1995, 74th Leg., ch. 20, § 1, eff. April 20, 1995.

§ 104.003. Prerecorded Videotaped Testimony of Child

(a) The court may, on the motion of a party to the proceeding, order that the testimony of the child be taken outside the courtroom and be recorded for showing in the courtroom before the court, the finder of fact, and the parties to the proceeding.

(b) Only an attorney for each party, an attorney ad litem for the child or other person whose presence would contribute to the welfare and well-being of the child, and persons necessary to operate the equipment may be present in the room with the child during the child's testimony.

(c) Only the attorneys for the parties may question the child.

(d) The persons operating the equipment shall be placed in a manner that prevents the child from seeing or hearing them.

(e) The court shall ensure that:

(1) the recording is both visual and aural and is recorded on film or videotape or by other electronic means;

(2) the recording equipment was capable of making an accurate recording, the operator was competent, and the recording is accurate and is not altered;

(3) each voice on the recording is identified; and

(4) each party to the proceeding is afforded an opportunity to view the recording before it is shown in the courtroom.

Added by Acts 1995, 74th Leg., ch. 20, § 1, eff. April 20, 1995.

§ 104.004. Remote Televised Broadcast of Testimony of Child

(a) If in a suit a child 12 years of age or younger is alleged to have been abused, the court may, on the motion of a party to the proceeding, order that the testimony of the child be taken in a room other than the courtroom and be televised by closed-circuit equipment in the courtroom to be viewed by the court and the parties.

(b) The procedures that apply to prerecorded videotaped testimony of a child apply to the remote broadcast of testimony of a child.

Added by Acts 1995, 74th Leg., ch. 20, § 1, eff. April 20, 1995.

§ 104.005. Substitution for In-Court Testimony of Child

(a) If the testimony of a child is taken as provided by this chapter, the child may not be compelled to testify in court during the proceeding.

(b) The court may allow the testimony of a child of any age to be taken in any manner provided by this chapter if the child, because of a medical condition, is incapable of testifying in open court.

Added by Acts 1995, 74th Leg., ch. 20, § 1, eff. April 20, 1995. Amended by Acts 1995, 74th Leg., ch. 751, § 11, eff. Sept. 1, 1995.

§ 104.006. Hearsay Statement of Child Abuse Victim

In a suit affecting the parent-child relationship, a statement made by a child 12 years of age or younger that describes alleged abuse against the child, without regard to whether the statement is otherwise inadmissible as hearsay, is admissible as evidence if, in a hearing conducted outside the presence of the jury, the court finds that the time, content, and circumstances of the statement provide sufficient indications of the statement's reliability and:

(1) the child testifies or is available to testify at the proceeding in court or in any other manner provided for by law; or

(2) the court determines that the use of the statement in lieu of the child's testimony is necessary to protect the welfare of the child.

Added by Acts 1997, 75th Leg., ch. 575, § 4, eff. Sept. 1, 1997.

For application provisions of Acts 1997, 75th Leg., ch. 575, see note following V.T.C.A., Family Code § 102.003.

CHAPTER 105. SETTINGS, HEARINGS, AND ORDERS

Section

§ 105.001. Temporary Orders Before Final Order

(a) In a suit, the court may make a temporary order, including the modification of a prior temporary order, for the safety and welfare of the child, including an order:

(1) for the temporary conservatorship of the child;

(2) for the temporary support of the child;

(3) restraining a party from molesting or disturbing the peace of the child or another party;

(4) prohibiting a person from removing the child beyond a geographical area identified by the court; or

(5) for payment of reasonable attorney's fees and expenses.

(b) Except as provided by Subsection (c), temporary restraining orders and temporary injunctions under this section shall be granted without the necessity of an affidavit or verified pleading stating specific facts showing that immediate and irreparable injury, loss, or damage will result before notice can be served and a hearing can be held. Except as provided by Subsection (h), an order may not be rendered under Subsection (a)(1), (2), or (5) except after notice and a hearing. A temporary restraining order granted under this section need not:

(1) define the injury or state why it is irreparable; or

(2) state why the order was granted without notice.

(c) Except on a verified pleading or an affidavit in accordance with the Texas Rules of Civil Procedure, an order may not be rendered:

(1) attaching the body of the child;

(2) taking the child into the possession of the court or of a parent designated by the court; or

(3) excluding a parent from possession of or access to a child.

(d) In a suit, the court may dispense with the necessity of:

(1) a bond in connection with temporary orders in behalf of the child; and

(2) setting the cause for trial on the merits with respect to the ultimate relief requested.

(e) Temporary orders rendered under this section are not subject to interlocutory appeal.

(f) The violation of a temporary restraining order, temporary injunction, or other temporary order rendered under this section is punishable by contempt and the order is subject to and enforceable under Chapter 157.

(g) The rebuttable presumptions established in favor of the application of the guidelines for a child support order and for the standard possession order under Chapters 153 and 154 apply to temporary orders. The presumptions do not limit the authority of the court to render other temporary orders.

(h) An order under Subsection (a)(1) may be rendered without notice and an adversary hearing if the order is an emergency order sought by a governmental entity under Chapter 262.

Added by Acts 1995, 74th Leg., ch. 20, § 1, eff. April 20, 1995. Amended by Acts 1997, 75th Leg., ch. 575, § 5, eff. Sept. 1, 1997.

For application provisions of Acts 1997, 75th Leg., ch. 575, see note following V.T.C.A., Family Code § 102.003.

§ 105.002. Jury

(a) Except as provided by Subsection (b), a party may demand a jury trial.

(b) A party may not demand a jury trial in a suit in which adoption is sought, including a trial on the issue of denial or revocation of consent to the adoption by the managing conservator.

(c) In a jury trial:

(1) a party is entitled to a verdict by the jury on the issues of:

(A) the appointment of a managing conservator;

(B) the appointment of joint managing conservators;

(C) the appointment of a possessory conservator; and

(D) the determination of the primary residence of the child;

(2) a party is not entitled to a jury verdict on the issues of:

(A) child support;

(B) a specific term or condition of possession of or access to the child; or

(C) any right or duty of a possessory or managing conservator, other than the issue of primary residence determined under Subdivision (1)(D); and

(3) the court may submit to the jury an issue described by Subdivision (2).

(d) The court may not contravene a jury verdict on an issue submitted under Subsection (c)(1). A jury verdict on an issue submitted under Subsection (c)(3) is advisory only.

Added by Acts 1995, 74th Leg., ch. 20, § 1, eff. April 20, 1995. Amended by Acts 1995, 74th Leg., ch. 751, § 12, eff. Sept. 1, 1995; Acts 1997, 75th Leg., ch. 180, § 1, eff. Sept. 1, 1997.

Section 2 of Acts 1997, 75th Leg., ch. 180, provides:

"This Act takes effect September 1, 1997, and applies only to a suit in which the trial on the merits has not begun on that date, a suit in which a trial has been held and a new trial is ordered on or after that date, and a suit filed on or after that date. The fact of the enactment of this Act is not a ground for a new trial."

§ 105.003. Procedure for Contested Hearing

(a) Except as otherwise provided by this title, proceedings shall be as in civil cases generally.

(b) On the agreement of all parties to the suit, the court may limit attendance at the hearing to only those persons who have a direct interest in the suit or in the work of the court.

(c) A record shall be made as in civil cases generally unless waived by the parties with the consent of the court.

(d) When information contained in a report, study, or examination is before the court, the person making the report, study, or examination is subject to both direct examination and cross-examination as in civil cases generally.

(e) The hearing may be adjourned from time to time.

Added by Acts 1995, 74th Leg., ch. 20, § 1, eff. April 20, 1995.

§ 105.004. Preferential Setting

After a hearing, the court may:

(1) grant a motion filed by a party or the attorney or guardian ad litem for the child for a preferential setting for a trial on the merits; and

(2) give precedence to that hearing over other civil cases if the court finds that the delay created by ordinary scheduling practices will unreasonably affect the best interest of the child.

Added by Acts 1995, 74th Leg., ch. 20, § 1, eff. April 20, 1995.

§ 105.005. Findings

Except as otherwise provided by this title, the court's findings shall be based on a preponderance of the evidence.

Added by Acts 1995, 74th Leg., ch. 20, § 1, eff. April 20, 1995.

§ 105.006. Contents of Final Order

(a) A final order must contain:

(1) the social security number and driver's license number of each party to the suit, including the child, except that the child's social security number or driver's license number is not required if the child has not been assigned a social security number or driver's license number; and

(2) each party's current residence address, mailing address, home telephone number, name of employer, address of employment, and work telephone number, except as provided by Subsection (c).

(b) Except as provided by Subsection (c), the court shall order each party to inform each other party, the court that rendered the order, and the state case registry under Chapter 234 of an intended change in any of the information required by this section as long as any person, as a result of the order, is under an obligation to pay child support or is entitled to possession of or access to a child. The court shall order that notice of the intended change be given at the earlier of:

(1) the 60th day before the date the party intends to make the change; or

(2) the fifth day after the date that the party knew of the change, if the party did not know or could not have known of the change in sufficient time to comply with Subdivision (1).

(c) If a court finds after notice and hearing that requiring a party to provide the information required by this section to another party is likely to cause the child or a conservator harassment, abuse, serious harm, or injury, the court may:

(1) order the information not to be disclosed to another party; or

(2) render any other order the court considers necessary.

(d) An order in a suit that orders child support or possession of or access to a child must contain the following notice in bold-faced type or in capital letters:

"FAILURE TO OBEY A COURT ORDER FOR CHILD SUPPORT OR FOR POSSESSION OF OR ACCESS TO A CHILD MAY RESULT IN FURTHER LITIGATION TO ENFORCE THE ORDER, INCLUDING CONTEMPT OF COURT. A FINDING OF CONTEMPT MAY BE PUNISHED BY CONFINEMENT IN JAIL FOR UP TO SIX MONTHS, A FINE OF UP TO $500 FOR EACH VIOLATION, AND A MONEY JUDGMENT FOR PAYMENT OF ATTORNEY'S FEES AND COURT COSTS.

"FAILURE OF A PARTY TO MAKE A CHILD SUPPORT PAYMENT TO THE PLACE AND IN THE MANNER REQUIRED BY A COURT ORDER MAY RESULT IN THE PARTY NOT RECEIVING CREDIT FOR MAKING THE PAYMENT.

"FAILURE OF A PARTY TO PAY CHILD SUPPORT DOES NOT JUSTIFY DENYING THAT PARTY COURT–ORDERED POSSESSION OF OR ACCESS TO A CHILD. REFUSAL BY A PARTY TO ALLOW POSSESSION OF OR ACCESS TO A CHILD DOES NOT JUSTIFY FAILURE TO PAY COURT–ORDERED CHILD SUPPORT TO THAT PARTY."

(e) Except as provided by Subsection (c), an order in a suit that orders child support or possession of or access to a child must also contain the following notice in bold-faced type or in capital letters:

"EACH PERSON WHO IS A PARTY TO THIS ORDER IS ORDERED TO NOTIFY EACH OTHER PARTY, THE COURT, AND THE STATE CASE REGISTRY OF ANY CHANGE IN THE PARTY'S CURRENT RESIDENCE ADDRESS, MAILING ADDRESS, HOME TELEPHONE NUMBER, NAME OF EMPLOYER, ADDRESS OF EMPLOYMENT, DRIVER'S LICENSE NUMBER, AND WORK TELEPHONE NUMBER. THE PARTY IS ORDERED TO GIVE NOTICE OF AN INTENDED CHANGE IN ANY OF THE REQUIRED INFORMATION TO EACH OTHER PARTY, THE COURT, AND THE STATE CASE REGISTRY ON OR BEFORE THE 60TH DAY BEFORE THE INTENDED CHANGE. IF THE PARTY DOES NOT KNOW OR COULD NOT HAVE KNOWN OF THE CHANGE IN SUFFICIENT TIME TO PROVIDE 60-DAY NOTICE, THE PARTY IS ORDERED TO GIVE NOTICE OF THE CHANGE ON OR BEFORE THE FIFTH DAY AFTER THE DATE THAT THE PARTY KNOWS OF THE CHANGE.

"THE DUTY TO FURNISH THIS INFORMATION TO EACH OTHER PARTY, THE COURT, AND THE STATE CASE REGISTRY CONTINUES AS LONG AS ANY PERSON, BY VIRTUE OF THIS ORDER, IS UNDER AN OBLIGATION TO PAY CHILD SUPPORT OR ENTITLED TO POSSESSION OF OR ACCESS TO A CHILD.

"FAILURE BY A PARTY TO OBEY THE ORDER OF THIS COURT TO PROVIDE EACH OTHER PARTY, THE COURT, AND THE STATE CASE REGISTRY WITH THE CHANGE IN THE REQUIRED INFORMATION MAY RESULT IN FURTHER LITIGATION TO ENFORCE THE OR-

DER, INCLUDING CONTEMPT OF COURT. A FINDING OF CONTEMPT MAY BE PUNISHED BY CONFINEMENT IN JAIL FOR UP TO SIX MONTHS, A FINE OF UP TO $500 FOR EACH VIOLATION, AND A MONEY JUDGMENT FOR PAYMENT OF ATTORNEY'S FEES AND COURT COSTS."

Text of subsec. (f) as added by Acts 1997, 75th Leg., ch. 786, § 1

(f) The court may include in a final order in a suit in which a party to the suit makes an allegation of child abuse or neglect a finding on whether the party who made the allegation knew that the allegation was false. This finding shall not constitute collateral estoppel for any criminal proceeding. The court may impose on a party found to have made a false allegation of child abuse or neglect any civil sanction permitted under law, including attorney's fees, costs of experts, and any other costs.

Text of subsec. (f) as added by Acts 1997, 75th Leg., ch. 911, § 6

(f) Except for an action in which contempt is sought, in any subsequent child support enforcement action, the court may, on a showing that diligent effort has been made to determine the location of a party, consider due process requirements for notice and service of process to be met with respect to that party on delivery of written notice to the most recent residential or employer address filed by that party with the court and the state case registry.

(g) The Title IV-D agency shall promulgate and provide forms for a party to use in reporting to the court and, when established, to the state case registry under Chapter 234 the information required under this section.

Added by Acts 1995, 74th Leg., ch. 20, § 1, eff. April 20, 1995. Amended by Acts 1995, 74th Leg., ch. 751, §§ 13, 128, eff. Sept. 1, 1995; Acts 1997, 75th Leg., ch. 786, § 1, eff. Sept. 1, 1997; Acts 1997, 75th Leg., ch. 911, § 6, eff. Sept. 1, 1997.

Section 129 of Acts 1995, 74th Leg., ch. 751 provides:

"This Act takes effect September 1, 1995, and applies to a pending suit affecting the parent-child relationship without regard to whether the suit was commenced before, on, or after the effective date of this Act."

Section 3 of Acts 1997, 75th Leg., ch. 786 provides:

"This Act takes effect September 1, 1997, and applies only to a suit affecting the parent-child relationship filed on or after that date. A suit affecting the parent-child relationship filed before the effective date of this Act is governed by the law in effect on the date the suit was filed, and the former law is continued in effect for that purpose."

For application and effectiveness provisions of Acts 1997, 75th Leg., ch. 911, see note following V.T.C.A., Family Code § 101.011.

§ 105.007. Compliance With Order Requiring Notice of Change of Required Information

(a) A party shall comply with the order by giving written notice to each other party of an intended change in the party's current residence address, mailing address, home telephone number, name of employer, address of employment, and work telephone number.

(b) The party must give written notice by registered or certified mail of an intended change in the required information to each other party on or before the 60th day before the change is made. If the party does not know or could not have known of the change in sufficient time to provide 60-day notice, the party shall provide the written notice of the change on or before the fifth day after the date that the party knew of the change.

(c) The court may waive the notice required by this section on motion by a party if it finds that the giving of notice of a change of the required information would be likely to expose the child or the party to harassment, abuse, serious harm, or injury.

Added by Acts 1995, 74th Leg., ch. 20, § 1, eff. April 20, 1995. Amended by Acts 1995, 74th Leg., ch. 751, § 14, eff. Sept. 1, 1995.

§ 105.008. Record of Support Order for State Case Registry

(a) The clerk of the court shall provide the state case registry with a record of a court order for child support as required by procedures adopted under Section 234.003. The record of an order shall include information provided by the parties on a form developed by the Title IV-D agency. The form shall be completed by the petitioner and submitted to the clerk at the time the order is filed for record.

(b) To the extent federal funds are available, the Title IV-D agency shall reimburse the clerk of the court for the costs incurred in providing the record of support order required under this section.

Added by Acts 1997, 75th Leg., ch. 911, § 7, eff. Sept. 1, 1997.

CHAPTER 106. COSTS AND ATTORNEY'S FEES

Section

§ 106.001. Costs

The court may award costs in a suit or motion under this title and in a habeas corpus proceeding.

Added by Acts 1995, 74th Leg., ch. 20, § 1, eff. April 20, 1995. Amended by Acts 1997, 75th Leg., ch. 15, § 1, eff. Sept. 1, 1997.

Section 4 of Acts 1997, 75th Leg., ch. 15 provides:

"This Act takes effect September 1, 1997, and applies to a pending suit affecting the parent-child relationship without regard to whether the suit was commenced before, on, or after the effective date of this Act."

§ 106.002. Attorney's Fees

(a) In a suit under this title, the court may order reasonable attorney's fees as costs and order the fees to be paid directly to an attorney.

(b) An award of attorney's fees may be enforced in the attorney's name by any means available for the enforcement of a judgment for debt.

Added by Acts 1995, 74th Leg., ch. 20, § 1, eff. April 20, 1995. Amended by Acts 1997, 75th Leg., ch. 15, § 2, eff. Sept. 1, 1997.

For application provisions of Acts 1997, 75th Leg., ch. 15, see notes following V.T.C.A., Family Code § 106.001.

CHAPTER 107. SPECIAL APPOINTMENTS AND SOCIAL STUDIES

Chapter 107, which as added by Acts 1995, 74th Leg., ch. 20, consisted of §§ 107.001 to 107.005, was amended by Acts 1995, 74th Leg., ch. 751, § 15.

SUBCHAPTER A. GUARDIAN AD LITEM REPRESENTATION

§ 107.001. Appointment of Guardian ad Litem

(a) In a suit in which termination of the parent-child relationship is requested, the court or an associate judge shall appoint a guardian ad litem to represent the interests of the child immediately after the filing of the petition but before the full adversary hearing to ensure adequate representation of the child, unless:

(1) the child is a petitioner;

(2) an attorney ad litem has been appointed for the child; or

(3) the court or an associate judge finds that the interests of the child will be represented adequately by a party to the suit and are not adverse to that party.

(b) In a suit filed by a governmental entity in which the entity requests the termination of the parent-child relationship or to be named conservator of a child, the court or an associate judge shall appoint a guardian ad litem to represent the best interests of the child immediately after the filing of the petition but before the full adversary hearing to ensure adequate representation of the child.

(c) In any other suit, the court or an associate judge may appoint a guardian ad litem.

(d) A guardian ad litem appointed under this section may be an attorney, a volunteer advocate appointed under Section 107.031, or another adult having the competence, training, and expertise determined by the court to be sufficient to represent the best interests of the child.

(e) The managing conservator may be appointed guardian ad litem if the managing conservator:

(1) is not a parent of the child or a person petitioning for adoption of the child; and

(2) has no personal interest in the suit.

(f) A guardian ad litem shall be appointed to represent any other person entitled to service of citation under this code if the person is incompetent or a child, unless the person has executed an affidavit of relinquishment of parental rights or an affidavit of waiver of interest in child containing a waiver of service of citation.

Amended by Acts 1995, 74th Leg., ch. 751, § 15, eff. Sept. 1, 1995; Acts 1997, 75th Leg., ch. 1294, § 1, eff. Sept. 1, 1997.

Section 10 of Acts 1997, 75th Leg., ch. 1294 provides:

"This Act takes effect September 1, 1997, and applies to a suit affecting the parent-child relationship pending on that date or filed on or after that date."

Section 129 of Acts 1995, 74th Leg., ch. 751 provides:

"This Act takes effect September 1, 1995, and applies to a pending suit affecting the parent-child relationship without regard to whether the suit was commenced before, on, or after the effective date of this Act."

§ 107.002. Powers and Duties of Guardian ad Litem

(a) A guardian ad litem appointed under this subchapter is not a party to the suit but may:

(1) conduct an investigation to the extent that the guardian ad litem considers necessary to determine the best interest of the child for whom the guardian is appointed; and

(2) obtain and review copies of the child's relevant medical, psychological, and school records.

(b) A guardian ad litem appointed under this subchapter shall, within a reasonable time after the appointment, interview:

(1) the child, if the child is four years of age or older; and

(2) each individual that the guardian ad litem considers likely to have significant knowledge of the child's history and condition.

(c) A guardian ad litem appointed under this subchapter is not a party to the suit but is entitled to:

(1) receive a copy of each pleading or other paper filed with the court in the case in which the guardian ad litem is appointed;

(2) receive notice of each hearing in the case;

(3) participate in case staffings by an authorized agency concerning the child;

(4) attend all legal proceedings in the case but may not call or question a witness unless the ad litem is a licensed attorney;

(5) review and sign or decline to sign any agreed order affecting the child; and

(6) testify in court, except as provided by Subsection (d), regarding the recommendations concerning the actions that the guardian ad litem considers to be in the best interest of the child, including giving reasons for the guardian ad litem's opposition if the guardian ad litem does not agree to the terms of a proposed order.

(d) An attorney who is appointed as attorney ad litem and guardian ad litem for a child may not testify under Subsection (c)(6).

(e) An attorney who is appointed as attorney ad litem and guardian ad litem for a child shall:

(1) become familiar with the American Bar Association's standards of practice for lawyers who represent children in abuse and neglect cases; and

(2) comply with the requirements of the Texas Disciplinary Rules of Professional Conduct.

(f) An attorney who is appointed as attorney ad litem and guardian ad litem for a child and who determines that a conflict exists by performing both roles shall:

(1) withdraw as the child's guardian ad litem;

(2) continue to serve as the child's attorney ad litem; and

(3) request appointment of a new guardian ad litem for the child without revealing the reason a new appointment is required.

Added by Acts 1995, 74th Leg., ch. 20, § 1, eff. Sept. 1, 1995. Amended by Acts 1995, 74th Leg., ch. 943, § 10, eff. Sept. 1, 1995; Acts 1997, 75th Leg., ch. 1294, § 2, eff. Sept. 1, 1997.

For application provisions of Acts 1997, 75th Leg., ch. 1294, see note following V.T.C.A., Family Code § 107.001.

§ 107.003. Immunity

(a) A guardian ad litem appointed under this subchapter is not liable for civil damages arising from a recommendation made or an opinion given in the capacity of guardian ad litem.

(b) Subsection (a) does not apply to a recommendation or opinion that is:

(1) wilfully wrongful;

(2) given with conscious indifference or reckless disregard to the safety of another;

(3) given in bad faith or with malice; or

(4) grossly negligent.

Added by Acts 1997, 75th Leg., ch. 1294, § 3, eff. Sept. 1, 1997.

For application provisions of Acts 1997, 75th Leg., ch. 1294, see note following V.T.C.A., Family Code § 107.001.

§§ 107.003 to 107.005. Deleted by Acts 1995, 74th Leg., ch. 751, § 15, eff. Sept. 1, 1995

§ 107.006. Guardian Ad Litem and Attorney Ad Litem Pool; Qualifications

(a) The local administrative district judge in each county in a Department of Protective and Regulatory Services region for child protective services that contains a county having a population of 2.8 million or more shall establish a pool from which guardians ad litem and attorneys ad litem are appointed for proceedings in the district courts of the county. A local administrative district judge in any other county may establish a pool from which guardians ad litem and attorneys ad litem are appointed for proceedings in the district courts of that county. To be eligible for a pool established under this subsection, a person must:

(1) complete training approved by the State Bar of Texas in family law and the responsibilities of ad litems;

(2) complete as part of the person's annual continuing legal education requirement not fewer than three hours in family law issues; and

(3) meet other requirements established by the local administrative district judge.

(b) Before appointment as a guardian ad litem or an attorney ad litem, the person must have read, acknowledged by signing, and filed with the local administrative judge a written statement prepared by the local administrative district judge that lists the responsibilities of an ad litem, some or all of which may be appropriate to the person's specific case. The court shall retain a copy of the acknowledgment for two years. To continue to receive appointments under this section, the person must execute a new statement at least every two years.

(c) A party to a proceeding in which a person is appointed as a guardian ad litem or an attorney ad litem may object to appointment of the person at any time before the date of the trial of the proceeding. A party may object under this subsection by filing a written motion stating the grounds and facts on which the party believes that the person appointed lacks objectivity or is failing to fulfill the person's responsibilities as an ad litem as outlined in the written statement of ad litem responsibilities. The court shall promptly rule on an objection raised under this subsection and shall order the removal of the guardian ad litem or attorney ad litem if the court finds that the objection is justifiable.

(d) A person appointed as a guardian ad litem or attorney ad litem shall complete and submit to the court a voucher or claim for payment that includes the fees charged and hours worked by the ad litem. Information submitted under this section is subject to disclosure under Chapter 552, Government Code.

(e) The Bureau of Vital Statistics may compile information submitted under Subsection (d) for a county that maintains that information on an electronic database. On the request of the bureau, the county shall provide the information. Information compiled by the bureau under this section shall be made available to the Department of Protective and Regulatory Services.

Added by Acts 1995, 74th Leg., ch. 943, § 11, eff. Sept. 1, 1995. Amended by Acts 1997, 75th Leg., ch. 1294, § 4, eff. Sept. 1, 1997.

Section 13(a) of the 1995 Act provides:

"This Act takes effect September 1, 1995, and applies to a proceeding in which an investigation of the abuse of a child is pending on or after that date."

For application provisions of Acts 1997, 75th Leg., ch. 1294, see note following V.T.C.A., Family Code § 107.001.

[Sections 107.007 to 107.010 reserved for expansion]

SUBCHAPTER B. ATTORNEY AD LITEM

§ 107.011. Discretionary Appointment of Attorney Ad Litem

(a) An associate judge shall recommend the appointment of an attorney ad litem for any party in a case in which the associate judge deems representation necessary to protect the interests of the child who is the subject matter of the suit.

(b) The court shall appoint an attorney ad litem for any party in a case in which the court deems representation necessary to protect the interests of the child who is the subject matter of the suit.

Added by Acts 1995, 74th Leg., ch. 751, § 15, eff. Sept. 1, 1995.

§ 107.012. Mandatory Appointment of Attorney Ad Litem for Child

In a suit filed by a governmental entity requesting termination of the parent-child relationship or to be named conservator of a child, the court shall appoint an attorney ad litem to represent the interests of the child immediately after the filing, but before the full adversary hearing, to ensure adequate representation of the child.

Added by Acts 1995, 74th Leg., ch. 751, § 15, eff. Sept. 1, 1995.

§ 107.013. Mandatory Appointment of Attorney ad Litem for Parent

(a) In a suit in which termination of the parent-child relationship is requested, the court shall appoint an attorney ad litem to represent the interests of:

(1) an indigent parent of the child who responds in opposition to the termination;

(2) a parent served by citation by publication;

(3) an alleged father who failed to register with the registry under Subchapter D, Chapter 160, and whose identity or location is unknown; and

(4) an alleged father who registered with the paternity registry under Subchapter D, Chapter 160,[1] but the petitioner's attempt to personally serve citation at the address provided to the registry and at any other address for the alleged father known by the petitioner has been unsuccessful.

(b) If both parents of the child are entitled to the appointment of an attorney ad litem under this section and the court finds that the interests of the parents are not in conflict, the court may appoint a single attorney ad litem to represent the interests of both parents.

Added by Acts 1995, 74th Leg., ch. 751, § 15, eff. Sept. 1, 1995. Amended by Acts 1997, 75th Leg., ch. 561, § 3, eff. Sept. 1, 1997.

[1] V.T.C.A., Family Code § 160.251 et seq.

For application provisions of Acts 1997, 75th Leg., ch. 561, see notes following V.T.C.A., Family Code § 102.009.

§ 107.0135. Appointment of Attorney ad Litem Not Required; Certain Cases

A court is not required under this section to appoint an attorney ad litem in a proceeding in which:

(1) a suit for the dissolution of a marriage is uncontested; or

(2) the issues of possession of and access to a child are agreed to by both parents.

Added by Acts 1997, 75th Leg., ch. 1294, § 5, eff. Sept. 1, 1997.

For application provisions of Acts 1997, 75th Leg., ch. 1294, see note following V.T.C.A., Family Code § 107.001.

§ 107.014. Powers and Duties of Attorney Ad Litem for Child

(a) An attorney ad litem appointed under this subchapter to represent a child:

(1) shall investigate to the extent the attorney ad litem considers appropriate to determine the facts of the case;

(2) shall obtain and review copies of all of the child's relevant medical, psychological, and school records; and

(3) may call, examine, or cross-examine witnesses.

(b) An attorney ad litem appointed to represent a child shall within a reasonable time after the appointment:

(1) interview the child if the child is four years of age or older;

(2) interview individuals with significant knowledge of the child's history and condition; and

(3) interview all parties to the suit.

Added by Acts 1995, 74th Leg., ch. 751, § 15, eff. Sept. 1, 1995. Amended by Acts 1997, 75th Leg., ch. 650, § 1, eff. Sept. 1, 1997.

Section 2 of Acts 1997, 75th Leg., ch. 650 provides:

"This Act takes effect September 1, 1997, and applies only to an attorney ad litem appointed on or after that date. An attorney ad litem appointed before the effective date of this Act is governed by the law in effect on the date the attorney ad litem was appointed, and the former law is continued in effect for that purpose."

§ 107.015. Ad Litem Fees

(a) An attorney appointed to represent a child or parent as authorized by this subchapter is entitled to a reasonable fee in the amount set by the court to be paid by the parents of the child unless the parents are indigent.

(b) If the court or associate judge determines that the parties or litigants are able to defray the costs of an ad litem's compensation as determined by the reasonable and customary fees for similar services in the county of jurisdiction, the costs may be ordered paid by either or both parties, or the court or associate judge may order either or both parties, prior to final hearing, to pay the sums into the registry of the court or into an account authorized by the court for the use and benefit of the ad litem on order of the court. The sums may be taxed as costs to be assessed against one or more of the parties.

(c) If indigency of the parents is shown, an attorney appointed to represent a child or parent in a suit to terminate the parent-child relationship shall be paid from the general funds of the county according to the fee schedule that applies to an attorney appointed to represent a child in a suit under Title 3 as provided by Chapter 51.

Added by Acts 1995, 74th Leg., ch. 751, § 15, eff. Sept. 1, 1995.

§ 107.016. Continued Representation

In a suit brought by a governmental entity seeking termination of the parent-child relationship or appointment of the entity as conservator of the child, an order appointing the Department of Protective and Regulatory Services as the child's managing conservator may provide for the continuation of the attorney ad litem appointment for the child for any period set by the court.

Added by Acts 1995, 74th Leg., ch. 751, § 15, eff. Sept. 1, 1995. Amended by Acts 1997, 75th Leg., ch. 575, § 6, eff. Sept. 1, 1997.

For application provisions of Acts 1997, 75th Leg., ch. 575, see note following V.T.C.A., Family Code § 102.003.

[Sections 107.017 to 107.030 reserved for expansion]

SUBCHAPTER C. OTHER COURT APPOINTMENTS

§ 107.031. Volunteer Advocates

(a) In a suit filed by a governmental entity, the court may appoint a person who has received the court's approved training and who has been certified by the court to appear at court hearings as a volunteer advocate on behalf of the child.

(b) In addition, the court may appoint a group of court-certified volunteers to serve as an administrative review board to advise the court as to the conservatorship appointment and the placement of the child by the Department of Protective and Regulatory Services or authorized agency in substitute care.

(c) A court-appointed volunteer, a board member or employee of a volunteer advocate charitable organization, or a member of an administrative review board is not liable for civil damages for a recommendation made or opinion rendered while serving or having served as a court-appointed volunteer, board member or employee of a volunteer advocate charitable organization, or member of an administrative review board under this section unless the act or failure to act is wilfully wrongful, committed with conscious indifference or reckless disregard for the safety of another, committed in bad faith or with malice, or is grossly negligent.

(d) This section does not prohibit the court from appointing as a guardian ad litem for a child under Section 107.001 a court-certified volunteer advocate appointed for the child under this section.

Added by Acts 1995, 74th Leg., ch. 751, § 15, eff. Sept. 1, 1995. Amended by Acts 1997, 75th Leg., ch. 1294, § 6, eff. Sept. 1, 1997.

For application provisions of Acts 1997, 75th Leg., ch. 1294, see note following V.T.C.A., Family Code § 107.001.

[Sections 107.032 to 107.050 reserved for expansion]

SUBCHAPTER D. SOCIAL STUDY

§ 107.051. Order for Social Study

(a) The court may order the preparation of a social study into the circumstances and condition of the child and of the home of any person requesting managing conservatorship or possession of the child.

(b) The social study may be made by a state agency, including the Department of Protective and Regulatory Services, or a person appointed by the court.

(c) In a suit in which adoption is requested or possession of or access to the child is an issue and in which the Department of Protective and Regulatory Services is not a party or has no interest, the court shall appoint a private agency or person to conduct the social study.

Added by Acts 1995, 74th Leg., ch. 751, § 15, eff. Sept. 1, 1995.

§ 107.052. Standards for Conducting Social Study

(a) The court may appoint an investigator to conduct the social study required by this section who has the qualifications established by the rules of the Department of Protective and Regulatory Services providing minimum qualifications for persons who may conduct social studies. If the Department of Protective and Regulatory Services or another governmental entity is appointed, the person who conducts the investigation and makes the report must also have those qualifications.

(b) A study made under this section shall comply with the rules of the Department of Protective and Regulatory Services establishing minimum standards, guidelines, and procedures for social studies or the criteria established by the court.

(c) The social study shall contain any history of physical, sexual, or emotional abuse suffered by the child.

Added by Acts 1995, 74th Leg., ch. 751, § 15, eff. Sept. 1, 1995.

§ 107.053. Prospective Adoptive Parents to Receive Copy

In all adoptions a copy of the report shall be made available to the prospective adoptive parents prior to a final order of adoption.

Added by Acts 1995, 74th Leg., ch. 751, § 15, eff. Sept. 1, 1995.

§ 107.054. Report Filed With Court

The agency or person making the social study shall file with the court on a date set by the court a report containing its findings and conclusions. The report shall be made a part of the record of the suit.

Added by Acts 1995, 74th Leg., ch. 751, § 15, eff. Sept. 1, 1995.

§ 107.055. Introduction of Report at Trial

(a) Disclosure to the jury of the contents of a report to the court of a social study is subject to the rules of evidence.

(b) In a contested case, the agency or person making the social study shall furnish copies of the report to the attorneys for the parties before the earlier of:

(1) the seventh day after the date the social study is completed; or

(2) the fifth day before the date of commencement of the trial.

(c) The court may compel the attendance of witnesses necessary for the proper disposition of the suit, including a representative of the agency making the social study, who may be compelled to testify.

Added by Acts 1995, 74th Leg., ch. 751, § 15, eff. Sept. 1, 1995.

§ 107.056. Preparation Fee

If the court orders a social study to be conducted and a report to be prepared, the court shall award the agency or other person a reasonable fee for the preparation of the study that shall be taxed as costs and paid directly to the agency or other person. The person or agency may enforce the order for the fee.

Added by Acts 1995, 74th Leg., ch. 751, § 15, eff. Sept. 1, 1995.

CHAPTER 108. CENTRAL RECORD FILE; VITAL STATISTICS

Section

§ 108.001. Transmittal of Records of Suit by Clerk

(a) Except as provided by this chapter, the clerk of the court shall transmit to the bureau of vital statistics a certified record of the order rendered in a suit, together with the name and all prior names, birth date, and place of birth of the child prepared by the petitioner on a form provided by the bureau.

(b) The bureau of vital statistics shall maintain these records in a central file according to the name, birth date, and place of birth of the child, the court that rendered the order, and the docket number of the suit.

(c) All the records required under this section to be maintained by the bureau of vital statistics and the records of a child-placing agency that has ceased operations are confidential and no person is entitled to access to or information from these records except for good cause on an order of the court that rendered the order.

Added by Acts 1995, 74th Leg., ch. 20, § 1, eff. April 20, 1995. Amended by Acts 1995, 74th Leg., ch. 751, § 16, eff. Sept. 1, 1995.

§ 108.002. Dissolution of Marriage Records Maintained by Clerk

A clerk may not transmit to the central record file the pleadings, papers, studies, and records relating to a suit for divorce or annulment or to declare a marriage void.

Added by Acts 1995, 74th Leg., ch. 20, § 1, eff. April 20, 1995.

§ 108.003. Transmittal of Information Regarding Adoption

(a) The clerk of a court that renders a decree of adoption shall, not later than the 10th day of the first month after the month in which the adoption is rendered, transmit to the central registry of the bureau of vital statistics certified report of adoption that includes:

(1) the name of the adopted child after adoption as shown in the adoption order;

(2) the birth date of the adopted child;

(3) the docket number of the adoption suit;

(4) the identity of the court rendering the adoption;

(5) the date of the adoption order;

(6) the name and address of each parent, guardian, managing conservator, or other person whose consent to adoption was required or waived under Chapter 159, or whose parental rights were terminated in the adoption suit;

(7) the identity of the licensed child placing agency, if any, through which the adopted child was placed for adoption; and

(8) the identity, address, and telephone number of the registry through which the adopted child may register as an adoptee.

(b) Except for good cause shown or on an order of the court that granted the adoption or terminated the proceedings under Section 155.001, the records concerning a child maintained by the district clerk after rendition of a decree of adoption, the records of a child-placing agency that has ceased operations, and the records required under this section to be maintained by the bureau of vital statistics are confidential, and no person is entitled to access to or information from these records.

Added by Acts 1995, 74th Leg., ch. 20, § 1, eff. April 20, 1995. Amended by Acts 1995, 74th Leg., ch. 751, § 17, eff. Sept. 1, 1995.

§ 108.004. Transmittal of Files on Loss of Jurisdiction

On the loss of jurisdiction of a court under Chapter 155, the clerk of the court shall transmit to the central registry of the bureau of vital statistics a certified record, on a form provided by the bureau, stating that jurisdiction has been lost, the reason for the loss of jurisdiction, and the name and all previous names, date of birth, and place of birth of the child.

Added by Acts 1995, 74th Leg., ch. 20, § 1, eff. April 20, 1995. Amended by Acts 1995, 74th Leg., ch. 751, § 18, eff. Sept. 1, 1995.

§ 108.005. Adoption Records Received by Bureau of Vital Statistics

(a) When the bureau of vital statistics receives records from the district clerk, the bureau shall close the records concerning that child. Except for statistical purposes, the bureau may not disclose any information concerning the prior proceedings affecting the child. Except as provided in Chapter 162, any subsequent inquiry concerning the child who has been adopted shall be handled as though the child had not been previously the subject of a suit affecting the parent-child relationship. The bureau shall provide to the Department of Protective and Regulatory Services registry information as necessary for the department to comply with federal law or regulations regarding the compilation or reporting of adoption information to federal officials and other information as necessary for the department to administer the central registry as provided in Subchapter E, Chapter 162.[1]

(b) On the receipt of additional records concerning a child who has been the subject of a suit affecting the parent-child relationship in which the records have been closed, a new file shall be made and maintained.

Added by Acts 1995, 74th Leg., ch. 20, § 1, eff. April 20, 1995. Amended by Acts 1995, 74th Leg., ch. 751, § 19, eff. Sept. 1, 1995.

[1] V.T.C.A., Family Code § 162.401 et seq.

Repeal

Without reference to the amendment of this section by Acts 1995, 74th Leg., ch. 751, § 19, Acts 1995, 74th Leg., ch. 968, § 11 repealed this section effective Sept. 1, 1995.

§ 108.006. Fees

(a) The bureau of vital statistics may charge a reasonable fee to cover the cost of determining and sending information concerning the identity of the court with continuing, exclusive jurisdiction.

(b) On the filing of a suit requesting the adoption of a child, the clerk of the court shall collect an additional fee of $15.

(c) The clerk shall send the fees collected under Subsection (b) to the bureau of vital statistics for deposit in a special fund in the state treasury from which the legislature may appropriate money only to operate and maintain the central file and central registry of the bureau.

(d) The receipts from the fees charged under Subsection (a) shall be deposited in a financial institution as determined by the director of the bureau of vital statistics and withdrawn as necessary for the sole purpose of operating and maintaining the central record file.

Added by Acts 1995, 74th Leg., ch. 20, § 1, eff. April 20, 1995. Amended by Acts 1995, 74th Leg., ch. 751, § 20, eff. Sept. 1, 1995.

§ 108.007. Microfilm

(a) The bureau of vital statistics may use microfilm or other suitable means for maintaining the central record file.

(b) A certified reproduction of a document maintained by the bureau of vital statistics is admissible in evidence as the original document.

Added by Acts 1995, 74th Leg., ch. 20, § 1, eff. April 20, 1995. Amended by Acts 1995, 74th Leg., ch. 751, § 21, eff. Sept. 1, 1995.

§ 108.008. Filing Information After Determination of Paternity

(a) On a determination of paternity, the petitioner shall provide the clerk of the court in which the order was rendered the information necessary to prepare the declaration. The clerk shall:

(1) prepare the declaration on a form provided by the Bureau of Vital Statistics; and

(2) complete the declaration immediately after the order becomes final.

(b) Not later than the 10th day of each month, the clerk of the court shall forward to the state registrar a declaration for each order that became final in that court during the preceding month.

Added by Acts 1995, 74th Leg., ch. 20, § 1, eff. April 20, 1995.

§ 108.009. Birth Certificate

(a) The state registrar shall substitute a new birth certificate for the original based on the order in accordance with laws or rules that permit the correction or substitution of birth certificates for adopted children or children presumed to be biological children by the subsequent marriage of their parents.

(b) The new certificate may not show that the father and child relationship was established after the child's birth but may show the child's actual place and date of birth.

Added by Acts 1995, 74th Leg., ch. 20, § 1, eff. April 20, 1995.

CHAPTER 109. APPEALS

§ 109.001. Temporary Orders During Pendency of Appeal

(a) Not later than the 30th day after the date an appeal is perfected, on the motion of any party or on the court's own motion and after notice and hearing, the court may make any order necessary to preserve and protect the safety and welfare of the child during the pendency of the appeal as the court may deem necessary and equitable. In addition to other matters, an order may:

(1) appoint temporary conservators for the child and provide for possession of the child;

(2) require the temporary support of the child by a party;

(3) restrain a party from molesting or disturbing the peace of the child or another party;

(4) prohibit a person from removing the child beyond a geographical area identified by the court;

(5) require payment of reasonable attorney's fees and expenses; or

(6) suspend the operation of the order or judgment that is being appealed.

(b) A court retains jurisdiction to enforce its orders rendered under this section unless the appellate court, on a proper showing, supersedes the court's order.

(c) A temporary order rendered under this section is not subject to interlocutory appeal.

Added by Acts 1995, 74th Leg., ch. 20, § 1, eff. April 20, 1995.

§ 109.002. Appeal

(a) An appeal from a final order rendered in a suit, when allowed under this section or under other provisions of law, shall be as in civil cases generally. An appeal in a suit in which termination of the parent-child relationship is in issue shall be given precedence over other civil cases by the appellate courts.

(b) An appeal may be taken by any party to a suit from a final order rendered under this subtitle.

(c) An appeal from a final order, with or without a supersedeas bond, does not suspend the order unless suspension is ordered by the court rendering the order. The appellate court, on a proper showing, may permit the order to be suspended.

(d) On the motion of the parties or on the court's own motion, the appellate court in its opinion may identify the parties by fictitious names or by their initials only.

Added by Acts 1995, 74th Leg., ch. 20, § 1, eff. April 20, 1995.

§ 109.003. Payment for Statement of Facts

(a) If the party requesting a statement of facts in an appeal of a suit has filed an affidavit stating the party's inability to pay costs as provided by Rule 40, Texas Rules of Appellate Procedure, and the affidavit is approved by the trial court, the trial court may order the county in which the trial was held to pay the costs of preparing the statement of facts.

(b) Nothing in this section shall be construed to permit an official court reporter to be paid more than once for the preparation of the statement of facts.

Added by Acts 1995, 74th Leg., ch. 20, § 1, eff. April 20, 1995. Amended by Acts 1995, 74th Leg., ch. 472, § 1, eff. Sept. 1, 1995.

Section 2 of Acts 1995, 74th Leg., ch. 472 provides:

"(a) This Act takes effect September 1, 1995, and applies only to payment for a statement of facts in a suit affecting the parent-child relationship in which an affidavit stating a party's inability to pay costs is filed on or after the effective date of this Act.

"(b) Payment for a statement of facts in a suit affecting the parent-child relationship in which an affidavit stating a party's inability to pay costs is filed before the effective date of this Act is covered by the law in effect when the affidavit was filed, and the former law is continued in effect for that purpose."

CHAPTER 110. COURT FEES

§ 110.001. General Rule

Except as provided by this chapter, fees in a matter covered by this title shall be as in civil cases generally.

Added by Acts 1995, 74th Leg., ch. 20, § 1, eff. April 20, 1995.

§ 110.002. Filing Fees and Deposits

(a) The clerk of the court may collect a filing fee of $15 in a suit for filing:

(1) a suit for modification;

(2) a motion for enforcement;

(3) a notice of application for judicial writ of withholding;

(4) a motion to transfer.

(5) a petition for license suspension; or

(6) a motion to revoke a stay of license suspension.

(b) No other filing fee may be collected or required for an action described in this section.

(c) The clerk may collect a deposit as in other cases, in the amount set by the clerk for payment of expected costs and other expenses arising in the proceeding.

Added by Acts 1995, 74th Leg., ch. 20, § 1, eff. April 20, 1995. Amended by Acts 1997, 75th Leg., ch. 911, § 8, eff. Sept. 1, 1997; Acts 1997, 75th Leg., ch. 976, § 6, eff. Sept. 1, 1997.

For application and effectiveness provisions of Acts 1997, 75th Leg., ch. 911, see note following V.T.C.A., Family Code § 101.011.

Section 10(a) of Acts 1997, 75th Leg., ch. 976 provides:

"This Act takes effect September 1, 1997, and applies to a fee collected on or after that date, except as provided by Subsection (b) of this section.

§ 110.003. No Separate or Additional Filing Fee

The clerk of the court may not require:

(1) a separate filing fee in a suit joined with a suit for dissolution of marriage under Title 1; or

(2) an additional filing fee if more than one form of relief is requested in a suit.

Added by Acts 1995, 74th Leg., ch. 20, § 1, eff. April 20, 1995.

§ 110.004. Fee for Issuing and Delivering Withholding Order or Writ

The clerk of the court may charge a reasonable fee, not to exceed $15, for each order or writ of income withholding issued by the clerk and delivered to an employer.

Added by Acts 1995, 74th Leg., ch. 20, § 1, eff. April 20, 1995. Amended by Acts 1997, 75th Leg., ch. 911, § 9, eff. Sept. 1, 1997.

For application and effectiveness provisions of Acts 1997, 75th Leg., ch. 911, see note following V.T.C.A., Family Code § 101.011.

§ 110.005. Transfer Fee

(a) The fee for filing a transferred case is $45 payable to the clerk of the court to which the case is transferred. No portion of this fee may be sent to the state.

(b) A party may not be assessed any other fee, cost, charge, or expense by the clerk of the court or other public official in connection with filing of the transferred case.

(c) The fee limitation in this section does not affect a fee payable to the court transferring the case.

Added by Acts 1995, 74th Leg., ch. 20, § 1, eff. April 20, 1995.

§ 110.006. Domestic Relations Office Operations Fee

If an administering entity of a domestic relations office adopts an initial operations fee under Section 203.005(a)(1), the clerk of the court shall collect the fee at the time the suit is filed and send the fee to the domestic relations office.

Added by Acts 1997, 75th Leg., ch. 702, § 1, eff. Sept. 1, 1997.

Section 15(b) of Acts 1997, 75th Leg., ch. 702 provides:

"The change in law made by this Act by the addition of Section 110.006, Family Code, applies only to a suit affecting the parent-child relationship filed on or after the effective date of this Act. A suit filed before the effective date of this Act is governed by the law in effect on the date the suit was filed, and the former law is continued in effect for that purpose."

CHAPTER 111. GUIDELINES FOR POSSESSION AND CHILD SUPPORT

§ 111.001. Appointment of Advisory Committee

(a) The supreme court shall appoint an advisory committee consisting of not fewer than 25 persons, composed of legislators, judges, lawyers, and laypersons, to assist the legislature in making a periodic review of and suggested revisions, if any, to the guidelines in this title:

(1) for the possession of a child by a parent under Chapter 153; and

(2) for the support of a child under Chapter 154.

(b) Not fewer than five members of this committee must be or have been:

(1) managing conservators;

(2) possessory conservators;

(3) ordered to pay child support; or

(4) entitled to receive child support.

(c) The guidelines shall be reviewed at least once every four years.

Added by Acts 1995, 74th Leg., ch. 20, § 1, eff. April 20, 1995.

§ 111.002. Guidelines Supersede Court Rules

(a) The guidelines in this title supersede local court rules and rules of the supreme court that conflict with the guidelines.

(b) Notwithstanding other law, the guidelines may not be repealed or modified by a rule adopted by the supreme court.

Added by Acts 1995, 74th Leg., ch. 20, § 1, eff. April 20, 1995.

§ 111.003. Posting Guidelines

A copy of the guidelines for possession of and access to a child under Chapter 153 and a copy of the guidelines for the support of a child under Chapter 154 shall be prominently displayed at or near the entrance to the courtroom of every court having jurisdiction of a suit.

Added by Acts 1995, 74th Leg., ch. 20, § 1, eff. April 20, 1995.

[Chapters 112 to 150 reserved for expansion]

SUBTITLE B. SUITS AFFECTING THE PARENT–CHILD RELATIONSHIP

CHAPTER 151. THE PARENT–CHILD RELATIONSHIP

SUBCHAPTER A. GENERAL PROVISIONS

SUBCHAPTER A. GENERAL PROVISIONS

§ 151.001. Relation of Child to Mother and Father

(a) The parent-child relationship may be established between a child and:

(1) the biological mother by proof of her having given birth to the child;

(2) the biological father as provided by this code; and

(3) an adoptive parent by proof of adoption.

(b) The parent-child relationship extends equally to every child and parent regardless of the marital status of the parents.

Added by Acts 1995, 74th Leg., ch. 20, § 1, eff. April 20, 1995.

§ 151.002. Presumption of Paternity

(a) A man is presumed to be the biological father of a child if:

(1) he and the child's biological mother are or have been married to each other and the child is born during the marriage or not more than 300 days after the date the marriage terminated by death, annulment, or divorce or by having been declared void;

(2) before the child's birth, he and the child's biological mother attempted to marry each other by a marriage in apparent compliance with law, although the attempted marriage is or could be declared void, and the child is born during the attempted marriage or not more than 300 days after the date the attempted marriage terminated by death, annulment, or divorce or by having been declared void;

(3) after the child's birth, he and the child's biological mother have married or attempted to marry each other by a marriage in apparent compliance with law, although the attempted marriage is or could be declared void or voided by annulment, and:

(A) he has filed a written acknowledgment of his paternity of the child under Chapter 160;

(B) he consents in writing to be named and is named as the child's father on the child's birth certificate; or

(C) he is obligated to support the child under a written voluntary promise or by court order;

(4) without attempting to marry the mother, he consents in writing to be named as the child's father on the child's birth certificate; or

(5) before the child reaches the age of majority, he receives the child into his home and openly holds out the child as his biological child.

(b) A presumption under this section may be rebutted as provided by Section 160.110.

Added by Acts 1995, 74th Leg., ch. 20, § 1, eff. April 20, 1995. Amended by Acts 1995, 74th Leg., ch. 751, § 22, eff. Sept. 1, 1995.

§ 151.003. Rights and Duties of Parent

(a) A parent of a child has the following rights and duties:

(1) the right to have physical possession, to direct the moral and religious training, and to establish the residence of the child;

(2) the duty of care, control, protection, and reasonable discipline of the child;

(3) the duty to support the child, including providing the child with clothing, food, shelter, medical and dental care, and education;

(4) the duty, except when a guardian of the child's estate has been appointed, to manage the estate of the child, including the right as an agent of the child to act in relation to the child's estate if the child's action is required by a state, the United States, or a foreign government;

(5) the right to the services and earnings of the child;

(6) the right to consent to the child's marriage, enlistment in the armed forces of the United States, medical and dental care, and psychiatric, psychological, and surgical treatment;

(7) the right to represent the child in legal action and to make other decisions of substantial legal significance concerning the child;

(8) the right to receive and give receipt for payments for the support of the child and to hold or disburse funds for the benefit of the child;

(9) the right to inherit from and through the child;

(10) the right to make decisions concerning the child's education; and

(11) any other right or duty existing between a parent and child by virtue of law.

(b) The duty of a parent to support his or her child exists while the child is an unemancipated minor and continues as long as the child is fully enrolled in an accredited secondary school in a program leading toward a high school diploma until the end of the school year in which the child graduates.

(c) A parent who fails to discharge the duty of support is liable to a person who provides necessaries to those to whom support is owed.

(d) The rights and duties of a parent are subject to:

(1) a court order affecting the rights and duties;

(2) an affidavit of relinquishment of parental rights; and

(3) an affidavit by the parent designating another person or agency to act as managing conservator.

Added by Acts 1995, 74th Leg., ch. 20, § 1, eff. April 20, 1995. Amended by Acts 1995, 74th Leg., ch. 751, § 23, eff. Sept. 1, 1995.

§ 151.004. Rights of a Living Child After an Abortion or Premature Birth

(a) A living human child born alive after an abortion or premature birth is entitled to the same rights, powers, and privileges as are granted by the laws of this state to any other child born alive after the normal gestation period.

(b) In this code, "born alive" means the complete expulsion or extraction from its mother of a product of conception, irrespective of the duration of pregnancy, which, after such separation, breathes or shows any other evidence of life such as beating of the heart, pulsation of the umbilical cord, or definite movement of voluntary muscles, whether or not the umbilical cord has been cut or the placenta is attached. Each product of the birth is considered born alive.

Added by Acts 1995, 74th Leg., ch. 20, § 1, eff. April 20, 1995.

[Sections 151.005 to 151.100 reserved for expansion]

SUBCHAPTER B. ASSISTED CONCEPTION

§ 151.101. Artificial Insemination

(a) If a husband consents to the artificial insemination of his wife, any resulting child is the child of both of them. The consent must be in writing and must be acknowledged.

(b) If a woman is artificially inseminated, the resulting child is not the child of the donor unless he is the husband.

Added by Acts 1995, 74th Leg., ch. 20, § 1, eff. April 20, 1995.

§ 151.102. Oocyte Donation

(a) If a husband consents to provide sperm to fertilize a donor oocyte by in vitro fertilization or other assisted reproductive techniques and the wife consents to have a donor oocyte that has been fertilized with her husband's sperm, pursuant to his consent, placed in her uterus, a resulting child is the child of both of them. The consent of each must be in writing.

(b) If a donor oocyte that has been fertilized with her husband's sperm implants in a wife's uterus, a resulting child is not the child of the donor of the oocyte.

Added by Acts 1995, 74th Leg., ch. 20, § 1, eff. April 20, 1995.

§ 151.103. Embryo Donation

(a) If, with the consent of the husband and the wife, a donated preimplantation embryo implants in the uterus of the wife, a resulting child is the child of both of them. The consent must be in writing.

(b) If, with the consent of the husband and the wife, a donated preimplantation embryo implants in the uterus of the wife, a resulting child is not the child of the donor or donors of the preimplantation embryo.

(c) Subsections (a) and (b) apply whether the donated preimplantation embryo is the result of separate egg and sperm donations or the result of donation of an embryo created for the purpose of assisting the reproduction of the donating couple.

Added by Acts 1995, 74th Leg., ch. 20, § 1, eff. April 20, 1995.

CHAPTER 152. UNIFORM CHILD CUSTODY JURISDICTION ACT

Section

§ 152.001. Purposes; Construction of Provisions

(a) The general purposes of this chapter are to:

(1) avoid jurisdictional competition and conflict with courts of other states in matters of child custody that have in the past resulted in the shifting of children from state to state with harmful effects on their well-being;

(2) promote cooperation with the courts of other states to the end that a custody decree is rendered in the state that can best decide the case in the interest of the child;

(3) ensure that litigation concerning the custody of a child takes place ordinarily in the state with which the child and the child's family have the closest connection and where significant evidence concerning the child's care, protection, training, and personal relationships is most readily available, and that courts of this state decline the exercise of jurisdiction when the child and the child's family have a closer connection with another state;

(4) discourage continuing controversies over child custody in the interest of greater stability of home environment and of secure family relationships for the child;

(5) deter abductions and other unilateral removals of children undertaken to obtain custody awards;

(6) avoid relitigation of custody decisions of other states in this state insofar as is feasible;

(7) facilitate the enforcement of custody decrees of other states;

(8) promote and expand the exchange of information and other forms of mutual assistance between the courts of this state and those of other states concerned with the same child; and

(9) make uniform the law of those states that enact it.

(b) This chapter shall be construed to promote the general purposes stated in this section.

Added by Acts 1995, 74th Leg., ch. 20, § 1, eff. April 20, 1995.

§ 152.002. Definitions

In this chapter:

(1) "Contestant" means a person, including a parent, who claims a right to custody or visitation rights with respect to a child.

(2) "Custody" means managing conservatorship of a child.

(3) "Custody determination" means a court decision and court orders and instructions providing for the custody of a child, including visitation rights, but does not include a decision relating to child support or any other monetary obligation of any person.

(4) "Custody proceeding" includes a proceeding in which a custody determination is one of several issues, such as an action for divorce or separation, and includes child neglect and dependency proceedings.

(5) "Decree" or "custody decree" means a custody determination contained in a judicial decree or order made in a custody proceeding and includes an initial decree and a modification decree.

(6) "Home state" means the state in which the child, preceding the time involved, lived with the child's parents, a parent, or a person acting as parent for at least six consecutive months and, in the case of a child less than six months old, the state in which the child lived from birth with any of the persons mentioned. Periods of temporary absence of any of the named persons are counted as part of the six-month or other period.

(7) "Initial decree" means the first custody decree concerning a particular child.

(8) "Modification decree" means a custody decree that modifies or replaces a prior decree, whether made by the court that rendered the prior decree or by another court.

(9) "Physical custody" means actual possession and control of a child.

(10) "Person acting as parent" means a person, other than a parent, who has physical custody of a child and who either has been awarded custody by a court or claims a right to custody.

(11) "Visitation" means possession of or access to a child.

Added by Acts 1995, 74th Leg., ch. 20, § 1, eff. April 20, 1995.

§ 152.003. Jurisdiction

(a) A court of this state that is competent to decide child custody matters has jurisdiction to make a child custody determination by initial decree or modification decree or order if:

(1) this state:

(A) is the home state of the child on the date of the commencement of the proceeding; or

(B) had been the child's home state within six months before the date of the commencement of the proceeding and the child is absent from this state because of the child's removal or retention by a person claiming the child's custody or for other reasons, and a parent or person acting as parent continues to live in this state;

(2) it appears that no other state would have jurisdiction under Subdivision (1) and it is in the best interest of the child that a court of this state assume jurisdiction because:

(A) the child and the child's parents or the child and at least one contestant have a significant connection with this state other than mere physical presence in this state; and

(B) there is available in this state substantial evidence concerning the child's present or future care, protection, training, and personal relationships;

(3) the child is physically present in this state and:

(A) the child has been abandoned; or

(B) it is necessary in an emergency to protect the child because the child has been subjected to or threatened with mistreatment or abuse or is otherwise neglected or there is a serious and immediate question concerning the welfare of the child; or

(4) it is in the best interest of the child that the court assume jurisdiction and:

(A) it appears that no other state would have jurisdiction under prerequisites substantially in accordance with Subdivision (1), (2), or (3); or

(B) another state has declined to exercise jurisdiction on the ground that this state is the more appropriate forum to determine the custody of the child.

(b) Except under Subsections (a)(3) and (4), physical presence in this state of the child or of the child and one of the contestants is not alone sufficient to confer jurisdiction on a court of this state to make a child custody determination.

(c) Physical presence of the child, while desirable, is not a prerequisite for jurisdiction to determine the child's custody.

(d) Except on written agreement of all the parties, a court may not exercise its continuing jurisdiction to modify custody if the child and the party with custody have established another home state unless the action to modify was filed before the new home state was acquired.

(e) A court that has jurisdiction of a suit under Subsection (a)(3) for which a court in another state may exercise jurisdiction under prerequisites substantially in accordance with Subsection (a)(1) or (2) may enter only a temporary order to protect the child. The suit shall be dismissed in this state on the date a court of competent jurisdiction in another state signs an order in the suit or on the 91st day after the date the court in this state exercised its jurisdiction, whichever date occurs first. This subsection does not apply to a suit brought under Chapter 262.

Added by Acts 1995, 74th Leg., ch. 20, § 1, eff. April 20, 1995. Amended by Acts 1995, 74th Leg., ch. 751, § 24, eff. Sept. 1, 1995; Acts 1997, 75th Leg., ch. 575, § 7, eff. Sept. 1, 1997.

For application provisions of Acts 1997, 75th Leg., ch. 575, see note following V.T.C.A., Family Code § 102.003.

§ 152.004. Notice and Opportunity to be Heard

Before making a custody decree based on jurisdiction established under this chapter, reasonable notice and opportunity to be heard must be given to the contestants, to any parent whose parental rights have not been previously terminated, and to any person who has physical custody of the child. If any of these persons is outside this state, notice and opportunity to be heard must be given as provided under Section 152.005.

Added by Acts 1995, 74th Leg., ch. 20, § 1, eff. April 20, 1995.

§ 152.005. Notice to Persons Outside This State; Submission to Jurisdiction

(a) Notice required for the exercise of jurisdiction over a person outside this state must be given in a manner reasonably calculated to give actual notice and may be given:

(1) by personal delivery outside this state in the manner prescribed for service of process within this state;

(2) in the manner prescribed by the law of the place in which the service is made for service of process in that place in an action in any of its courts of general jurisdiction;

(3) by any form of mail addressed to the person to be served and requesting a receipt, subject to the requirements of the Texas Rules of Civil Procedure; or

(4) as directed by the court, including publication, if other means of notification are ineffective, subject to the requirements of the Texas Rules of Civil Procedure.

(b) Notice under this section must be delivered, mailed, or published with sufficient time to allow for filing of an answer before any hearing in this state, in accordance with the Texas Rules of Civil Procedure applicable to the filing of an original lawsuit. Each party whose rights, privileges, duties, or powers may be affected by the action is entitled to receive notice by citation and shall be commanded to appear by filing a written answer. Thereafter, the proceedings shall be as in civil cases generally.

(c) Proof of service outside this state may be made by the affidavit of the individual who made the service or in the manner prescribed by the law of this state, by the order under which the service is made, or by the law of the place in which the service is made. If service is made by mail, proof may be a receipt signed by the addressee or other evidence of delivery to the addressee.

(d) Notice is not required if a person submits to the jurisdiction of the court.

Added by Acts 1995, 74th Leg., ch. 20, § 1, eff. April 20, 1995.

§ 152.006. Simultaneous Proceedings in Other State

(a) A court of this state may not exercise its jurisdiction under this chapter if, at the time of filing the petition, a proceeding concerning the custody of the child was pending in a court of another state exercising jurisdiction substantially in conformity with this chapter, unless the proceeding is stayed by the court of the other state because this state is a more appropriate forum or for other reasons.

(b) Before hearing the petition in a custody proceeding, the court shall examine the pleadings and other information supplied by the parties under Section 152.009 and shall consult the child custody registry established under Section 152.016 concerning the pendency of proceedings with respect to the child in other states. If the court has reason to believe that proceedings may be pending in another state, it shall direct an inquiry to the state court administrator or other appropriate official of the other state.

(c) If the court is informed during the course of the proceeding that a proceeding concerning the custody of the child was pending in another state before the court assumed jurisdiction, it shall stay the proceeding and communicate with the court in which the other proceeding is pending to the end that the issue may be litigated in the more appropriate forum and that information may be exchanged in accordance with Sections 152.019–152.022. If a court of this state has made a custody decree before being informed of a pending proceeding in a court of another state, it shall immediately inform that court of the fact. If the court is informed that a proceeding was commenced in another state after it assumed jurisdiction, it shall likewise inform the other court to the end that the issues may be litigated in the more appropriate forum.

Added by Acts 1995, 74th Leg., ch. 20, § 1, eff. April 20, 1995.

§ 152.007. Inconvenient Forum

(a) A court that has jurisdiction under this chapter to make an initial or modification decree may decline to exercise its jurisdiction any time before making a decree if it finds that it is an inconvenient forum to make a custody determination under the circumstances of the case and that a court of another state is a more appropriate forum.

(b) A finding of inconvenient forum may be made on the court's own motion or on the motion of a party or a guardian ad litem or other representative of the child.

(c) In determining whether it is an inconvenient forum, the court shall consider whether it is in the best interest of the child that another state assume jurisdiction. For this purpose, the court may take into account the following factors, among others:

(1) whether another state is or recently was the child's home state;

(2) whether another state has a closer connection with the child and the child's family or with the child and one or more of the contestants;

(3) whether substantial evidence concerning the child's present or future care, protection, training, and personal relationships is more readily available in another state;

(4) whether the parties have agreed on another forum that is no less appropriate; and

(5) whether the exercise of jurisdiction by a court of this state would contravene any of the purposes stated in Section 152.001.

(d) Before determining whether to decline or retain jurisdiction, the court may communicate with a court of another state and exchange information pertinent to the assumption of jurisdiction by either court with a view to ensuring that jurisdiction will be exercised by the more appropriate court and that a forum will be available to the parties.

(e) If the court finds that it is an inconvenient forum and that a court of another state is a more appropriate forum, it may dismiss the proceedings, or it may stay the proceedings on condition that a custody proceeding be promptly commenced in another named state or on any other condition that may be just and proper, including the condition that a moving party stipulate the party's consent and submission to the jurisdiction of the other forum.

(f) The court may decline to exercise its jurisdiction under this chapter if a custody determination is incidental to an action for divorce or another proceeding while retaining jurisdiction over the divorce or other proceeding.

(g) If it appears to the court that it is clearly an inappropriate forum, the court may require the party who commenced the proceedings to pay, in addition to the costs of the proceedings in this state, necessary travel and other expenses, including attorney's fees, incurred by other parties or their witnesses.

(h) On dismissal or stay of proceedings under this section, the court shall inform the court found to be the more appropriate forum of this fact or, if the court that would have jurisdiction in the other state is not certainly known, shall transmit the information to the court administrator or other appropriate official for forwarding to the appropriate court.

(i) Any communication received from another state informing this state of a finding of inconvenient forum because a court of this state is the more appropriate forum shall be filed in the custody registry of the appropriate court. On assuming jurisdiction, the court of this state shall inform the original court of this fact.

Added by Acts 1995, 74th Leg., ch. 20, § 1, eff. April 20, 1995. Amended by Acts 1997, 75th Leg., ch. 15, § 3, eff. Sept. 1, 1997.

Section 2 of Acts 1997, 75th Leg., ch. 15 provides:

"This Act takes effect September 1, 1997, and applies to a pending suit affecting the parent-child relationship without regard to whether the suit was commenced before, on, or after the effective date of this Act."

§ 152.008. Jurisdiction Declined by Reason of Conduct

(a) If the petitioner for an initial decree has wrongfully taken the child from another state or has engaged in similar reprehensible conduct, the court may decline to exercise jurisdiction if just and proper under the circumstances.

(b) Unless required in the interest of the child, the court may not exercise its jurisdiction to modify a custody decree of another state if the petitioner, without consent of the person entitled to custody, has improperly removed the child from the physical custody of the person entitled to custody or has improperly retained the child after a visit or other temporary relinquishment of physical custody. If the petitioner has violated any other provision of a custody decree of another state, the court may decline to exercise its jurisdiction if just and proper under the circumstances.

(c) In an appropriate case, a court dismissing a petition under this section may charge the petitioner with necessary travel and other expenses, including attorney's fees, incurred by other parties or their witnesses.

Added by Acts 1995, 74th Leg., ch. 20, § 1, eff. April 20, 1995.

§ 152.009. Information Under Oath to be Submitted to the Court

(a) Unless all the contestants are residing in this state, every party in a custody proceeding in the party's first pleading or in an affidavit attached to that pleading shall give information under oath as to the child's present address, the places where the child has lived within the last five years, and the names and present addresses of the persons with whom the child has lived during that period. In this pleading or affidavit every party shall further declare under oath whether the party:

(1) has participated (as a party, as a witness, or in any other capacity) in any other litigation concerning the custody of the same child in this or any other state;

(2) has information of any proceeding concerning the child pending in a court of this or any other state; and

(3) knows of any person not a party to the proceedings who has physical custody of the child or claims to have custody or visitation rights with respect to the child.

(b) If the declaration as to any of the items in Subsection (a) is in the affirmative, the declarant shall give additional information under oath as required by the court. The court may examine the parties under oath as to details of the information furnished and as to other matters pertinent to the court's jurisdiction and the disposition of the case.

(c) Each party has a continuing duty to inform the court of any custody proceeding concerning the child in this or any other state of which the party obtained information during the proceeding.

Added by Acts 1995, 74th Leg., ch. 20, § 1, eff. April 20, 1995.

§ 152.010. Additional Parties

(a) If the court learns from information furnished by the parties under Section 152.009 or from other sources that a person not a party to the custody proceeding has physical custody of the child or claims to have custody or visitation rights with respect to the child, it shall order that the person:

(1) be joined as a party; and

(2) be notified of the pendency of the proceeding and of the person's joinder as a party.

(b) If the person joined as a party is outside this state, the person must be served with process or otherwise notified in accordance with Section 152.005.

Added by Acts 1995, 74th Leg., ch. 20, § 1, eff. April 20, 1995.

§ 152.011. Appearance of Parties and Child

(a) The court may order any party to the proceeding who is in this state to appear personally before the court. If that party has physical custody of the child, the court may order that the party appear personally with the child.

(b) If a party to the proceeding whose presence is desired by the court is outside this state, with or without the child, the court may order that the notice given under Section 152.005 include a statement directing that party to appear personally, with or without the child, and declaring that failure to appear may result in a decision adverse to that party.

(c) If a party to the proceeding who is outside this state is directed to appear under Subsection (b) or desires to appear personally before the court, with or without the child, the court may require another party to pay to the clerk of the court travel and other necessary expenses of the party appearing and of the child if just and proper under the circumstances.

Added by Acts 1995, 74th Leg., ch. 20, § 1, eff. April 20, 1995.

§ 152.012. Binding Force and Res Judicata Effect of Custody Decree

A custody decree of a court of this state that has jurisdiction under Section 152.003 binds all parties who have been served in this state or notified in accordance with Section 152.005 or who have submitted to the jurisdiction of the court and who have been given an opportunity to be heard. As to these parties, the custody decree is conclusive as to all issues of law and fact decided and as to the custody determination made, unless and until that determination is modified.

Added by Acts 1995, 74th Leg., ch. 20, § 1, eff. April 20, 1995.

§ 152.013. Recognition of Out-of-State Custody Decrees

The courts of this state shall recognize and enforce an initial or modification decree of a court of another state that had assumed jurisdiction under statutory provisions substantially in accordance with this chapter or that was made under factual circumstances meeting the jurisdictional standards of this chapter, so long as the decree has not been modified in accordance with jurisdictional standards substantially similar to those of this chapter.

Added by Acts 1995, 74th Leg., ch. 20, § 1, eff. April 20, 1995.

§ 152.014. Modification of Custody Decree of Another State

(a) If a court of another state has made a custody decree, a court of this state may not modify the decree unless:

(1) it appears to the court of this state that the court that rendered the decree does not have jurisdiction under jurisdictional prerequisites substantially in accordance with this chapter or has declined to assume jurisdiction to modify the decree; and

(2) the court of this state has jurisdiction.

(b) If a court of this state is authorized under Subsection (a) and Section 152.008 to modify a custody decree of another state, it shall give due consideration to the transcript of the record and other documents of all previous proceedings submitted to it in accordance with Section 152.022.

Added by Acts 1995, 74th Leg., ch. 20, § 1, eff. April 20, 1995.

§ 152.015. Filing and Enforcement of Custody Decree of Another State

(a) On payment of proper fees, a certified copy of a custody decree of another state may be filed in the office of the clerk of any district court or other appropriate court of this state. The clerk shall treat the decree in the same manner as a custody decree of a district court or other appropriate court of this state. A custody decree filed under this section has the same effect and shall be enforced in the same manner as a custody decree rendered by a court of this state.

(b) A person whose violation of a custody decree of another state makes it necessary to enforce the decree in this state may be required to pay necessary travel and other expenses, including attorney's fees, incurred by the party entitled to the custody or the party's witnesses.

Added by Acts 1995, 74th Leg., ch. 20, § 1, eff. April 20, 1995.

§ 152.016. Registry of Out-of-State Custody Decrees and Proceedings

The clerk of each district court or other appropriate court shall maintain a registry in which the clerk shall enter:

(1) certified copies of custody decrees of other states received for filing;

(2) communications as to the pendency of custody proceedings in other states;

(3) communications concerning a finding of inconvenient forum by a court of another state; and

(4) other communications or documents concerning custody proceedings in another state that may affect the jurisdiction of a court of this state or the disposition to be made by it in a custody proceeding.

Added by Acts 1995, 74th Leg., ch. 20, § 1, eff. April 20, 1995.

§ 152.017. Certified Copies of Custody Decree

The clerk of the district court or other appropriate court of this state, at the request of the court of another state or at the request of a person who is affected by or has a legitimate interest in a custody decree, shall, on payment of proper fees, certify and forward a copy of the decree to that court or person.

Added by Acts 1995, 74th Leg., ch. 20, § 1, eff. April 20, 1995.

§ 152.018. Taking Testimony in Another State

In addition to other procedural devices available to a party, a party to the proceeding or a guardian ad litem or other representative of the child may adduce testimony of witnesses, including parties and the child, by deposition or otherwise, in another state. The court on its own motion may direct that the testimony of a person be taken in another state and may prescribe the manner in which and the terms on which the testimony shall be taken.

Added by Acts 1995, 74th Leg., ch. 20, § 1, eff. April 20, 1995.

§ 152.019. Hearings and Studies in Another State; Orders to Appear

(a) A court of this state may request the appropriate court of another state to hold a hearing to adduce evidence, to order a party to produce or give evidence under other procedures of that state, to have social studies made with respect to the custody of a child involved in proceedings pending in the court of this state, and to forward to the court of this state certified copies of the transcript of the record of the hearing, the evidence otherwise adduced, or any social studies prepared in compliance with the request. The cost of the services may be assessed against the parties or, if necessary, ordered paid by the state as costs of court.

(b) A court of this state may request the appropriate court of another state to order a party to custody proceedings pending in the court of this state to appear in the proceedings and, if that party has physical custody of the child, to appear with the child. The request may state that travel and other necessary expenses of the party and of the child whose appearance is desired will be assessed against another party or will otherwise be paid.

Added by Acts 1995, 74th Leg., ch. 20, § 1, eff. April 20, 1995.

§ 152.020. Assistance to Courts of Other States

(a) On request of the court of another state, the courts of this state that are competent to hear custody matters may order a person in this state to appear at a hearing to adduce evidence or to produce or give evidence under other procedures available in this state or may order social studies to be made for use in a custody proceeding in another state. A certified copy of the transcript of the record of the hearing or the evidence otherwise adduced and any social studies prepared shall be forwarded by the clerk of the court to the requesting court.

(b) A person in this state may voluntarily give the person's testimony or statement in this state for use in a custody proceeding outside this state.

(c) On request of the court of another state, a competent court of this state may order a person in this state to appear alone or with the child in a custody proceeding in another state. The court may condition compliance with the request on assurance by the other state that state travel and other necessary expenses will be advanced or reimbursed.

Added by Acts 1995, 74th Leg., ch. 20, § 1, eff. April 20, 1995.

§ 152.021. Preservation of Documents for use in Other States

In a custody proceeding in this state, the court shall preserve the pleadings, orders, and decrees, a record that has been made of its hearings, social studies, and other pertinent documents until the child reaches 18 years of age or in accordance with the law of this state. On appropriate request of the court of another state and payment of proper fees, the court shall forward to the other court certified copies of the documents.

Added by Acts 1995, 74th Leg., ch. 20, § 1, eff. April 20, 1995.

§ 152.022. Request for Court Records of Another State

If a custody decree has been rendered in another state concerning a child involved in a custody proceeding pending in a court of this state, the court of this state on taking jurisdiction of the case may request of the court of the other state a certified copy of the transcript of a court record and other documents listed in Section 152.021.

Added by Acts 1995, 74th Leg., ch. 20, § 1, eff. April 20, 1995.

§ 152.023. International Application

The general policies of this chapter extend to the international area. The provisions of this chapter relating to the recognition and enforcement of custody decrees of other states apply to custody decrees and decrees involving legal institutions similar in nature to custody institutions rendered by appropriate authorities of other nations if reasonable notice and opportunity to be heard were given to all affected persons.

Added by Acts 1995, 74th Leg., ch. 20, § 1, eff. April 20, 1995.

§ 152.024. Priority

On the request of a party to a custody proceeding that raises a question of existence or exercise of jurisdiction under this chapter, the case shall be given calendar priority and handled expeditiously.

Added by Acts 1995, 74th Leg., ch. 20, § 1, eff. April 20, 1995.

§ 152.025. Short Title

This chapter may be cited as the Uniform Child Custody Jurisdiction Act.

Added by Acts 1995, 74th Leg., ch. 20, § 1, eff. April 20, 1995.

CHAPTER 153. CONSERVATORSHIP, POSSESSION, AND ACCESS

SUBCHAPTER A. GENERAL PROVISIONS

§ 153.001. Public Policy

(a) The public policy of this state is to:

(1) assure that children will have frequent and continuing contact with parents who have shown the ability to act in the best interest of the child;

(2) provide a stable environment for the child; and

(3) encourage parents to share in the rights and duties of raising their child after the parents have separated or dissolved their marriage.

(b) A court may not render an order that conditions the right of a conservator to possession of or access to a child on the payment of child support.

Added by Acts 1995, 74th Leg., ch. 20, § 1, eff. April 20, 1995. Amended by Acts 1995, 74th Leg., ch. 751, § 25, eff. Sept. 1, 1995.

§ 153.002. Best Interest of Child

The best interest of the child shall always be the primary consideration of the court in determining the issues of conservatorship and possession of and access to the child.

Added by Acts 1995, 74th Leg., ch. 20, § 1, eff. April 20, 1995.

§ 153.003. No Discrimination Based on Sex or Marital Status

The court shall consider the qualifications of the parties without regard to their marital status or to the sex of the party or the child in determining:

(1) which party to appoint as sole managing conservator;

(2) whether to appoint a party as joint managing conservator; and

(3) the terms and conditions of conservatorship and possession of and access to the child.

Added by Acts 1995, 74th Leg., ch. 20, § 1, eff. April 20, 1995.

§ 153.004. History of Domestic Violence

(a) In determining whether to appoint a party as a sole or joint managing conservator, the court shall consider evidence of the intentional use of abusive physical force by a party against the party's spouse or against any person younger than 18 years of age committed within a two-year period preceding the filing of the suit or during the pendency of the suit.

(b) The court may not appoint joint managing conservators if credible evidence is presented of a history or pattern of past or present child neglect, or physical or sexual abuse by one parent directed against the other parent, a spouse, or a child.

(c) The court shall consider the commission of family violence in determining whether to deny, restrict, or limit the possession of a child by a parent who is appointed as a possessory conservator.

Added by Acts 1995, 74th Leg., ch. 20, § 1, eff. April 20, 1995.

§ 153.005. Appointment of Sole or Joint Managing Conservator

(a) In a suit, the court may appoint a sole managing conservator or may appoint joint managing conservators. If the parents are or will be separated, the court shall appoint at least one managing conservator.

(b) A managing conservator must be a parent, a competent adult, an authorized agency, or a licensed child-placing agency.

Added by Acts 1995, 74th Leg., ch. 20, § 1, eff. April 20, 1995.

§ 153.006. Appointment of Possessory Conservator

(a) If a managing conservator is appointed, the court may appoint one or more possessory conservators.

(b) The court shall specify the rights and duties of a person appointed possessory conservator.

(c) The court shall specify and expressly state in the order the times and conditions for possession of or access to the child, unless a party shows good cause why specific orders would not be in the best interest of the child.

Added by Acts 1995, 74th Leg., ch. 20, § 1, eff. April 20, 1995.

§ 153.007. Agreement Concerning Conservatorship

(a) To promote the amicable settlement of disputes between the parties to a suit, the parties may enter into a written agreement containing provisions for conservatorship and possession of the child and for modification of the agreement, including variations from the standard possession order.

(b) If the court finds that the agreement is in the child's best interest, the court shall render an order in accordance with the agreement.

(c) Terms of the agreement contained in the order or incorporated by reference regarding conservatorship or support of or access to a child in an order may be enforced by all remedies available for enforcement of a judgment, including contempt, but are not enforceable as a contract.

(d) If the court finds the agreement is not in the child's best interest, the court may request the parties to submit a revised agreement or the court may render an order for the conservatorship and possession of the child.

Added by Acts 1995, 74th Leg., ch. 20, § 1, eff. April 20, 1995. Amended by Acts 1995, 74th Leg., ch. 751, § 26, eff. Sept. 1, 1995.

§ 153.0071. Alternate Dispute Resolution Procedures

(a) On written agreement of the parties, the court may refer a suit affecting the parent-child relationship to arbitration. The agreement must state whether the arbitration is binding or non-binding.

(b) If the parties agree to binding arbitration, the court shall render an order reflecting the arbitrator's award unless the court determines at a non-jury hearing that the award is not in the best interest of the child. The burden of proof at a hearing under this subsection is on the party seeking to avoid rendition of an order based on the arbitrator's award.

(c) On the written agreement of the parties or on the court's own motion, the court may refer a suit affecting the parent-child relationship to mediation.

(d) A mediated settlement agreement is binding on the parties if the agreement:

(1) provides in a separate paragraph an underlined statement that the agreement is not subject to revocation;

(2) is signed by each party to the agreement; and

(3) is signed by the party's attorney, if any, who is present at the time the agreement is signed.

(e) If a mediated settlement agreement meets the requirements of Subsection (d), a party is entitled to judgment on the mediated settlement agreement notwithstanding Rule 11, Texas Rules of Civil Procedure, or another rule of law.

(f) Repealed by Acts 1997, 75th Leg., ch. 937, § 3, eff. Sept. 1, 1997.

Added by Acts 1995, 74th Leg., ch. 751, § 27, eff. Sept. 1, 1995. Amended by Acts 1997, 75th Leg., ch. 937, § 3, eff. Sept. 1, 1997.

Section 4 of Acts 1997, 75th Leg., ch. 937 provides:

"This Act takes effect September 1, 1997, and applies only to a suit filed under Title 1, Family Code, or Chapter 151, 153, 154, 156, 157, 160, 161, or 262, Family Code, on or after that date."

Section 129 of the 1995 Act provides:

"This Act takes effect September 1, 1995, and applies to a pending suit affecting the parent-child relationship without regard to whether the suit was commenced before, on, or after the effective date of this Act."

§ 153.008. Child's Choice of Managing Conservator

If the child is 12 years of age or older, the child may, by writing filed with the court, choose the managing conservator, subject to the approval of the court.

Added by Acts 1995, 74th Leg., ch. 20, § 1, eff. April 20, 1995.

§ 153.009. Interview of Child in Chambers

(a) In a nonjury trial the court may interview the child in chambers to determine the child's wishes as to conservatorship.

(b) When the issue of managing conservatorship is contested, on the application of a party, the court shall interview a child 10 years of age or older and may interview a child under 10 years of age. Interviewing a child does not diminish the discretion of the court.

(c) The court may permit the attorney for a party or the attorney ad litem for the child to be present at the interview.

(d) On the motion of a party or on the court's own motion, the court shall cause a record of the interview to be made when the child is 10 years of age or older. A record of the interview shall be part of the record in the case.

Added by Acts 1995, 74th Leg., ch. 20, § 1, eff. April 20, 1995. Amended by Acts 1997, 75th Leg., ch. 781, § 1, eff. Sept. 1, 1997.

§ 153.010. Order for Family Counseling

(a) If the court finds at the time of a hearing that the parties have a history of conflict in resolving an issue of conservatorship or possession of or access to the child, the court may order a party to:

(1) participate in counseling with a mental health professional who:

(A) has a background in family therapy;

(B) has a mental health license that requires as a minimum a master's degree; and

(C) has training in domestic violence if the court determines that the training is relevant to the type of counseling needed; and

(2) pay the cost of counseling.

(b) If a person possessing the requirements of Subsection (a)(1) is not available in the county in which the court presides, the court may appoint a person the court believes is qualified to conduct the counseling ordered under Subsection (a).

Added by Acts 1995, 74th Leg., ch. 20, § 1, eff. April 20, 1995. Amended by Acts 1997, 75th Leg., ch. 645, § 1, eff. Sept. 1, 1997.

§ 153.011. Security Bond

If the court finds that a person who has a possessory interest in a child may violate the court order relating to the interest, the court may order the party to execute a bond or deposit security. The court shall set the amount and condition the bond or security on compliance with the order.

Added by Acts 1995, 74th Leg., ch. 20, § 1, eff. April 20, 1995.

§ 153.012. Right to Privacy; Deletion of Personal Information in Records

The court may order the custodian of records to delete all references in the records to the place of residence of either party appointed as a conservator of the child before the release of the records to another party appointed as a conservator.

Added by Acts 1995, 74th Leg., ch. 20, § 1, eff. April 20, 1995.

§ 153.013. False Report of Child Abuse

(a) If a party to a pending suit affecting the parent-child relationship makes a report alleging child abuse by another party to the suit that the reporting party knows lacks a factual foundation, the court shall deem the report to be a knowingly false report.

(b) Evidence of a false report of child abuse is admissible in a suit between the involved parties regarding the terms of conservatorship of a child.

(c) If the court makes a finding under Subsection (a), the court shall impose a civil penalty not to exceed $500.

Added by Acts 1995, 74th Leg., ch. 751, § 28, eff. Sept. 1, 1995. Amended by Acts 1997, 75th Leg., ch. 786, § 2, eff. Sept. 1, 1997.

Section 3 of Acts 1997, 75th Leg., ch. 786 provides:

"This Act takes effect September 1, 1997, and applies only to a suit affecting the parent-child relationship filed on or after that date. A suit affecting the parent-child relationship filed before the effective date of this Act is governed by the law in effect on the date the suit was filed, and the former law is continued in effect for that purpose."

[Sections 153.014 to 153.070 reserved for expansion]

SUBCHAPTER B. PARENT APPOINTED AS CONSERVATOR: IN GENERAL

§ 153.071. Court to Specify Rights and Duties of Parent Appointed a Conservator

If both parents are appointed as conservators of the child, the court shall specify the rights and duties of a parent that are to be exercised:

(1) by each parent independently;

(2) by the joint agreement of the parents; and

(3) exclusively by one parent.

Added by Acts 1995, 74th Leg., ch. 20, § 1, eff. April 20, 1995.

§ 153.072. Written Finding Required to Limit Parental Rights and Duties

The court may limit the rights and duties of a parent appointed as a conservator if the court makes a written finding that the limitation is in the best interest of the child.

Added by Acts 1995, 74th Leg., ch. 20, § 1, eff. April 20, 1995.

§ 153.073. Rights of Parent at All Times

(a) Unless limited by court order, a parent appointed as a conservator of a child has at all times the right:

(1) as specified by court order:

(A) to receive information from the other parent concerning the health, education, and welfare of the child; and

(B) to confer with the other parent to the extent possible before making a decision concerning the health, education, and welfare of the child;

(2) of access to medical, dental, psychological, and educational records of the child;

(3) to consult with a physician, dentist, or psychologist of the child;

(4) to consult with school officials concerning the child's welfare and educational status, including school activities;

(5) to attend school activities;

(6) to be designated on the child's records as a person to be notified in case of an emergency;

(7) to consent to medical, dental, and surgical treatment during an emergency involving an immediate danger to the health and safety of the child; and

(8) to manage the estate of the child to the extent the estate has been created by the parent or the parent's family.

(b) The court shall specify in the order the rights that a parent retains at all times.

Added by Acts 1995, 74th Leg., ch. 20, § 1, eff. April 20, 1995. Amended by Acts 1995, 74th Leg., ch. 751, § 29, eff. Sept. 1, 1995.

§ 153.074. Rights and Duties During Period of Possession

Unless limited by court order, a parent appointed as a conservator of a child has the following rights and duties during the period that the parent has possession of the child:

(1) the duty of care, control, protection, and reasonable discipline of the child;

(2) the duty to support the child, including providing the child with clothing, food, shelter, and medical and dental care not involving an invasive procedure;

(3) the right to consent for the child to medical and dental care not involving an invasive procedure;

(4) the right to consent for the child to medical, dental, and surgical treatment during an emergency involving immediate danger to the health and safety of the child; and

(5) the right to direct the moral and religious training of the child.

Added by Acts 1995, 74th Leg., ch. 20, § 1, eff. April 20, 1995. Amended by Acts 1995, 74th Leg., ch. 751, § 30, eff. Sept. 1, 1995.

§ 153.075. Duties of Parent Not Appointed Conservator

The court may order a parent not appointed as a managing or a possessory conservator to perform other parental duties, including paying child support.

Added by Acts 1995, 74th Leg., ch. 20, § 1, eff. April 20, 1995.

§ 153.076. Parents' Duty to Provide Information

If both parents are appointed as conservators of the child, the court shall order that each parent has a duty to inform the other parent in a timely manner of significant information concerning the health, education, and welfare of the child.

Added by Acts 1995, 74th Leg., ch. 751, § 31, eff. Sept. 1, 1995.

[Sections 153.077 to 153.130 reserved for expansion]

SUBCHAPTER C. PARENT APPOINTED AS SOLE OR JOINT MANAGING CONSERVATOR

§ 153.131. Presumption That Parent to be Appointed Managing Conservator

(a) Subject to the prohibition in Section 153.004, unless the court finds that appointment of the parent or parents would not be in the best interest of the child because the appointment would significantly impair the child's physical health or emotional development, a parent shall be appointed sole managing conservator or both parents shall be appointed as joint managing conservators of the child.

(b) It is a rebuttable presumption that the appointment of the parents of a child as joint managing conservators is in the best interest of the child. A finding of a history of family violence involving the parents of a child removes the presumption under this subsection.

Added by Acts 1995, 74th Leg., ch. 20, § 1, eff. April 20, 1995. Amended by Acts 1995, 74th Leg., ch. 751, § 32, eff. Sept. 1, 1995; Acts 1997, 75th Leg., ch. 1193, § 20, eff. Sept. 1, 1997.

§ 153.132. Rights and Duties of Parent Appointed Sole Managing Conservator

Unless limited by court order, a parent appointed as sole managing conservator of a child has the rights and duties provided by Subchapter B [1] and the following exclusive rights:

(1) the right to establish the primary residence of the child;

(2) the right to consent to medical, dental, and surgical treatment involving invasive procedures, and to consent to psychiatric and psychological treatment;

(3) the right to receive and give receipt for periodic payments for the support of the child and to hold or disburse these funds for the benefit of the child;

(4) the right to represent the child in legal action and to make other decisions of substantial legal significance concerning the child;

(5) the right to consent to marriage and to enlistment in the armed forces of the United States;

(6) the right to make decisions concerning the child's education;

(7) the right to the services and earnings of the child; and

(8) except when a guardian of the child's estate or a guardian or attorney ad litem has been appointed for the child, the right to act as an agent of the child in relation to the child's estate if the child's action is required by a state, the United States, or a foreign government.

Added by Acts 1995, 74th Leg., ch. 20, § 1, eff. April 20, 1995. Amended by Acts 1995, 74th Leg., ch. 751, § 33, eff. Sept. 1, 1995.

[1] V.T.C.A., Family Code § 153.071 et seq.

§ 153.133. Agreement for Joint Managing Conservatorship

(a) If a written agreement of the parents is filed with the court, the court shall render an order appointing the parents as joint managing conservators only if the agreement:

(1) establishes the county of residence of the child until modified by further order, or designates

the conservator who has the exclusive right to establish the primary residence of the child;

(2) specifies the rights and duties of each parent regarding the child's physical care, support, and education;

(3) includes provisions to minimize disruption of the child's education, daily routine, and association with friends;

(4) allocates between the parents, independently, jointly, or exclusively, all of the remaining rights and duties of a parent provided by Chapter 151;

(5) is voluntarily and knowingly made by each parent and has not been repudiated by either parent at the time the order is rendered; and

(6) is in the best interest of the child.

(b) The agreement may contain an alternative dispute resolution procedure that the parties agree to use before requesting enforcement or modification of the terms and conditions of the joint conservatorship through litigation, except in an emergency.

Added by Acts 1995, 74th Leg., ch. 20, § 1, eff. April 20, 1995.

§ 153.134. Court-Ordered Joint Conservatorship

(a) If a written agreement of the parents is not filed with the court, the court may render an order appointing the parents joint managing conservators only if the appointment is in the best interest of the child, considering the following factors:

(1) whether the physical, psychological, or emotional needs and development of the child will benefit from the appointment of joint managing conservators;

(2) the ability of the parents to give first priority to the welfare of the child and reach shared decisions in the child's best interest;

(3) whether each parent can encourage and accept a positive relationship between the child and the other parent;

(4) whether both parents participated in child rearing before the filing of the suit;

(5) the geographical proximity of the parents' residences;

(6) if the child is 12 years of age or older, the child's preference, if any, regarding the appointment of joint managing conservators; and

(7) any other relevant factor.

(b) In rendering an order appointing joint managing conservators, the court shall:

(1) establish the county of residence of the child until altered by further order, or designate the conservator who has the exclusive right to determine the primary residence of the child;

(2) specify the rights and duties of each parent regarding the child's physical care, support, and education;

(3) include provisions to minimize disruption of the child's education, daily routine, and association with friends;

(4) allocate between the parents, independently, jointly, or exclusively, all of the remaining rights and duties of a parent as provided by Chapter 151; and

(5) if feasible, recommend that the parties use an alternative dispute resolution method before requesting enforcement or modification of the terms and conditions of the joint conservatorship through litigation, except in an emergency.

Added by Acts 1995, 74th Leg., ch. 20, § 1, eff. April 20, 1995.

§ 153.135. Equal Possession Not Required

Joint managing conservatorship does not require the award of equal or nearly equal periods of physical possession of and access to the child to each of the joint conservators.

Added by Acts 1995, 74th Leg., ch. 20, § 1, eff. April 20, 1995.

§ 153.136. Court Designation of Primary Physical Residence

If joint managing conservatorship is ordered, the best interest of the child ordinarily requires the court to designate a primary physical residence for the child.

Added by Acts 1995, 74th Leg., ch. 20, § 1, eff. April 20, 1995.

§ 153.137. Guidelines for the Possession of Child by Parent Named as Joint Managing Conservator

The standard possession order provided by Subchapter F[1] constitutes a presumptive minimum amount of time for possession of a child by a parent named as a joint managing conservator who is not awarded the primary physical residence of the child in a suit.

Added by Acts 1995, 74th Leg., ch. 20, § 1, eff. April 20, 1995.

[1] V.T.C.A., Family Code § 153.311 et seq.

§ 153.138. Child Support Order Affecting Joint Conservators

The appointment of joint managing conservators does not impair or limit the authority of the court to order a joint managing conservator to pay child support to another joint managing conservator.

Added by Acts 1995, 74th Leg., ch. 20, § 1, eff. April 20, 1995.

§ 153.139. Repealed by Acts 1997, 75th Leg., ch. 561, § 30, eff. Sept. 1, 1997

[Sections 153.140 to 153.190 reserved for expansion]

SUBCHAPTER D. PARENT APPOINTED AS POSSESSORY CONSERVATOR

§ 153.191. Presumption that Parent to be Appointed Possessory Conservator

The court shall appoint as a possessory conservator a parent who is not appointed as a sole or joint managing conservator unless it finds that the appointment is not in the best interest of the child and that parental possession or access would endanger the physical or emotional welfare of the child.

Added by Acts 1995, 74th Leg., ch. 20, § 1, eff. April 20, 1995.

§ 153.192. Rights and Duties of Parent Appointed Possessory Conservator

(a) Unless limited by court order, a parent appointed as possessory conservator of a child has the rights and duties provided by Subchapter B [1] and any other right or duty expressly granted to the possessory conservator in the order.

(b) In ordering the terms and conditions for possession of a child by a parent appointed possessory conservator, the court shall be guided by the guidelines in Subchapter E.[2]

Added by Acts 1995, 74th Leg., ch. 20, § 1, eff. April 20, 1995.

[1] V.T.C.A., Family Code § 153.071 et seq.

[2] V.T.C.A., Family Code § 153.251 et seq.

§ 153.193. Minimal Restriction on Parent's Possession or Access

The terms of an order that denies possession of a child to a parent or imposes restrictions or limitations on a parent's right to possession of or access to a child may not exceed those that are required to protect the best interest of the child.

Added by Acts 1995, 74th Leg., ch. 20, § 1, eff. April 20, 1995.

[Sections 153.194 to 153.250 reserved for expansion]

SUBCHAPTER E. GUIDELINES FOR THE POSSESSION OF A CHILD BY A PARENT NAMED AS POSSESSORY CONSERVATOR

§ 153.251. Policy and General Application of Guidelines

(a) The guidelines established in the standard possession order are intended to guide the courts in ordering the terms and conditions for possession of a child by a parent named as a possessory conservator or as the minimum possession for a joint managing conservator.

(b) It is the policy of this state to encourage frequent contact between a child and each parent for periods of possession that optimize the development of a close and continuing relationship between each parent and child.

(c) It is preferable for all children in a family to be together during periods of possession.

(d) The standard possession order is designed to apply to a child three years of age or older.

Added by Acts 1995, 74th Leg., ch. 20, § 1, eff. April 20, 1995.

§ 153.252. Rebuttable Presumption

In a suit, there is a rebuttable presumption that the standard possession order in Subchapter F:[1]

(1) provides reasonable minimum possession of a child for a parent named as a possessory conservator or joint managing conservator; and

(2) is in the best interest of the child.

Added by Acts 1995, 74th Leg., ch. 20, § 1, eff. April 20, 1995.

[1] V.T.C.A., Family Code § 153.311 et seq.

§ 153.253. Standard Possession Order Inappropriate or Unworkable

The court shall render an order that grants periods of possession of the child as similar as possible to those provided by the standard possession order if the work schedule or other special circumstances of the managing conservator, the possessory conservator, or the child, or the year-round school schedule of the child, make the standard order unworkable or inappropriate.

Added by Acts 1995, 74th Leg., ch. 20, § 1, eff. April 20, 1995.

§ 153.254. Child Less Than Three Years of Age

(a) The court shall render an order appropriate under the circumstances for possession of a child less than three years of age.

(b) The court shall render a prospective order to take effect on the child's third birthday, which presumptively will be the standard possession order.

Added by Acts 1995, 74th Leg., ch. 20, § 1, eff. April 20, 1995.

§ 153.255. Agreement

The court may render an order for periods of possession of a child that vary from the standard possession order based on the agreement of the parties.

Added by Acts 1995, 74th Leg., ch. 20, § 1, eff. April 20, 1995.

§ 153.256. Factors for Court to Consider

In ordering the terms of possession of a child under an order other than a standard possession order, the court shall be guided by the guidelines established by the standard possession order and may consider:

(1) the age, developmental status, circumstances, needs, and best interest of the child;

(2) the circumstances of the managing conservator and of the parent named as a possessory conservator; and

(3) any other relevant factor.

Added by Acts 1995, 74th Leg., ch. 20, § 1, eff. April 20, 1995. Amended by Acts 1995, 74th Leg., ch. 751, § 35, eff. Sept. 1, 1995.

§ 153.257. Means of Travel

In an order providing for the terms and conditions of possession of a child, the court may restrict the means of travel of the child by a legal mode of transportation only after a showing of good cause contained in the record and a finding by the court that the restriction is in the best interest of the child. The court shall specify the duties of the conservators to provide transportation to and from the transportation facilities.

Added by Acts 1995, 74th Leg., ch. 20, § 1, eff. April 20, 1995.

§ 153.258. Request for Findings When Order Varies From Standard Order

Without regard to Rules 296 through 299, Texas Rules of Civil Procedure, in all cases in which possession of a child by a parent is contested and the possession of the child varies from the standard possession order, on written request made or filed with the court not later than 10 days after the date of the hearing or on oral request made in open court during the hearing, the court shall state in the order the specific reasons for the variance from the standard order.

Added by Acts 1995, 74th Leg., ch. 20, § 1, eff. April 20, 1995.

[Sections 153.259 to 153.310 reserved for expansion]

SUBCHAPTER F. STANDARD POSSESSION ORDER

§ 153.311. Mutual Agreement or Specified Terms for Possession

The court shall specify in a standard possession order that the parties may have possession of the child at times mutually agreed to in advance by the parties and, in the absence of mutual agreement, shall have possession of the child under the specified terms set out in the standard order.

Added by Acts 1995, 74th Leg., ch. 20, § 1, eff. April 20, 1995.

§ 153.312. Parents Who Reside 100 Miles or Less Apart

(a) If the possessory conservator resides 100 miles or less from the primary residence of the child, the possessory conservator shall have the right to possession of the child as follows:

(1) on weekends beginning at 6 p.m. on the first, third, and fifth Friday of each month and ending at 6 p.m. on the following Sunday or, at the possessory conservator's election made before or at the time of the rendition of the original or modification order, and as specified in the original or modification order, beginning at the time the child's school is regularly dismissed and ending at 6 p.m. on the following Sunday; and

(2) on Wednesdays of each week during the regular school term beginning at 6 p.m. and ending at 8 p.m., or, at the possessory conservator's election made before or at the time of the rendition of the original or modification order, and as specified in the original or modification order, beginning at the time the child's school is regularly dismissed and

ending at the time the child's school resumes, unless the court finds that visitation under this subdivision is not in the best interest of the child.

(b) The following provisions govern possession of the child for vacations and certain specific holidays and supersede conflicting weekend or Wednesday periods of possession. The possessory conservator and the managing conservator shall have rights of possession of the child as follows:

(1) the possessory conservator shall have possession in even-numbered years, beginning at 6 p.m. on the day the child is dismissed from school for the school's spring vacation and ending at 6 p.m. on the day before school resumes after that vacation, and the managing conservator shall have possession for the same period in odd-numbered years;

(2) if a possessory conservator:

(A) gives the managing conservator written notice by May 1 of each year specifying an extended period or periods of summer possession, the possessory conservator shall have possession of the child for 30 days beginning not earlier than the day after the child's school is dismissed for the summer vacation and ending not later than seven days before school resumes at the end of the summer vacation, to be exercised in not more than two separate periods of at least seven consecutive days each; or

(B) does not give the managing conservator written notice by May 1 of each year specifying an extended period or periods of summer possession, the possessory conservator shall have possession of the child for 30 consecutive days beginning at 6 p.m. on July 1 and ending at 6 p.m. on July 31;

(3) if the managing conservator gives the possessory conservator written notice by June 1 of each year, the managing conservator shall have possession of the child on any one weekend beginning Friday at 6 p.m. and ending at 6 p.m. on the following Sunday during one period of possession by the possessory conservator under Subdivision (2), provided that the managing conservator picks up the child from the possessory conservator and returns the child to that same place; and

(4) if the managing conservator gives the possessory conservator written notice by May 15 of each year or gives the possessory conservator 14 days' written notice on or after May 16 of each year, the managing conservator may designate one weekend beginning not earlier than the day after the child's school is dismissed for the summer vacation and ending not later than seven days before school resumes at the end of the summer vacation, during which an otherwise scheduled weekend period of possession by the possessory conservator will not take place, provided that the weekend designated does not interfere with the possessory conservator's period or periods of extended summer possession or with Father's Day if the possessory conservator is the father of the child.

Added by Acts 1995, 74th Leg., ch. 20, § 1, eff. April 20, 1995. Amended by Acts 1997, 75th Leg., ch. 802, § 1, eff. Sept. 1, 1997.

Section 2 of Acts 1997, 75th Leg., ch. 802 provides:

"This Act takes effect September 1, 1997, and applies only to a possession order rendered on or after that date."

§ 153.313. Parents Who Reside Over 100 Miles Apart

If the possessory conservator resides more than 100 miles from the residence of the child, the possessory conservator shall have the right to possession of the child as follows:

(1) either regular weekend possession beginning on the first, third, and fifth Friday as provided under the terms applicable to parents who reside 100 miles or less apart or not more than one weekend per month of the possessory conservator's choice beginning at 6 p.m. on the day school recesses for the weekend and ending at 6 p.m. on the day before school resumes after the weekend, provided that the possessory conservator gives the managing conservator 14 days' written or telephonic notice preceding a designated weekend, and provided that the possessory conservator elects an option for this alternative period of possession by written notice given to the managing conservator within 90 days after the parties begin to reside more than 100 miles apart, as applicable;

(2) each year beginning on the day the child is dismissed from school for the school's spring vacation and ending at 6 p.m. on the day before school resumes after that vacation;

(3) if the possessory conservator:

(A) gives the managing conservator written notice by May 1 of each year specifying an extended period or periods of summer possession, the possessory conservator shall have possession of the child for 42 days beginning not earlier than the day after the child's school is dismissed for the summer vacation and ending not later than seven days before school resumes at the end of the summer vacation, to be exercised in not more than two separate periods of at least seven consecutive days each; or

(B) does not give the managing conservator written notice by May 1 of each year specifying an extended period or periods of summer possession, the possessory conservator shall have possession of the child for 42 consecutive days beginning at 6 p.m. on June 15 and ending at 6 p.m. on July 27;

(4) if the managing conservator gives the possessory conservator written notice by June 1 of each year the managing conservator shall have possession of the child on one weekend beginning Friday at 6 p.m. and ending at 6 p.m. on the following Sunday during one period of possession by the possessory conservator under Subdivision (3), provided that if a period of possession by the possessory conservator exceeds 30 days, the managing conservator may have possession of the child under the terms of this subdivision on two nonconsecutive weekends during that time period, and further provided that the managing conservator picks up the child from the possessory conservator and returns the child to that same place; and

(5) if the managing conservator gives the possessory conservator written notice by June 1 of each year, the managing conservator may designate 21 days beginning not earlier than the day after the child's school is dismissed for the summer vacation and ending not later than seven days before school resumes at the end of the summer vacation, to be exercised in not more than two separate periods of at least seven consecutive days each, during which the possessory conservator may not have possession of the child, provided that the period or periods so designated do not interfere with the possessory conservator's period or periods of extended summer possession or with Father's Day if the possessory conservator is the father of the child.

Added by Acts 1995, 74th Leg., ch. 20, § 1, eff. April 20, 1995. Amended by Acts 1995, 74th Leg., ch. 751, § 36, eff. Sept. 1, 1995.

§ 153.314. Holiday Possession Unaffected by Distance Parents Reside Apart

The following provisions govern possession of the child for certain specific holidays and supersede conflicting weekend or Wednesday periods of possession without regard to the distance the parents reside apart. The possessory conservator and the managing conservator shall have rights of possession of the child as follows:

(1) the possessory conservator shall have possession of the child in even-numbered years beginning at 6 p.m. on the day the child is dismissed from school for the Christmas school vacation and ending at noon on December 26, and the managing conservator shall have possession for the same period in odd-numbered years;

(2) the possessory conservator shall have possession of the child in odd-numbered years beginning at noon on December 26 and ending at 6 p.m. on the day before school resumes after that vacation, and the managing conservator shall have possession for the same period in even-numbered years;

(3) the possessory conservator shall have possession of the child in odd-numbered years, beginning at 6 p.m. on the day the child is dismissed from school before Thanksgiving and ending at 6 p.m. on the following Sunday, and the managing conservator shall have possession for the same period in even-numbered years;

(4) the parent not otherwise entitled under this standard order to present possession of a child on the child's birthday shall have possession of the child beginning at 6 p.m. and ending at 8 p.m. on that day, provided that the parent picks up the child from the residence of the conservator entitled to possession and returns the child to that same place;

(5) if a conservator, the father shall have possession of the child beginning at 6 p.m. on the Friday preceding Father's Day and ending on Father's Day at 6 p.m., provided that, if he is not otherwise entitled under this standard order to present possession of the child, he picks up the child from the residence of the conservator entitled to possession and returns the child to that same place; and

(6) if a conservator, the mother shall have possession of the child beginning at 6 p.m. on the Friday preceding Mother's Day and ending on Mother's Day at 6 p.m., provided that, if she is not otherwise entitled under this standard order to present possession of the child, she picks up the child from the residence of the conservator entitled to possession and returns the child to that same place.

Added by Acts 1995, 74th Leg., ch. 20, § 1, eff. April 20, 1995.

§ 153.315. Weekend Possession Extended by Holiday

(a) If a weekend period of possession of the possessory conservator coincides with a school holiday during the regular school term or with a federal, state, or local holiday during the summer months in which school is not in session, the weekend possession shall end at 6 p.m. on a Monday holiday or school holiday or shall begin at 6 p.m. Thursday for a Friday holiday or school holiday, as applicable.

(b) At the possessory conservator's election, made before or at the time of the rendition of the original or modification order, and as specified in the original or modification order, periods of possession extended by a holiday may begin at the time the child's school is regularly dismissed.

Added by Acts 1995, 74th Leg., ch. 20, § 1, eff. April 20, 1995.

§ 153.316. General Terms and Conditions

The court shall order the following general terms and conditions of possession of a child to apply without regard to the distance between the residence of a parent and the child:

(1) the managing conservator shall surrender the child to the possessory conservator at the beginning of each period of the possessory conservator's possession at the residence of the managing conservator;

(2) if the possessory conservator elects to begin a period of possession at the time the child's school is regularly dismissed, the managing conservator shall surrender the child to the possessory conservator at the beginning of each period of possession at the school in which the child is enrolled;

(3) the possessory conservator shall be ordered to do one of the following:

(A) the possessory conservator shall surrender the child to the managing conservator at the end of each period of possession at the residence of the possessory conservator; or

(B) the possessory conservator shall return the child to the residence of the managing conservator at the end of each period of possession, except that the order shall provide that the possessory conservator shall surrender the child to the managing conservator at the end of each period of possession at the residence of the possessory conservator if:

(i) at the time the original order or a modification of an order establishing terms and conditions of possession or access the possessory conservator and the managing conservator lived in the same county, the possessory conservator's county of residence remains the same after the rendition of the order, and the managing conservator's county of residence changes, effective on the date of the change of residence by the managing conservator; or

(ii) the possessory conservator and managing conservator lived in the same residence at any time during a six-month period preceding the date on which a suit for dissolution of the marriage was filed and the possessory conservator's county of residence remains the same and the managing conservator's county of residence changes after they no longer live in the same residence, effective on the date the order is rendered;

(4) if the possessory conservator elects to end a period of possession at the time the child's school resumes, the possessory conservator shall surrender the child to the managing conservator at the end of each period of possession at the school in which the child is enrolled;

(5) each conservator shall return with the child the personal effects that the child brought at the beginning of the period of possession;

(6) either parent may designate a competent adult to pick up and return the child, as applicable; a parent or a designated competent adult shall be present when the child is picked up or returned;

(7) a parent shall give notice to the person in possession of the child on each occasion that the parent will be unable to exercise that parent's right of possession for a specified period;

(8) written notice shall be deemed to have been timely made if received or postmarked before or at the time that notice is due; and

(9) if a conservator's time of possession of a child ends at the time school resumes and for any reason the child is not or will not be returned to school, the conservator in possession of the child shall immediately notify the school and the other conservator that the child will not be or has not been returned to school.

Added by Acts 1995, 74th Leg., ch. 20, § 1, eff. April 20, 1995. Amended by Acts 1995, 74th Leg., ch. 751, § 37, eff. Sept. 1, 1995; Acts 1997, 75th Leg., ch. 9, § 1, eff. Sept. 1, 1997.

Section 2 of Acts 1997, 75th Leg., ch. 9 provides:

"The changes made by this Act to orders for the possession of a child apply only to an order rendered on or after the effective date of this Act. This Act does not affect the terms or conditions of an order made before that date."

§ 153.317. Alternative Possession Times

If a child is enrolled in school and the possessory conservator elects before or at the time of the rendition of the original or modification order, the standard order must expressly provide that the possessory conservator's period of possession shall begin or end, or both, at a different time expressly set in the standard order under and within the range of alternative times provided by one or both of the following subdivisions:

(1) instead of a period of possession by a possessory conservator beginning at 6 p.m. on the day school recesses, the period of possession may be set in the standard possession order to begin at the time the child's school is regularly dismissed or at any time between the time the child's school is regularly dismissed and 6 p.m.; and

(2) except for Wednesday evening possession, instead of a period of possession by a possessory conservator ending at 6 p.m. on the day before school resumes, the period of possession may be set in the standard order to end at the time school resumes.

Added by Acts 1995, 74th Leg., ch. 20, § 1, eff. April 20, 1995. Amended by Acts 1997, 75th Leg., ch. 9, § 1, eff. Sept. 1, 1997.

[Sections 153.318 to 153.370 reserved for expansion]

SUBCHAPTER G. APPOINTMENT OF NONPARENT AS CONSERVATOR

§ 153.371. Rights and Duties of Nonparent Appointed as Sole Managing Conservator

Unless limited by court order or other provisions of this chapter, a nonparent, licensed child-placing agency, or authorized agency appointed as a managing conservator of the child has the following rights and duties:

(1) the right to have physical possession and to direct the moral and religious training of the child;

(2) the duty of care, control, protection, and reasonable discipline of the child;

(3) the duty to provide the child with clothing, food, shelter, education, and medical, psychological, and dental care;

(4) the right to consent for the child to medical, psychiatric, psychological, dental, and surgical treatment;

(5) the right to receive and give receipt for payments for the support of the child and to hold or disburse funds for the benefit of the child;

(6) the right to the services and earnings of the child;

(7) the right to consent to marriage and to enlistment in the armed forces of the United States;

(8) the right to represent the child in legal action and to make other decisions of substantial legal significance concerning the child;

(9) except when a guardian of the child's estate or a guardian or attorney ad litem has been appointed for the child, the right to act as an agent of the child in relation to the child's estate if the child's action is required by a state, the United States, or a foreign government;

(10) the right to establish the primary residence of the child and to make decisions regarding the child's education; and

(11) if the parent-child relationship has been terminated with respect to the parents, or only living parent, or if there is no living parent, the right to consent to the adoption of the child and to make any other decision concerning the child that a parent could make.

Added by Acts 1995, 74th Leg., ch. 20, § 1, eff. April 20, 1995. Amended by Acts 1995, 74th Leg., ch. 751, § 34, eff. Sept. 1, 1995.

§ 153.372. Nonparent Appointed as Joint Managing Conservator

(a) A nonparent, authorized agency, or licensed child-placing agency appointed as a joint managing conservator may serve in that capacity with either another nonparent or with a parent of the child.

(b) The procedural and substantive standards regarding an agreed or court-ordered joint managing conservatorship provided by Subchapter C [1] apply to a nonparent joint managing conservator.

Added by Acts 1995, 74th Leg., ch. 20, § 1, eff. April 20, 1995.

[1] V.T.C.A., Family Code § 153.131 et seq.

§ 153.373. Voluntary Surrender of Possession Rebuts Parental Presumption

The presumption that a parent should be appointed or retained as managing conservator of the child is rebutted if the court finds that:

(1) the parent has voluntarily relinquished actual care, control, and possession of the child to a nonparent, licensed child-placing agency, or authorized agency for a period of one year or more, a portion of which was within 90 days preceding the date of intervention in or filing of the suit; and

(2) the appointment of the nonparent or agency as managing conservator is in the best interest of the child.

Added by Acts 1995, 74th Leg., ch. 20, § 1, eff. April 20, 1995.

§ 153.374. Designation of Managing Conservator in Affidavit of Relinquishment

(a) A parent may designate a competent person, authorized agency, or licensed child-placing agency to serve as managing conservator of the child in an unrevoked or irrevocable affidavit of relinquishment of parental rights executed as provided by Chapter 161.

(b) The person or agency designated to serve as managing conservator shall be appointed managing conservator unless the court finds that the appointment would not be in the best interest of the child.

Added by Acts 1995, 74th Leg., ch. 20, § 1, eff. April 20, 1995. Amended by Acts 1995, 74th Leg., ch. 751, § 38, eff. Sept. 1, 1995.

§ 153.375. Annual Report by Nonparent Managing Conservator

(a) A nonparent appointed as a managing conservator of a child shall each 12 months after the appointment file with the court a report of facts concerning the child's welfare, including the child's whereabouts and physical condition.

(b) The report may not be admitted in evidence in a subsequent suit.

Added by Acts 1995, 74th Leg., ch. 20, § 1, eff. April 20, 1995.

§ 153.376. Rights and Duties of Nonparent Possessory Conservator

(a) Unless limited by court order or other provisions of this chapter, a nonparent, licensed child-placing agency, or authorized agency appointed as a possessory conservator has the following rights and duties during the period of possession:

(1) the duty of care, control, protection, and reasonable discipline of the child;

(2) the duty to provide the child with clothing, food, and shelter; and

(3) the right to consent to medical, dental, and surgical treatment during an emergency involving an immediate danger to the health and safety of the child.

(b) A nonparent possessory conservator has any other right or duty specified in the order.

Added by Acts 1995, 74th Leg., ch. 20, § 1, eff. April 20, 1995.

§ 153.377. Access to Child's Records

A nonparent possessory conservator has the right of access to medical, dental, psychological, and educational records of the child to the same extent as the managing conservator, without regard to whether the right is specified in the order.

Added by Acts 1995, 74th Leg., ch. 20, § 1, eff. April 20, 1995.

[Sections 153.378 to 153.430 reserved for expansion]

SUBCHAPTER H. RIGHTS OF GRANDPARENT

§ 153.431. Grandparental Appointment as Managing Conservators

If the parents are deceased, the grandparents may be considered for appointment as managing conservators, but consideration does not alter or diminish the discretionary power of the court.

Added by Acts 1995, 74th Leg., ch. 20, § 1, eff. April 20, 1995.

§ 153.432. Suit for Access

(a) A biological or adoptive grandparent may request access to a grandchild by filing:

(1) an original suit; or

(2) a suit for modification as provided by Chapter 156.

(b) A grandparent may request access to a grandchild in a suit filed for the sole purpose of requesting the relief, without regard to whether the appointment of a managing conservator is an issue in the suit.

Added by Acts 1995, 74th Leg., ch. 20, § 1, eff. April 20, 1995.

§ 153.433. Possession of and Access to Grandchild

The court shall order reasonable access to a grandchild by a grandparent if:

(1) at the time the relief is requested, at least one biological or adoptive parent of the child has not had that parent's parental rights terminated; and

(2) access is in the best interest of the child, and at least one of the following facts is present:

(A) the grandparent requesting access to the child is a parent of a parent of the child and that parent of the child has been incarcerated in jail or prison during the three-month period preceding the filing of the petition or has been found by a court to be incompetent or is dead;

(B) the parents of the child are divorced or have been living apart for the three-month period preceding the filing of the petition or a suit for the dissolution of the parents' marriage is pending;

(C) the child has been abused or neglected by a parent of the child;

(D) the child has been adjudicated to be a child in need of supervision or a delinquent child under Title 3;

(E) the grandparent requesting access to the child is the parent of a person whose parent-child relationship with the child has been terminated by court order; or

(F) the child has resided with the grandparent requesting access to the child for at least six months within the 24-month period preceding the filing of the petition.

Added by Acts 1995, 74th Leg., ch. 20, § 1, eff. April 20, 1995. Amended by Acts 1997, 75th Leg., ch. 1397, § 1, eff. Sept. 1, 1997.

§ 153.434. Limitation on Right to Request Access

A biological or adoptive grandparent may not request possession of or access to a grandchild if:

(1) the grandparent is a parent of a person whose parental rights with the child have been terminated by court order or by death; or

(2) the grandparent is a parent of a person who has executed an affidavit of waiver of interest in child or an affidavit of relinquishment of parental rights under Chapter 161 and the affidavit designates an authorized agency, licensed child-placing agency, or person other than the child's stepparent as the managing conservator of the child; and

(3) the other biological parent has died, has executed an affidavit of waiver of interest in child or an affidavit of relinquishment of parental rights under Chapter 161, or has had that parent's parental rights terminated and the grandchild has been adopted by a person other than the child's stepparent.

Added by Acts 1995, 74th Leg., ch. 20, § 1, eff. April 20, 1995. Amended by Acts 1997, 75th Leg., ch. 561, § 4, eff. Sept. 1, 1997.

For application provisions of Acts 1997, 75th Leg., ch. 561, see notes following V.T.C.A., Family Code § 102.009.

CHAPTER 154. CHILD SUPPORT

SUBCHAPTER A. COURT-ORDERED CHILD SUPPORT

SUBCHAPTER B. COMPUTING NET RESOURCES AVAILABLE FOR PAYMENT OF CHILD SUPPORT

SUBCHAPTER C. CHILD SUPPORT GUIDELINES

SUBCHAPTER D. MEDICAL SUPPORT FOR CHILD

SUBCHAPTER E. LOCAL CHILD SUPPORT REGISTRY

SUBCHAPTER A. COURT–ORDERED CHILD SUPPORT

§ 154.001. Support of Child

(a) The court may order either or both parents to support a child in the manner specified by the order:

(1) until the child is 18 years of age or until graduation from high school, whichever occurs later;

(2) until the child is emancipated through marriage, through removal of the disabilities of minority by court order, or by other operation of law;

(3) until the death of the child; or

(4) if the child is disabled as defined in this chapter, for an indefinite period.

(b) The court may order either or both parents to make periodic payments for the support of a child in a proceeding in which the Department of Protective and Regulatory Services is named temporary managing conservator. In a proceeding in which the Department of Protective and Regulatory Services is named permanent managing conservator of a child whose parents' rights have not been terminated, the court shall order each parent that is financially able to make periodic payments for the support of the child.

Added by Acts 1995, 74th Leg., ch. 20, § 1, eff. April 20, 1995. Amended by Acts 1995, 74th Leg., ch. 751, § 39, eff. Sept. 1, 1995.

§ 154.002. Child Support Through High School Graduation

(a) If the child is fully enrolled in an accredited secondary school in a program leading toward a high school diploma, the court may render an original support order or modify an existing order providing child support past the 18th birthday of the child.

(b) The request for a support order through high school graduation may be filed before or after the child's 18th birthday.

(c) The order for periodic support may provide that payments continue through the end of the month in which the child graduates.

Added by Acts 1995, 74th Leg., ch. 20, § 1, eff. April 20, 1995.

§ 154.003. Manner of Payment

The court may order that child support be paid by:

(1) periodic payments;

(2) a lump-sum payment;

(3) an annuity purchase;

(4) the setting aside of property to be administered for the support of the child as specified in the order; or

(5) any combination of periodic payments, lump-sum payments, annuity purchases, or setting aside of property.

Added by Acts 1995, 74th Leg., ch. 20, § 1, eff. April 20, 1995.

§ 154.004. Place of Payment

(a) Except as agreed by the parties, the court shall order the payment of child support through a local registry or through the Title IV–D agency.

(b) In a Title IV–D case, the court shall order that income withheld for child support be paid:

(1) to the Title IV–D agency through a local registry, which shall forward the payment to the Title IV–D agency; or

(2) directly to the Title IV–D agency.

Added by Acts 1995, 74th Leg., ch. 20, § 1, eff. April 20, 1995.

§ 154.005. Payments of Support Obligation by Trust

(a) The court may order the trustees of a spendthrift or other trust to make disbursements for the support of a child to the extent the trustees are required to make payments to a beneficiary who is required to make child support payments as provided by this chapter.

(b) If disbursement of the assets of the trust is discretionary, the court may order child support payments from the income of the trust but not from the principal.

Added by Acts 1995, 74th Leg., ch. 20, § 1, eff. April 20, 1995.

§ 154.006. Termination of Duty of Support

Unless otherwise agreed in writing or expressly provided in the order, the child support order terminates on the marriage of the child, removal of the child's disabilities for general purposes, or death of the child or a parent ordered to pay child support.

Added by Acts 1995, 74th Leg., ch. 20, § 1, eff. April 20, 1995.

§ 154.007. Order to Withhold Child Support From Income

(a) In a proceeding in which periodic payments of child support are ordered, modified, or enforced, the court or Title IV-D agency shall order that income be withheld from the disposable earnings of the obligor as provided by Chapter 158.

(b) If the court does not order income withholding, an order for support must contain a provision for income withholding to ensure that withholding may be effected if a delinquency occurs.

(c) A child support order must be construed to contain a withholding provision even if the provision has been omitted from the written order.

(d) If the order was rendered or last modified before January 1, 1987, the order is presumed to contain a provision for income withholding procedures to take effect in the event a delinquency occurs without further amendment to the order or future action by the court.

Added by Acts 1995, 74th Leg., ch. 20, § 1, eff. April 20, 1995. Amended by Acts 1997, 75th Leg., ch. 911, § 10, eff. Sept. 1, 1997.

For application and effectiveness provisions of Acts 1997, 75th Leg., ch. 911, see note following V.T.C.A., Family Code § 101.011.

§ 154.008. Provision for Health Insurance Coverage

The court shall order health insurance coverage for the child as provided by Subchapters B and D.[1]

Added by Acts 1995, 74th Leg., ch. 20, § 1, eff. April 20, 1995.

[1] V.T.C.A., Family Code § 154.061 et seq. and V.T.C.A., Family Code § 154.181 et seq.

§ 154.009. Retroactive Child Support

(a) The court may order a parent to pay retroactive child support if the parent:

(1) has not previously been ordered to pay support for the child; and

(2) was not a party to a suit in which support was ordered.

(b) In ordering retroactive child support, the court shall apply the child support guidelines provided by this chapter.

(c) Unless the Title IV–D agency is a party to an agreement concerning support or purporting to settle past, present, or future support obligations by prepayment or otherwise, an agreement between the parties does not reduce or terminate retroactive support that the agency may request.

Added by Acts 1995, 74th Leg., ch. 20, § 1, eff. April 20, 1995.

§ 154.010. No Discrimination Based on Marital Status of Parents or Sex

The amount of support ordered for the benefit of a child shall be determined without regard to:

(1) the sex of the obligor, obligee, or child; or

(2) the marital status of the parents of the child.

Added by Acts 1995, 74th Leg., ch. 20, § 1, eff. April 20, 1995.

§ 154.011. Support Not Conditioned on Possession or Access

A court may not render an order that conditions the payment of child support on whether a managing conservator allows a possessory conservator to have possession of or access to a child.

Added by Acts 1995, 74th Leg., ch. 751, § 40, eff. Sept. 1, 1995.

[Sections 154.012 to 154.060 reserved for expansion]

SUBCHAPTER B. COMPUTING NET RESOURCES AVAILABLE FOR PAYMENT OF CHILD SUPPORT

§ 154.061. Computing Net Monthly Income

(a) Whenever feasible, gross income should first be computed on an annual basis and then should be recalculated to determine average monthly gross income.

(b) The Title IV–D agency shall annually promulgate tax charts to compute net monthly income, subtracting from gross income social security taxes and federal income tax withholding for a single person claiming one personal exemption and the standard deduction.

Added by Acts 1995, 74th Leg., ch. 20, § 1, eff. April 20, 1995.

OFFICE OF THE ATTORNEY GENERAL
1997 TAX CHARTS

Pursuant to Section 154.061(b) of the Texas Family Code, the Attorney General of Texas, as the Title IV–D agency has promulgated the following tax charts for 1997 to assist courts in establishing the amount of a child support order. These tax charts are applicable to employed and self-employed persons in computing net monthly income.

INSTRUCTIONS FOR USE

To use these tables, first compute the obligor's annual gross income. Then recompute to determine the obligor's average monthly gross income. These tables provide a method for calculating "monthly net income" for child support purposes, subtracting from monthly gross income the social security taxes and the federal income tax withholding for a single person claiming one personal exemption and the standard deduction.

Thereafter, in many cases the guidelines call for a number of additional steps to complete the necessary calculations. For example, Sections 154.061 through 154.068 provide for appropriate additions to "income" as that term is defined for federal income tax purposes, and for certain subtractions from monthly net income, in order to arrive at the net resources of the obligor available for child support purposes. Computation of the obligee's net resources should follow similar steps.

EMPLOYED PERSONS
1997 TAX CHART

	Social Security Taxes			
Monthly Gross Wages	Old–Age, Survivors and Disability Insurance Taxes (6.2%) *	Hospital (Medicare) Insurance Taxes (1.45%) *	Federal Income Taxes **	Net Monthly Income
100.00	6.20	1.45	–0–	92.35
200.00	12.40	2.90	–0–	184.70
300.00	18.60	4.35	–0–	277.05
400.00	24.80	5.80	–0–	369.40
500.00	31.00	7.25	–0–	461.75
600.00	37.20	8.70	5.00	549.10
700.00	43.40	10.15	20.00	626.45
800.00	49.60	11.60	35.00	703.80
900.00	55.80	13.05	50.00	781.15
1,000.00	62.00	14.50	65.00	858.50
1,100.00	68.20	15.95	80.00	935.85
1,200.00	74.40	17.40	95.00	1,013.20
1,300.00	80.60	18.85	110.00	1,090.55
1,400.00	86.80	20.30	125.00	1,167.90
1,500.00	93.00	21.75	140.00	1,245.25
1,600.00	99.20	23.20	155.00	1,322.60
1,700.00	105.40	24.65	170.00	1,399.95
1,800.00	111.60	26.10	185.00	1,477.30
1,900.00	117.80	27.55	200.00	1,554.65
2,000.00	124.00	29.00	215.00	1,632.00
2,100.00	130.20	30.45	230.00	1,709.35
2,200.00	136.40	31.90	245.00	1,786.70
2,300.00	142.60	33.35	260.00	1,864.05
2,400.00	148.80	34.80	275.00	1,941.40
2,500.00	155.00	36.25	290.00	2,018.75
2,600.00	161.20	37.70	305.00	2,096.10
2,700.00	167.40	39.15	330.29	2,163.16
2,800.00	173.60	40.60	358.29	2,227.51
2,900.00	179.80	42.05	386.29	2,291.86
3,000.00	186.00	43.50	414.29	2,356.21
3,100.00	192.20	44.95	442.29	2,420.56
3,200.00	198.40	46.40	470.29	2,484.91
3,300.00	204.60	47.85	498.29	2,549.26
3,400.00	210.80	49.30	526.29	2,613.61
3,500.00	217.00	50.75	554.29	2,677.96
3,600.00	223.20	52.20	582.29	2,742.31
3,700.00	229.40	53.65	610.29	2,806.66
3,800.00	235.60	55.10	638.29	2,871.01
3,900.00	241.80	56.55	666.29	2,935.36
4,000.00	248.00	58.00	694.29	2,999.71
4,250.00	263.50	61.63	764.29	3,160.58
4,500.00	279.00	65.25	834.29	3,321.46

Monthly Gross Wages	Social Security Taxes: Old–Age, Survivors and Disability Insurance Taxes (6.2%) *	Social Security Taxes: Hospital (Medicare) Insurance Taxes (1.45%) *	Federal Income Taxes **	Net Monthly Income
4,750.00	294.50	68.88	904.29	3,482.33
5,000.00	310.00	72.50	974.29	3,643.21
5,250.00	325.50	76.13	1,044.29	3,804.08
5,500.00	337.90***	79.75	1,114.29	3,968.06
5,750.00	337.90	83.38	1,190.42	4,138.30
6,000.00	337.90	87.00	1,267.92	4,307.18
6,250.00	337.90	90.63	1,345.42	4,476.05
6,500.00	337.90	94.25	1,422.92	4,644.93
6,750.00	337.90	97.88	1,500.42	4,813.80
7,000.00	337.90	101.50	1,577.92	4,982.68
7,500.00	337.90	108.75	1,732.92	5,320.43
8,000.00	337.90	116.00	1,887.92	5,658.18
8,500.00	337.90	123.25	2,042.92	5,995.93
9,000.00	337.90	130.50	2,197.92	6,333.68
9,500.00	337.90	137.75	2,352.92	6,671.43
10,000.00	337.90	145.00	2,507.92	7,009.18
10,500.00	337.90	152.25	2,665.66	7,344.19
11,000.00	337.90	159.50	2,828.16	7,674.44
11,500.00	337.90	166.75	3,011.34	7,984.01
12,000.00	337.90	174.00	3,196.11	8,291.99
12,500.00	337.90	181.25	3,379.29	8,601.56
13,000.00	337.90	188.50	3,562.47	8,911.13

Footnotes to Employed Persons 1997 Tax Chart:

* An employed person not subject to the Old–age, Survivors and Disability Insurance/Hospital (Medicare) Insurance taxes will be allowed the reductions reflected in these columns, unless it is shown that such person has no similar contributory plan such as teacher retirement, federal railroad retirement, federal civil service retirement, etc.

** These amounts represent one-twelfth of the annual Federal income tax calculated for a single taxpayer claiming one personal exemption ($2,650.00, subject to reduction in certain cases, as described in the next paragraph of this footnote) and taking the standard deduction ($4,150.00).

For a single taxpayer with an adjusted gross income in excess of $121,200.00, the deduction for the personal exemption is reduced by two percent (2.0%) for each $2,500.00 or fraction thereof by which adjusted gross income exceeds $121,200.00. The reduction is completed (i.e., the deduction for the personal exemption is eliminated) for adjusted gross income in excess of $243,700.00. In no case is the deduction for the personal exemption reduced by more than 100%. For example, monthly gross wages of $12,000.00 times 12 months equals $144,000.00. The excess over $121,200.00 is $22,800.00. $22,800.00 divided by $2,500.00 equals 9.12. The 9.12 amount is rounded up to 10. The reduction percentage is 20% (10 × 2.0% = 20%). The $2,650.00 deduction for one personal exemption is reduced by $530.00 ($2,650.00 × 20% = $530.00) to $2,120.00 ($2,650.00 − $530.00 = $2,120.00).

*** For annual gross wages above $65,400.00, this amount represents a monthly average of the Old–Age, Survivors and Disability Insurance tax based on the 1997 maximum Old–Age, Survivors and Disability Insurance tax of $4,054.80 per person (6.2% of the first $65,400.00 of annual gross wages equals $4,054.80). One-twelfth of $4,054.80 equals $337.90.

* *

References Relating to Employed Persons 1997 Tax Chart:

1. Old–Age, Survivors and Disability Insurance Tax
   (a) Contribution Base
      (1) Social Security Administration's notice dated October 18, 1996, and appearing in 61 Fed.Reg. 55,346 (October 25, 1996)
      (2) Section 3121(a)(1) of the Internal Revenue Code of 1986, as amended (26 U.S.C. § 3121(a)(1))
      (3) Section 230 of the Social Security Act, as amended (42 U.S.C. § 430)
   (b) Tax Rate
      (1) Section 3101(a) of the Internal Revenue Code of 1986, as amended (26 U.S.C. § 3101(a))
2. Hospital (Medicare) Insurance Tax
   (a) Contribution Base
      (1) Omnibus Budget Reconciliation Act of 1993, Pub.L.No. 103–66, § 13207, 107 Stat. 312, 467–69 (1993)
   (b) Tax Rate
      (1) Section 3101(b) of the Internal Revenue Code of 1986, as amended (26 U.S.C. § 3101(b))
3. Federal Income Tax

(a) Inflation Adjusted Tax Rate Table for 1997 for Single Taxpayers
   (1) Revenue Procedure 96–59, Section 3.01, Table 3, which appears at pages 18–19 of Internal Revenue Bulletin 1996–53, dated December 30, 1996
   (2) Section 1(c) and (f) of the Internal Revenue Code of 1986, as amended (26 U.S.C. § 1(c) and (f))
(b) Standard Deduction
   (1) Revenue Procedure 96–59, Section 3.05, which appears at page 20 of Internal Revenue Bulletin 1996–53, dated December 30, 1996
   (2) Section 63(c) of the Internal Revenue Code of 1986, as amended (26 U.S.C. § 63(c))
(c) Personal Exemption
   (1) Revenue Procedure 96–59, Section 3.09, which appears at page 21 of Internal Revenue Bulletin 1996–53, dated December 30, 1996
   (2) Section 151(d)of the Internal Revenue Code of 1986, as amended (26 U.S.C. § 151(d))

SELF–EMPLOYED PERSONS
1997 TAX CHART

	Social Security Taxes			
Monthly Net Earnings From Self–Employment *	Old–Age, Survivors and Disability Insurance Taxes (12.4%) **	Hospital (Medicare) Insurance Taxes (2.9%) **	Federal Income Taxes ***	Net Monthly Income
100.00	11.45	2.68	–0–	85.87
200.00	22.90	5.36	–0–	171.74
300.00	34.35	8.03	–0–	257.62
400.00	45.81	10.71	–0–	343.48
500.00	57.26	13.39	–0–	429.35
600.00	68.71	–0–	1.77	515.22
700.00	80.16	18.75	12.58	588.51
800.00	91.61	21.43	26.52	660.44
900.00	103.06	24.10	40.46	732.38
1,000.00	114.51	26.78	54.40	804.31
1,100.00	125.97	29.46	68.34	876.23
1,200.00	137.42	32.14	82.28	948.16
1,300.00	148.87	34.82	96.22	1,020.09
1,400.00	160.32	37.49	110.16	1,092.03
1,500.00	171.77	40.17	124.10	1,163.96
1,600.00	183.22	42.85	138.04	1,235.89
1,700.00	194.67	45.53	151.98	1,307.82
1,800.00	206.13	48.21	165.93	1,379.73
1,900.00	217.58	50.88	179.87	1,451.67
2,000.00	229.03	53.56	193.81	1,523.60
2,100.00	240.48	56.24	207.75	1,595.53
2,200.00	251.93	58.92	221.69	1,667.46
2,300.00	263.38	61.60	235.63	1,739.39
2,400.00	274.83	64.28	249.57	1,811.32
2,500.00	286.29	66.95	263.51	1,883.25
2,600.00	297.74	69.63	277.45	1,955.18
2,700.00	309.19	72.31	291.39	2,027.11
2,800.00	320.64	74.99	305.33	2,099.04
2,900.00	332.09	77.67	328.93	2,161.31
3,000.00	343.54	80.34	354.95	2,221.17
3,100.00	354.99	83.02	380.97	2,281.02
3,200.00	366.44	85.70	406.99	2,340.87
3,300.00	377.90	88.38	433.01	2,400.71
3,400.00	389.35	91.06	459.04	2,460.55
3,500.00	400.80	93.74	485.06	2,520.40
3,600.00	412.25	96.41	511.08	2,580.26
3,700.00	423.70	99.09	537.10	2,640.11
3,800.00	435.15	101.77	563.12	2,699.96
3,900.00	446.60	104.45	589.14	2,759.81
4,000.00	458.06	107.13	615.17	2,819.64
4,250.00	486.68	113.82	680.22	2,969.28
4,500.00	515.31	120.52	745.28	3,118.89
4,750.00	543.94	127.21	810.33	3,268.52
5,000.00	572.57	133.91	875.38	3,418.14
5,250.00	601.20	140.60	940.44	3,567.76

Monthly Net Earnings From Self-Employment *	Social Security Taxes: Old–Age, Survivors and Disability Insurance Taxes (12.4%) **	Social Security Taxes: Hospital (Medicare) Insurance Taxes (2.9%) **	Federal Income Taxes ***	Net Monthly Income
5,500.00	629.83	147.30	1,005.49	3,717.38
5,750.00	658.46	153.99	1,070.55	3,867.00
6,000.00	675.80****	160.69	1,138.26	4,025.25
6,250.00	675.80	167.38	1,214.72	4,192.10
6,500.00	675.80	174.08	1,291.19	4,358.93
6,750.00	675.80	180.78	1,367.65	4,525.77
7,000.00	675.80	187.47	1,444.11	4,692.62
7,500.00	675.80	200.86	1,597.03	5,026.31
8,000.00	675.80	214.25	1,749.96	5,359.99
8,500.00	675.80	227.64	1,902.88	5,693.68
9,000.00	675.80	241.03	2,055.81	6,027.36
9,500.00	675.80	254.42	2,208.73	6,361.05
10,000.00	675.80	267.82	2,361.66	6,694.72
10,500.00	675.80	281.21	2,514.58	7,028.41
11,000.00	675.80	294.60	2,670.24	7,359.36
11,500.00	675.80	307.99	2,831.08	7,685.13
12,000.00	675.80	321.38	3,011.85	7,990.97
12,500.00	675.80	334.77	3,194.21	8,295.22
13,000.00	675.80	348.16	3,374.98	8,601.06

Footnotes to Self–Employed Persons 1997 Tax Chart:

* Determined without regard to Section 1402(a)(12) of the Internal Revenue Code of 1986, as amended (26 U.S.C.) (the "Code").

** In calculating each of the Old–Age, Survivors and Disability Insurance tax and the Hospital (Medicare) Insurance tax, net earnings from self-employment are reduced by the deduction under Section 1402(a)(12) of the Code. The deduction under Section 1402(a)(12) of the Code is equal to net earnings from self-employment (determined without regard to Section 1402(a)(12) of the Code) multiplied by one-half of the sum of the Old–Age, Survivors and Disability Insurance tax rate (12.4%) and the Hospital (Medicare) Insurance tax rate (2.9%). The sum of these rates is 15.3% (12.4% + 2.9% = 15.3%). One-half of the combined rate is 7.65% (15.3% × ½ = 7.65%). The deduction can be computed by multiplying the net earnings from self-employment (determined without regard to Section 1402(a)(12) of the Code) by 92.35%. This gives the same deduction as multiplying the net earnings from self-employment (determined without regard to Section 1402(a)(12) of the Code) by 7.65% and then subtracting the result.

For example, the Social Security taxes imposed on monthly net earnings from self-employment (determined without regard to Section 1402(a)(12) of the Code) of $2,500.00 are calculated as follows:

(i) Old–Age, Survivors and Disability Insurance Taxes:
$2,500.00 × 92.35% × 12.4% = $286.29

(ii) Hospital (Medicare) Insurance Taxes:
$2,500.00 × 92.35% × 2.9% = $66.95

*** These amounts represent one-twelfth of the annual Federal income tax calculated for a single taxpayer claiming one personal exemption ($2,650.00, subject to reduction in certain cases, as described below in this footnote) and taking the standard deduction ($4,150.00).

In calculating the annual Federal income tax, gross income is reduced by the deduction under Section 164(f) of the Code. The deduction under Section 164(f) of the Code is equal to one-half of the self-employment taxes imposed by Section 1401 of the Code for the taxable year. For example, monthly net earnings from self-employment of $12,000.00 times 12 months equals $144,000.00. The Old–Age, Survivors and Disability Insurance taxes imposed by Section 1401 of the Code for the taxable year equal $8,109.60 ($65,400.00 × 12.4% = $8,109.60). The Hospital (Medicare) Insurance taxes imposed by Section 1401 of the Code for the taxable year equal $3,856.54 ($144,000.00 × .9235 × 2.9% = $3,856.54). The sum of the taxes imposed by Section 1401 of the Code for the taxable year equals $11,966.14 ($8,109.60 + $3,856.54 = $11,966.14). The deduction under Section 164(f) of the Code is equal to one-half of $11,966.14 or $5,983.07.

For a single taxpayer with an adjusted gross income in excess of $121,200.00, the deduction for the personal exemption is reduced by two percent (2.0%) for each $2,500.00 or fraction thereof by which adjusted gross income exceeds $121,200.00. The reduction is completed (i.e., the deduction of the personal exemption is eliminated) for adjusted gross income in excess of $243,700.00. In no case is the deduction for the personal exemption reduced by more than 100%. For example, monthly net earnings from self-employment of $12,000.00 times 12 months equals $144,000.00.

The $144,000.00 amount is reduced by $5,983.07 (i.e., the deduction under Section 164(f) of the Code —see the immediately preceding paragraph of this footnote for the computation) to arrive at adjusted gross income of $138,016.93. The excess over $121,200.00 is $16,816.93. $16,816.93 divided by $2,500.00 equals 6.73. The 6.73 amount is rounded up to 7. The reduction percentage is 14% (7 × 2.0% = 14%). The $2,650.00 deduction for one personal exemption is reduced by $371.00 ($2,650.00 × 14% = $371.00) to $2,279.00 ($2,650.00 − $371.00 = $2,279.00).

**** For annual net earnings from self-employment (determined with regard to Section 1402(a)(12) of the Code) above $65,400.00, this amount represents a monthly average of the Old–Age, Survivors and Disability Insurance tax based on the 1997 maximum Old–Age, Survivors and Disability Insurance tax of $8,109.60 per person (12.4% of the first $65,400.00 of net earnings from self-employment (determined with regard to Section 1402(a)(12) of the Code) equals $8,109.60). One-twelfth of $8,109.60 equals $675.80.

* *

References Relating to Self–Employed Persons 1997 Tax Chart:

1. Old–Age, Survivors and Disability Insurance Tax
   (a) Contribution Base
      (1) Social Security Administration's notice dated October 18, 1996, and appearing in 61 Fed.Reg. 55,346 (October 25, 1996)
      (2) Section 1402(b)(1) of the Internal Revenue Code of 1986, as amended (26 U.S.C. § 1402(b)(1))
      (3) Section 230 of the Social Security Act, as amended (42 U.S.C. § 430)
   (b) Tax Rate
      (1) Section 1401(a) of the Internal Revenue Code of 1986, as amended (26 U.S.C. § 1401(a))
   (c) Deduction Under Section 1402(a)(12)
      (1) Section 1402(a)(12) of the Internal Revenue Code of 1986, as amended (26 U.S.C. § 1402(a)(12))
2. Hospital (Medicare) Insurance Tax
   (a) Contribution Base
      (1) Omnibus Budget Reconciliation Act of 1993, Pub.L.No. 103–66, § 13207, 107 Stat. 312, 467–69 (1993)
   (b) Tax Rate
      (1) Section 1401(b) of the Internal Revenue Code of 1986, as amended (26 U.S.C. § 1401(b))
   (c) Deduction Under Section 1402(a)(12)
      (1) Section 1402(a)(12) of the Internal Revenue Code of 1986, as amended (26 U.S.C. § 1402(a)(12))
3. Federal Income Tax
   (a) Inflation Adjusted Tax Rate Table for 1997 for Single Taxpayers
      (1) Revenue Procedure 96–59, Section 3.01, Table 3, which appears at pages 18–19 of Internal Revenue Bulletin 1996–53, dated December 30, 1996
      (2) Section 1(c) and (f) of the Internal Revenue Code of 1986, as amended (26 U.S.C. § 1(c) and (f))
   (b) Standard Deduction
      (1) Revenue Procedure 96–59, Section 3.05, which appears at page 20 of Internal Revenue Bulletin 1996–53, dated December 30, 1996
      (2) Section 63(c) of the Internal Revenue Code of 1986, as amended (26 U.S.C. § 63(c))
   (c) Personal Exemption
      (1) Revenue Procedure 96–59, Section 3.09, which appears at page 21 of Internal Revenue Bulletin 1996–53, dated December 30, 1996
      (2) Section 151(d) of the Internal Revenue Code of 1986, as amended (26 U.S.C. § 151(d))
   (d) Deduction Under Section 164(f)
      (1) Section 164(f) of the Internal Revenue Code of 1986, as amended (26 U.S.C. § 164(f))

§ 154.062. Net Resources

(a) The court shall calculate net resources for the purpose of determining child support liability as provided by this section.

(b) Resources include:

(1) 100 percent of all wage and salary income and other compensation for personal services (including commissions, overtime pay, tips, and bonuses);

(2) interest, dividends, and royalty income;

(3) self-employment income;

(4) net rental income (defined as rent after deducting operating expenses and mortgage payments, but not including noncash items such as depreciation); and

(5) all other income actually being received, including severance pay, retirement benefits, pensions, trust income, annuities, capital gains, social security benefits, unemployment benefits, disability and workers' compensation benefits, interest income

from notes regardless of the source, gifts and prizes, spousal maintenance, and alimony.

(c) Resources do not include:

(1) return of principal or capital;

(2) accounts receivable; or

(3) benefits paid in accordance with aid for families with dependent children.

(d) The court shall deduct the following items from resources to determine the net resources available for child support:

(1) social security taxes;

(2) federal income tax based on the tax rate for a single person claiming one personal exemption and the standard deduction;

(3) state income tax;

(4) union dues; and

(5) expenses for health insurance coverage for the obligor's child.

Added by Acts 1995, 74th Leg., ch. 20, § 1, eff. April 20, 1995. Amended by Acts 1995, 74th Leg., ch. 751, § 41, eff. Sept. 1, 1995.

§ 154.063. Party to Furnish Information

The court shall require a party to:

(1) furnish information sufficient to accurately identify that party's net resources and ability to pay child support; and

(2) produce copies of income tax returns for the past two years, a financial statement, and current pay stubs.

Added by Acts 1995, 74th Leg., ch. 20, § 1, eff. April 20, 1995.

§ 154.064. Health Insurance for Child Presumptively Provided by Obligor

The guidelines for support of a child are based on the assumption that the court will order the obligor to provide health insurance coverage for the child in addition to the amount of child support calculated in accordance with those guidelines.

Added by Acts 1995, 74th Leg., ch. 20, § 1, eff. April 20, 1995.

§ 154.065. Self-Employment Income

(a) Income from self-employment, whether positive or negative, includes benefits allocated to an individual from a business or undertaking in the form of a proprietorship, partnership, joint venture, close corporation, agency, or independent contractor, less ordinary and necessary expenses required to produce that income.

(b) In its discretion, the court may exclude from self-employment income amounts allowable under federal income tax law as depreciation, tax credits, or any other business expenses shown by the evidence to be inappropriate in making the determination of income available for the purpose of calculating child support.

Added by Acts 1995, 74th Leg., ch. 20, § 1, eff. April 20, 1995.

§ 154.066. Intentional Unemployment or Underemployment

If the actual income of the obligor is significantly less than what the obligor could earn because of intentional unemployment or underemployment, the court may apply the support guidelines to the earning potential of the obligor.

Added by Acts 1995, 74th Leg., ch. 20, § 1, eff. April 20, 1995.

§ 154.067. Deemed Income

(a) When appropriate, in order to determine the net resources available for child support, the court may assign a reasonable amount of deemed income attributable to assets that do not currently produce income. The court shall also consider whether certain property that is not producing income can be liquidated without an unreasonable financial sacrifice because of cyclical or other market conditions. If there is no effective market for the property, the carrying costs of such an investment, including property taxes and note payments, shall be offset against the income attributed to the property.

(b) The court may assign a reasonable amount of deemed income to income-producing assets that a party has voluntarily transferred or on which earnings have intentionally been reduced.

Added by Acts 1995, 74th Leg., ch. 20, § 1, eff. April 20, 1995.

§ 154.068. Wage and Salary Presumption

In the absence of evidence of the wage and salary income of a party, the court shall presume that the party has wages or salary equal to the federal minimum wage for a 40–hour week.

Added by Acts 1995, 74th Leg., ch. 20, § 1, eff. April 20, 1995.

§ 154.069. Net Resources of Spouse

(a) The court may not add any portion of the net resources of a spouse to the net resources of an obligor or obligee in order to calculate the amount of child support to be ordered.

(b) The court may not subtract the needs of a spouse, or of a dependent of a spouse, from the net resources of the obligor or obligee.

Added by Acts 1995, 74th Leg., ch. 20, § 1, eff. April 20, 1995.

§ 154.070. Child Support Received by Obligor

In a situation involving multiple households due child support, child support received by an obligor shall be added to the obligor's net resources to compute the net resources before determining the child support credit or applying the percentages in the multiple household table in this chapter.

Added by Acts 1995, 74th Leg., ch. 20, § 1, eff. April 20, 1995.

[Sections 154.071 to 154.120 reserved for expansion]

SUBCHAPTER C. CHILD SUPPORT GUIDELINES

§ 154.121. Guidelines for the Support of a Child

The child support guidelines in this subchapter are intended to guide the court in determining an equitable amount of child support.

Added by Acts 1995, 74th Leg., ch. 20, § 1, eff. April 20, 1995.

§ 154.122. Application of Guidelines Rebuttably Presumed in Best Interest of Child

(a) The amount of a periodic child support payment established by the child support guidelines in effect in this state at the time of the hearing is presumed to be reasonable, and an order of support conforming to the guidelines is presumed to be in the best interest of the child.

(b) A court may determine that the application of the guidelines would be unjust or inappropriate under the circumstances.

Added by Acts 1995, 74th Leg., ch. 20, § 1, eff. April 20, 1995.

§ 154.123. Additional Factors for Court to Consider

(a) The court may order periodic child support payments in an amount other than that established by the guidelines if the evidence rebuts the presumption that application of the guidelines is in the best interest of the child and justifies a variance from the guidelines.

(b) In determining whether application of the guidelines would be unjust or inappropriate under the circumstances, the court shall consider evidence of all relevant factors, including:

(1) the age and needs of the child;

(2) the ability of the parents to contribute to the support of the child;

(3) any financial resources available for the support of the child;

(4) the amount of time of possession of and access to a child;

(5) the amount of the obligee's net resources, including the earning potential of the obligee if the actual income of the obligee is significantly less than what the obligee could earn because the obligee is intentionally unemployed or underemployed and including an increase or decrease in the income of the obligee or income that may be attributed to the property and assets of the obligee;

(6) child care expenses incurred by either party in order to maintain gainful employment;

(7) whether either party has the managing conservatorship or actual physical custody of another child;

(8) the amount of alimony or spousal maintenance actually and currently being paid or received by a party;

(9) the expenses for a son or daughter for education beyond secondary school;

(10) whether the obligor or obligee has an automobile, housing, or other benefits furnished by his or her employer, another person, or a business entity;

(11) the amount of other deductions from the wage or salary income and from other compensation for personal services of the parties;

(12) provision for health care insurance and payment of uninsured medical expenses;

(13) special or extraordinary educational, health care, or other expenses of the parties or of the child;

(14) the cost of travel in order to exercise possession of and access to a child;

(15) positive or negative cash flow from any real and personal property and assets, including a business and investments;

(16) debts or debt service assumed by either party; and

(17) any other reason consistent with the best interest of the child, taking into consideration the circumstances of the parents.

Added by Acts 1995, 74th Leg., ch. 20, § 1, eff. April 20, 1995.

§ 154.124. Agreement Concerning Support

(a) To promote the amicable settlement of disputes between the parties to a suit, the parties may enter into a written agreement containing provisions for support of the child and for modification of the agreement, including variations from the child support guidelines provided by Subchapter C.[1]

(b) If the court finds that the agreement is in the child's best interest, the court shall render an order in accordance with the agreement.

(c) Terms of the agreement in the order may be enforced by all remedies available for enforcement of a judgment, including contempt, but are not enforceable as contract terms unless provided by the agreement.

(d) If the court finds the agreement is not in the child's best interest, the court may request the parties to submit a revised agreement or the court may render an order for the support of the child.

Added by Acts 1995, 74th Leg., ch. 20, § 1, eff. April 20, 1995.

[1] V.T.C.A., Family Code § 154.121 et seq.

§ 154.125. Application of Guidelines to Net Resources of $6,000 or Less

(a) The guidelines for the support of a child in this section are specifically designed to apply to situations in which the obligor's monthly net resources are $6,000 or less.

(b) If the obligor's monthly net resources are $6,000 or less, the court shall presumptively apply the following schedule in rendering the child support order:

CHILD SUPPORT GUIDELINES

BASED ON THE MONTHLY NET RESOURCES OF THE OBLIGOR

1 child	20% of Obligor's Net Resources
2 children	25% of Obligor's Net Resources
3 children	30% of Obligor's Net Resources
4 children	35% of Obligor's Net Resources
5 children	40% of Obligor's Net Resources
6+ children	Not less than the amount for 5 children

Added by Acts 1995, 74th Leg., ch. 20, § 1, eff. April 20, 1995.

§ 154.126. Application of Guidelines to Net Resources of More Than $6,000 Monthly

(a) If the obligor's net resources exceed $6,000 per month, the court shall presumptively apply the percentage guidelines to the first $6,000 of the obligor's net resources. Without further reference to the percentage recommended by these guidelines, the court may order additional amounts of child support as appropriate, depending on the income of the parties and the proven needs of the child.

(b) The proper calculation of a child support order that exceeds the presumptive amount established for the first $6,000 of the obligor's net resources requires that the entire amount of the presumptive award be subtracted from the proven total needs of the child. After the presumptive award is subtracted, the court shall allocate between the parties the responsibility to meet the additional needs of the child according to the circumstances of the parties. However, in no event may the obligor be required to pay more child support than the greater of the presumptive amount or the amount equal to 100 percent of the proven needs of the child.

Added by Acts 1995, 74th Leg., ch. 20, § 1, eff. April 20, 1995.

§ 154.127. Partial Termination of Support Obligation

A child support order for more than one child shall provide that, on the termination of support for a child, the level of support for the remaining child or children is in accordance with the child support guidelines.

Added by Acts 1995, 74th Leg., ch. 20, § 1, eff. April 20, 1995.

§ 154.128. Computing Support for Children in More Than One Household

(a) In applying the child support guidelines for an obligor who has children in more than one household, the court shall apply the percentage guidelines in this subchapter by making the following computation:

(1) determine the amount of child support that would be ordered if all children whom the obligor has the legal duty to support lived in one household by applying the schedule in this subchapter;

(2) compute a child support credit for the obligor's children who are not before the court by dividing the amount determined under Subdivision (1) by the total number of children whom the obligor is obligated to support and multiplying that number by the number of the obligor's children who are not before the court;

(3) determine the adjusted net resources of the obligor by subtracting the child support credit computed under Subdivision (2) from the net resources of the obligor; and

(4) determine the child support amount for the children before the court by applying the percentage guidelines for one household for the number of children of the obligor before the court to the obligor's adjusted net resources.

(b) For the purpose of determining a child support credit, the total number of an obligor's children includes the children before the court for the establishment or modification of a support order and any other children, including children residing with the obligor, whom the obligor has the legal duty of support.

(c) The child support credit with respect to children for whom the obligor is obligated by an order to pay support is computed, regardless of whether the obligor is delinquent in child support payments, without regard to the amount of the order.

Added by Acts 1995, 74th Leg., ch. 20, § 1, eff. April 20, 1995.

§ 154.129. Alternative Method of Computing Support for Children in More Than One Household

In lieu of performing the computation under the preceding section, the court may determine the child support amount for the children before the court by applying the percentages in the table below to the obligor's net resources:

MULTIPLE FAMILY ADJUSTED GUIDELINES
(% OF NET RESOURCES)

		Number of children before the court						
		1	2	3	4	5	6	7
Number of	0	20.00	25.00	30.00	35.00	40.00	40.00	40.00
other	1	17.50	22.50	27.38	32.20	37.33	37.71	38.00
children for	2	16.00	20.63	25.20	30.33	35.43	36.00	36.44
whom the	3	14.75	19.00	24.00	29.00	34.00	34.67	35.20
obligor	4	13.60	18.33	23.14	28.00	32.89	33.60	34.18
has a	5	13.33	17.86	22.50	27.22	32.00	32.73	33.33
duty of	6	13.14	17.50	22.00	26.60	31.27	32.00	32.62
support	7	13.00	17.22	21.60	26.09	30.67	31.38	32.00

Added by Acts 1995, 74th Leg., ch. 20, § 1, eff. April 20, 1995.

§ 154.130. Findings in Child Support Order

(a) Without regard to Rules 296 through 299, Texas Rules of Civil Procedure, in rendering an order of child support, the court shall make the findings required by Subsection (b) if:

(1) a party files a written request with the court not later than 10 days after the date of the hearing;

(2) a party makes an oral request in open court during the hearing; or

(3) the amount of child support ordered by the court varies from the amount computed by applying the percentage guidelines.

(b) If findings are required by this section, the court shall state whether the application of the guidelines would be unjust or inappropriate and shall state the following in the child support order:

"(1) the monthly net resources of the obligor per month are $______;

"(2) the monthly net resources of the obligee per month are $______;

"(3) the percentage applied to the obligor's net resources for child support by the actual order rendered by the court is ______%;

"(4) the amount of child support if the percentage guidelines are applied to the first $6,000 of the obligor's net resources is $______;

"(5) if applicable, the specific reasons that the amount of child support per month ordered by the court varies from the amount stated in Subdivision (4) are: ______; and

"(6) if applicable, the obligor is obligated to support children in more than one household, and:

"(A) the number of children before the court is ______;

"(B) the number of children not before the court residing in the same household with the obligor is ______; and

"(C) the number of children not before the court for whom the obligor is obligated by a court order to pay support, without regard to whether the obligor is delinquent in child support payments, and who are not counted under Paragraph (A) or (B) is ______."

Added by Acts 1995, 74th Leg., ch. 20, § 1, eff. April 20, 1995.

§ 154.131. Application of Guidelines to Retroactive Support

(a) The child support guidelines are intended to guide the court in determining the amount of retroactive child support, if any, to be ordered.

(b) In ordering retroactive child support, the court shall consider the net resources of the obligor during the relevant time period and whether:

(1) the mother of the child had made any previous attempts to notify the biological father of his paternity or probable paternity;

(2) the biological father had knowledge of his paternity or probable paternity;

(3) the order of retroactive child support will impose an undue financial hardship on the obligor or the obligor's family; and

(4) the obligor has provided actual support or other necessaries before the filing of the action.

Added by Acts 1995, 74th Leg., ch. 20, § 1, eff. April 20, 1995.

[Sections 154.132 to 154.180 reserved for expansion]

SUBCHAPTER D. MEDICAL SUPPORT FOR CHILD

§ 154.181. Medical Support Order

In a suit affecting the parent-child relationship or in a proceeding under Chapter 159, the court shall render an order for the medical support of the child.

Added by Acts 1995, 74th Leg., ch. 20, § 1, eff. April 20, 1995.

§ 154.182. Health Insurance

(a) The court shall consider the cost and quality of health insurance coverage available to the parties and shall give priority to health insurance coverage available through the employment of one of the parties.

(b) Except as provided for by Subdivision (6), in determining the manner in which health insurance for the child is to be ordered, the court shall render its order in accordance with the following priorities, unless a party shows good cause why a particular order would not be in the best interest of the child:

(1) if health insurance is available for the child through the obligor's employment or membership in a union, trade association, or other organization, the court shall order the obligor to include the child in the obligor's health insurance;

(2) if health insurance is not available for the child through the obligor's employment but is available for the child through the obligee's employment or membership in a union, trade association, or other organization, the court may order the obligee to provide health insurance for the child, and, in such event, shall order the obligor to pay additional child support to be withheld from earnings under Chapter 158 to the obligee for the actual cost of the health insurance for the child;

(3) if health insurance is not available for the child under Subdivision (1) or (2), the court shall order the obligor to provide health insurance for the child if the court finds that health insurance is available for the child from another source and that the obligor is financially able to provide it;

(4) if health insurance is not available for the child under Subdivision (1), (2), or (3), the court shall order the obligor to apply for coverage through the Texas Healthy Kids Corporation established under Chapter 109, Health and Safety Code;

(5) if health coverage is not available for the child under Subdivision (1), (2), (3), or (4), the court shall order the obligor to pay the obligee, in addition to any amount ordered under the guidelines for child support, a reasonable amount each month as medical support for the child to be withheld from earnings under Chapter 158; or

(6) notwithstanding Subdivisions (1) through (3), an obligor whose employer, union, trade association, or other organization does not offer a child/children coverage option in lieu of a spouse/child/children option of health insurance coverage may elect to apply for coverage through the Texas Healthy Kids Corporation. An obligor required to pay additional child support to an obligee for health insurance coverage may elect to apply for coverage through the Texas Healthy Kids Corporation if the obligee's employer, union, trade association, or other organization does not offer a child/children coverage option in lieu of a spouse/child/children option of health insurance coverage.

(c) In establishing the amount of additional medical child support under Subsection (b)(5), the court shall presume that $38 each month is a reasonable amount for a child but may order a greater or lesser amount as appropriate under the circumstances. The Health and Human Services Commission may promulgate guidelines for the dollar amounts of medical child support that the court may presumptively apply in circumstances in which the obligor is responsible for medical child support for more than one child.

Added by Acts 1995, 74th Leg., ch. 20, § 1, eff. April 20, 1995. Amended by Acts 1997, 75th Leg., ch. 550, § 2, eff. June 2, 1997.

Sections 9 and 10 of Acts 1997, 75th Leg., ch. 550 provide:

"Sec. 9. A court may not order that coverage be provided to a child through the Texas Healthy Kids Corporation under Section 154.182, Family Code, as amended by this Act, before the date that corporation first offers coverage under a health benefit plan in the applicable region of the state.

"Sec. 10. As soon as practicable after the effective date of this Act, the Title IV-D agency shall seek the modification of child support orders that are enforced by the agency and to which Section 154.182(b)(5), Family Code, as added by this Act, applies to obtain additional medical child support under that subdivision."

§ 154.183. Health Insurance Additional Support Duty of Obligor

(a) An amount that an obligor is required to pay for health insurance for the child:

(1) is in addition to the amount that the obligor is required to pay for child support under the guidelines for child support;

(2) is a child support obligation; and

(3) may be enforced as a child support obligation.

(b) If the court finds and states in the child support order that the obligee will maintain health insurance coverage for the child at the obligee's expense, the court may increase the amount of child support to be paid by the obligor in an amount not exceeding the total expense to the obligee for maintaining health insurance coverage.

(c) As additional child support, the court shall allocate between the parties, according to their circumstances, the reasonable and necessary health care expenses of a child that are not reimbursed by health insurance.

Added by Acts 1995, 74th Leg., ch. 20, § 1, eff. April 20, 1995.

§ 154.184. Effect of Order

(a) Receipt of a medical support order requiring that health insurance be provided for a child shall be considered a change in the family circumstances of the employee or member, for health insurance purposes, equivalent to the birth or adoption of a child.

(b) If the employee or member is eligible for dependent health coverage, the employer shall automatically enroll the child for the first 31 days after the receipt of the order or notice of the medical support order under Section 154.186 on the same terms and conditions as apply to any other dependent child.

(c) The employer shall notify the insurer of the automatic enrollment.

(d) During the 31–day period, the employer and insurer shall complete all necessary forms and procedures to make the enrollment permanent or shall report in accordance with this subchapter the reasons the coverage cannot be made permanent.

Added by Acts 1995, 74th Leg., ch. 20, § 1, eff. April 20, 1995. Amended by Acts 1995, 74th Leg., ch. 341, § 4.03, eff. Sept. 1, 1995; Acts 1997, 75th Leg., ch. 911, § 11, eff. Sept. 1, 1997.

For application and effectiveness provisions of Acts 1997, 75th Leg., ch. 911, see note following V.T.C.A., Family Code § 101.011.

§ 154.185. Parent to Furnish Information

(a) The court shall order a parent providing health insurance to furnish to either the obligee, obligor, local domestic relations office, or Title IV–D agency the following information not later than the 30th day after the date the notice of rendition of the order is received:

(1) the social security number of the parent;

(2) the name and address of the parent's employer;

(3) whether the employer is self-insured or has health insurance available;

(4) proof that health insurance has been provided for the child;

(5) if the employer has health insurance available, the name of the health insurance carrier, the number of the policy, a copy of the policy and schedule of benefits, a health insurance membership card, claim forms, and any other information necessary to submit a claim; and

(6) if the employer is self-insured, a copy of the schedule of benefits, a membership card, claim forms, and any other information necessary to submit a claim.

(b) The court shall also order a parent providing health insurance to furnish the obligor, obligee, local domestic relations office, or Title IV–D agency with additional information regarding health insurance coverage not later than the 15th day after the date the information is received by the parent.

Added by Acts 1995, 74th Leg., ch. 20, § 1, eff. April 20, 1995.

§ 154.186. Notice to Employer Concerning Medical Support

The obligee, obligor, or a child support agency may send to the employer a copy of the order requiring an employee to provide health insurance coverage for a child or may include notice of the medical support order in an order or writ of withholding sent to the employer in accordance with Chapter 158.

Added by Acts 1995, 74th Leg., ch. 20, § 1, eff. April 20, 1995. Amended by Acts 1995, 74th Leg., ch. 341, § 4.04, eff. Sept. 1, 1995; Acts 1997, 75th Leg., ch. 911, § 12, eff. Sept. 1, 1997.

For application and effectiveness provisions of Acts 1997, 75th Leg., ch. 911, see note following V.T.C.A., Family Code § 101.011.

§ 154.187. Duties of Employer

(a) An order or notice under this subchapter to an employer directing that health insurance coverage be provided to a child of an employee or member is binding on a current or subsequent employer on receipt without regard to the date the order was rendered. If the employee or member is eligible for dependent health coverage for the child, the employer shall immediately enroll the child in a health insurance plan regardless of whether the employee is enrolled in the plan. If dependent coverage is not available to the employee or member through the employer's health insurance plan or enrollment cannot be made permanent or if the employer is not responsible or otherwise liable for providing such coverage, the employer shall provide notice to the sender in accordance with Subsection (c).

(b) If additional premiums are incurred as a result of adding the child to the health insurance plan, the employer shall deduct the health insurance premium from the earnings of the employee in accordance with Chapter 158 and apply the amount withheld to payment of the insurance premium.

(c) An employer who has received an order or notice under this subchapter shall provide to the sender, by first class mail not later than the 30th day after the date the employer receives the order or notice, a statement that the child:

(1) has been enrolled in a health insurance plan; or

(2) cannot be enrolled or cannot be enrolled permanently in a health insurance plan and provide the reason why coverage or permanent coverage cannot be provided.

(d) If the employee ceases employment or if the health insurance coverage lapses, the employer shall provide to the sender, by first class mail not later than the 15th day after the date of the termination of employment or the lapse of the coverage, notice of the termination or lapse and of the availability of any conversion privileges.

(e) On request, the employer shall release to the sender information concerning the available health insurance coverage, including the name of the health insurance carrier, the policy number, a copy of the policy and schedule of benefits, a health insurance membership card, and claim forms.

(f) In this section, "sender" means the person sending the order under Section 154.186.

(g) An employer who fails to enroll a child, fails to withhold or remit premiums or cash medical support, or discriminates in hiring or employment on the basis of a medical support order shall be subject to the penalties and fines in Subchapter C, Chapter 158.[1]

Added by Acts 1995, 74th Leg., ch. 20, § 1, eff. April 20, 1995. Amended by Acts 1995, 74th Leg., ch. 341, § 4.05, eff. Sept. 1, 1995; Acts 1997, 75th Leg., ch. 911, § 13, eff. Sept. 1, 1997.

[1] V.T.C.A., Family Code § 158.201 et seq.

For application and effectiveness provisions of Acts 1997, 75th Leg., ch. 911, see note following V.T.C.A., Family Code § 101.011.

§ 154.188. Failure to Provide Required Health Insurance

A parent ordered to provide health insurance who fails to do so is liable for necessary medical expenses of the child, without regard to whether the expenses would have been paid if health insurance had been provided.

Added by Acts 1995, 74th Leg., ch. 20, § 1, eff. April 20, 1995.

§ 154.189. Notice of Termination or Lapse of Insurance Coverage

(a) An obligor ordered to provide health insurance coverage for a child must notify the obligee and any child support agency enforcing a support obligation against the obligor of the:

(1) termination or lapse of health insurance coverage for the child not later than the 15th day after the date of a termination or lapse; and

(2) availability of additional health insurance to the obligor for the child after a termination or lapse of coverage not later than the 15th day after the date the insurance becomes available.

(b) If termination of coverage results from a change of employers, the obligor, the obligee, or the child support agency may send the new employer a copy of the order requiring the employee to provide health insurance for a child or notice of the medical support order as provided by this subchapter.

Added by Acts 1995, 74th Leg., ch. 20, § 1, eff. April 20, 1995. Amended by Acts 1997, 75th Leg., ch. 911, § 14, eff. Sept. 1, 1997.

For application and effectiveness provisions of Acts 1997, 75th Leg., ch. 911, see note following V.T.C.A., Family Code § 101.011.

§ 154.190. Reenrolling Child for Insurance Coverage

After health insurance has been terminated or has lapsed, an obligor ordered to provide health insurance coverage for the child must enroll the child in a health insurance plan at the next available enrollment period.

Added by Acts 1995, 74th Leg., ch. 20, § 1, eff. April 20, 1995.

§ 154.191. Remedy Not Exclusive

(a) This subchapter does not limit the rights of the obligor, obligee, local domestic relations office, or Title IV–D agency to enforce, modify, or clarify the medical support order.

(b) This subchapter does not limit the authority of the court to render or modify a medical support order containing a provision for payment of uninsured health expenses, health care costs, or health insurance premiums that are in addition to and inconsistent with this subchapter.

Added by Acts 1995, 74th Leg., ch. 20, § 1, eff. April 20, 1995.

§ 154.192. Cancellation or Elimination of Insurance Coverage for Child

(a) Unless the employee or member ceases to be eligible for dependent coverage, or the employer has eliminated dependent health coverage for all of the employer's employees or members, the employer may not cancel or eliminate coverage of a child enrolled under this subchapter until the employer is provided satisfactory written evidence that:

(1) the court order or administrative order requiring the coverage is no longer in effect; or

(2) the child is enrolled in comparable health insurance coverage or will be enrolled in comparable coverage that will take effect not later than the effective date of the cancellation or elimination of the employer's coverage.

Added by Acts 1995, 74th Leg., ch. 20, § 1, eff. April 20, 1995. Amended by Acts 1995, 74th Leg., ch. 341, § 4.06, eff. Sept. 1, 1995.

§ 154.193. Medical Support Order Not Qualified

(a) If a plan administrator or other person acting in an equivalent position determines that a medical support order issued under this subchapter does not qualify for enforcement under federal law, the tribunal may, on its own motion or the motion of a party, render an order that qualifies for enforcement under federal law.

(b) The procedure for filing a motion for enforcement of a final order applies to a motion under this section. Service of citation is not required, and a person is not entitled to a jury in a proceeding under this section.

(c) The employer or plan administrator is not a necessary party to a proceeding under this section.

Added by Acts 1997, 75th Leg., ch. 911, § 15, eff. Sept. 1, 1997.

[Sections 154.193 to 154.240 reserved for expansion]

SUBCHAPTER E. LOCAL CHILD SUPPORT REGISTRY

§ 154.241. Local Registry

(a) A local registry shall receive a court-ordered child support payment or a payment otherwise authorized by law and shall forward the payment, as appropriate, to the Title IV–D agency, local domestic relations office, or obligee within two working days after the date the local registry receives the payment.

(b) A local registry may not require an obligor, obligee, or other party or entity to furnish a certified copy of a court order as a condition of processing child support payments and shall accept as sufficient authority to process the payments a photocopy, facsimile copy, or conformed copy of the court's order.

(c) A local registry shall include with each payment it forwards to the Title IV–D agency the date it received the payment and the withholding date furnished by the employer.

(d) A local registry shall accept child support payments made by personal check, money order, or cashier's check. A local registry may refuse payment by personal check if a pattern of abuse regarding the use of personal checks has been established. Abuse includes checks drawn on insufficient funds, abusive or offensive language written on the check, intentional mutilation of the instrument, or other actions that delay or disrupt the registry's operation.

(e) Subject to Section 154.004, at the request of an obligee, a local registry shall redirect and forward a child support payment to an address and in care of a person or entity designated by the obligee. A local registry may require that the obligee's request be in writing or be made on a form provided by the local registry for that purpose, but may not charge a fee for receiving the request or redirecting the payments as requested.

Added by Acts 1995, 74th Leg., ch. 20, § 1, eff. April 20, 1995. Amended by Acts 1995, 74th Leg., ch. 751, § 42, eff. Sept. 1, 1995.

§ 154.242. Payment or Transfer of Child Support Payments by Electronic Funds Transfer

(a) A child support payment may be made by electronic funds transfer to the Title IV–D agency or a local registry if the registry agrees to accept electronic payment.

(b) A local registry may transmit child support payments to the Title IV-D agency by electronic funds transfer if the Title IV-D agency agrees to accept electronic payment. An obligor may make payments, with the approval of the court entering the order, directly to the bank account of the obligee by electronic transfer and provide verification of the deposit to the local registry. A local registry in a county that makes deposits into personal bank accounts by electronic funds transfer as of April 1, 1995, may transmit a child support payment to an obligee by electronic funds transfer if the obligee maintains a bank account. The obligee shall furnish to the local registry the necessary bank account information to complete electronic payment if the Title IV-D agency agrees to accept electronic payment.

Added by Acts 1995, 74th Leg., ch. 20, § 1, eff. April 20, 1995. Amended by Acts 1995, 74th Leg., ch. 597, § 1, eff. Jan. 1, 1996; Acts 1997, 75th Leg., ch. 702, § 2, eff. Jan. 1, 1998; Acts 1997, 75th Leg., ch. 1053, § 2, eff. Sept. 1, 1997.

§ 154.243. Production of Child Support Payment Record

The Title IV–D agency or a local registry may comply with a subpoena or other order directing the production of a child support payment record by sending a certified copy of the record to the court that directed production of the record.

Added by Acts 1995, 74th Leg., ch. 20, § 1, eff. April 20, 1995.

[Sections 154.244 to 154.300 reserved for expansion]

SUBCHAPTER F. SUPPORT FOR A MINOR OR ADULT DISABLED CHILD

§ 154.301. Definitions

In this subchapter:

(1) "Adult child" means a child 18 years of age or older.

(2) "Child" means a son or daughter of any age.

Added by Acts 1995, 74th Leg., ch. 20, § 1, eff. April 20, 1995.

§ 154.302. Court-Ordered Support for Disabled Child

(a) The court may order either or both parents to provide for the support of a child for an indefinite period and may determine the rights and duties of the parents if the court finds that:

(1) the child, whether institutionalized or not, requires substantial care and personal supervision because of a mental or physical disability and will not be capable of self-support; and

(2) the disability exists, or the cause of the disability is known to exist, on or before the 18th birthday of the child.

(b) A court that orders support under this section shall designate a parent of the child or another person having physical custody or guardianship of the child under a court order to receive the support for the child. The court may designate a child who is 18 years of age or older to receive the support directly.

Added by Acts 1995, 74th Leg., ch. 20, § 1, eff. April 20, 1995. Amended by Acts 1997, 75th Leg., ch. 1173, § 1, eff. Sept. 1, 1997.

§ 154.303. Standing to Sue

(a) A suit provided by this subchapter may be filed only by:

(1) a parent of the child or another person having physical custody or guardianship of the child under a court order; or

(2) the child if the child:

(A) is 18 years of age or older;

(B) does not have a mental disability; and

(C) is determined by the court to be capable of managing the child's financial affairs.

(b) The parent, the child, if the child is 18 years of age or older, or other person may not transfer or assign the cause of action to any person, including a governmental or private entity or agency, except for an assignment made to the Title IV-D agency.

Added by Acts 1995, 74th Leg., ch. 20, § 1, eff. April 20, 1995. Amended by Acts 1997, 75th Leg., ch. 1173, § 2, eff. Sept. 1, 1997.

§ 154.304. General Procedure

Except as otherwise provided by this subchapter, the substantive and procedural rights and remedies in a suit affecting the parent-child relationship relating to the establishment, modification, or enforcement of a child support order apply to a suit filed and an order rendered under this subchapter.

Added by Acts 1995, 74th Leg., ch. 20, § 1, eff. April 20, 1995.

§ 154.305. Specific Procedures

(a) A suit under this subchapter may be filed:

(1) regardless of the age of the child; and

(2) as an independent cause of action or joined with any other claim or remedy provided by this code.

(b) If no court has continuing, exclusive jurisdiction of the child, an action under this subchapter may be filed as an original suit affecting the parent-child relationship.

(c) If there is a court of continuing, exclusive jurisdiction, an action under this subchapter may be filed as a suit for modification as provided by Chapter 156.

Added by Acts 1995, 74th Leg., ch. 20, § 1, eff. April 20, 1995.

§ 154.306. Amount of Support After Age 18

In determining the amount of support to be paid after a child's 18th birthday, the specific terms and conditions of that support, and the rights and duties of both parents with respect to the support of the child, the court shall determine and give special consideration to:

(1) any existing or future needs of the adult child directly related to the adult child's mental or physical disability and the substantial care and personal supervision directly required by or related to that disability;

(2) whether the parent pays for or will pay for the care or supervision of the adult child or provides or will provide substantial care or personal supervision of the adult child;

(3) the financial resources available to both parents for the support, care, and supervision of the adult child; and

(4) any other financial resources or other resources or programs available for the support, care, and supervision of the adult child.

Added by Acts 1995, 74th Leg., ch. 20, § 1, eff. April 20, 1995.

§ 154.307. Modification and Enforcement

An order provided by this subchapter may contain provisions governing the rights and duties of both parents with respect to the support of the child and may be modified or enforced in the same manner as any other order provided by this title.

Added by Acts 1995, 74th Leg., ch. 20, § 1, eff. April 20, 1995.

§ 154.308. Remedy Not Exclusive

(a) This subchapter does not affect a parent's:

(1) cause of action for the support of a disabled child under any other law; or

(2) ability to contract for the support of a disabled child.

(b) This subchapter does not affect the substantive or procedural rights or remedies of a person other than a parent, including a governmental or private entity or agency, with respect to the support of a disabled child under any other law.

Added by Acts 1995, 74th Leg., ch. 20, § 1, eff. April 20, 1995.

§ 154.309. Possession of or Access to Adult Disabled Child

(a) A court may render an order for the possession of or access to an adult disabled child that is appropriate under the circumstances.

(b) Possession of or access to an adult disabled child is enforceable in the manner provided by Chapter 157. An adult disabled child may refuse possession or access if the adult disabled child is mentally competent.

(c) A court that obtains continuing, exclusive jurisdiction of a suit affecting the parent-child relationship involving a disabled person who is a child retains continuing, exclusive jurisdiction of subsequent proceedings involving the person, including proceedings after the person is an adult.

Added by Acts 1995, 74th Leg., ch. 751, § 43, eff. Sept. 1, 1995.

CHAPTER 155. CONTINUING, EXCLUSIVE JURISDICTION; TRANSFER

SUBCHAPTER A. CONTINUING, EXCLUSIVE JURISDICTION

Section

SUBCHAPTER A. CONTINUING, EXCLUSIVE JURISDICTION

§ 155.001. Acquiring Continuing, Exclusive Jurisdiction

(a) Except as otherwise provided by this section, a court acquires continuing, exclusive jurisdiction over the matters provided for by this subtitle in connection with a child on the rendition of a final order.

(b) The following final orders do not create continuing, exclusive jurisdiction in a court:

(1) a voluntary or involuntary dismissal of a suit affecting the parent-child relationship;

(2) in a suit to determine parentage, a final order finding that an alleged or presumed father is not the biological father of the child, except that the jurisdiction of the court is not affected if the child was subject to the jurisdiction of the court or some other court in a suit affecting the parent-child relationship before the commencement of the suit to determine parentage; and

(3) a final order of adoption, after which a subsequent suit affecting the child must be commenced as though the child had not been the subject of a suit for adoption or any other suit affecting the parent-child relationship before the adoption.

(c) If a court of this state has acquired continuing, exclusive jurisdiction, no other court of this state has jurisdiction of a suit with regard to that child except as provided by this chapter or Chapter 262.

(d) Unless a final order has been rendered by a court of continuing, exclusive jurisdiction, a subsequent suit shall be commenced as an original proceeding.

Added by Acts 1995, 74th Leg., ch. 20, § 1, eff. April 20, 1995.

§ 155.002. Retaining Continuing, Exclusive Jurisdiction

Except as otherwise provided by this subchapter, a court with continuing, exclusive jurisdiction retains jurisdiction of the parties and matters provided by this subtitle.

Added by Acts 1995, 74th Leg., ch. 20, § 1, eff. April 20, 1995.

§ 155.003. Exercise of Continuing, Exclusive Jurisdiction

(a) Except as otherwise provided by this section, a court with continuing, exclusive jurisdiction may exercise its jurisdiction to modify its order regarding managing conservatorship, possessory conservatorship, possession of and access to the child, and support of the child.

(b) A court of this state may not exercise its continuing, exclusive jurisdiction to modify managing conservatorship if:

(1) the child's home state is other than this state; or

(2) modification is precluded by Chapter 152.

(c) A court of this state may not exercise its continuing, exclusive jurisdiction to modify possessory conservatorship or possession of or access to a child if:

(1) the child's home state is other than this state and all parties have established and continue to maintain their principal residence outside this state; or

(2) each individual party has filed written consent with the tribunal of this state for a tribunal of another state to modify the order and assume continuing, exclusive jurisdiction of the suit.

(d) A court of this state may not exercise its continuing, exclusive jurisdiction to modify its child support order if modification is precluded by Chapter 159.

Added by Acts 1995, 74th Leg., ch. 20, § 1, eff. April 20, 1995.

§ 155.004. Loss of Continuing, Exclusive Jurisdiction

(a) A court of this state loses its continuing, exclusive jurisdiction to modify its order if:

(1) an order of adoption is rendered after the court acquires continuing, exclusive jurisdiction of the suit;

(2) the parents of the child have remarried each other after the dissolution of a previous marriage between them and file a suit for the dissolution of their subsequent marriage combined with a suit affecting the parent-child relationship as if there had not been a prior court with continuing, exclusive jurisdiction over the child; or

(3) another court assumed jurisdiction over a suit and rendered a final order based on incorrect information received from the bureau of vital statistics that there was no court of continuing, exclusive jurisdiction.

(b) This section does not affect the power of the court to enforce its order for a violation that occurred before the time continuing, exclusive jurisdiction was lost under this section.

Added by Acts 1995, 74th Leg., ch. 20, § 1, eff. April 20, 1995. Amended by Acts 1997, 75th Leg., ch. 575, § 8, eff. Sept. 1, 1997.

For application provisions of Acts 1997, 75th Leg., ch. 575, see note following V.T.C.A., Family Code § 102.003.

§ 155.005. Jurisdiction Pending Transfer

(a) During the transfer of a suit from a court with continuing, exclusive jurisdiction, the transferring court retains jurisdiction to render temporary orders.

(b) The jurisdiction of the transferring court terminates on the docketing of the case in the transferee court.

Added by Acts 1995, 74th Leg., ch. 20, § 1, eff. April 20, 1995.

[Sections 155.006 to 155.100 reserved for expansion]

SUBCHAPTER B. IDENTIFICATION OF COURT OF CONTINUING, EXCLUSIVE JURISDICTION

§ 155.101. Request for Identification of Court of Continuing, Exclusive Jurisdiction

(a) The petitioner or the court shall request from the bureau of vital statistics identification of the court that last had continuing, exclusive jurisdiction of the child in a suit unless:

(1) the petition alleges that no court has continuing, exclusive jurisdiction of the child and the issue is not disputed by the pleadings; or

(2) the petition alleges that the court in which the suit, petition for further remedy, or petition to modify has been filed has acquired and retains continuing, exclusive jurisdiction of the child as the result of a prior proceeding and the issue is not disputed by the pleadings.

(b) The bureau of vital statistics shall, on the written request of the court, an attorney, or a party:

(1) identify the court that last had continuing, exclusive jurisdiction of the child in a suit and give the docket number of the suit; or

(2) state that the child has not been the subject of a suit.

(c) The child shall be identified in the request by name, birthdate, and place of birth.

(d) The bureau of vital statistics shall transmit the information not later than the 10th day after the date on which the request is received.

Added by Acts 1995, 74th Leg., ch. 20, § 1, eff. April 20, 1995. Amended by Acts 1995, 74th Leg., ch. 751, § 44, eff. Sept. 1, 1995.

§ 155.102. Dismissal

If a court in which a suit is filed determines that another court has continuing, exclusive jurisdiction of the child, the court in which the suit is filed shall dismiss the suit without prejudice.

Added by Acts 1995, 74th Leg., ch. 20, § 1, eff. April 20, 1995.

§ 155.103. Reliance on Bureau of Vital Statistics Information

(a) A court shall have jurisdiction over a suit if it has been, correctly or incorrectly, informed by the bureau of vital statistics that the child has not been the subject of a suit and the petition states that no other court has continuing, exclusive jurisdiction over the child.

(b) If the bureau of vital statistics notifies the court that the bureau has furnished incorrect information regarding the existence of another court with continuing, exclusive jurisdiction before the rendition of a final order, the provisions of this chapter apply.

Added by Acts 1995, 74th Leg., ch. 20, § 1, eff. April 20, 1995. Amended by Acts 1995, 74th Leg., ch. 751, § 45, eff. Sept. 1, 1995.

§ 155.104. Voidable Order

(a) If a request for information from the bureau of vital statistics relating to the identity of the court having continuing, exclusive jurisdiction of the child has been made under this subchapter, a final order, except an order of dismissal, may not be rendered until the information is filed with the court.

(b) If a final order is rendered in the absence of the filing of the information from the bureau of vital statistics, the order is voidable on a showing that a court other than the court that rendered the order had continuing, exclusive jurisdiction.

Added by Acts 1995, 74th Leg., ch. 20, § 1, eff. April 20, 1995. Amended by Acts 1995, 74th Leg., ch. 751, § 46, eff. Sept. 1, 1995.

[Sections 155.105 to 155.200 reserved for expansion]

SUBCHAPTER C. TRANSFER OF CONTINUING, EXCLUSIVE JURISDICTION

§ 155.201. Mandatory Transfer

(a) On a showing that a suit for dissolution of the marriage of the child's parents has been filed in another court, the court having continuing, exclusive jurisdiction of a suit affecting the parent-child relationship shall transfer the proceedings to the court in which the dissolution of the marriage is pending.

(b) If a suit to modify or a motion to enforce an order is filed in the court having continuing, exclusive jurisdiction of a suit, on the timely motion of a party the court shall transfer the proceeding to another county in this state if the child has resided in the other county for six months or longer.

Added by Acts 1995, 74th Leg., ch. 20, § 1, eff. April 20, 1995.

§ 155.202. Discretionary Transfer

(a) If the basis of a motion to transfer a proceeding under this subchapter is that the child resides in another county, the court may deny the motion if it is shown that the child has resided in that county for less than six months at the time the proceeding is commenced.

(b) For the convenience of the parties and witnesses and in the interest of justice, the court, on the timely motion of a party, may transfer the proceeding to a proper court in another county in the state.

Added by Acts 1995, 74th Leg., ch. 20, § 1, eff. April 20, 1995.

§ 155.203. Determining County of Child's Residence

In computing the time during which the child has resided in a county, the court may not require that the period of residence be continuous and uninterrupted but shall look to the child's principal residence during the six-month period preceding the commencement of the suit.

Added by Acts 1995, 74th Leg., ch. 20, § 1, eff. April 20, 1995.

§ 155.204. Procedure for Transfer

(a) A motion to transfer by a petitioner or movant is timely if it is made at the time the initial pleadings are filed. A motion to transfer by another party is timely if it is made on or before the first Monday after the 20th day after the date of service of citation or notice of the suit or before the commencement of the hearing, whichever is sooner. If a timely motion to transfer has been filed and no controverting affidavit is filed within the period allowed for its filing, the proceeding shall be transferred promptly without a hearing to the proper court.

(b) On or before the first Monday after the 20th day after the date of notice of a motion to transfer is served, a party desiring to contest the motion must file a controverting affidavit denying that grounds for the transfer exist.

(c) If a controverting affidavit contesting the motion to transfer is filed, each party is entitled to notice not less than 10 days before the date of the hearing on the motion to transfer.

(d) Only evidence pertaining to the transfer may be taken at the hearing.

(e) An order transferring or refusing to transfer the proceeding is not subject to interlocutory appeal.

Added by Acts 1995, 74th Leg., ch. 20, § 1, eff. April 20, 1995.

§ 155.205. Transfer of Child Support Registry

(a) On rendition of an order transferring continuing, exclusive jurisdiction to another court, the transferring court shall also order that all future payments of child support be made to the local registry of the transferee court.

(b) The transferring court's local registry shall continue to receive, record, and disburse child support payments to the payee until it receives notice that the transferred case has been docketed by the transferee court.

(c) After receiving notice of docketing from the transferee court, the transferring court's local registry shall send a certified copy of the child support payment record to the clerk of the transferee court and shall forward any payments received to the transferee court's local registry.

Added by Acts 1995, 74th Leg., ch. 20, § 1, eff. April 20, 1995.

§ 155.206. Effect of Transfer

(a) A court to which a transfer is made becomes the court of continuing, exclusive jurisdiction and all proceedings in the suit are continued as if it were brought there originally.

(b) A judgment or order transferred has the same effect and shall be enforced as if originally rendered in the transferee court.

(c) The transferee court shall enforce a judgment or order of the transferring court by contempt or by any other means by which the transferring court could have enforced its judgment or order. The transferee court shall have the power to punish disobedience of the transferring court's order, whether occurring before or after the transfer, by contempt.

(d) After the transfer, the transferring court does not retain jurisdiction of the child who is the subject of the suit, nor does it have jurisdiction to enforce its order for a violation occurring before or after the transfer of jurisdiction.

Added by Acts 1995, 74th Leg., ch. 20, § 1, eff. April 20, 1995.

§ 155.207. Transfer of Court Files

(a) On rendition of an order of transfer, the clerk of the court transferring a proceeding shall send to the proper court in the county to which transfer is being made:

(1) the complete files in all matters affecting the child;

(2) certified copies of all entries in the minutes;

(3) a certified copy of any order of dissolution of marriage rendered in a suit joined with the suit affecting the parent-child relationship; and

(4) a certified copy of each order rendered.

(b) The clerk of the transferring court shall keep a copy of the transferred files. If the transferring court retains jurisdiction of another child who was the subject of the suit, the clerk shall send a copy of the complete files to the court to which the transfer is made and shall keep the original files.

(c) On receipt of the files, documents, and orders from the transferring court, the clerk of the transferee court shall docket the suit and shall notify all parties, the clerk of the transferring court, and the transferring court's local registry that the suit has been docketed.

(d) The clerk of the transferring court shall send a certified copy of the order directing payments to the transferee court, to any party or employer affected by that order, and to the local registry of the transferee court.

Added by Acts 1995, 74th Leg., ch. 20, § 1, eff. April 20, 1995.

[Sections 155.208 to 155.300 reserved for expansion]

SUBCHAPTER D. TRANSFER OF PROCEEDINGS WITHIN THE STATE WHEN PARTY OR CHILD RESIDES OUTSIDE THE STATE

§ 155.301. Authority to Transfer

(a) A court of this state with continuing, exclusive jurisdiction over a suit or an action for child support under Chapter 159 shall transfer the proceeding to the county of residence of the resident party if one party is a resident of this state and all other parties including the child or all of the children affected by the proceedings reside outside this state.

(b) If one or more of the parties affected by the proceedings reside outside the state and if more than one party or one or more children affected by the proceeding reside in this state in different counties, the court shall transfer the proceeding according to the following priorities:

(1) to the court of continuing, exclusive jurisdiction, if any;

(2) to the county of residence of the child, if applicable, provided that:

(A) Subdivision (1) is inapplicable; or

(B) the court of continuing, exclusive jurisdiction finds that neither a party nor a child affected by the proceeding resides in the county of the court of continuing, exclusive jurisdiction; or

(3) if Subdivisions (1) and (2) are inapplicable, to the county most appropriate to serve the convenience of the resident parties, the witnesses, and the interest of justice.

(c) If a transfer of continuing, exclusive jurisdiction is sought under this section, the procedures for determining and effecting a transfer of proceedings provided by this chapter apply.

Added by Acts 1995, 74th Leg., ch. 20, § 1, eff. April 20, 1995.

CHAPTER 156. MODIFICATION

SUBCHAPTER A. GENERAL PROVISIONS

§ 156.001. Orders Subject to Modification

A court with continuing, exclusive jurisdiction may modify an order that provides for the conservatorship, support, or possession of and access to a child.

Added by Acts 1995, 74th Leg., ch. 20, § 1, eff. April 20, 1995.

§ 156.002. Who can File

(a) A party affected by an order may file a suit for modification in the court with continuing, exclusive jurisdiction.

(b) A person or entity who, at the time of filing, has standing to sue under Chapter 102 may file a suit for modification in the court with continuing, exclusive jurisdiction.

Added by Acts 1995, 74th Leg., ch. 20, § 1, eff. April 20, 1995.

§ 156.003. Notice

A party whose rights, privileges, duties, or powers may be affected by a suit for modification is entitled to receive notice by service of citation.

Added by Acts 1995, 74th Leg., ch. 20, § 1, eff. April 20, 1995.

§ 156.004. Procedure

The Texas Rules of Civil Procedure applicable to the filing of an original lawsuit apply to a suit for modification under this chapter.

Added by Acts 1995, 74th Leg., ch. 20, § 1, eff. April 20, 1995.

§ 156.005. Frivolous Filing of Suit for Modification

If the court finds that a suit for modification is filed frivolously or is designed to harass a party, the court shall tax attorney's fees as costs against the offending party.

Added by Acts 1995, 74th Leg., ch. 20, § 1, eff. April 20, 1995.

§ 156.006. Temporary Orders

(a) Except as provided by Subsection (b), the court may render a temporary order in a suit for modification.

(b) While a suit for modification is pending, the court may not render a temporary order that has the effect of changing the designation of a sole or joint managing conservator appointed in a final order unless:

(1) the order is necessary because the child's present living environment may endanger the child's physical health or significantly impair the child's emotional development;

(2) the child's managing conservator has voluntarily relinquished the actual care, control, and possession of the child for more than six months and the temporary order is in the best interest of the child; or

(3) the child is 12 years of age or older and has filed with the court in writing the name of the person who is the child's choice for managing conservator and the temporary order naming that person as managing conservator is in the best interest of the child.

Added by Acts 1995, 74th Leg., ch. 20, § 1, eff. April 20, 1995.

[Sections 156.007 to 156.100 reserved for expansion]

SUBCHAPTER B. MODIFICATION OF SOLE MANAGING CONSERVATORSHIP

§ 156.101. Grounds for Modification of Sole Managing Conservatorship

(a) The court may modify an order that designates a sole managing conservator of a child of any age if:

(1) the circumstances of the child, sole managing conservator, possessory conservator, or other party affected by the order have materially and substantially changed since the date of the rendition of the order; and

(2) the appointment of the new sole managing conservator would be a positive improvement for the child.

(b) The court may modify an order that designates a sole managing conservator of a child 12 years of age or older if:

(1) the child has filed with the court in writing the name of the person who is the child's choice for managing conservator; and

(2) the court finds that the appointment of the named person is in the best interest of the child.

Added by Acts 1995, 74th Leg., ch. 20, § 1, eff. April 20, 1995. Amended by Acts 1995, 74th Leg., ch. 751, § 47, eff. Sept. 1, 1995.

§ 156.102. Modification of Sole Managing Conservatorship Within One Year of Order

(a) If a suit seeking to modify sole managing conservatorship is filed not later than one year after the date of rendition of the order, the person filing the suit shall execute and attach an affidavit as provided by Subsection (b).

(b) The affidavit must contain, along with supporting facts, at least one of the following allegations:

(1) that the child's present environment may endanger the child's physical health or significantly impair the child's emotional development;

(2) that the sole managing conservator is the person seeking or consenting to the modification and the modification is in the best interest of the child; or

(3) that the child's sole managing conservator has voluntarily relinquished the actual care, control, and possession of the child for not less than six months and the modification is in the best interest of the child.

(c) The court shall deny the relief sought and refuse to schedule a hearing for modification under this section unless the court determines, on the basis of the affidavit, that facts adequate to support an allegation listed in Subsection (b) are stated in the affidavit. If the court determines that the facts stated are adequate to support an allegation, the court shall set a time and place for the hearing.

Added by Acts 1995, 74th Leg., ch. 20, § 1, eff. April 20, 1995.

§ 156.103. Voluntary Relinquishment

The court may modify an order that designates a sole managing conservator if the sole managing conservator has voluntarily relinquished actual care, control, and possession of the child for a period of not less than six months and the modification is in the best interest of the child.

Added by Acts 1995, 74th Leg., ch. 20, § 1, eff. April 20, 1995.

§ 156.104. Modification From Sole Managing Conservatorship to Joint Managing Conservatorship

(a) The court may modify an order that designates a sole managing conservator if a parent of the child requests appointment as a joint managing conservator and the court finds that:

(1) the circumstances of the child or the sole managing conservator have materially and substantially changed since the rendition of the order;

(2) retention of a sole managing conservatorship would be detrimental to the welfare of the child; and

(3) the appointment of the parent as a joint managing conservator would be a positive improvement for and in the best interest of the child.

(b) An order of joint conservatorship, in and of itself, does not constitute grounds for modifying a support order.

Added by Acts 1995, 74th Leg., ch. 20, § 1, eff. April 20, 1995.

§ 156.105. Statutory Change of Circumstance

(a) The power of the court to order a joint managing conservatorship under Chapter 153 is a material and substantial change of circumstances sufficient to justify a modification of an existing sole managing conservatorship to a joint managing conservatorship if the sole managing conservatorship was ordered in a suit affecting the parent-child relationship in which a final order was rendered on or after September 1, 1987.

(b) The power of the court to order a joint managing conservatorship is not a material and substantial change of circumstances sufficient to justify a modification of an existing sole managing conservatorship to a joint managing conservatorship if the sole managing conservatorship was ordered in a suit affecting the parent-child relationship in which a final order was rendered before September 1, 1987.

Added by Acts 1995, 74th Leg., ch. 20, § 1, eff. April 20, 1995.

[Sections 156.106 to 156.200 reserved for expansion]

SUBCHAPTER C. MODIFICATION OF JOINT MANAGING CONSERVATORSHIP

§ 156.201. Written Agreement to Modify Joint Managing Conservatorship

The joint managing conservators may enter into a written agreement to modify the terms and conditions of an existing joint conservatorship order, and the court may modify the existing order according to the agreement if the court finds that the modification meets the standards for joint managing conservatorship in Chapter 153.

Added by Acts 1995, 74th Leg., ch. 20, § 1, eff. April 20, 1995.

§ 156.202. Modification of Terms and Conditions of Joint Managing Conservatorship

The court may modify the terms and conditions of a joint conservatorship order if:

(1)(A) the circumstances of the child or of one or both of the joint managing conservators have materially and substantially changed since the rendition of the order; or

(B) the order has become unworkable or inappropriate under existing circumstances; and

(2) a modification of the terms and conditions of the order would be a positive improvement for and in the best interest of the child.

Added by Acts 1995, 74th Leg., ch. 20, § 1, eff. April 20, 1995.

§ 156.203. Modification From Joint Managing Conservatorship to Sole Managing Conservatorship

The court may replace a joint managing conservatorship with a sole managing conservatorship if:

(1)(A) the child's present living environment may endanger the child's physical health or significantly impair the child's emotional development;

(B) there has been a substantial and unexcused violation of the terms and conditions established in the existing conservatorship order; or

(C) the circumstances of the child or of one or both of the joint managing conservators have so materially and substantially changed since the rendition of the order that it has become unworkable or inappropriate under existing circumstances; and

(2) the appointment of a sole managing conservator would be a positive improvement for and in the best interest of the child.

Added by Acts 1995, 74th Leg., ch. 20, § 1, eff. April 20, 1995. Amended by Acts 1995, 74th Leg., ch. 751, § 48, eff. Sept. 1, 1995.

[Sections 156.204 to 156.300 reserved for expansion]

SUBCHAPTER D. MODIFICATION OF POSSESSION OF OR ACCESS TO CHILD

§ 156.301. Grounds for Modification of Possession and Access

The court may modify an order that sets the terms and conditions for possession of or access to a child or that prescribes the relative rights, privileges, duties, and powers of conservators if:

(1) the circumstances of the child or a person affected by the order have materially and substantially changed since the date of the rendition of the order;

(2) the order has become unworkable or inappropriate under existing circumstances;

(3) the notice of change of a conservator's residence required by Chapter 153 was not given or there was a change in a conservator's residence to a place outside this state; or

(4) a conservator has repeatedly failed to give notice of an inability to exercise possessory rights.

Added by Acts 1995, 74th Leg., ch. 20, § 1, eff. April 20, 1995.

§ 156.302. Effect of Guidelines

(a) The court may consider the guidelines for possession of and access to a child in Chapter 153 to determine if there has been a material and substantial change in circumstances or if the order has become unworkable or inappropriate under this subchapter in determining whether a modification of the existing order for possession of or access to a child by a parent is in the best interest of the child.

(b) The court may modify an order for possession of and access to a child that does not substantially conform to the standard possession order if the modification is in the best interest of the child.

Added by Acts 1995, 74th Leg., ch. 20, § 1, eff. April 20, 1995.

§ 156.303. Increased Expenses Because of Change of Residence

(a) If a change of residence results in increased expenses for a party having possession of or access to a child, the court may render appropriate orders to allocate those increased costs on a fair and equitable basis, taking into account the cause of the increased costs and the best interest of the child.

(b) The payment of increased costs by the party whose residence is changed is rebuttably presumed to be in the best interest of the child.

(c) The court may render an order without regard to whether another change in the terms and conditions of possession of or access to the child is made.

Added by Acts 1995, 74th Leg., ch. 20, § 1, eff. April 20, 1995.

§ 156.304. Modification of Order on Conviction for Child Abuse

(a) The conviction or an order deferring adjudication of an individual who is a possessory conservator or a sole or joint managing conservator for an offense involving the abuse of a child under Section 21.11, 22.011, or 22.021, Penal Code, is a material and substantial change of circumstances sufficient to justify a modification of an existing court order or portion of a decree that provides for the appointment of a conservator or that sets the terms and conditions of conservatorship for or access to a child.

(b) A person commits an offense if the person files a motion to modify an order or portion of a decree under this section and the person knows that the person against whom the motion is filed has not been convicted of or received deferred adjudication for an offense under Section 21.11, 22.011, or 22.021, Penal Code. An offense under this subsection is a Class B misdemeanor.

Added by Acts 1995, 74th Leg., ch. 602, § 1, eff. Sept. 1, 1995.

Section 2 of the 1995 Act provides:

"This Act takes effect September 1, 1995, and applies to any order or portion of a decree appointing a managing conservator, a possessory conservator, or a joint managing conservator without regard to whether the order or decree was entered before, on, or after the effective date of this Act."

[Sections 156.305 to 156.400 reserved for expansion]

SUBCHAPTER E. MODIFICATION OF CHILD SUPPORT

§ 156.401. Grounds for Modification of Child Support

(a) Except as provided by Subsection (b), the court may modify an order that provides for the support of a child if:

(1) the circumstances of the child or a person affected by the order have materially and substantially changed since the date of the order's rendition; or

(2) it has been three years since the order was rendered or last modified and the monthly amount of the child support award under the order differs by either 20 percent or $100 from the amount that would be awarded in accordance with the child support guidelines.

(b) A support order may be modified only as to obligations accruing after the earlier of:

(1) the date of service of citation; or

(2) an appearance in the suit to modify.

(c) An order of joint conservatorship, in and of itself, does not constitute grounds for modifying a support order.

Added by Acts 1995, 74th Leg., ch. 20, § 1, eff. April 20, 1995. Amended by Acts 1997, 75th Leg., ch. 911, § 16, eff. Sept. 1, 1997.

Section 98(b) and (c) of Acts 1997, 75th Leg., ch. 911 provides:

"(b) The change in law made by this Act does not affect a proceeding under the Family Code pending on the effective date of this Act. A proceeding pending on the effective date of this Act is governed by the law in effect at the time the proceeding was commenced, and the former law is continued in effect for that purpose.

"(c) The enactment of this Act does not by itself constitute a material and substantial change of circumstances sufficient to warrant modification of a court order or portion of a decree that provides for the support of or possession of or access to a child entered before the effective date of this Act."

§ 156.402. Effect of Guidelines

(a) The court may consider the child support guidelines in Chapter 153 [1] to determine whether there has been a material or substantial change of circumstances under this chapter that warrants a modification of an existing child support order if the modification is in the best interest of the child.

(b) If the amount of support contained in the order does not substantially conform with the guidelines, the court may modify the order to substantially conform with the guidelines if the modification is in the best interest of the child. A court may consider other relevant evidence in addition to the factors listed in the guidelines.

Added by Acts 1995, 74th Leg., ch. 20, § 1, eff. April 20, 1995.

[1] So in enrolled bill, probably should read "Chapter 154."

§ 156.403. Voluntary Additional Support

A history of support voluntarily provided in excess of the court order does not constitute cause to increase the amount of an existing child support order.

Added by Acts 1995, 74th Leg., ch. 20, § 1, eff. April 20, 1995.

§ 156.404. Net Resources of New Spouse

(a) The court may not add any portion of the net resources of a new spouse to the net resources of an obligor or obligee in order to calculate the amount of child support to be ordered in a suit for modification.

(b) The court may not subtract the needs of a new spouse, or of a dependent of a new spouse, from the net resources of the obligor or obligee in a suit for modification.

Added by Acts 1995, 74th Leg., ch. 20, § 1, eff. April 20, 1995.

§ 156.405. Change in Lifestyle

An increase in the needs, standard of living, or lifestyle of the obligee since the rendition of the existing order does not warrant an increase in the obligor's child support obligation.

Added by Acts 1995, 74th Leg., ch. 20, § 1, eff. April 20, 1995.

§ 156.406. Use of Guidelines for Children in More Than One Household

In applying the child support guidelines in a suit under this subchapter, if the obligor has the duty to support children in more than one household, the court shall apply the percentage guidelines for multiple families in Chapter 153 [1].

Added by Acts 1995, 74th Leg., ch. 20, § 1, eff. April 20, 1995.

[1] So in enrolled bill, probably should read "Chapter 154."

§ 156.407. Assignment of Child Support Right

A notice of assignment filed under Chapter 231 does not constitute a modification of an order to pay child support.

Added by Acts 1995, 74th Leg., ch. 20, § 1, eff. April 20, 1995.

§ 156.408. Modification of Support Order Rendered by Another State

(a) Unless both parties and the child reside in this state, a court of this state may modify an order of child support rendered by an appropriate tribunal of another state only as provided by Chapter 159.

(b) If both parties and the child reside in this state, a court of this state may modify an order of child support rendered by an appropriate tribunal of another state and any aspect of conservatorship as provided by this chapter without reference to Chapter 159.

Added by Acts 1995, 74th Leg., ch. 20, § 1, eff. April 20, 1995.

CHAPTER 157. ENFORCEMENT

SUBCHAPTER A. PLEADINGS AND DEFENSES

SUBCHAPTER B. PROCEDURE

SUBCHAPTER C. FAILURE TO APPEAR; BOND OR SECURITY

SUBCHAPTER A. PLEADINGS AND DEFENSES

§ 157.001. Motion for Enforcement

(a) A motion for enforcement as provided in this chapter may be filed to enforce a final order for conservatorship, child support, possession of or access to a child, or other provisions of a final order.

(b) The court may enforce by contempt a final order for possession of and access to a child as provided in this chapter.

(c) The court may enforce a final order for child support as provided in this chapter or Chapter 158.

(d) A motion for enforcement shall be filed in the court of continuing, exclusive jurisdiction.

Added by Acts 1995, 74th Leg., ch. 20, § 1, eff. April 20, 1995.

§ 157.002. Contents of Motion

(a) A motion for enforcement must, in ordinary and concise language:

(1) identify the provision of the order allegedly violated and sought to be enforced;

(2) state the manner of the respondent's alleged noncompliance;

(3) state the relief requested by the movant; and

(4) contain the signature of the movant or the movant's attorney.

(b) A motion for enforcement of child support:

(1) must include the amount owed as provided in the order, the amount paid, and the amount of arrearages;

(2) if contempt is requested, must include the portion of the order allegedly violated and, for each date of alleged contempt, the amount due and the amount paid, if any;

(3) may include as an attachment a copy of a record of child support payments maintained by the Title IV-D registry or a local registry; and

(4) if the obligor owes arrearages for a child receiving assistance under Part A of Title IV of the federal Social Security Act (42 U.S.C. Section 601 et seq.), may include a request that:

(A) the obligor pay the arrearages in accordance with a plan approved by the court; or

(B) if the obligor is already subject to a plan and is not incapacitated, the obligor participate in work activities, as defined under 42 U.S.C. Section 607(d), that the court determines appropriate.

(c) A motion for enforcement of the terms and conditions of conservatorship or possession of or access to a child must include the date, place, and, if applicable, the time of each occasion of the respondent's failure to comply with the order.

(d) The movant is not required to plead that the underlying order is enforceable by contempt to obtain other appropriate enforcement remedies.

(e) The movant may allege repeated past violations of the order and that future violations of a similar nature may occur before the date of the hearing.

Added by Acts 1995, 74th Leg., ch. 20, § 1, eff. April 20, 1995. Amended by Acts 1997, 75th Leg., ch. 911, § 17, eff. Sept. 1, 1997.

For application and effectiveness provisions of Acts 1997, 75th Leg., ch. 911, see note following V.T.C.A., Family Code § 156.401.

§ 157.003. Joinder of Claims and Remedies; No Election of Remedies

(a) A party requesting enforcement may join in the same proceeding any claim and remedy provided for in this chapter, other provisions of this subtitle, or other rules of law.

(b) A motion for enforcement does not constitute an election of remedies that limits or precludes:

(1) the use of any other civil or criminal proceeding to enforce a final order; or

(2) a suit for damages under Chapter 42.

Added by Acts 1995, 74th Leg., ch. 20, § 1, eff. April 20, 1995.

§ 157.004. Time Limitations; Enforcement of Possession

The court retains jurisdiction to render a contempt order for failure to comply with the order of possession and access if the motion for enforcement is filed not later than the sixth month after the date:

(1) the child becomes an adult; or

(2) on which the right of possession and access terminates under the order or by operation of law.

Added by Acts 1995, 74th Leg., ch. 20, § 1, eff. April 20, 1995.

§ 157.005. Time Limitations; Enforcement of Child Support

(a) The court retains jurisdiction to render a contempt order for failure to comply with the child support order if the motion for enforcement is filed not later than the sixth month after the date:

(1) the child becomes an adult; or

(2) on which the child support obligation terminates under the order or by operation of law.

(b) The court retains jurisdiction to confirm the total amount of child support arrearages and render judgment for past-due child support if a motion for enforcement requesting a money judgment is filed not later than the fourth anniversary after the date:

(1) the child becomes an adult; or

(2) on which the child support obligation terminates under the order or by operation of law.

Added by Acts 1995, 74th Leg., ch. 20, § 1, eff. April 20, 1995.

§ 157.006. Affirmative Defense to Motion for Enforcement

(a) The issue of the existence of an affirmative defense to a motion for enforcement does not arise unless evidence is admitted supporting the defense.

(b) The respondent must prove the affirmative defense by a preponderance of the evidence.

Added by Acts 1995, 74th Leg., ch. 20, § 1, eff. April 20, 1995.

§ 157.007. Affirmative Defense to Motion for Enforcement of Possession or Access

(a) The respondent may plead as an affirmative defense to contempt for failure to comply with an order for possession or access to a child that the movant voluntarily relinquished actual possession and control of the child.

(b) The voluntary relinquishment must have been for the time encompassed by the court-ordered periods during which the respondent is alleged to have interfered.

Added by Acts 1995, 74th Leg., ch. 20, § 1, eff. April 20, 1995.

§ 157.008. Affirmative Defense to Motion for Enforcement of Child Support

(a) An obligor may plead as an affirmative defense in whole or in part to a motion for enforcement of child support that the obligee voluntarily relinquished to the obligor actual possession and control of a child.

(b) The voluntary relinquishment must have been for a time period in excess of any court-ordered periods of possession of and access to the child and actual support must have been supplied by the obligor.

(c) An obligor may plead as an affirmative defense to an allegation of contempt or of the violation of a condition of community service requiring payment of child support that the obligor:

(1) lacked the ability to provide support in the amount ordered;

(2) lacked property that could be sold, mortgaged, or otherwise pledged to raise the funds needed;

(3) attempted unsuccessfully to borrow the funds needed; and

(4) knew of no source from which the money could have been borrowed or legally obtained.

(d) An obligor who has provided actual support to the child during a time subject to an affirmative defense under this section may request reimbursement for that support as a counterclaim or offset against the claim of the obligee.

(e) An action against the obligee for support supplied to a child is limited to the amount of periodic payments previously ordered by the court.

Added by Acts 1995, 74th Leg., ch. 20, § 1, eff. April 20, 1995.

[Sections 157.009 to 157.060 reserved for expansion]

SUBCHAPTER B. PROCEDURE

§ 157.061. Setting Hearing

(a) On filing a motion for enforcement requesting contempt, the court shall set the date, time, and place of the hearing and order the respondent to personally appear and respond to the motion.

(b) If the motion for enforcement does not request contempt, the court shall set the motion for hearing on the request of a party.

(c) The court shall give preference to a motion for enforcement of child support in setting a hearing date and may not delay the hearing because a suit for modification of the order requested to be enforced has been or may be filed.

Added by Acts 1995, 74th Leg., ch. 20, § 1, eff. April 20, 1995.

§ 157.062. Notice of Hearing

(a) The notice of hearing must include the date, time, and place of the hearing.

(b) The notice of hearing need not repeat the allegations contained in the motion for enforcement.

(c) Notice of hearing on a motion for enforcement of an existing order providing for child support or possession of or access to a child shall be given to the respondent by personal service of a copy of the motion and notice not later than the 10th day before the date of the hearing.

(d) If a motion for enforcement is joined with another claim:

(1) the hearing may not be held before 10 a.m. on the first Monday after the 20th day after the date of service; and

(2) the provisions of the Texas Rules of Civil Procedure applicable to the filing of an original lawsuit apply.

Added by Acts 1995, 74th Leg., ch. 20, § 1, eff. April 20, 1995. Amended by Acts 1995, 74th Leg., ch. 751, § 49, eff. Sept. 1, 1995.

§ 157.063. Appearance

A party makes a general appearance for all purposes in an enforcement proceeding if:

(1) the party appears at the hearing or is present when the case is called; and

(2) the party does not object to the court's jurisdiction or the form or manner of the notice of hearing.

Added by Acts 1995, 74th Leg., ch. 20, § 1, eff. April 20, 1995.

§ 157.064. Special Exception

(a) If a respondent specially excepts to the motion for enforcement or moves to strike, the court shall rule on the exception or the motion to strike before it hears the motion for enforcement.

(b) If an exception is sustained, the court shall give the movant an opportunity to replead and continue the hearing to a designated date and time without the requirement of additional service.

Added by Acts 1995, 74th Leg., ch. 20, § 1, eff. April 20, 1995.

§ 157.065. Notice of Hearing, First Class Mail

(a) If a party has been ordered under Chapter 105 to provide the court and the state case registry with the party's current mailing address, notice of a motion for enforcement may be served by mailing a copy of the notice to the respondent, together with a copy of the motion, by first class mail to the last mailing address of the respondent on file with the court and the registry.

(b) The notice may be sent by the clerk of the court, the movant's attorney, or any person entitled to the address information as provided in Chapter 105.

(c) A person who sends the notice shall file of record a certificate of service showing the date of mailing and the name of the person who sent the notice.

(d) Repealed by Acts 1997, 75th Leg., ch. 911, § 97(a), eff. Sept. 1, 1997.

Added by Acts 1995, 74th Leg., ch. 20, § 1, eff. April 20, 1995. Amended by Acts 1997, 75th Leg., ch. 911, §§ 18, 97(a), eff. Sept. 1, 1997.

For application and effectiveness provisions of Acts 1997, 75th Leg., ch. 911, see note following V.T.C.A., Family Code § 156.401.

§ 157.066. Failure to Appear

If a respondent who has been personally served with notice to appear at a hearing does not appear at the designated time, place, and date to respond to a motion for enforcement of an existing court order, regardless of whether the motion is joined with other claims or remedies, the court may not hold the respondent in contempt but may, on proper proof, grant a default judgment for the relief sought and issue a capias for the arrest of the respondent.

Added by Acts 1995, 74th Leg., ch. 20, § 1, eff. April 20, 1995. Amended by Acts 1995, 74th Leg., ch. 751, § 50, eff. Sept. 1, 1995.

[Sections 157.067 to 157.100 reserved for expansion]

SUBCHAPTER C. FAILURE TO APPEAR; BOND OR SECURITY

§ 157.101. Bond or Security for Release of Respondent

(a) When the court orders the issuance of a capias as provided in this chapter, the court shall also set an appearance bond or security, payable to the obligee or to a person designated by the court, in a reasonable amount.

(b) An appearance bond or security in the amount of $1,000 or a cash bond in the amount of $250 is presumed to be reasonable. Evidence that the respondent has attempted to evade service of process, has previously been found guilty of contempt, or has accrued arrearages over $1,000 is sufficient to rebut the presumption. If the presumption is rebutted, the court shall set a reasonable bond.

Added by Acts 1995, 74th Leg., ch. 20, § 1, eff. April 20, 1995.

§ 157.102. Capias; Duty of Law Enforcement Officials

Law enforcement officials shall treat the capias in the same manner as an arrest warrant for a criminal offense and shall enter the capias in the computer records for outstanding warrants maintained by the local police, sheriff, and Department of Public Safety. The capias may be forwarded to and disseminated by the Texas Crime Information Center and the National Crime Information Center.

Added by Acts 1995, 74th Leg., ch. 20, § 1, eff. April 20, 1995. Amended by Acts 1997, 75th Leg., ch. 702, § 3, eff. Sept. 1, 1997.

§ 157.103. Capias Fees

(a) The fee for issuing a capias as provided in this chapter is the same as the fee for issuance of a writ of attachment.

(b) The fee for serving a capias is the same as the fee for service of a writ in civil cases generally.

Added by Acts 1995, 74th Leg., ch. 20, § 1, eff. April 20, 1995.

§ 157.104. Conditional Release

If the respondent is taken into custody and released on bond, the court shall condition the bond on the respondent's promise to appear in court for a hearing as required by the court without the necessity of further personal service of notice on the respondent.

Added by Acts 1995, 74th Leg., ch. 20, § 1, eff. April 20, 1995.

§ 157.105. Release Hearing

(a) If the respondent is taken into custody and not released on bond, the respondent shall be brought before the court that issued the capias on or before the first working day after the arrest. The court shall determine whether the respondent's appearance in court at a designated time and place can be assured by a method other than by posting the bond or security previously established.

(b) If the respondent is released without posting bond or security, the court shall set a hearing on the alleged contempt at a designated date, time, and place and give the respondent notice of hearing in open court. No other notice to the respondent is required.

(c) If the court is not satisfied that the respondent's appearance in court can be assured and the respondent remains in custody, a hearing on the alleged contempt shall be held as soon as practicable, but not later than the fifth day after the date that the respondent was taken into custody, unless the respondent and the respondent's attorney waive the accelerated hearing.

Added by Acts 1995, 74th Leg., ch. 20, § 1, eff. April 20, 1995.

§ 157.106. Cash Bond as Support

(a) If the respondent has posted a cash bond and is found to be in arrears in the payment of court-ordered child support, the court shall order that the proceeds of the cash bond be paid to the child support obligee or to a person designated by the court, not to exceed the amount of child support arrearages determined to exist.

(b) This section applies without regard to whether the respondent appears at the hearing.

Added by Acts 1995, 74th Leg., ch. 20, § 1, eff. April 20, 1995.

§ 157.107. Appearance Bond or Security Other Than Cash Bond as Support

(a) If the respondent fails to appear at the hearing as directed, the court shall order that the appearance bond or security be forfeited and that the proceeds of any judgment on the bond or security, not to exceed the amount of child support arrearages determined to exist, be paid to the obligee or to a person designated by the court.

(b) The obligee may file suit on the bond.

Added by Acts 1995, 74th Leg., ch. 20, § 1, eff. April 20, 1995.

§ 157.108. Cash Bond as Property of Respondent

A court shall treat a cash bond posted for the benefit of the respondent as the property of the respondent. A person who posts the cash bond does not have recourse in relation to an order regarding the bond other than against the respondent.

Added by Acts 1995, 74th Leg., ch. 20, § 1, eff. April 20, 1995.

§ 157.109. Security for Compliance With Order

(a) The court may order the respondent to execute a bond or post security if the court finds that the respondent:

(1) has on two or more occasions denied possession of or access to a child who is the subject of the order; or

(2) is employed by an employer not subject to the jurisdiction of the court or for whom income withholding is unworkable or inappropriate.

(b) The court shall set the amount of the bond or security and condition the bond or security on compliance with the court order permitting possession or access or the payment of past-due or future child support.

(c) The court shall order the bond or security payable through the registry of the court:

(1) to the obligee or other person or entity entitled to receive child support payments designated by the court if enforcement of child support is requested; or

(2) to the person who is entitled to possession or access if enforcement of possession or access is requested.

Added by Acts 1995, 74th Leg., ch. 20, § 1, eff. April 20, 1995.

§ 157.110. Forfeiture of Security for Failure to Comply With Order

(a) On the motion of a person or entity for whose benefit a bond has been executed or security deposited, the court may forfeit all or part of the bond or security deposit on a finding that the person who furnished the bond or security:

(1) has violated the court order for possession of and access to a child; or

(2) failed to make child support payments.

(b) The court shall order the registry to pay the funds from a forfeited bond or security deposit to the obligee or person or entity entitled to receive child support payments in an amount that does not exceed the child support arrearages or, in the case of possession of or access to a child, to the person entitled to possession or access.

(c) The court may order that all or part of the forfeited amount be applied to pay attorney's fees and costs incurred by the person or entity bringing the motion for contempt or motion for forfeiture.

Added by Acts 1995, 74th Leg., ch. 20, § 1, eff. April 20, 1995.

§ 157.111. Forfeiture Not Defense to Contempt

The forfeiture of bond or security is not a defense in a contempt proceeding.

Added by Acts 1995, 74th Leg., ch. 20, § 1, eff. April 20, 1995.

§ 157.112. Joinder of Forfeiture and Contempt Proceedings

A motion for enforcement requesting contempt may be joined with a forfeiture proceeding.

Added by Acts 1995, 74th Leg., ch. 20, § 1, eff. April 20, 1995.

§ 157.113. Application of Bond Pending Writ

If the obligor requests to execute a bond or to post security pending a hearing by an appellate court on a writ, the bond or security on forfeiture shall be payable to the obligee.

Added by Acts 1995, 74th Leg., ch. 20, § 1, eff. April 20, 1995.

§ 157.114. Failure to Appear

The court may order a capias to be issued for the arrest of the respondent if:

(1) the motion for enforcement requests contempt;

(2) the respondent was personally served; and

(3) the respondent fails to appear.

Added by Acts 1995, 74th Leg., ch. 20, § 1, eff. April 20, 1995.

§ 157.115. Default Judgment

(a) The court may render a default order for the relief requested if the respondent:

(1) has been personally served, has filed an answer, or has entered an appearance; and

(2) does not appear at the designated time, place, and date to respond to the motion.

(b) If the respondent fails to appear, the court may not hold the respondent in contempt but may order a capias to be issued.

Added by Acts 1995, 74th Leg., ch. 20, § 1, eff. April 20, 1995. Amended by Acts 1995, 74th Leg., ch. 751, § 51, eff. Sept. 1, 1995.

[Sections 157.116 to 157.160 reserved for expansion]

SUBCHAPTER D. HEARING AND ENFORCEMENT ORDER

§ 157.161. Record

(a) Except as provided by Subsection (b), a record of the hearing in a motion for enforcement shall be made by a court reporter or as provided by Chapter 201.

(b) A record is not required if:

(1) the parties agree to an order; or

(2) the motion does not request incarceration and the parties waive the requirement of a record at the time of hearing, either in writing or in open court, and the court approves waiver.

Added by Acts 1995, 74th Leg., ch. 20, § 1, eff. April 20, 1995.

§ 157.162. Proof

(a) The movant is not required to prove that the underlying order is enforceable by contempt to obtain other appropriate enforcement remedies.

(b) A finding that the respondent is not in contempt does not preclude the court from ordering any other enforcement remedy, including rendering a money judgment, posting a bond or other security, or withholding income.

(c) A copy of the payment record attached to the motion is evidence of the facts asserted in the payment record and is admissible to show whether payments were made. The respondent may offer controverting evidence.

Added by Acts 1995, 74th Leg., ch. 20, § 1, eff. April 20, 1995.

§ 157.163. Appointment of Attorney

(a) In a motion for enforcement or motion to revoke community service, the court must first determine whether incarceration of the respondent is a possible result of the proceedings.

(b) If the court determines that incarceration is a possible result of the proceedings, the court shall inform a respondent not represented by an attorney of the right to be represented by an attorney and, if the respondent is indigent, of the right to the appointment of an attorney.

(c) If the court determines that the respondent will not be incarcerated as a result of the proceedings, the court may require a respondent who is indigent to proceed without an attorney.

(d) If the respondent claims indigency and requests the appointment of an attorney, the court shall require the respondent to file an affidavit of indigency. The court may hear evidence to determine the issue of indigency.

(e) Except as provided by Subsection (c), the court shall appoint an attorney to represent the respondent if the court determines that the respondent is indigent.

(f) If the respondent is not in custody, an appointed attorney is entitled to not less than 10 days from the date of the attorney's appointment to respond to the movant's pleadings and prepare for the hearing.

(g) If the respondent is in custody, an appointed attorney is entitled to not less than five days from the date the respondent was taken into custody to respond to the movant's pleadings and prepare for the hearing.

(h) The court may shorten or extend the time for preparation if the respondent and the respondent's attorney sign a waiver of the time limit.

(i) The scope of the court appointment of an attorney to represent the respondent is limited to the allegation of contempt or of violation of community supervision contained in the motion for enforcement or motion to revoke community supervision.

Added by Acts 1995, 74th Leg., ch. 20, § 1, eff. April 20, 1995.

§ 157.164. Payment of Appointed Attorney

(a) An attorney appointed to represent an indigent respondent is entitled to a reasonable fee for services within the scope of the appointment in the amount set by the court.

(b) The fee shall be paid from the general funds of the county according to the schedule for the compensation of counsel appointed to defend criminal defendants as provided in the Code of Criminal Procedure.

(c) For purposes of this section, a proceeding in a court of appeals or the Supreme Court of Texas is considered the equivalent of a bona fide appeal to the Texas Court of Criminal Appeals.

Added by Acts 1995, 74th Leg., ch. 20, § 1, eff. April 20, 1995.

§ 157.165. Probation of Contempt Order

The court may place the respondent on community supervision and suspend commitment if the court finds that the respondent is in contempt of court for failure or refusal to obey an order rendered as provided in this subtitle.

Added by Acts 1995, 74th Leg., ch. 20, § 1, eff. April 20, 1995.

§ 157.166. Contents of Enforcement Order

(a) An enforcement order must include:

(1) in ordinary and concise language the provisions of the order for which enforcement was requested;

(2) the acts or omissions that are the subject of the order;

(3) the manner of the respondent's noncompliance; and

(4) the relief granted by the court.

(b) If the order imposes incarceration or a fine, an enforcement order must contain findings setting out or incorporating by reference the provisions of the order for which enforcement was requested and the date of each occasion when the respondent failed to comply with the order.

Added by Acts 1995, 74th Leg., ch. 20, § 1, eff. April 20, 1995.

§ 157.167. Respondent to Pay Attorney's Fees and Costs

(a) If the court finds that the respondent has failed to make child support payments, the court shall order the respondent to pay the movant's reasonable attorney's fees and all court costs in addition to the arrearages.

(b) For good cause shown, the court may waive the requirement that the respondent pay attorney's fees and costs if the court states the reasons supporting that finding.

Added by Acts 1995, 74th Leg., ch. 20, § 1, eff. April 20, 1995.

§ 157.168. Additional Periods of Possession or Access

(a) A court may order additional periods of possession of or access to a child to compensate for the denial of court-ordered possession or access. The additional periods of possession or access:

(1) must be of the same type and duration of the possession or access that was denied;

(2) may include weekend, holiday, and summer possession or access; and

(3) must occur on or before the first anniversary of the date the court finds that court-ordered possession or access has been denied.

(b) The person denied possession or access is entitled to decide the time of the additional possession or access, subject to the provisions of Subsection (a)(1).

Added by Acts 1995, 74th Leg., ch. 751, § 52, eff. Sept. 1, 1995. Amended by Acts 1997, 75th Leg., ch. 974, § 1, eff. Sept. 1, 1997.

Section 2 of Acts 1997, 75th Leg., ch. 974 provides:

"This Act takes effect September 1, 1997, and applies only to an order for additional periods of possession of or access to a child made on or after that date."

[Sections 157.169 to 157.210 reserved for expansion]

SUBCHAPTER E. COMMUNITY SUPERVISION

§ 157.211. Conditions of Community Supervision

If the court places the respondent on community supervision and suspends commitment, the terms and conditions of community supervision may include the requirement that the respondent:

(1) report to the community supervision and corrections department officer as directed;

(2) permit the community supervision and corrections department officer to visit the respondent at the respondent's home or elsewhere;

(3) obtain counseling on financial planning, budget management, alcohol or drug abuse, or other matters causing the respondent to fail to obey the order;

(4) pay required child support and any child support arrearages; and

(5) pay court costs and attorney's fees ordered by the court.

Added by Acts 1995, 74th Leg., ch. 20, § 1, eff. April 20, 1995. Amended by Acts 1997, 75th Leg., ch. 702, § 4, eff. Sept. 1, 1997.

§ 157.212. Term of Community Supervision

The community supervision period may not exceed five years.

Added by Acts 1995, 74th Leg., ch. 20, § 1, eff. April 20, 1995.

§ 157.213. Community Supervision Fees

(a) The court may require the respondent to pay a fee to the court in an amount equal to that required of a criminal defendant subject to community supervision.

(b) The court may make payment of the fee a condition of granting or continuing community supervision.

(c) The court shall deposit the fees received under this subchapter in the special fund of the county treasury provided by the Code of Criminal Procedure to be used for community supervision.

Added by Acts 1995, 74th Leg., ch. 20, § 1, eff. April 20, 1995.

§ 157.214. Motion to Revoke Community Supervision

A prosecuting attorney, the Title IV–D agency, or a party affected by the order may file a verified motion alleging specifically that certain conduct of the respondent constitutes a violation of the terms and conditions of community supervision.

Added by Acts 1995, 74th Leg., ch. 20, § 1, eff. April 20, 1995.

§ 157.215. Arrest for Alleged Violation of Community Supervision

(a) If the motion to revoke community supervision alleges a prima facie case that the respondent has violated a term or condition of community supervision, the court may order the respondent's arrest by warrant.

(b) The respondent shall be brought promptly before the court ordering the arrest.

Added by Acts 1995, 74th Leg., ch. 20, § 1, eff. April 20, 1995.

§ 157.216. Hearing on Motion to Revoke Community Supervision

(a) The court shall hold a hearing without a jury on or before the first working day after the date the respondent is arrested under Section 157.215. If the court is unavailable for a hearing on that date, the hearing shall be held not later than the first working day after the date the court becomes available.

(b) The hearing under this section may not be held later than the third working day after the date the respondent is arrested.

(c) After the hearing, the court may continue, modify, or revoke the community supervision.

Added by Acts 1995, 74th Leg., ch. 20, § 1, eff. April 20, 1995.

§ 157.217. Discharge From Community Supervision

(a) When a community supervision period has been satisfactorily completed, the court on its own motion shall discharge the respondent from community supervision.

(b) The court may discharge the respondent from community supervision on the motion of the respondent if the court finds that the respondent:

(1) has satisfactorily completed one year of community supervision; and

(2) has fully complied with the community supervision order.

Added by Acts 1995, 74th Leg., ch. 20, § 1, eff. April 20, 1995.

[Sections 157.218 to 157.260 reserved for expansion]

SUBCHAPTER F. JUDGMENT AND INTEREST

§ 157.261. Unpaid Child Support as Judgment

(a) A child support payment not timely made constitutes a final judgment for the amount due and owing, including interest as provided in this chapter.

(b) For the purposes of this subchapter, interest begins to accrue on the date the judge signs the order for the judgment unless the order contains a statement that the order is rendered on another specific date.

Added by Acts 1995, 74th Leg., ch. 20, § 1, eff. April 20, 1995. Amended by Acts 1997, 75th Leg., ch. 702, § 5, eff. Sept. 1, 1997.

§ 157.262. Reduction of Arrearages

(a) In a contempt proceeding or in rendering a money judgment, the court may not reduce or modify the amount of child support arrearages.

(b) The money judgment for arrearages rendered by the court may be subject to a counterclaim or offset as provided by this subchapter.

Added by Acts 1995, 74th Leg., ch. 20, § 1, eff. April 20, 1995.

§ 157.263. Confirmation of Arrearages

(a) If a motion for enforcement of child support requests a money judgment for arrearages, the court shall confirm the amount of arrearages and render one cumulative money judgment.

(b) A cumulative money judgment includes:

(1) unpaid child support not previously confirmed;

(2) the balance owed on previously confirmed arrearages or lump sum or retroactive support judgments;

(3) interest on the arrearages; and

(4) a statement that it is a cumulative judgment.

Added by Acts 1995, 74th Leg., ch. 20, § 1, eff. April 20, 1995.

§ 157.264. Enforcement by Income Withholding

A money judgment rendered as provided in this subchapter may be enforced by any means available for the enforcement of a judgment for debts and by an order requiring that income be withheld from the disposable earnings of the obligor.

Added by Acts 1995, 74th Leg., ch. 20, § 1, eff. April 20, 1995.

§ 157.265. Accrual of Interest on Child Support

(a) Interest accrues on delinquent child support at the rate of 12 percent simple interest per year from the date the support is delinquent until the date the support is paid or the arrearages are confirmed and reduced to money judgment.

(b) Interest accrues on child support arrearages that have been confirmed and reduced to money judgment as provided in this subchapter at the rate of 12 percent simple interest per year from the date the order is rendered until the date the judgment is paid.

(c) Interest accrues on a money judgment for retroactive or lump-sum child support at the annual rate of 12 percent simple interest from the date the order is rendered until the judgment is paid.

Added by Acts 1995, 74th Leg., ch. 20, § 1, eff. April 20, 1995. Amended by Acts 1995, 74th Leg., ch. 751, § 53, eff. Sept. 1, 1995.

§ 157.266. Date of Delinquency

(a) A child support payment is delinquent for the purpose of accrual of interest if the payment is not received before the 31st day after the payment date stated in the order by:

(1) the local registry or Title IV–D registry; or

(2) the obligee or entity specified in the order, if payments are not made through a registry.

(b) If a payment date is not stated in the order, a child support payment is delinquent if payment is not received by the registry or the obligee or entity specified in the order on the date that an amount equal to the support payable for one month becomes past due.

Added by Acts 1995, 74th Leg., ch. 20, § 1, eff. April 20, 1995.

§ 157.267. Interest Enforced as Child Support

Accrued interest is part of the child support obligation and may be enforced by any means provided for the collection of child support.

Added by Acts 1995, 74th Leg., ch. 20, § 1, eff. April 20, 1995.

§ 157.268. Application of Child Support Payment

Child support collected shall be applied in the following order of priority:

(1) current child support;

(2) non-delinquent child support owed;

(3) interest on the principal amounts specified in Subdivisions (4) and (5);

(4) the principal amount of child support that has not been confirmed and reduced to money judgment; and

(5) the principal amount of child support that has been confirmed and reduced to money judgment.

Added by Acts 1995, 74th Leg., ch. 20, § 1, eff. April 20, 1995.

§ 157.269. Retention of Jurisdiction

A court that renders an order providing for the payment of child support arrearages retains jurisdiction until the arrearages are paid in full as required by the court order.

Added by Acts 1995, 74th Leg., ch. 751, § 54, eff. Sept. 1, 1995.

[Sections 157.270 to 157.310 reserved for expansion]

SUBCHAPTER G. CHILD SUPPORT LIEN

§ 157.311. Definitions

In this subchapter:

(1) "Claimant" means:

(A) the obligee or a private attorney representing the obligee;

(B) the Title IV-D agency providing child support services;

(C) a domestic relations office or local registry; or

(D) an attorney appointed as a friend of the court.

(2) "Court having continuing jurisdiction" is the court of continuing, exclusive jurisdiction in this state or a tribunal of another state having jurisdiction under the Uniform Interstate Family Support Act or a substantially similar act.

(3) "Lien" means a child support lien.

Added by Acts 1995, 74th Leg., ch. 20, § 1, eff. April 20, 1995. Amended by Acts 1997, 75th Leg., ch. 420, § 1, eff. Sept. 1, 1997; Acts 1997, 75th Leg., ch. 911, § 19, eff. Sept. 1, 1997.

For application and effectiveness provisions of Acts 1997, 75th Leg., ch. 911, see note following V.T.C.A., Family Code § 156.401.

§ 157.312. General Provisions

(a) A claimant may enforce child support by a lien as provided in this subchapter.

(b) The remedies provided by this subchapter do not affect the availability of other remedies provided by law.

(c) The lien is in addition to any other lien provided by law.

(d) A child support lien arises:

(1) by operation of law against real and personal property of an obligor for all amounts of overdue support, regardless of whether the amounts have been adjudicated or otherwise determined, subject to the requirements of this subchapter for recording and notice; or

(2) when a court having continuing jurisdiction or, in a Title IV-D case,[1] the Title IV-D agency determines an amount of arrears[2] owed by a child support obligor.

(e) A child support lien arising in another state may be enforced in the same manner and to the same extent as a lien arising in this state.

(f) A foreclosure action under this subchapter is not required as a prerequisite to levy and execution on a judgment or an administrative determination of arrears[2] rendered after notice and opportunity for hearing.

Added by Acts 1995, 74th Leg., ch. 20, § 1, eff. April 20, 1995. Amended by Acts 1997, 75th Leg., ch. 420, § 2, eff. Sept. 1, 1997; Acts 1997, 75th Leg., ch. 911, § 20, eff. Sept. 1, 1997.

[1] Acts 1997, 75th Leg., ch. 420, § 2 here read "in Title IV-D cases" in lieu of "in a Title IV-D case".

[2] Acts 1997, 75th Leg., ch. 420, § 2 here read "arrearage" in lieu of "arrears".

Section 31 of Acts 1997, 75th Leg., ch. 420 provides:

"(a) The change in law made by this Act applies only to a child support lien notice or suit filed on or after the effective date of this Act.

"(b) A child support lien notice or suit filed before the effective date of this Act is covered by the law in effect on the date the lien notice or suit was filed, and the former law is continued in effect for that purpose."

For application and effectiveness provisions of Acts 1997, 75th Leg., ch. 911, see note following V.T.C.A., Family Code § 156.401.

§ 157.313. Contents of Lien Notice

(a) A child support lien notice must contain:

(1) the style, docket number, and identity of the tribunal of this or another state having continuing jurisdiction of the child support action;

(2) the name, address, and, if available, the birth date, driver's license number, and social security number of the obligor;

(3) the name and social security number, if available, of the obligee and the child;

(4) the amount of child support arrearages owed by the obligor and the date of the signing of the court order, administrative order, or writ that determined the arrearages or the date and manner in which the arrearages were determined;

(5) the rate of interest specified in the court order, administrative order, or writ or, in the absence of a specified interest rate, the rate provided for by law;

(6) the name and address of the person or agency asserting the lien; and

(7) the motor vehicle identification number as shown on the obligor's title if the property is a motor vehicle.

(b) A claimant may include any other information that the claimant considers necessary.

(c) The lien notice must be verified.

(d) A claimant must file a notice for each after-acquired motor vehicle.

Added by Acts 1995, 74th Leg., ch. 20, § 1, eff. April 20, 1995. Amended by Acts 1997, 75th Leg., ch. 420, § 3, eff. Sept. 1, 1997; Acts 1997, 75th Leg., ch. 911, § 21, eff. Sept. 1, 1997.

For application and effectiveness provisions of Acts 1997, 75th Leg., ch. 911, see note following V.T.C.A., Family Code § 156.401.

§ 157.314. Filing Lien Notice or Abstract of Judgment

(a) A child support lien notice or an abstract of judgment for past due child support may be filed by the claimant with the county clerk of:

(1) any county in which the obligor is believed to own nonexempt real or personal property;

(2) the county in which the obligor resides; or

(3) the county in which the court having continuing jurisdiction has venue of the suit affecting the parent-child relationship.

(b) A child support lien notice may be filed with:

(1) the clerk of the court in which a claim, counterclaim, or suit by, or on behalf of, the obligor, including a claim or potential right to proceeds from an estate as an heir, beneficiary, or creditor, is pending, provided that a copy of the lien is mailed to the attorney of record for the obligor, if any;

(2) an attorney who represents the obligor in a claim or counterclaim that has not been filed with a court;

(3) any other individual or organization believed to be in possession of real or personal property of the obligor; or

(4) any governmental unit or agency that issues or records certificates, titles, or other indicia of property ownership.

Added by Acts 1995, 74th Leg., ch. 20, § 1, eff. April 20, 1995. Amended by Acts 1997, 75th Leg., ch. 420, § 4, eff. Sept. 1, 1997; Acts 1997, 75th Leg., ch. 911, § 22, eff. Sept. 1, 1997.

For application and effectiveness provisions of Acts 1997, 75th Leg., ch. 911, see note following V.T.C.A., Family Code § 156.401.

§ 157.315. Recording and Indexing Lien

(a) On receipt of a lien notice, the county clerk shall record the notice in the county judgment records as provided in Chapter 52, Property Code.

(b) The county clerk may not charge the Title IV–D agency, a domestic relations office, or a friend of the court a fee for recording the notice or for release of the lien. The county clerk shall collect the fees for recording the notice and for the release of the lien from the obligor before filing the release.

Added by Acts 1995, 74th Leg., ch. 20, § 1, eff. April 20, 1995.

§ 157.316. Perfection of Child Support Lien

(a) Except as provided by Subsection (b), a child support lien is perfected when an abstract of judgment for past due child support or a child support lien notice is filed with the county clerk as provided by this subchapter.

(b) If a lien established under this subchapter attaches to a motor vehicle, the lien must be perfected in the manner provided by Chapter 501, Transportation Code, and the court or Title IV-D agency that rendered the order of child support shall include in the order a requirement that the obligor surrender to the court or Title IV-D agency evidence of the legal ownership of the motor vehicle against which the lien may attach. A lien against a motor vehicle under this subchapter is not perfected until the obligor's title to the vehicle has been surrendered to the court or Title IV-D agency and the Texas Department of Transportation has issued a subsequent title that discloses on its face the fact that the vehicle is subject to a child support lien under this subchapter.

Added by Acts 1995, 74th Leg., ch. 20, § 1, eff. April 20, 1995. Amended by Acts 1997, 75th Leg., ch. 420, § 5, eff. Sept. 1, 1997; Acts 1997, 75th Leg., ch. 911, § 23, eff. Sept. 1, 1997.

For application and effectiveness provisions of Acts 1997, 75th Leg., ch. 911, see note following V.T.C.A., Family Code § 156.401.

§ 157.317. Property to Which Lien Attaches

(a) A lien attaches to all real and personal property not exempt under the Texas Constitution, including a claim for negligence, personal injury, or workers' compensation, or an insurance award for the claim, owned by the obligor on or after the date the lien notice or abstract of judgment is filed with the county clerk of the county in which the property is located, with the court clerk as to property or claims in litigation, or, as to property of the obligor in the possession or control of a third party, from the date the lien notice is filed with that party.

(b) A lien attaches to all nonhomestead real property of the obligor but does not attach to a homestead exempt under the Texas Constitution or the Property Code.

Added by Acts 1995, 74th Leg., ch. 20, § 1, eff. April 20, 1995. Amended by Acts 1997, 75th Leg., ch. 420, § 6, eff. Sept. 1, 1997; Acts 1997, 75th Leg., ch. 911, § 24, eff. Sept. 1, 1997.

For application and effectiveness provisions of Acts 1997, 75th Leg., ch. 911, see note following V.T.C.A., Family Code § 156.401.

§ 157.318. Duration and Effect of Child Support Lien

(a) A lien is effective until all current support and child support arrearages, including interest, have been paid or the lien is otherwise released as provided by[1] this subchapter.

(b) The lien secures payment of all child support arrearages[2] owed by the obligor under the underlying support order, including arrearages that accrue after the administrative or judicial determination of arrearages stated in the lien notice.

(c) The filing of a lien notice or abstract of judgment with the county clerk is a record of the notice and has the same effect as any other lien notice with respect to real property records.

Added by Acts 1995, 74th Leg., ch. 20, § 1, eff. April 20, 1995. Amended by Acts 1997, 75th Leg., ch. 420, § 7, eff. Sept. 1, 1997; Acts 1997, 75th Leg., ch. 911, § 25, eff. Sept. 1, 1997.

[1] Acts 1997, 75th Leg., ch. 420, § 7 here read "in" in lieu of "by".

[2] Acts 1997, 75th Leg., ch. 911, § 25 here read "arrears" in lieu of "arrearages".

For application and effectiveness provisions of Acts 1997, 75th Leg., ch. 911, see note following V.T.C.A., Family Code § 156.401.

§ 157.319. Effect of Lien Notice

(a) If a person having actual notice of the lien possesses nonexempt personal property of the obligor that may be subject to the lien, the property may not be paid over, released, sold, transferred, encumbered, or conveyed unless:

(1) a release of lien signed by the claimant is delivered to the person in possession; or

(2) a court, after notice to the claimant and hearing, has ordered the release of the lien because arrearages do not exist.

(b) A person having notice of a child support lien who violates this section may be joined as a party to a foreclosure action under this chapter and is subject to the penalties [1] provided by this subchapter.

Added by Acts 1995, 74th Leg., ch. 20, § 1, eff. April 20, 1995. Amended by Acts 1997, 75th Leg., ch. 420, § 8, eff. Sept. 1, 1997; Acts 1997, 75th Leg., ch. 911, § 26, eff. Sept. 1, 1997.

[1] Acts 1997, 75th Leg., ch. 420, § 8 here read "remedies" in lieu of "penalties".

For application and effectiveness provisions of Acts 1997, 75th Leg., ch. 911, see note following V.T.C.A., Family Code § 156.401.

§ 157.320. Priority of Lien as to Real Property

(a) A lien created under this subchapter does not have priority over a lien or conveyance of an interest in the nonexempt real property recorded before the child support lien notice is recorded in the county where the real property is located.

(b) A lien created under this subchapter has priority over any lien or conveyance of an interest in the nonexempt real property recorded after the child support lien notice is recorded in the county clerk's office in the county where the property of the obligor is located.

(c) A conveyance of real property by the obligor after a lien notice has been recorded in the county where the real property is located is subject to the lien and may not impair the enforceability of the lien against the real property.

(d) A lien created under this subchapter is subordinate to a vendor's lien retained in a conveyance to the obligor.

Added by Acts 1995, 74th Leg., ch. 20, § 1, eff. April 20, 1995. Amended by Acts 1997, 75th Leg., ch. 911, § 27, eff. Sept. 1, 1997.

For application and effectiveness provisions of Acts 1997, 75th Leg., ch. 911, see note following V.T.C.A., Family Code § 156.401.

§ 157.321. Discretionary Release of Lien

A claimant may at any time release a lien on all or part of the property of the obligor or return seized property, without liability, if assurance of payment is considered adequate by the claimant or if the release or return will facilitate the collection of the arrearages. The release or return may not operate to prevent future action to collect from the same or other property owned by the obligor.

Added by Acts 1995, 74th Leg., ch. 20, § 1, eff. April 20, 1995. Amended by Acts 1997, 75th Leg., ch. 420, § 9, eff. Sept. 1, 1997; Acts 1997, 75th Leg., ch. 911, § 28, eff. Sept. 1, 1997.

For application and effectiveness provisions of Acts 1997, 75th Leg., ch. 911, see note following V.T.C.A., Family Code § 156.401.

§ 157.322. Mandatory Release of Lien

(a) On payment in full of the amount of child support due, together with any costs and reasonable attorney's fees, the claimant shall execute and deliver to the obligor or the obligor's attorney a release of the child support lien.

(b) The release of lien is effective when filed with the county clerk with whom the lien notice or abstract of judgment was filed. A copy of the release of lien may be filed with any other individual or organization that may have been served with a lien notice under this subchapter.

(c) to (e) Repealed by Acts 1997, 75th Leg., ch. 911, § 97(a), eff. Sept. 1, 1997.

Added by Acts 1995, 74th Leg., ch. 20, § 1, eff. April 20, 1995. Amended by Acts 1997, 75th Leg., ch. 420, § 10, eff. Sept. 1, 1997; Acts 1997, 75th Leg., ch. 911, §§ 29, 97(a), eff. Sept. 1, 1997.

For application and effectiveness provisions of Acts 1997, 75th Leg., ch. 911, see note following V.T.C.A., Family Code § 156.401.

§ 157.323. Foreclosure or Suit to Determine Arrearages

(a) In addition to any other remedy provided by law, an action to foreclose a child support lien or to dispute the amount of arrearages stated in the lien may be brought in the court of continuing jurisdiction or, if there is no court of continuing jurisdiction in this state, in the district court of the county in which the property is or was located and the lien was filed.

(b) The procedures provided by Subchapter B [1] apply to a foreclosure action under this section, except that a person or organization in possession of the property of the obligor may be joined as an additional respondent.

(c) If arrearages are owed by the obligor, the court shall:

(1) render judgment against the obligor for the amount due, plus costs and reasonable attorney's fees;

(2) order any official authorized to levy execution to satisfy the lien, costs, and attorney's fees by selling any property on which a lien is established under this subchapter; or

(3) order an individual or organization in possession of nonexempt personal property or cash owned by the obligor to dispose of the property as the court may direct.

(d) For execution and sale under this section, publication of notice is necessary only for three consecutive weeks in a newspaper published in the county where the property is located or, if there is no newspaper in that county, in the most convenient newspaper in circulation in the county.

Added by Acts 1995, 74th Leg., ch. 20, § 1, eff. April 20, 1995. Amended by Acts 1997, 75th Leg., ch. 420, § 11, eff. Sept. 1, 1997; Acts 1997, 75th Leg., ch. 911, § 30, eff. Sept. 1, 1997.

[1] V.T.C.A., Family Code § 157.061 et seq.

For application and effectiveness provisions of Acts 1997, 75th Leg., ch. 911, see note following V.T.C.A., Family Code § 156.401.

§ 157.324. Liability for Failure to Comply With Order or Lien

A person who knowingly disposes of property subject to a lien or who, after a foreclosure hearing, fails to surrender on demand nonexempt personal property as directed by a court or administrative order under this subchapter is liable to the claimant in an amount equal to the arrearages for which the foreclosure judgment was issued.

Added by Acts 1995, 74th Leg., ch. 20, § 1, eff. April 20, 1995. Amended by Acts 1997, 75th Leg., ch. 420, § 12, eff. Sept. 1, 1997; Acts 1997, 75th Leg., ch. 911, § 31, eff. Sept. 1, 1997.

For application and effectiveness provisions of Acts 1997, 75th Leg., ch. 911, see note following V.T.C.A., Family Code § 156.401.

§ 157.325. Release of Excess Funds to Debtor or Obligor

(a) If a person has in the person's possession earnings, deposits, accounts, or balances in excess of the amount of arrearages specified in the child support lien, the holder of the nonexempt personal property or the obligor may request that the claimant release any excess amount from the lien. The claimant shall grant the request and discharge any lien on the excess unless the security for the arrearages would be impaired.

(b) If the claimant refuses the request, the holder of the personal property or the obligor may file suit under this subchapter for an order determining the amount of arrearages and discharging excess personal property or money from the lien.

Added by Acts 1995, 74th Leg., ch. 20, § 1, eff. April 20, 1995. Amended by Acts 1997, 75th Leg., ch. 420, § 13, eff. Sept. 1, 1997; Acts 1997, 75th Leg., ch. 911, § 32, eff. Sept. 1, 1997.

For application and effectiveness provisions of Acts 1997, 75th Leg., ch. 911, see note following V.T.C.A., Family Code § 156.401.

§ 157.326. Interest of Obligor's Spouse

(a) A spouse of an obligor may file an affidavit with the court of continuing jurisdiction or, if there is no court of continuing jurisdiction in this state, in the district court of the county in which the property is or was located and the lien was filed requesting that the court determine the extent, if any, of the spouse's interest in real or personal property that is subject to:

(1) a lien perfected under this subchapter; or

(2) an action to foreclose under this subchapter.

(b) After notice to the obligor, the obligor's spouse, the claimant, and the obligee, the court shall conduct a hearing and determine the extent, if any, of the ownership interest in the property held by the obligor's spouse. If the court finds that:

(1) the property is the separate property of the obligor's spouse, the court shall order that the lien against the property be released and that any action to foreclose on the property be dismissed; or

(2) the property is jointly owned by the obligor and the obligor's spouse, the court shall determine whether the sale of the obligor's interest in the property would result in an unreasonable hardship on the obligor's spouse or family and:

(A) if so, the court shall render an order that the obligor's interest in the property not be sold and that the lien against the property should be released; or

(B) if not, the court shall render an order partitioning the property and directing that the property be sold and the proceeds applied to the child support arrearages.

(c) In a proceeding under this section, the spouse claiming an ownership interest in the property has the burden to prove the extent of that ownership interest.

Added by Acts 1995, 74th Leg., ch. 20, § 1, eff. April 20, 1995. Amended by Acts 1997, 75th Leg., ch. 420, § 14, eff. Sept. 1, 1997; Acts 1997, 75th Leg., ch. 911, § 33, eff. Sept. 1, 1997.

For application and effectiveness provisions of Acts 1997, 75th Leg., ch. 911, see note following V.T.C.A., Family Code § 156.401.

[Sections 157.327 to 157.370 reserved for expansion]

SUBCHAPTER H. HABEAS CORPUS

§ 157.371. Jurisdiction

(a) The relator may file a petition for a writ of habeas corpus in either the court of continuing, exclusive jurisdiction or in a court with jurisdiction to issue a writ of habeas corpus in the county in which the child is found.

(b) Although a habeas corpus proceeding is not a suit affecting the parent-child relationship, the court may refer to the provisions of this title for definitions and procedures as appropriate.

Added by Acts 1995, 74th Leg., ch. 20, § 1, eff. April 20, 1995.

§ 157.372. Return of Child

(a) Subject to Chapter 152 and the Parental Kidnapping Prevention Act (28 U.S.C. Section 1738A), if the right to possession of a child is governed by a court order, the court in a habeas corpus proceeding involving the right to possession of the child shall compel return of the child to the relator only if the court finds that the relator is entitled to possession under the order.

(b) If the court finds that the previous order was granted by a court that did not give the contestants reasonable notice of the proceeding and an opportunity to be heard, the court may not render an order in the habeas corpus proceeding compelling return of the child on the basis of that order.

Added by Acts 1995, 74th Leg., ch. 20, § 1, eff. April 20, 1995.

§ 157.373. Relator Relinquished Possession; Temporary Orders

(a) If the relator has by consent or acquiescence relinquished actual possession and control of the child for not less than 6 months preceding the date of the filing of the petition for the writ, the court may either compel or refuse to order return of the child.

(b) The court may disregard brief periods of possession and control by the relator during the 6-month period.

(c) In a suit in which the court does not compel return of the child, the court may issue temporary orders under Chapter 105 if a suit affecting the parent-child relationship is pending and the parties have received notice of a hearing on temporary orders set for the same time as the habeas corpus proceeding.

Added by Acts 1995, 74th Leg., ch. 20, § 1, eff. April 20, 1995.

§ 157.374. Welfare of Child

Notwithstanding any other provision of this subchapter, the court may render an appropriate temporary order if there is a serious immediate question concerning the welfare of the child.

Added by Acts 1995, 74th Leg., ch. 20, § 1, eff. April 20, 1995.

§ 157.375. Immunity to Civil Process

(a) While in this state for the sole purpose of compelling the return of a child through a habeas corpus proceeding, the relator is not amenable to civil process and is not subject to the jurisdiction of any civil court except the court in which the writ is pending. The relator is subject to process and jurisdiction in that court only for the purpose of prosecuting the writ.

(b) A request by the relator for costs, attorney's fees, and necessary travel and other expenses under Chapter 106 or 152 is not a waiver of immunity to civil process.

Added by Acts 1995, 74th Leg., ch. 20, § 1, eff. April 20, 1995.

§ 157.376. No Existing Order

(a) If the right to possession of a child is not governed by an order, the court in a habeas corpus proceeding involving the right of possession of the child:

(1) shall compel return of the child to the parent if the right of possession is between a parent and a nonparent and a suit affecting the parent-child relationship has not been filed; or

(2) may either compel return of the child or issue temporary orders under Chapter 105 if a suit affecting the parent-child relationship is pending and the parties have received notice of a hearing on temporary orders set for the same time as the habeas corpus proceeding.

(b) The court may not use a habeas corpus proceeding to adjudicate the right of possession of a child between two parents or between two or more nonparents.

Added by Acts 1995, 74th Leg., ch. 20, § 1, eff. April 20, 1995.

[Sections 157.377 to 157.420 reserved for expansion]

SUBCHAPTER I. CLARIFICATION OF ORDERS

§ 157.421. Clarifying Nonspecific Order

(a) A court may clarify an order rendered by the court in a proceeding under this title if the court finds, on the motion of a party or on the court's own motion, that the order is not specific enough to be enforced by contempt.

(b) The court shall clarify the order by rendering an order that is specific enough to be enforced by contempt.

(c) A clarified order does not affect the finality of the order that it clarifies.

Added by Acts 1995, 74th Leg., ch. 20, § 1, eff. April 20, 1995.

§ 157.422. Procedure

(a) The procedure for filing a motion for enforcement of a final order applies to a motion for clarification.

(b) A person is not entitled to a jury in a proceeding under this subchapter.

Added by Acts 1995, 74th Leg., ch. 20, § 1, eff. April 20, 1995.

§ 157.423. Substantive Change Not Enforceable

(a) A court may not change the substantive provisions of an order to be clarified under this subchapter.

(b) A substantive change made by a clarification order is not enforceable.

Added by Acts 1995, 74th Leg., ch. 20, § 1, eff. April 20, 1995.

§ 157.424. Relation to Motion for Contempt

The court may render a clarification order before a motion for contempt is made or heard, in conjunction with a motion for contempt, or after the denial of a motion for contempt.

Added by Acts 1995, 74th Leg., ch. 20, § 1, eff. April 20, 1995.

§ 157.425. Order Not Retroactive

The court may not provide that a clarification order is retroactive for the purpose of enforcement by contempt.

Added by Acts 1995, 74th Leg., ch. 20, § 1, eff. April 20, 1995.

§ 157.426. Time Allowed to Comply

(a) In a clarification order, the court shall provide a reasonable time for compliance.

(b) The clarification order may be enforced by contempt after the time for compliance has expired.

Added by Acts 1995, 74th Leg., ch. 20, § 1, eff. April 20, 1995.

CHAPTER 158. WITHHOLDING FROM EARNINGS FOR CHILD SUPPORT

SUBCHAPTER A. INCOME WITHHOLDING REQUIRED; GENERAL PROVISIONS

§ 158.001. Income Withholding; General Rule

In a proceeding in which periodic payments of child support are ordered, modified, or enforced, the court or the Title IV-D agency shall order that income be withheld from the disposable earnings of the obligor as provided by this chapter.

Added by Acts 1995, 74th Leg., ch. 20, § 1, eff. April 20, 1995. Amended by Acts 1997, 75th Leg., ch. 911, § 34, eff. Sept. 1, 1997.

For application and effectiveness provisions of Acts 1997, 75th Leg., ch. 911, see note following V.T.C.A., Family Code § 156.401.

§ 158.002. Suspension Of Income Withholding

Except in a Title IV-D case, the court may provide, for good cause shown or on agreement of the parties, that the order withholding income need not be issued or delivered to an employer until:

(1) the obligor has been in arrears for an amount due for more than 30 days;

(2) the amount of the arrearages is an amount equal to or greater than the amount due for a one-month period; or

(3) any other violation of the child support order has occurred.

Added by Acts 1995, 74th Leg., ch. 20, § 1, eff. April 20, 1995. Amended by Acts 1997, 75th Leg., ch. 911, § 35, eff. Sept. 1, 1997.

For application and effectiveness provisions of Acts 1997, 75th Leg., ch. 911, see note following V.T.C.A., Family Code § 156.401.

§ 158.003. Withholding for Arrearages in Addition to Current Support

(a) In addition to income withheld for the current support of a child, the court shall order that income be withheld from the disposable earnings of the obligor to be applied toward the liquidation of any child support arrearages, including accrued interest as provided in Chapter 157.

(b) The additional amount to be withheld for arrearages shall be an amount sufficient to discharge those arrearages in not more than two years or an additional 20 percent added to the amount of the current monthly support order, whichever amount will result in the arrearages being discharged in the least amount of time.

Added by Acts 1995, 74th Leg., ch. 20, § 1, eff. April 20, 1995.

§ 158.004. Withholding for Arrearages When no Current Support is Due

If current support is no longer owed, the court shall order that income be withheld for arrearages, including accrued interest as provided in Chapter 157, in an amount sufficient to discharge those arrearages in not more than two years.

Added by Acts 1995, 74th Leg., ch. 20, § 1, eff. April 20, 1995.

§ 158.005. Withholding to Satisfy Judgment for Arrearages

In rendering a cumulative judgment for arrearages, the court shall order that a reasonable amount of income be withheld from the disposable earnings of the obligor to be applied toward the satisfaction of the judgment.

Added by Acts 1995, 74th Leg., ch. 20, § 1, eff. April 20, 1995.

§ 158.006. Income Withholding in Title IV-D Suits

In a Title IV-D case, the court or the Title IV-D agency shall order that income be withheld from the disposable earnings of the obligor and may not suspend, stay, or delay issuance of the order or of a judicial or administrative writ of withholding.

Added by Acts 1995, 74th Leg., ch. 20, § 1, eff. April 20, 1995. Amended by Acts 1997, 75th Leg., ch. 911, § 36, eff. Sept. 1, 1997.

For application and effectiveness provisions of Acts 1997, 75th Leg., ch. 911, see note following V.T.C.A., Family Code § 156.401.

§ 158.007. Extension of Repayment Schedule by Court; Unreasonable Hardship

If the court finds that the schedule for discharging arrearages would cause the obligor, the obligor's family, or children for whom support is due from the obligor to suffer unreasonable hardship, the court may extend the payment period for a reasonable length of time.

Added by Acts 1995, 74th Leg., ch. 20, § 1, eff. April 20, 1995.

§ 158.008. Priority of Withholding

An order or writ of withholding has priority over any garnishment, attachment, execution, or other assignment or order affecting disposable earnings.

Added by Acts 1995, 74th Leg., ch. 20, § 1, eff. April 20, 1995.

§ 158.009. Maximum Amount Withheld From Earnings

An order or writ of withholding shall direct that any employer of the obligor withhold from the obligor's disposable earnings the amount specified up to a maximum amount of 50 percent of the obligor's disposable earnings.

Added by Acts 1995, 74th Leg., ch. 20, § 1, eff. April 20, 1995. Amended by Acts 1997, 75th Leg., ch. 911, § 37, eff. Sept. 1, 1997.

For application and effectiveness provisions of Acts 1997, 75th Leg., ch. 911, see note following V.T.C.A., Family Code § 156.401.

§ 158.010. Order or Writ Binding on Employer Doing Business in State

An order or writ of withholding issued under this chapter and delivered to an employer doing business in this state is binding on the employer without regard to whether the obligor resides or works outside this state.

Added by Acts 1995, 74th Leg., ch. 20, § 1, eff. April 20, 1995. Amended by Acts 1997, 75th Leg., ch. 911, § 38, eff. Sept. 1, 1997.

For application and effectiveness provisions of Acts 1997, 75th Leg., ch. 911, see note following V.T.C.A., Family Code § 156.401.

§ 158.011. Voluntary Withholding by Obligor

(a) An obligor may file with the clerk of the court a notarized or acknowledged request signed by the obligor and the obligee for the issuance and delivery to the obligor's employer of a writ of withholding. A notarized or acknowledged request may be filed under this section regardless of whether a writ or order has been served on any party or of the existence or amount of an arrearage.

(b) On receipt of a request under this section, the clerk shall issue and deliver a writ of withholding in the manner provided by this chapter.

(c) An employer that receives a writ of withholding issued under this section may request a hearing in the same manner and according to the same terms provided by Section 158.205.

(d) An obligor whose employer receives a writ of withholding issued under this section may request a hearing in the manner provided by Section 158.309.

(e) An obligee may contest a writ of withholding issued under this section by requesting, not later than the 180th day after the date on which the obligee discovers that the writ has been issued, a hearing in the manner provided by Section 158.309.

(f) A writ of withholding under this section may not reduce the total amount of child support, including arrearages, owed by the obligor.

Added by Acts 1995, 74th Leg., ch. 751, § 55, eff. Sept. 1, 1995. Amended by Acts 1997, 75th Leg., ch. 911, § 39, eff. Sept. 1, 1997.

For application and effectiveness provisions of Acts 1997, 75th Leg., ch. 911, see note following V.T.C.A., Family Code § 156.401.

[Sections 158.012 to 158.100 reserved for expansion]

SUBCHAPTER B. PROCEDURE

§ 158.101. Applicability of Procedure

Except as otherwise provided in this chapter, the procedure for a motion for enforcement of child support as provided in Chapter 157 applies to an action for income withholding.

Added by Acts 1995, 74th Leg., ch. 20, § 1, eff. April 20, 1995.

§ 158.102. Time Limitations

The court retains jurisdiction to render an order that provides for income to be withheld from the disposable earnings of the obligor until all current support and child support arrearages, including interest, have been paid.

Added by Acts 1995, 74th Leg., ch. 20, § 1, eff. April 20, 1995. Amended by Acts 1997, 75th Leg., ch. 911, § 40, eff. Sept. 1, 1997.

For application and effectiveness provisions of Acts 1997, 75th Leg., ch. 911, see note following V.T.C.A., Family Code § 156.401.

§ 158.103. Contents of Order of Withholding

An order of withholding shall state:

(1) the style, cause number, and court having continuing jurisdiction of the suit;

(2) the name, address, and, if available, the social security number of the obligor;

(3) the amount and duration of the child support payments and medical support payments or other provisions for medical support;

(4) the name, address, and, if available, the social security numbers of the child and the obligee;

(5) the name and address of the person or agency to whom the payments shall be made;

(6) that the obligor is required to notify the court promptly of any change affecting the order; and

(7) that the ordered amount shall be paid to a local registry or the Title IV-D agency.

Added by Acts 1995, 74th Leg., ch. 20, § 1, eff. April 20, 1995. Amended by Acts 1997, 75th Leg., ch. 911, § 41, eff. Sept. 1, 1997.

For application and effectiveness provisions of Acts 1997, 75th Leg., ch. 911, see note following V.T.C.A., Family Code § 156.401.

§ 158.104. Request for Issuance of Order or Writ of Withholding

A request for issuance of an order or writ of withholding may be filed with the clerk of the court by the prosecuting attorney, the Title IV-D agency, the friend of the court, the obligor, or the obligee.

Added by Acts 1995, 74th Leg., ch. 20, § 1, eff. April 20, 1995. Amended by Acts 1997, 75th Leg., ch. 702, § 6, eff. Sept. 1, 1997.

§ 158.105. Issuance and Delivery of Order or Writ of Withholding

(a) On filing a request for issuance of an order or writ of withholding, the clerk of the court shall cause a certified copy of the order or writ to be delivered to the obligor's current employer or to any subsequent employer of the obligor.

(b) In order to inform the employer, the clerk shall attach a copy of Subchapter C [1] to the order or writ.

(c) The clerk shall issue and mail the certified copy of the order or writ not later than the fourth working day after the date the order is signed or the request is filed, whichever is later.

(d) An order or writ of withholding shall be delivered to the employer by certified or registered mail, return receipt requested, or by service of citation to:

(1) the person authorized to receive service of process for the employer in civil cases generally; or

(2) a person designated by the employer, by written notice to the clerk, to receive orders or notices of withholding.

Added by Acts 1995, 74th Leg., ch. 20, § 1, eff. April 20, 1995. Amended by Acts 1997, 75th Leg., ch. 702, § 7, eff. Sept. 1, 1997.

[1] V.T.C.A., Family Code § 158.201 et seq.

§ 158.106. Forms for Income Withholding

(a) The Title IV-D agency shall prescribe forms for:

(1) an order of withholding that is sufficient if rendered in substantially the prescribed manner;

(2) a notice of application for judicial writ of withholding;

(3) a judicial writ of withholding as provided by Subchapter D;[1] and

(4) an administrative writ of withholding, including forms and procedures for electronic issuance of the writ, as provided by Subchapter F.[2]

(b) The Title IV–D agency shall make the appropriate forms available to obligors, obligees, domestic relations offices, friends of the court, and private attorneys.

(c) The Title IV–D agency may prescribe additional forms for the efficient collection of child support and to promote the administration of justice for all parties.

Added by Acts 1995, 74th Leg., ch. 20, § 1, eff. April 20, 1995. Amended by Acts 1997, 75th Leg., ch. 911, § 42, eff. Sept. 1, 1997.

[1] V.T.C.A., Family Code § 158.301 et seq.

[2] V.T.C.A., Family Code § 158.501 et seq.

For application and effectiveness provisions of Acts 1997, 75th Leg., ch. 911, see note following V.T.C.A., Family Code § 156.401.

§ 158.107. Repealed by Acts 1997, 75th Leg., ch. 911, § 97(a), eff. Sept. 1, 1997

[Sections 158.108 to 158.200 reserved for expansion]

SUBCHAPTER C. RIGHTS AND DUTIES OF EMPLOYER

§ 158.201. Order or Writ Binding on Employer

(a) An employer required to withhold income from earnings is not entitled to notice of the proceedings before the order is rendered or writ of withholding is issued.

(b) An order or writ of withholding is binding on an employer regardless of whether the employer is specifically named in the order or writ.

Added by Acts 1995, 74th Leg., ch. 20, § 1, eff. April 20, 1995. Amended by Acts 1997, 75th Leg., ch. 911, § 43, eff. Sept. 1, 1997.

For application and effectiveness provisions of Acts 1997, 75th Leg., ch. 911, see note following V.T.C.A., Family Code § 156.401.

§ 158.202. Effective Date of and Duration of Withholding

An employer shall begin to withhold income in accordance with an order or writ of withholding not later than the first pay period following the date on which the order or writ was delivered to the employer and shall continue to withhold income as required by the order or writ as long as the obligor is employed by the employer.

Added by Acts 1995, 74th Leg., ch. 20, § 1, eff. April 20, 1995. Amended by Acts 1997, 75th Leg., ch. 911, § 44, eff. Sept. 1, 1997.

For application and effectiveness provisions of Acts 1997, 75th Leg., ch. 911, see note following V.T.C.A., Family Code § 156.401.

§ 158.203. Remitting Withheld Payments

(a) The employer shall remit the amount to be withheld to the person or office named in the order or writ on each pay date. The payment must include the date on which the withholding occurred.

(b) The employer shall include with each payment transmitted:

(1) the number assigned by the Title IV-D agency, if available, the county identification number, if available, or the cause number of the suit under which withholding is required;

(2) the payor's name; and

(3) the payee's name, unless the payment is transmitted by electronic funds transfer.

Added by Acts 1995, 74th Leg., ch. 20, § 1, eff. April 20, 1995. Amended by Acts 1997, 75th Leg., ch. 702, § 8, eff. Jan. 1, 1998.

§ 158.204. Employer May Deduct Fee From Earnings

An employer may deduct an administrative fee of not more than $5 each month from the obligor's disposable earnings in addition to the amount to be withheld as child support.

Added by Acts 1995, 74th Leg., ch. 20, § 1, eff. April 20, 1995.

§ 158.205. Hearing Requested by Employer

(a) Not later than the 20th day after the date an order or writ of withholding is delivered, the employer may, as appropriate, file a motion with the court or file a request with the Title IV-D agency for a hearing on the applicability of the order or writ to the employer. The Title IV-D agency by rule shall establish procedures for an agency hearing under this section.

(b) The hearing under this section shall be held not later than the 15th day after the date the motion or request was made.

(c) An order or writ of withholding remains binding and payments shall continue to be made pending further order of the court or, in the case of an administrative writ, action of the Title IV-D agency.

Added by Acts 1995, 74th Leg., ch. 20, § 1, eff. April 20, 1995. Amended by Acts 1997, 75th Leg., ch. 911, § 45, eff. Sept. 1, 1997.

For application and effectiveness provisions of Acts 1997, 75th Leg., ch. 911, see note following V.T.C.A., Family Code § 156.401.

§ 158.206. Liability and Obligation of Employer for Payments

(a) An employer receiving an order or a writ of withholding under this chapter, including an order or writ directing that health insurance be provided to a child, who complies with the order or writ is not liable to the obligor for the amount of income withheld and paid as required by the order or writ.

(b) An employer receiving an order or writ of withholding who does not comply with the order or writ is liable:

(1) to the obligee for the amount not paid in compliance with the order or writ, including the amount the obligor is required to pay for health insurance under Chapter 154;

(2) to the obligor for the amount withheld and not paid; and

(3) for reasonable attorney's fees and court costs.

Added by Acts 1995, 74th Leg., ch. 20, § 1, eff. April 20, 1995. Amended by Acts 1995, 74th Leg., ch. 341, § 4.07, eff. Sept. 1, 1995; Acts 1997, 75th Leg., ch. 911, § 46, eff. Sept. 1, 1997.

For application and effectiveness provisions of Acts 1997, 75th Leg., ch. 911, see note following V.T.C.A., Family Code § 156.401.

§ 158.207. Employer Receiving More Than One Order or Writ

(a) An employer receiving two or more orders or writs for one obligor shall comply with each order or writ to the extent possible.

(b) If the total amount due under the orders or writs exceeds the maximum amount allowed to be withheld under Section 158.009, the employer shall pay an equal amount towards the current support in each order or writ until the employer has complied fully with each current support obligation and, thereafter, equal amounts on the arrearages until the employer has complied with each order or writ, or until the maximum total amount of allowed withholding is reached, whichever occurs first.

Added by Acts 1995, 74th Leg., ch. 20, § 1, eff. April 20, 1995. Amended by Acts 1997, 75th Leg., ch. 911, § 47, eff. Sept. 1, 1997.

For application and effectiveness provisions of Acts 1997, 75th Leg., ch. 911, see note following V.T.C.A., Family Code § 156.401.

§ 158.208. Employer may Combine Amounts Withheld

An employer required to withhold from more than one obligor may combine the amounts withheld and make a single payment to each agency designated if the employer separately identifies the amount of the payment that is attributable to each obligor.

Added by Acts 1995, 74th Leg., ch. 20, § 1, eff. April 20, 1995.

§ 158.209. Employer's Penalty for Discriminatory Hiring or Discharge

(a) An employer may not use an order or writ of withholding as grounds in whole or part for the termination of employment or for any other disciplinary action against an employee.

(b) An employer may not refuse to hire an employee because of an order or writ of withholding.

(c) If an employer intentionally discharges an employee in violation of this section, the employer continues to be liable to the employee for current wages and other benefits and for reasonable attorney's fees and court costs incurred in enforcing the employee's rights as provided in this section.

(d) An action under this section may be brought by the employee, a friend of the court, the domestic relations office, or the Title IV-D agency.

Added by Acts 1995, 74th Leg., ch. 20, § 1, eff. April 20, 1995. Amended by Acts 1997, 75th Leg., ch. 911, § 48, eff. Sept. 1, 1997.

For application and effectiveness provisions of Acts 1997, 75th Leg., ch. 911, see note following V.T.C.A., Family Code § 156.401.

§ 158.210. Fine for Noncompliance

(a) In addition to the civil remedies provided by this subchapter or any other remedy provided by law, an employer who knowingly violates the provisions of this chapter may be subject to a fine not to exceed $200 for each occurrence in which the employer fails to withhold.

(b) A fine recovered under this section shall be paid to the county in which the obligee resides and shall be used by the county to improve child support services.

Added by Acts 1995, 74th Leg., ch. 20, § 1, eff. April 20, 1995. Amended by Acts 1997, 75th Leg., ch. 420, § 15, eff. Sept. 1, 1997.

§ 158.211. Notice of Termination of Employment and of New Employment

(a) If an obligor terminates employment with an employer who has been withholding income, both the obligor and the employer shall notify the court and the obligee of that fact not later than the seventh day after the date employment terminated and shall provide the obligor's last known address and the name and address of the obligor's new employer, if known.

(b) The obligor has a continuing duty to inform any subsequent employer of the order or writ of withholding after obtaining employment.

Added by Acts 1995, 74th Leg., ch. 20, § 1, eff. April 20, 1995.

[Sections 158.212 to 158.300 reserved for expansion]

SUBCHAPTER D. JUDICIAL WRIT OF WITHHOLDING ISSUED BY CLERK

Acts 1997, 75th Leg., ch. 911, § 49, in the subchapter heading, inserted "judicial" and "issued by clerk".

§ 158.301. Notice of Application for Judicial Writ Of Withholding; Filing

(a) A notice of application for judicial writ of withholding may be filed if:

(1) a delinquency occurs in child support payments in an amount equal to or greater than the total support due for one month; or

(2) income withholding was not ordered at the time child support was ordered.

(b) The notice of application for judicial writ of withholding may be filed in the court of continuing jurisdiction by:

(1) the Title IV-D agency;

(2) the attorney representing the local domestic relations office;

(3) the attorney appointed a friend of the court as provided in Chapter 202;

(4) the obligor or obligee; or

(5) a private attorney representing the obligor or obligee.

(c) The Title IV-D agency may in a Title IV-D case file a notice of application for judicial writ of withholding on request of the obligor or obligee.

Added by Acts 1995, 74th Leg., ch. 20, § 1, eff. April 20, 1995. Amended by Acts 1995, 74th Leg., ch. 751, § 57, eff. Sept. 1, 1995; Acts 1997, 75th Leg., ch. 911, § 50, eff. Sept. 1, 1997.

For application and effectiveness provisions of Acts 1997, 75th Leg., ch. 911, see note following V.T.C.A., Family Code § 156.401.

§ 158.302. Contents of Notice of application for Judicial Writ Of Withholding

The notice of application for judicial writ of withholding shall be verified and:

(1) state the amount of monthly support due, including medical support, the amount of arrearages or anticipated arrearages, including accrued interest, and the amount of wages that will be withheld in accordance with a judicial writ of withholding;

(2) state that the withholding applies to each current or subsequent employer or period of employment;

(3) state that if the obligor does not contest the withholding within 10 days after the date of receipt of the notice, the obligor's employer will be notified to begin the withholding;

(4) describe the procedures for contesting the issuance and delivery of a writ of withholding;

(5) state that if the obligor contests the withholding, the obligor will be afforded an opportunity for a hearing by the court not later than the 30th day after the date of receipt of the notice of contest;

(6) state that the sole ground for successfully contesting the issuance of a writ of withholding is a dispute concerning the identity of the obligor or the existence or amount of the arrearages, including accrued interest;

(7) describe the actions that may be taken if the obligor contests the notice of application for judicial writ of withholding, including the procedures for suspending issuance of a writ of withholding; and

(8) include with the notice a suggested form for the motion to stay issuance and delivery of the

judicial writ of withholding that the obligor may file with the clerk of the appropriate court.

Added by Acts 1995, 74th Leg., ch. 20, § 1, eff. April 20, 1995. Amended by Acts 1997, 75th Leg., ch. 911, § 51, eff. Sept. 1, 1997.

For application and effectiveness provisions of Acts 1997, 75th Leg., ch. 911, see note following V.T.C.A., Family Code § 156.401.

§ 158.303. Interstate Request for Income Withholding

(a) The registration of a foreign support order as provided in Chapter 159 is sufficient for the filing of a notice of application for judicial writ of withholding.

(b) The notice shall be filed with the clerk of the court having venue as provided in Chapter 159.

(c) Notice of application for judicial writ of withholding may be delivered to the obligor at the same time that an order is filed for registration under Chapter 159.

Added by Acts 1995, 74th Leg., ch. 20, § 1, eff. April 20, 1995. Amended by Acts 1995, 74th Leg., ch. 751, § 58, eff. Sept. 1, 1995; Acts 1997, 75th Leg., ch. 911, § 52, eff. Sept. 1, 1997.

For application and effectiveness provisions of Acts 1997, 75th Leg., ch. 911, see note following V.T.C.A., Family Code § 156.401.

§ 158.304. Additional Arrearages

If the notice of application for judicial writ of withholding states that the obligor has repeatedly failed to pay support in accordance with the underlying support order, the judicial writ may include arrearages that accrue between the filing of the notice and the date of the hearing or the issuance of a judicial writ of withholding.

Added by Acts 1995, 74th Leg., ch. 20, § 1, eff. April 20, 1995. Amended by Acts 1997, 75th Leg., ch. 911, § 53, eff. Sept. 1, 1997.

For application and effectiveness provisions of Acts 1997, 75th Leg., ch. 911, see note following V.T.C.A., Family Code § 156.401.

§ 158.305. Repealed by Acts 1997, 75th Leg., ch. 911, § 97(a), eff. Sept. 1, 1997

§ 158.306. Delivery of Notice of Application for Judicial Writ Of Withholding; Time of Delivery

(a) A notice of application for judicial writ of withholding may be delivered to the obligor by:

(1) hand delivery by a person designated by the Title IV-D agency or local domestic relations office;

(2) first-class or certified mail, return receipt requested, addressed to the obligor's last known address or place of employment; or

(3) by service of citation as in civil cases generally.

(b) If the notice is delivered by mailing or hand delivery, the party who filed the notice shall file with the court a certificate stating the name, address, and date on which the mailing or hand delivery was made.

(c) Notice is considered to have been received by the obligor:

(1) if hand delivered, on the date of delivery;

(2) if mailed by certified mail, on the date of receipt;

(3) if mailed by first-class mail, on the 10th day after the date the notice was mailed; or

(4) if delivered by service of citation, on the date of service.

Added by Acts 1995, 74th Leg., ch. 20, § 1, eff. April 20, 1995. Amended by Acts 1997, 75th Leg., ch. 911, § 54, eff. Sept. 1, 1997.

For application and effectiveness provisions of Acts 1997, 75th Leg., ch. 911, see note following V.T.C.A., Family Code § 156.401.

§ 158.307. Motion to Stay Issuance of Writ of Withholding

(a) The obligor may stay issuance of a judicial writ of withholding by filing a motion to stay with the clerk of court not later than the 10th day after the date the notice of application for judicial writ of withholding was received.

(b) The grounds for filing a motion to stay issuance are limited to a dispute concerning the identity of the obligor or the existence or the amount of the arrearages.

(c) The obligor shall verify that statements of fact in the motion to stay issuance of the writ are true and correct.

Added by Acts 1995, 74th Leg., ch. 20, § 1, eff. April 20, 1995. Amended by Acts 1997, 75th Leg., ch. 911, § 55, eff. Sept. 1, 1997.

For application and effectiveness provisions of Acts 1997, 75th Leg., ch. 911, see note following V.T.C.A., Family Code § 156.401.

§ 158.308. Effect of Filing Motion to Stay

The filing of a motion to stay by an obligor in the manner provided by Section 158.307 prohibits the clerk of court from delivering the judicial writ of withholding to any employer of the obligor before a hearing is held.

Added by Acts 1995, 74th Leg., ch. 20, § 1, eff. April 20, 1995. Amended by Acts 1997, 75th Leg., ch. 911, § 56, eff. Sept. 1, 1997.

For application and effectiveness provisions of Acts 1997, 75th Leg., ch. 911, see note following V.T.C.A., Family Code § 156.401.

§ 158.309. Hearing on Motion to Stay

(a) If a motion to stay is filed in the manner provided by Section 158.307, the court shall set a hearing on the motion and the clerk of court shall notify the obligor, obligee, or their authorized representatives, and the party who filed the application for judicial writ of withholding of the date, time, and place of the hearing.

(b) The court shall hold a hearing on the motion to stay not later than the 30th day after the date the motion was filed, except that a hearing may be held later than the 30th day after filing if both the obligor and obligee agree and waive the right to have the motion heard within 30 days.

(c) Upon hearing, the court shall:

(1) render an order for income withholding that includes a determination of the amount of child support arrearages, including medical support and interest; or

(2) grant the motion to stay.

Added by Acts 1995, 74th Leg., ch. 20, § 1, eff. April 20, 1995. Amended by Acts 1995, 74th Leg., ch. 751, § 59, eff. Sept. 1, 1995; Acts 1997, 75th Leg., ch. 911, § 57, eff. Sept. 1, 1997.

For application and effectiveness provisions of Acts 1997, 75th Leg., ch. 911, see note following V.T.C.A., Family Code § 156.401.

§ 158.310. Special Exceptions

(a) A defect in a notice of application for judicial writ of withholding is waived unless the respondent specially excepts in writing and cites with particularity the alleged defect, obscurity, or other ambiguity in the notice.

(b) A special exception under this section must be heard by the court before hearing the motion to stay issuance.

(c) If the court sustains an exception, the court shall provide the party filing the notice an opportunity to refile and the court shall continue the hearing to a date certain without the requirement of additional service.

Added by Acts 1995, 74th Leg., ch. 20, § 1, eff. April 20, 1995. Amended by Acts 1997, 75th Leg., ch. 911, § 58, eff. Sept. 1, 1997.

For application and effectiveness provisions of Acts 1997, 75th Leg., ch. 911, see note following V.T.C.A., Family Code § 156.401.

§ 158.311. Arrearages

(a) Payment of arrearages after receipt of notice of application for judicial writ of withholding may not be the sole basis for the court to refuse to order withholding.

(b) The court shall order that a reasonable amount of income be withheld to be applied toward the liquidation of arrearages, even though a judgment confirming arrearages has been rendered against the obligor.

Added by Acts 1995, 74th Leg., ch. 20, § 1, eff. April 20, 1995. Amended by Acts 1997, 75th Leg., ch. 911, § 59, eff. Sept. 1, 1997.

For application and effectiveness provisions of Acts 1997, 75th Leg., ch. 911, see note following V.T.C.A., Family Code § 156.401.

§ 158.312. Request for Issuance and Delivery of Writ of Withholding

(a) If a notice of application for judicial writ of withholding is delivered and a motion to stay is not filed within the time limits provided by Section 158.307, the party who filed the notice shall file with the clerk of the court a request for issuance of the writ of withholding stating the amount of current support, including medical support, the amount of arrearages, and the amount to be withheld from the obligor's income.

(b) The request for issuance may not be filed before the 11th day after the date of receipt of the notice of withholding by the obligor.

Added by Acts 1995, 74th Leg., ch. 20, § 1, eff. April 20, 1995. Amended by Acts 1997, 75th Leg., ch. 911, § 60, eff. Sept. 1, 1997.

For application and effectiveness provisions of Acts 1997, 75th Leg., ch. 911, see note following V.T.C.A., Family Code § 156.401.

§ 158.313. Issuance and Delivery of Writ of Withholding

(a) On the filing of a request for issuance of a writ of withholding, the clerk of the court shall issue the writ.

(b) The writ shall be delivered as provided by Subchapter B.[1]

(c) The clerk shall issue and mail the writ not later than the second working day after the date the request is filed.

Added by Acts 1995, 74th Leg., ch. 20, § 1, eff. April 20, 1995.

[1] V.T.C.A., Family Code § 158.101 et seq.

§ 158.314. Contents of Writ of Withholding

The judicial writ of income withholding issued by the clerk must direct that the employer or a subsequent employer withhold from the obligor's disposable income for current child support, including medical support, and child support arrearages an amount that is consistent with the provisions of this chapter regarding orders of withholding.

Added by Acts 1995, 74th Leg., ch. 20, § 1, eff. April 20, 1995. Amended by Acts 1997, 75th Leg., ch. 911, § 61, eff. Sept. 1, 1997.

For application and effectiveness provisions of Acts 1997, 75th Leg., ch. 911, see note following V.T.C.A., Family Code § 156.401.

§ 158.315. Extension of Repayment Schedule by Party; Unreasonable Hardship

If the party who filed the notice of application for judicial writ of withholding finds that the schedule for repaying arrearages would cause the obligor, the obligor's family, or the children for whom the support is due from the obligor to suffer unreasonable hardship, the party may extend the payment period in the writ.

Added by Acts 1995, 74th Leg., ch. 20, § 1, eff. April 20, 1995. Amended by Acts 1997, 75th Leg., ch. 911, § 62, eff. Sept. 1, 1997.

For application and effectiveness provisions of Acts 1997, 75th Leg., ch. 911, see note following V.T.C.A., Family Code § 156.401.

§ 158.316. Payment of Amount to be Withheld

The amount to be withheld shall be paid to the person or office named in the writ on each pay date and shall include with the payment the date on which the withholding occurred.

Added by Acts 1995, 74th Leg., ch. 20, § 1, eff. April 20, 1995.

§ 158.317. Failure to Receive Notice of Application for Judicial Writ Of Withholding

(a) Not later than the 30th day after the date of the first pay period following the date of delivery of the writ of withholding to the obligor's employer, the obligor may file an affidavit with the court that a motion to stay was not timely filed because the notice of application for judicial writ of withholding was not received by the obligor and that grounds exist for a motion to stay.

(b) Concurrently with the filing of the affidavit, the obligor may file a motion to withdraw the writ of withholding and request a hearing on the applicability of the writ.

(c) Income withholding may not be interrupted until after the hearing at which the court renders an order denying or modifying withholding.

Added by Acts 1995, 74th Leg., ch. 20, § 1, eff. April 20, 1995. Amended by Acts 1997, 75th Leg., ch. 911, § 63, eff. Sept. 1, 1997.

For application and effectiveness provisions of Acts 1997, 75th Leg., ch. 911, see note following V.T.C.A., Family Code § 156.401.

[Section 158.318 reserved for expansion]

§ 158.319. Issuance and Delivery of Judicial Writ of Withholding to Subsequent Employer

(a) After the issuance of a judicial writ of withholding by the clerk, a party authorized to file a notice of application for judicial writ of withholding under this subchapter may issue the judicial writ of withholding to a subsequent employer of the obligor by delivering to the employer by certified mail a copy of the writ.

(b) The judicial writ of withholding must include the name, address, and signature of the party and clearly indicate that the writ is being issued to a subsequent employer.

(c) The party shall file a copy of the judicial writ of withholding with the clerk not later than the third working day following delivery of the writ to the subsequent employer. The party shall pay the clerk a fee of $15 at the time the copy of the writ is filed.

(d) The party shall file the postal return receipt from the delivery to the subsequent employer not later than the third working day after the party receives the receipt.

Added by Acts 1995, 74th Leg., ch. 751, § 60, eff. Sept. 1, 1995. Amended by Acts 1997, 75th Leg., ch. 911, § 64, eff. Sept. 1, 1997.

For application and effectiveness provisions of Acts 1997, 75th Leg., ch. 911, see note following V.T.C.A., Family Code § 156.401.

[Sections 158.320 to 158.400 reserved for expansion]

SUBCHAPTER E. MODIFICATION, REDUCTION, OR TERMINATION OF WITHHOLDING

§ 158.401. Modifications to or Termination of Withholding by Title IV–D Agency

(a) The Title IV–D agency shall establish procedures for the reduction in the amount of or termination of withholding from income on the liquidation of an arrearages or the termination of the obligation of support in Title IV–D cases. The procedures shall provide that the payment of overdue support may not be used as the sole basis for terminating withholding.

(b) At the request of the Title IV-D agency, the clerk of the court shall issue a judicial writ of withholding to the obligor's employer reflecting any modification or changes in the amount to be withheld or the termination of withholding.

Added by Acts 1995, 74th Leg., ch. 20, § 1, eff. April 20, 1995. Amended by Acts 1997, 75th Leg., ch. 911, § 65, eff. Sept. 1, 1997.

For application and effectiveness provisions of Acts 1997, 75th Leg., ch. 911, see note following V.T.C.A., Family Code § 156.401.

§ 158.402. Agreement by Parties Regarding Amount or Duration of Withholding

(a) An obligor and obligee may agree on a reduction in or termination of income withholding for child support on the occurrence of one of the following contingencies stated in the order:

(1) the child becomes 18 years of age or is graduated from high school, whichever is later;

(2) the child's disabilities of minority are removed by marriage, court order, or other operation of law; or

(3) the child dies.

(b) The obligor and obligee may file a notarized or acknowledged request with the clerk of the court under Section 158.011 for a revised judicial writ of withholding, including the termination of withholding.

(c) The clerk shall issue and deliver to an employer of the obligor a judicial writ of withholding that reflects the agreed revision or termination of withholding.

(d) An agreement by the parties under this section does not modify the terms of a support order.

Added by Acts 1995, 74th Leg., ch. 751, § 61, eff. Sept. 1, 1995. Amended by Acts 1997, 75th Leg., ch. 911, § 66, eff. Sept. 1, 1997.

For application and effectiveness provisions of Acts 1997, 75th Leg., ch. 911, see note following V.T.C.A., Family Code § 156.401.

§ 158.403. Modifications to or Termination of Withholding in Voluntary Withholding Cases

(a) If an obligor initiates voluntary withholding under Section 158.011, the obligee or an agency providing child support services may file with the clerk of the court a notarized request signed by the obligor and the obligee or agency, as appropriate, for the issuance and delivery to the obligor of a:

(1) modified writ of withholding that reduces the amount of withholding; or

(2) notice of termination of withholding.

(b) On receipt of a request under this section, the clerk shall issue and deliver a modified writ of withholding or notice of termination in the manner provided by Section 158.402.

(c) The clerk may charge a reasonable fee not to exceed $15 for filing the request.

(d) An obligee may contest a modified writ of withholding or notice of termination issued under this section by requesting a hearing in the manner provided by Section 158.309 not later than the 180th day after the date the obligee discovers that the writ or notice has been issued.

Added by Acts 1995, 74th Leg., ch. 751, § 61, eff. Sept. 1, 1995.

§ 158.404. Delivery of Order of Reduction or Termination of Withholding

If a court has rendered an order that reduces the amount of child support to be withheld or terminates withholding for child support, any person or governmental entity may deliver to the employer a certified copy of the order without the requirement that the clerk of the court deliver the order.

Added by Acts 1995, 74th Leg., ch. 20, § 1, eff. April 20, 1995. Renumbered from § 158.402 by Acts 1995, 74th Leg., ch. 751, § 61, eff. Sept. 1, 1995.

§ 158.405. Liability of Employers

The provisions of this chapter regarding the liability of employers for withholding apply to an order that reduces or terminates withholding.

Added by Acts 1995, 74th Leg., ch. 20, § 1, eff. April 20, 1995. Renumbered from § 158.403 by Acts 1995, 74th Leg., ch. 751, § 61, eff. Sept. 1, 1995.

SUBCHAPTER F. ADMINISTRATIVE WRIT OF WITHHOLDING IN TITLE IV-D CASES

§ 158.501. Issuance of Administrative Writ of Withholding

The Title IV-D agency may initiate income withholding by issuing an administrative writ of withholding for the enforcement of an existing order as authorized by this subchapter.

Added by Acts 1997, 75th Leg., ch. 911, § 67, eff. Sept. 1, 1997.

§ 158.502. When Administrative Writ of Withholding May be Issued

An administrative writ of withholding under this subchapter may be issued at any time until all current support, including medical support, and child support arrearages have been paid.

Added by Acts 1997, 75th Leg., ch. 911, § 67, eff. Sept. 1, 1997.

§ 158.503. Delivery of Administrative Writ to Employer; Filing With Court

(a) An administrative writ of withholding issued under this subchapter may be delivered to an employer by mail or by electronic transmission.

(b) Not later than the third business day after the date of delivery of the administrative writ of withholding to an employer, the Title IV-D agency shall file a copy of the writ, together with a certificate of service, in the court of continuing jurisdiction.

(c) The copy of the administrative writ of withholding filed with the clerk of court must include:

(1) the name, address, and signature of the authorized attorney or individual that issued the writ;

(2) the name and address of the employer served with the writ; and

(3) a true copy of the information provided to the employer.

Added by Acts 1997, 75th Leg., ch. 911, § 67, eff. Sept. 1, 1997.

§ 158.504. Contents of Administrative Writ of Withholding

(a) The administrative writ of withholding must be in the form prescribed by the Title IV-D agency as required by this chapter and in a standard format authorized by the United States Department of Health and Human Services.

(b) An administrative writ of withholding issued under this subchapter may contain only the information that is necessary for the employer to comply with the existing withholding order, including the amount of current support and medical support, the amount of arrearages, accrued interest, and the amount of earnings to be withheld.

Added by Acts 1997, 75th Leg., ch. 911, § 67, eff. Sept. 1, 1997.

§ 158.505. Notice to Obligor

(a) On issuance of an administrative writ of withholding, the Title IV-D agency shall send the obligor:

(1) notice that the withholding has commenced;

(2) notice of the procedures to follow if the obligor desires to contest withholding on the grounds that the identity of the obligor or the existence or amount of arrearages is incorrect; and

(3) a copy of the administrative writ, including the information concerning income withholding provided in the original writ to the employer.

(b) The notice required under this section may be sent to the obligor by:

(1) personal delivery by a person designated by the Title IV-D agency;

(2) first-class mail or certified mail, return receipt requested, addressed to the obligor's last known address; or

(3) service of citation as in civil cases generally.

(c) The copy of the administrative writ of withholding delivered to the obligor shall include the information concerning income withholding provided in the original writ to the employer.

Added by Acts 1997, 75th Leg., ch. 911, § 67, eff. Sept. 1, 1997.

§ 158.506. Contest by Obligor to Administrative Writ of Withholding

(a) An obligor receiving the notice under Section 158.503 may request a review by the Title IV-D agency to resolve any issue in dispute regarding the identity of the obligor or the existence or amount of arrearages. The Title IV-D agency shall provide an opportunity for a review, by telephonic conference or in person, as may be appropriate under the circumstances.

(b) After a review under this section, the Title IV-D agency may issue a new administrative writ of withholding to the employer, including a writ modifying the amount to be withheld or terminating withholding.

(c) If a review under this section fails to resolve any issue in dispute, the obligor is entitled to the remedies provided by Section 158.317 for cases in which a notice of an application for judicial writ of withholding was not received. The obligor may file a motion with the court to withdraw the administrative writ and request a hearing with the court not later than the 30th day after receiving notice of the agency's determination. Income withholding may not be interrupted pending a hearing by the court.

Added by Acts 1997, 75th Leg., ch. 911, § 67, eff. Sept. 1, 1997.

§ 158.507. Administrative Writ Terminating Withholding

An administrative writ to terminate withholding may be issued and delivered to an employer by the Title IV-D agency when all current support, including medical support, and child support arrearages have been paid.

Added by Acts 1997, 75th Leg., ch. 911, § 67, eff. Sept. 1, 1997.

§ 158.508. Interstate Request for Income Withholding

An administrative writ of withholding may be issued in a Title IV-D interstate case on registration of a foreign support order as provided in Chapter 159.

Added by Acts 1997, 75th Leg., ch. 911, § 67, eff. Sept. 1, 1997.

CHAPTER 159. UNIFORM INTERSTATE FAMILY SUPPORT ACT

SUBCHAPTER A. CONFLICTS BETWEEN PROVISIONS

§ 159.001. Conflicts Between Provisions

If a provision of this chapter conflicts with a provision of this title or another statute or rule of this state and the conflict cannot be reconciled, this chapter prevails.

Added by Acts 1995, 74th Leg., ch. 20, § 1, eff. April 20, 1995.

[Sections 159.002 to 159.100 reserved for expansion]

SUBCHAPTER B. GENERAL PROVISIONS

§ 159.101. Definitions

In this chapter:

(1) "Child" means an individual, whether over or under the age of majority, who:

(A) is or is alleged to be owed a duty of support by the individual's parent; or

(B) is or is alleged to be the beneficiary of a support order directed to the parent.

(2) "Child support order" means a support order for a child, including a child who has attained the age of majority under the law of the issuing state.

(3) "Duty of support" means an obligation imposed or imposable by law to provide support for a child, spouse, or former spouse, including an unsatisfied obligation to provide support.

(4) "Home state" means the state in which a child lived with a parent or a person acting as parent for at least six consecutive months preceding the time of filing of a petition or a comparable pleading for support and, if a child is less than six months old, the state in which the child lived with a parent or a person acting as parent from the time of birth. A period of temporary absence of any of them is counted as part of the six-month or other period.

(5) "Income" includes earnings or other periodic entitlements to money from any source and any other property subject to withholding for support under the law of this state.

(6) "Income-withholding order" means an order or other legal process directed to an obligor's employer, as provided in Chapter 158, to withhold support from the income of the obligor.

(7) "Initiating state" means a state from which a proceeding is forwarded or in which a proceeding is filed for forwarding to a responding state under this chapter or a law or procedure substantially similar to this chapter, the Uniform Reciprocal Enforcement of Support Act, or the Revised Uniform Reciprocal Enforcement of Support Act.

(8) "Initiating tribunal" means the authorized tribunal in an initiating state.

(9) "Issuing state" means the state in which a tribunal issues a support order or renders a judgment determining parentage.

(10) "Issuing tribunal" means the tribunal that issues a support order or renders a judgment determining parentage.

(11) "Law" includes decisional and statutory law and rules and regulations having the force of law.

(12) "Obligee" means:

(A) an individual to whom a duty of support is or is alleged to be owed or in whose favor a support order has been issued or a judgment determining parentage has been rendered;

(B) a state or political subdivision to which the rights under a duty of support or support order have been assigned or that has independent claims based on financial assistance provided to an individual obligee; or

(C) an individual seeking a judgment determining parentage of the individual's child.

(13) "Obligor" means an individual or the estate of a decedent:

(A) who owes or is alleged to owe a duty of support;

(B) who is alleged but has not been adjudicated to be a parent of a child; or

(C) who is liable under a support order.

(14) "Register" means to file a support order or judgment determining parentage in the registry of foreign support orders.

(15) "Registering tribunal" means a tribunal in which a support order is registered.

(16) "Responding state" means a state in which a proceeding is filed or to which a proceeding is forwarded for filing from an initiating state under this chapter or a law or procedure substantially similar to this chapter, the Uniform Reciprocal Enforcement of Support Act, or the Revised Uniform Reciprocal Enforcement of Support Act.

(17) "Responding tribunal" means the authorized tribunal in a responding state.

(18) "Spousal support order" means a support order for a spouse or former spouse of the obligor.

(19) "State" means a state of the United States, the District of Columbia, Puerto Rico, the United States Virgin Islands, or any territory or insular possession subject to the jurisdiction of the United States. The term includes:

(A) an Indian tribe; and

(B) a foreign jurisdiction that has enacted a law or established procedures for issuance and enforcement of support orders that are substantially similar to the procedures under this chapter, the Uniform Reciprocal Enforcement of Support Act, or the Revised Uniform Reciprocal Enforcement of Support Act.

(20) "Support enforcement agency" means a public official or agency authorized to seek:

(A) enforcement of support orders or laws relating to the duty of support;

(B) establishment or modification of child support;

(C) determination of parentage; or

(D) the location of obligors or their assets.

"Support enforcement agency" does not include a domestic relations office unless that office has entered into a cooperative agreement with the Title IV–D agency to perform duties under this chapter.

(21) "Support order" means a judgment, decree, or order, whether temporary, final, or subject to modification, for the benefit of a child, a spouse, or a former spouse that provides for monetary support, health care, arrearages, or reimbursement and may include related costs and fees, interest, income withholding, attorney's fees, and other relief.

(22) "Tribunal" means a court, administrative agency, or quasi-judicial entity authorized to establish, enforce, or modify support orders or to determine parentage.

Added by Acts 1995, 74th Leg., ch. 20, § 1, eff. April 20, 1995. Amended by Acts 1997, 75th Leg., ch. 607, § 1, eff. Sept. 1, 1997.

Section 19 of Acts 1997, 75th Leg., ch. 607 provides:

"This Act takes effect September 1, 1997, and applies only to an order, decree, or judgment entered on or after that date."

§ 159.102. Tribunal of State

The court is the tribunal of this state.

Added by Acts 1995, 74th Leg., ch. 20, § 1, eff. April 20, 1995. Amended by Acts 1997, 75th Leg., ch. 607, § 2, eff. Sept. 1, 1997.

For application provisions of Acts 1997, 75th Leg., ch. 607, see note following V.T.C.A., Family Code § 159.101.

§ 159.103. Remedies Cumulative

Remedies provided in this chapter are cumulative and do not affect the availability of remedies under other law.

Added by Acts 1995, 74th Leg., ch. 20, § 1, eff. April 20, 1995.

[Sections 159.104 to 159.200 reserved for expansion]

SUBCHAPTER C. JURISDICTION

§ 159.201. Bases for Jurisdiction Over Nonresident

In a proceeding to establish, enforce, or modify a support order or to determine parentage, a tribunal of this state may exercise personal jurisdiction over a nonresident individual or the individual's guardian or conservator if:

(1) the individual is personally served with citation in this state;

(2) the individual submits to the jurisdiction of this state by consent, by entering a general appearance, or by filing a responsive document having the effect of waiving any contest to personal jurisdiction;

(3) the individual resided with the child in this state;

(4) the individual resided in this state and provided prenatal expenses or support for the child;

(5) the child resides in this state as a result of the acts or directives of the individual;

(6) the individual engaged in sexual intercourse in this state and the child may have been conceived by that act of intercourse;

(7) the individual asserted parentage in the paternity registry maintained in this state by the bureau of vital statistics; or

(8) there is any other basis consistent with the constitutions of this state and the United States for the exercise of personal jurisdiction.

Added by Acts 1995, 74th Leg., ch. 20, § 1, eff. April 20, 1995. Amended by Acts 1997, 75th Leg., ch. 561, § 5, eff. Sept. 1, 1997.

For application provisions of Acts 1997, 75th Leg., ch. 561, see notes following V.T.C.A., Family Code § 160.251.

§ 159.202. Procedure When Exercising Jurisdiction Over Nonresident

A tribunal of this state exercising personal jurisdiction over a nonresident under Section 159.201 may apply Section 159.316 to receive evidence from another state and Section 159.318 to obtain discovery through a tribunal of another state. In all other respects, Subchapters D–H[1] do not apply and the tribunal shall apply the procedural and substantive law of this state, including the rules on choice of law other than those established by this chapter.

Added by Acts 1995, 74th Leg., ch. 20, § 1, eff. April 20, 1995.

[1] V.T.C.A., Family Code § 159.301 et seq.; V.T.C.A., Family Code § 159.401 et seq.; V.T.C.A., Family Code § 159.501 et seq.; V.T.C.A., Family Code § 159.601 et seq.; and V.T.C.A., Family Code § 159.701 et seq.

§ 159.203. Initiating and Responding Tribunal of State

Under this chapter, a tribunal of this state may serve as an initiating tribunal to forward proceedings to another state and as a responding tribunal for proceedings initiated in another state.

Added by Acts 1995, 74th Leg., ch. 20, § 1, eff. April 20, 1995. Amended by Acts 1997, 75th Leg., ch. 607, § 3, eff. Sept. 1, 1997.

For application provisions of Acts 1997, 75th Leg., ch. 607, see note following V.T.C.A., Family Code § 159.101.

§ 159.204. Simultaneous Proceedings in Another State

(a) A tribunal of this state may exercise jurisdiction to establish a support order if the petition or comparable pleading is filed after a pleading is filed in another state only if:

(1) the petition or comparable pleading in this state is filed before the expiration of the time allowed in the other state for filing a responsive pleading challenging the exercise of jurisdiction by the other state;

(2) the contesting party timely challenges the exercise of jurisdiction in the other state; and

(3) if relevant, this state is the home state of the child.

(b) A tribunal of this state may not exercise jurisdiction to establish a support order if the petition or comparable pleading is filed before a petition or comparable pleading is filed in another state if:

(1) the petition or comparable pleading in the other state is filed before the expiration of the time allowed in this state for filing a responsive pleading challenging the exercise of jurisdiction by this state;

(2) the contesting party timely challenges the exercise of jurisdiction in this state; and

(3) if relevant, the other state is the home state of the child.

Added by Acts 1995, 74th Leg., ch. 20, § 1, eff. April 20, 1995.

§ 159.205. Continuing, Exclusive Jurisdiction

(a) A tribunal of this state issuing a support order consistent with the law of this state has continuing, exclusive jurisdiction over a child support order:

(1) as long as this state remains the residence of the obligor, the individual obligee, or the child for whose benefit the support order is issued; or

(2) until all of the parties who are individuals have filed written consents with the tribunal of this state for a tribunal of another state to modify the order and assume continuing, exclusive jurisdiction.

(b) A tribunal of this state issuing a child support order consistent with the law of this state may not exercise its continuing jurisdiction to modify the order if the order has been modified by a tribunal of another state under a law substantially similar to this chapter.

(c) If a child support order of this state is modified by a tribunal of another state under a law substantially similar to this chapter, a tribunal of this state loses its continuing, exclusive jurisdiction with regard to prospective enforcement of the order issued in this state and may only:

(1) enforce the order that was modified as to amounts accruing before the modification;

(2) enforce nonmodifiable aspects of that order; and

(3) provide other appropriate relief for violations of that order that occurred before the effective date of the modification.

(d) A tribunal of this state shall recognize the continuing, exclusive jurisdiction of a tribunal of another state that issued a child support order under a law substantially similar to this chapter.

(e) A temporary support order issued ex parte or pending resolution of a jurisdictional conflict does not create continuing, exclusive jurisdiction in the issuing tribunal.

(f) A tribunal of this state issuing a support order consistent with the law of this state has continuing, exclusive jurisdiction over a spousal support order throughout the existence of the support obligation. A tribunal of this state may not modify a spousal support order issued by a tribunal of another state having continuing, exclusive jurisdiction over that order under the law of that state.

Added by Acts 1995, 74th Leg., ch. 20, § 1, eff. April 20, 1995. Amended by Acts 1997, 75th Leg., ch. 607, § 4, eff. Sept. 1, 1997.

For application provisions of Acts 1997, 75th Leg., ch. 607, see note following V.T.C.A., Family Code § 159.101.

§ 159.206. Enforcement and Modification of Support Order by Tribunal Having Continuing Jurisdiction

(a) A tribunal of this state may serve as an initiating tribunal to request a tribunal of another state to enforce or modify a support order issued in that state.

(b) A tribunal of this state having continuing, exclusive jurisdiction over a support order may act as a responding tribunal to enforce or modify the order. If a party subject to the tribunal's continuing, exclusive jurisdiction no longer resides in the issuing state, in subsequent proceedings the tribunal may apply Section 159.316 to receive evidence from another state and Section 159.318 to obtain discovery through a tribunal of another state.

(c) A tribunal of this state that lacks continuing, exclusive jurisdiction over a spousal support order may not serve as a responding tribunal to modify a spousal support order of another state.

Added by Acts 1995, 74th Leg., ch. 20, § 1, eff. April 20, 1995.

§ 159.207. Recognition of Controlling Child Support Order

(a) If a proceeding is brought under this chapter and only one tribunal has issued a child support order, the order of that tribunal controls and must be so recognized.

(b) If a proceeding is brought under this chapter and two or more child support orders have been issued by tribunals of this state or another state with regard to the same obligor and child, a tribunal of this state shall apply the following rules in determining which order to recognize for purposes of continuing, exclusive jurisdiction:

(1) if only one of the tribunals would have continuing, exclusive jurisdiction under this chapter, the order of that tribunal controls and must be so recognized;

(2) if more than one of the tribunals would have continuing, exclusive jurisdiction under this chapter, an order issued by a tribunal in the current home state of the child controls and must be so recognized, but if an order has not been issued in the current home state of the child, the order most recently issued controls and must be so recognized; and

(3) if none of the tribunals would have continuing, exclusive jurisdiction under this chapter, the tribunal of this state having jurisdiction over the parties shall issue a child support order that controls and must be so recognized.

(c) If two or more child support orders have been issued for the same obligor and child and if the obligor or the individual obligee resides in this state, a party may request a tribunal of this state to determine which order controls and must be so recognized under Subsection (b). The request must be accompanied by a certified copy of every support order in effect. The requesting party shall give notice of the request to each party whose rights may be affected by the determination.

(d) The tribunal that issued the controlling order under Subsection (a), (b), or (c) is the tribunal that has continuing, exclusive jurisdiction under Section 159.205.

(e) A tribunal of this state that determines by order the identity of the controlling order under Subsection (b)(1) or (2) or that issues a new controlling order under Subsection (b)(3) shall state in that order the basis upon which the tribunal made its determination.

(f) Within 30 days after issuance of an order determining the identity of the controlling order, the party obtaining the order shall file a certified copy of it with each tribunal that issued or registered an earlier order of child support. A party who obtains the order and fails to file a certified copy is subject to appropriate sanctions by a tribunal in which the issue of failure to file arises. The failure to file does not affect the validity or enforceability of the controlling order.

Added by Acts 1995, 74th Leg., ch. 20, § 1, eff. April 20, 1995. Amended by Acts 1997, 75th Leg., ch. 607, § 5, eff. Sept. 1, 1997.

For application provisions of Acts 1997, 75th Leg., ch. 607, see note following V.T.C.A., Family Code § 159.101.

§ 159.208. Multiple Child Support Orders for Two or More Obligees

In responding to multiple registrations or petitions for enforcement of two or more child support orders in effect at the same time with regard to the same obligor and different individual obligees, at least one of which was issued by a tribunal of another state, a tribunal of this state shall enforce those orders in the same manner as if the multiple orders had been issued by a tribunal of this state.

Added by Acts 1995, 74th Leg., ch. 20, § 1, eff. April 20, 1995.

§ 159.209. Credit for Payments

Amounts collected and credited for a particular period under a support order issued by a tribunal of another state must be credited against the amounts accruing or accrued for the same period under a support order issued by the tribunal of this state.

Added by Acts 1995, 74th Leg., ch. 20, § 1, eff. April 20, 1995.

[Sections 159.210 to 159.300 reserved for expansion]

SUBCHAPTER D. CIVIL PROVISIONS OF GENERAL APPLICATION

§ 159.301. Proceedings Under Chapter

(a) Except as otherwise provided in this chapter, this subchapter applies to all proceedings under this chapter.

(b) This chapter provides for the following proceedings:

(1) establishment of an order for spousal support or child support pursuant to Section 159.401;

(2) enforcement of a support order and income-withholding order of another state without registration pursuant to Sections 159.501 through 159.507;

(3) registration of an order for spousal support or child support of another state for enforcement pursuant to Sections 159.601 through 159.608;

(4) modification of an order for child support or spousal support issued by a tribunal of this state pursuant to Sections 159.203 through 159.205;

(5) registration of an order for child support of another state for modification pursuant to Sections 159.609 through 159.614;

(6) determination of parentage pursuant to Section 159.701; and

(7) assertion of jurisdiction over nonresidents pursuant to Sections 159.201 and 159.202.

(c) An individual or a support enforcement agency may commence a proceeding authorized under this chapter by filing a petition in an initiating tribunal for forwarding to a responding tribunal or by filing a petition or a comparable pleading directly in a tribunal of another state that has or that can obtain personal jurisdiction over the respondent.

Added by Acts 1995, 74th Leg., ch. 20, § 1, eff. April 20, 1995. Amended by Acts 1997, 75th Leg., ch. 607, § 6, eff. Sept. 1, 1997.

For application provisions of Acts 1997, 75th Leg., ch. 607, see note following V.T.C.A., Family Code § 159.101.

§ 159.302. Action by Minor Parent

A minor parent or a guardian or other legal representative of a minor parent may maintain a proceeding on behalf of or for the benefit of the minor's child.

Added by Acts 1995, 74th Leg., ch. 20, § 1, eff. April 20, 1995.

§ 159.303. Application of Law of State

Except as otherwise provided in this chapter, a responding tribunal of this state shall:

(1) apply the procedural and substantive law, including the rules on choice of law, generally applicable to similar proceedings originating in this state and may exercise all powers and provide all remedies available in those proceedings; and

(2) determine the duty of support and the amount payable in accordance with the law and support guidelines of this state.

Added by Acts 1995, 74th Leg., ch. 20, § 1, eff. April 20, 1995. Amended by Acts 1997, 75th Leg., ch. 607, § 7, eff. Sept. 1, 1997.

For application provisions of Acts 1997, 75th Leg., ch. 607, see note following V.T.C.A., Family Code § 159.101.

§ 159.304. Duties of Initiating Tribunal

(a) On the filing of a petition authorized by this chapter, an initiating tribunal of this state shall forward three copies of the petition and its accompanying documents:

(1) to the responding tribunal or appropriate support enforcement agency in the responding state; or

(2) if the identity of the responding tribunal is unknown, to the state information agency of the responding state with a request that they be forwarded to the appropriate tribunal and that receipt be acknowledged.

(b) If a responding state has not enacted the Uniform Interstate Family Support Act or a law or procedure substantially similar to that Act, a tribunal of this state may issue a certificate or other document and make findings required by the law of the responding state. If the responding state is a foreign jurisdiction, the tribunal may specify the amount of support sought and provide other documents necessary to satisfy the requirements of the responding state.

Added by Acts 1995, 74th Leg., ch. 20, § 1, eff. April 20, 1995. Amended by Acts 1997, 75th Leg., ch. 607, § 8, eff. Sept. 1, 1997.

For application provisions of Acts 1997, 75th Leg., ch. 607, see note following V.T.C.A., Family Code § 159.101.

§ 159.305. Duties and Powers of Responding Tribunal

(a) When a responding tribunal of this state receives a petition or comparable pleading from an initiating tribunal or directly under Section 159.301(c), the responding tribunal shall cause the petition or pleading to be filed and notify the petitioner where and when it was filed.

(b) A responding tribunal of this state, to the extent otherwise authorized by law, may do one or more of the following:

(1) issue or enforce a support order, modify a child support order, or render a judgment to determine parentage;

(2) order an obligor to comply with a support order and specify the amount and the manner of compliance;

(3) order income withholding;

(4) determine the amount of any arrearages and specify a method of payment;

(5) enforce orders by civil or criminal contempt, or both;

(6) set aside property for satisfaction of the support order;

(7) place liens and order execution on the obligor's property;

(8) order an obligor to keep the tribunal informed of the obligor's current residential address, telephone number, employer, address of employment, and telephone number at the place of employment;

(9) issue a bench warrant or capias for an obligor who has failed after proper notice to appear at a hearing ordered by the tribunal and enter the bench warrant or capias in any local and state computer systems for criminal warrants;

(10) order the obligor to seek appropriate employment by specified methods;

(11) award reasonable attorney's fees and other fees and costs; and

(12) grant any other available remedy.

(c) A responding tribunal of this state shall include in a support order issued under this chapter, or in the documents accompanying the order, the calculations on which the support order is based.

(d) A responding tribunal of this state may not condition the payment of a support order issued under this chapter on compliance by a party with provisions for visitation.

(e) If a responding tribunal of this state issues an order under this chapter, the tribunal shall send a copy of the order to the petitioner and the respondent and to the initiating tribunal, if any.

Added by Acts 1995, 74th Leg., ch. 20, § 1, eff. April 20, 1995. Amended by Acts 1997, 75th Leg., ch. 607, § 9, eff. Sept. 1, 1997.

For application provisions of Acts 1997, 75th Leg., ch. 607, see note following V.T.C.A., Family Code § 159.101.

§ 159.306. Inappropriate Tribunal

If a petition or comparable pleading is received by an inappropriate tribunal of this state, that tribunal shall forward the pleading and accompanying documents to an appropriate tribunal in this state or another state and notify the petitioner where and when the pleading was sent.

Added by Acts 1995, 74th Leg., ch. 20, § 1, eff. April 20, 1995. Amended by Acts 1997, 75th Leg., ch. 607, § 10, eff. Sept. 1, 1997.

For application provisions of Acts 1997, 75th Leg., ch. 607, see note following V.T.C.A., Family Code § 159.101.

§ 159.307. Duties of Support Enforcement Agency

(a) A support enforcement agency of this state, on request, shall provide services to a petitioner in a proceeding under this chapter.

(b) A support enforcement agency that provides services to the petitioner as appropriate shall:

(1) take all steps necessary to enable an appropriate tribunal in this state or another state to obtain jurisdiction over the respondent;

(2) request an appropriate tribunal to set a date, time, and place for a hearing;

(3) make a reasonable effort to obtain all relevant information, including information as to income and property of the parties;

(4) not later than the second day, excluding Saturdays, Sundays, and legal holidays, after the date of receipt of a written notice from an initiating, responding, or registering tribunal, send a copy of the notice to the petitioner;

(5) not later than the second day, excluding Saturdays, Sundays, and legal holidays, after the date of receipt of a written communication from the respondent or the respondent's attorney, send a copy of the communication to the petitioner; and

(6) notify the petitioner if jurisdiction over the respondent cannot be obtained.

(c) This chapter does not create or negate a relationship of attorney and client or other fiduciary relationship between a support enforcement agency or the attorney for the agency and the individual being assisted by the agency.

Added by Acts 1995, 74th Leg., ch. 20, § 1, eff. April 20, 1995. Amended by Acts 1997, 75th Leg., ch. 607, § 11, eff. Sept. 1, 1997.

For application provisions of Acts 1997, 75th Leg., ch. 607, see note following V.T.C.A., Family Code § 159.101.

§ 159.308. Duty of Attorney General

If the attorney general determines that the support enforcement agency is neglecting or refusing to provide services to an individual, the attorney general may order the agency to perform its duties under this chapter or may provide those services directly to the individual.

Added by Acts 1995, 74th Leg., ch. 20, § 1, eff. April 20, 1995.

§ 159.309. Private Counsel

An individual may employ private counsel to represent the individual in proceedings authorized by this chapter.

Added by Acts 1995, 74th Leg., ch. 20, § 1, eff. April 20, 1995.

§ 159.310. Duties of State Information Agency

(a) The Title IV–D agency is the state information agency under this chapter.

(b) The state information agency shall:

(1) compile and maintain a current list, including addresses, of the tribunals in this state that have jurisdiction under this chapter and any support enforcement agencies in this state and send a copy to the state information agency of every other state;

(2) maintain a register of tribunals and support enforcement agencies received from other states;

(3) forward to the appropriate tribunal in the place in this state where the individual obligee or the obligor resides, or where the obligor's property is believed to be located, all documents concerning a proceeding under this chapter received from an initiating tribunal or the state information agency of the initiating state; and

(4) obtain information concerning the location of the obligor and the obligor's property in this state not exempt from execution, by such means as postal verification and federal or state locator services, examination of telephone directories, requests for the obligor's address from employers, and examination of governmental records, including, to the extent not prohibited by other law, those relating to real property, vital statistics, law enforcement, taxation, motor vehicles, driver's licenses, and social security.

Added by Acts 1995, 74th Leg., ch. 20, § 1, eff. April 20, 1995.

§ 159.311. Pleadings and Accompanying Documents

(a) A petitioner seeking to establish or modify a support order or to determine parentage in a proceeding under this chapter must verify the petition. Unless otherwise ordered under Section 159.312, the petition or accompanying documents must provide, so far as known, the name, residential address, and social security numbers of the obligor and the obligee and the name, sex, residential address, social security number, and date of birth of each child for whom support is sought. The petition must be accompanied by a certified copy of any support order in effect. The petition may include any other information that may assist in locating or identifying the respondent.

(b) The petition must specify the relief sought. The petition and accompanying documents must conform substantially with the requirements imposed by the forms mandated by federal law for use in cases filed by a support enforcement agency.

Added by Acts 1995, 74th Leg., ch. 20, § 1, eff. April 20, 1995.

§ 159.312. Nondisclosure of Information in Exceptional Circumstances

On a finding, which may be made ex parte, that the health, safety, or liberty of a party or child would be unreasonably put at risk by the disclosure of identifying information or if an existing order so provides, a tribunal shall order that the address of the child or party or other identifying information not be disclosed in a pleading or other document filed in a proceeding under this chapter.

Added by Acts 1995, 74th Leg., ch. 20, § 1, eff. April 20, 1995.

§ 159.313. Costs and Fees

(a) The petitioner may not be required to pay a filing fee or other costs.

(b) If an obligee prevails, a responding tribunal may assess against an obligor filing fees, reasonable attorney's fees, other costs, and necessary travel and other reasonable expenses incurred by the obligee and the obligee's witnesses. The tribunal may not assess fees, costs, or expenses against the obligee or the support enforcement agency of either the initiating state or the responding state, except as provided by other law. Attorney's fees may be taxed as costs and may be ordered paid directly to the attorney, who may enforce the order in the attorney's own name. Payment of support owed to the obligee has priority over fees, costs, and expenses.

(c) The tribunal shall order the payment of costs and reasonable attorney's fees if it determines that a hearing was requested primarily for delay. In a proceeding pursuant to Sections 159.601 through 159.608, a hearing is presumed to have been requested primarily for delay if a registered support order is confirmed or enforced without change.

Added by Acts 1995, 74th Leg., ch. 20, § 1, eff. April 20, 1995. Amended by Acts 1997, 75th Leg., ch. 607, § 12, eff. Sept. 1, 1997.

For application provisions of Acts 1997, 75th Leg., ch. 607, see note following V.T.C.A., Family Code § 159.101.

§ 159.314. Limited Immunity of Petitioner

(a) Participation by a petitioner in a proceeding before a responding tribunal, whether in person, by private attorney, or through services provided by the support enforcement agency, does not confer personal jurisdiction over the petitioner in another proceeding.

(b) A petitioner is not amenable to service of civil process while physically present in this state to participate in a proceeding under this chapter.

(c) The immunity granted by this section does not extend to civil litigation based on acts unrelated to a proceeding under this chapter committed by a party while present in this state to participate in the proceeding.

Added by Acts 1995, 74th Leg., ch. 20, § 1, eff. April 20, 1995.

§ 159.315. Nonparentage as Defense

A party whose parentage of a child has been previously determined by or under law may not plead nonparentage as a defense to a proceeding under this chapter.

Added by Acts 1995, 74th Leg., ch. 20, § 1, eff. April 20, 1995.

§ 159.316. Special Rules of Evidence and Procedure

(a) The physical presence of the petitioner in a responding tribunal of this state is not required for the establishment, enforcement, or modification of a support order or the rendition of a judgment determining parentage.

(b) A verified petition, affidavit, document substantially complying with federally mandated forms, and a document incorporated by reference in the petition, affidavit, or document, not excluded under the hearsay rule if given in person, are admissible in evidence if given under oath by a party or witness residing in another state.

(c) A copy of the record of child support payments certified as a true copy of the original by the custodian of the record may be forwarded to a responding tribunal. The copy is evidence of facts asserted in it and is admissible to show whether payments were made.

(d) Copies of bills for testing for parentage and for prenatal and postnatal health care of the mother and child that are furnished to the adverse party not less than 10 days before the date of trial are admissible in evidence to prove the amount of the charges billed and that the charges were reasonable, necessary, and customary.

(e) Documentary evidence sent from another state to a tribunal of this state by telephone, telecopier, or another means that does not provide an original writing may not be excluded from evidence on an objection based on the means of transmission.

(f) In a proceeding under this chapter, a tribunal of this state may permit a party or witness residing in another state to be deposed or to testify by telephone, audiovisual means, or other electronic means at a designated tribunal or other location in that state. A tribunal of this state shall cooperate with a tribunal of another state in designating an appropriate location for the deposition or testimony.

(g) If a party called to testify at a civil hearing refuses to answer on the ground that the testimony may be self-incriminating, the trier of fact may draw an adverse inference from the refusal.

(h) A privilege against disclosure of communications between spouses does not apply in a proceeding under this chapter.

(i) The defense of immunity based on the relationship of husband and wife or parent and child does not apply in a proceeding under this chapter.

Added by Acts 1995, 74th Leg., ch. 20, § 1, eff. April 20, 1995.

§ 159.317. Communications Between Tribunals

A tribunal of this state may communicate with a tribunal of another state in writing, by telephone, or by another means, to obtain information concerning the laws of that state, the legal effect of a judgment, decree, or order of that tribunal, and the status of a proceeding in the other state. A tribunal of this state may furnish similar information by similar means to a tribunal of another state.

Added by Acts 1995, 74th Leg., ch. 20, § 1, eff. April 20, 1995.

§ 159.318. Assistance With Discovery

A tribunal of this state may:

(1) request a tribunal of another state to assist in obtaining discovery; and

(2) on request, compel a person over whom the tribunal has jurisdiction to respond to a discovery order issued by a tribunal of another state.

Added by Acts 1995, 74th Leg., ch. 20, § 1, eff. April 20, 1995.

§ 159.319. Receipt and Disbursement of Payments

A support enforcement agency or tribunal of this state shall disburse promptly any amounts received under a support order, as directed by the order. The agency or tribunal shall furnish to a requesting party or tribunal of another state a certified statement by the custodian of the record of the amounts and dates of all payments received.

Added by Acts 1995, 74th Leg., ch. 20, § 1, eff. April 20, 1995.

[Sections 159.320 to 159.400 reserved for expansion]

SUBCHAPTER E. ESTABLISHMENT OF SUPPORT ORDER

§ 159.401. Petition to Establish Support Order

(a) If a support order entitled to recognition under this chapter has not been issued, a responding tribunal of this state may issue a support order if:

(1) the individual seeking the order resides in another state; or

(2) the support enforcement agency seeking the order is located in another state.

(b) The tribunal may issue a temporary child support order if:

(1) the respondent has signed a verified statement acknowledging parentage;

(2) the respondent has been determined by or under law to be the parent; or

(3) there is other clear and convincing evidence that the respondent is the child's parent.

(c) On finding, after notice and an opportunity to be heard, that an obligor owes a duty of support, the tribunal shall issue a support order directed to the obligor and may issue other orders under Section 159.305.

Added by Acts 1995, 74th Leg., ch. 20, § 1, eff. April 20, 1995.

[Sections 159.402 to 159.500 reserved for expansion]

SUBCHAPTER F. ENFORCEMENT OF ORDER OF ANOTHER STATE WITHOUT REGISTRATION

Acts 1997, 75th Leg., ch. 607, § 13 amended Subchapter F.

§ 159.501. Employer's Receipt of Income-Withholding Order of Another State

An income-withholding order issued in another state may be sent to the obligor's employer under Chapter 158 without first filing a petition or comparable pleading or registering the order with a tribunal of this state.

Amended by Acts 1997, 75th Leg., ch. 607, § 13, eff. Sept. 1, 1997.

For application provisions of Acts 1997, 75th Leg., ch. 607, see note following V.T.C.A., Family Code § 159.101.

§ 159.502. Employer's Compliance With Income-Withholding Order of Another State

(a) On receipt of an income-withholding order, the obligor's employer shall immediately provide a copy of the order to the obligor.

(b) The employer shall treat an income-withholding order issued in another state that appears regular on its face as if the order had been issued by a tribunal of this state.

(c) Except as otherwise provided in Subsection (d) and Section 159.503, the employer shall withhold and distribute the funds as directed in the withholding order by complying with terms of the order that specify:

(1) the duration and amount of periodic payments of current child support, stated as a sum certain;

(2) the person or agency designated to receive payments and the address to which the payments are to be forwarded;

(3) medical support, whether in the form of periodic cash payments, stated as a sum certain, or ordering the obligor to provide health insurance coverage for the child under a policy available through the obligor's employment;

(4) the amount of periodic payments of fees and costs for a support enforcement agency, the issuing tribunal, and the obligee's attorney, stated as sums certain; and

(5) the amount of periodic payments of arrearages and interest on arrearages, stated as sums certain.

(d) An employer shall comply with the law of the state of the obligor's principal place of employment for withholding from income with respect to:

(1) the employer's fee for processing an income-withholding order;

(2) the maximum amount permitted to be withheld from the obligor's income; and

(3) the times within which the employer must implement the withholding order and forward the child support payment.

Amended by Acts 1997, 75th Leg., ch. 607, § 13, eff. Sept. 1, 1997.

For application provisions of Acts 1997, 75th Leg., ch. 607, see note following V.T.C.A., Family Code § 159.101.

§ 159.503. Compliance With Multiple Income-Withholding Orders

If an obligor's employer receives multiple income-withholding orders with respect to the earnings of the same obligor, the employer satisfies the terms of the multiple orders if the employer complies with the law of the state of the obligor's principal place of employment to establish the priorities for withholding and allocating income withheld for multiple child support obligees.

Added by Acts 1997, 75th Leg., ch. 607, § 13, eff. Sept. 1, 1997.

For application provisions of Acts 1997, 75th Leg., ch. 607, see note following V.T.C.A., Family Code § 159.101.

§ 159.504. Immunity From Civil Liability

An employer who complies with an income-withholding order issued in another state in accordance with this subchapter is not subject to civil liability to an individual or agency with regard to the employer's withholding of child support from the obligor's income.

Added by Acts 1997, 75th Leg., ch. 607, § 13, eff. Sept. 1, 1997.

For application provisions of Acts 1997, 75th Leg., ch. 607, see note following V.T.C.A., Family Code § 159.101.

§ 159.505. Penalties for Noncompliance

An employer who wilfully fails to comply with an income-withholding order issued by another state and received for enforcement is subject to the same penalties that may be imposed for noncompliance with an order issued by a tribunal of this state.

Added by Acts 1997, 75th Leg., ch. 607, § 13, eff. Sept. 1, 1997.

For application provisions of Acts 1997, 75th Leg., ch. 607, see note following V.T.C.A., Family Code § 159.101.

§ 159.506. Contest by Obligor

(a) An obligor may contest the validity or enforcement of an income-withholding order issued in another state and received directly by an employer in this state in the same manner as if the order had been issued by a tribunal of this state. Section 159.604 applies to the contest.

(b) The obligor shall give notice of the contest to:

(1) a support enforcement agency providing services to the obligee;

(2) each employer that has directly received an income-withholding order; and

(3) the person or agency designated to receive payments in the income-withholding order or to the obligee, if no person or agency is designated.

Added by Acts 1997, 75th Leg., ch. 607, § 13, eff. Sept. 1, 1997.

For application provisions of Acts 1997, 75th Leg., ch. 607, see note following V.T.C.A., Family Code § 159.101.

§ 159.507. Administrative Enforcement of Orders

(a) A party seeking to enforce a support order or an income-withholding order, or both, issued by a tribunal of another state may send the documents required for registering the order to a support enforcement agency of this state.

(b) On receipt of the documents, the support enforcement agency, without initially seeking to register the order, shall consider and, if appropriate, use any administrative procedure authorized by the law of this state to enforce a support order or an income-withholding order, or both. If the obligor does not contest administrative enforcement, the order need not be registered. If the obligor contests the validity or administrative enforcement of the order, the support enforcement agency shall register the order under this chapter.

Added by Acts 1997, 75th Leg., ch. 607, § 13, eff. Sept. 1, 1997.

For application provisions of Acts 1997, 75th Leg., ch. 607, see note following V.T.C.A., Family Code § 159.101.

[Sections 159.503 to 159.600 reserved for expansion]

SUBCHAPTER G. ENFORCEMENT AND MODIFICATION OF SUPPORT ORDER AFTER REGISTRATION

§ 159.601. Registration of Order for Enforcement

A support order or income-withholding order issued by a tribunal of another state may be registered in this state for enforcement.

Added by Acts 1995, 74th Leg., ch. 20, § 1, eff. April 20, 1995.

§ 159.602. Procedure to Register Order for Enforcement

(a) A support order or income-withholding order of another state may be registered in this state by sending to the appropriate tribunal in this state:

(1) a letter of transmittal to the tribunal requesting registration and enforcement;

(2) two copies, including one certified copy, of all orders to be registered, including any modification of an order;

(3) a sworn statement by the party seeking registration or a certified statement by the custodian of the records showing the amount of any arrearage;

(4) the name of the obligor and, if known:

(A) the obligor's address and social security number;

(B) the name and address of the obligor's employer and any other source of income of the obligor; and

(C) a description of and the location of property of the obligor in this state not exempt from execution; and

(5) the name and address of the obligee and, if applicable, the agency or person to whom support payments are to be remitted.

(b) On receipt of a request for registration, the registering tribunal shall cause the order to be filed as a foreign judgment, together with one copy of the documents and information, regardless of their form.

(c) A petition or comparable pleading seeking a remedy that must be affirmatively sought under other law of this state may be filed at the same time as the request for registration or later. The pleading must specify the grounds for the remedy sought.

Added by Acts 1995, 74th Leg., ch. 20, § 1, eff. April 20, 1995.

§ 159.603. Effect of Registration for Enforcement

(a) A support order or income-withholding order issued in another state is registered when the order is filed in the registering tribunal of this state.

(b) A registered order issued in another state is enforceable in the same manner and is subject to the same procedures as an order issued by a tribunal of this state.

(c) Except as otherwise provided in this subchapter, a tribunal of this state shall recognize and enforce, but may not modify, a registered order if the issuing tribunal had jurisdiction.

Added by Acts 1995, 74th Leg., ch. 20, § 1, eff. April 20, 1995.

§ 159.604. Choice of Law

(a) The law of the issuing state governs the nature, extent, amount, and duration of current payments and other obligations of support and the payment of arrearages under the order.

(b) In a proceeding for arrearages, the statute of limitation under the laws of this state or of the issuing state, whichever statute of limitation is longer, applies.

Added by Acts 1995, 74th Leg., ch. 20, § 1, eff. April 20, 1995. Amended by Acts 1997, 75th Leg., ch. 607, § 14, eff. Sept. 1, 1997.

For application provisions of Acts 1997, 75th Leg., ch. 607, see note following V.T.C.A., Family Code § 159.101.

§ 159.605. Notice of Registration of Order

(a) When a support order or income-withholding order issued in another state is registered, the registering tribunal shall notify the nonregistering party. The notice must be accompanied by a copy of the registered order and the documents and relevant information accompanying the order.

(b) The notice must inform the nonregistering party:

(1) that a registered order is enforceable as of the date of registration in the same manner as an order issued by a tribunal of this state;

(2) that a hearing to contest the validity or enforcement of the registered order must be requested within 20 days after notice;

(3) that failure to contest the validity or enforcement of the registered order in a timely manner:

(A) will result in confirmation of the order and enforcement of the order and the alleged arrearages; and

(B) precludes further contest of that order with respect to any matter that could have been asserted; and

(4) of the amount of any alleged arrearages.

(c) On registration of an income-withholding order for enforcement, the registering tribunal shall notify the obligor's employer under Chapter 158.

Added by Acts 1995, 74th Leg., ch. 20, § 1, eff. April 20, 1995. Amended by Acts 1997, 75th Leg., ch. 607, § 15, eff. Sept. 1, 1997.

For application provisions of Acts 1997, 75th Leg., ch. 607, see note following V.T.C.A., Family Code § 159.101.

§ 159.606. Procedure to Contest Validity or Enforcement of Registered Order

(a) A nonregistering party seeking to contest the validity or enforcement of a registered order in this state shall request a hearing within 20 days after notice of the registration. The nonregistering party may seek under Section 159.607 to:

(1) vacate the registration;

(2) assert any defense to an allegation of noncompliance with the registered order; or

(3) contest the remedies being sought or the amount of any alleged arrearages.

(b) If the nonregistering party fails to contest the validity or enforcement of the registered order in a timely manner, the order is confirmed by operation of law.

(c) If a nonregistering party requests a hearing to contest the validity or enforcement of the registered order, the registering tribunal shall schedule the matter for hearing and give notice to the parties of the date, time, and place of the hearing.

Added by Acts 1995, 74th Leg., ch. 20, § 1, eff. April 20, 1995. Amended by Acts 1997, 75th Leg., ch. 607, § 16, eff. Sept. 1, 1997.

For application provisions of Acts 1997, 75th Leg., ch. 607, see note following V.T.C.A., Family Code § 159.101.

§ 159.607. Contest of Registration or Enforcement

(a) A party contesting the validity or enforcement of a registered order or seeking to vacate the registration has the burden of proving one or more of the following defenses:

(1) the issuing tribunal lacked personal jurisdiction over the contesting party;

(2) the order was obtained by fraud;

(3) the order has been vacated, suspended, or modified by a later order;

(4) the issuing tribunal has stayed the order pending appeal;

(5) there is a defense under the law of this state to the remedy sought;

(6) full or partial payment has been made; or

(7) the statute of limitation under Section 159.604 precludes enforcement of some or all of the arrearages.

(b) If a party presents evidence establishing a full or partial defense under Subsection (a), a tribunal may stay enforcement of the registered order, continue the proceeding to permit production of additional relevant evidence, and issue other appropriate orders. An uncontested portion of the registered order may be enforced by all remedies available under the law of this state.

(c) If the contesting party does not establish a defense under Subsection (a) to the validity or enforcement of the order, the registering tribunal shall issue an order confirming the order.

Added by Acts 1995, 74th Leg., ch. 20, § 1, eff. April 20, 1995.

§ 159.608. Confirmed Order

Confirmation of a registered order, whether by operation of law or after notice and hearing, precludes further contest of the order with respect to any matter that could have been asserted at the time of registration.

Added by Acts 1995, 74th Leg., ch. 20, § 1, eff. April 20, 1995.

§ 159.609. Procedure to Register Child Support Order of Another State for Modification

A party or support enforcement agency seeking to modify or to modify and enforce a child support order issued in another state shall register that order in this state in the same manner provided in Sections 159.601–159.604 if the order has not been registered. A petition for modification may be filed at the same time as a request for registration or later. The pleading must specify the grounds for modification.

Added by Acts 1995, 74th Leg., ch. 20, § 1, eff. April 20, 1995.

§ 159.610. Effect of Registration for Modification

A tribunal of this state may enforce a child support order of another state registered for purposes of modification in the same manner as if the order had been issued by a tribunal of this state, but the registered order may be modified only if the requirements of Section 159.611 have been met.

Added by Acts 1995, 74th Leg., ch. 20, § 1, eff. April 20, 1995.

§ 159.611. Modification of Child Support Order of Another State

(a) After a child support order issued in another state has been registered in this state, the responding tribunal of this state may modify the order only if Section 159.613 does not apply and after notice and hearing the tribunal finds that:

(1) the following requirements are met:

(A) the child, the individual obligee, and the obligor do not reside in the issuing state;

(B) a petitioner who is a nonresident of this state seeks modification; and

(C) the respondent is subject to the personal jurisdiction of the tribunal of this state; or

(2) the child, or a party who is an individual, is subject to the personal jurisdiction of the tribunal of this state and all of the parties who are individuals have filed in the issuing tribunal written consents for a tribunal of this state to modify the support

order and assume continuing, exclusive jurisdiction over the order; however, for the purposes of this subdivision, if the issuing state is a foreign jurisdiction that has not enacted a law or established procedures substantially similar to the procedures under this chapter, the consent otherwise required of an individual residing in this state is not required for the tribunal to assume jurisdiction to modify the child support order.

(b) Modification of a registered child support order is subject to the same requirements, procedures, and defenses that apply to the modification of an order issued by a tribunal of this state, and the order may be enforced and satisfied in the same manner.

(c) A tribunal of this state may not modify any aspect of a child support order that may not be modified under the law of the issuing state. If two or more tribunals have issued child support orders for the same obligor and child, the order that controls and must be so recognized under Section 159.207 establishes the aspects of the support order that are nonmodifiable.

(d) On issuance of an order modifying a child support order issued in another state, a tribunal of this state becomes the tribunal of continuing, exclusive jurisdiction.

(e) Not later than the 30th day after the date a modified child support order is issued, the party obtaining the modification shall file a certified copy of the order:

(1) with the issuing tribunal that had continuing, exclusive jurisdiction over the earlier order; and

(2) in each tribunal in which the party knows that the earlier order has been registered.

Added by Acts 1995, 74th Leg., ch. 20, § 1, eff. April 20, 1995. Amended by Acts 1997, 75th Leg., ch. 607, § 17, eff. Sept. 1, 1997.

For application provisions of Acts 1997, 75th Leg., ch. 607, see note following V.T.C.A., Family Code § 159.101.

§ 159.612. Recognition of Order Modified in Another State

A tribunal of this state shall recognize a modification of its earlier child support order by a tribunal of another state that assumed jurisdiction under a law substantially similar to this chapter and, except as otherwise provided in this chapter, shall on request:

(1) enforce the order that was modified only as to amounts accruing before the modification;

(2) enforce only nonmodifiable aspects of the order;

(3) provide other appropriate relief only for a violation of the order that occurred before the effective date of the modification; and

(4) recognize the modifying order of the other state, on registration, for the purpose of enforcement.

Added by Acts 1995, 74th Leg., ch. 20, § 1, eff. April 20, 1995.

§ 159.613. Jurisdiction to Modify Child Support Order of Another State When Individual Parties Reside in This State

(a) If all of the parties who are individuals reside in this state and the child does not reside in the issuing state, a tribunal of this state has jurisdiction to enforce and to modify the issuing state's child support order in a proceeding to register that order.

(b) A tribunal of this state exercising jurisdiction under this section shall apply the provisions of Sections 159.101 through 159.209 and 159.601 through 159.614 and the procedural and substantive law of this state to the proceeding for enforcement or modification. Sections 159.301 through 159.507 and 159.701 through 159.802 do not apply.

Added by Acts 1997, 75th Leg., ch. 607, § 18, eff. Sept. 1, 1997.

For application provisions of Acts 1997, 75th Leg., ch. 607, see notes following V.T.C.A., Family Code § 159.101.

§ 159.614. Notice to Issuing Tribunal of Modification

Within 30 days after issuance of a modified child support order, the party obtaining the modification shall file a certified copy of the order with the issuing tribunal that had continuing, exclusive jurisdiction over the earlier order and in each tribunal in which the party knows the earlier order has been registered. A party who obtains the order and fails to file a certified copy is subject to appropriate sanctions by a tribunal in which the issue of failure to file arises. The failure to file does not affect the validity or enforceability of the modified order of the new tribunal having continuing, exclusive jurisdiction.

Added by Acts 1997, 75th Leg., ch. 607, § 18, eff. Sept. 1, 1997.

For application provisions of Acts 1997, 75th Leg., ch. 607, see notes following V.T.C.A., Family Code § 159.101.

[Sections 159.613 to 159.700 reserved for expansion]

SUBCHAPTER H. DETERMINATION OF PARENTAGE

§ 159.701. Proceeding to Determine Parentage

(a) A tribunal of this state may serve as an initiating or responding tribunal in a proceeding brought under this chapter or a law substantially similar to this chapter, the Uniform Reciprocal Enforcement of Support Act, or the Revised Uniform Reciprocal Enforcement of Support Act to determine that the petitioner is a parent of a particular child or to determine that a respondent is a parent of that child.

(b) In a proceeding to determine parentage, a responding tribunal of this state shall apply the procedural and substantive law of this state and the rules of this state on choice of law.

Added by Acts 1995, 74th Leg., ch. 20, § 1, eff. April 20, 1995.

[Sections 159.702 to 159.800 reserved for expansion]

SUBCHAPTER I. INTERSTATE RENDITION

§ 159.801. Grounds for Rendition

(a) In this subchapter, "governor" includes an individual performing the functions of governor or the executive authority of a state covered by this chapter.

(b) The governor of this state may:

(1) demand that the governor of another state surrender an individual found in the other state who is charged criminally in this state with having failed to provide for the support of an obligee; or

(2) on the demand by the governor of another state, surrender an individual found in this state who is charged criminally in the other state with having failed to provide for the support of an obligee.

(c) A provision for extradition of individuals not inconsistent with this chapter applies to the demand even if the individual whose surrender is demanded was not in the demanding state when the crime was allegedly committed and has not fled from that state.

Added by Acts 1995, 74th Leg., ch. 20, § 1, eff. April 20, 1995.

§ 159.802. Conditions of Rendition

(a) Before making a demand that the governor of another state surrender an individual charged criminally in this state with having failed to provide for the support of an obligee, the governor may require a prosecutor of this state to demonstrate:

(1) that not less than 60 days before the date of the demand, the obligee had initiated proceedings for support under this chapter; or

(2) that initiating the proceeding would be of no avail.

(b) If, under this chapter or a law substantially similar to this chapter, the Uniform Reciprocal Enforcement of Support Act, or the Revised Uniform Reciprocal Enforcement of Support Act, the governor of another state makes a demand that the governor of this state surrender an individual charged criminally in that state with having failed to provide for the support of a child or other individual to whom a duty of support is owed, the governor may require a prosecutor to investigate the demand and report whether a proceeding for support has been initiated or would be effective. If it appears that a proceeding would be effective but has not been initiated, the governor may delay honoring the demand for a reasonable time to permit the initiation of a proceeding.

(c) If a proceeding for support has been initiated and the individual whose rendition is demanded prevails, the governor may decline to honor the demand. If the petitioner prevails and the individual whose rendition is demanded is subject to a support order, the governor may decline to honor the demand if the individual is complying with the support order.

Added by Acts 1995, 74th Leg., ch. 20, § 1, eff. April 20, 1995.

[Sections 159.803 to 159.900 reserved for expansion]

SUBCHAPTER J. MISCELLANEOUS PROVISIONS

§ 159.901. Uniformity of Application and Construction

This chapter shall be applied and construed to effectuate its general purpose to make uniform the law with respect to the subject of this chapter among states enacting it.

Added by Acts 1995, 74th Leg., ch. 20, § 1, eff. April 20, 1995.

§ 159.902. Short Title

This chapter may be cited as the Uniform Interstate Family Support Act.

Added by Acts 1995, 74th Leg., ch. 20, § 1, eff. April 20, 1995.

CHAPTER 160. DETERMINATION OF PARENTAGE

SUBCHAPTER A. GENERAL PROVISIONS

Section

SUBCHAPTER A. GENERAL PROVISIONS

§ 160.001. Applicability

This chapter governs a suit affecting the parent-child relationship in which the parentage of the biological mother or biological father is sought to be adjudicated.

Added by Acts 1995, 74th Leg., ch. 20, § 1, eff. April 20, 1995.

§ 160.002. Time in Which to Bring Suit to Determine Parentage

(a) A suit affecting the parent-child relationship to determine parentage under Subchapter B [1] may be brought before the birth of the child, but must be brought on or before the second anniversary of the date the child becomes an adult, or the suit is barred.

(b) This section applies to a child for whom a parentage suit was brought but dismissed because a statute of limitations of less than 18 years was then in effect.

(c) A suit to establish paternity under Subchapter C [2] may be brought at any time.

Added by Acts 1995, 74th Leg., ch. 20, § 1, eff. April 20, 1995.

[1] V.T.C.A., Family Code § 160.101 et seq.
[2] V.T.C.A., Family Code § 160.201 et seq.

§ 160.003. Necessary Party: Representation of Child

(a) The child is not a necessary party to a suit under this chapter.

(b) It is rebuttably presumed in a trial on the merits before a judge or jury that the interests of the child will be adequately represented by the party bringing suit to determine parentage of the child. If the court finds that the interests of the child will not be adequately represented by a party to the suit or are adverse to that party, the court shall appoint an attorney ad litem to represent the child.

(c) The child shall be represented in a settlement agreement, dismissal, or nonsuit by a guardian ad litem or an attorney ad litem appointed by the court, unless the court finds on the record that the interests of the child will be adequately represented by a party to the suit or are not adverse to that party, and that the court approves the settlement agreement, dismissal, or nonsuit.

Added by Acts 1995, 74th Leg., ch. 20, § 1, eff. April 20, 1995.

§ 160.004. Temporary Orders

The court may render a temporary order authorized in a suit under this title, including an order for temporary support of a child, if the person ordered to pay support:

(1) is a presumed parent under Chapter 151;

(2) is an alleged father petitioning to have his paternity adjudicated or who admits paternity in pleadings filed with the court; or

(3) is found by the court at the pretrial conference authorized by this chapter not to be excluded as the biological father of the child, with the court finding that at least 99 percent of the male population is excluded from being the biological father of the child.

Added by Acts 1995, 74th Leg., ch. 20, § 1, eff. April 20, 1995.

§ 160.005. Conservatorship, Support, and Payments

(a) In a suit in which a determination of parentage is sought, the court may provide for the managing and possessory conservatorship and support of and access to the child.

(b) On a finding of parentage, the court may order support retroactive to the time of the birth of the child and, on a proper showing, may order a party to pay an equitable portion of all prenatal and postnatal health care expenses of the mother and child.

(c) In making an order for retroactive child support under this section, the court shall use the child support guidelines provided by Chapter 154 together with any relevant factors.

Added by Acts 1995, 74th Leg., ch. 20, § 1, eff. April 20, 1995.

§ 160.006. Final Order Regarding Parentage

(a) On a verdict of the jury, or on a finding of the court if there is no jury, the court shall render a final order declaring whether an alleged parent is the biological parent of the child.

(b) The effect of an order declaring that an alleged parent is the biological parent of the child is to confirm or create the parent-child relationship between the parent and the child for all purposes.

(c) If parentage is established, the order shall state the name of the child.

Added by Acts 1995, 74th Leg., ch. 20, § 1, eff. April 20, 1995.

§ 160.007. Suit Barred

(a) Except as provided by Subsection (b), a suit under this chapter with respect to a child is barred if final judgment has been rendered by a court of competent jurisdiction:

(1) adjudicating a named individual to be the biological father of the child; or

(2) terminating the parent-child relationship between the child and each living parent of the child; or

(3) granting a petition for the adoption of the child.

(b) During the pendency of an appeal or direct attack on a judgment described by Subsection (a), a suit under this chapter may be filed but shall, on motion of a party, be stayed pending the final disposition of the appeal or direct attack on the judgment.

Added by Acts 1995, 74th Leg., ch. 20, § 1, eff. April 20, 1995.

[Sections 160.008 to 160.100 reserved for expansion]

SUBCHAPTER B. PARENTAGE SUIT

§ 160.101. Denial of Paternity

(a) The presumption that a man is the biological father of a child under Chapter 151 may be contested by:

(1) the biological mother of the child;

(2) a person related within the second degree of consanguinity to the biological mother of the child, if the biological mother of the child is deceased;

(3) a man presumed to be the father of the child, who may contest his own or another man's presumed paternity;

(4) a man alleging himself to be the biological father of the child; or

(5) a governmental entity, authorized agency, or a licensed child-placing agency.

(b) A contest of paternity must be raised by an express statement denying paternity of the child in a party's pleadings in the suit, without regard to whether the presumed father or biological mother is a petitioner or respondent.

(c) In a suit in which a question of paternity is raised, the court shall conduct the pretrial proceedings and order scientifically accepted paternity testing as provided by this chapter.

Added by Acts 1995, 74th Leg., ch. 20, § 1, eff. April 20, 1995. Amended by Acts 1995, 74th Leg., ch. 751, § 62, eff. Sept. 1, 1995; Acts 1997, 75th Leg., ch. 962, § 1, eff. Sept. 1, 1997.

§ 160.102. Order for Parentage Testing

(a) When the respondent appears in a parentage suit, the court shall order the mother, an alleged father, and the child to submit to the taking of blood, body fluid, or tissue samples for the purpose of scientifically accepted parentage testing.

(b) If the respondent fails to appear and wholly defaults or if the allegation of parentage is admitted, the court may waive parentage testing.

Added by Acts 1995, 74th Leg., ch. 20, § 1, eff. April 20, 1995.

§ 160.103. Requirements of Testing

The court shall require in its order testing necessary to ascertain the possibility of an alleged father's paternity and shall require that the tests exclude at least 99 percent of the male population from the possibility of being the father of the child, except that the court shall permit the omission of any further testing if the testing has been conducted sufficiently to establish that an alleged father is not the father of the child, or if the costs of testing have reached an amount that the court determines to be the greatest amount that may reasonably be borne by one or more parties to the suit. If the appearance is before the birth of the child, the court shall order the taking of blood, body fluid, or tissue samples to be made as soon as medically practical after the birth.

Added by Acts 1995, 74th Leg., ch. 20, § 1, eff. April 20, 1995.

§ 160.104. Appointment of Experts

(a) The court shall:

(1) appoint one or more experts qualified in parentage testing to perform the tests;

(2) determine the number and qualifications of the experts; and

(3) prescribe the arrangements for conducting the tests.

(b) The court may:

(1) order a reasonable fee for each court-appointed expert; and

(2) require the fee to be paid by any or all of the parties in the amounts and in the manner directed or tax all, part, or none of the fee as costs in the suit.

(c) A party may employ other experts qualified in parentage testing. The court may order blood, body fluid, or tissue samples made available to these experts if requested.

Added by Acts 1995, 74th Leg., ch. 20, § 1, eff. April 20, 1995.

§ 160.105. Pretrial Conference

(a) After completion of parentage testing, the court shall order all parties to appear, either in person or by attorney, at a pretrial conference.

(b) Either party may call a parentage testing expert to testify in person or by deposition about the expert's tests and findings.

(c) A witness at a pretrial conference is governed by the Texas Rules of Civil Evidence.

(d) A verified written report of a parentage testing expert is admissible at the pretrial conference as evidence of the truth of the matters it contains.

(e) All evidence admitted at the pretrial conference is a part of the record of the case.

(f) Parentage test results offered at a pretrial conference are admissible as evidence if the tests were conducted under a court order or by agreement without regard to whether the tests were performed before or after the filing of a suit.

Added by Acts 1995, 74th Leg., ch. 20, § 1, eff. April 20, 1995.

§ 160.106. Effect of Parentage Tests

(a) At the conclusion of the pretrial conference, if the court finds that the tests show by clear and convincing evidence that an alleged or presumed father is not the father of the child, the court shall dismiss with prejudice the parentage suit as to that man.

(b) If the court finds that the parentage tests do not exclude an alleged father as the father of the child, the court shall set the suit for trial.

(c) If the court finds that at least 99 percent of the male population is excluded by the tests and that an alleged father is not excluded from the possibility of being the child's father, the burden of proof at trial is on the party opposing the establishment of the alleged father's parentage.

Added by Acts 1995, 74th Leg., ch. 20, § 1, eff. April 20, 1995.

§ 160.107. Effect of Refusing Parentage Testing

(a) An order for parentage testing is enforceable by contempt and:

(1) if the petitioner is the mother or an alleged father and refuses to submit to parentage testing, the court may dismiss the suit; or

(2) if a party refuses to submit to court-ordered parentage testing, on proof sufficient to render a default judgment the court may resolve the question of parentage against that party.

(b) If a parent or an alleged parent refuses to submit to parentage testing, the fact of refusal may be introduced as evidence as provided by this subchapter.

Added by Acts 1995, 74th Leg., ch. 20, § 1, eff. April 20, 1995.

§ 160.108. Preferential Trial Setting

(a) In a suit provided by this chapter, after a hearing the court shall grant a motion for a preferential setting for trial on the merits filed by a party to the suit or by the attorney or guardian ad litem for the child. The court shall give precedence to that trial over other civil cases if discovery has been completed or sufficient time has elapsed since the filing of the suit for the completion of all necessary and reasonable discovery if diligently pursued.

(b) The provisions of this section regarding preferential setting apply to trial on the merits without regard to whether the suit is set for a trial before the court or before a jury.

Added by Acts 1995, 74th Leg., ch. 20, § 1, eff. April 20, 1995.

§ 160.109. Evidence at Trial

(a) A party may call a parentage testing expert to testify at the trial in person or by deposition.

(b) A verified written report of a parentage testing expert is admissible at the trial as evidence of the truth of the matters it contains.

(c) If the parentage tests show the possibility of an alleged father's paternity, the court shall admit this evidence if offered at the trial.

(d) Parentage test results offered at the trial shall be admissible as evidence if the tests were conducted under court order or by agreement, without regard to whether the tests were performed before or after the filing of a suit.

(e) The party seeking to establish an alleged father's paternity retains the right to open and close at trial without regard to whether the court has shifted the burden of proof to the opposing party.

(f) If a copy is provided to the adverse party and to the court at the pretrial conference, submission of a copy of a medical bill for the prenatal and postnatal health care expenses of the mother and child or for charges directly related to the parentage testing constitutes a prima facie showing that the charges are reasonable, necessary, and customary and may be admitted as evidence of the truth of the matters stated in the bill.

Added by Acts 1995, 74th Leg., ch. 20, § 1, eff. April 20, 1995.

§ 160.110. Presumptions; Burden of Proof

(a) In a suit in which there is a presumption of parentage under Chapter 151, the party denying a presumed father's paternity of the child has the burden of rebutting the presumption of paternity by clear and convincing evidence.

(b) If the parentage tests show the possibility of an alleged father's paternity and that at least 99 percent of the male population is excluded from the possibility of being the father, evidence of these facts constitutes a prima facie showing of an alleged father's paternity, and the party opposing the establishment of the alleged father's paternity has the burden of proving that the alleged father is not the father of the child.

(c) A party who refuses to submit to parentage testing has the burden of proving that an alleged father is not the father of the child.

(d) The court shall dismiss with prejudice a claim regarding a presumed father whose paternity is excluded by scientifically accepted paternity testing.

(e) If two or more presumptions are in conflict, the presumption that is founded on the weightier considerations of policy and logic controls. The court shall find that the weightier presumption of paternity is that of a presumed father who is not excluded as the biological father of the child by scientifically accepted paternity testing that shows that at least 99 percent of the male population is excluded.

(f) The court shall dismiss a suit contesting a presumption of paternity filed by a man who is not a presumed father, but who alleges himself to be the biological father of a child, if:

(1) the suit is filed after the second anniversary of the later of:

(A) the date of birth of the child; or

(B) the time the presumption of paternity came into existence after the child was born; and

(2) the presumed father:

(A) has resided in the same household as the child in a father-child relationship or has established a father-child relationship with the child through his other actions; and

(B) requests an order designating him as the father of the child.

(g) A suit contesting a presumption that a man is the biological father of a child may be filed at any time during the minority of the child by:

(1) the biological mother of the child;

(2) a person related within the second degree of consanguinity to the biological mother of the child, if the biological mother of the child is deceased;

(3) a presumed father; or

(4) a governmental entity, authorized agency, or licensed child-placing agency.

(h) If a presumption of paternity is rebutted, the court shall enter an order finding that the man presumed to be the father of the child is not the biological father.

Added by Acts 1995, 74th Leg., ch. 20, § 1, eff. April 20, 1995. Amended by Acts 1995, 74th Leg., ch. 751, § 63, eff. Sept. 1, 1995; Acts 1997, 75th Leg., ch. 962, § 2, eff. Sept. 1, 1997.

[Sections 160.111 to 160.200 reserved for expansion]

SUBCHAPTER C. VOLUNTARY PATERNITY

Acts 1995, 74th Leg., ch. 751, § 64 amended Subchapter C.

§ 160.201. Voluntary Paternity

(a) If a statement of paternity has been executed by a man claiming to be the biological father of a child who has no presumed father, he, the mother of the child, or the child through a representative authorized by the court or a governmental entity may file a petition for an order adjudicating him as a parent of the child. The statement of paternity must be attached to or filed with the petition.

(b) The court shall render an order adjudicating the child to be the biological child of the child's father and the father to be a parent of the child if the court finds that the statement of paternity was executed as provided by this chapter, and the facts stated are true.

(c) A suit for voluntary paternity may be joined with a suit for termination under Chapter 161.

Added by Acts 1995, 74th Leg., ch. 20, § 1, eff. April 20, 1995. Amended by Acts 1995, 74th Leg., ch. 751, § 64, eff. Sept. 1, 1995.

§ 160.202. Statement of Paternity

(a) The statement of paternity authorized to be used by this subchapter must:

(1) be in writing;

(2) be signed by the man alleging himself to be the father of the child;

(3) state whether the man alleging himself to be the father is a minor; and

(4) clearly state that the man signing the statement acknowledges the child as his biological child.

(b) The statement may include a waiver of citation in a suit to establish the parent-child relationship and may include a waiver of the right to notice of the proceedings.

(c) The statement must be executed before a person authorized to administer oaths under the laws of this state.

(d) The statement may be signed before the birth of the child.

(e) The statement must include the social security number of the father.

Added by Acts 1995, 74th Leg., ch. 20, § 1, eff. April 20, 1995. Amended by Acts 1995, 74th Leg., ch. 751, § 64, eff. Sept. 1, 1995.

§ 160.203. Effect of Statement of Paternity

(a) A statement of paternity executed as provided by this subchapter is prima facie evidence that the child is the child of the person executing the statement and that the person has an obligation to support the child.

(b) If an alleged father's address is unknown or he is outside the jurisdiction of the court at the time a suit is instituted under this subchapter, his statement of paternity, in the absence of controverting evidence, is sufficient for the court to render an order establishing his paternity of the child.

Added by Acts 1995, 74th Leg., ch. 20, § 1, eff. April 20, 1995. Amended by Acts 1995, 74th Leg., ch. 751, § 64, eff. Sept. 1, 1995.

§ 160.204. Disputed Parentage

If the paternity of the child is uncertain or is disputed by a party in a suit filed under this subchapter, the provisions of Subchapter B [1] apply.

Added by Acts 1995, 74th Leg., ch. 20, § 1, eff. April 20, 1995. Renumbered from § 160.205 by Acts 1995, 74th Leg., ch. 751, § 64, eff. Sept. 1, 1995.

[1] V.T.C.A., Family Code § 160.101 et seq.

§ 160.205. Validation of Prior Statements

A statement acknowledging paternity or an obligation to support a child that was signed by the father before January 1, 1974, is valid and binding even though the statement is not executed as provided by this subchapter.

Added by Acts 1995, 74th Leg., ch. 20, § 1, eff. April 20, 1995. Renumbered from § 160.206 by Acts 1995, 74th Leg., ch. 751, § 64, eff. Sept. 1, 1995.

§ 160.206. Renumbered as § 160.205 by Acts 1995, 74th Leg., ch. 751, § 64, eff. Sept. 1, 1995

SUBCHAPTER D. PATERNITY REGISTRY

§ 160.251. Paternity Registry; Purpose

(a) The bureau of vital statistics shall establish a paternity registry.

(b) The bureau of vital statistics shall administer the registry to:

(1) protect the parental rights of fathers who affirmatively assume responsibility for children they may have fathered; and

(2) expedite adoptions of children whose biological fathers are unwilling to assume responsibility for their children by registering with the registry or otherwise acknowledging their children.

(c) The registry does not relieve a mother of the obligation to identify the known father of her child.

(d) A man is not required to register with the paternity registry if he:

(1) is presumed to be the biological father of a child under Chapter 151; or

(2) has been adjudicated to be the biological father of a child by a court of competent jurisdiction.

Added by Acts 1997, 75th Leg., ch. 561, § 6, eff. Sept. 1, 1997.

Section 32(b) to (d) of Acts 1997, 75th Leg., ch. 561 provides:

"(b) Except as otherwise provided by this section, the change in law made by this Act applies only to a suit affecting the parent-child relationship commenced on or after the effective date of this Act. A suit affecting the parent-child relationship commenced before the effective date of this Act is governed by the law in effect on the date it was commenced, and the former law is continued in effect for that purpose.

"(c) The change in law made by this Act pertaining to the termination of the parent-child relationship applies only to an affidavit to relinquish parental rights or an affidavit of waiver of interest in a child executed on or after the effective date of this Act. An affidavit executed before the effective date of this Act is governed by the law in effect on the date the affidavit was executed, and the former law is continued in effect for that purpose.

"(d) The change in law made by this Act pertaining to adoptions applies only to petitions for adoptions filed on or after the effective date of this Act. A petition for adoption filed before the effective date of this Act is governed by the law in effect on the date the petition was filed, and the former law is continued in effect for that purpose; except that for these purposes a petition for adoption shall be considered to be filed at the time that the original petition was filed or at the time that an amended petition seeking the adoption was filed if the amended petition is filed in a cause that has previously been filed and where the court has continuing jurisdiction over the child."

§ 160.252. Required Information

A man registering with the registry shall provide:

(1) the name, last known address, driver's license number, and social security number, if known, of the mother of the child;

(2) the name of the child and the location and date of birth of the child, if known, or the probable month and year of the expected birth of the child;

(3) the man's name, address, driver's license number, and social security number; and

(4) a statement in which the man claims to be the father of the child identified by the man.

Added by Acts 1997, 75th Leg., ch. 561, § 6, eff. Sept. 1, 1997.

For application provisions of Acts 1997, 75th Leg., ch. 561, see notes following V.T.C.A., Family Code § 160.251.

§ 160.253. Information Maintained by Registry

The registry shall record the name, address, driver's license number, and social security number of a man who claims to be the father of a child whose paternity has not been adjudicated by a court of competent jurisdiction by giving notice of intent to claim paternity, as provided by this subchapter.

Added by Acts 1997, 75th Leg., ch. 561, § 6, eff. Sept. 1, 1997.

For application provisions of Acts 1997, 75th Leg., ch. 561, see notes following V.T.C.A., Family Code § 160.251.

§ 160.254. Knowledge of Pregnancy

(a) A person who has sexual intercourse with a person of the opposite sex is deemed to have knowledge that sexual intercourse can result in the woman's pregnancy.

(b) Except as provided by this subchapter, a man who claims to be the father of a child shall file a notice of intent to assert as provided by this subchapter his right to establish paternity of a child that may result from the sexual intercourse.

(c) Ignorance of a pregnancy is not a sufficient reason for failing to register with the registry to claim paternity of the child born of the pregnancy.

Added by Acts 1997, 75th Leg., ch. 561, § 6, eff. Sept. 1, 1997.

For application provisions of Acts 1997, 75th Leg., ch. 561, see notes following V.T.C.A., Family Code § 160.251.

§ 160.255. Furnishing of Registry Information; Confidentiality; Offense

(a) If the mother's address has been provided, the registry shall send a copy of the notice of intent to claim paternity to the mother as notification that a man has registered with the paternity registry claiming to be the father of the mother's child.

(b) Information contained in the registry is confidential and may be released on request only to:

(1) a court;

(2) the mother of a child;

(3) an authorized agency;

(4) a licensed child-placing agency;

(5) an attorney at law in this state who is participating or assisting in a suit affecting the parent-

child relationship, including termination of the parent-child relationship or a suit for the adoption of the child that the registrant claims to have fathered; or

(6) any other person or entity the bureau of vital statistics considers to have a legitimate interest in the information.

(c) The registry shall furnish registry information by electronic data exchange or any other means to the state's Title IV-D agency and the Department of Protective and Regulatory Services.

(d) A person commits an offense if the person intentionally and unlawfully releases information from the registry to the public or makes any other unlawful use of the information in violation of this subchapter. An offense under this subsection is a Class B misdemeanor.

Added by Acts 1997, 75th Leg., ch. 561, § 6, eff. Sept. 1, 1997.

Section 32(e) of Acts 1997, 75th Leg., ch. 561 provides:

"The change in law made by this Act pertaining to a criminal offense applies only to an offense committed on or after the effective date of this Act. For purposes of this subsection, an offense is committed before the effective date of this Act if any element of the offense occurs before that date. An offense committed before the effective date of this Act is covered by the law in effect when the offense was committed, and the former law is continued in effect for that purpose."

For other application provisions of Acts 1997, 75th Leg., ch. 561, see notes following V.T.C.A., Family Code § 160.251.

§ 160.256. Notice of Intent to Claim Paternity

(a) Except as provided by Subsection (d), a person may register as provided by this subchapter by filing a notice of intent to claim paternity on a form provided by the bureau of vital statistics. This form shall be signed and acknowledged before a notary public.

(b) The bureau shall make registration forms available to all:

(1) hospitals and other birthing places in this state;

(2) licensed child-placing agencies;

(3) county and district clerks;

(4) municipal clerks;

(5) justices of the peace;

(6) jails;

(7) prisons; and

(8) facilities of the Texas Department of Criminal Justice and Texas Youth Commission.

(c) A notice of intent to claim paternity may be filed before the birth of the child but may not be filed after the 30th day after the date of birth of the child.

(d) If the bureau of vital statistics has received from the clerk of the court notice under Chapter 108 of a decree terminating the parent-child relationship between the person applying to register and the child, the bureau shall notify the person that the person's parent-child relationship with the child has been terminated and may not enter into the registry a notice of intent to claim paternity filed by the person.

Added by Acts 1997, 75th Leg., ch. 561, § 6, eff. Sept. 1, 1997.

For application provisions of Acts 1997, 75th Leg., ch. 561, see notes following V.T.C.A., Family Code § 160.251.

§ 160.257. Denial of Registrant's Paternity; Notification

(a) Not later than the 30th day after the date of the receipt of notification from the bureau of vital statistics that a notice of intent to claim paternity has been filed, the mother of the child may deny the registrant's claim of paternity on a form provided by the bureau and signed and acknowledged before a notary public.

(b) If the mother denies that the registrant is the father of the child, the bureau of vital statistics shall immediately notify the registrant of the denial and of the registrant's right to file a legal action to establish paternity.

Added by Acts 1997, 75th Leg., ch. 561, § 6, eff. Sept. 1, 1997.

For application provisions of Acts 1997, 75th Leg., ch. 561, see notes following V.T.C.A., Family Code § 160.251.

§ 160.258. Effect of Failure to File Notice of Intent

Except as provided by Chapter 102 and Chapter 161, a man who fails to file a notice of intent to claim paternity before the 30th day after the date of the birth of the child may not assert an interest in the child other than by filing a suit to establish paternity before the termination of the man's parental rights.

Added by Acts 1997, 75th Leg., ch. 561, § 6, eff. Sept. 1, 1997.

For application provisions of Acts 1997, 75th Leg., ch. 561, see notes following V.T.C.A., Family Code § 160.251.

§ 160.259. Change or Revocation of Registry Information

(a) A man who files a notice of intent to claim paternity with the registry shall promptly notify the registry in writing of any change in the information, including a change of address.

(b) A man who files a notice of intent to claim paternity may at any time revoke the notice by sending the registry a written statement signed and acknowledged by the registrant before a notary public. The statement must include a declaration that, to the best of the registrant's knowledge and belief:

(1) the registrant is not the father of the named child; or

(2) a court has adjudicated paternity and a person other than the registrant has been determined to be the father of the child.

Added by Acts 1997, 75th Leg., ch. 561, § 6, eff. Sept. 1, 1997.

For application provisions of Acts 1997, 75th Leg., ch. 561, see notes following V.T.C.A., Family Code § 160.251.

§ 160.260. Furnishing of Certificate of Registry Search

On request, the bureau of vital statistics shall furnish a certificate, signed by the state registrar of vital statistics, attesting to the results of a search of the registry regarding a notice of intent to claim paternity to:

(1) a court;

(2) the mother of a child;

(3) an authorized agency;

(4) a licensed child-placing agency;

(5) an attorney licensed to practice law in this state who is participating or assisting in an adoption; or

(6) any other person or entity the bureau of vital statistics considers to have a legitimate interest in the information.

Added by Acts 1997, 75th Leg., ch. 561, § 6, eff. Sept. 1, 1997.

For application provisions of Acts 1997, 75th Leg., ch. 561, see notes following V.T.C.A., Family Code § 160.251.

§ 160.261. Removal of Registrant's Name

If a court determines that a registrant is not the father of the child, the court shall order the bureau of vital statistics to remove the registrant's name from the registry. On receipt of an order for the removal of a registrant's name, the bureau of vital statistics shall remove the name from the registry.

Added by Acts 1997, 75th Leg., ch. 561, § 6, eff. Sept. 1, 1997.

For application provisions of Acts 1997, 75th Leg., ch. 561, see notes following V.T.C.A., Family Code § 160.251.

§ 160.262. Registry Fees

(a) A fee may not be charged for filing with the registry a notice of intent to claim paternity of a child or a denial of a registrant's paternity.

(b) Except as provided by Subsection (c), the Texas Department of Health may charge a fee for processing a search of the paternity registry and for furnishing a certificate under Section 160.260.

(c) The Department of Protective and Regulatory Services and the Title IV-D agency are not required to pay a fee under Subsection (b).

Added by Acts 1997, 75th Leg., ch. 561, § 6, eff. Sept. 1, 1997.

For application provisions of Acts 1997, 75th Leg., ch. 561, see notes following V.T.C.A., Family Code § 160.251.

§ 160.263. Admissibility of Information Maintained by Registry

Information maintained by the paternity registry is admissible in a proceeding in a court or administrative tribunal of this state for any purpose, including for the establishment of the registrant's paternity or an action to terminate parental rights.

Added by Acts 1997, 75th Leg., ch. 561, § 6, eff. Sept. 1, 1997.

For application provisions of Acts 1997, 75th Leg., ch. 561, see notes following V.T.C.A., Family Code § 160.251.

CHAPTER 161. TERMINATION OF THE PARENT–CHILD RELATIONSHIP

SUBCHAPTER A. GROUNDS

161.211. Direct or Collateral Attack on Termination Order.

SUBCHAPTER A. GROUNDS

§ 161.001. Involuntary Termination of Parent-Child Relationship

The court may order termination of the parent-child relationship if the court finds by clear and convincing evidence:

(1) that the parent has:

(A) voluntarily left the child alone or in the possession of another not the parent and expressed an intent not to return;

(B) voluntarily left the child alone or in the possession of another not the parent without expressing an intent to return, without providing for the adequate support of the child, and remained away for a period of at least three months;

(C) voluntarily left the child alone or in the possession of another without providing adequate support of the child and remained away for a period of at least six months;

(D) knowingly placed or knowingly allowed the child to remain in conditions or surroundings which endanger the physical or emotional well-being of the child;

(E) engaged in conduct or knowingly placed the child with persons who engaged in conduct which endangers the physical or emotional well-being of the child;

(F) failed to support the child in accordance with the parent's ability during a period of one year ending within six months of the date of the filing of the petition;

(G) abandoned the child without identifying the child or furnishing means of identification, and the child's identity cannot be ascertained by the exercise of reasonable diligence;

(H) voluntarily, and with knowledge of the pregnancy, abandoned the mother of the child beginning at a time during her pregnancy with the child and continuing through the birth, failed to provide adequate support or medical care for the mother during the period of abandonment before the birth of the child, and remained apart from the child or failed to support the child since the birth;

(I) contumaciously refused to submit to a reasonable and lawful order of a court under Chapter 264;

(J) been the major cause of:

(i) the failure of the child to be enrolled in school as required by the Education Code; or

(ii) the child's absence from the child's home without the consent of the parents or guardian for a substantial length of time or without the intent to return;

(K) executed before or after the suit is filed an unrevoked or irrevocable affidavit of relinquishment of parental rights as provided by this chapter;

(L) been convicted or has been placed on community supervision, including deferred adjudication community supervision, for being criminally responsible for the death or serious injury of a child under the following sections of the Penal Code or adjudicated under Title 3 for conduct that caused the death or serious injury of a child and that would constitute a violation of one of the following Penal Code sections:

(i) Section 19.02 (murder);

(ii) Section 19.03 (capital murder);

(iii) Section 21.11 (indecency with a child);

(iv) Section 22.01 (assault);

(v) Section 22.011 (sexual assault);

(vi) Section 22.02 (aggravated assault);

(vii) Section 22.021 (aggravated sexual assault);

(viii) Section 22.04 (injury to a child, elderly individual, or disabled individual);

(ix) Section 22.041 (abandoning or endangering child);

(x) Section 25.02 (prohibited sexual conduct);

(xi) Section 43.25 (sexual performance by a child); and

(xii) Section 43.26 (possession or promotion of child pornography);

(M) had his or her parent-child relationship terminated with respect to another child based on a finding that the parent's conduct was in violation of Paragraph (D) or (E) or substantially equivalent provisions of the law of another state;

(N) constructively abandoned the child who has been in the permanent or temporary managing conservatorship of the Department of Protective and Regulatory Services or an authorized agency for not less than six months, and:

(i) the department or authorized agency has made reasonable efforts to return the child to the parent;

(ii) the parent has not regularly visited or maintained significant contact with the child; and

(iii) the parent has demonstrated an inability to provide the child with a safe environment;

(O) failed to comply with the provisions of a court order that specifically established the actions necessary for the parent to obtain the return of the child who has been in the permanent or temporary managing conservatorship of the Department of Protective and Regulatory Services for not less than nine months as a result of the child's removal from the parent under Chapter 262 for the abuse or neglect of the child;

(P) used a controlled substance, as defined by Chapter 481, Health and Safety Code:

(i) in a manner that endangered the health or safety of the child, and failed to complete a court-ordered substance abuse treatment program; or

(ii) repeatedly, after completion of a court-ordered substance treatment program, in a manner that endangered the health or safety of the child;

(Q) knowingly engaged in criminal conduct that results in the parent's imprisonment and inability to care for the child for not less than two years from the date of filing the petition; or

(R) been the cause of the child being born addicted to alcohol or a controlled substance, other than a controlled substance legally obtained by prescription, as defined by Section 261.001(7); and

(2) that termination is in the best interest of the child.

Added by Acts 1995, 74th Leg., ch. 20, § 1, eff. April 20, 1995. Amended by Acts 1995, 74th Leg., ch. 709, § 1, eff. Sept. 1, 1995; Acts 1995, 74th Leg., ch. 751, § 65, eff. Sept. 1, 1995; Acts 1997, 75th Leg., ch. 575, § 9, eff. Sept. 1, 1997; Acts 1997, 75th Leg., ch. 1022, § 60, eff. Sept. 1, 1997.

For application provisions of Acts 1997, 75th Leg., ch. 575, see note following V.T.C.A., Family Code § 102.003.

Section 105(h) of Acts 1997, 75th Leg., ch. 1022 provides:

"The change in law made by this Act regarding the termination of the parent-child relationship applies only to a suit affecting the parent-child relationship in which termination of the parent-child relationship is sought filed on or after the effective date of this Act. A suit affecting the parent-child relationship in which termination of the parent-child relationship is sought filed before the effective date of this Act is governed by the law in effect on the date the suit was filed, and the former law is continued in effect for that purpose."

§ 161.002. Termination of the Rights of an Alleged Biological Father

(a) The procedural and substantive standards for termination of parental rights apply to the termination of the rights of an alleged biological father.

(b) The rights of an alleged biological father may be terminated if:

(1) after being served with citation, he does not respond by timely filing an admission of paternity or a counterclaim for paternity under Chapter 160 prior to the final hearing in the suit;

(2) he has not registered with the paternity registry under Subchapter D, Chapter 160,[1] and after the exercise of due diligence by the petitioner:

(A) his identity and location are unknown; or

(B) his identity is known but he cannot be located; or

(3) he has registered with the paternity registry under Subchapter D, Chapter 160, but the petitioner's attempt to personally serve citation at the address provided to the registry and at any other address for the alleged father known by the petitioner has been unsuccessful, despite the due diligence of the petitioner.

(c) The termination of the rights of an alleged biological father under Subsection (b)(2) rendered on or after January 1, 1998, does not require personal service of citation or citation by publication on the alleged father.

(d) The termination of rights of an alleged biological father under Subsection (b)(3) does not require service of citation by publication on the alleged father.

(e) The court shall not render an order terminating parental rights under Subsection (b)(2) unless the court, after reviewing the petitioner's sworn affidavit describing the petitioner's effort to identify and locate the alleged biological father and considering any evidence submitted by the attorney ad litem for the alleged biological father, has found that the petitioner exercised due diligence in attempting to identify and locate the alleged biological father. The order shall contain specific findings regarding due diligence of the petitioner.

(f) The court shall not render an order terminating parental rights under Subsection (b)(3) unless the court, after reviewing the petitioner's sworn affidavit describing the petitioner's effort to obtain personal service of citation on the alleged father and considering any evidence submitted by the attorney ad litem for the alleged father, has found that the petitioner exercised due diligence in attempting to obtain service on the alleged father. The order shall contain specific findings regarding the exercise of due diligence of the petitioner.

Added by Acts 1995, 74th Leg., ch. 20, § 1, eff. April 20, 1995. Amended by Acts 1995, 74th Leg., ch. 751, § 66, eff. Sept. 1, 1995; Acts 1997, 75th Leg., ch. 561, § 7, eff. Sept. 1, 1997.

[1] V.T.C.A., Family Code § 160.251 et seq.

For application provisions of Acts 1997, 75th Leg., ch. 561, see notes following V.T.C.A., Family Code § 160.251.

§ 161.003. Involuntary Termination: Inability to Care for Child

(a) The court may order termination of the parent-child relationship in a suit filed by the Department of Protective and Regulatory Services if the court finds that:

(1) the parent has a mental or emotional illness or a mental deficiency that renders the parent unable to provide for the physical, emotional, and mental needs of the child;

(2) the illness or deficiency, in all reasonable probability, proved by clear and convincing evidence, will continue to render the parent unable to provide for the child's needs until the 18th birthday of the child;

(3) the department has been the temporary or sole managing conservator of the child of the parent for the six months preceding the filing of the petition;

(4) the department has made reasonable efforts to return the child to the parent; and

(5) the termination is in the best interest of the child.

(b) Immediately after the filing of a suit under this section, the court shall appoint an attorney ad litem to represent the interests of the parent against whom the suit is brought.

(c) A hearing on the termination may not be held earlier than 180 days after the date on which the suit was filed.

(d) An attorney appointed under Subsection (b) shall represent the parent for the duration of the suit unless the parent, with the permission of the court, retains another attorney.

Added by Acts 1995, 74th Leg., ch. 20, § 1, eff. April 20, 1995. Amended by Acts 1995, 74th Leg., ch. 751, § 67, eff. Sept. 1, 1995.

§ 161.004. Termination of Parental Rights After Denial of Prior Petition to Terminate

(a) The court may terminate the parent-child relationship after rendition of an order that previously denied termination of the parent-child relationship if:

(1) the petition under this section is filed after the date the order denying termination was rendered;

(2) the circumstances of the child, parent, sole managing conservator, possessory conservator, or other party affected by the order denying termination have materially and substantially changed since the date that the order was rendered;

(3) the parent committed an act listed under Section 161.001 before the date the order denying termination was rendered; and

(4) termination is in the best interest of the child.

(b) At a hearing under this section, the court may consider evidence presented at a previous hearing in a suit for termination of the parent-child relationship of the parent with respect to the same child.

Added by Acts 1995, 74th Leg., ch. 20, § 1, eff. April 20, 1995.

§ 161.005. Termination When Parent is Petitioner

(a) A parent may file a suit for termination of the petitioner's parent-child relationship. The court may order termination if termination is in the best interest of the child.

(b) If the petition designates the Department of Protective and Regulatory Services as managing conservator, the department shall be given service of citation. The court shall notify the department if the court appoints the department as the managing conservator of the child.

Added by Acts 1995, 74th Leg., ch. 20, § 1, eff. April 20, 1995. Amended by Acts 1995, 74th Leg., ch. 751, § 68, eff. Sept. 1, 1995.

§ 161.006. Termination After Abortion

(a) A petition requesting termination of the parent-child relationship with respect to a parent who is not the petitioner may be granted if the child was born alive as the result of an abortion.

(b) In this code, "abortion" means an intentional expulsion of a human fetus from the body of a woman induced by any means for the purpose of causing the death of the fetus.

(c) The court or the jury may not terminate the parent-child relationship under this section with respect to a parent who:

(1) had no knowledge of the abortion; or

(2) participated in or consented to the abortion for the sole purpose of preventing the death of the mother.

Added by Acts 1995, 74th Leg., ch. 20, § 1, eff. April 20, 1995.

§ 161.007. Termination When Pregnancy Results From Criminal Act

The court may order the termination of the parent-child relationship of a parent and a child if the court finds that:

(1) the parent has been convicted of an offense committed under Section 22.011, 22.021, or 25.02, Penal Code;

(2) as a direct result of the commission of the offense by the parent, the victim of the offense became pregnant with the parent's child; and

(3) termination is in the best interest of the child.

Added by Acts 1997, 75th Leg., ch. 561, § 8, eff. Sept. 1, 1997.

Section 32(e) of Acts 1997, 75th Leg., ch. 561 provides:

"The change in law made by this Act pertaining to a criminal offense applies only to an offense committed on or after the effective date of this Act. For purposes of this subsection, an offense is committed before the effective date of this Act if any element of the offense occurs before that date. An offense committed before the effective date of this Act is covered by the law in effect when the offense was committed, and the former law is continued in effect for that purpose."

For other application provisions of Acts 1997, 75th Leg., ch. 561, see notes following V.T.C.A., Family Code § 160.251.

[Sections 161.007 to 161.100 reserved for expansion]

SUBCHAPTER B. PROCEDURES

§ 161.101. Petition Allegations

A petition for the termination of the parent-child relationship is sufficient without the necessity of specifying the underlying facts if the petition alleges in the statutory language the ground for the termination and that termination is in the best interest of the child.

Added by Acts 1995, 74th Leg., ch. 20, § 1, eff. April 20, 1995.

§ 161.102. Filing Suit for Termination Before Birth

(a) A suit for termination may be filed before the birth of the child.

(b) If the suit is filed before the birth of the child, the petition shall be styled "In the Interest of an Unborn Child." After the birth, the clerk shall change the style of the case to conform to the requirements of Section 102.008.

Added by Acts 1995, 74th Leg., ch. 20, § 1, eff. April 20, 1995.

§ 161.103. Affidavit of Voluntary Relinquishment of Parental Rights

(a) An affidavit for voluntary relinquishment of parental rights must be:

(1) signed after the birth of the child, but not before 48 hours after the birth of the child, by the parent, whether or not a minor, whose parental rights are to be relinquished;

(2) witnessed by two credible persons; and

(3) verified before a person authorized to take oaths.

(b) The affidavit must contain:

(1) the name, address, and age of the parent whose parental rights are being relinquished;

(2) the name, age, and birth date of the child;

(3) the names and addresses of the guardians of the person and estate of the child, if any;

(4) a statement that the affiant is or is not presently obligated by court order to make payments for the support of the child;

(5) a full description and statement of value of all property owned or possessed by the child;

(6) an allegation that termination of the parent-child relationship is in the best interest of the child;

(7) one of the following, as applicable:

(A) the name and address of the other parent;

(B) a statement that the parental rights of the other parent have been terminated by death or court order; or

(C) a statement that the child has no presumed father and that an affidavit of status of the child has been executed as provided by this chapter;

(8) a statement that the parent has been informed of parental rights and duties;

(9) a statement that the relinquishment is revocable, that the relinquishment is irrevocable, or that the relinquishment is irrevocable for a stated period of time;

(10) if the relinquishment is revocable, a statement in boldfaced type concerning the right of the parent signing the affidavit to revoke the relinquishment only if the revocation is made before the 11th day after the date the affidavit is executed;

(11) if the relinquishment is revocable, the name and address of a person to whom the revocation is to be delivered; and

(12) the designation of a prospective adoptive parent, the Department of Protective and Regulatory Services, if the department has consented in writing to the designation, or a licensed child-placing agency to serve as managing conservator of the child and the address of the person or agency.

(c) The affidavit may contain:

(1) a waiver of process in a suit to terminate the parent-child relationship filed under this chapter or in a suit to terminate joined with a petition for adoption; and

(2) a consent to the placement of the child for adoption by the Department of Protective and Regulatory Services or by a licensed child-placing agency.

(d) A copy of the affidavit shall be provided to the parent at the time the parent signs the affidavit.

(e) The relinquishment in an affidavit that designates the Department of Protective and Regulatory Services or a licensed child-placing agency to serve as the managing conservator is irrevocable. A relinquishment in any other affidavit of relinquishment is revocable unless it expressly provides that it is irrevocable for a stated period of time not to exceed 60 days after the date of its execution.

(f) A relinquishment in an affidavit of relinquishment of parental rights that fails to state that the relinquishment is irrevocable for a stated time is revocable as provided by Section 161.1035.

(g) To revoke a relinquishment under Subsection (e) the parent must sign a statement witnessed by two credible persons and verified before a person authorized to take oaths. A copy of the revocation shall be delivered to the person designated in the affidavit. If a parent attempting to revoke a relinquishment under this subsection has knowledge that a suit for termination of the parent-child relationship has been filed based on the parent's affidavit of relinquishment of parental rights, the parent shall file a copy of the revocation with the clerk of the court.

Added by Acts 1995, 74th Leg., ch. 20, § 1, eff. April 20, 1995. Amended by Acts 1995, 74th Leg., ch. 751, § 69, eff. Sept. 1, 1995; Acts 1997, 75th Leg., ch. 561, § 9, eff. Sept. 1, 1997.

Section 32(b) to (d) of Acts 1997, 75th Leg., ch. 561 provides:

"(b) Except as otherwise provided by this section, the change in law made by this Act applies only to a suit affecting the parent-child relationship commenced on or after the effective date of this Act. A suit affecting the parent-child relationship commenced before the effective date of this Act is governed by the law in effect on the date it was commenced, and the former law is continued in effect for that purpose.

"(c) The change in law made by this Act pertaining to the termination of the parent-child relationship applies only to an affidavit to relinquish parental rights or an affidavit of waiver of interest in a child executed on or after the effective date of this Act. An affidavit executed before the effective date of this Act is governed by the law in effect on the date the affidavit was executed, and the former law is continued in effect for that purpose.

"(d) The change in law made by this Act pertaining to adoptions applies only to petitions for adoptions filed on or after the effective date of this Act. A petition for adoption filed before the effective date of this Act is governed by the law in effect on the date the petition was filed, and the former law is continued in effect for that purpose; except that for these purposes a petition for adoption shall be considered to be filed at the time that the original petition was filed or at the time that an amended petition seeking the adoption was filed if the amended petition is filed in a cause that has previously been filed and where the court has continuing jurisdiction over the child."

§ 161.1035. Revocability of Certain Affidavits

An affidavit of relinquishment of parental rights or affidavit of waiver of interest in a child that fails to state that the relinquishment or waiver is irrevocable for a stated time is:

(1) revocable only if the revocation is made before the 11th day after the date the affidavit is executed; and

(2) irrevocable on or after the 11th day after the date the affidavit is executed.

Added by Acts 1997, 75th Leg., ch. 561, § 10, eff. Sept. 1, 1997.

For application provisions of Acts 1997, 75th Leg., ch. 561, see notes following V.T.C.A., Family Code § 161.103.

§ 161.104. Rights of Designated Managing Conservator Pending Court Appointment

A person, licensed child-placing agency, or authorized agency designated managing conservator of a child in an irrevocable or unrevoked affidavit of relinquishment has a right to possession of the child superior to the right of the person executing the affidavit, the right to consent to medical, surgical, dental, and psychological treatment of the child, and the rights and duties given by Chapter 153 to a possessory conservator until such time as these rights and duties are modified or terminated by court order.

Added by Acts 1995, 74th Leg., ch. 20, § 1, eff. April 20, 1995. Amended by Acts 1995, 74th Leg., ch. 751, § 70, eff. Sept. 1, 1995.

§ 161.105. Affidavit of Status of Child

(a) If the child has no presumed father, an affidavit shall be:

(1) signed by the mother, whether or not a minor;

(2) witnessed by two credible persons; and

(3) verified before a person authorized to take oaths.

(b) The affidavit must:

(1) state that the mother is not and has not been married to the alleged father of the child;

(2) state that the mother and alleged father have not attempted to marry under the laws of this state or another state or nation;

(3) state that paternity has not been established under the laws of any state or nation; and

(4) contain one of the following, as applicable:

(A) the name and whereabouts of a man alleged to be the father;

(B) the name of an alleged father and a statement that the affiant does not know the whereabouts of the father;

(C) a statement that an alleged father has executed a statement of paternity under Chapter 160 and an affidavit of relinquishment of parental rights under this chapter and that both affidavits have been filed with the court; or

(D) a statement that the name of an alleged father is unknown.

(c) The affidavit of status of child may be executed at any time after the first trimester of the pregnancy of the mother.

Added by Acts 1995, 74th Leg., ch. 20, § 1, eff. April 20, 1995.

§ 161.106. Affidavit of Waiver of Interest in Child

(a) A man may sign an affidavit disclaiming any interest in a child and waiving notice or the service of citation in any suit filed or to be filed affecting the parent-child relationship with respect to the child.

(b) The affidavit may be signed before the birth of the child.

(c) The affidavit shall be:

(1) signed by the man, whether or not a minor;

(2) witnessed by two credible persons; and

(3) verified before a person authorized to take oaths.

(d) The affidavit may contain a statement that the affiant does not admit being the father of the child or having had a sexual relationship with the mother of the child.

(e) An affidavit of waiver of interest in a child may be used in a suit in which the affiant attempts to establish an interest in the child. The affidavit may not be used in a suit brought by another person, licensed child-placing agency, or authorized agency to establish the affiant's paternity of the child.

(f) A waiver in an affidavit under this section that designates the Department of Protective and Regulatory Services or a licensed child-placing agency to serve as the managing conservator is irrevocable. A waiver in any other affidavit under this section is revocable unless it expressly provides that it is irrevocable for a stated period not to exceed 60 days after the date of execution.

(g) A waiver in an affidavit under this section that fails to state that the waiver is irrevocable for a stated time is revocable as provided by Section 161.1035.

(h) An affidavit under this section that contains a waiver that is revocable must contain:

(1) a statement in boldfaced type concerning the right of the person who executed the affidavit to revoke the affidavit only if the revocation is made before the 11th day after the date the affidavit is executed; and

(2) the name and address of the person to whom the revocation is to be delivered.

(i) A copy of the affidavit shall be provided to the person who executed the affidavit at the time the person signs the affidavit.

(j) To revoke a waiver, the person who executed the affidavit must sign a statement witnessed by two credible persons and verified before a person authorized to take oaths. A copy of the revocation shall be delivered to the person designated in the affidavit of waiver of interest in a child. If a person attempting to revoke an affidavit under this subsection has knowledge that a suit for termination of the parent-child relationship based on the person's waiver of interest in a child has been filed, the person shall file a copy of the revocation with the clerk of the court.

Added by Acts 1995, 74th Leg., ch. 20, § 1, eff. April 20, 1995. Amended by Acts 1997, 75th Leg., ch. 561, § 11, eff. Sept. 1, 1997.

For application provisions of Acts 1997, 75th Leg., ch. 561, see notes following V.T.C.A., Family Code § 161.103.

§ 161.107. Missing Parent or Relative

(a) In this section:

(1) "Parent" means a parent whose parent-child relationship with a child has not been terminated.

(2) "Relative" means a parent, grandparent, or adult sibling or child.

(b) If a parent of the child has not been personally served in a suit in which the Department of Protective and Regulatory Services seeks termination, the department must make a diligent effort to locate that parent.

(c) If a parent has not been personally served and cannot be located, the department shall make a diligent effort to locate a relative of the missing parent to give the relative an opportunity to request appointment as the child's managing conservator.

(d) If the department is not able to locate a missing parent or a relative of that parent and sufficient information is available concerning the physical whereabouts of the parent or relative, the department shall request the state agency designated to administer a statewide plan for child support to use the parental locator service established under 42 U.S.C. Section 653 to determine the location of the missing parent or relative.

(e) The department shall be required to provide evidence to the court to show what actions were taken by the department in making a diligent effort to locate the missing parent and relative of the missing parent.

Added by Acts 1995, 74th Leg., ch. 20, § 1, eff. April 20, 1995. Amended by Acts 1995, 74th Leg., ch. 751, § 71, eff. Sept. 1, 1995.

§ 161.108. Release of Child From Hospital or Birthing Center

(a) Before or at the time an affidavit of relinquishment of parental rights under Section 161.103 is executed, the mother of a newborn child may authorize the release of the child from the hospital or birthing center to a licensed child-placing agency, the Department of Protective and Regulatory Services, or another designated person.

(b) A release under this section must be:

(1) executed in writing;

(2) witnessed by two credible adults; and

(3) verified before a person authorized to take oaths.

(c) A hospital or birthing center shall comply with the terms of a release executed under this section without requiring a court order.

Added by Acts 1997, 75th Leg., ch. 561, § 12, eff. Sept. 1, 1997.

For application provisions of Acts 1997, 75th Leg., ch. 561, see notes following V.T.C.A., Family Code § 161.103.

§ 161.109. Requirement of Paternity Registry Certificate

(a) If an affidavit of status of child as provided by this chapter states that the father of the child is unknown and no probable father is known, a certificate from the bureau of vital statistics signed by the registrar that a diligent search has been made of the paternity registry maintained by the bureau and that a registration has not been found pertaining to the father of the child in question must be filed with the court before a trial on the merits in the suit for termination may be held.

(b) In a proceeding to terminate parental rights in which the alleged or probable father has not been personally served with citation or signed an affidavit of relinquishment or an affidavit of waiver of interest, the court may not terminate the parental rights of the alleged or probable father, whether known or unknown, unless a certificate from the bureau of vital statistics signed by the registrar states that a diligent search has been made of the paternity registry maintained by the bureau and that a filing or registration has not been found pertaining to the father of the child in question.

Added by Acts 1997, 75th Leg., ch. 561, § 12, eff. Sept. 1, 1997.

For application provisions of Acts 1997, 75th Leg., ch. 561, see notes following V.T.C.A., Family Code § 161.103.

[Sections 161.108 to 161.200 reserved for expansion]

SUBCHAPTER C. HEARING AND ORDER

§ 161.201. No Final Order Until Child Five Days Old

If the petition in a suit for termination is filed before the birth of the child, the court may not conduct a hearing in the suit nor render an order other than a temporary order until the child is at least five days old.

Added by Acts 1995, 74th Leg., ch. 20, § 1, eff. April 20, 1995.

§ 161.2011. Continuance; Access to Child

(a) The court shall not proceed to final trial in a suit to terminate the parent-child relationship during the time that any criminal charges filed against a parent whose rights are subject to termination in the suit are pending if the criminal charges are directly related to the grounds for which termination of the parent's rights are sought unless it determines that it is in the best interest of the child.

(b) Nothing in this section precludes the court from issuing appropriate temporary orders as authorized in this code.

(c) The court in which a suit to terminate the parent-child relationship is pending may render an order denying a parent access to a child if the parent is indicted for criminal activity that constitutes a ground for terminating the parent-child relationship under Section 161.001. The denial of access under this section shall continue until the date the criminal charges for which the parent was indicted are resolved and the court renders an order providing for access to the child by the parent.

Added by Acts 1997, 75th Leg., ch. 1022, § 61, eff. Sept. 1, 1997.

§ 161.202. Preferential Setting; Suit by Governmental Entity

In a termination suit filed by a governmental entity, licensed child-placing agency, or authorized agency, after a hearing, the court shall grant a motion for a preferential setting for a final hearing on the merits filed by a party to the suit or by the attorney or guardian ad litem for the child and shall give precedence to that hearing over other civil cases if:

(1) termination would make the child eligible for adoption; and

(2) discovery has been completed or sufficient time has elapsed since the filing of the suit for the completion of all necessary and reasonable discovery if diligently pursued.

Added by Acts 1995, 74th Leg., ch. 20, § 1, eff. April 20, 1995.

§ 161.203. Dismissal of Petition

A suit to terminate may not be dismissed nor may a nonsuit be taken unless the dismissal or nonsuit is approved by the court.

Added by Acts 1995, 74th Leg., ch. 20, § 1, eff. April 20, 1995.

§ 161.204. Termination Based on Affidavit of Waiver of Interest

In a suit for termination, the court may render an order terminating all legal relationships and rights which exist or may exist between a child and a man who has signed an affidavit of waiver of interest in the child, if the termination is in the best interest of the child.

Added by Acts 1995, 74th Leg., ch. 20, § 1, eff. April 20, 1995.

§ 161.205. Order Denying Termination

If the court does not order termination of the parent-child relationship, it shall:

(1) dismiss the petition; or

(2) render any order in the best interest of the child.

Added by Acts 1995, 74th Leg., ch. 20, § 1, eff. April 20, 1995.

§ 161.206. Order Terminating Parental Rights

(a) If the court finds by clear and convincing evidence grounds for termination of the parent-child relationship,[1] it shall render an order terminating the parent-child relationship.

(b) An order terminating the parent-child relationship divests the parent and the child of all legal rights and duties with respect to each other, except that the child retains the right to inherit from and through the parent unless the court otherwise provides.

(c) Nothing in this chapter precludes or affects the rights of a biological or adoptive maternal or paternal grandparent to reasonable access under Chapter 153.

Added by Acts 1995, 74th Leg., ch. 20, § 1, eff. April 20, 1995. Amended by Acts 1995, 74th Leg., ch. 709, § 2, eff. Sept. 1, 1995; Acts 1995, 74th Leg., ch. 751, § 72, eff. Sept. 1, 1995.

[1] Acts 1995, 74th Leg., ch. 751 inserted "by clear and convincing evidence" following "relationship".

§ 161.207. Appointment of Managing Conservator on Termination

(a) If the court terminates the parent-child relationship with respect to both parents or to the only living parent, the court shall appoint a suitable, competent adult, the Department of Protective and Regulatory Services, a licensed child-placing agency, or an authorized agency as managing conservator of the child. An agency designated managing conservator in an unrevoked or irrevocable affidavit of relinquishment shall be appointed managing conservator.

(b) The order of appointment may refer to the docket number of the suit and need not refer to the parties nor be accompanied by any other papers in the record.

Added by Acts 1995, 74th Leg., ch. 20, § 1, eff. April 20, 1995.

§ 161.208. Appointment of Department of Protective and Regulatory Services as Managing Conservator

If a parent of the child has not been personally served in a suit in which the Department of Protective and Regulatory Services seeks termination, the court that terminates a parent-child relationship may not appoint the Department of Protective and Regulatory Services as permanent managing conservator of the child unless the court determines that:

(1) the department has made a diligent effort to locate a missing parent who has not been personally served and a relative of that parent; and

(2) a relative located by the department has had a reasonable opportunity to request appointment as managing conservator of the child or the department has not been able to locate the missing parent or a relative of the missing parent.

Added by Acts 1995, 74th Leg., ch. 20, § 1, eff. April 20, 1995.

§ 161.209. Copy of Order of Termination

A copy of an order of termination rendered under Section 161.206 is not required to be mailed to parties as provided by Rules 119a and 239a, Texas Rules of Civil Procedure.

Added by Acts 1995, 74th Leg., ch. 20, § 1, eff. April 20, 1995.

§ 161.210. Sealing of File

The court, on the motion of a party or on the court's own motion, may order the sealing of the file, the minutes of the court, or both, in a suit for termination.

Added by Acts 1995, 74th Leg., ch. 20, § 1, eff. April 20, 1995.

§ 161.211. Direct or Collateral Attack on Termination Order

Text of section as added by Acts 1997, 75th Leg., ch. 600, § 1

(a) Notwithstanding Rule 329, Texas Rules of Civil Procedure, the validity of an order terminating the parental rights of a person who has been personally served or who has executed an affidavit of relinquishment of parental rights or an affidavit of waiver of interest in a child or whose rights have been terminated under Section 161.002(b) is not subject to collateral or direct attack after the sixth month after the date the order was rendered.

(b) The validity of an order terminating the parental rights of a person who is served by citation by publication is not subject to collateral or direct attack after the sixth month after the date the order was rendered.

(c) A direct or collateral attack on an order terminating parental rights based on an unrevoked affidavit of relinquishment of parental rights or affidavit of waiver of interest in a child is limited to issues relating to fraud, duress, or coercion in the execution of the affidavit.

Added by Acts 1997, 75th Leg., ch. 600, § 1, eff. Sept. 1, 1997.

For text of section as added by Acts 1997, 75th Leg., ch. 601, § 2, see § 161.211, post.

§ 161.211. Direct or Collateral Attack on Termination Order

Text of section as added by Acts 1997, 75th Leg., ch. 601, § 2

(a) Notwithstanding Rule 329, Texas Rules of Civil Procedure, the validity of an order terminating the parental rights of a person who has been personally served or who has executed an affidavit of relinquishment of parental rights or an affidavit of waiver of interest in a child is not subject to collateral or direct attack after the sixth month after the date the order was signed.

(b) Notwithstanding Rule 329, Texas Rules of Civil Procedure, the validity of an order terminating the parental rights of a person who is served by citation by publication is not subject to collateral or direct attack after the sixth month after the date the order was signed.

(c) A direct or collateral attack on an order terminating parental rights based on an unrevoked affidavit of relinquishment of parental rights or affidavit of waiver of interest in a child is limited to issues relating to fraud, duress, or coercion in the execution of the affidavit.

Added by Acts 1997, 75th Leg., ch. 601, § 2, eff. Sept. 1, 1997.

For text of section as added by Acts 1997, 75th Leg., ch. 600, § 1, see § 161.211, ante.

For application provisions of Acts 1997, 75th Leg., ch. 601, see note following V.T.C.A., Family Code § 162.012.

CHAPTER 162. ADOPTION

SUBCHAPTER A. ADOPTION OF A CHILD

SUBCHAPTER A. ADOPTION OF A CHILD

§ 162.001. Who May Adopt and be Adopted

(a) Subject to the requirements for standing to sue in Chapter 102, an adult may petition to adopt a child who may be adopted.

(b) A child residing in this state may be adopted if:

(1) the parent-child relationship as to each living parent of the child has been terminated or a suit for termination is joined with the suit for adoption;

(2) the parent whose rights have not been terminated is presently the spouse of the petitioner and the proceeding is for a stepparent adoption;

(3) the child is at least two years old, the parent-child relationship has been terminated with respect to one parent, the person seeking the adoption is the child's former stepparent and has been a managing conservator or has had actual care, possession, and control of the child for a period of six

months preceding the adoption, and the nonterminated parent consents to the adoption; or

(4) the child is at least two years old, the parent-child relationship has been terminated with respect to one parent, and the person seeking the adoption is the child's former stepparent and has been a managing conservator or has had actual care, possession, and control of the child for a period of one year preceding the adoption.

(c) If an affidavit of relinquishment of parental rights contains a consent for the Department of Protective and Regulatory Services or a licensed child-placing agency to place the child for adoption and appoints the department or agency managing conservator of the child, further consent by the parent is not required and the adoption order shall terminate all rights of the parent without further termination proceedings.

Added by Acts 1995, 74th Leg., ch. 20, § 1, eff. April 20, 1995. Amended by Acts 1997, 75th Leg., ch. 561, § 14, eff. Sept. 1, 1997.

Section 32(b) to (d) of Acts 1997, 75th Leg., ch. 561 provides:

"(b) Except as otherwise provided by this section, the change in law made by this Act applies only to a suit affecting the parent-child relationship commenced on or after the effective date of this Act. A suit affecting the parent-child relationship commenced before the effective date of this Act is governed by the law in effect on the date it was commenced, and the former law is continued in effect for that purpose.

"(c) The change in law made by this Act pertaining to the termination of the parent-child relationship applies only to an affidavit to relinquish parental rights or an affidavit of waiver of interest in a child executed on or after the effective date of this Act. An affidavit executed before the effective date of this Act is governed by the law in effect on the date the affidavit was executed, and the former law is continued in effect for that purpose.

"(d) The change in law made by this Act pertaining to adoptions applies only to petitions for adoptions filed on or after the effective date of this Act. A petition for adoption filed before the effective date of this Act is governed by the law in effect on the date the petition was filed, and the former law is continued in effect for that purpose; except that for these purposes a petition for adoption shall be considered to be filed at the time that the original petition was filed or at the time that an amended petition seeking the adoption was filed if the amended petition is filed in a cause that has previously been filed and where the court has continuing jurisdiction over the child."

§ 162.002. Prerequisites to Petition

(a) If a petitioner is married, both spouses must join in the petition for adoption.

(b) A petition in a suit for adoption or a suit for appointment of a nonparent managing conservator with authority to consent to adoption of a child must include:

(1) a verified allegation that there has been compliance with Subchapter B [1]; or

(2) if there has not been compliance with Subchapter B, a verified statement of the particular reasons for noncompliance.

Added by Acts 1995, 74th Leg., ch. 20, § 1, eff. April 20, 1995.

[1] V.T.C.A., Family Code § 162.101 et seq.

§ 162.0025. Adoptive Home Screening

(a) The court shall order an adoptive home screening to evaluate each party who requests the adoption. The screening must be completed before a child may be placed in an applicant's home unless the child is being adopted by a member of the child's family related by the second degree of consanguinity or affinity. The screening must comply with the rules adopted by the Board of Protective and Regulatory Services providing minimum requirements for the screening.

(b) The court may appoint an investigator to conduct the screening required by this section who has the qualifications established by rule of the Board of Protective and Regulatory Services providing minimum qualifications for persons who may perform adoptive home screenings.

(c) The cost of an adoptive home study shall be paid by an applicant who seeks to adopt a child.

Added by Acts 1997, 75th Leg., ch. 561, § 13, eff. Sept. 1, 1997.

For application provisions of Acts 1997, 75th Leg., ch. 561, see notes following V.T.C.A., Family Code § 162.001.

§ 162.003. Social Study

(a) In a suit for adoption, including a suit in which a private agency or individual is responsible for placing the child for adoption, the court shall order a social study as provided in Chapter 107.

(b) The social study required by this section must include a complete investigation of the circumstances and condition of the home of a person petitioning for the adoption of a child under this chapter.

(c) The court shall order that the cost of the social study be paid by the person seeking to adopt the child who is the subject of the social study.

Added by Acts 1995, 74th Leg., ch. 20, § 1, eff. April 20, 1995. Amended by Acts 1995, 74th Leg., ch. 751, § 73, eff. Sept. 1, 1995; Acts 1995, 74th Leg., ch. 800, § 1, eff. Sept. 1, 1995.

Section 2 of Acts 1995, 74th Leg., ch. 800 provides:

"This Act takes effect September 1, 1995, and applies only to a social study ordered by a court under Section 162.003, Family Code, as amended by this Act, on or after the effective date of this Act in a suit affecting the parent-child relationship in which an adoption is sought, without regard to whether the suit is filed before, on, or after the effective date of this Act."

§ 162.004. Time for Hearing

(a) The court shall set the date for the hearing on the adoption at a time not before the 40th day or later than the 60th day after the later of the date the social study is ordered or the date criminal history record information is requested under Section 162.0085.

Text of subsec. (b) as amended by Acts 1995, 74th Leg., ch. 751, § 74

(b) For good cause shown, the court may set the hearing at any date after the report is filed and the court has been notified of the criminal history record information for a person seeking to adopt the child.

Text of subsec. (b) as amended by Acts 1995, 74th Leg., ch. 908, § 1

(b) For good cause shown, the court may set the hearing at any time that provides adequate time for filing the social study and notifying the court of the criminal history record information for a person seeking to adopt the child.

Added by Acts 1995, 74th Leg., ch. 20, § 1, eff. April 20, 1995. Amended by Acts 1995, 74th Leg., ch. 751, § 74, eff. Sept. 1, 1995; Acts 1995, 74th Leg., ch. 908, § 1, eff. Sept. 1, 1995.

Section 4 of Acts 1995, 74th Leg., ch. 908, provides:

"The change in law made by this Act applies only to a suit affecting the parent-child relationship in which an adoption is sought that is filed on or after the effective date of this Act. A suit that is filed before the effective date of this Act is covered by the law in effect when the suit was filed, and the former law is continued in effect for that purpose."

§ 162.0045. Preferential Setting

The court shall grant a motion for a preferential setting for a final hearing on an adoption and shall give precedence to that hearing over all other civil cases not given preference by other law if the social study has been filed and the criminal history for the person seeking to adopt the child has been obtained.

Added by Acts 1997, 75th Leg., ch. 561, § 15, eff. Sept. 1, 1997.

For application provisions of Acts 1997, 75th Leg., ch. 561, see notes following V.T.C.A., Family Code § 162.001.

§ 162.005. Preparation of Health, Social, Educational, and Genetic History Report

(a) This section does not apply to an adoption by the child's:

(1) grandparent;

(2) aunt or uncle by birth, marriage, or prior adoption; or

(3) stepparent.

(b) Before placing a child for adoption, the Department of Protective and Regulatory Services, a licensed child-placing agency, or the child's parent or guardian shall compile a report on the available health, social, educational, and genetic history of the child to be adopted.

(c) The report shall include a history of physical, sexual, or emotional abuse suffered by the child, if any.

(d) If the child has been placed for adoption by a person or entity other than the department, a licensed child-placing agency, or the child's parent or guardian, it is the duty of the person or entity who places the child for adoption to prepare the report.

(e) The person or entity who places the child for adoption shall provide the prospective adoptive parents a copy of the report as early as practicable before the first meeting of the adoptive parents with the child. The copy of the report shall be edited to protect the identity of birth parents and their families.

(f) The department, licensed child-placing agency, parent, guardian, person, or entity who prepares and files the original report is required to furnish supplemental medical, psychological, and psychiatric information to the adoptive parents if that information becomes available and to file the supplemental information where the original report is filed. The supplemental information shall be retained for as long as the original report is required to be retained.

Added by Acts 1995, 74th Leg., ch. 20, § 1, eff. April 20, 1995.

§ 162.006. Right to Examine Records

(a) The department, licensed child-placing agency, person, or entity placing a child for adoption shall inform the prospective adoptive parents of their right to examine the records and other information relating to the history of the child. The person or entity placing the child for adoption shall edit the records and information to protect the identity of the biological parents and any other person whose identity is confidential.

(b) The department, licensed child-placing agency, or court retaining a copy of the report shall provide a copy of the report that has been edited to protect the identity of the birth parents and any other person whose identity is confidential to the following persons on request:

(1) an adoptive parent of the adopted child;

(2) the managing conservator, guardian of the person, or legal custodian of the adopted child;

(3) the adopted child, after the child is an adult;

(4) the surviving spouse of the adopted child if the adopted child is dead and the spouse is the parent or guardian of a child of the deceased adopted child; or

(5) a progeny of the adopted child if the adopted child is dead and the progeny is an adult.

(c) A copy of the report may not be furnished to a person who cannot furnish satisfactory proof of identity and legal entitlement to receive a copy.

(d) A person requesting a copy of the report shall pay the actual and reasonable costs of providing a copy and verifying entitlement to the copy.

(e) The report shall be retained for 99 years from the date of the adoption by the department or licensed child-placing agency placing the child for adoption. If the agency ceases to function as a child-placing agency, the agency shall transfer all the reports to the department or, after giving notice to the department, to a transferee agency that is assuming responsibility for the preservation of the agency's adoption records. If the child has not been placed for adoption by the department or a licensed child-placing agency and if the child is being adopted by a person other than the child's stepparent, grandparent, aunt, or uncle by birth, marriage, or prior adoption, the person or entity who places the child for adoption shall file the report with the department, which shall retain the copies for 99 years from the date of the adoption.

Added by Acts 1995, 74th Leg., ch. 20, § 1, eff. April 20, 1995.

§ 162.007. Contents of Health, Social, Educational, and Genetic History Report

(a) The health history of the child must include information about:

(1) the child's health status at the time of placement;

(2) the child's birth, neonatal, and other medical, psychological, psychiatric, and dental history information;

(3) a record of immunizations for the child; and

(4) the available results of medical, psychological, psychiatric, and dental examinations of the child.

(b) The social history of the child must include information, to the extent known, about past and existing relationships between the child and the child's siblings, parents by birth, extended family, and other persons who have had physical possession of or legal access to the child.

(c) The educational history of the child must include, to the extent known, information about:

(1) the enrollment and performance of the child in educational institutions;

(2) results of educational testing and standardized tests for the child; and

(3) special educational needs, if any, of the child.

(d) The genetic history of the child must include a description of the child's parents by birth and their parents, any other child born to either of the child's parents, and extended family members and must include, to the extent the information is available, information about:

(1) their health and medical history, including any genetic diseases and disorders;

(2) their health status at the time of placement;

(3) the cause of and their age at death;

(4) their height, weight, and eye and hair color;

(5) their nationality and ethnic background;

(6) their general levels of educational and professional achievements, if any;

(7) their religious backgrounds, if any;

(8) any psychological, psychiatric, or social evaluations, including the date of the evaluation, any diagnosis, and a summary of any findings;

(9) any criminal conviction records relating to a misdemeanor or felony classified as an offense against the person or family or public indecency or a felony violation of a statute intended to control the possession or distribution of a substance included in Chapter 481, Health and Safety Code; and

(10) any information necessary to determine whether the child is entitled to or otherwise eligible for state or federal financial, medical, or other assistance.

Added by Acts 1995, 74th Leg., ch. 20, § 1, eff. April 20, 1995.

§ 162.008. Filing of Health, Social, Educational, and Genetic History Report

(a) This section does not apply to an adoption by the child's:

(1) grandparent;

(2) aunt or uncle by birth, marriage, or prior adoption; or

(3) stepparent.

(b) A petition for adoption may not be granted until the following documents have been filed:

(1) a copy of the health, social, educational, and genetic history report signed by the child's adoptive parents; and

(2) if the report is required to be submitted to the department by Section 162.006(e), a certificate from the department acknowledging receipt of the report.

(c) A court having jurisdiction of a suit affecting the parent-child relationship may by order waive the making and filing of a report under this section if the child's biological parents cannot be located and their absence results in insufficient information being available to compile the report.

Added by Acts 1995, 74th Leg., ch. 20, § 1, eff. April 20, 1995.

§ 162.0085. Criminal History Report Required

(a) In a suit affecting the parent-child relationship in which an adoption is sought, the court shall order each person seeking to adopt the child to obtain that person's own criminal history record information. The court shall accept under this section a person's criminal history record information that is provided by the Department of Protective and Regulatory Services or by a licensed child-placing agency that received the information from the department if the information was obtained not more than one year before the date the court ordered the history to be obtained.

(b) A person required to obtain information under Subsection (a) shall obtain the information in the manner provided by Section 411.128, Government Code.

Added by Acts 1995, 74th Leg., ch. 751, § 75, eff. Sept. 1, 1995; Acts 1995, 74th Leg., ch. 908, § 2, eff. Sept. 1, 1995. Amended by Acts 1997, 75th Leg., ch. 561, § 16, eff. Sept. 1, 1997.

For application provisions of Acts 1997, 75th Leg., ch. 561, see notes following V.T.C.A., Family Code § 162.001.

Section 4 of Acts 1995, 74th Leg., ch. 908 provides:

"The change in law made by this Act applies only to a suit affecting the parent-child relationship in which an adoption is sought that is filed on or after the effective date of this Act. A suit that is filed before the effective date of this Act is covered by the law in effect when the suit was filed, and the former law is continued in effect for that purpose."

§ 162.009. Residence With Petitioner

(a) The court may not grant an adoption until the child has resided with the petitioner for not less than six months.

(b) On request of the petitioner, the court may waive the residence requirement if the waiver is in the best interest of the child.

Added by Acts 1995, 74th Leg., ch. 20, § 1, eff. April 20, 1995.

§ 162.010. Consent Required

(a) Unless the managing conservator is the petitioner, the written consent of a managing conservator to the adoption must be filed. The court may waive the requirement of consent by the managing conservator if the court finds that the consent is being refused or has been revoked without good cause. A hearing on the issue of consent shall be conducted by the court without a jury.

(b) If a parent of the child is presently the spouse of the petitioner, that parent must join in the petition for adoption and further consent of that parent is not required.

(c) A child 12 years of age or older must consent to the adoption in writing or in court. The court may waive this requirement if it would serve the child's best interest.

Added by Acts 1995, 74th Leg., ch. 20, § 1, eff. April 20, 1995. Amended by Acts 1995, 74th Leg., ch. 751, § 76, eff. Sept. 1, 1995.

§ 162.011. Revocation of Consent

At any time before an order granting the adoption of the child is rendered, a consent required by Section 162.010 may be revoked by filing a signed revocation.

Added by Acts 1995, 74th Leg., ch. 20, § 1, eff. April 20, 1995.

§ 162.012. Direct or Collateral Attack

(a) Notwithstanding Rule 329, Texas Rules of Civil Procedure, the validity of an adoption order is not subject to attack after six months after the date the order was signed.

(b) The validity of a final adoption order is not subject to attack because a health, social, educational, and genetic history was not filed.

Added by Acts 1995, 74th Leg., ch. 20, § 1, eff. April 20, 1995. Amended by Acts 1997, 75th Leg., ch. 600, § 2, eff. Jan. 1, 1998; Acts 1997, 75th Leg., ch. 601, § 1, eff. Sept. 1, 1997.

Section 22 of Acts 1997, 75th Leg., ch. 600 provides:

"(a) The change in law made by Sections 2 through 16 of this Act takes effect January 1, 1998.

"(b) Except as provided by Subsection (c) of this section, Sections 2 through 16 of this Act apply to a pending suit affecting the parent-child relationship regardless of whether the suit was commenced before, on, or after the effective date of this Act.

"(c) If the Department of Protective and Regulatory Services has been appointed temporary managing conservator of a child before January 1, 1998, the court shall at the first hearing conducted on or after that date under Chapter 263, Family Code, establish a date for dismissal of the suit not later than the second anniversary of the date of the hearing, unless the court has rendered a final order before the dismissal date."

Section 3 of Acts 1997, 75th Leg., ch. 601 provides:

"This Act takes effect September 1, 1997. This Act applies only to an adoption order or order terminating parental rights signed on or after the effective date of this Act. An adoption order or order terminating parental rights signed before the effective date of this Act is governed by the law as it existed before the effective date of this Act, and that law is continued in effect for that purpose."

§ 162.013. Abatement or Dismissal

(a) If the sole petitioner dies or the joint petitioners die, the court shall dismiss the suit for adoption.

(b) If one of the joint petitioners dies, the proceeding shall continue uninterrupted.

(c) If the joint petitioners divorce, the court shall abate the suit for adoption. The court shall dismiss the petition unless the petition is amended to request adoption by one of the original petitioners.

Added by Acts 1995, 74th Leg., ch. 20, § 1, eff. April 20, 1995.

§ 162.014. Attendance at Hearing Required

(a) If the joint petitioners are husband and wife and it would be unduly difficult for one of the petitioners to appear at the hearing, the court may waive the attendance of that petitioner if the other spouse is present.

(b) A child to be adopted who is 12 years of age or older shall attend the hearing. The court may waive this requirement in the best interest of the child.

Added by Acts 1995, 74th Leg., ch. 20, § 1, eff. April 20, 1995.

§ 162.015. Race or Ethnicity

(a) In determining the best interest of the child, the court may not deny or delay the adoption or otherwise discriminate on the basis of race or ethnicity of the child or the prospective adoptive parents.

(b) This section does not apply to a person, entity, tribe, organization, or child custody proceeding subject to the Indian Child Welfare Act of 1978 (25 U.S.C. Section 1901 et seq.). In this subsection "child custody proceeding" has the meaning provided by 25 U.S.C. Section 1903.

Added by Acts 1995, 74th Leg., ch. 20, § 1, eff. April 20, 1995. Amended by Acts 1995, 74th Leg., ch. 751, § 77, eff. Sept. 1, 1995.

§ 162.016. Adoption Order

(a) If a petition requesting termination has been joined with a petition requesting adoption, the court shall also terminate the parent-child relationship at the same time the adoption order is rendered. The court must make separate findings that the termination is in the best interest of the child and that the adoption is in the best interest of the child.

(b) If the court finds that the requirements for adoption have been met and the adoption is in the best interest of the child, the court shall grant the adoption.

(c) The name of the child may be changed in the order if requested.

Added by Acts 1995, 74th Leg., ch. 20, § 1, eff. April 20, 1995.

§ 162.017. Effect of Adoption

(a) An order of adoption creates the parent-child relationship between the adoptive parent and the child for all purposes.

(b) An adopted child is entitled to inherit from and through the child's adoptive parents as though the child were the biological child of the parents.

(c) The terms "child," "descendant," "issue," and other terms indicating the relationship of parent and child include an adopted child unless the context or express language clearly indicates otherwise.

(d) Nothing in this chapter precludes or affects the rights of a biological or adoptive maternal or paternal grandparent to reasonable access, as provided in Chapter 153.

Added by Acts 1995, 74th Leg., ch. 20, § 1, eff. April 20, 1995.

§ 162.018. Access to Information

(a) The adoptive parents are entitled to receive copies of the records and other information relating to the history of the child maintained by the department, licensed child-placing agency, person, or entity placing the child for adoption.

(b) The adoptive parents and the adopted child, after the child is an adult, are entitled to receive copies of the records that have been edited to protect the identity of the biological parents and any other person whose identity is confidential and other information relating to the history of the child maintained by the department, licensed child-placing agency, person, or entity placing the child for adoption.

(c) It is the duty of the person or entity placing the child for adoption to edit the records and information to protect the identity of the biological parents and any other person whose identity is confidential.

(d) At the time an adoption order is rendered, the court shall provide to the parents of an adopted child information provided by the bureau of vital statistics that describes the functions of the voluntary adoption registry under Subchapter E.[1] The licensed child-placing agency shall provide to each of the child's biological parents known to the agency, the information when the parent signs an affidavit of relinquishment of parental rights, affidavit of status of child, or affidavit of waiver of interest in a child. The information shall include the right of the child or biological parent to refuse to participate in the registry. If the adopted child is 14 years old or older the court shall provide the information to the child.

Added by Acts 1995, 74th Leg., ch. 20, § 1, eff. April 20, 1995. Amended by Acts 1997, 75th Leg., ch. 561, § 17, eff. Sept. 1, 1997.

[1] V.T.C.A., Family Code § 162.401 et seq.

For application provisions of Acts 1997, 75th Leg., ch. 561, see notes following V.T.C.A., Family Code § 162.001.

§ 162.019. Copy of Order

A copy of the adoption order is not required to be mailed to the parties as provided in Rules 119a and 239a, Texas Rules of Civil Procedure.

Added by Acts 1995, 74th Leg., ch. 20, § 1, eff. April 20, 1995.

§ 162.020. Withdrawal or Denial of Petition

If a petition requesting adoption is withdrawn or denied, the court may order the removal of the child from the proposed adoptive home if removal is in the child's best interest and may enter any order necessary for the welfare of the child.

Added by Acts 1995, 74th Leg., ch. 20, § 1, eff. April 20, 1995.

§ 162.021. Sealing File

(a) The court, on the motion of a party or on the court's own motion, may order the sealing of the file and the minutes of the court, or both, in a suit requesting an adoption.

(b) Rendition of the order does not relieve the clerk from the duty to send information regarding adoption to the bureau of vital statistics as required by this subchapter and Chapter 108.

Added by Acts 1995, 74th Leg., ch. 20, § 1, eff. April 20, 1995. Amended by Acts 1995, 74th Leg., ch. 751, § 78, eff. Sept. 1, 1995.

§ 162.022. Confidentiality Maintained by Clerk

The records concerning a child maintained by the district clerk after entry of an order of adoption are confidential. No person is entitled to access to the records or may obtain information from the records except for good cause under an order of the court that issued the order.

Added by Acts 1995, 74th Leg., ch. 20, § 1, eff. April 20, 1995.

§§ 162.023, 162.024. Repealed by Acts 1995, 74th Leg., ch. 751, § 128, eff. Sept. 1, 1995

§ 162.025. Placement by Unauthorized Person; Offense

(a) A person who is not the natural or adoptive parent of the child, the legal guardian of the child, or a child-placing agency licensed under Chapter 42, Human Resources Code, commits an offense if the person:

(1) serves as an intermediary between a prospective adoptive parent and an expectant parent or parent of a minor child to identify the parties to each other; or

(2) places a child for adoption.

(b) It is not an offense under this section if a professional provides legal or medical services to:

(1) a parent who identifies the prospective adoptive parent and places the child for adoption without the assistance of the professional; or

(2) a prospective adoptive parent who identifies a parent and receives placement of a child for adoption without the assistance of the professional.

(c) An offense under this section is a Class B misdemeanor.

Added by Acts 1995, 74th Leg., ch. 411, § 1, eff. Sept. 1, 1995. Amended by Acts 1997, 75th Leg., ch. 561, § 18, eff. Sept. 1, 1997.

Section 32(e) of Acts 1997, 75th Leg., ch. 561 provides:

"The change in law made by this Act pertaining to a criminal offense applies only to an offense committed on or after the effective date of this Act. For purposes of this subsection, an offense is committed before the effective date of this Act if any element of the offense occurs before that date. An offense committed before the effective date of this Act is covered by the law in effect when the offense was committed, and the former law is continued in effect for that purpose."

For other application provisions of Acts 1997, 75th Leg., ch. 561, see notes following V.T.C.A., Family Code § 162.001.

[Sections 162.026 to 162.100 reserved for expansion]

SUBCHAPTER B. INTERSTATE COMPACT ON THE PLACEMENT OF CHILDREN

Acts 1995, 74th Leg., ch. 846, § 1 amended the Subchapter heading

§ 162.101. Definitions

In this subchapter:

(1) "Appropriate public authorities," with reference to this state, means the executive director.

(2) "Appropriate authority in the receiving state," with reference to this state, means the executive director.

(3) "Compact" means the Interstate Compact on the Placement of Children.

(4) "Executive head," with reference to this state, means the governor.

Added by Acts 1995, 74th Leg., ch. 20, § 1, eff. April 20, 1995. Amended by Acts 1995, 74th Leg., ch. 846, § 2, eff. June 16, 1995.

§ 162.102. Adoption of Compact; Text

The Interstate Compact on the Placement of Children is adopted by this state and entered into with all other jurisdictions in form substantially as provided by this subchapter.

INTERSTATE COMPACT ON THE PLACEMENT OF CHILDREN

ARTICLE I. PURPOSE AND POLICY

It is the purpose and policy of the party states to cooperate with each other in the interstate placement of children to the end that:

(a) Each child requiring placement shall receive the maximum opportunity to be placed in a suitable environment and with persons or institutions having appropriate qualifications and facilities to provide a necessary and desirable degree and type of care.

(b) The appropriate authorities in a state where a child is to be placed may have full opportunity to ascertain the circumstances of the proposed placement, thereby promoting full compliance with applicable requirements for the protection of the child.

(c) The proper authorities of the state from which the placement is made may obtain the most complete information on the basis on which to evaluate a projected placement before it is made.

(d) Appropriate jurisdictional arrangements for the care of children will be promoted.

ARTICLE II. DEFINITIONS

As used in this compact:

(a) "Child" means a person who, by reason of minority, is legally subject to parental, guardianship, or similar control.

(b) "Sending agency" means a party state, officer, or employee thereof; a subdivision of a party state, or officer or employee thereof; a court of a party state; a person, corporation, association, charitable agency, or other entity which sends, brings, or causes to be sent or brought any child to another party state.

(c) "Receiving state" means the state to which a child is sent, brought, or caused to be sent or brought, whether by public authorities or private persons or agencies, and whether for placement with state or local public authorities or for placement with private agencies or persons.

(d) "Placement" means the arrangement for the care of a child in a family free or boarding home or in a child-caring agency or institution but does not include any institution caring for the mentally ill, mentally defective, or epileptic or any institution primarily educational in character, and any hospital or other medical facility.

ARTICLE III. CONDITIONS FOR PLACEMENT

(a) No sending agency shall send, bring, or cause to be sent or brought into any other party state any child for placement in foster care or as a preliminary to a possible adoption unless the sending agency shall comply with each and every requirement set forth in this article and with the applicable laws of the receiving state governing the placement of children therein.

(b) Prior to sending, bringing, or causing any child to be sent or brought into a receiving state for placement in foster care or as a preliminary to a possible adoption, the sending agency shall furnish the appropriate public authorities in the receiving state written notice of the intention to send, bring, or place the child in the receiving state. The notice shall contain:

(1) the name, date, and place of birth of the child;

(2) the identity and address or addresses of the parents or legal guardian;

(3) the name and address of the person, agency, or institution to or with which the sending agency proposes to send, bring, or place the child;

(4) a full statement of the reasons for such proposed action and evidence of the authority pursuant to which the placement is proposed to be made.

(c) Any public officer or agency in a receiving state which is in receipt of a notice pursuant to Paragraph (b) of this article may request of the sending agency, or any other appropriate officer or agency of or in the sending agency's state, and shall be entitled to receive therefrom, such supporting or additional information as it may deem necessary under the circumstances to carry out the purpose and policy of this compact.

(d) The child shall not be sent, brought, or caused to be sent or brought into the receiving state until the appropriate public authorities in the receiving state shall notify the sending agency, in writing, to the effect that the proposed placement does not appear to be contrary to the interests of the child.

ARTICLE IV. PENALTY FOR ILLEGAL PLACEMENT

The sending, bringing, or causing to be sent or brought into any receiving state of a child in violation of the terms of this compact shall constitute a violation of the laws respecting the placement of children of both the state in which the sending agency is located or from which it sends or brings the child and of the receiving state. Such violation may be punished or subjected to penalty in either jurisdiction in accordance with its laws. In addition to liability for any such punishment or penalty, any such violation shall constitute full and sufficient grounds for the suspension or revocation of any license, permit, or other legal authorization held by the sending agency which empowers or allows it to place or care for children.

ARTICLE V. RETENTION OF JURISDICTION

(a) The sending agency shall retain jurisdiction over the child sufficient to determine all matters in relation to the custody, supervision, care, treatment, and disposition of the child which it would have had if the child had remained in the sending agency's state, until the child is adopted, reaches majority, becomes self-supporting, or is discharged with the concurrence of the appropriate authority in the receiving state. Such jurisdiction shall also include the power to effect or cause the return of the child or its transfer to another location and custody pursuant to law. The sending agency shall continue to have financial responsibility for support and maintenance of the child during the period of the placement. Nothing contained herein shall defeat a claim of jurisdiction by a receiving state sufficient to deal with an act of delinquency or crime committed therein.

(b) When the sending agency is a public agency, it may enter into an agreement with an authorized public or private agency in the receiving state providing for the performance of one or more services in respect of such case by the latter as agent for the sending agency.

(c) Nothing in this compact shall be construed to prevent a private charitable agency authorized to place children in the receiving state from performing services or acting as agent in that state for a private charitable agency of the sending state; nor to prevent the agency in the receiving state from discharging financial responsibility for the support and maintenance of a child who has been placed on behalf of the sending agency without relieving the responsibility set forth in Paragraph (a) hereof.

ARTICLE VI. INSTITUTIONAL CARE OF DELINQUENT CHILDREN

A child adjudicated delinquent may be placed in an institution in another party jurisdiction pursuant to this compact but no such placement shall be made unless the child is given a court hearing on notice to the parent or guardian with opportunity to be heard, prior to his being sent to such other party jurisdiction for institutional care and the court finds that:

(1) equivalent facilities for the child are not available in the sending agency's jurisdiction; and

(2) institutional care in the other jurisdiction is in the best interest of the child and will not produce undue hardship.

ARTICLE VII. COMPACT ADMINISTRATOR

The executive head of each jurisdiction party to this compact shall designate an officer who shall be general coordinator of activities under this compact in his jurisdiction and who, acting jointly with like officers of other party jurisdictions, shall have power to promulgate rules and regulations to carry out more effectively the terms and provisions of this compact.

ARTICLE VIII. LIMITATIONS

This compact shall not apply to:

(a) the sending or bringing of a child into a receiving state by his parent, stepparent, grandparent, adult brother or sister, adult uncle or aunt, or his guardian and leaving the child with any such relative or nonagency guardian in the receiving state; or

(b) any placement, sending, or bringing of a child into a receiving state pursuant to any other interstate compact to which both the state from which the child is sent or brought and the receiving state are party, or to any other agreement between said states which has the force of law.

ARTICLE IX. ENACTMENT AND WITHDRAWAL

This compact shall be open to joinder by any state, territory, or possession of the United States, the District of Columbia, the Commonwealth of Puerto Rico, and, with the consent of congress, the government of Canada or any province thereof. It shall become effective with respect to any such jurisdiction when such jurisdiction has enacted the same into law. Withdrawal from this compact shall be by the enactment of a statute repealing the same, but shall not take effect until two years after the effective date of such statute and until written notice of the withdrawal has been given by the withdrawing state to the governor of each other party jurisdiction. Withdrawal of a party state shall not affect the rights, duties, and obligations under this compact of any sending agency therein with respect to a placement made prior to the effective date of withdrawal.

ARTICLE X. CONSTRUCTION AND SEVERABILITY

The provisions of this compact shall be liberally construed to effectuate the purposes thereof. The provisions of this compact shall be severable and if any phrase, clause, sentence, or provision of this compact is declared to be contrary to the constitution of any party state or of the United States or the applicability thereof to any government, agency, person, or circumstance is held invalid, the validity of the remainder of this compact and the applicability thereof to any government, agency, person, or circumstance shall not be affected thereby. If this compact shall be held contrary to the constitution of any state party thereto, the compact shall remain in full force and effect as to the remaining states and in full force and effect as to the state affected as to all severable matters.

Added by Acts 1995, 74th Leg., ch. 20, § 1, eff. April 20, 1995. Renumbered from V.T.C.A., Family Code § 162.108 and amended by Acts 1995, 74th Leg., ch. 846, § 3, eff. June 16, 1995.

§ 162.103. Financial Responsibility for Child

(a) Financial responsibility for a child placed as provided in the compact is determined, in the first instance, as provided in Article V of the compact. After partial or complete default of performance under the provisions of Article V assigning financial responsibility, the executive director may bring suit under Chapter 154 and may file a complaint with the appropriate prosecuting attorney, claiming a violation of Section 25.05, Penal Code.

(b) After default, if the executive director determines that financial responsibility is unlikely to be assumed by the sending agency or the child's parents, the executive director may cause the child to be returned to the sending agency.

(c) After default, the department shall assume financial responsibility for the child until it is assumed by the child's parents or until the child is safely returned to the sending agency.

Added by Acts 1995, 74th Leg., ch. 20, § 1, eff. April 20, 1995. Renumbered from V.T.C.A., Family Code § 162.109 and amended by Acts 1995, 74th Leg., ch. 846, § 4, eff. June 16, 1995.

§ 162.104. Approval of Placement

The executive director may not approve the placement of a child in this state without the concurrence of the individuals with whom the child is proposed to be placed or the head of an institution with which the child is proposed to be placed.

Added by Acts 1995, 74th Leg., ch. 20, § 1, eff. April 20, 1995. Renumbered from V.T.C.A., Family Code § 162.110 and amended by Acts 1995, 74th Leg., ch. 846, § 5, eff. June 16, 1995.

§ 162.105. Placement in Another State

A juvenile court may place a delinquent child in an institution in another state as provided by Article VI of the compact. After placement in another state, the court retains jurisdiction of the child as provided by Article V of the compact.

Added by Acts 1995, 74th Leg., ch. 20, § 1, eff. April 20, 1995. Renumbered from V.T.C.A., Family Code § 162.111 by Acts 1995, 74th Leg., ch. 846, § 6, eff. June 16, 1995.

§ 162.106. Compact Authority

(a) The governor shall appoint the executive director of the Department of Protective and Regulatory Services as compact administrator.

(b) The executive director shall designate a deputy compact administrator and staff necessary to execute the terms of the compact in this state.

Added by Acts 1995, 74th Leg., ch. 20, § 1, eff. April 20, 1995. Renumbered from V.T.C.A., Family Code § 162.112 and amended by Acts 1995, 74th Leg., ch. 846, § 7, eff. June 16, 1995.

§ 162.107. Offenses; Penalties

(a) An individual, agency, corporation, or child-care facility that violates a provision of the compact commits an offense. An offense under this subsection is a Class B misdemeanor.

(b) An individual, agency, corporation, child-care facility, or child-care institution in this state that violates Article IV of the compact commits an offense. An offense under this subsection is a Class B misdemeanor. On conviction, the court shall revoke any license to operate as a child-care facility or child-care institution issued by the department to the entity convicted and shall revoke any license or certification of the individual, agency, or corporation necessary to practice in the state.

Added by Acts 1995, 74th Leg., ch. 20, § 1, eff. April 20, 1995. Renumbered from V.T.C.A., Family Code § 162.113 and amended by Acts 1995, 74th Leg., ch. 846, § 8, eff. June 16, 1995.

§§ 162.108 to 162.113. Renumbered as V.T.C.A., Family Code §§ 162.102 to 162.107 by Acts 1995, 74th Leg., ch. 846, §§ 3 to 8, eff. June 16, 1995

§ 162.114. Repealed by Acts 1995, 74th Leg., ch. 846, § 10, eff. June 16, 1995

[Sections 162.115 to 162.200 reserved for expansion]

SUBCHAPTER C. INTERSTATE COMPACT ON ADOPTION AND MEDICAL ASSISTANCE

§ 162.201. Adoption of Compact; Text

The Interstate Compact on Adoption and Medical Assistance is adopted by this state and entered into with all other jurisdictions joining in the compact in form substantially as provided under this subchapter.

INTERSTATE COMPACT ON ADOPTION AND MEDICAL ASSISTANCE

ARTICLE I. FINDINGS

The legislature finds that:

(a) Finding adoptive families for children for whom state assistance is desirable, under Subchapter D, Chapter 162,[1] and assuring the protection of the interest of the children affected during the entire assistance period require special measures when the adoptive parents move to other states or are residents of another state.

(b) The provision of medical and other necessary services for children, with state assistance, encounters special difficulties when the provision of services takes place in other states.

ARTICLE II. PURPOSES

The purposes of the compact are to:

(a) authorize the Department of Protective and Regulatory Services, with the concurrence of the Health and Human Services Commission, to enter into interstate agreements with agencies of other states for the protection of children on behalf of whom adoption assistance is being provided by the Department of Protective and Regulatory Services; and

(b) provide procedures for interstate children's adoption assistance payments, including medical payments.

ARTICLE III. DEFINITIONS

In this compact:

(a) "Adoption assistance state" means the state that signs an adoption assistance agreement in a particular case.

(b) "Residence state" means the state in which the child resides by virtue of the residence of the adoptive parents.

(c) "State" means a state of the United States, the District of Columbia, the Commonwealth of Puerto Rico, the Virgin Islands, Guam, the Commonwealth of the Northern Mariana Islands, or a territory or possession of or a territory or possession administered by the United States.

ARTICLE IV. COMPACTS AUTHORIZED

The Department of Protective and Regulatory Services, through its executive director, is authorized to develop, participate in the development of, negotiate, and enter into one or more interstate compacts on behalf of this state with other states to implement one or more of the purposes of this compact. An interstate compact authorized by this article has the force and effect of law.

ARTICLE V. CONTENTS OF COMPACTS

A compact entered into under the authority conferred by this compact shall contain:

(1) a provision making the compact available for joinder by all states;

(2) a provision for withdrawal from the compact on written notice to the parties, with a period of one year between the date of the notice and the effective date of the withdrawal;

(3) a requirement that protections under the compact continue for the duration of the adoption assistance and apply to all children and their adoptive parents who on the effective date of the withdrawal are receiving adoption assistance from a party state other than the one in which they reside and have their principal place of abode;

(4) a requirement that each case of adoption assistance to which the compact applies be covered by a written adoption assistance agreement between the adoptive parents and the state child welfare agency of the state that provides the adoption assistance and that the agreement be expressly for the benefit of the adopted child and enforceable by the adoptive parents and the state agency providing the adoption assistance; and

(5) other provisions that are appropriate for the proper administration of the compact.

ARTICLE VI. OPTIONAL CONTENTS OF COMPACTS

A compact entered into under the authority conferred by this compact may contain the following provisions, in addition to those required under Article V of this compact:

(1) provisions establishing procedures and entitlement to medical, developmental, child-care, or other social services for the child in accordance with applicable laws, even if the child and the adoptive parents are in a state other than the one responsible for or providing the services or the funds to defray part or all of the costs thereof; and

(2) other provisions that are appropriate or incidental to the proper administration of the compact.

ARTICLE VII. MEDICAL ASSISTANCE

(a) A child with special needs who resides in this state and who is the subject of an adoption assistance agreement with another state is entitled to receive a medical assistance identification from this state on the filing in the state medical assistance agency of a certified copy of the adoption assistance agreement obtained from the adoption assistance state. In accordance with rules of the state medical assistance agency, the adoptive parents, at least annually, shall show that the agreement is still in effect or has been renewed.

(b) The state medical assistance agency shall consider the holder of a medical assistance identification under this article as any other holder of a medical assistance identification under the laws of this state and shall process and make payment on claims on the holder's account in the same manner and under the same conditions and procedures as for other recipients of medical assistance.

(c) The state medical assistance agency shall provide coverage and benefits for a child who is in another state and who is covered by an adoption assistance agreement made by the Department of Protective and Regulatory Services for the coverage or benefits, if any, not provided by the residence state. The adoptive parents acting for the child may submit evidence of payment for services or benefit amounts not payable in the residence state and shall be reimbursed for those amounts. Services or benefit amounts covered under any insurance or other third-party medical contract or arrangement held by the child or the adoptive parents may not be reimbursed. The state medical assistance agency shall adopt rules implementing this subsection. The additional coverage and benefit amounts provided under this subsection are for services for which there is no federal contribution or services that, if federally aided, are not provided by the residence state. The rules shall include procedures for obtaining prior approval for services in cases in which prior approval is required for the assistance.

(d) The submission of a false, misleading, or fraudulent claim for payment or reimbursement for services or benefits under this article or the making of a false, misleading, or fraudulent statement in connection with the claim is an offense under this subsection if the person submitting the claim or making the statement knows or should know that the claim or statement is false, misleading, or fraudulent. A person who commits an offense under this subsection may be liable for a fine not to exceed $10,000 or imprisonment for not more than two years, or both the fine and the imprisonment. An offense under this subsection that also constitutes an offense under other law may be punished under either this subsection or the other applicable law.

(e) This article applies only to medical assistance for children under adoption assistance agreements with states that have entered into a compact with this state under which the other state provides medical assistance to children with special needs under adoption assistance agreements made by this state. All other children entitled to medical assistance under adoption assistance agreements entered into by this state are eligible to receive the medical assistance in accordance with the laws and procedures that apply to the agreement.

ARTICLE VIII. FEDERAL PARTICIPATION

Consistent with federal law, the Department of Protective and Regulatory Services and the Health and Human Services Commission, in connection with the administration of this compact or a compact authorized by this compact, shall include the provision of adoption assistance and medical assistance for which the federal government pays some or all of the cost in any state plan made under the Adoption Assistance and Child Welfare Act of 1980 (Pub. L. No. 96–272), Titles IV-E and XIX of the Social Security Act, and other applicable federal laws. The Department of Protective and Regulatory Services and the Health and Human Services Commission shall apply for and administer all relevant federal aid in accordance with law.

Added by Acts 1995, 74th Leg., ch. 846, § 9, eff. June 16, 1995.

[1] V.T.C.A., Family Code § 162.301 et seq.

§ 162.202. Authority of Department of Protective and Regulatory Services

The Department of Protective and Regulatory Services, with the concurrence of the Health and Human Services Commission, may develop, participate in the development of, negotiate, and enter into one or more interstate compacts on behalf of this state with other states to implement one or more of the purposes of this subchapter. An interstate compact authorized by this article has the force and effect of law.

Added by Acts 1995, 74th Leg., ch. 846, § 9, eff. June 16, 1995.

§ 162.203. Compact Administration

The executive director of the Department of Protective and Regulatory Services shall serve as the compact administrator. The administrator shall cooperate with all departments, agencies, and officers of this state and its subdivisions in facilitating the proper administration of the compact and any supplemental agreements entered into by this state. The executive director and the commissioner of human services shall designate deputy compact administrators to represent adoption assistance services and medical assistance services provided under Title XIX of the Social Security Act.

Added by Acts 1995, 74th Leg., ch. 846, § 9, eff. June 16, 1995.

§ 162.204. Supplementary Agreements

The compact administrator may enter into supplementary agreements with appropriate officials of other states under the compact. If a supplementary agreement requires or authorizes the use of any institution or facility of this state or requires or authorizes the provision of a service by this state, the supplementary agreement does not take effect until approved by the head of the department or agency under whose jurisdiction the institution or facility is operated or whose department or agency will be charged with rendering the service.

Added by Acts 1995, 74th Leg., ch. 846, § 9, eff. June 16, 1995.

§ 162.205. Payments by State

The compact administrator, subject to the approval of the chief state fiscal officer, may make or arrange for payments necessary to discharge financial obligations imposed on this state by the compact or by a supplementary agreement entered into under the compact.

Added by Acts 1995, 74th Leg., ch. 846, § 9, eff. June 16, 1995.

§ 162.206. Penalties

A person who, under a compact entered into under this subchapter, knowingly obtains or attempts to obtain or aids or abets any person in obtaining, by means of a wilfully false statement or representation or by impersonation or other fraudulent device, any assistance on behalf of a child or other person to which the child or other person is not entitled, or assistance in an amount greater than that to which the child or other person is entitled, commits an offense. An offense under this section is a Class B misdemeanor. An offense under this section that also constitutes an offense under other law may be punished under either this section or the other applicable law.

Added by Acts 1995, 74th Leg., ch. 846, § 9, eff. June 16, 1995.

[Sections 162.207 to 162.300 reserved for expansion]

SUBCHAPTER D. ADOPTION SERVICES BY THE DEPARTMENT OF PROTECTIVE AND REGULATORY SERVICES

§ 162.301. Definitions

In this subchapter:

(1) "Adoption assistance agreement" means a written agreement, binding on the parties to the agreement, between the department and the prospective adoptive parents that specifies the nature and amount of any payment, services, or assistance to be provided under the agreement and stipulates that the agreement will remain in effect without regard to the state in which the prospective adoptive parents reside at any particular time.

(2) "Child" means a child who cannot be placed for adoption with appropriate adoptive parents without the provision of adoption assistance because of factors including ethnic background, age, membership in a minority or sibling group, the presence of a medical condition, or a physical, mental, or emotional disability.

(3) "Department" means the Department of Protective and Regulatory Services.

Added by Acts 1995, 74th Leg., ch. 20, § 1, eff. April 20, 1995. Amended by Acts 1995, 74th Leg., ch. 412, § 1, eff. Aug. 28, 1995.

§ 162.302. Adoption Assistance Program

(a) The department shall administer a program designed to promote the adoption of children by providing information to prospective adoptive parents concerning the availability and needs of the children, assisting the parents in completing the adoption process, and providing adoption assistance necessary for the parents to adopt the children.

(b) The legislature intends that the program benefit children residing in foster homes at state or county expense by providing them with the stability and security of permanent homes and that the costs paid by the state and counties for foster home care for the children be reduced.

(c) The program shall be carried out by licensed child-placing agencies or county child-care or welfare units under rules adopted by the department.

(d) The department shall keep records necessary to evaluate the program's effectiveness in encouraging and promoting the adoption of children.

Added by Acts 1995, 74th Leg., ch. 20, § 1, eff. April 20, 1995. Amended by Acts 1995, 74th Leg., ch. 412, § 2, eff. Aug. 28, 1995.

§ 162.303. Dissemination of Information

The department, county child-care or welfare units, and licensed child-placing agencies shall disseminate information to prospective adoptive parents concerning the availability and needs of children for adoption and the existence of adoption assistance for parents who adopt them. Special effort shall be made to disseminate the information to families that have lower income levels or that belong to disadvantaged groups.

Added by Acts 1995, 74th Leg., ch. 20, § 1, eff. April 20, 1995. Amended by Acts 1995, 74th Leg., ch. 412, § 3, eff. Aug. 28, 1995.

§ 162.304. Financial and Medical Assistance

(a) The department shall enter into adoption assistance agreements with the adoptive parents of a child as authorized by Part E of Title IV of the federal Social Security Act, as amended (42 U.S.C. Section 673).

(b) The adoption of a child may be subsidized by the department. The need for and amount of the subsidy shall be determined by the department under its rules.

(c) In addition to the subsidy under Subsection (b), the department may subsidize the cost of medical care for a child. The department shall determine the amount and need for the subsidy.

(d) The county may pay a subsidy under Subsection (b) or (c) if the county is responsible for the child's foster care at the time of the child's adoptive placement.

(e) If the child is receiving supplemental security income from the federal government, the state may pay the subsidy regardless of whether the state is the managing conservator for the child.

Added by Acts 1995, 74th Leg., ch. 20, § 1, eff. April 20, 1995. Amended by Acts 1995, 74th Leg., ch. 412, § 4, eff. Aug. 28, 1995.

§ 162.305. Funds

The department and other state agencies shall actively seek and use federal funds available for the purposes of this subchapter.

Added by Acts 1995, 74th Leg., ch. 20, § 1, eff. April 20, 1995. Amended by Acts 1995, 74th Leg., ch. 412, § 5, eff. Aug. 28, 1995.

§ 162.306. Postadoption Services

(a) The department may provide services after adoption to adoptees and adoptive families for whom the department provided services before the adoption.

(b) The department may provide services under this section directly or through contract.

(c) The services may include financial assistance, respite care, placement services, parenting programs, support groups, counseling services, crisis intervention, and medical aid.

Added by Acts 1995, 74th Leg., ch. 20, § 1, eff. April 20, 1995. Amended by Acts 1995, 74th Leg., ch. 412, § 6, eff. Aug. 28, 1995.

§ 162.307. Repealed by Acts 1995, 74th Leg., ch. 412, § 7, eff. Aug. 28, 1995

Section 7 of the 1995 repealing act provides:

"Section 162.307, Family Code, as added by H.B. No. 655, Acts of the 74th Legislature, Regular Session, 1995, is repealed, and the postadoption services advisory committee established under that section is abolished on the effective date of this Act."

§ 162.308. Race or Ethnicity

(a) The department, a county child-care or welfare unit, or a licensed child-placing agency may not make an adoption placement decision on the presumption that placing a child in a family of the same race or ethnicity as the race or ethnicity of the child is in the best interest of the child.

(b) Unless an independent psychological evaluation specific to a child indicates that placement with a family of a particular race or ethnicity would be detrimental to the child, the department, county child-care or welfare unit, or licensed child-placing agency may not deny, delay, or prohibit the adoption of a child because the department, county, or agency is attempting to locate a family of a particular race or ethnicity.

(c) This section does not prevent or limit the recruitment of minority families as adoptive families, but the recruitment of minority families may not be a reason to delay placement of a child with an available family of a race or ethnicity different from that of the child.

(d) A state or county employee who violates this section is subject to immediate dismissal. A licensed child-placing agency that violates this section is subject to action by the licensing agency as a ground for revocation or suspension of the agency's license.

(e) A district court, on the application for an injunction or the filing of a petition complaining of a violation of this section by any person residing in the county in which the court has jurisdiction, shall enforce this section by issuing appropriate orders. An action for an injunction is in addition to any other action, proceeding, or remedy authorized by law. An applicant or petitioner who is granted an injunction or given other appropriate relief under this section is entitled to the costs of the suit, including reasonable attorney's fees.

Added by Acts 1995, 74th Leg., ch. 20, § 1, eff. April 20, 1995. Amended by Acts 1995, 74th Leg., ch. 879, § 1, eff. June 16, 1995.

§ 162.309. Advisory Committee on Promoting Adoption of Minority Children

(a) An advisory committee on promoting the adoption of and provision of services to minority children is established within the department.

(b) The committee is composed of 12 members appointed by the board of the Department of Protective and Regulatory Services. The board shall appoint to the committee individuals who in the aggregate have knowledge of and experience in community education, cultural relations, family support, counseling, and parenting skills and education. At least six members must be ordained members of the clergy.

(c) A committee member serves for a two-year term and may be appointed for additional terms.

(d) A member of the committee receives no compensation but is entitled to reimbursement for actual and necessary expenses incurred in performing the member's duties under this section.

(e) The committee shall elect one member to serve as presiding officer. The presiding officer serves for a two-year term and may be elected for additional terms.

(f) The department shall set the time and place of the first committee meeting. The committee shall meet at least quarterly.

(g) The department shall pay the expenses of the committee and shall supply necessary personnel and supplies.

(h) To promote the adoption of and provision of services to minority children, the committee shall:

(1) study, develop, and evaluate programs and projects relating to community awareness and education, family support, counseling, parenting skills and education, and reform of the child welfare system;

(2) consult with churches and other cultural and civic organizations; and

(3) report to the department at least annually the committee's recommendations for department programs and projects that will promote the adoption of and provision of services to minority children.

(i) On receiving the committee's recommendations, the department may adopt rules to implement a program or project recommended under this section. The department may solicit, accept, and use gifts and donations to implement a program or project recommended by the committee.

(j) The department shall report to the legislature not later than November 1 of each even-numbered year following the first year in which it receives recommendations under this section regarding committee recommendations and action taken by the department under this section.

(k) The recruitment of minority families may not be a reason to delay placement of a child with an available family of a race or ethnicity different from that of the child.

Added by Acts 1997, 75th Leg., ch. 165, § 7.17(a), eff. Sept. 1, 1997.

[Sections 162.310 to 162.400 reserved for expansion]

SUBCHAPTER E. VOLUNTARY ADOPTION REGISTRIES

§ 162.401. Purpose

The purpose of this subchapter is to provide for the establishment of mutual consent voluntary adoption registries through which adoptees, birth parents, and biological siblings may voluntarily locate each other. It is not the purpose of this subchapter to inhibit or prohibit persons from locating each other through other legal means or to inhibit or affect in any way the provision of postadoptive services and education, by adoption agencies or others, that go further than the procedures set out for registries established under this subchapter.

Added by Acts 1995, 74th Leg., ch. 20, § 1, eff. April 20, 1995.

§ 162.402. Definitions

In this subchapter:

(1) "Administrator" means the administrator of a mutual consent voluntary adoption registry established under this subchapter.

(2) "Adoptee" means a person 18 years of age or older who has been legally adopted in this state or another state or country.

(3) "Adoption" means the act of creating the legal relationship of parent and child between a person and a child who is not the biological child of that person. The term does not include the act of establishing the legal relationship of parent and child between a man and a child through proof of paternity or voluntary legitimation proceedings.

(4) "Adoption agency" means a person, other than a natural parent or guardian of a child, who plans for the placement of or places a child in the home of a prospective adoptive parent.

(5) "Adoptive parent" means an adult who is a parent of an adoptee through a legal process of adoption.

(6) "Alleged father" means a man who is not deemed by law to be or who has not been adjudicated to be the biological father of an adoptee and who claims or is alleged to be the adoptee's biological father.

(7) "Authorized agency" means a public agency authorized to care for or to place children for adoption or a private entity approved for that purpose by the department through a license, certification, or other means. The term includes a licensed child-placing agency or a previously licensed child-placing agency that has ceased operations and has transferred its adoption records to the bureau or an agency authorized by the department to place children for adoption and a licensed child-placing agency that has been acquired by, merged with, or otherwise succeeded by an agency authorized by the department to place children for adoption.

(8) "Biological parent" means a man or woman who is the father or mother of genetic origin of a child.

(9) "Biological siblings" means persons who share a common birth parent.

(10) "Birth parent" means:

(A) the biological mother of an adoptee;

(B) the man adjudicated or presumed under Chapter 151 to be the biological father of an adoptee; and

(C) a man who has signed a consent to adoption, affidavit of relinquishment, affidavit of waiver of interest in child, or other written instrument releasing the adoptee for adoption, unless the consent, affidavit, or other instrument includes a sworn refusal to admit or a denial of paternity. The term includes a birth mother and birth father but does not include a person adjudicated by a court of competent jurisdiction as not being the biological parent of an adoptee.

(11) "Central registry" means the mutual consent voluntary adoption registry established and maintained by the bureau under this subchapter.

(12) "Department" means the Department of Protective and Regulatory Services.

(13) "Registry" means a mutual consent voluntary adoption registry established under this subchapter.

(14) "Bureau" means the bureau of vital statistics.

Added by Acts 1995, 74th Leg., ch. 20, § 1, eff. April 20, 1995. Amended by Acts 1995, 74th Leg., ch. 968, §§ 1, 11, eff. Sept. 1, 1995; Acts 1997, 75th Leg., ch. 561, § 19, eff. Sept. 1, 1997.

Section 32(f) of Acts 1997, 75th Leg., ch. 561 provides:

"The change in law made by this Act transferring the administration of the central voluntary adoption registry from the Department of Protective and Regulatory Services to the bureau of vital statistics takes effect January 1, 1998. On that date, the powers, duties, obligations, rights, contracts, records, personnel, property, and unexpended appropriations dedicated to the department for the operation of the registry are transferred to the bureau. The department and the bureau shall develop and implement a plan before that date for the transfer of the registry."

§ 162.403. Establishment of Voluntary Adoption Registries

(a) The bureau shall establish and maintain a mutual consent voluntary adoption registry.

(b) Except as provided by Subsection (c), an agency authorized by the department to place children for adoption and an association comprised exclusively of those agencies may establish a mutual consent voluntary adoption registry. An agency may contract with any other agency authorized by the department to place children for adoption or with an association comprised exclusively of those agencies to perform registry services on its behalf.

(c) An authorized agency that did not directly or by contract provide registry services as required by this subchapter on January 1, 1984, may not provide its own registry service. The bureau shall operate through the central registry those services for agencies not permitted to provide a registry under this section.

Added by Acts 1995, 74th Leg., ch. 20, § 1, eff. April 20, 1995. Amended by Acts 1997, 75th Leg., ch. 561, § 20, eff. Sept. 1, 1997.

For transition provisions of Acts 1997, 75th Leg., ch. 561, see notes following V.T.C.A., Family Code § 162.402.

§ 162.404. Requirement to Send Information to Central Registry

An authorized agency that is permitted to provide a registry under this subchapter or that participates in a mutual consent voluntary adoption registry with an association of authorized agencies shall send to the central registry a duplicate of all information the registry maintains in the agency's registry or sends to the registry in which the agency participates.

Added by Acts 1997, 75th Leg., ch. 561, § 21, eff. Sept. 1, 1997.

For transition provisions of Acts 1997, 75th Leg., ch. 561, see notes following V.T.C.A., Family Code § 162.402.

§ 162.405. Determination of Appropriate Registry

(a) The administrator of the central registry shall determine the appropriate registry to which an applicant is entitled to apply.

(b) On receiving an inquiry by an adoptee, birth parent, or sibling who has provided satisfactory proof of age and identity and paid all required inquiry fees, the administrator of the central registry shall review the information on file in the central index and consult with the administrators of other registries in the state to determine the identity of any appropriate registry through which the adoptee, birth parent, or sibling may register.

(c) Each administrator shall, not later than the 30th day after the date of receiving an inquiry from the administrator of the central registry, respond in writing to the inquiry that the registrant was not placed for adoption by an agency served by that registry or that the registrant was placed for adoption by an agency served by that registry. If the registrant was placed for adoption by an agency served by the registry, the administrator shall file a report with the administrator of the central registry including:

(1) the name of the adopted child as shown in the final adoption decree;

(2) the birth date of the adopted child;

(3) the docket number of the adoption suit;

(4) the identity of the court that granted the adoption;

(5) the date of the final adoption decree;

(6) the identity of the agency, if any, through which the adopted child was placed; and

(7) the identity, address, and telephone number of the registry through which the adopted child may register as an adoptee.

(d) After completing the investigation, the administrator of the central registry shall issue an official certificate stating:

(1) the identity of the registry through which the adoptee, birth parent, or biological sibling may apply for registration, if known; or

(2) if the administrator cannot make a conclusive determination, that the adoptee, birth parent, or biological sibling is entitled to apply for registration through the central registry.

Added by Acts 1995, 74th Leg., ch. 20, § 1, eff. April 20, 1995. Amended by Acts 1995, 74th Leg., ch. 751, § 79, eff. Sept. 1, 1995; Acts 1995, 74th Leg., ch. 968, § 2, eff. Sept. 1, 1995.

§ 162.406. Registration Eligibility

(a) An adoptee who is 18 years of age or older may apply to a registry for information about the adoptee's birth parents and biological siblings.

(b) A birth parent who is 18 years of age or older may apply to a registry for information about an adoptee who is a child by birth of the birth parent.

(c) An alleged father who is 18 years of age or older and who acknowledges paternity but is not, at the time of application, a birth father may register as a birth father but may not otherwise be recognized as a birth father for the purposes of this subchapter unless:

(1) the adoptee's birth mother in her application identifies him as the adoptee's biological father; and

(2) additional information concerning the adoptee obtained from other sources is not inconsistent with his claim of paternity.

(d) A biological sibling who is 18 years of age or older may apply to a registry for information about the person's adopted biological siblings.

(e) Only birth parents, adoptees, and biological siblings may apply for information through a registry.

(f) A person, including an authorized agency, may not apply for information through a registry as an agent, attorney, or representative of an adoptee, birth parent, or biological sibling.

Added by Acts 1995, 74th Leg., ch. 20, § 1, eff. April 20, 1995. Amended by Acts 1995, 74th Leg., ch. 968, § 3, eff. Sept. 1, 1995.

§ 162.407. Registration

(a) The administrator shall require each registration applicant to sign a written application.

(b) An adoptee adopted or placed through an authorized agency may register through the registry maintained by that agency or the registry to which the agency has delegated registry services or through the central registry maintained by the bureau.

(c) Birth parents and biological siblings shall register through:

(1) the registry of the authorized agency through which the adoptee was adopted or placed; or

(2) the central registry.

(d) The administrator may not accept an application for registration unless the applicant:

(1) provides proof of identity as provided by Section 162.408;

(2) establishes the applicant's eligibility to register; and

(3) pays all required registration fees.

(e) A registration remains in effect until the 99th anniversary of the date the registration is accepted unless a shorter period is specified by the applicant or the registration is withdrawn before that time.

(f) A registrant may withdraw the registrant's registration in writing without charge at any time.

(g) After a registration is withdrawn or expires, the registrant shall be treated as if the person has not previously registered.

(h) A completed registry application must be accepted or rejected before the 46th day after the date the application is received. If an application is rejected, the administrator shall provide the applicant with a written statement of the reason for the rejection.

Added by Acts 1995, 74th Leg., ch. 20, § 1, eff. April 20, 1995. Amended by Acts 1995, 74th Leg., ch. 968, § 4, eff. Sept. 1, 1995; Acts 1997, 75th Leg., ch. 561, § 22, eff. Sept. 1, 1997.

For transition provisions of Acts 1997, 75th Leg., ch. 561, see notes following V.T.C.A., Family Code § 162.402.

§ 162.408. Proof of Identity

The rules and minimum standards of the Texas Board of Health for the bureau must provide for proof of identity in order to facilitate the purposes of this subchapter and to protect the privacy rights of adoptees, adoptive parents, birth parents, biological siblings, and their families.

Added by Acts 1995, 74th Leg., ch. 20, § 1, eff. April 20, 1995. Amended by Acts 1997, 75th Leg., ch. 561, § 23, eff. Sept. 1, 1997.

For transition provisions of Acts 1997, 75th Leg., ch. 561, see notes following V.T.C.A., Family Code § 162.402.

§ 162.409. Application

(a) An application must contain:

(1) the name, address, and telephone number of the applicant;

(2) any other name or alias by which the applicant has been known;

(3) the age, date of birth, and place of birth of the applicant;

(4) the original name of the adoptee, if known;

(5) the adoptive name of the adoptee, if known;

(6) a statement that the applicant is willing to allow the applicant's identity to be disclosed to a registrant who is eligible to learn the applicant's identity;

(7) the name, address, and telephone number of the agency or other entity, organization, or person placing the adoptee for adoption, if known, or, if not known, a statement that the applicant does not know that information;

(8) an authorization to the administrator and the administrator's designees to inspect all vital statistics records, court records, and agency records, including confidential records, relating to the birth, adoption, marriage, and divorce of the applicant or to the birth and death of any child or sibling by birth or adoption of the applicant;

(9) the specific address to which the applicant wishes notice of a successful match to be mailed;

(10) a statement that the applicant either does or does not consent to disclosure of identifying information about the applicant after the applicant's death;

(11) a statement that the registration is to be effective for 99 years or for a stated shorter period selected by the applicant; and

(12) a statement that the adoptee applicant either does or does not desire to be informed that registry records indicate that the applicant has a biological sibling who has registered under this subchapter.

(b) The application may contain the applicant's social security number if the applicant, after being advised of the right not to supply the number, voluntarily furnishes it.

(c) The application of a birth parent must include:

(1) the original name and date of birth or approximate date of birth of each adoptee with respect to whom the parent is registering;

(2) the names of all other birth children, including maiden names, aliases, dates and places of birth, and names of the birth parents;

(3) each name known or thought by the applicant to have been used by the adoptee's other birth parent;

(4) the last known address of the adoptee's other birth parent; and

(5) other available information through which the other birth parent may be identified.

(d) The application of a biological sibling must include:

(1) a statement explaining the applicant's basis for believing that the applicant has one or more biological siblings;

(2) the names, including maiden and married names, and aliases of all the applicant's siblings by birth and adoption and their dates and places of birth, if known;

(3) the names of the applicant's legal parents;

(4) the names of the applicant's birth parents, if known; and

(5) any other information known to the applicant through which the existence and identity of the applicant's biological siblings can be confirmed.

(e) An application may also contain additional information through which the applicant's identity and eligibility to register may be ascertained.

(f) The administrator shall assist the applicant in filling out the application if the applicant is unable to complete the application without assistance, but the administrator may not furnish the applicant with any substantive information necessary to complete the application.

Added by Acts 1995, 74th Leg., ch. 20, § 1, eff. April 20, 1995. Amended by Acts 1995, 74th Leg., ch. 968, § 5, eff. Sept. 1, 1995.

§ 162.410. Repealed by Acts 1995, 74th Leg., ch. 968, § 11, eff. Sept. 1, 1995

§ 162.411. Fees

(a) The costs of establishing, operating, and maintaining a registry may be recovered in whole or in part through users' fees charged to applicants and registrants.

(b) Each registry shall establish a schedule of fees for services provided by the registry. The fees shall be reasonably related to the direct and indirect costs of establishing, operating, and maintaining the registry.

(c) A fee may not be charged for withdrawing a registration.

(d) The fees collected by the bureau shall be deposited in a special fund in the general revenue fund. Funds in the special fund may be appropriated only for the administration of the central registry.

(e) The administrator may waive users' fees in whole or in part if the applicant provides satisfactory proof of financial inability to pay the fees.

Added by Acts 1995, 74th Leg., ch. 20, § 1, eff. April 20, 1995. Amended by Acts 1995, 74th Leg., ch. 968, § 6, eff. Sept. 1, 1995; Acts 1997, 75th Leg., ch. 561, § 24, eff. Sept. 1, 1997.

For transition provisions of Acts 1997, 75th Leg., ch. 561, see notes following V.T.C.A., Family Code § 162.402.

§ 162.412. Supplemental Information

(a) A registrant may amend the registrant's registration and submit additional information to the administrator. A registrant shall notify the administrator of any change in the registrant's name or address that occurs after acceptance of the application.

(b) The administrator does not have a duty to search for a registrant who fails to register a change of name or address.

Added by Acts 1995, 74th Leg., ch. 20, § 1, eff. April 20, 1995.

§ 162.413. Counseling

The applicant must participate in counseling for not less than one hour with a social worker or mental health professional with expertise in postadoption counseling after the administrator has accepted the application for registration and before the release of confidential information.

Added by Acts 1995, 74th Leg., ch. 20, § 1, eff. April 20, 1995. Amended by Acts 1995, 74th Leg., ch. 968, § 7, eff. Sept. 1, 1995.

§ 162.414. Matching Procedures

(a) The administrator shall process each registration in an attempt to match the adoptee and the adoptee's birth parents or the adoptee and the adoptee's biological siblings.

(b) The administrator shall determine that there is a match if the adult adoptee and the birth mother or the birth father have registered or if a biological sibling has registered.

(c) To establish or corroborate a match, the administrator shall request confirmation of a possible match from the bureau. If the agency operating the registry has in its own records sufficient information through which the match may be confirmed, the administrator may, but is not required to, request confirmation from the bureau. The bureau may confirm or deny the match without breaching the duty of confidentiality to the adoptee, adoptive parents, birth parents, or biological siblings and without a court order.

(d) To establish a match, the administrator may also request confirmation of a possible match from the agency, if any, that has possession of records concerning the adoption of an adoptee or from the court that granted the adoption, the hospital where the adoptee or any biological sibling was born, the physician who delivered the adoptee or biological sibling, or any other person who has knowledge of the relevant facts. The agency, court, hospital, physician, or person with knowledge may confirm or deny the match without breaching any duty of confidentiality to the adoptee, adoptive parents, birth parents, or biological siblings.

(e) If a match is denied by a source contacted under Subsection (d), the administrator shall make a full and complete investigation into the reliability of the denial. If the match is corroborated by other reliable sources and the administrator is satisfied that the denial is erroneous, the administrator may make disclosures but shall report to the adoptee, birth parents, and biological siblings involved that the match was not confirmed by all information sources.

Added by Acts 1995, 74th Leg., ch. 20, § 1, eff. April 20, 1995. Amended by Acts 1995, 74th Leg., ch. 968, § 8, eff. Sept. 1, 1995; Acts 1997, 75th Leg., ch. 561, § 25, eff. Sept. 1, 1997.

For transition provisions of Acts 1997, 75th Leg., ch. 561, see notes following V.T.C.A., Family Code § 162.402.

§ 162.415. Repealed by Acts 1995, 74th Leg., ch. 968, § 11, eff. Sept. 1, 1995

§ 162.416. Disclosure of Identifying Information

(a) When a match has been made and confirmed to the administrator's satisfaction, the administrator shall mail to each registrant, at the registrant's last known address, by fax or registered or certified mail, return receipt requested, delivery restricted to addressee only, a written notice:

(1) informing the registrant that a match has been made and confirmed;

(2) reminding the registrant that the registrant may withdraw the registration before disclosures are made, if desired; and

(3) notifying the registrant that before any identifying disclosures are made, the registrant must:

(A) sign a written consent to disclosure that allows the disclosure of identifying information about the other registrants to the registrant and allows the disclosure of identifying information about the registrant to other registrants;

(B) participate in counseling for not less than one hour with a social worker or mental health professional who has expertise in postadoption counseling; and

(C) provide the administrator with written certification that the counseling required under Subdivision (B) has been completed.

(b) Identifying information about a registrant shall be released without the registrant's having consented after the match to disclosure if the registrant is dead, the registrant's registration was valid at the time of death, and the registrant had in writing specifically authorized the postdeath disclosure in the registrant's application or in a supplemental statement filed with the administrator.

(c) Identifying information about a deceased birth parent may not be released until each surviving child of the deceased birth parent is an adult or until each child's surviving parent, guardian, managing conservator, or legal custodian consents in writing to the disclosure.

(d) The administrator shall prepare and release written disclosure statements identifying information about each of the registrants if the registrants complied with Subsection (a) and, before the 60th day after the date notification of match was mailed, the registrant or registrants have not withdrawn their registrations.

(e) If the administrator establishes that a match cannot be made because of the death of an adoptee, birth parent, or biological sibling, the administrator shall promptly notify the affected registrant. The administrator shall disclose the reason why a match cannot be made and may disclose nonidentifying information concerning the circumstances of the person's death.

Added by Acts 1995, 74th Leg., ch. 20, § 1, eff. April 20, 1995. Amended by Acts 1995, 74th Leg., ch. 968, § 9, eff. Sept. 1, 1995.

§§ 162.417, 162.418. Repealed by Acts 1995, 74th Leg., ch. 968, § 11, eff. Sept. 1, 1995

§ 162.419. Registry Records Confidential

(a) All applications, registrations, records, and other information submitted to, obtained by, or otherwise acquired by a registry are confidential and may not be disclosed to any person or entity except in the manner authorized by this subchapter.

(b) Information acquired by a registry may not be disclosed under freedom of information or sunshine legislation, rules, or practice.

(c) A person may not file or prosecute a class action litigation to force a registry to disclose identifying information.

Added by Acts 1995, 74th Leg., ch. 20, § 1, eff. April 20, 1995.

§ 162.420. Rulemaking

(a) The Texas Board of Health shall make rules and adopt minimum standards for the bureau to:

(1) administer the provisions of this subchapter; and

(2) ensure that each registry respects the right to privacy and confidentiality of an adoptee, birth parent, and biological sibling who does not desire to disclose the person's identity.

(b) The bureau shall conduct a comprehensive review of all rules and standards adopted under this subchapter not less than every six years.

(c) In order to provide the administrators an opportunity to review proposed rules and standards and send written suggestions to the Texas Board of Health, the board shall, before adopting rules and minimum standards, send a copy of the proposed rules and standards not less than 60 days before the date they take effect to:

(1) the administrator of each registry established under this subchapter; and

(2) the administrator of each agency authorized by the department to place children for adoption.

Added by Acts 1995, 74th Leg., ch. 20, § 1, eff. April 20, 1995. Amended by Acts 1997, 75th Leg., ch. 561, § 26, eff. Sept. 1, 1997.

For transition provisions of Acts 1997, 75th Leg., ch. 561, see notes following V.T.C.A., Family Code § 162.402.

§ 162.421. Prohibited Acts; Criminal Penalties

(a) This subchapter does not prevent the bureau from making known to the public, by appropriate means, the existence of voluntary adoption registries.

(b) Information received by or in connection with the operation of a registry may not be stored in a data bank used for any purpose other than operation of the registry.

(c) A person commits an offense if the person knowingly or recklessly discloses information from a registry application, registration, record, or other information submitted to, obtained by, or otherwise acquired by a registry in violation of this subchapter. This subsection may not be construed to penalize the disclosure of information from adoption agency records. An offense under this subsection is a felony of the second degree.

(d) A person commits an offense if the person with criminal negligence causes or permits the disclosure of information from a registry application, registration, record, or other information submitted to, obtained by, or otherwise acquired by a registry in violation of this subchapter. This subsection may not be construed to penalize the disclosure of information from adoption agency records. An offense under this subsection is a Class A misdemeanor.

(e) A person commits an offense if the person impersonates an adoptee, birth parent, or biological sibling with the intent to secure confidential information from a registry established under this subchapter. An offense under this subsection is a felony of the second degree.

(f) A person commits an offense if the person impersonates an administrator, agent, or employee of a registry with the intent to secure confidential information from a registry established under this subchapter. An offense under this subsection is a felony of the second degree.

(g) A person commits an offense if the person, with intent to deceive and with knowledge of the statement's meaning, makes a false statement under oath in connection with the operation of a registry. An offense under this subsection is a felony of the third degree.

Added by Acts 1995, 74th Leg., ch. 20, § 1, eff. April 20, 1995. Amended by Acts 1995, 74th Leg., ch. 968, § 10, eff. Sept. 1, 1995; Acts 1997, 75th Leg., ch. 561, § 27, eff. Sept. 1, 1997.

For transition provisions of Acts 1997, 75th Leg., ch. 561, see notes following V.T.C.A., Family Code § 162.402.

§ 162.422. Immunity From Liability

(a) The bureau or authorized agency establishing or operating a registry is not liable to any person for obtaining or disclosing identifying information about a birth parent, adoptee, or biological sibling within the scope of this subchapter and under its provisions.

(b) An employee or agent of the bureau or of an authorized agency establishing or operating a registry under this subchapter is not liable to any person for obtaining or disclosing identifying information about a birth parent, adoptee, or biological sibling within the scope of this subchapter and under its provisions.

(c) A person or entity furnishing information to the administrator or an employee or agent of a registry is not liable to any person for disclosing information about a birth parent, adoptee, or biological sibling within the scope of this subchapter and under its provisions.

(d) A person or entity is not immune from liability for performing an act prohibited by Section 162.421.

Added by Acts 1995, 74th Leg., ch. 20, § 1, eff. April 20, 1995. Amended by Acts 1997, 75th Leg., ch. 561, § 28, eff. Sept. 1, 1997.

For transition provisions of Acts 1997, 75th Leg., ch. 561, see notes following V.T.C.A., Family Code § 162.402.

[Sections 162.423 to 162.500 reserved for expansion]

SUBCHAPTER F. ADOPTION OF AN ADULT

§ 162.501. Adoption of Adult

The court may grant the petition of an adult residing in this state to adopt another adult according to this subchapter.

Added by Acts 1995, 74th Leg., ch. 20, § 1, eff. April 20, 1995.

§ 162.502. Jurisdiction

The petitioner shall file a suit to adopt an adult in the district court or a statutory county court granted jurisdiction in family law cases and proceedings by Chapter 25, Government Code, in the county of the petitioner's residence.

Added by Acts 1995, 74th Leg., ch. 20, § 1, eff. April 20, 1995.

§ 162.503. Requirements of Petition

(a) A petition to adopt an adult shall be entitled "In the Interest of __________, An Adult."

(b) If the petitioner is married, both spouses must join in the petition for adoption.

Added by Acts 1995, 74th Leg., ch. 20, § 1, eff. April 20, 1995.

§ 162.504. Consent

A court may not grant an adoption unless the adult consents in writing to be adopted by the petitioner.

Added by Acts 1995, 74th Leg., ch. 20, § 1, eff. April 20, 1995.

§ 162.505. Attendance Required

The petitioner and the adult to be adopted must attend the hearing. For good cause shown, the court may waive this requirement, by written order, if the petitioner or adult to be adopted is unable to attend.

Added by Acts 1995, 74th Leg., ch. 20, § 1, eff. April 20, 1995.

§ 162.506. Adoption Order

The court shall grant the adoption if the court finds that the requirements for adoption of an adult are met.

Added by Acts 1995, 74th Leg., ch. 20, § 1, eff. April 20, 1995.

§ 162.507. Effect of Adoption

(a) The adopted adult is the son or daughter of the adoptive parents for all purposes.

(b) The adopted adult is entitled to inherit from and through the adopted adult's adoptive parents as though the adopted adult were the biological child of the adoptive parents.

(c) The adopted adult retains the right to inherit from the adult's biological parents. However, a biological parent may not inherit from or through an adopted adult.

Added by Acts 1995, 74th Leg., ch. 20, § 1, eff. April 20, 1995.

SUBCHAPTER G. MISCELLANEOUS PROVISIONS

§ 162.601. Incentives for Licensed Child-Placing Agencies

(a) Subject to the availability of funds, the Department of Protective and Regulatory Services shall pay, in addition to any other amounts due, a monetary incentive to a licensed child-placing agency for the completion of an adoption:

(1) of a child, as defined by Section 162.301, receiving or entitled to receive foster care at department expense; and

(2) arranged with the assistance of the agency.

(b) The incentive may not exceed 25 percent of the amount the department would have spent to provide one year of foster care for the child, determined according to the child's level of care at the time the adoption is completed.

(c) For purposes of this section, an adoption is completed on the date on which the court issues the adoption order.

Added by Acts 1997, 75th Leg., ch. 1309, § 1, eff. Sept. 1, 1997.

Section 2 of Acts 1997, 75th Leg., ch. 1309 provides:

"This Act applies to an adoption that becomes final on or after the effective date of this Act. For purposes of this section, an adoption becomes final on the date the court issues the adoption order."

[Chapters 163 to 200 reserved for expansion]

SUBTITLE C. JUDICIAL RESOURCES AND SERVICES

CHAPTER 201. ASSOCIATE JUDGE; CHILD SUPPORT MASTER

SUBCHAPTER A. ASSOCIATE JUDGE

SUBCHAPTER A. ASSOCIATE JUDGE

§ 201.001. Appointment

(a) A judge of a court having jurisdiction of a suit under this title or Title 1 or 4 may appoint a full-time or part-time associate judge to perform the duties authorized by this chapter if the commissioners court of a county in which the court has jurisdiction authorizes the employment of an associate judge.

(b) If a court has jurisdiction in more than one county, an associate judge appointed by that court may serve only in a county in which the commissioners court has authorized the associate judge's appointment.

(c) If more than one court in a county has jurisdiction of a suit under this title or Title 1 or 4 the commissioners court may authorize the appointment of an associate judge for each court or may authorize one or more associate judges to share service with two or more courts.

(d) If an associate judge serves more than one court, the associate judge's appointment must be made with the unanimous approval of all the judges under whom the associate judge serves.

(e) This section does not apply to a master appointed under Subchapter B.[1]

Added by Acts 1995, 74th Leg., ch. 20, § 1, eff. April 20, 1995.

[1] V.T.C.A., Family Code § 201.101 et seq.

§ 201.002. Qualifications

To be eligible for appointment as an associate judge, a person must meet the requirements and qualifications to serve as a judge of the court or courts for which the associate judge is appointed.

Added by Acts 1995, 74th Leg., ch. 20, § 1, eff. April 20, 1995.

§ 201.003. Compensation

(a) An associate judge shall be paid a salary determined by the commissioners court of the county in which the associate judge serves.

(b) If an associate judge serves in more than one county, the associate judge shall be paid a salary as determined by agreement of the commissioners courts of the counties in which the associate judge serves.

(c) The associate judge's salary is paid from the county fund available for payment of officers' salaries.

(d) This section does not apply to a master appointed under Subchapter B.[1]

Added by Acts 1995, 74th Leg., ch. 20, § 1, eff. April 20, 1995.

[1] V.T.C.A., Family Code § 201.101 et seq.

§ 201.004. Termination of Associate Judge

(a) An associate judge who serves a single court serves at the will of the judge of that court.

(b) The employment of an associate judge who serves more than two courts may only be terminated by a majority vote of all the judges of the courts which the associate judge serves.

(c) The employment of an associate judge who serves two courts may be terminated by either of the judges of the courts which the associate judge serves.

(d) This section does not apply to a master appointed under Subchapter B.[1]

Added by Acts 1995, 74th Leg., ch. 20, § 1, eff. April 20, 1995.

[1] V.T.C.A., Family Code § 201.101 et seq.

§ 201.005. Cases That May Be Referred

(a) Except as provided by this section, a judge of a court may refer to an associate judge any aspect of a suit over which the court has jurisdiction under this title or Title 1 or 4 including any matter ancillary to the suit.

(b) Unless a party files a written objection to the associate judge hearing a trial on the merits, the judge may refer the trial to the associate judge. A trial on the merits is any final adjudication from which an appeal may be taken to a court of appeals.

(c) A party must file an objection to an associate judge hearing a trial on the merits not later than the 10th day after the date the party receives notice that the associate judge will hear the trial. If an objection is filed, the referring court shall hear the trial on the merits.

(d) Unless all parties consent in writing to an associate judge hearing a contested trial on the merits to terminate parental rights, the court may not refer the trial to the associate judge. If the parties do not consent in writing to the associate judge conducting the trial on the merits to terminate parental rights, any order terminating parental rights rendered under an associate judge's report is void.

(e) If a jury trial is demanded and a jury fee paid in a trial on the merits, the associate judge shall refer any matters requiring a jury back to the referring court for a trial before the referring court and jury.

Added by Acts 1995, 74th Leg., ch. 20, § 1, eff. April 20, 1995.

§ 201.006. Order of Referral

(a) In referring a case to an associate judge, the judge of the referring court shall render:

(1) an individual order of referral; or

(2) a general order of referral specifying the class and type of cases to be heard by the associate judge.

(b) The order of referral may limit the power or duties of an associate judge.

Added by Acts 1995, 74th Leg., ch. 20, § 1, eff. April 20, 1995.

§ 201.007. Powers of Associate Judge

Except as limited by an order of referral, an associate judge may:

(1) conduct a hearing;

(2) hear evidence;

(3) compel production of relevant evidence;

(4) rule on the admissibility of evidence;

(5) issue a summons for the appearance of witnesses;

(6) examine a witness;

(7) swear a witness for a hearing;

(8) make findings of fact on evidence;

(9) formulate conclusions of law;

(10) recommend an order to be rendered in a case;

(11) regulate all proceedings in a hearing before the associate judge; and

(12) take action as necessary and proper for the efficient performance of the associate judge's duties.

Added by Acts 1995, 74th Leg., ch. 20, § 1, eff. April 20, 1995.

§ 201.008. Attendance of Bailiff

A bailiff may attend a hearing by an associate judge if directed by the referring court.

Added by Acts 1995, 74th Leg., ch. 20, § 1, eff. April 20, 1995.

§ 201.009. Court Reporter

(a) A court reporter is not required during a hearing held by an associate judge appointed under this chapter.

(b) A party, the associate judge, or the referring court may provide for a reporter during the hearing.

(c) The record may be preserved by any other means approved by the associate judge.

(d) The referring court or associate judge may tax the expense of preserving the record as costs.

Added by Acts 1995, 74th Leg., ch. 20, § 1, eff. April 20, 1995.

§ 201.010. Witness

(a) A witness appearing before an associate judge is subject to the penalties for perjury provided by law.

(b) A referring court may fine or imprison a witness who:

(1) failed to appear before an associate judge after being summoned; or

(2) improperly refused to answer questions if the refusal has been certified to the court by the associate judge.

Added by Acts 1995, 74th Leg., ch. 20, § 1, eff. April 20, 1995.

§ 201.011. Report

(a) The associate judge's report may contain the associate judge's findings, conclusions, or recommendations. The associate judge's report must be in writing in the form directed by the referring court. The form may be a notation on the referring court's docket sheet.

(b) After a hearing, the associate judge shall provide the parties participating in the hearing notice of the substance of the associate judge's report.

(c) Notice may be given to the parties:

(1) in open court, by an oral statement or a copy of the associate judge's written report; or

(2) by certified mail, return receipt requested.

(d) The associate judge shall certify the date of mailing of notice by certified mail. Notice is considered given on the third day after the date of mailing.

(e) After a hearing conducted by an associate judge, the associate judge shall send the associate judge's signed and dated report and all other papers relating to the case to the referring court.

Added by Acts 1995, 74th Leg., ch. 20, § 1, eff. April 20, 1995.

§ 201.012. Notice of Right to Appeal

(a) Notice of the right of appeal to the judge of the referring court shall be given to all parties.

(b) The notice may be given:

(1) by oral statement in open court;

(2) by posting inside or outside the courtroom of the referring court; or

(3) as otherwise directed by the referring court.

Added by Acts 1995, 74th Leg., ch. 20, § 1, eff. April 20, 1995.

§ 201.013. Order of Court

(a) Pending appeal of the associate judge's report to the referring court, the decisions and recommendations of the associate judge are in full force and effect and are enforceable as an order of the referring court, except for orders providing for incarceration or for the appointment of a receiver.

(b) If an appeal to the referring court is not filed or the right to an appeal to the referring court is waived, the findings and recommendations of the associate judge become the order of the referring court only on the referring court's signing an order conforming to the associate judge's report.

Added by Acts 1995, 74th Leg., ch. 20, § 1, eff. April 20, 1995.

§ 201.014. Judicial Action on Associate Judge's Report

Unless a party files a written notice of appeal, the referring court may:

(1) adopt, modify, or reject the associate judge's report;

(2) hear further evidence; or

(3) recommit the matter to the associate judge for further proceedings.

Added by Acts 1995, 74th Leg., ch. 20, § 1, eff. April 20, 1995.

§ 201.015. Appeal to Referring Court

(a) A party may appeal an associate judge's report by filing notice of appeal not later than the third day after the date the party receives notice of the substance of the associate judge's report as provided by Section 201.011.

(b) An appeal to the referring court must be in writing specifying the findings and conclusions of the associate judge to which the party objects. The appeal is limited to the specified findings and conclusions.

(c) On appeal to the referring court, the parties may present witnesses as in a hearing de novo on the issues raised in the appeal.

(d) Notice of an appeal to the referring court shall be given to the opposing attorney under Rule 21a, Texas Rules of Civil Procedure.

(e) If an appeal to the referring court is filed by a party, any other party may file an appeal to the referring court not later than the seventh day after the date the initial appeal was filed.

(f) The referring court, after notice to the parties, shall hold a hearing on all appeals not later than the 30th day after the date on which the initial appeal was filed with the referring court.

(g) Before the start of a hearing by an associate judge, the parties may waive the right of appeal to the referring court in writing or on the record.

Added by Acts 1995, 74th Leg., ch. 20, § 1, eff. April 20, 1995.

§ 201.016. Appellate Review

(a) Failure to appeal to the referring court, by waiver or otherwise, the approval by the referring court of an associate judge's report does not deprive a party of the right to appeal to or request other relief from a court of appeals or the supreme court.

(b) The date an order or judgment by the referring court is signed is the controlling date for the purposes of appeal to or request for other relief from a court of appeals or the supreme court.

Added by Acts 1995, 74th Leg., ch. 20, § 1, eff. April 20, 1995.

§ 201.017. Immunity

An associate judge appointed under this subchapter has the judicial immunity of a district judge. All existing immunity granted an associate judge by law, express or implied, continues in full force and effect.

Added by Acts 1995, 74th Leg., ch. 20, § 1, eff. April 20, 1995.

[Sections 201.018 to 201.100 reserved for expansion]

SUBCHAPTER B. CHILD SUPPORT MASTER

§ 201.101. Authority of Presiding Judge

(a) The presiding judge of each administrative judicial region, after conferring with the judges of courts in the region having jurisdiction of Title IV–D cases, shall determine which courts require the appointment of a full-time or part-time master to complete each Title IV–D case within the time specified in this subchapter.

(b) The presiding judge may limit the appointment to a specified time period and may terminate an appointment at any time.

(c) A master appointed under this subchapter may be appointed to serve more than one court. Two or more judges of administrative judicial regions may jointly appoint one or more masters to serve the regions.

(d) If the presiding judge determines that a court requires a master, the presiding judge shall appoint a master. If a master is appointed for a court, all Title IV–D cases shall be referred to the master by a general order for each county issued by the judge of the court for which the master is appointed, or, in the absence of that order, by a general order issued by the presiding judge who appointed the master. Referral of Title IV–D cases may not be made for individual cases or case by case.

Added by Acts 1995, 74th Leg., ch. 20, § 1, eff. April 20, 1995.

§ 201.102. Application of Law Governing Associate Judges

(a) The provisions of Subchapter A relating to the qualifications, powers, and immunity of an associate judge apply to a master appointed under this subchapter, except that a master:

(1) may reside anywhere within the administrative judicial region in which the court to which the master is appointed is located or, if a master is appointed to serve in two or more administrative judicial regions, may reside anywhere within the regions; and

(2) may not be designated as an associate judge.

(b) Except as provided by this subchapter, the following provisions of Subchapter A relating to an associate judge apply to a master appointed under this subchapter:

(1) the appearance of a party or witness before an associate judge;

(2) the papers transmitted to the judge by the associate judge;

(3) judicial action taken on an associate judge's report;

(4) hearings before the judge;

(5) an appeal;

(6) the effect of the associate judge's report pending an appeal;

(7) a jury trial;

(8) the attendance of a bailiff; and

(9) the presence of a court reporter.

Added by Acts 1995, 74th Leg., ch. 20, § 1, eff. April 20, 1995.

§ 201.103. Designation of Host County

(a) The presiding judges of the administrative judicial regions by majority vote shall determine the host county of a master appointed under this subchapter.

(b) The host county shall provide an adequate courtroom and quarters, including furniture, necessary utilities, and telephone equipment and service, for the master and other personnel assisting the master.

(c) A master is not required to reside in the host county.

Added by Acts 1995, 74th Leg., ch. 20, § 1, eff. April 20, 1995.

§ 201.104. Other Powers and Duties of Master

(a) On motion of a party, a master may refer a complex case back to the judge for final disposition after the master has recommended temporary support.

(b) A master shall take testimony and make a record in all Title IV–D cases as provided by this chapter.

Added by Acts 1995, 74th Leg., ch. 20, § 1, eff. April 20, 1995.

§ 201.105. Compensation of Master

(a) A master appointed under this subchapter is entitled to a salary to be determined by a majority vote of the presiding judges of the administrative judicial regions. The salary may not exceed 90 percent of the salary paid to a district judge as set by the state general appropriations act.

(b) The master's salary shall be paid from the county fund available for payment of officers' salaries or from funds available from the state and federal government as provided in Section 201.107.

Added by Acts 1995, 74th Leg., ch. 20, § 1, eff. April 20, 1995.

§ 201.106. Personnel

(a) The presiding judge of an administrative judicial region or the presiding judges of the administrative judicial regions, by majority vote, may appoint other personnel as needed to implement and administer the provisions of this subchapter.

(b) The salary of the personnel shall be paid from the county fund available for payment of officers' salaries or from funds available from the state and federal government as provided by Section 201.107.

Added by Acts 1995, 74th Leg., ch. 20, § 1, eff. April 20, 1995.

§ 201.107. State and Federal Funds

(a) The office of court administration may contract with the Title IV–D agency for available state and federal funds under Title IV–D and may employ personnel needed to implement and administer this subchapter. A master and other personnel appointed under this subsection are state employees for all purposes, including accrual of leave time, insurance benefits, retirement benefits, and travel regulations.

(b) The presiding judges of the administrative judicial regions, state agencies, and counties may contract with the Title IV–D agency for available federal funds under Title IV–D to reimburse costs and salaries associated with masters and personnel appointed under this section and may also use available state funds and public or private grants.

(c) The presiding judges and the Title IV–D agency shall act and are authorized to take any action necessary to maximize the amount of federal funds available under the Title IV–D program.

Added by Acts 1995, 74th Leg., ch. 20, § 1, eff. April 20, 1995.

§ 201.108. Mandatory Appointment of Master

The presiding judge shall appoint a master for each court handling Title IV–D cases for which the state has not been granted an exemption from the expedited process of Title IV–D cases required by federal law.

Added by Acts 1995, 74th Leg., ch. 20, § 1, eff. April 20, 1995.

§ 201.1085. Discretionary Appointment of Master for Child Protection Cases

Text of section as added by Acts 1997, 75th Leg., ch. 600, § 3

The presiding judge of an administrative judicial region may appoint a master for a court handling child protection cases if the court needs assistance in order to process the cases in a reasonable time.

Added by Acts 1997, 75th Leg., ch. 600, § 3, eff. Jan. 1, 1998.

For text of section as added by Acts 1997, 75th Leg., ch. 1022, § 62, see § 201.1085, post

For application provision of Acts 1997, 75th Leg., ch. 600, see notes following V.T.C.A., Family Code § 162.012.

§ 201.1085. Discretionary Appointment of Master for Child Protection Cases

Text of section as added by Acts 1997, 75th Leg., ch. 1022, § 62

The presiding judge may appoint a master for a court handling child protection cases if the court needs assistance in order to process the cases in a reasonable time.

Added by Acts 1997, 75th Leg., ch. 1022, § 62, eff. Sept. 1, 1997.

For text of section as added by Acts 1997, 75th Leg., ch. 600, § 3, see § 201.1085, ante

Section 116 of Acts 1997, 75th Leg., ch. 1022 provides:

"The Department of Protective and Regulatory Services shall establish a working group to coordinate the processing of child protection cases. The working group shall consist of representatives from the Office of Court Administration, the Texas Supreme Court, and district and county attorneys' offices. The working group shall report its recommendations to the Texas Supreme Court not later than September 1, 1998. After considering the recommendations of the working group, the Texas Supreme Court shall adopt rules regarding the processing of child protection cases."

§ 201.109. Exemption From Appointment of Master

(a) If a presiding judge of an administrative judicial region does not require the appointment of a master for a court, the presiding judge shall provide to the Title IV–D agency the information required by the secretary of health and human services to grant the court an exemption from the expedited process requirement for Title IV–D cases.

(b) On receipt of sufficient information, the Title IV–D agency shall immediately apply to the secretary for an exemption from the expedited process requirement for Title IV–D cases for the district court.

(c) The Title IV–D agency shall promptly notify the presiding judge of the administrative judicial region in which the court is located of any information received from the secretary concerning the application for the exemption.

(d) If the secretary does not grant an exemption for a court or if the secretary revokes an exemption for a court, the presiding judge of the administrative judicial region in which the court is located shall appoint a master as prescribed by this subchapter not later than the 30th day after the date the judge receives notice that the exemption was denied or revoked.

(e) The presiding judge of an administrative judicial region shall require each court within the judicial region to provide information and data to the presiding judge, the office of court administration, and the Title IV–D agency regarding the processing of Title IV–D cases necessary to:

(1) establish the need for an exemption as provided by Subsection (a); and

(2) comply with federal law.

(f) The Title IV–D agency and the office of court administration shall provide assistance to the presiding judge in obtaining and storing the information and data provided under this section.

(g) Any information or data required under this section may be provided as required by the presiding judge.

Added by Acts 1995, 74th Leg., ch. 20, § 1, eff. April 20, 1995.

§ 201.110. Time for Disposition of Title IV–D Cases

(a) Title IV–D cases must be completed from the time of successful service to the time of disposition within the following time:

(1) 90 percent within three months;

(2) 98 percent within six months; and

(3) 100 percent within one year.

(b) Title IV–D cases shall be given priority over other cases.

(c) A clerk or judge may not restrict the number of Title IV–D cases that are filed or heard in the courts.

Added by Acts 1995, 74th Leg., ch. 20, § 1, eff. April 20, 1995.

§ 201.111. Time to Act on Master's Report

(a) Except as provided by Subsection (b), not later than the 30th day after the date a master's report is filed, the referring court shall:

(1) adopt, approve, or reject the master's report;

(2) hear further evidence; or

(3) recommit the matter for further proceedings.

(b) The time limit in Subsection (a) does not apply if a party has filed a written notice of appeal to the referring court.

Added by Acts 1995, 74th Leg., ch. 751, § 80, eff. Sept. 1, 1995.

CHAPTER 202. FRIEND OF THE COURT

Section

§ 202.001. Appointment

(a) After an order for child support or possession of or access to a child has been rendered, a court may appoint a friend of the court on:

(1) the request of a person alleging that the order has been violated; or

(2) its own motion.

(b) A court may appoint a friend of the court in a proceeding under Part D of Title IV of the federal Social Security Act (42 U.S.C. Section 651 et seq.) only if the Title IV–D agency agrees in writing to the appointment.

(c) The duration of the appointment of a friend of the court is as determined by the court.

(d) In the appointment of a friend of the court, the court shall give preference to:

(1) a local domestic relations office;

(2) a local child support collection office;

(3) the local court official designated to enforce actions as provided in Chapter 159; or

(4) an attorney in good standing with the State Bar of Texas.

(e) In the execution of a friend of the court's duties under this subchapter, a friend of the court shall represent the court to ensure compliance with the court's order.

Added by Acts 1995, 74th Leg., ch. 20, § 1, eff. April 20, 1995.

§ 202.002. Authority and Duties

(a) A friend of the court may coordinate nonjudicial efforts to improve compliance with a court order relating to child support or possession of or access to a child by use of:

(1) telephone communication;

(2) written communication;

(3) one or more volunteer advocates under Chapter 107;

(4) informal pretrial consultation;

(5) one or more of the alternate dispute resolution methods under Chapter 154, Civil Practice and Remedies Code;

(6) a certified social worker;

(7) a family mediator; and

(8) employment agencies, retraining programs, and any similar resources to ensure that both parents can meet their financial obligations to the child.

(b) A friend of the court, not later than the 15th day of the month following the reporting month:

(1) shall report to the court or monitor reports made to the court on:

(A) the amount of child support collected as a percentage of the amount ordered; and

(B) efforts to ensure compliance with orders relating to possession of or access to a child; and

(2) may file an action to enforce, clarify, or modify a court order relating to child support or possession of or access to a child.

(c) A friend of the court may file a notice of delinquency and a request for a writ of income withholding under Chapter 158 in order to enforce a child support order.

Added by Acts 1995, 74th Leg., ch. 20, § 1, eff. April 20, 1995. Amended by Acts 1995, 74th Leg., ch. 751, § 81, eff. Sept. 1, 1995; Acts 1997, 75th Leg., ch. 702, § 9, eff. Sept. 1, 1997.

§ 202.003. Duty of Local Offices and Officials to Report

A local domestic relations office, a local registry, or a court official designated to receive child support under a court order shall, if ordered by the court, report to the court or a friend of the court on a monthly basis:

(1) any delinquency and arrearage in child support payments; and

(2) any violation of an order relating to possession of or access to a child.

Added by Acts 1995, 74th Leg., ch. 20, § 1, eff. April 20, 1995.

§ 202.004. Access to Information

A friend of the court may arrange access to child support payment records by electronic means if the records are computerized.

Added by Acts 1995, 74th Leg., ch. 20, § 1, eff. April 20, 1995.

§ 202.005. Compensation

(a) A friend of the court is entitled to compensation for services rendered and for expenses incurred in rendering the services.

(b) The court may assess the amount that the friend of the court receives in compensation against a party to the suit in the same manner as the court awards costs under Chapter 106.

(c) A friend of the court or a person who acts as the court's custodian of child support records, including the clerk of a court, may apply for and receive funds from the child support and court management account under Section 21.007, Government Code.

(d) A friend of the court who receives funds under Subsection (c) shall use the funds to reimburse any compensation the friend of the court received under Subsection (b).

Added by Acts 1995, 74th Leg., ch. 20, § 1, eff. April 20, 1995.

CHAPTER 203. DOMESTIC RELATIONS OFFICES

Chapter 203, formerly Domestic Relations Office, consisting of §§ 203.001 to 203.012, was amended by Acts 1995, 74th Leg., ch. 475, § 1.

§ 203.001. Definitions

In this chapter:

(1) "Administering entity" means a commissioners court, juvenile board, or other entity responsible for administering a domestic relations office under this chapter.

(2) "Domestic relations office" means a county office that serves families, county departments, and courts to ensure effective implementation of this title.

Added by Acts 1995, 74th Leg., ch. 20, § 1, eff. April 20, 1995. Amended by Acts 1995, 74th Leg., ch. 475, § 1, eff. Sept. 1, 1995.

Section 2(b) and (c) of Acts 1995, 74th Leg., ch. 475 provides:

"(b) A domestic relations office created before the effective date of this Act that is in existence on that date may continue to operate after that date but may operate only as provided by this Act.

"(c) The enactment of this Act does not affect the validity or enforcement of a court order entered before the effective date of this Act that provides for a service to be performed by a domestic relations office. A domestic relations office performing services under a court order entered before the effective date of this Act shall perform the services as provided by this Act."

§ 203.002. Establishment of Domestic Relations Office

A commissioners court may establish a domestic relations office.

Added by Acts 1995, 74th Leg., ch. 20, § 1, eff. April 20, 1995. Renumbered from § 203.003 and amended by Acts 1995, 74th Leg., ch. 475, § 1, eff. Sept. 1, 1995.

Section 2(b) and (c) of Acts 1995, 74th Leg., ch. 475 provides:

"(b) A domestic relations office created before the effective date of this Act that is in existence on that date may continue to operate after that date but may operate only as provided by this Act.

"(c) The enactment of this Act does not affect the validity or enforcement of a court order entered before the effective date of this Act that provides for a service to be performed by a domestic relations office. A domestic relations office performing services under a court order entered before the effective date of this Act shall perform the services as provided by this Act."

§ 203.003. Administration

(a) A domestic relations office shall be administered:

(1) as provided by the commissioners court; or

(2) if the commissioners court does not otherwise provide for the administration of the office, by the juvenile board that serves the county in which the domestic relations office is located.

(b) The administering entity shall appoint and assign the duties of a director who shall be responsible for the day-to-day administration of the office. A director serves at the pleasure of the administering entity.

(c) The administering entity shall determine the amount of money needed to operate the office.

(d) A commissioners court that establishes a domestic relations office under this chapter may execute a bond for the office. A bond under this subsection must be:

(1) executed with a solvent surety company authorized to do business in the state; and

(2) conditioned on the faithful performance of the duties of the office.

(e) The administering entity shall establish procedures for the acceptance and use of a grant or donation to the office.

Added by Acts 1995, 74th Leg., ch. 20, § 1, eff. April 20, 1995. Renumbered from § 203.004 and amended by Acts 1995, 74th Leg., ch. 475, § 1, eff. Sept. 1, 1995.

Section 2(b) and (c) of Acts 1995, 74th Leg., ch. 475 provides:

"(b) A domestic relations office created before the effective date of this Act that is in existence on that date may continue to operate after that date but may operate only as provided by this Act.

"(c) The enactment of this Act does not affect the validity or enforcement of a court order entered before the effective date of this Act that provides for a service to be performed by a domestic relations office. A domestic relations office performing services under a court order entered before the effective date of this Act shall perform the services as provided by this Act."

§ 203.004. Powers and Duties

(a) A domestic relations office may:

(1) collect and disburse child support payments that are ordered by a court to be paid through a domestic relations registry;

(2) maintain records of payments and disbursements made under Subdivision (1);

(3) file a suit, including a suit to:

(A) establish paternity;

(B) enforce a court order for child support or for possession of and access to a child; and

(C) modify or clarify an existing child support order;

(4) provide an informal forum in which mediation is used to resolve disputes in an action under Subdivision (3);

(5) prepare a court-ordered social study;

(6) represent a child as guardian ad litem in a suit in which:

(A) termination of the parent-child relationship is sought; or

(B) conservatorship of or access to a child is contested;

(7) serve as a friend of the court;

(8) provide predivorce counseling ordered by a court;

(9) provide community supervision services under Chapter 157; and

(10) provide information to assist a party in understanding, complying with, or enforcing the party's duties and obligations under Subdivision (3).

(b) A court having jurisdiction in a proceeding under this title, Title 3, or Section 25.05, Penal Code, may order that child support payments be made through a domestic relations office.

(c) A domestic relations office may hire or contract for the services of attorneys to assist the office in providing services under this chapter.

Added by Acts 1995, 74th Leg., ch. 20, § 1, eff. April 20, 1995. Renumbered from § 203.005 and amended by Acts 1995, 74th Leg., ch. 475, § 1, eff. Sept. 1, 1995. Amended by Acts 1997, 75th Leg., ch. 702, § 10, eff. Sept. 1, 1997.

Section 2(b) and (c) of Acts 1995, 74th Leg., ch. 475 provides:

"(b) A domestic relations office created before the effective date of this Act that is in existence on that date may continue to operate after that date but may operate only as provided by this Act.

"(c) The enactment of this Act does not affect the validity or enforcement of a court order entered before the effective date of this Act that provides for a service to be performed by a domestic relations office. A domestic relations office performing services under a court order entered before the effective date of this Act shall perform the services as provided by this Act."

§ 203.005. Fees and Charges

(a) The administering entity may authorize a domestic relations office to assess and collect:

(1) an initial operations fee not to exceed $15 to be paid to the domestic relations office on the filing of a suit;

(2) a reasonable application fee to be paid by an applicant requesting services from the office;

(3) a reasonable attorney's fee and court costs incurred or ordered by the court;

(4) a monthly child support service fee not to exceed $3 to be paid by a managing conservator and possessory conservator for whom the domestic relations office acts as a local child support registry;

(5) community supervision fees as provided by Chapter 157 if community supervision officers are employed by the domestic relations office; and

(6) a reasonable fee for preparation of a court-ordered social study.

(b) The first payment of a fee under Subsection (a)(4) is due on the date that the person required to pay support is ordered to begin child support, alimony, or separate maintenance payments. Subsequent payments of the fee are due annually and in advance.

(c) The director of a domestic relations office shall attempt to collect all fees in an efficient manner.

(d) The administering entity may provide for an exemption from the payment of a fee authorized under this section if payment of the fee is not practical or in the interest of justice. Fees that may be exempted under this subsection include fees related to:

(1) spousal and child support payments made under an interstate pact;

(2) a suit brought by the Texas Department of Human Services;

(3) activities performed by the Department of Protective and Regulatory Services or another governmental agency, a private adoption agency, or a charitable organization; and

(4) services for a person who has applied for or who receives public assistance under the laws of this state.

Added by Acts 1995, 74th Leg., ch. 20, § 1, eff. April 20, 1995. Renumbered from § 203.009 and amended by Acts 1995, 74th Leg., ch. 475, § 1, eff. Sept. 1, 1995.

Section 2(b) and (c) of Acts 1995, 74th Leg., ch. 475 provides:

"(b) A domestic relations office created before the effective date of this Act that is in existence on that date may continue to operate after that date but may operate only as provided by this Act.

"(c) The enactment of this Act does not affect the validity or enforcement of a court order entered before the effective date of this Act that provides for a service to be performed by a domestic relations office. A domestic relations office performing services under a court order entered before the effective date of this Act shall perform the services as provided by this Act."

§ 203.006. Fund

(a) As determined by the administering entity, fees collected or received by a domestic relations office shall be deposited in:

(1) the general fund for the county in which the domestic relations office is located; or

(2) the office fund established for the domestic relations office.

(b) The administering entity shall use the domestic relations office fund to provide money for services authorized by this chapter.

(c) A domestic relations office fund may be supplemented as necessary from the county's general fund or from other money available from the county.

Added by Acts 1995, 74th Leg., ch. 20, § 1, eff. April 20, 1995. Renumbered from § 203.010 and amended by Acts 1995, 74th Leg., ch. 475, § 1, eff. Sept. 1, 1995. Amended by Acts 1997, 75th Leg., ch. 702, § 11, eff. Sept. 1, 1997.

Section 2(b) and (c) of Acts 1995, 74th Leg., ch. 475 provides:

"(b) A domestic relations office created before the effective date of this Act that is in existence on that date may continue to operate after that date but may operate only as provided by this Act.

"(c) The enactment of this Act does not affect the validity or enforcement of a court order entered before the effective date of this Act that provides for a service to be performed by a domestic relations office. A domestic relations office performing services under a court order entered before the effective date of this Act shall perform the services as provided by this Act."

§ 203.007. Access to Records; Offense

(a) A domestic relations office may obtain the records described by Subsections (b) and (c) that relate to a person who has:

(1) been ordered to pay child support;

(2) been designated as a possessory conservator or managing conservator of a child;

(3) been designated to be the father of a child; or

(4) executed a statement of paternity.

(b) A domestic relations office is entitled to obtain from the Department of Public Safety records that relate to:

(1) a person's date of birth;

(2) a person's most recent address;

(3) a person's current driver's license status;

(4) motor vehicle accidents involving a person; and

(5) reported traffic-law violations of which a person has been convicted.

(c) A domestic relations office is entitled to obtain from the Texas Employment Commission records that relate to:

(1) a person's address;

(2) a person's employment status and earnings;

(3) the name and address of a person's current or former employer; and

(4) unemployment compensation benefits received by a person.

(d) An agency required to provide records under this section may charge a domestic relations office a fee for providing the records in an amount that does not exceed the amount paid for those records by the agency responsible for Title IV-D cases.

(e) The Department of Public Safety, the Texas Employment Commission, or the office of the secretary of state may charge a domestic relations office a fee not to exceed the charge paid by the Title IV-D agency for furnishing records under this section.

(f) Information obtained by a domestic relations office under this section that is confidential under a constitution, statute, judicial decision, or rule is privileged and may be used only by that office.

(g) A person commits an offense if the person releases or discloses confidential information obtained under this section without the consent of the person to whom the information relates. An offense under this subsection is a Class C misdemeanor.

(h) A domestic relations office is entitled to obtain from the office of the secretary of state the following information about a registered voter to the extent that the information is available:

(1) complete name;

(2) current and former street and mailing address;

(3) sex;

(4) date of birth;

(5) social security number; and

(6) telephone number.

Added by Acts 1995, 74th Leg., ch. 20, § 1, eff. April 20, 1995. Renumbered from § 203.012 and amended by Acts 1995, 74th Leg., ch. 475, § 1, eff. Sept. 1, 1995. Amended by Acts 1995, 74th Leg., ch. 803, § 1, eff. Sept. 1, 1995; Acts 1997, 75th Leg., ch. 165, § 7.18, eff. Sept. 1, 1997.

Section 2(b) and (c) of Acts 1995, 74th Leg., ch. 475 provides:

"(b) A domestic relations office created before the effective date of this Act that is in existence on that date may continue to operate after that date but may operate only as provided by this Act.

"(c) The enactment of this Act does not affect the validity or enforcement of a court order entered before the effective date of this Act that provides for a service to be performed by a domestic relations office. A domestic relations office performing services under a court order entered before the effective date of this Act shall perform the services as provided by this Act."

§ 203.008. Deleted by Acts 1995, 74th Leg., ch. 475, § 1, eff. Sept. 1, 1995

§ 203.009. Renumbered as § 203.005 by Acts 1995, 74th Leg., ch. 475, § 1, eff. Sept. 1, 1995

§ 203.010. Renumbered as § 203.006 by Acts 1995, 74th Leg., ch. 475, § 1, eff. Sept. 1, 1995

§ 203.011. Deleted by Acts 1995, 74th Leg., ch. 475, § 1, eff. Sept. 1, 1995

§ 203.012. Renumbered as § 203.007 by Acts 1995, 74th Leg., ch. 475, § 1, eff. Sept. 1, 1995

[Chapters 204 to 230 reserved for expansion]

SUBTITLE D. ADMINISTRATIVE SERVICES

CHAPTER 231. TITLE IV–D SERVICES

SUBCHAPTER A. ADMINISTRATION OF TITLE IV–D PROGRAM

Section

SUBCHAPTER B. SERVICES PROVIDED BY TITLE IV–D PROGRAM

Section

SUBCHAPTER C. PAYMENT OF FEES AND COSTS

SUBCHAPTER D. LOCATION OF PARENTS AND RESOURCES

SUBCHAPTER E. CHILD SUPPORT REVIEW PROCESS TO ESTABLISH OR ENFORCE SUPPORT OBLIGATIONS [REDESIGNATED]

SUBCHAPTER A. ADMINISTRATION OF TITLE IV–D PROGRAM

§ 231.001. Designation of Title IV–D Agency

The office of the attorney general is designated as the state's Title IV–D agency.

Added by Acts 1995, 74th Leg., ch. 20, § 1, eff. April 20, 1995.

§ 231.0011. Development of Statewide Integrated System for Child Support and Medical Support Enforcement

(a) The attorney general, as the Title IV–D agency for the State of Texas shall have final approval authority on any contract or proposal for delivery of Title IV–D services under this section and in coordination with the Texas Judicial Council, the Office of Court Administration of the Texas Judicial System, the federal Office of Child Support Enforcement, and state, county, and local officials, shall develop and implement a statewide integrated system for child support and medical support enforcement, employing federal, state, local, and private resources to:

(1) unify child support registry functions;

(2) record and track all child support orders entered in the state;

(3) establish an automated enforcement process which will use delinquency monitoring, billing, and other enforcement techniques to ensure the payment of current support;

(4) incorporate existing enforcement resources into the system to obtain maximum benefit from state and federal funding; and

(5) ensure accountability for all participants in the process, including state, county, and local officials, private contractors, and the judiciary.

(b) The attorney general shall convene a work group to determine a process and develop a timetable for implementation of a unified registry system and to identify any barriers to completion of the project. The work group shall include representatives of the judiciary, district clerks, and domestic relations offices, as well as other interested agencies, organizations, and individuals. The work group shall report the results of its deliberations to the governor, lieutenant governor, speaker of the house of representatives, and attorney general on or before January 15, 1996.

(c) The attorney general shall, in cooperation with the work group established by this section, develop technical standards for participation in the unified child support system, including standard required data elements for effective monitoring of child support and medical support orders and for the imposition of interest on delinquent child support.

(d) Counties and other providers of child support services shall be required, as a condition of participation in the unified system, to enter into a contract with the attorney general, to comply with all federal requirements for the Title IV–D program, and to maintain at least the current level of funding for activities which are proposed to be included in the integrated child support system.

(e) The attorney general shall identify federal requirements, apply for necessary federal waivers, and provide technical system requirements and other information concerning participation in the system to counties and other providers of child support services not later than January 15, 1996. Counties shall notify the attorney general of existing resources and options for participation not later than May 1, 1996.

(f) Not later than June 1, 1996, the attorney general shall produce a procurement and implementation plan for hardware and software necessary to implement in phases a unified statewide registry and enforcement system.

(g) Effective January 15, 1996, the attorney general may contract with any county meeting technical system requirements necessary to comply with federal law for provision of Title IV–D services in that county. All new cases in which support orders are entered in such county after the effective date of a monitoring contract shall be Title IV–D cases. Any other case in the county, subject to federal requirements and the agreement of the county and the attorney general, may be included as a Title IV–D case. Any obligee under a support order may refuse Title IV–D enforcement services unless required to accept such services pursuant to other law.

(h) Counties participating in the unified enforcement system shall monitor all child support registry cases and on delinquency may, subject to the approval of the Title IV–D agency, provide enforcement services through:

(1) direct provision of services by county personnel;

(2) subcontracting all or portions of the services to private entities or attorneys; or

(3) such other methods as may be approved by the Title IV–D agency.

(i) The attorney general shall undertake a least-cost review of its child support operations and shall use the information developed in such review to determine what, if any, contribution of program funds generated through other Title IV–D activities should be made to the participating counties. The attorney general, in cooperation with the counties and the federal Office of Child Support Enforcement shall develop a cost allocation methodology to assist the counties in identifying county contributions which may qualify for federal financial participation.

(j) The attorney general may phase in the integrated child support registry and enforcement system, and the requirement to implement the system shall be contingent on the receipt of locally generated funds and federal reimbursement. Locally generated funds include but are not limited to funds contributed by counties and cities.

(k) The attorney general shall adopt rules to implement this section.

(*l*) Participation in the statewide integrated system for child support and medical support enforcement by a county is voluntary, and nothing in this section shall be construed to mandate participation.

(m) This section does not limit the ability of the Title IV-D agency to enter into an agreement with a county for the provision of services as authorized under Section 231.002.

Added by Acts 1995, 74th Leg., ch. 341, § 1.01, eff. Sept. 1, 1995. Amended by Acts 1997, 75th Leg., ch. 702, § 12, eff. Sept. 1, 1997.

Section 30 of Acts 1997, 75th Leg., ch. 420 provides:

"(a) The involvement of the attorney general's office in matters related to the enforcement of child support is subject to review under Chapter 325, Government Code (Texas Sunset Act), as if the attorney general's involvement in matters relating to the enforcement of child support were a state agency under that chapter. The involvement of the attorney general's office in matters related to child support enforcement is not abolished under Chapter 325, Government Code (Texas Sunset Act).

"(b) To the extent Chapter 325, Government Code (Texas Sunset Act), imposes a duty on a state agency under review, the attorney general's office shall perform the duty as it applies to the attorney general's involvement in matters related to child support enforcement.

"(c) The Sunset Advisory Commission shall select an independent firm with experience in evaluating government programs to conduct a comprehensive analysis of, and to make recommendations to the commission concerning, the structure, efficiency, and effectiveness of the attorney general's involvement in matters relating to child support enforcement. In performing the analysis under this subsection, the firm shall consider and recommend whether programs related to the enforcement of child support should remain as part of the attorney general's office, be privatized, or be transferred to an independent state agency established to operate child support enforcement programs. The commission may prescribe additional matters to be evaluated by the firm selected under this subsection. The attorney general's office shall pay the costs of the analysis by the firm selected under this subsection from funds appropriated to the attorney general's office for the enforcement of child support.

"(d) The office of the state auditor, the Texas Legislative Council, and the Department of Information Resources shall assist the Sunset Advisory Commission in performing the commission's review of the attorney general's involvement in matters relating to the enforcement of child support.

"(e) The Sunset Advisory Commission shall report its findings as required under Section 325.010, Government Code, to the 76th Legislature, Regular Session, 1999."

§ 231.0012. Child Support Enforcement Management

The person appointed by the attorney general as the person responsible for managing the Title IV-D agency's child support enforcement duties shall report directly to the attorney general.

Added by Acts 1997, 75th Leg., ch. 420, § 16, eff. Sept. 1, 1997.

§ 231.0013. Dedication of Funds

Appropriations made to the Title IV-D agency for child support enforcement may be expended only for the purposes for which the money was appropriated.

Added by Acts 1997, 75th Leg., ch. 420, § 16, eff. Sept. 1, 1997.

§ 231.002. Powers and Duties

(a) The Title IV–D agency may:

(1) accept, transfer, and expend funds, subject to the General Appropriations Act, made available by the federal or state government or by another public or private source for the purpose of carrying out this chapter;

(2) adopt rules for the provision of child support services;

(3) initiate legal actions needed to implement this chapter; and

(4) enter into contracts or agreements necessary to administer this chapter.

(b) The Title IV–D agency may perform the duties and functions necessary for locating children under agreements with the federal government as provided by 42 U.S.C. Section 663.

(c) The Title IV–D agency may enter into agreements or contracts with federal, state, or other public or private agencies or individuals for the purpose of carrying out this chapter. The agreements or contracts between the agency and other state agencies or political subdivisions of the state are not subject to Chapter 771 or Chapter 783, Government Code.

(d) Consistent with federal law and any international treaty or convention to which the United States is a party and that has been ratified by the United States Congress, the Title IV-D agency may:

(1) on approval by and in cooperation with the governor, pursue negotiations and enter into reciprocal arrangements with the federal government, another state, or a foreign country or a political subdivision of the federal government, state, or foreign country to:

(A) establish and enforce child support obligations; and

(B) establish mechanisms to enforce an order providing for possession of or access to a child rendered under Chapter 153;

(2) spend money appropriated to the agency for child support enforcement to engage in international child support enforcement; and

(3) spend other money appropriated to the agency necessary for the agency to conduct the agency's activities under Subdivision (1).

Text of subsec. (e) as relettered by Acts 1997, 75th Leg., ch. 874, § 1, and amended by Acts 1997, 75th Leg., ch. 911, § 68

(e) The Title IV-D agency may take the following administrative actions with respect to the location of a parent, the determination of parentage, and the establishment, modification, and enforcement of child support and medical support orders required by 42 U.S.C. Section 666(c), without obtaining an order from any other judicial or administrative tribunal:

(1) issue an administrative subpoena, as provided by Section 231.303, to obtain financial or other information;

(2) order genetic testing for parentage determination, as provided by Chapter 233;

(3) order income withholding, as provided by Chapter 233, and issue an administrative writ of withholding, as provided by Chapter 158; and

(4) take any action with respect to execution, collection, and release of a judgment or lien for child support necessary to satisfy the judgment or lien, as provided by Chapter 157.

Text of subsec. (e) as added by Acts 1997, 75th Leg., ch. 911, § 68

(e) The Title IV-D agency shall recognize and enforce the authority of the Title IV-D agency of another state to take actions similar to the actions listed in Subsection (d).

(f) The Title IV-D agency shall develop and use procedures for the administrative enforcement of interstate cases meeting the requirements of 42 U.S.C. Section 666(a)(14) under which the agency:

(1) shall respond within five business days to a request made by another state for assistance in a Title IV-D case; and

(2) may, by electronic or other means, transmit to another state a request for assistance in a Title IV-D case.

Added by Acts 1995, 74th Leg., ch. 20, § 1, eff. April 20, 1995. Amended by Acts 1997, 75th Leg., ch. 874, § 1, eff. Sept. 1, 1997; Acts 1997, 75th Leg., ch. 911, § 68, eff. Sept. 1, 1997.

For application and effectiveness provisions of Acts 1997, 75th Leg., ch. 911, see note following V.T.C.A., Family Code § 156.401.

§ 231.003. Forms and Procedures

The Title IV–D agency shall by rule promulgate any forms and procedures necessary to comply fully with the intent of this chapter.

Added by Acts 1995, 74th Leg., ch. 20, § 1, eff. April 20, 1995.

§ 231.004. Repealed by Acts 1997, 75th Leg., ch. 911, § 97(a), eff. Sept. 1, 1997

§ 231.005. Biennial Report Required

The Title IV–D agency shall report to the legislature each biennium on the effectiveness of the agency's child support enforcement activity in reducing the state's public assistance obligations. The agency shall develop a method for estimating the costs and benefits of the child support enforcement program and the effect of the program on appropriations for public assistance.

Added by Acts 1995, 74th Leg., ch. 20, § 1, eff. April 20, 1995.

§ 231.006. Ineligibility to Receive State Grants or Loans or Receive Payment on State Contracts

(a) A child support obligor who is more than 30 days delinquent in paying child support and a business entity in which the obligor is a sole proprietor, partner, shareholder, or owner with an ownership interest of at least 25 percent is not eligible to:

(1) receive payments from state funds under a contract to provide property, materials, or services; or

(2) receive a state-funded grant or loan.

(b) A child support obligor or business entity ineligible to receive payments under Subsection (a) remains ineligible until:

(1) all arrearages have been paid; or

(2) the obligor is in compliance with a written repayment agreement or court order as to any existing delinquency.

(c) A bid or an application for a contract, grant, or loan paid from state funds must include the name and social security number of the individual or sole proprietor and each partner, shareholder, or owner with an ownership interest of at least 25 percent of the business entity submitting the bid or application.

(d) A contract, bid, or application subject to the requirements of this section must include the following statement:

"Under Section 231.006, Family Code, the vendor or applicant certifies that the individual or business entity named in this contract, bid, or application is not ineligible to receive the specified grant, loan, or payment and acknowledges that this contract may be terminated and payment may be withheld if this certification is inaccurate."

(e) If a state agency determines that an individual or business entity holding a state contract is ineligible to receive payment under Subsection (a), the contract may be terminated.

(f) If the certificate required under Subsection (d) is shown to be false, the vendor is liable to the state for attorney's fees, the costs necessary to complete the contract, including the cost of advertising and awarding a second contract, and any other damages provided by law or contract.

(g) This section does not create a cause of action to contest a bid or award of a state grant, loan, or contract. This section does not impose a duty on the Title IV-D agency to collect information to send to the comptroller to withhold a payment to a business entity. The Title IV-D agency and other affected agencies are encouraged to develop a system by which the Title IV-D agency may identify a business entity that is ineligible to receive a state payment under Subsection (a) and to ensure that a state payment to the entity is not made. This system should be implemented using existing funds and only if the Title IV-D agency, comptroller, and other affected agencies determine that it will be cost-effective.

(h) This section does not apply to a contract between governmental entities.

(i) The Title IV-D agency may adopt rules or prescribe forms to implement any provision of this section.

Added by Acts 1995, 74th Leg., ch. 20, § 1, eff. April 20, 1995. Amended by Acts 1995, 74th Leg., ch. 751, § 82, eff. Sept. 1, 1995.

§ 231.007. Debts to State

(a) A person obligated to pay child support in a case in which the Title IV–D agency is providing services under this chapter who does not pay the required child support is in debt to the state for the purposes of Section 403.055, Government Code.

(b) The debt of a person in debt to the state as provided by Subsection (a) is equal to the amount of the child support that is past due and not paid and any interest, fees, court costs, or other amounts owed by the person as a result of the person's failure to pay the child support.

(c) The Title IV–D agency is an assignee of all payments, including compensation, by the state to a person in debt to the state as provided by this section. The assignment takes effect before the date the person's debt to the state arose.

(d) A person in debt to the state as provided by this section may eliminate the person's debt by:

(1) paying the entire amount of the debt; or

(2) resolving the debt in a manner acceptable to the Title IV–D agency.

(e) The comptroller may rely on a representation by the Title IV–D agency that:

(1) a person is in debt to the state as provided by this section; or

(2) a person who was in debt to the state has eliminated the person's debt as provided by this section.

(f) In this section, the payment of workers' compensation benefits to a person in debt to the state is the same as any other payment made to the person by the state. Notwithstanding Section 408.203, Labor Code, an order or writ to withhold income from workers' compensation benefits is not required under this section.

(g) The amount of weekly workers' compensation benefits that may be withheld or assigned under this section may not exceed the percentage of the person's benefits that would apply if the benefits equalled the person's monthly net resources as provided by Chapter 154, except that in no event may more than 50 percent of the person's weekly compensation benefits be withheld or assigned.

(h) Notwithstanding Sections 403.055(c) and (e)(4), Government Code, the comptroller may not issue a warrant to a state officer or employee who is in debt to the state as provided by this section.

(i) In this section, "compensation" has the meaning assigned by Section 403.055(f)(1), Government Code, and includes the payment of workers' compensation benefits.

Added by Acts 1995, 74th Leg., ch. 20, § 1, eff. April 20, 1995. Amended by Acts 1995, 74th Leg., ch. 751, § 83, eff. Sept. 1, 1995; Acts 1997, 75th Leg., ch. 165, § 7.19, eff. Sept. 1, 1997.

§ 231.008. Disposition of Funds

(a) The Title IV–D agency shall deposit money received under assignments or as fees in a special fund in the state treasury. The agency may spend money in the fund for the administration of this chapter, subject to the General Appropriations Act.

(b) All other money received under this chapter shall be deposited in a special fund in the state treasury.

(c) Sections 403.094 [1] and 403.095, Government Code, do not apply to a fund described by this section.

Added by Acts 1995, 74th Leg., ch. 20, § 1, eff. April 20, 1995.

[1] Repealed.

§ 231.009. Payment of Penalties

From funds appropriated for the Title IV–D agency, the agency shall reimburse the Texas Department of Human Services for any penalty assessed under Title IV–A of the federal Social Security Act (42 U.S.C. Section 651 et seq.) that is assessed because of the agency's administration of this chapter.

Added by Acts 1995, 74th Leg., ch. 20, § 1, eff. April 20, 1995.

§ 231.010. Case Processing Pilot Program

(a) As part of the development of a statewide integrated system for child support and medical support enforcement under Section 231.0011, the Title IV-D agency shall establish a pilot program to improve the efficiency of court processing of family welfare cases, including child support, medical support, and foster care cases. The Title IV-D agency shall consult with the Department of Protective and Regulatory Services in establishing the pilot program with respect to the processing of foster care cases.

(b) The Title IV-D agency shall identify at least two counties that have a population of more than one million and that are voluntarily participating in the statewide integrated system under Section 231.0011 for the development and establishment of pilot programs during each fiscal year of the 1998–1999 biennium. A county shall be selected on the basis of the county's ability to achieve the automation goals of the pilot program.

(c) A pilot program must include processes for:

(1) electronic case filing;

(2) automated reporting of appropriate orders to the state case registry required under 42 U.S.C. Section 654a;

(3) automated case tracking;

(4) automated child support delinquency monitoring; and

(5) automated statistical reporting to the state case registry.

(d) The pilot program authorized under this section shall be developed and implemented in cooperation with representatives of the counties identified under Subsection (b), including representatives of the county's judiciary.

(e) As part of the pilot program, the Title IV-D agency shall review county assessments of needs related to processing child support, medical support, and foster care cases and shall provide technical assistance to county and district clerks as requested.

(f) The Title IV-D agency shall provide funding for the pilot program from funds appropriated to operate the agency and from any available federal funds.

(g) Not later than January 15, 1999, the agency shall submit a report regarding the status of the pilot program to the governor, the lieutenant governor, the speaker of the house of representatives, and the comptroller. On request, the Title IV-D agency shall make the report available to any member of the legislature.

Added by Acts 1997, 75th Leg., ch. 420, § 17, eff. Sept. 1, 1997.

[Sections 231.010 to 231.100 reserved for expansion]

SUBCHAPTER B. SERVICES PROVIDED BY TITLE IV–D PROGRAM

§ 231.101. Title IV–D Child Support Services

(a) The Title IV–D agency may provide all services required or authorized to be provided by Part D of Title IV of the federal Social Security Act (42 U.S.C. Section 651 et seq.), including:

(1) parent locator services;

(2) paternity determination;

(3) child support and medical support establishment;

(4) review and adjustment of child support orders;

(5) enforcement of child support and medical support orders; and

(6) collection and distribution of child support payments.

(b) At the request of either the obligee or obligor, the Title IV-D agency shall review a child support order once every three years and, if appropriate, adjust the support amount to meet the requirements of the child support guidelines under Chapter 154.

Text of subsec. (c) as added by Acts 1997, 75th Leg., ch. 702, § 13

(c) The Title IV-D agency shall distribute a child support payment received by the agency from an employer within two working days after the date the agency receives the payment.

Text of subsec. (c) as added by Acts 1997, 75th Leg., ch. 911, § 69

(c) Except as notice is included in the child support order, a party subject to a support order shall be provided notice not less than once every three years of the party's right to request that the Title IV-D agency review and, if appropriate, adjust the amount of ordered support.

(d) The Title IV-D agency may review a support order at any time on a showing of a material and substantial change in circumstances, taking into consideration the best interests of the child.

Added by Acts 1995, 74th Leg., ch. 20, § 1, eff. April 20, 1995. Amended by Acts 1997, 75th Leg., ch. 702, § 13, eff. Sept. 1, 1997; Acts 1997, 75th Leg., ch. 911, § 69, eff. Sept. 1, 1997.

Section 15(d) of Acts 1997, 75th Leg., ch. 702 provides:

"The change in law made by this Act by the addition of Subsection (c), Section 231.101, Family Code, applies only to a child support payment made on or after October 1, 1999, or the date the state disbursement unit begins to operate, whichever date is earlier. A child support payment made before that date is governed by the law in effect on the date the payment was made, and the former law is continued in effect for that purpose."

For application and effectiveness provisions of Acts 1997, 75th Leg., ch. 911, see note following V.T.C.A., Family Code § 156.401.

§ 231.102. Eligibility for Child Support Services

The Title IV–D agency on application or as otherwise authorized by law may provide services for the benefit of a child without regard to whether the child has received public assistance.

Added by Acts 1995, 74th Leg., ch. 20, § 1, eff. April 20, 1995.

§ 231.103. Application Fee

(a) The Title IV–D agency may charge a reasonable application fee and recover costs for the services provided.

(b) An application fee may not be charged in a case in which the Title IV–D agency provides services because the family receives public assistance.

(c) An application fee may not exceed a maximum amount established by federal law.

Added by Acts 1995, 74th Leg., ch. 20, § 1, eff. April 20, 1995.

§ 231.104. Assignment of Right to Support

(a) To the extent authorized by law, the approval of an application for or the receipt of financial assistance as provided by Chapter 31, Human Resources Code, constitutes an assignment to the Title IV-D agency of any rights to support from any other person that the applicant or recipient may have personally or for a child for whom the applicant or recipient is claiming assistance, including the right to the amount accrued at the time the application is filed or the assistance is received.

(b) An application for child support services is an assignment of support rights, to the extent permitted by federal law, to enable the Title IV–D agency to establish and enforce child support and medical support obligations, but an assignment is not a condition of eligibility for services.

Added by Acts 1995, 74th Leg., ch. 20, § 1, eff. April 20, 1995. Amended by Acts 1997, 75th Leg., ch. 911, § 70, eff. Sept. 1, 1997.

For application and effectiveness provisions of Acts 1997, 75th Leg., ch. 911, see note following V.T.C.A., Family Code § 156.401.

§ 231.105. Notice of Change of Payee

(a) Child support payments for the benefit of a child whose support rights have been assigned to the Title IV-D agency shall be made payable to and transmitted to the Title IV-D agency.

(b) If a court has ordered support payments to be made to an applicant for or recipient of financial assistance or to a person other than the applicant or recipient, the Title IV-D agency shall, on providing notice to the obligee and the obligor, direct the obligor or other payor to make support payments payable to the Title IV-D agency and to transmit the payments to the agency. The Title IV-D agency shall file a copy of the notice with the court ordering the payments and with the child support registry. The notice must include:

(1) a statement that the child is an applicant for or recipient of financial assistance, or a child other than a recipient child for whom services are provided;

(2) the name of the child and the caretaker for whom support has been ordered by the court;

(3) the style and cause number of the case in which support was ordered; and

(4) instructions for the payment of ordered support to the agency.

(c) On receipt of a copy of the notice under Subsection (b), the clerk of the court shall file the notice in the appropriate case file.

Added by Acts 1995, 74th Leg., ch. 20, § 1, eff. April 20, 1995. Amended by Acts 1997, 75th Leg., ch. 911, § 71, eff. Sept. 1, 1997.

For application and effectiveness provisions of Acts 1997, 75th Leg., ch. 911, see note following V.T.C.A., Family Code § 156.401.

§ 231.106. Notice of Termination of Assignment

(a) On termination of support rights to the Title IV-D agency, the Title IV-D agency shall, after providing notice to the obligee and the obligor, send a notice of termination of assignment to the obligor or other payor, which may direct that all or a portion of the payments be made payable to the agency and to other persons who are entitled to receive the payments.

(b) The Title IV-D agency shall send a copy of the notice of termination of assignment to the court ordering the support and to the child support registry, and on receipt of the notice the clerk of the court shall file the notice in the appropriate case file.

Added by Acts 1995, 74th Leg., ch. 20, § 1, eff. April 20, 1995. Amended by Acts 1997, 75th Leg., ch. 911, § 72, eff. Sept. 1, 1997.

For application and effectiveness provisions of Acts 1997, 75th Leg., ch. 911, see note following V.T.C.A., Family Code § 156.401.

§ 231.107. Certificate of Assignment or of Termination of Assignment

If an abstract of judgment or a child support lien on support amounts assigned to the Title IV-D agency under this chapter has previously been filed of record, the agency shall file for recordation, with the county clerk of each county in which such abstract or lien has been filed, a certificate that a notice of change of payee or a notice of termination of assignment has been issued by the agency.

Added by Acts 1995, 74th Leg., ch. 20, § 1, eff. April 20, 1995. Amended by Acts 1997, 75th Leg., ch. 911, § 73, eff. Sept. 1, 1997.

For application and effectiveness provisions of Acts 1997, 75th Leg., ch. 911, see note following V.T.C.A., Family Code § 156.401.

§ 231.108. Confidentiality of Records and Privileged Communications

(a) Except as provided by Subsection (c), all files and records of services provided under this chapter, including information concerning a custodial parent, noncustodial parent, child, and an alleged or presumed father, are confidential.

(b) Except as provided by Subsection (c), all communications made by a recipient of financial assistance under Chapter 31, Human Resources Code, or an applicant for or recipient of services under this chapter are privileged.

(c) The Title IV–D agency may use or release information from the files and records, including information that results from a communication made by a recipient of financial assistance under Chapter 31, Human Resources Code, or by an applicant for or recipient of services under this chapter, for purposes directly connected with the administration of the child support, paternity determination, parent locator, or aid to families with dependent children programs. The Title IV–D agency may release information from the files and records to a consumer reporting agency in accordance with Section 231.114.

(d) The Title IV–D agency by rule may provide for the release of information to public officials.

(e) The Title IV-D agency may not release information on the physical location of a person if:

(1) a protective order has been entered with respect to the person; or

(2) there is reason to believe that the release of information may result in physical or emotional harm to the person.

Added by Acts 1995, 74th Leg., ch. 20, § 1, eff. April 20, 1995. Amended by Acts 1995, 74th Leg., ch. 341, § 1.08, eff. Sept. 1, 1995; Acts 1997, 75th Leg., ch. 911, § 74, eff. Sept. 1, 1997.

For application and effectiveness provisions of Acts 1997, 75th Leg., ch. 911, see note following V.T.C.A., Family Code § 156.401.

§ 231.109. Attorneys Representing State

(a) Attorneys employed by the Title IV–D agency may represent this state or another state in an action brought under the authority of federal law or this chapter.

(b) The Title IV–D agency may contract with private attorneys, other private entities, or political subdivisions of the state to provide services in Title IV–D cases.

(c) The Title IV–D agency shall provide copies of all contracts entered into under this section to the Legislative Budget Board and the Governor's Office of Budget and Planning, along with a written justification of the need for each contract, within 60 days after the execution of the contract.

(d) An attorney employed to provide Title IV-D services represents the interest of the state and not the interest of any other party. The provision of services by an attorney under this chapter does not create an attorney-client relationship between the attorney and any other party. The agency shall, at the time an application for child support services is made, inform the applicant that neither the Title IV–D agency nor any attorney who provides services under this chapter is the applicant's attorney and that the attorney providing services under this chapter does not provide legal representation to the applicant.

(e) An attorney employed by the Title IV–D agency or as otherwise provided by this chapter may not be appointed or act as a guardian ad litem or attorney ad litem for a child or another party.

Added by Acts 1995, 74th Leg., ch. 20, § 1, eff. April 20, 1995. Amended by Acts 1995, 74th Leg., ch. 341, § 1.02, eff. Sept. 1, 1995.

§ 231.110. Authorization of Service

The provision of services by the Title IV–D agency under this chapter or Part D of Title IV of the federal Social Security Act (42 U.S.C. Section 651 et seq.) does not authorize service on the agency of any legal notice that is required to be served on any party other than the agency.

Added by Acts 1995, 74th Leg., ch. 20, § 1, eff. April 20, 1995.

§ 231.111. Disqualification of Agency

A court shall not disqualify the Title IV–D agency in a legal action filed under this chapter or Part D of Title IV of the federal Social Security Act (42 U.S.C. Section 651 et seq.) on the basis that the agency has previously provided services to a party whose interests may now be adverse to the relief requested.

Added by Acts 1995, 74th Leg., ch. 20, § 1, eff. April 20, 1995.

§ 231.112. Information on Paternity Establishment

On notification by the state registrar under Section 192.005(d), Health and Safety Code, that the items relating to the child's father are not completed on a birth certificate filed with the state registrar, the Title IV–D agency may provide to:

(1) the child's mother and, if possible, the man claiming to be the child's biological father written information necessary for the man to complete a statement of paternity as provided by Chapter 160; and

(2) the child's mother written information:

(A) explaining the benefits of having the child's paternity established; and

(B) regarding the availability of paternity establishment and child support enforcement services.

Added by Acts 1995, 74th Leg., ch. 20, § 1, eff. April 20, 1995.

§ 231.113. Enforcement of Support Obligations in Public Assistance Cases

To the extent possible, the Title IV–D agency shall enforce a child support obligation in a case involving a child who receives financial assistance under Chapter 31, Human Resources Code, not later than the first anniversary of the date the agency receives from the Texas Department of Human Services the information the department is required to provide to assist in the enforcement of that obligation.

Added by Acts 1995, 74th Leg., ch. 341, § 1.03, eff. Sept. 1, 1995.

§ 231.114. Reports of Child Support Payments to Consumer Reporting Agencies

(a) The Title IV–D agency shall make information available in accordance with this section to a consumer reporting agency regarding the amount of child support owed and the amount paid by an obligor in a Title IV–D case.

(b) Before disclosing the information to consumer reporting agencies, the Title IV–D agency shall send the obligor a notice by mail to the obligor's last known address. The notice must include:

(1) the information to be released, including the amount of the obligor's child support obligation and delinquency, if any, that will be reported;

(2) the procedure available for the obligor to contest the accuracy of the information; and

(3) a statement that the information will be released if the obligor fails to contest the disclosure before the 30th day after the date of mailing of the notice.

(c) If the obligor does not contest the disclosure within the period specified by Subsection (b), the Title IV–D agency shall make the information available to the consumer reporting agency.

(d) The Title IV–D agency shall regularly update the information released to a consumer reporting agency under this section to ensure the accuracy of the released information.

(e) The Title IV–D agency may charge a consumer reporting agency a reasonable fee for making information available under this section, including all applicable mailing costs.

(f) In this section:

(1) "Consumer reporting agency" means any person that regularly engages in whole or in part in the practice of assembling or evaluating consumer credit information or other information on consumers for monetary fees, for dues, or on a cooperative nonprofit basis, to furnish consumer reports to third parties.

(2) "Obligor" means any person required to make payments under the terms of a support order for a child.

(3) "Title IV–D case" means a case in which services are being provided by the Title IV–D agency under Part D of Title IV of the federal Social Security Act (42 U.S.C. Section 651 et seq.) seeking to locate an absent parent, determine parentage, or establish, modify, enforce, or monitor a child support obligation.

Added by Acts 1995, 74th Leg., ch. 341, § 1.03, eff. Sept. 1, 1995.

§ 231.115. Unemployed Noncustodial Parents

Text of section as added by Acts 1997, 75th Leg., ch. 165, § 7.20(a)

(a) The Title IV-D agency shall refer to appropriate state and local entities that assist unemployed noncustodial parents in gaining employment any unemployed noncustodial parent who is in arrears in court-ordered child support payments to a child who:

(1) receives financial assistance under Chapter 31, Human Resources Code; or

(2) is otherwise eligible to receive financial assistance under Chapter 31, Human Resources Code, and for whom the Department of Protective and Regulatory Services is providing substitute care.

(b) A referral under Subsection (a) may include:

(1) skills training and job placement through:

(A) the Texas Workforce Commission; or

(B) the agency responsible for the food stamp employment and training program (7 U.S.C. Section 2015(d));

(2) referrals to education and literacy classes; and

(3) counseling regarding:

(A) substance abuse;

(B) parenting skills;

(C) life skills; and

(D) mediation techniques.

(c) The Title IV-D agency may require an unemployed noncustodial parent to complete the training, classes, or counseling the parent is referred to under this section. The agency shall suspend under Chapter 232 the license of a parent who fails to comply with the requirements of this subsection.

Added by Acts 1997, 75th Leg., ch. 165, § 7.20(a), eff. Sept. 1, 1997.

For text of section as added by Acts 1997, 75th Leg., ch. 911, § 75, see § 231.115, post.

§ 231.115. Noncooperation by Recipient of Public Assistance

Text of section as added by Acts 1997, 75th Leg., ch. 911, § 75

(a) The failure by a person who is a recipient of public assistance under Chapter 31, Human Resources Code, to provide accurate information as required by Section 31.0315, Human Resources Code, shall serve as the basis for a determination by the Title IV-D agency that the person did not cooperate with the Title IV-D agency.

(b) The Title IV-D agency shall adopt rules establishing the actions or failures to act by a recipient of public assistance that constitute noncooperation with the Title IV-D agency.

(c) In adopting rules under this section that establish the basis for determining that a person has failed to cooperate with the Title IV-D agency, the Title IV-D agency shall consider whether:

(1) good cause exists for the failure to cooperate;

(2) the person has failed to disclose the name and location of an alleged or probable parent of the child, if known by the person, at the time of applying for public assistance or at a subsequent time; and

(3) the person named a man as the alleged father and the man was subsequently excluded by parentage testing as being the father if the person has previously named another man as the child's father.

Added by Acts 1997, 75th Leg., ch. 911, § 75, eff. Sept. 1, 1997.

For text of section as added by Acts 1997, 75th Leg., ch. 165, § 7.20(a), see § 231.115, ante.

§ 231.116. Information on Internet

The Title IV-D agency shall place on the Internet for public access child support information to assist the public in child support matters, including application forms, child support collection in other states, and profiles of certain obligors who are in arrears in paying child support.

Added by Acts 1997, 75th Leg., ch. 420, § 18, eff. Sept. 1, 1997.

[Sections 231.115 to 231.200 reserved for expansion]

SUBCHAPTER C. PAYMENT OF FEES AND COSTS

§ 231.201. Definitions

In this subchapter:

(1) "Federal share" means the portion of allowable expenses for fees and other costs that will be reimbursed by the federal government under federal law and regulations regarding the administration of the Title IV–D program.

(2) "State share" means the portion of allowable expenses for fees and other costs that remain after receipt of the federal share of reimbursement and that is to be reimbursed by the state or may be contributed by certified public expenditure by a county.

Added by Acts 1995, 74th Leg., ch. 20, § 1, eff. April 20, 1995.

§ 231.202. Authorized Costs and Fees in Title IV–D Cases

In a Title IV-D case filed under this title, the Title IV-D agency shall pay:

(1) filing fees and fees for issuance and service of process as provided by Chapter 110 of this code and by Sections 51.317, 51.318(b)(2), and 51.319(2), Government Code;

(2) fees for transfer as provided by Chapter 110;

(3) fees for the issuance and delivery of orders and writs of income withholding in the amounts provided by Chapter 110; and

(4) a fee of $45 for each item of process to each individual on whom service is required, including service by certified or registered mail, to be paid to a sheriff, constable, or clerk whenever service of process is required.

Added by Acts 1995, 74th Leg., ch. 20, § 1, eff. April 20, 1995. Amended by Acts 1995, 74th Leg., ch. 341, § 1.04, eff. Sept. 1, 1995; Acts 1997, 75th Leg., ch. 165, § 7.21(a), eff. Sept. 1, 1997.

§ 231.2025. Contingency Fees

The Title IV-D agency may pay a contingency fee in a contract or agreement between the agency and a private agency or individual authorized under Section 231.002(c).

Added by Acts 1997, 75th Leg., ch. 420, § 19, eff. Sept. 1, 1997.

§ 231.203. State Exemption From Bond Not Affected

This subchapter does not affect, nor is this subchapter affected by, the exemption from bond provided by Section 6.001, Civil Practice and Remedies Code.

Added by Acts 1995, 74th Leg., ch. 20, § 1, eff. April 20, 1995.

§ 231.204. Prohibited Fees in Title IV–D Cases

Except as provided by this subchapter, a district or county clerk, sheriff, constable, or other government officer or employee may not charge the Title IV–D agency or a private attorney or political subdivision that has entered into a contract to provide Title IV–D services any fees or other amounts otherwise imposed by law for services rendered in, or in connection with, a Title IV–D case, including:

(1) a fee payable to a district clerk for:

(A) performing services related to the estates of deceased persons or minors;

(B) certifying copies; or

(C) comparing copies to originals;

(2) a court reporter fee, except as provided by Section 231.209;

(3) a judicial fund fee;

(4) a fee for a child support registry, enforcement office, or domestic relations office; and

(5) a fee for alternative dispute resolution services.

Added by Acts 1995, 74th Leg., ch. 20, § 1, eff. April 20, 1995.

§ 231.205. Limitations on Liability of Attorney General for Authorized Fees and Costs

(a) The Title IV–D agency is liable for a fee or cost under this subchapter only to the extent that an express, specific appropriation is made to the agency exclusively for that purpose. To the extent that state funds are not available, the amount of costs and fees that are not reimbursed by the federal government and that represent the state share shall be paid by certified public expenditure by the county through the clerk of the court, sheriff, or constable. This section does not prohibit the agency from spending other funds appropriated for child support enforcement to provide the initial expenditures necessary to qualify for the federal share.

(b) The Title IV–D agency is liable for the payment of the federal share of reimbursement for fees and costs under this subchapter only to the extent that the federal share is received, and if an amount is paid by the agency and that amount is disallowed by the federal government or the federal share is not otherwise received, the clerk of the court, sheriff, or constable to whom the payment was made shall return the amount to the agency not later than the 30th day after the date on which notice is given by the agency.

Added by Acts 1995, 74th Leg., ch. 20, § 1, eff. April 20, 1995.

§ 231.206. Restriction on Fees for Child Support or Registry Services in Title IV-D Cases

A district clerk, a county child support registry or enforcement office, or a domestic relations office may not assess or collect fees for processing child support payments or for child support services from the Title IV-D agency, a managing conservator, or a possessory conservator in a Title IV-D case, except as provided by this subchapter.

Added by Acts 1995, 74th Leg., ch. 20, § 1, eff. April 20, 1995.

§ 231.207. Method of Billing for Allowable Fees

(a) To be entitled to reimbursement under this subchapter, the clerk of the court, sheriff, or constable must submit one monthly billing to the Title IV-D agency.

(b) The monthly billing must be in the form and manner prescribed by the Title IV-D agency and be approved by the clerk, sheriff, or constable.

Added by Acts 1995, 74th Leg., ch. 20, § 1, eff. April 20, 1995.

§ 231.208. Agreements for Reimbursement in Lieu of Fees

(a) The Title IV-D agency and a qualified county may enter into a written agreement under which reimbursement for salaries and certain other actual costs incurred by the clerk, sheriff, or constable in Title IV-D cases is provided to the county.

(b) A county may not enter into an agreement for reimbursement under this section unless the clerk, sheriff, or constable providing service has at least two full-time employees each devoted exclusively to providing services in Title IV-D cases.

(c) Reimbursement made under this section is in lieu of all costs and fees provided by this subchapter.

Added by Acts 1995, 74th Leg., ch. 20, § 1, eff. April 20, 1995.

§ 231.209. Payment for Services Not Affected by This Subchapter

Without regard to this subchapter and specifically Section 231.205, the Title IV-D agency may pay the costs for:

(1) the services of an official court reporter for the preparation of statements of facts;

(2) the costs for the publication of citation served by publication; and

(3) mileage or other reasonable travel costs incurred by a sheriff or constable when traveling out of the county to execute an outstanding warrant or capias, to be reimbursed at a rate not to exceed the rate provided for mileage or other costs incurred by state employees in the General Appropriations Act.

Added by Acts 1995, 74th Leg., ch. 20, § 1, eff. April 20, 1995. Amended by Acts 1995, 74th Leg., ch. 341, § 1.05, eff. Sept. 1, 1995.

§ 231.210. Authority to Pay Litigation Expenses

(a) The Title IV-D agency may pay all fees, expenses, costs, and bills necessary to secure evidence and to take the testimony of a witness, including advance payments or purchases for transportation, lodging, meals, and incidental expenses of custodians of evidence or witnesses whose transportation is necessary and proper for the production of evidence or the taking of testimony in a Title IV-D case.

(b) In making payments under this section, the Title IV-D agency shall present vouchers to the comptroller that have been sworn to by the custodian or witness and approved by the agency. The voucher shall be sufficient to authorize payment without the necessity of a written contract.

(c) The Title IV-D agency may directly pay a commercial transportation company or commercial lodging establishment for the expense of transportation or lodging of a custodian or witness.

Added by Acts 1995, 74th Leg., ch. 20, § 1, eff. April 20, 1995.

§ 231.211. Award of Cost Against Nonprevailing Party in Title IV-D Case

(a) At the conclusion of a Title IV-D case, the court may assess attorney's fees and all court costs as authorized by law against the nonprevailing party, except that the court may not assess those amounts against the Title IV-D agency or a private attorney or political subdivision that has entered into a contract under this chapter or any party to whom the agency has provided services under this chapter. Such fees and costs may not exceed reasonable and necessary costs as determined by the court.

(b) The clerk of the court may take any action necessary to collect any fees or costs assessed under this section.

Added by Acts 1995, 74th Leg., ch. 20, § 1, eff. April 20, 1995.

[Sections 231.212 to 231.300 reserved for expansion]

SUBCHAPTER D. LOCATION OF PARENTS AND RESOURCES

§ 231.301. Title IV-D Parent Locator Services

The parent locator service conducted by the Title IV-D agency shall be used to obtain information for child support enforcement purposes regarding the identity, social security number, location, employer and employment benefits, income, and assets or debts of any individual under an obligation to pay child or medical support or to whom a support obligation is owed.

Added by Acts 1995, 74th Leg., ch. 20, § 1, eff. April 20, 1995. Amended by Acts 1997, 75th Leg., ch. 911, § 76, eff. Sept. 1, 1997.

For application and effectiveness provisions of Acts 1997, 75th Leg., ch. 911, see note following V.T.C.A., Family Code § 156.401.

§ 231.302. Information to Assist in Location of Persons or Property

(a) The Title IV-D agency of this or another state may request and obtain information relating to the identity, location, employment, compensation, benefits, income, and property holdings or other assets of any person from a state or local government agency, private company, institution, or other entity as necessary to establish, modify, or enforce a support order.

Text of subsec. (b) as amended by Acts 1997, 75th Leg., ch. 420, § 20

(b) A government agency, private company, institution, or other entity shall provide the information requested under Subsection (a) and shall, subject to safeguards on privacy and information security, provide the information in the most efficient and expeditious manner available, including electronic or automated transfer and interface. Any individual or entity disclosing information under this section in response to a request from a Title IV-D agency may not be held liable in any civil action or proceeding to any person for the disclosure of information under this subsection.

Text of subsec. (b) as amended by Acts 1997, 75th Leg., ch. 911, § 77

(b) A government agency, private company, institution, or other entity shall provide the information requested under Subsection (a) and shall provide the information, subject to safeguards for privacy and information security, in the most efficient and expeditious manner available, including electronic or automated transfer and interface. An individual or entity disclosing information under this section in response to a request from a Title IV-D agency may not be held liable in a civil action or proceeding for the disclosure of the information.

(c) To assist in the administration of laws relating to child support enforcement under Parts A and D of Title IV of the federal Social Security Act (42 U.S.C. Sections 601–617 and 651–669):

(1) each licensing authority shall request and each applicant for a license shall provide the applicant's social security number;

(2) each agency administering a contract that provides for a payment of state funds shall request and each individual or entity bidding on a state contract shall provide the individual's or entity's social security number as required by Section 231.006, Family Code; and

(3) each agency administering a state-funded grant or loan program shall request and each applicant for a grant or loan shall provide the applicant's social security number as required by Section 231.006, Family Code.

(d) This section does not limit the right of an agency or licensing authority to collect and use a social security number under another provision of law.

(e) Except as provided by Subsection (d), a social security number provided under this section is confidential and may be disclosed only for the purposes of responding to a request for information from an agency operating under the provisions of Part A or D of Title IV of the federal Social Security Act (42 U.S.C. Sections 601 et seq. and 651 et seq).

(f) Information collected by the Title IV-D agency under this section may be used only for child support purposes.

(g) In this section, "licensing authority" has the meaning assigned by Section 232.001.

Added by Acts 1995, 74th Leg., ch. 20, § 1, eff. April 20, 1995. Amended by Acts 1995, 74th Leg., ch. 751, § 84, eff. Sept. 1, 1995; Acts 1997, 75th Leg., ch. 420, § 20, eff. Sept. 1, 1997; Acts 1997, 75th Leg., ch. 911, § 77, eff. Sept. 1, 1997.

For application and effectiveness provisions of Acts 1997, 75th Leg., ch. 911, see note following V.T.C.A., Family Code § 156.401.

§ 231.303. Title IV-D Administrative Subpoena

(a) The Title IV-D agency of this state or another state may issue an administrative subpoena to any individual or private or public entity in this state to furnish information necessary to carry out the purposes of child support enforcement under 42 U.S.C. Section 651 et seq. or this chapter.

(b) An individual or entity receiving an administrative subpoena under this section shall comply with the subpoena. The Title IV-D agency may impose a fine in an amount not to exceed $500 on an individual or entity that fails without good cause to comply with an administrative subpoena. An alleged or presumed father or a parent who fails to comply with a subpoena without good cause may also be subject to license suspension under Chapter 232.

(c) A court may compel compliance with an administrative subpoena and with any administrative fine for failure to comply with the subpoena and may award attorney's fees and costs to the Title IV-D agency in enforcing an administrative subpoena on proof that an individual or organization failed without good cause to comply with the subpoena.

(d) An individual or organization may not be liable in a civil action or proceeding for disclosing financial or other information to a Title IV-D agency under this section. The Title IV-D agency may disclose information in a financial record obtained from a financial institution only to the extent necessary to establish, modify, or enforce a child support obligation.

Added by Acts 1995, 74th Leg., ch. 20, § 1, eff. April 20, 1995. Amended by Acts 1997, 75th Leg., ch. 911, § 78, eff. Sept. 1, 1997.

For application and effectiveness provisions of Acts 1997, 75th Leg., ch. 911, see note following V.T.C.A., Family Code § 156.401.

§ 231.304. Employer New Hire Reporting Program

Text of section effective until October 1, 1998

(a) In this section, "ENHR program" means an Employer New Hire Reporting program.

(b) The Title IV–D agency, the Texas Department of Human Services, the Texas Workers' Compensation Commission, and the Texas Employment Commission shall create and develop a voluntary ENHR program to provide a means for employers to assist in the state's efforts to prevent fraud in the welfare, workers' compensation, and unemployment insurance programs, locate absent parents who owe child support, and collect support from those parents by reporting information concerning newly hired and rehired employees directly to a centralized state database. In order to encourage use of the ENHR program, employer reporting requirements shall be simplified and standardized.

(c) To ensure timely receipt of information, the ENHR program shall provide that employers participating in the program report the hiring or rehiring of persons not later than the 10th working day after the hiring date.

(d) The ENHR program shall apply to a person who will:

(1) be employed for more than one month's duration;

(2) be paid for more than 350 hours during a continuous six-month period; or

(3) have gross earnings of more than $300 in each month of employment.

(e) An employer doing business in this state may voluntarily participate in the ENHR program by reporting to the Title IV–D agency the:

(1) hiring of a person who resides or works in this state to whom the employer anticipates paying earnings; or

(2) rehiring or return to work of an employee who was laid off, furloughed, separated, granted leave without pay, or terminated from employment.

(f) Employers participating in the ENHR program may provide information to the Title IV–D agency by:

(1) sending a copy of the new employee's W–4 form;

(2) completing a form supplied by the agency; or

(3) any other means authorized by the agency for conveying information, including electronic transmission or delivery of data tapes containing the employee's name, address, social security number, date of birth, and salary information, and the employer's name, address, and employer identification number.

(g) An employer participating in the ENHR program may disclose the information described above and is not liable to the employee for the disclosure or a later use by the Title IV–D agency of the information.

(h) Subject to approval of the agencies involved and any requirements of federal law, the centralized database shall make the information on each employee reported under the ENHR program available for:

(1) purposes directly connected with the administration of a plan or program for unemployment benefits, workers' compensation benefits, child support, or public assistance;

(2) an investigation or a civil or criminal prosecution relating to the administration of such plan or program; or

(3) the administration of any other federal or federally assisted program which provides assistance, in cash or in kind, or services, directly to individuals on the basis of need.

(i) In cooperation with the Texas Employment Commission and representatives of the private sector, the Title IV–D agency may develop a plan for phasing in implementation of the ENHR program, acknowledging employer participation in the program, and publicizing the availability of the program to employers in this state.

(j) An employer participating in the ENHR program is strongly encouraged to report information about health insurance coverage available through the employer in which a dependent child may be enrolled under Subchapter D, Chapter 154.[1]

(k) To expand the ENHR program, the Title IV–D agency shall work closely with the Texas Employment Commission, the Texas Workers' Compensation Commission, the comptroller, the Texas Department of Commerce,[2] the secretary of state, and employer groups. Efforts to expand the program shall include:

(1) regularly sending to employers solicitations for participation in the program and promotional information about the program that includes information on:

(A) the program's impact on child support and medical support enforcement;

(B) savings in public assistance payments attributable to the program;

(C) benefits to employers and taxpayers of the fraud prevention aspects of the program;

(D) participation requirements; and

(E) awards available for business participation; and

(2) developing a public awareness program that:

(A) stresses the importance of securing financial support for all children; and

(B) informs the public about the ENHR program.

(*l*) The affected agencies may pool resources, develop a cost allocation plan, determine the most cost-effective means of establishing and funding the required database, and issue rules, solicit bids, or enter into contracts to carry out the purposes of this section.

(m) The affected agencies shall implement the plan to create the ENHR database, if cost-effective, using existing funding and considering savings and revenue gains that may result from the use of such system.

Added by Acts 1995, 74th Leg., ch. 20, § 1, eff. April 20, 1995. Amended by Acts 1995, 74th Leg., ch. 341, § 1.06, eff. Sept. 1, 1995.

[1] V.T.C.A., Family Code § 154.181 et seq.

[2] The Texas Department of Commerce is abolished and its powers and duties are transferred to the Texas Department of Economic Development. A reference in law to the Texas Department of Commerce means the Texas Department of Economic Development.

Repeal

Acts 1997, 75th Leg., ch. 911, § 97(b) repeals this section effective October 1, 1998.

§ 231.305. Memorandum of Understanding on Child Support for Children Receiving Public Assistance

(a) The Title IV–D agency and the Texas Department of Human Services by rule shall adopt a memorandum of understanding governing the establishment and enforcement of court-ordered child support in cases involving children who receive financial assistance under Chapter 31, Human Resources Code. The memorandum shall require the agency and the department to:

(1) develop procedures to ensure that the information the department is required to collect to establish and enforce child support:

(A) is collected from the person applying to receive the financial assistance at the time the application is filed;

(B) is accurate and complete when the department forwards the information to the agency; and

(C) is not information previously reported to the agency;

(2) develop procedures to ensure that the agency does not duplicate the efforts of the department in gathering necessary information;

(3) clarify each agency's responsibilities in the establishment and enforcement of child support; and

(4) develop guidelines for use by eligibility workers and child support enforcement officers in obtaining from an applicant the information required to establish and enforce child support for that child.

(b) The Title IV–D agency and the Texas Department of Human Services semiannually shall review and renew or modify the memorandum as necessary.

Added by Acts 1995, 74th Leg., ch. 341, § 1.07, eff. Sept. 1, 1995.

§ 231.306. Maximizing Medical Support Establishment and Collection by the Title IV–D Agency

(a) On the installation of an automated child support enforcement system, the Title IV–D agency is strongly encouraged to:

(1) maximize the collection of medical support; and

(2) establish cash medical support orders for children eligible for medical assistance under the state Medicaid program for whom private insurance coverage is not available.

(b) In this section, "medical support" has the meaning assigned by Section 101.020.

Added by Acts 1995, 74th Leg., ch. 341, § 2.03, eff. Sept. 1, 1995.

§ 231.307. Financial Institution Data Matches

(a) The Title IV-D agency shall develop a system meeting the requirements of 42 U.S.C. Section 666(a)(17) for the quarterly exchange of data with financial institutions doing business in the state to identify an account of an obligor owing past-due child support and enforce support obligations against the obligor.

(b) The Title IV-D agency by rule shall establish procedures for data matches authorized under this section.

(c) A financial institution providing information or responding to a notice of child support lien provided under Subchapter G, Chapter 157,[1] or otherwise acting in good faith to comply with the Title IV-D agency's procedures under this section may not be liable under any federal or state law for any damages that arise from those acts.

(d) In this section:

(1) "Financial institution" has the meaning assigned by 42 U.S.C. Section 669a(d)(1); and

(2) "Account" means a demand deposit account, checking or negotiable withdrawal order account, savings account, time deposit account, or money market mutual fund account.

Added by Acts 1997, 75th Leg., ch. 911, § 79, eff. Sept. 1, 1997.

[1] V.T.C.A., Family Code § 157.311 et seq.

§ 231.308. Public Identification of Certain Obligors

(a) The Title IV-D agency shall develop a program to identify publicly certain child support obligors who are delinquent in the payment of child support. The program shall include the displaying of photographs and profiles of obligors in public and private locations. The Title IV-D agency shall use posters, the news media, and other cost-effective methods to display photographs and profiles of certain obligors who are in arrears in paying child support. The Title IV-D agency shall divide the state into at least six regions for local identification of certain child support obligors who are delinquent in the payment of child support.

(b) The Title IV-D agency may not disclose information under this section that is by law required to remain confidential.

Added by Acts 1997, 75th Leg., ch. 420, § 21, eff. Sept. 1, 1997.

§ 231.309. Rewards for Information

(a) The Title IV-D agency may offer a reward to an individual who provides information to the agency that leads to the collection of child support owed by an obligor who is delinquent in paying support.

(b) The Title IV-D agency shall adopt rules providing for the amounts of rewards offered under this section and the circumstances under which an individual providing information described in Subsection (a) is entitled to receive a reward.

(c) A reward paid under this section shall be paid from the child support retained collections account.

Added by Acts 1997, 75th Leg., ch. 420, § 21, eff. Sept. 1, 1997.

[Sections 231.307 to 231.400 reserved for expansion]

SUBCHAPTER E. CHILD SUPPORT REVIEW PROCESS TO ESTABLISH OR ENFORCE SUPPORT OBLIGATIONS [REDESIGNATED]

Acts 1997, 75th Leg., ch. 911, § 80 redesignated and amended V.T.C.A., Family Code Chapter 231, Subchapter E, consisting of §§ 231.401 to 231.429, to be V.T.C.A., Family Code Chapter 233.

§§ 231.401 to 231.429. Redesignated as V.T.C.A., Family Code §§ 233.001 to 233.029 by Acts 1997, 75th Leg., ch. 911, § 80, eff. Sept. 1, 1997

§§ 231.430, 231.431. Repealed by Acts 1997, 75th Leg., ch. 911, § 97(a), eff. Sept. 1, 1997

CHAPTER 232. SUSPENSION OF LICENSE FOR FAILURE TO PAY CHILD SUPPORT OR COMPLY WITH SUBPOENA

Acts 1997, 75th Leg., ch. 911, § 81, in the Chapter heading, added "or comply with subpoena".

Section

§ 232.001. Definitions

In this chapter:

(1) "License" means a license, certificate, registration, permit, or other authorization that:

(A) is issued by a licensing authority;

(B) is subject before expiration to suspension, revocation, forfeiture, or termination by the issuing licensing authority; and

(C) a person must obtain [1] to:

(i) practice or engage in a particular business, occupation, or profession;

(ii) operate a motor vehicle; or

(iii) engage in any other regulated activity, including hunting, fishing, or other recreational activity for which a license or permit is required.

(2) "Licensing authority" means a department, commission, board, office, or other agency of the state or a political subdivision of the state that issues a license.

(3) "Order suspending license" means an order issued by the Title IV-D agency or a court directing a licensing authority to suspend a license.

(4) "Subpoena" means a subpoena issued in a parentage determination or child support proceeding under this title.

Added by Acts 1995, 74th Leg., ch. 655, § 5.03, eff. Sept. 1, 1995; Acts 1995, 74th Leg., ch. 751, § 85, eff. Sept. 1, 1995. Amended by Acts 1997, 75th Leg., ch. 911, § 82, eff. Sept. 1, 1997.

[1] Acts 1995, 74th Leg., ch. 655, § 5.03 here read "is necessary for a person" in lieu of "a person must obtain".

For application and effectiveness provisions of Acts 1997, 75th Leg., ch. 911, see note following V.T.C.A., Family Code § 156.401.

§ 232.002. Licensing Authorities Subject to Chapter

The following state agencies are licensing authorities subject to this chapter:

(1) Department of Agriculture;

(2) Texas Commission on Alcohol and Drug Abuse;

(3) Texas Alcoholic Beverage Commission;

(4) Texas Appraiser Licensing and Certification Board;

(5) Texas Board of Architectural Examiners;

(6) State Board of Barber Examiners;

(7) Texas Board of Chiropractic Examiners;

(8) Comptroller of Public Accounts;

(9) Texas Cosmetology Commission;

(10) Court Reporters Certification Board;

(11) State Board of Dental Examiners;

(12) Texas State Board of Examiners of Dietitians;

(13) Texas Funeral Service Commission;

(14) Texas Department of Health;

(15) Texas Department of Human Services;

(16) Texas Board of Professional Land Surveying;

(17) Texas Department of Licensing and Regulation;

(18) Texas State Board of Examiners of Marriage and Family Therapists;

(19) Texas State Board of Medical Examiners;

(20) Midwifery Board;

(21) Texas Natural Resource Conservation Commission;

(22) Board of Nurse Examiners;

(23) Texas Board of Occupational Therapy Examiners;

(24) Texas Optometry Board;

(25) Parks and Wildlife Department;

(26) Texas State Board of Examiners of Perfusionists;

(27) Texas State Board of Pharmacy;

(28) Texas Board of Physical Therapy Examiners;

(29) Texas State Board of Plumbing Examiners;

(30) Texas State Board of Podiatric Medical Examiners;

(31) Polygraph Examiners Board;

(32) Texas Board of Private Investigators and Private Security Agencies;

(33) Texas State Board of Examiners of Professional Counselors;

(34) State Board of Registration for Professional Engineers;

(35) Department of Protective and Regulatory Services;

(36) Texas State Board of Examiners of Psychologists;

(37) Texas State Board of Public Accountancy;

(38) Department of Public Safety of the State of Texas;

(39) Public Utility Commission of Texas;

(40) Railroad Commission of Texas;

(41) Texas Real Estate Commission;

(42) State Bar of Texas;

(43) Texas State Board of Social Worker Examiners;

(44) State Board of Examiners for Speech-Language Pathology and Audiology;

(45) Texas Structural Pest Control Board;

(46) Board of Tax Professional Examiners;

(47) Secretary of State;

(48) Supreme Court of Texas;

(49) Texas Transportation Commission;

(50) State Board of Veterinary Medical Examiners;

(51) Board of Vocational Nurse Examiners;

(52) Texas Ethics Commission;

(53) Advisory Board of Athletic Trainers;

(54) State Committee of Examiners in the Fitting and Dispensing of Hearing Instruments;

(55) Texas Board of Licensure for Professional Medical Physicists; and

(56) Texas Department of Insurance.

(57) Texas Board of Orthotics and Prosthetics.

Added by Acts 1995, 74th Leg., ch. 655, § 5.03, eff. Sept. 1, 1995; Acts 1995, 74th Leg., ch. 751, § 85, eff. Sept. 1, 1995. Amended by Acts 1997, 75th Leg., ch. 165, § 7.22, eff. Sept. 1, 1997; Acts 1997, 75th Leg., ch. 1280, § 1.02, eff. Sept. 1, 1997; Acts 1997, 75th Leg., ch. 1288, § 2, eff. Sept. 1, 1997.

§ 232.003. Suspension of License

(a) A court or the Title IV-D agency may issue an order suspending a license as provided by this chapter if an individual who is an obligor:

(1) has a child support arrearage equal to or greater than the total support due for 90 days under a support order;

(2) has been provided an opportunity to make payments toward the child support arrearage under an agreed or court-ordered repayment schedule, without regard to whether the repayment schedule was agreed to or ordered before or after the date the petition for suspension of a license was filed; and

(3) has failed to comply with the repayment schedule.

(b) A court or the Title IV-D agency may issue an order suspending license as provided by this chapter if an individual has failed, after receiving appropriate notice, to comply with a subpoena.

Added by Acts 1995, 74th Leg., ch. 655, § 5.03, eff. Sept. 1, 1995; Acts 1995, 74th Leg., ch. 751, § 85, eff. Sept. 1, 1995. Amended by Acts 1997, 75th Leg., ch. 420, §§ 22, 23, eff. Sept. 1, 1997; Acts 1997, 75th Leg., ch. 911, § 83, eff. Sept. 1, 1997.

For application and effectiveness provisions of Acts 1997, 75th Leg., ch. 911, see note following V.T.C.A., Family Code § 156.401.

§ 232.004. Petition for Suspension of License

(a) A child support agency or obligee may file a petition to suspend, as provided by this chapter, a license of an obligor who has an arrearage equal to or greater than the total support due for 90 days under a support order.

(b) In a Title IV-D case, the petition shall be filed with the Title IV-D agency.

(c) In a case other than a Title IV-D case, the petition shall be filed in the court of continuing jurisdiction or the court in which a child support order has been registered under Chapter 159.

(d) A proceeding in a case filed with the Title IV-D agency under this chapter is governed by the contested case provisions of Chapter 2001, Government Code, except that Section 2001.054 does not apply to the proceeding. The director of the Title IV-D agency or the director's designee may render a final decision in a contested case proceeding under this chapter.

Added by Acts 1995, 74th Leg., ch. 655, § 5.03, eff. Sept. 1, 1995; Acts 1995, 74th Leg., ch. 751, § 85, eff. Sept. 1, 1995. Amended by Acts 1997, 75th Leg., ch. 420, § 24, eff. Sept. 1, 1997; Acts 1997, 75th Leg., ch. 911, § 84, eff. Sept. 1, 1997.

For application and effectiveness provisions of Acts 1997, 75th Leg., ch. 911, see note following V.T.C.A., Family Code § 156.401.

§ 232.005. Contents of Petition

(a) A petition under this chapter must state that license suspension is required under Section 232.003 and allege:

(1) the name and, if known, social security number of the individual;

(2) the type, and if known, number of any license the individual is believed to hold and the name of the licensing authority that issued the license; and

(3) the amount of arrearages owed under the child support order or the facts associated with the individual's failure to comply with a subpoena.

(b) A petition under this chapter may include as an attachment a copy of:

(1) the record of child support payments maintained by the Title IV-D registry or local registry; or

(2) the subpoena with which the individual has failed to comply, together with proof of service of the subpoena.

Added by Acts 1995, 74th Leg., ch. 655, § 5.03, eff. Sept. 1, 1995; Acts 1995, 74th Leg., ch. 751, § 85, eff. Sept. 1, 1995. Amended by Acts 1997, 75th Leg., ch. 911, § 85, eff. Sept. 1, 1997.

For application and effectiveness provisions of Acts 1997, 75th Leg., ch. 911, see note following V.T.C.A., Family Code § 156.401.

§ 232.006. Notice

(a) On the filing of a petition under Section 232.004, the clerk of the court or the Title IV-D agency shall deliver to the individual:

(1) notice of the individual's right to a hearing before the court or agency;

(2) notice of the deadline for requesting a hearing; and

(3) a hearing request form if the proceeding is in a Title IV-D case.

(b) Notice under this section may be served as in civil cases generally.

(c) The notice must contain the following statement in bold-faced type or capital letters:

"AN ACTION TO SUSPEND ONE OR MORE LICENSES ISSUED TO YOU HAS BEEN FILED. YOU MAY EMPLOY AN ATTORNEY TO REPRESENT YOU IN THIS ACTION. IF YOU OR YOUR ATTORNEY DO NOT REQUEST A HEARING BEFORE THE 21ST DAY AFTER THE DATE OF SERVICE OF THIS NOTICE, AN ORDER OF LICENSE SUSPENSION MAY BE RENDERED."

Added by Acts 1995, 74th Leg., ch. 655, § 5.03, eff. Sept. 1, 1995; Acts 1995, 74th Leg., ch. 751, § 85, eff. Sept. 1, 1995. Amended by Acts 1997, 75th Leg., ch. 911, § 86, eff. Sept. 1, 1997; Acts 1997, 75th Leg., ch. 976, § 7, eff. Sept. 1, 1997.

For application and effectiveness provisions of Acts 1997, 75th Leg., ch. 911, see note following V.T.C.A., Family Code § 156.401.

Section 10 of Acts 1997, 75th Leg., ch. 976 provides:

"(a) This Act takes effect September 1, 1997, and applies to a fee collected on or after that date, except as provided by Subsection (b) of this section.

"(b) Section 3 of this Act takes effect January 1, 1998, and applies to a fee collected on or after that date."

§ 232.007. Hearing on Petition to Suspend License

(a) A request for a hearing and motion to stay suspension must be filed with the court or Title IV-D agency by the individual not later than the 20th day after the date of service of the notice under Section 232.006.

(b) If a request for a hearing is filed, the court or Title IV-D agency shall:

(1) promptly schedule a hearing;

(2) notify each party of the date, time, and location of the hearing; and

(3) stay suspension pending the hearing.

(c) In a case involving support arrearages, a record of child support payments made by the Title IV-D agency or a local registry is evidence of whether the payments were made. A copy of the record appearing regular on its face shall be admitted as evidence at a hearing under this chapter, including a hearing on a motion to revoke a stay. Either party may offer controverting evidence.

(d) In a case in which an individual has failed to comply with a subpoena, proof of service is evidence of delivery of the subpoena.

Added by Acts 1995, 74th Leg., ch. 655, § 5.03, eff. Sept. 1, 1995; Acts 1995, 74th Leg., ch. 751, § 85, eff. Sept. 1, 1995. Amended by Acts 1997, 75th Leg., ch. 911, § 87, eff. Sept. 1, 1997.

For application and effectiveness provisions of Acts 1997, 75th Leg., ch. 911, see note following V.T.C.A., Family Code § 156.401.

§ 232.008. Order Suspending License for Failure to Pay Child Support

(a) On making the findings required by Section 232.003, the court or Title IV-D agency shall render an order suspending the license unless the individual:

(1) proves that all arrearages and the current month's support have been paid; or

(2) shows good cause for failure to comply with the subpoena.

(b) The court or Title IV-D agency may stay an order suspending a license conditioned on the individual's compliance with:

(1) a reasonable repayment schedule that is incorporated in the order; or

(2) the requirements of a reissued and delivered subpoena.

(c) An order suspending a license with a stay of the suspension may not be served on the licensing authority unless the stay is revoked as provided by this chapter.

(d) A final order suspending license rendered by a court or the Title IV-D agency shall be forwarded to the appropriate licensing authority by the clerk of the court or Title IV-D agency. The clerk shall collect from an obligor a fee of $5 for each order mailed.

(e) If the court or Title IV-D agency renders an order suspending license, the individual may also be ordered not to engage in the licensed activity.

(f) If the court or Title IV-D agency finds that the petition for suspension should be denied, the petition shall be dismissed without prejudice, and an order suspending license may not be rendered.

Added by Acts 1995, 74th Leg., ch. 655, § 5.03, eff. Sept. 1, 1995; Acts 1995, 74th Leg., ch. 751, § 85, eff. Sept. 1, 1995. Amended by Acts 1997, 75th Leg., ch. 911, § 88, eff. Sept. 1, 1997; Acts 1997, 75th Leg., ch. 976, § 8, eff. Sept. 1, 1997.

For application and effectiveness provisions of Acts 1997, 75th Leg., ch. 911, see note following V.T.C.A., Family Code § 156.401.

Section 10 of Acts 1997, 75th Leg., ch. 976 provides:

"(a) This Act takes effect September 1, 1997, and applies to a fee collected on or after that date, except as provided by Subsection (b) of this section.

"(b) Section 3 of this Act takes effect January 1, 1998, and applies to a fee collected on or after that date."

§ 232.009. Default Order

The court or Title IV-D agency shall consider the allegations of the petition for suspension to be admitted and shall render an order suspending the license of an obligor without the requirement of a hearing if the court or Title IV-D agency determines that the individual failed to:

(1) respond to a notice issued under Section 232.006;

(2) request a hearing; or

(3) appear at a hearing.

Added by Acts 1995, 74th Leg., ch. 655, § 5.03, eff. Sept. 1, 1995; Acts 1995, 74th Leg., ch. 751, § 85, eff. Sept. 1, 1995. Amended by Acts 1997, 75th Leg., ch. 420, § 25, eff. Sept. 1, 1997; Acts 1997, 75th Leg., ch. 911, § 89, eff. Sept. 1, 1997.

For application and effectiveness provisions of Acts 1997, 75th Leg., ch. 911, see note following V.T.C.A., Family Code § 156.401.

§ 232.010. Review of Final Administrative Order

An order issued by a Title IV-D agency under this chapter is a final agency decision and is subject to review under the substantial evidence rule as provided by Chapter 2001, Government Code.

Added by Acts 1995, 74th Leg., ch. 655, § 5.03, eff. Sept. 1, 1995; Acts 1995, 74th Leg., ch. 751, § 85, eff. Sept. 1, 1995.

§ 232.011. Action by Licensing Authority

(a) On receipt of a final order suspending license, the licensing authority shall immediately determine if the authority has issued a license to the individual named on the order and, if a license has been issued:

(1) record the suspension of the license in the licensing authority's records;

(2) report the suspension as appropriate; and

(3) demand surrender of the suspended license if required by law for other cases in which a license is suspended.

(b) A licensing authority shall implement the terms of a final order suspending license without additional review or hearing. The authority may provide notice as appropriate to the license holder or to others concerned with the license.

(c) A licensing authority may not modify, remand, reverse, vacate, or stay an order suspending license issued under this chapter and may not review, vacate, or reconsider the terms of a final order suspending license.

(d) An individual who is the subject of a final order suspending license is not entitled to a refund for any fee or deposit paid to the licensing authority.

(e) An individual who continues to engage in the business, occupation, profession, or other licensed activity after the implementation of the order suspending license by the licensing authority is liable for the same civil and criminal penalties provided for engaging in the licensed activity without a license or while a license is suspended that apply to any other license holder of that licensing authority.

(f) A licensing authority is exempt from liability to a license holder for any act authorized under this chapter performed by the authority.

(g) Except as provided by this chapter, an order suspending license or dismissing a petition for the suspension of a license does not affect the power of a licensing authority to grant, deny, suspend, revoke, terminate, or renew a license.

(h) The denial or suspension of a driver's license under this chapter is governed by this chapter and not by the general licensing provisions of Chapter 521, Transportation Code.

Added by Acts 1995, 74th Leg., ch. 655, § 5.03, eff. Sept. 1, 1995; Acts 1995, 74th Leg., ch. 751, § 85, eff. Sept. 1, 1995. Amended by Acts 1997, 75th Leg., ch. 165, § 30.184, eff. Sept. 1, 1997; Acts 1997, 75th Leg., ch. 911, § 90, eff. Sept. 1, 1997.

For application and effectiveness provisions of Acts 1997, 75th Leg., ch. 911, see note following V.T.C.A., Family Code § 156.401.

§ 232.012. Motion to Revoke Stay

(a) The obligee, support enforcement agency, court, or Title IV-D agency may file a motion to revoke the stay of an order suspending license if the individual who is subject of an order suspending license does not comply with:

(1) the terms of a reasonable repayment plan entered into by the individual; or

(2) the requirements of a reissued subpoena.

(b) Notice to the individual of a motion to revoke stay under this section may be given by personal service or by mail to the address provided by the individual, if any, in the order suspending license. The notice must include a notice of hearing. The notice must be provided to the individual not less than 10 days before the date of the hearing.

(c) A motion to revoke stay must allege the manner in which the individual failed to comply with the repayment plan or the reissued subpoena.

(d) If the court or Title IV-D agency finds that the individual is not in compliance with the terms of the repayment plan or reissued subpoena, the court or agency shall revoke the stay of the order suspending license and render a final order suspending license.

Added by Acts 1995, 74th Leg., ch. 655, § 5.03, eff. Sept. 1, 1995; Acts 1995, 74th Leg., ch. 751, § 85, eff. Sept. 1, 1995. Amended by Acts 1997, 75th Leg., ch. 911, § 91, eff. Sept. 1, 1997.

For application and effectiveness provisions of Acts 1997, 75th Leg., ch. 911, see note following V.T.C.A., Family Code § 156.401.

§ 232.013. Vacating or Staying Order Suspending License

(a) The court or Title IV-D agency may render an order vacating or staying an order suspending license if the individual has:

(1) paid all delinquent child support or has established a satisfactory payment record; or

(2) complied with the requirements of a reissued subpoena.

(b) The clerk of the court or Title IV-D agency shall promptly deliver an order vacating or staying an order suspending license to the appropriate licensing authority. The clerk shall collect from an obligor a fee of $5 for each order mailed.

(c) On receipt of an order vacating or staying an order suspending license, the licensing authority shall promptly issue the affected license to the individual if the individual is otherwise qualified for the license.

(d) An order rendered under this section does not affect the right of the child support agency or obligee to any other remedy provided by law, including the right to seek relief under this chapter. An order rendered under this section does not affect the power of a licensing authority to grant, deny, suspend, revoke, terminate, or renew a license as otherwise provided by law.

Added by Acts 1995, 74th Leg., ch. 655, § 5.03, eff. Sept. 1, 1995; Acts 1995, 74th Leg., ch. 751, § 85, eff. Sept. 1, 1995. Amended by Acts 1997, 75th Leg., ch. 911, § 92, eff. Sept. 1, 1997; Acts 1997, 75th Leg., ch. 976, § 9, eff. Sept. 1, 1997.

For application and effectiveness provisions of Acts 1997, 75th Leg., ch. 911, see note following V.T.C.A., Family Code § 156.401.

Section 10 of Acts 1997, 75th Leg., ch. 976 provides:

"(a) This Act takes effect September 1, 1997, and applies to a fee collected on or after that date, except as provided by Subsection (b) of this section.

"(b) Section 3 of this Act takes effect January 1, 1998, and applies to a fee collected on or after that date."

§ 232.014. Fee by Licensing Authority

A licensing authority may charge a fee to an individual who is the subject of an order suspending license in an amount sufficient to recover the administrative costs incurred by the authority under this chapter.

Added by Acts 1995, 74th Leg., ch. 655, § 5.03, eff. Sept. 1, 1995; Acts 1995, 74th Leg., ch. 751, § 85, eff. Sept. 1, 1995. Amended by Acts 1997, 75th Leg., ch. 911, § 93, eff. Sept. 1, 1997.

For application and effectiveness provisions of Acts 1997, 75th Leg., ch. 911, see note following V.T.C.A., Family Code § 156.401.

§ 232.015. Cooperation Between Licensing Authorities and Title IV–D Agency

(a) The Title IV-D agency may request from each licensing authority the name, address, social security number, license renewal date, and other identifying information for each individual who holds, applies for, or renews a license issued by the authority.

(b) A licensing authority shall provide the requested information in the manner agreed to by the Title IV-D agency and the licensing authority.

(c) The Title IV-D agency may enter into a cooperative agreement with a licensing authority to administer this chapter in a cost-effective manner.

(d) The Title IV-D agency may adopt a reasonable implementation schedule for the requirements of this section.

(e) The Title IV-D agency, the comptroller, and the Texas Alcoholic Beverage Commission shall by rule specify additional prerequisites for the suspension of licenses relating to state taxes collected under Title 2, Tax Code.[1] The joint rules must be adopted not later than March 1, 1996.

Added by Acts 1995, 74th Leg., ch. 751, § 85, eff. Sept. 1, 1995.

[1] V.T.C.A., Tax Code § 101.001 et seq.

§ 232.016. Rules, Forms, and Procedures

The Title IV-D agency by rule shall prescribe forms and procedures for the implementation of this chapter.

Added by Acts 1995, 74th Leg., ch. 655, § 5.03, eff. Sept. 1, 1995; Acts 1995, 74th Leg., ch. 751, § 85, eff. Sept. 1, 1995.

CHAPTER 233. SHARING INFORMATION IN STATE CASE REGISTRY

Chapter 233, Sharing Information in State Case Registry, consisting of §§ 233.001 to 233.004, was added by Acts 1997, 75th Leg., ch. 420, § 26.

For another Chapter 233, Child Support Review Process to Establish or Enforce Support Obligations, consisting of §§ 233.001 to 233.029, redesignated from V.T.C.A., Family Code Chapter 231, Subchapter E by Acts 1997, 75th Leg., ch. 911, § 80, see § 233.001 et seq., post.

§ 233.001. Request for Information

(a) The state case registry shall provide information under this chapter on the written request of a custodial parent whose case:

(1) is included in the state case registry established under 42 U.S.C. Section 654a and for whom the Title IV-D agency is not providing enforcement services; or

(2) would otherwise not be required to be included in the state case registry under 42 U.S.C. Section 654a but who has applied for inclusion under Section 233.002.

(b) The state case registry shall provide to a custodial parent under Subsection (a) who makes a request for information or to an attorney, friend of the court, guardian ad litem, or domestic relations office designated by the parent any information in the registry concerning the parent's case, including:

(1) the noncustodial parent's address, social security number, and employer's name and address;

(2) the amount and location of real and personal property owned by the noncustodial parent;

(3) the name and address of financial institutions in which the noncustodial parent has an account and each account number; and

(4) any other information the disclosure of which is not specifically prohibited by federal law.

Added by Acts 1997, 75th Leg., ch. 420, § 26, eff. Sept. 1, 1997.

§ 233.002. Request to Include Case in Registry

The case of a custodial parent whose case would otherwise not be included in the state case registry under 42 U.S.C. Section 654a may be included in the state case registry by making a written request to the registry either directly or through an attorney, friend of the court, guardian ad litem, or domestic relations office designated by the custodial parent. The request must be accompanied by a certified copy of the court order requiring the payment of child support.

Added by Acts 1997, 75th Leg., ch. 420, § 26, eff. Sept. 1, 1997.

For application and effectiveness provisions of Acts 1997, 75th Leg., ch. 420, see note following V.T.C.A., Family Code § 157.312.

§ 233.003. Application for Services Not Required

The Title IV-D agency may not require an application for services as a condition for:

(1) releasing information under Section 233.001 to a custodial parent or to the person designated by the parent; or

(2) including a case in the state case registry under Section 233.002.

Added by Acts 1997, 75th Leg., ch. 420, § 26, eff. Sept. 1, 1997.

§ 233.004. Fees

(a) The state case registry may charge a fee for:

(1) including in the registry a child support case entered in the registry under Section 233.002; and

(2) providing information concerning a case as authorized by Section 233.001.

(b) The amount of a fee under this section may not exceed the actual costs incurred by the state case registry in providing the services.

Added by Acts 1997, 75th Leg., ch. 420, § 26, eff. Sept. 1, 1997.

CHAPTER 233. CHILD SUPPORT REVIEW PROCESS TO ESTABLISH OR ENFORCE SUPPORT OBLIGATIONS

Section

Chapter 233, Child Support Review Process to Establish or Enforce Support Obligations, consisting of §§ 233.001 to 233.029, was redesignated from V.T.C.A., Family Code Chapter 231, Subchapter E and amended by Acts 1997, 75th Leg., ch. 911, § 80.

For another Chapter 233, Sharing Information in State Case Registry, consisting of §§ 233.001 to 233.004, added by Acts 1997, 75th Leg., ch. 420, § 26, see V.T.C.A., Family Code § 233.001 et seq., ante.

§ 233.001. Purpose

(a) The purpose of the procedures specified in the child support review process authorized by this chapter is to enable the Title IV-D agency to take expedited administrative actions to establish, modify, and enforce child support and medical support obligations, to determine parentage, or to take any other action authorized or required under Part D, Title IV, of the federal Social Security Act (42 U.S.C. Section 651 et seq.), and Chapter 231.

(b) A child support review order issued under this chapter and confirmed by a court constitutes an order of the court and is enforceable by any means available for the enforcement of child support obligations under this code, including withholding income, filing a child support lien, and suspending a license under Chapter 232.

Added by Acts 1995, 74th Leg., ch. 20, § 1, eff. April 20, 1995. Amended by Acts 1995, 74th Leg., ch. 341, § 2.04, eff. Sept. 1, 1995. Redesignated from V.T.C.A., Family Code § 231.401 and amended by Acts 1997 75th Leg., ch. 911, § 80, eff. Sept. 1, 1997.

For application and effectiveness provisions of Acts 1997, 75th Leg., ch. 911, see note following V.T.C.A., Family Code § 156.401.

§ 233.002. Agreements Encouraged

To the extent permitted by this chapter, the Title IV-D agency shall encourage agreement of the parties.

Added by Acts 1995, 74th Leg., ch. 20, § 1, eff. April 20, 1995. Amended by Acts 1995, 74th Leg., ch. 341, § 2.04, eff. Sept. 1, 1995. Redesignated from V.T.C.A., Family Code § 231.402 and amended by Acts 1997, 75th Leg., ch. 911, § 80, eff. Sept. 1, 1997.

For application and effectiveness provisions of Acts 1997, 75th Leg., ch. 911, see note following V.T.C.A., Family Code § 156.401.

§ 233.003. Bilingual Forms Required

A notice or other form used to implement administrative procedures under this chapter shall be printed in both Spanish and English.

Added by Acts 1995, 74th Leg., ch. 20, § 1, eff. April 20, 1995. Amended by Acts 1995, 74th Leg., ch. 341, § 2.04, eff. Sept. 1, 1995. Redesignated from V.T.C.A., Family Code § 231.403 and amended by Acts 1997 75th Leg., ch. 911, § 80, eff. Sept. 1, 1997.

For application and effectiveness provisions of Acts 1997, 75th Leg., ch. 911, see note following V.T.C.A., Family Code § 156.401.

§ 233.004. Interpreter Required

If a party participating in an administrative proceeding under this chapter does not speak English or is hearing impaired, the Title IV-D agency shall provide for interpreter services at no charge to the party.

Added by Acts 1995, 74th Leg., ch. 20, § 1, eff. April 20, 1995. Amended by Acts 1995, 74th Leg., ch. 341, § 2.04, eff. Sept. 1, 1995. Redesignated from V.T.C.A., Family Code § 231.404 and amended by Acts 1997 75th Leg., ch. 911, § 80, eff. Sept. 1, 1997.

For application and effectiveness provisions of Acts 1997, 75th Leg., ch. 911, see note following V.T.C.A., Family Code § 156.401.

§ 233.005. Initiating Administrative Actions

An administrative action under this chapter may be initiated by issuing a notice of child support review under Section 233.006 or a notice of proposed child support review order under Section 233.009 to each party entitled to notice.

Added by Acts 1995, 74th Leg., ch. 20, § 1, eff. April 20, 1995. Amended by Acts 1995, 74th Leg., ch. 341, § 2.04, eff. Sept. 1, 1995. Redesignated from V.T.C.A., Family Code § 231.405 and amended by Acts 1997 75th Leg., ch. 911, § 80, eff. Sept. 1, 1997.

For application and effectiveness provisions of Acts 1997, 75th Leg., ch. 911, see note following V.T.C.A., Family Code § 156.401.

§ 233.006. Contents of Notice of Child Support Review

(a) The notice of child support review issued by the Title IV-D agency must:

(1) describe the procedure for a child support review, including the procedures for requesting a negotiation conference;

(2) inform the recipient that the recipient may be represented by legal counsel during the review process or at a court hearing;

(3) inform the recipient that the recipient may refuse to participate or cease participation in the child support review process, but that the refusal by the recipient to participate will not prevent the completion of the process or the filing of a child support review order;

(4) include an affidavit of financial resources to be executed by the recipient; and

(5) include a request that the recipient designate, on a form provided by the Title IV-D agency, an address for mailing any subsequent notice to the recipient.

(b) In addition to the information required by Subsection (a), the notice of child support review must inform the recipient that:

(1) the information requested on the form must be returned to the Title IV-D agency not later than the 15th day after the date the notice is received or delivered; and

(2) if the requested information is not returned as required, the agency may:

(A) proceed with the review using the information that is available to the agency; and

(B) file a legal action without further notice to the recipient, except as otherwise required by law.

Added by Acts 1995, 74th Leg., ch. 20, § 1, eff. April 20, 1995. Amended by Acts 1995, 74th Leg., ch. 341, § 2.04, eff. Sept. 1, 1995. Redesignated from V.T.C.A., Family Code § 231.406 and amended by Acts 1997 75th Leg., ch. 911, § 80, eff. Sept. 1, 1997.

For application and effectiveness provisions of Acts 1997, 75th Leg., ch. 911, see note following V.T.C.A., Family Code § 156.401.

§ 233.007. Service of Notice

(a) A notice required in an administrative action under this chapter may be delivered by personal service or first class mail on each party entitled to citation or notice as provided by Chapter 102.

(b) This section does not apply to notice required on filing of a child support review order or to later judicial actions.

Added by Acts 1995, 74th Leg., ch. 20, § 1, eff. April 20, 1995. Amended by Acts 1995, 74th Leg., ch. 341, § 2.04, eff. Sept. 1, 1995. Redesignated from V.T.C.A., Family Code § 231.407 and amended by Acts 1997 75th Leg., ch. 911, § 80, eff. Sept. 1, 1997.

For application and effectiveness provisions of Acts 1997, 75th Leg., ch. 911, see note following V.T.C.A., Family Code § 156.401.

§ 233.008. Administrative Subpoena in Child Support Review

In a child support review under this chapter, the Title IV-D agency may issue an administrative subpoena authorized under Chapter 231 to any individual or organization believed to have financial or other information needed to establish, modify, or enforce a support order.

Added by Acts 1995, 74th Leg., ch. 20, § 1, eff. April 20, 1995. Amended by Acts 1995, 74th Leg., ch. 341, § 2.04, eff. Sept. 1, 1995. Redesignated from V.T.C.A., Family Code § 231.408 and amended by Acts 1997 75th Leg., ch. 911, § 80, eff. Sept. 1, 1997.

For application and effectiveness provisions of Acts 1997, 75th Leg., ch. 911, see note following V.T.C.A., Family Code § 156.401.

§ 233.009. Notice of Proposed Child Support Review Order; Negotiation Conference

(a) After an investigation and assessment of financial resources, the Title IV-D agency may serve on the parties a notice of proposed child support review order in enforcing or modifying an existing order.

(b) The notice of proposed child support review order shall state:

(1) the amount of periodic payment of child support due, the amount of any overdue support that is owed as an arrearage as of the date of the notice, and the amounts that are to be paid by the obligor for current support due and in payment on the arrearage owed;

(2) that the person identified in the notice as the party responsible for payment of the support amounts may contest the notice order on the grounds that:

(A) the respondent is not the responsible party;

(B) the dependent child is no longer entitled to child support; or

(C) the amount of monthly support or arrearage is incorrectly stated; and

(3) that, if the person identified in the notice as the party responsible for payment of the support amounts does not contest the notice in writing or request a negotiation conference to discuss the notice not later than the 15th day after the date the notice was delivered, the Title IV-D agency may file a child support review order for child support and for medical support for the child as provided by Chapter 154 according to the information available to the agency.

(c) The Title IV-D agency may schedule a negotiation conference without a request from a party.

(d) The Title IV-D agency shall schedule a negotiation conference on the timely request of a party.

(e) The agency may conduct a negotiation conference, or any part of a negotiation conference, by telephone conference call, by video conference, as well as in person and may adjourn the conference for a reasonable time to permit mediation of issues that cannot be resolved by the parties and the agency.

Added by Acts 1995, 74th Leg., ch. 20, § 1, eff. April 20, 1995. Amended by Acts 1995, 74th Leg., ch. 341, § 2.04, eff. Sept. 1, 1995. Redesignated from V.T.C.A., Family Code § 231.409 and amended by Acts 1997 75th Leg., ch. 911, § 80, eff. Sept. 1, 1997.

For application and effectiveness provisions of Acts 1997, 75th Leg., ch. 911, see note following V.T.C.A., Family Code § 156.401.

§ 233.010. Notice of Negotiation Conference; Failure to Attend Conference

(a) The Title IV-D agency shall notify all parties entitled to notice of the negotiation conference of the date, time, and place of the conference not later than the 10th day before the date of the conference.

(b) If a party fails to attend the scheduled conference, the agency may proceed with the review and file a child support review order according to the information available to the agency.

Added by Acts 1995, 74th Leg., ch. 20, § 1, eff. April 20, 1995. Amended by Acts 1995, 74th Leg., ch. 341, § 2.04, eff. Sept. 1, 1995. Redesignated from V.T.C.A., Family Code § 231.410 and amended by Acts 1997 75th Leg., ch. 911, § 80, eff. Sept. 1, 1997.

For application and effectiveness provisions of Acts 1997, 75th Leg., ch. 911, see note following V.T.C.A., Family Code § 156.401.

§ 233.011. Rescheduling Negotiation Conference; Notice Required

(a) The Title IV-D agency may reschedule or adjourn a negotiation conference on the request of any party.

(b) The Title IV-D agency shall give all parties notice of a rescheduled conference not later than the third day before the date of the rescheduled conference.

Added by Acts 1995, 74th Leg., ch. 20, § 1, eff. April 20, 1995. Amended by Acts 1995, 74th Leg., ch. 341, § 2.04, eff. Sept. 1, 1995. Redesignated from V.T.C.A., Family Code § 231.411 and amended by Acts 1997 75th Leg., ch. 911, § 80, eff. Sept. 1, 1997.

For application and effectiveness provisions of Acts 1997, 75th Leg., ch. 911, see note following V.T.C.A., Family Code § 156.401.

§ 233.012. Information Required to be Provided at Negotiation Conference

At the beginning of the negotiation conference, the child support review officer shall review with the parties participating in the conference information provided in the notice of child support review and inform the parties that:

(1) the purpose of the negotiation conference is to provide an opportunity to reach an agreement on a child support order;

(2) if the parties reach an agreement, the review officer will prepare an agreed review order to be effective immediately on being confirmed by the court, as provided by Section 233.024;

(3) a party does not have to sign a review order prepared by the child support review officer but that the Title IV-D agency may file a review order without the agreement of the parties;

(4) the parties may sign a waiver of the right to service of process;

(5) a party may request a court hearing on a nonagreed order at any time before the 20th day

after the date a petition for confirmation of the order is filed; and

(6) a party may file a motion for a new trial at any time before the 30th day after an order is confirmed by the court.

Added by Acts 1995, 74th Leg., ch. 20, § 1, eff. April 20, 1995. Amended by Acts 1995, 74th Leg., ch. 341, § 2.04, eff. Sept. 1, 1995. Redesignated from V.T.C.A., Family Code § 231.412 and amended by Acts 1997 75th Leg., ch. 911, § 80, eff. Sept. 1, 1997.

For application and effectiveness provisions of Acts 1997, 75th Leg., ch. 911, see note following V.T.C.A., Family Code § 156.401.

§ 233.013. Determining Support Amount; Modification

(a) The Title IV-D agency may use any information obtained by the agency from the parties or any other source and shall apply the child support guidelines provided by this code to determine the appropriate amount of child support.

(b) If it has been three years since a child support order was rendered or last modified and the amount of the child support award under the order differs by either 20 percent or $100 from the amount that would be awarded under the child support guidelines, the Title IV-D agency shall file an appropriate child support review order, including an order that has the effect of modifying an existing court or administrative order for child support without the necessity of filing a motion to modify.

Added by Acts 1995, 74th Leg., ch. 20, § 1, eff. April 20, 1995. Amended by Acts 1995, 74th Leg., ch. 341, § 2.04, eff. Sept. 1, 1995. Redesignated from V.T.C.A., Family Code § 231.413 and amended by Acts 1997 75th Leg., ch. 911, § 80, eff. Sept. 1, 1997.

For application and effectiveness provisions of Acts 1997, 75th Leg., ch. 911, see note following V.T.C.A., Family Code § 156.401.

§ 233.014. Record of Proceedings

(a) For the purposes of this chapter, documentary evidence relied on by the child support review officer, including an affidavit of a party, together with the child support review order is a sufficient record of the proceedings.

(b) The Title IV-D agency is not required to make any other record or transcript of the negotiation conference.

Added by Acts 1995, 74th Leg., ch. 20, § 1, eff. April 20, 1995. Amended by Acts 1995, 74th Leg., ch. 341, § 2.04, eff. Sept. 1, 1995. Redesignated from V.T.C.A., Family Code § 231.414 and amended by Acts 1997 75th Leg., ch. 911, § 80, eff. Sept. 1, 1997.

For application and effectiveness provisions of Acts 1997, 75th Leg., ch. 911, see note following V.T.C.A., Family Code § 156.401.

§ 233.015. Issuance of Child Support Review Order or Finding That No Order Should be Issued; Effect

(a) If a negotiation conference does not result in agreement by all parties to the child support review order, the Title IV-D agency shall render a final decision in the form of a child support review order or a determination that the agency should not issue a child support review order not later than the fifth day after the date of the negotiation conference.

(b) If the Title IV-D agency determines that the agency should not issue a child support order, the agency shall immediately provide each party with notice of the determination by personal delivery or by first class mail.

(c) A determination that a child support order should not be issued must include a statement of the reasons that an order is not being issued and a statement that the agency's determination does not affect the right of the Title IV-D agency or a party to request any other remedy provided by law.

Added by Acts 1995, 74th Leg., ch. 20, § 1, eff. April 20, 1995. Amended by Acts 1995, 74th Leg., ch. 341, § 2.04, eff. Sept. 1, 1995. Redesignated from V.T.C.A., Family Code § 231.415 and amended by Acts 1997 75th Leg., ch. 911, § 80, eff. Sept. 1, 1997.

For application and effectiveness provisions of Acts 1997, 75th Leg., ch. 911, see note following V.T.C.A., Family Code § 156.401.

§ 233.016. Vacating Child Support Review Order

(a) The Title IV-D agency may vacate a child support review order at any time before the order is filed with the court.

(b) A new negotiation conference, with notice to all parties, may be scheduled or the Title IV-D agency may make a determination that a child support review order should not be issued and give notice of that determination as provided by this chapter.

Added by Acts 1995, 74th Leg., ch. 20, § 1, eff. April 20, 1995. Amended by Acts 1995, 74th Leg., ch. 341, § 2.04, eff. Sept. 1, 1995. Redesignated from V.T.C.A., Family Code § 231.416 and amended by Acts 1997 75th Leg., ch. 911, § 80, eff. Sept. 1, 1997.

For application and effectiveness provisions of Acts 1997, 75th Leg., ch. 911, see note following V.T.C.A., Family Code § 156.401.

§ 233.017. Contents of Child Support Review Order

(a) An order issued under this chapter must be reviewed and signed by an attorney of the Title IV-D agency and must contain all provisions that are appropriate for an order under this title, including current child support, medical support, a determination of any arrearages or retroactive support, and, if not otherwise ordered, income withholding.

(b) A child support review order providing for the enforcement of an order may not contain a provision that imposes incarceration or a fine or contains a finding of contempt.

(c) A child support review order that establishes or modifies an amount of previously ordered support must include the findings required by Section 154.130.

(d) A child support review order that is not agreed to by all the parties may specify and reserve for the court at the confirmation hearing unresolved issues relating to conservatorship or possession of a child.

Added by Acts 1995, 74th Leg., ch. 20, § 1, eff. April 20, 1995. Amended by Acts 1995, 74th Leg., ch. 341, § 2.04, eff. Sept. 1, 1995. Redesignated from V.T.C.A., Family Code § 231.417 and amended by Acts 1997 75th Leg., ch. 911, § 80, eff. Sept. 1, 1997.

For application and effectiveness provisions of Acts 1997, 75th Leg., ch. 911, see note following V.T.C.A., Family Code § 156.401.

§ 233.018. Additional Contents of Agreed Child Support Review Order

If a negotiation conference results in an agreement of the parties, each party must sign the child support review order and the order must contain as to each party:

(1) a waiver by the party of the right to service of process and a court hearing and the making of a record on the petition for confirmation;

(2) the mailing address of the party; and

(3) the following statement printed on the order in boldface or in all capital letters:

"I KNOW THAT I DO NOT HAVE TO SIGN THIS CHILD SUPPORT REVIEW ORDER. I UNDERSTAND THAT IF I SIGN THIS ORDER, IT WILL BE CONFIRMED BY THE COURT WITHOUT FURTHER NOTICE TO ME. I KNOW THAT I HAVE A RIGHT TO REQUEST THAT A COURT RECONSIDER THE ORDER BY FILING A MOTION FOR A NEW TRIAL AT ANY TIME BEFORE THE 30TH DAY AFTER THE DATE OF THE CONFIRMATION OF THE ORDER BY THE COURT. I KNOW THAT IF I DO NOT OBEY THE TERMS OF THIS ORDER I MAY BE HELD IN CONTEMPT OF COURT."

Added by Acts 1995, 74th Leg., ch. 20, § 1, eff. April 20, 1995. Amended by Acts 1995, 74th Leg., ch. 341, § 2.04, eff. Sept. 1, 1995. Redesignated from V.T.C.A., Family Code § 231.418 and amended by Acts 1997 75th Leg., ch. 911, § 80, eff. Sept. 1, 1997.

For application and effectiveness provisions of Acts 1997, 75th Leg., ch. 911, see note following V.T.C.A., Family Code § 156.401.

§ 233.019. Filing of Agreed Review Order

(a) The Title IV-D agency shall file an agreed child support review order and a waiver of service signed by the parties with the clerk of the court having continuing jurisdiction of the child who is the subject of the order.

(b) If there is not a court of continuing jurisdiction, the Title IV-D agency shall file the agreed review order with the clerk of a court having jurisdiction under this title.

(c) If applicable, a statement of paternity or a written report of a parentage testing expert and any documentary evidence relied upon by the agency shall be filed with the agreed review order as an exhibit to the order.

Added by Acts 1995, 74th Leg., ch. 20, § 1, eff. April 20, 1995. Amended by Acts 1995, 74th Leg., ch. 341, § 2.04, eff. Sept. 1, 1995. Redesignated from V.T.C.A., Family Code § 231.419 and amended by Acts 1997 75th Leg., ch. 911, § 80, eff. Sept. 1, 1997.

For application and effectiveness provisions of Acts 1997, 75th Leg., ch. 911, see note following V.T.C.A., Family Code § 156.401.

§ 233.020. Contents of Petition for Confirmation of Nonagreed Order

(a) A petition for confirmation of a child support review order not agreed to by the parties must include the final review order as an attachment to the petition.

(b) Documentary evidence relied on by the Title IV-D agency, including, if applicable, a statement of paternity or a written report of a parentage testing expert, shall be filed with the clerk as exhibits to the petition, but are not required to be served on the parties. The petition must identify the exhibits that are filed with the clerk.

Added by Acts 1995, 74th Leg., ch. 20, § 1, eff. April 20, 1995. Amended by Acts 1995, 74th Leg., ch. 341, § 2.04, eff. Sept. 1, 1995. Redesignated from V.T.C.A., Family Code § 231.420 and amended by Acts 1997 75th Leg., ch. 911, § 80, eff. Sept. 1, 1997.

For application and effectiveness provisions of Acts 1997, 75th Leg., ch. 911, see note following V.T.C.A., Family Code § 156.401.

§ 233.021. Duties of Clerk of Court

(a) On the filing of an agreed child support review order or of a petition for confirmation of a nonagreed order issued by the Title IV-D agency, the clerk of court shall endorse on the order or petition the date and time the order or petition is filed.

(b) In an original action, the clerk shall endorse the appropriate court and cause number on the agreed review order or on the petition for confirmation of a nonagreed order.

(c) The clerk shall deliver by personal service a copy of the petition for confirmation of a nonagreed review order and a copy of the order, to each party entitled to service who has not waived service.

(d) A clerk of a district court is entitled to collect in a child support review case the fees authorized in a Title IV-D case by Chapter 231.

Added by Acts 1995, 74th Leg., ch. 20, § 1, eff. April 20, 1995. Amended by Acts 1995, 74th Leg., ch. 341, § 2.04, eff. Sept. 1, 1995. Redesignated from V.T.C.A., Family Code § 231.421 and amended by Acts 1997 75th Leg., ch. 911, § 80, eff. Sept. 1, 1997.

For application and effectiveness provisions of Acts 1997, 75th Leg., ch. 911, see note following V.T.C.A., Family Code § 156.401.

§ 233.022. Form to Request a Court Hearing on Nonagreed Order

(a) A court shall consider any responsive pleading that is intended as an objection to confirmation of a child support review order not agreed to by the parties, including a general denial, as a request for a court hearing.

(b) The Title IV-D agency shall:

(1) make available to each clerk of court copies of the form to request a court hearing on a nonagreed review order; and

(2) provide the form to request a court hearing to a party to the child support review proceeding on request of the party.

(c) The clerk shall furnish the form to a party to the child support review proceeding on the request of the party.

Added by Acts 1995, 74th Leg., ch. 20, § 1, eff. April 20, 1995. Amended by Acts 1995, 74th Leg., ch. 341, § 2.04, eff. Sept. 1, 1995. Redesignated from V.T.C.A., Family Code § 231.422 and amended by Acts 1997 75th Leg., ch. 911, § 80, eff. Sept. 1, 1997.

For application and effectiveness provisions of Acts 1997, 75th Leg., ch. 911, see note following V.T.C.A., Family Code § 156.401.

§ 233.023. Time to Request a Court Hearing

A party may file a request for a court hearing not later than the 20th day after the date the petition for confirmation of a nonagreed child support review order is delivered to the party.

Added by Acts 1995, 74th Leg., ch. 20, § 1, eff. April 20, 1995. Amended by Acts 1995, 74th Leg., ch. 341, § 2.04, eff. Sept. 1, 1995. Redesignated from V.T.C.A., Family Code § 231.423 and amended by Acts 1997 75th Leg., ch. 911, § 80, eff. Sept. 1, 1997.

For application and effectiveness provisions of Acts 1997, 75th Leg., ch. 911, see note following V.T.C.A., Family Code § 156.401.

§ 233.024. Confirmation of Agreed Order

(a) If the court finds that all parties have appropriately agreed to a child support review order and that there is waiver of service, the court shall sign the order not later than the third day after the filing of the order.

(b) On confirmation by the court, the Title IV-D agency shall immediately deliver to each party a copy of the signed agreed review order.

Added by Acts 1995, 74th Leg., ch. 20, § 1, eff. April 20, 1995. Amended by Acts 1995, 74th Leg., ch. 341, § 2.04, eff. Sept. 1, 1995. Redesignated from V.T.C.A., Family Code § 231.424 and amended by Acts 1997 75th Leg., ch. 911, § 80, eff. Sept. 1, 1997.

For application and effectiveness provisions of Acts 1997, 75th Leg., ch. 911, see note following V.T.C.A., Family Code § 156.401.

§ 233.025. Effect of Request for Hearing on Nonagreed Order; Pleading

(a) A request for hearing or an order setting a hearing on confirmation of a nonagreed child support review order stays confirmation of the order pending the hearing.

(b) At a hearing on confirmation, any issues in dispute shall be heard in a trial de novo.

(c) The petition for confirmation and the child support review order constitute a sufficient pleading by the Title IV-D agency for relief on any issue addressed in the petition and order.

(d) The request for hearing may limit the scope of the de novo hearing by specifying the issues that are in dispute.

Added by Acts 1995, 74th Leg., ch. 20, § 1, eff. April 20, 1995. Amended by Acts 1995, 74th Leg., ch. 341, § 2.04, eff. Sept. 1, 1995. Redesignated from V.T.C.A., Family Code § 231.425 and amended by Acts 1997 75th Leg., ch. 911, § 80, eff. Sept. 1, 1997.

For application and effectiveness provisions of Acts 1997, 75th Leg., ch. 911, see note following V.T.C.A., Family Code § 156.401.

§ 233.026. Time for Court Hearing

A court shall hold a hearing on the confirmation of a child support review order that has not been agreed to by the parties not later than the 30th day after the date the last party to be served files a timely request for a court hearing.

Added by Acts 1995, 74th Leg., ch. 20, § 1, eff. April 20, 1995. Amended by Acts 1995, 74th Leg., ch. 341, § 2.04, eff. Sept. 1, 1995. Redesignated from V.T.C.A., Family Code § 231.426 and amended by Acts 1997 75th Leg., ch. 911, § 80, eff. Sept. 1, 1997.

For application and effectiveness provisions of Acts 1997, 75th Leg., ch. 911, see note following V.T.C.A., Family Code § 156.401.

§ 233.027. Order After Hearing; Effect of Confirmation Order

(a) After the hearing on the confirmation of a nonagreed child support review order, the court shall:

(1) if the court finds that the order should be confirmed, immediately sign a confirmation order and enter the order as an order of the court;

(2) if the court finds that the relief granted in the child support review order is inappropriate, sign an appropriate order at the conclusion of the hearing or as soon after the conclusion of the hearing as is practical and enter the order as an order of the court; or

(3) if the court finds that all relief should be denied, enter an order that denies relief and includes specific findings explaining the reasons that relief is denied.

(b) On the signing of a confirmation order by the judge of the court, the child support review order becomes a final order of the court.

Added by Acts 1995, 74th Leg., ch. 20, § 1, eff. April 20, 1995. Amended by Acts 1995, 74th Leg., ch. 341, § 2.04, eff. Sept. 1, 1995. Redesignated from V.T.C.A., Family Code § 231.427 and amended by Acts 1997 75th Leg., ch. 911, § 80, eff. Sept. 1, 1997.

For application and effectiveness provisions of Acts 1997, 75th Leg., ch. 911, see note following V.T.C.A., Family Code § 156.401.

§ 233.0271. Confirmation of Nonagreed Order Without Hearing

(a) If a request for hearing has not been timely received, the court shall confirm and sign a nonagreed child support review order not later than the 30th day after the date the petition for confirmation was delivered to the last party entitled to service.

(b) The Title IV-D agency shall immediately deliver a copy of the confirmed nonagreed review order to each party, together with notice of right to file a motion for a new trial not later than the 30th day after the date the order was confirmed by the court.

Added by Acts 1997, 75th Leg., ch. 911, § 80, eff. Sept. 1, 1997.

For application and effectiveness provisions of Acts 1997, 75th Leg., ch. 911, see note following V.T.C.A., Family Code § 156.401.

§ 233.028. Special Child Support Review Procedures Relating to Establishment of Parentage

(a) If the parentage of a child has not been established, the notice of child support review delivered to the parties must include an allegation that the recipient is a biological parent of the child. The notice shall inform the parties that:

(1) not later than the 15th day after the date of delivery of the notice, the alleged parent of the child shall either sign a statement of paternity or an acknowledgment of paternity or deny in writing that the alleged parent is the biological parent of the child;

(2) either party may request that scientifically accepted parentage testing be conducted to assist in determining the identities of the child's parents;

(3) if the alleged parent timely denies parentage of the child, the Title IV-D agency shall order parentage testing; and

(4) if the alleged parent does not deny parentage of the child, the Title IV-D agency may conduct a negotiation conference.

(b) If all parties agree to the child's parentage, the agency may file an agreed child support review order as provided by this chapter.

(c) If a party denies parentage, the Title IV-D agency shall order parentage testing and give each party notice of the time and place of testing. If either party fails or refuses to participate in administrative parentage testing, the Title IV-D agency may file a child support review order resolving the question of parentage against that party. The court shall confirm the child support review order as a temporary or final order of the court only after an opportunity for parentage testing has been provided.

(d) If parentage testing does not exclude the alleged parent and the results of a verified written report of a parentage testing expert meet the requirements of Chapter 160 for issuing a temporary order, the Title IV-D agency may conduct a negotiation conference to resolve any issues of support and file with the court a child support review order.

(e) If the results of parentage testing exclude an alleged parent from being the biological parent of the child, the Title IV-D agency shall issue and provide to each party a child support review order that declares that the excluded person is not a parent of the child.

(f) Any party may file a petition for confirmation of a child support review order issued under this section.

Added by Acts 1995, 74th Leg., ch. 20, § 1, eff. April 20, 1995. Amended by Acts 1995, 74th Leg., ch. 341, § 2.04, eff. Sept. 1, 1995. Redesignated from V.T.C.A., Family Code § 231.428 and amended by Acts 1997 75th Leg., ch. 911, § 80, eff. Sept. 1, 1997.

For application and effectiveness provisions of Acts 1997, 75th Leg., ch. 911, see note following V.T.C.A., Family Code § 156.401.

§ 233.029. Administrative Procedure Law Not Applicable

The child support review process under this chapter is not governed by Chapter 2001, Government Code.

Added by Acts 1995, 74th Leg., ch. 20, § 1, eff. April 20, 1995. Amended by Acts 1995, 74th Leg., ch. 341, § 2.04, eff. Sept. 1, 1995. Redesignated from V.T.C.A., Family Code § 231.429 and amended by Acts 1997 75th Leg., ch. 911, § 80, eff. Sept. 1, 1997.

For application and effectiveness provisions of Acts 1997, 75th Leg., ch. 911, see note following V.T.C.A., Family Code § 156.401.

CHAPTER 234. COMPETITIVE BIDDING FOR CHILD SUPPORT COLLECTION SERVICES

Chapter 234, Competitive Bidding for Child Support Collection Services, consisting of §§ 234.001 to 234.003, was added by Acts 1997, 75th Leg., ch. 420, § 27.

For another Chapter 234, State Case Registry, Disbursement Unit, and Directory of New Hires, consisting of §§ 234.001 to 234.104, added by Acts 1997, 75th Leg., ch. 911, § 94, see V.T.C.A., Family Code § 234.001 et seq., post.

§ 234.001. Definition

In this chapter, "council" means the State Council on Competitive Government.

Added by Acts 1997, 75th Leg., ch. 420, § 27, eff. Sept. 1, 1997.

§ 234.002. Powers and Duties of Council

(a) The council shall:

(1) establish an initiative called "Kids Can't Wait" to increase child support enforcement;

(2) identify child support enforcement functions performed by the Title IV-D agency that may be competitively bid;

(3) establish guidelines for referral of child support enforcement cases to a contractor;

(4) after consulting with the Title IV-D agency, make recommendations regarding competitive bidding of child support enforcement functions that are identified under Subdivision (2);

(5) consider the benefits of the state's participation in an electronic parent locator network or a similar national service designed to locate parents who owe child support;

(6) study the feasibility of cost recovery options in child support collection actions for children who do not receive public assistance; and

(7) engage in other activities necessary for the administration of this chapter.

(b) The Title IV-D agency shall coordinate with the council regarding competitive bidding of child support enforcement functions identified under this section.

(c) A member of the council may designate an employee of the state agency represented by the member to perform any of the member's powers or duties under this section.

(d) The Title IV-D agency shall cooperate with the council if requested by the council.

(e) The council and the Title IV-D agency shall report not later than October 1, 1998, to the presiding officer of each house of the legislature the results of the council's efforts under this section.

Added by Acts 1997, 75th Leg., ch. 420, § 27, eff. Sept. 1, 1997.

§ 234.003. Child Support Collection Agreement

The Title IV-D agency or a contractor awarded a contract under this chapter to collect child support may enter into an agreement with a person liable for the payment of child support. The agreement may relate to any matter that may be adjudicated by a court, including:

(1) the determination of paternity;

(2) the determination of the amount of child support due;

(3) the method of making child support payments;

(4) the imposition of income garnishment or withholding;

(5) the payment of fees;

(6) the reimbursement of costs; and

(7) other child support enforcement matters permitted by state or federal law.

Added by Acts 1997, 75th Leg., ch. 420, § 27, eff. Sept. 1, 1997.

CHAPTER 234. STATE CASE REGISTRY, DISBURSEMENT UNIT, AND DIRECTORY OF NEW HIRES

SUBCHAPTER A. UNIFIED STATE CASE REGISTRY AND DISBURSEMENT UNIT

Chapter 234, State Case Registry, Disbursement Unit, and Directory of New Hires, consisting of §§ 234.001 to 234.104, was added by Acts 1997, 75th Leg., ch. 911, § 94.

For another Chapter 234, Competitive Bidding for Child Support Collection Services, consisting of §§ 234.001 to 234.003, added by Acts 1997, 75th Leg., ch. 420, § 27, see V.T.C.A., Family Code § 234.001 et seq., ante.

SUBCHAPTER A. UNIFIED STATE CASE REGISTRY AND DISBURSEMENT UNIT

§ 234.001. Establishment and Operation of Unified Registry and Disbursement Unit

The Title IV-D agency shall establish and operate a unified state case registry and state disbursement unit meeting the requirements of 42 U.S.C. Sections 654a(e) and 654b. The registry and unit shall:

(1) maintain records of child support orders in Title IV-D cases and in other cases in which a child support order has been established or modified in this state on or after October 1, 1998;

(2) receive, maintain, and furnish records of child support payments in Title IV-D cases and other cases as required by law;

(3) in a Title IV-D case, monitor support payments and initiate appropriate enforcement actions immediately on the occurrence of a delinquency in payment;

(4) distribute child support payments as required by law; and

(5) maintain custody of official child support payment records in the registry and disbursement unit.

Added by Acts 1997, 75th Leg., ch. 911, § 94, eff. Sept. 1, 1997.

§ 234.002. Integrated System for Child Support and Medical Support Enforcement

The statewide integrated system for child support and medical support enforcement under Chapter 231 shall be part of the unified state case registry and state disbursement unit authorized by this subchapter.

Added by Acts 1997, 75th Leg., ch. 911, § 94, eff. Sept. 1, 1997.

§ 234.003. Work Group; Cooperation Required

(a) The Title IV-D agency shall convene a work group to develop procedures for the establishment and operation of the unified state case registry and disbursement unit. The work group shall consist of representatives of the judiciary, district clerks, domestic relations offices, and the bureau of vital statistics, as well as other county and state agencies, and other appropriate entities, identified by the Title IV-D agency. To the extent possible, the work group shall consolidate the reporting of information relating to court orders required of clerks of courts under this title.

(b) The Title IV-D agency shall, in cooperation with the work group established under this section, adopt rules and prescribe forms to implement this subchapter.

Added by Acts 1997, 75th Leg., ch. 911, § 94, eff. Sept. 1, 1997.

§ 234.004. Contracts and Cooperative Agreements

The Title IV-D agency may enter into contracts and cooperative agreements as necessary to establish and operate the state case registry and state disbursement unit authorized under this subchapter.

Added by Acts 1997, 75th Leg., ch. 911, § 94, eff. Sept. 1, 1997.

§ 234.005. Application of Laws Requiring Reporting to Registry

Text of section effective until September 1, 1999

(a) The requirements in Sections 105.006(b) and 105.008(a) that certain information be provided to the state case registry do not apply until the registry is established under this subchapter.

(b) This section expires September 1, 1999.

Added by Acts 1997, 75th Leg., ch. 911, § 94, eff. Sept. 1, 1997.

[Sections 234.006 to 234.100 reserved for expansion]

SUBCHAPTER B. STATE DIRECTORY OF NEW HIRES

§ 234.101. Definitions

In this subchapter:

(1) "Employee" means an individual who is an employee within the meaning of Chapter 24 of the Internal Revenue Code of 1986 (26 U.S.C. Section 3401(c)). The term does not include an employee of a state agency performing intelligence or counterintelligence functions if the head of the agency has determined that reporting employee information under this subchapter could endanger the safety of the employee or compromise an ongoing investigation or intelligence activity.

(2) "Employer" has the meaning given that term by Section 3401(d) of the Internal Revenue Code of 1986 (26 U.S.C. Section 3401(d)) and includes a governmental entity and a labor organization, as that term is identified in Section 2(5) of the National Labor Relations Act (29 U.S.C. Section 152(5)), including an entity, also known as a "hiring hall," used by the labor organization and an employer to carry out requirements of an agreement between the organization and an employer described in Section 8(f)(3) of that Act (29 U.S.C. Section 158(f)(3)).

Added by Acts 1997, 75th Leg., ch. 911, § 94, eff. Sept. 1, 1997.

§ 234.102. Establishment and Operation of New Hire Directory [1]

In cooperation with the Texas Workforce Commission, the Title IV-D agency shall develop and operate a state directory to which employers in the state shall report each newly hired or rehired employee in accordance with the requirements of 42 U.S.C. Section 653a.

Added by Acts 1997, 75th Leg., ch. 911, § 94, eff. Sept. 1, 1997.

[1] Section heading editorially supplied.

Section 98(d) of Acts 1997, 75th Leg., ch. 911 provides:

"The requirement that an employer report a newly hired or rehired employee to the state directory of new hires under Subchapter B, Chapter 234, Family Code, as added by this Act, takes effect October 1, 1998."

§ 234.103. Contracts and Cooperative Agreements [1]

The Title IV-D agency may enter into cooperative agreements and contracts as necessary to create and operate the directory authorized under this subchapter.

Added by Acts 1997, 75th Leg., ch. 911, § 94, eff. Sept. 1, 1997.

[1] Section heading editorially supplied.

§ 234.104. Operation of Directory [1]

The Title IV-D agency by rule shall establish procedures for reporting employee information and for operating a state directory of new hires meeting the requirements of federal law.

Added by Acts 1997, 75th Leg., ch. 911, § 94, eff. Sept. 1, 1997.

[1] Section heading editorially supplied.

[Chapters 235 to 260 reserved for expansion]

SUBTITLE E. PROTECTION OF THE CHILD

CHAPTER 261. INVESTIGATION OF REPORT OF CHILD ABUSE OR NEGLECT

SUBCHAPTER A. GENERAL PROVISIONS

SUBCHAPTER A. GENERAL PROVISIONS

§ 261.001. Definitions

In this chapter:

(1) "Abuse" includes the following acts or omissions by a person:

(A) mental or emotional injury to a child that results in an observable and material impairment in the child's growth, development, or psychological functioning;

(B) causing or permitting the child to be in a situation in which the child sustains a mental or emotional injury that results in an observable and material impairment in the child's growth, development, or psychological functioning;

(C) physical injury that results in substantial harm to the child, or the genuine threat of substantial harm from physical injury to the child, including an injury that is at variance with the history or explanation given and excluding an accident or reasonable discipline by a parent, guardian, or managing or possessory conservator that does not expose the child to a substantial risk of harm;

(D) failure to make a reasonable effort to prevent an action by another person that results in physical injury that results in substantial harm to the child;

(E) sexual conduct harmful to a child's mental, emotional, or physical welfare;

(F) failure to make a reasonable effort to prevent sexual conduct harmful to a child;

(G) compelling or encouraging the child to engage in sexual conduct as defined by Section 43.01, Penal Code;

(H) causing, permitting, encouraging, engaging in, or allowing the photographing, filming, or depicting of the child if the person knew or should have known that the resulting photograph, film, or depiction of the child is obscene as defined by Section 43.21, Penal Code, or pornographic;

(I) the current use by a person of a controlled substance as defined by Chapter 481, Health and Safety Code, in a manner or to the extent that the use results in physical, mental, or emotional injury to a child; or

(J) causing, expressly permitting, or encouraging a child to use a controlled substance as defined by Chapter 481, Health and Safety Code.

(2) "Department" means the Department of Protective and Regulatory Services.

(3) "Designated agency" means the agency designated by the court as responsible for the protection of children.

(4) "Neglect" includes:

(A) the leaving of a child in a situation where the child would be exposed to a substantial risk of physical or mental harm, without arranging for necessary care for the child, and the demonstration of an intent not to return by a parent, guardian, or managing or possessory conservator of the child;

(B) the following acts or omissions by a person:

(i) placing a child in or failing to remove a child from a situation that a reasonable person would realize requires judgment or actions beyond the child's level of maturity, physical condition, or mental abilities and that results in bodily injury or a substantial risk of immediate harm to the child;

(ii) failing to seek, obtain, or follow through with medical care for a child, with the failure resulting in or presenting a substantial risk of death, disfigurement, or bodily injury or with the failure resulting in an observable and material impairment to the growth, development, or functioning of the child;

(iii) the failure to provide a child with food, clothing, or shelter necessary to sustain the life or health of the child, excluding failure caused primarily by financial inability unless relief services had been offered and refused; or

(iv) placing a child in or failing to remove the child from a situation in which the child would be exposed to a substantial risk of sexual conduct harmful to the child; or

(C) the failure by the person responsible for a child's care, custody, or welfare to permit the child to return to the child's home without arranging for the necessary care for the child after the child has been absent from the home for any reason, including having been in residential placement or having run away.

(5) "Person responsible for a child's care, custody, or welfare" means a person who traditionally is responsible for a child's care, custody, or welfare, including:

(A) a parent, guardian, managing or possessory conservator, or foster parent of the child;

(B) a member of the child's family or household as defined by Chapter 71;

(C) a person with whom the child's parent cohabits;

(D) school personnel or a volunteer at the child's school; or

(E) personnel or a volunteer at a public or private child-care facility that provides services for the child or at a public or private residential institution or facility where the child resides.

(6) "Report" means a report that alleged or suspected abuse or neglect of a child has occurred or may occur.

Text of subdivision (7) as added by Acts 1997, 75th Leg., ch. 575, § 10

(7) "Born addicted to alcohol or a controlled substance" means a child:

(A) who is born to a mother who during the pregnancy used a controlled substance, as defined by Chapter 481, Health and Safety Code, other than a controlled substance legally obtained by prescription, or alcohol; and

(B) who, after birth as a result of the mother's use of the controlled substance or alcohol:

(i) experiences observable withdrawal from the alcohol or controlled substance;

(ii) exhibits observable or harmful effects in the child's physical appearance or functioning; or

(iii) exhibits the demonstrable presence of alcohol or a controlled substance in the child's bodily fluids.

Text of subdivision (7) as added by Acts 1997, 75th Leg., ch. 1022, § 63

(7) "Board" means the Board of Protective and Regulatory Services.

Added by Acts 1995, 74th Leg., ch. 20, § 1, eff. April 20, 1995. Amended by Acts 1995, 74th Leg., ch. 751, § 86, eff. Sept. 1, 1995; Acts 1997, 75th Leg., ch. 575, § 10, eff. Sept. 1, 1997; Acts 1997, 75th Leg., ch. 1022, § 63, eff. Sept. 1, 1997.

For application provisions of Acts 1997, 75th Leg., ch. 575, see note following V.T.C.A., Family Code § 102.003.

§ 261.002. Central Registry

(a) The department shall establish and maintain in Austin a central registry of reported cases of child abuse or neglect.

(b) The department may adopt rules necessary to carry out this section. The rules shall provide for cooperation with local child service agencies, including hospitals, clinics, and schools, and cooperation with other states in exchanging reports to effect a national registration system.

Added by Acts 1995, 74th Leg., ch. 20, § 1, eff. April 20, 1995.

§ 261.003. Application to Students in School for Deaf or School for Blind and Visually Impaired

This chapter applies to the investigation of a report of abuse or neglect of a student, without regard to the age of the student, in the Texas School for the Deaf or the Texas School for the Blind and Visually Impaired.

Added by Acts 1995, 74th Leg., ch. 20, § 1, eff. April 20, 1995.

§ 261.004. Statistics of Abuse and Neglect of Children

(a) The department shall prepare and disseminate statistics by county relating to the department's activities under this subtitle and include the information specified in Subsection (b) in an annual report available to the public.

(b) The department shall report the following information:

(1) the number of initial phone calls received by the department alleging abuse and neglect;

(2) the number of children reported to the department as having been abused and neglected;

(3) the number of reports received by the department alleging abuse or neglect and assigned by the department for investigation;

(4) of the children to whom Subdivision (2) applies:

(A) the number for whom the report was substantiated;

(B) the number for whom the report was unsubstantiated;

(C) the number for whom the report was determined to be false;

(D) the number who did not receive services from the department under a state or federal program;

(E) the number who received services, including preventative services, from the department under a state or federal program; and

(F) the number who were removed from the child's home during the preceding year;

(5) the number of families in which the child was not removed, but the child or family received services from the department;

(6) the number of children who died during the preceding year as a result of child abuse or neglect;

(7) of the children to whom Subdivision (6) applies, the number who were in foster care at the time of death;

(8) the number of child protective services workers responsible for report intake, assessment, or investigation;

(9) the response time by the department with respect to conducting an initial investigation of a report of child abuse or neglect;

(10) the response time by the department with respect to commencing services to families and children for whom an allegation of abuse or neglect has been made;

(11) the number of children who were returned to their families or who received family preservation services and who, before the fifth anniversary of the date of return or receipt, were the victims of substantiated reports of child abuse or neglect, including abuse or neglect resulting in the death of the child;

(12) the number of cases pursued by the department in each stage of the judicial process, including civil and criminal proceedings and the results of each proceeding; and

(13) the number of children for whom a person was appointed by the court to represent the best interests of the child and the average number of out-of-court contacts between the person and the child.

(c) The department shall compile the information specified in Subsection (b) for the preceding year in a report to be submitted to the legislature and the general public not later than February 1 of each year.

Added by Acts 1997, 75th Leg., ch. 1022, § 64, eff. Sept. 1, 1997.

[Sections 261.005 to 261.100 reserved for expansion]

SUBCHAPTER B. REPORT OF ABUSE OR NEGLECT; IMMUNITIES

§ 261.101. Persons Required to Report; Time to Report

(a) A person having cause to believe that a child's physical or mental health or welfare has been adversely affected by abuse or neglect by any person shall immediately make a report as provided by this subchapter.

Text of subsection (b) as amended by Acts 1997, 75th Leg., ch. 162, § 1

(b) If a professional has cause to believe that a child has been or may be abused or neglected, the professional shall make a report not later than the 48th hour after the hour the professional first suspects that the child has been or may be abused or neglected. A professional may not delegate to or rely on another person to make the report. In this subsection, "professional" means an individual who is licensed or certified by the state or who is an employee of a facility licensed, certified, or operated by the state and who, in the normal course of official duties or duties for which a license or certification is required, has direct contact with children. The term includes teachers, nurses, doctors, day-care employees, juvenile probation officers, and juvenile detention or correctional officers.

Text of subsection (b) as amended by Acts 1997, 75th Leg., ch. 1022, § 65

(b) If a professional has cause to believe that a child has been abused or neglected or that a child is a victim of an offense under Section 21.11, Penal Code, and that the professional has cause to believe that the child has been abused as defined by Section 261.001, the professional shall make a report not later than the 48th hour after the hour the professional first suspects that the child has been or may be abused or neglected or is a victim of an offense under Section 21.11, Penal Code. A professional may not delegate to or rely on another person to make the report. In this subsection, "professional" means an individual who is licensed or certified by the state or who is an employee of a facility licensed, certified, or operated by the state and who, in the normal course of official duties or duties for which a license or certification is required, has direct contact with children. The term includes teachers, nurses, doctors, day-care employees, and employees of a clinic or health care facility that provides reproductive services.

(c) The requirement to report under this section applies without exception to an individual whose personal communications may otherwise be privileged, including an attorney, a member of the clergy, a medical practitioner, a social worker, a mental health professional, and an employee of a clinic or health care facility that provides reproductive services.

(d) The identity of an individual making a report under this chapter is confidential and may be disclosed only on the order of a court rendered under Section 261.201 or to a law enforcement officer for the purposes of conducting a criminal investigation of the report.

Added by Acts 1995, 74th Leg., ch. 20, § 1, eff. April 20, 1995. Amended by Acts 1995, 74th Leg., ch. 751, § 87, eff. Sept. 1, 1995; Acts 1997, 75th Leg., ch. 162, § 1, eff. Sept. 1, 1997; Acts 1997, 75th Leg., ch. 575, § 11, eff. Sept. 1, 1997; Acts 1997, 75th Leg., ch. 1022, § 65, eff. Sept. 1, 1997.

For application provisions of Acts 1997, 75th Leg., ch. 575, see note following V.T.C.A., Family Code § 102.003.

Section 109 of Acts 1997, 75th Leg., ch. 1022 provides:

"The change in law made by this Act to Section 261.101, Family Code, applies only to a report of child abuse or neglect made on or after the effective date of this Act. A report made before that date is governed by the law in effect on the date the report was made, and the former law is continued in effect for that purpose."

§ 261.102. Matters to be Reported

A report should reflect the reporter's belief that a child has been or may be abused or neglected or has died of abuse or neglect.

Added by Acts 1995, 74th Leg., ch. 20, § 1, eff. April 20, 1995. Amended by Acts 1995, 74th Leg., ch. 751, § 88, eff. Sept. 1, 1995.

§ 261.103. Report Made to Appropriate Agency

A report shall be made to:

(1) any local or state law enforcement agency;

(2) the department if the alleged or suspected abuse involves a person responsible for the care, custody, or welfare of the child;

(3) the state agency that operates, licenses, certifies, or registers the facility in which the alleged abuse or neglect occurred; or

(4) the agency designated by the court to be responsible for the protection of children.

Added by Acts 1995, 74th Leg., ch. 20, § 1, eff. April 20, 1995. Amended by Acts 1995, 74th Leg., ch. 751, § 89, eff. Sept. 1, 1995.

§ 261.104. Contents of Report

The person making a report shall identify, if known:

(1) the name and address of the child;

(2) the name and address of the person responsible for the care, custody, or welfare of the child; and

(3) any other pertinent information concerning the alleged or suspected abuse or neglect.

Added by Acts 1995, 74th Leg., ch. 20, § 1, eff. April 20, 1995. Amended by Acts 1995, 74th Leg., ch. 751, § 90, eff. Sept. 1, 1995.

§ 261.105. Referral of Report by Department or Law Enforcement

(a) All reports received by a local or state law enforcement agency that allege abuse or neglect by a person responsible for a child's care, custody, or welfare shall be referred immediately to the department or the designated agency.

(b) The department or designated agency shall immediately notify the appropriate state or local law enforcement agency of any report it receives, other than a report from a law enforcement agency, that concerns the suspected abuse or neglect of a child or death of a child from abuse or neglect.

(c) In addition to notifying a law enforcement agency, if the report relates to a child in a facility operated, licensed, certified, or registered by a state agency, the department shall refer the report to the agency for investigation.

(d) If the department initiates an investigation and determines that the abuse or neglect does not involve a person responsible for the child's care, custody, or welfare, the department shall refer the report to a law enforcement agency for further investigation.

Added by Acts 1995, 74th Leg., ch. 20, § 1, eff. April 20, 1995. Amended by Acts 1997, 75th Leg., ch. 1022, § 66, eff. Sept. 1, 1997.

§ 261.1055. Notification of District Attorneys

(a) A district attorney may inform the department or designated agency that the district attorney wishes to receive notification of some or all reports of suspected abuse or neglect of children who were in the county at the time the report was made or who were in the county at the time of the alleged abuse or neglect.

(b) If the district attorney makes the notification under this section, the department or designated agency shall, on receipt of a report of suspected abuse or neglect, immediately notify the district attorney as requested and the department or designated agency shall forward a copy of the reports to the district attorney on request.

Added by Acts 1997, 75th Leg., ch. 1022, § 67, eff. Sept. 1, 1997.

§ 261.106. Immunities

(a) A person acting in good faith who reports or assists in the investigation of a report of alleged child abuse or neglect or who testifies or otherwise participates in a judicial proceeding arising from a report, petition, or investigation of alleged child abuse or neglect is immune from civil or criminal liability that might otherwise be incurred or imposed.

(b) Immunity from civil and criminal liability extends to an authorized volunteer of the department or a law enforcement officer who participates at the request of the department in an investigation of alleged or suspected abuse or neglect or in an action arising from an investigation if the person was acting in good faith and in the scope of the person's responsibilities.

(c) A person who reports the person's own abuse or neglect of a child or who acts in bad faith or with malicious purpose in reporting alleged child abuse or neglect is not immune from civil or criminal liability.

Added by Acts 1995, 74th Leg., ch. 20, § 1, eff. April 20, 1995. Amended by Acts 1995, 74th Leg., ch. 751, § 91, eff. Sept. 1, 1995.

§ 261.107. False Report; Penalty

Text of section as amended by Acts 1997, 75th Leg., ch. 575, § 2

(a) A person commits an offense if the person knowingly or intentionally makes a report as provided in this chapter that the person knows is false or lacks factual foundation. The first offense under this section is a Class A misdemeanor; a subsequent offense under this section is a state jail felony.

(b) A report under this section which was made prior to or during a suit affecting the parent-child relationship and in which is contained accusations that the court determines the accuser knew to be false or lacking factual foundation, may be grounds for the court to modify the parent-child relationship to restrict further access to the child by the accuser.

(c) The respective prosecuting attorney shall be responsible for the prosecution of offenses under this section.

Added by Acts 1995, 74th Leg., ch. 20, § 1, eff. April 20, 1995. Amended by Acts 1995, 74th Leg., ch. 751, § 92, eff. Sept. 1, 1995; Acts 1997, 75th Leg., ch. 575, § 2, eff. Sept. 1, 1997.

For text of section as amended by Acts 1997, 75th Leg., ch. 1022, § 68, see § 261.107, post.

Sections 37 and 38 of Acts 1997, 75th Leg., ch. 575 provide:

"Sec. 37. (a) The change in law made by Section 2 of this Act applies only to an offense committed on or after the effective date of this Act. For the purpose of this section, an offense is committed before the effective date of this Act if any element of the offense occurs before that date.

"(b) An offense committed before the effective date of this Act is covered by the law in effect when the offense was committed, and the former law is continued in effect for that purpose.

"Sec. 38. This Act takes effect September 1, 1997, and applies to a suit affecting the parent-child relationship filed on or after that date. A suit filed before the effective date of this Act is governed by the law in effect on the date the suit was filed, and the former law is continued in effect for that purpose."

§ 261.107. False Report; Penalty

Text of section as amended by Acts 1997, 75th Leg., ch. 1022, § 68

(a) A person commits an offense if the person knowingly or intentionally makes a report as provided in this chapter that the person knows is false or lacks factual foundation. An offense under this section is a Class A misdemeanor unless it is shown on the trial of the offense that the person has previously been convicted under this section, in which case the offense is a state jail felony.

(b) A finding by a court in a suit affecting the parent-child relationship that a report made under this chapter before or during the suit was false or lacking factual foundation may be grounds for the court to modify an order providing for possession of or access to the child who was the subject of the report by restricting further access to the child by the person who made the report.

(c) The appropriate county prosecuting attorney shall be responsible for the prosecution of an offense under this section.

Added by Acts 1995, 74th Leg., ch. 20, § 1, eff. April 20, 1995. Amended by Acts 1995, 74th Leg., ch. 751, § 92, eff. Sept. 1, 1995; Acts 1997, 75th Leg., ch. 1022, § 68, eff. Sept. 1, 1997.

For text of section as amended by Acts 1997, 75th Leg., ch. 575, § 2, see § 261.107, ante.

§ 261.108. Frivolous Claims Against Person Reporting

(a) In this section:

(1) "Claim" means an action or claim by a party, including a plaintiff, counterclaimant, cross-claimant, or third-party plaintiff, requesting recovery of damages.

(2) "Defendant" means a party against whom a claim is made.

(b) A court shall award a defendant reasonable attorney's fees and other expenses related to the defense of a claim filed against the defendant for damages or other relief arising from reporting or assisting in the investigation of a report under this chapter or participating in a judicial proceeding resulting from the report if:

(1) the court finds that the claim is frivolous, unreasonable, or without foundation because the defendant is immune from liability under Section 261.106; and

(2) the claim is dismissed or judgment is rendered for the defendant.

(c) To recover under this section, the defendant must, at any time after the filing of a claim, file a written motion stating that:

(1) the claim is frivolous, unreasonable, or without foundation because the defendant is immune from liability under Section 261.106; and

(2) the defendant requests the court to award reasonable attorney's fees and other expenses related to the defense of the claim.

Added by Acts 1995, 74th Leg., ch. 20, § 1, eff. April 20, 1995.

§ 261.109. Failure to Report; Penalty

(a) A person commits an offense if the person has cause to believe that a child's physical or mental health or welfare has been or may be adversely affected by abuse or neglect and knowingly fails to report as provided in this chapter.

(b) An offense under this section is a Class B misdemeanor.

Added by Acts 1995, 74th Leg., ch. 20, § 1, eff. April 20, 1995.

[Sections 261.110 to 261.200 reserved for expansion]

SUBCHAPTER C. CONFIDENTIALITY AND PRIVILEGED COMMUNICATION

§ 261.201. Confidentiality and Disclosure of Information

(a) The following information is confidential, is not subject to public release under Chapter 552, Government Code, and may be disclosed only for purposes consistent with this code and applicable federal or state law or under rules adopted by an investigating agency:

(1) a report of alleged or suspected abuse or neglect made under this chapter and the identity of the person making the report; and

(2) except as otherwise provided in this section, the files, reports, records, communications, audiotapes, videotapes, and working papers used or developed in an investigation under this chapter or in providing services as a result of an investigation.

(b) A court may order the disclosure of information that is confidential under this section if:

(1) a motion has been filed with the court requesting the release of the information;

(2) a notice of hearing has been served on the investigating agency and all other interested parties; and

(3) after hearing and an in camera review of the requested information, the court determines that the disclosure of the requested information is:

(A) essential to the administration of justice; and

(B) not likely to endanger the life or safety of:

(i) a child who is the subject of the report of alleged or suspected abuse or neglect;

(ii) a person who makes a report of alleged or suspected abuse or neglect; or

(iii) any other person who participates in an investigation of reported abuse or neglect.

(c) In addition to Subsection (b), a court, on its own motion, may order disclosure of information that is confidential under this section if:

(1) the order is rendered at a hearing for which all parties have been given notice;

(2) the court finds that disclosure of the information is:

(A) essential to the administration of justice; and

(B) not likely to endanger the life or safety of:

(i) a child who is the subject of the report of alleged or suspected abuse or neglect;

(ii) a person who makes a report of alleged or suspected abuse or neglect; or

(iii) any other person who participates in an investigation of reported abuse or neglect; and

(3) the order is reduced to writing or made on the record in open court.

(d) The adoptive parents of a child who was the subject of an investigation and an adult who was the subject of an investigation as a child are entitled to examine and make copies of any report, record, working paper, or other information in the possession, custody, or control of the state that pertains to the history of the child. The department may edit the documents to protect the identity of the biological parents and any other person whose identity is confidential.

(e) Before placing a child who was the subject of an investigation, the department shall notify the prospective adoptive parents of their right to examine any report, record, working paper, or other information in the possession, custody, or control of the state that pertains to the history of the child.

(f) The department shall provide prospective adoptive parents an opportunity to examine information under this section as early as practicable before placing a child.

(g) Notwithstanding Subsection (b), the department, on request and subject to department rule, shall provide to the parent, managing conservator, or other legal representative of a child who is the subject of reported abuse or neglect information concerning the reported abuse or neglect that would otherwise be confidential under this section if the department has edited the information to protect the confidentiality of the identity of the person who made the report and any other person whose life or safety may be endangered by the disclosure.

Added by Acts 1995, 74th Leg., ch. 20, § 1, eff. April 20, 1995. Amended by Acts 1995, 74th Leg., ch. 751, § 93, eff. Sept. 1, 1995; Acts 1997, 75th Leg., ch. 575, § 12, eff. Sept. 1, 1997; Acts 1997, 75th Leg., ch. 1022, § 69, eff. Sept. 1, 1997.

For application provisions of Acts 1997, 75th Leg., ch. 575, see note following V.T.C.A., Family Code § 102.003.

§ 261.202. Privileged Communication

In a proceeding regarding the abuse or neglect of a child, evidence may not be excluded on the ground of privileged communication except in the case of communications between an attorney and client.

Added by Acts 1995, 74th Leg., ch. 20, § 1, eff. April 20, 1995.

[Sections 261.203 to 261.300 reserved for expansion]

SUBCHAPTER D. INVESTIGATIONS

§ 261.301. Investigation of Report

(a) With assistance from the appropriate state or local law enforcement agency, the department or designated agency shall make a prompt and thorough investigation of a report of child abuse or neglect allegedly committed by a person responsible for a child's care, custody, or welfare. The investigation shall be conducted without regard to any pending suit affecting the parent-child relationship.

(b) A state agency shall investigate a report that alleges abuse or neglect occurred in a facility operated, licensed, certified, or registered by that agency as provided by Subchapter E.[1]

(c) The department is not required to investigate a report that alleges child abuse or neglect by a person other than a person responsible for a child's care, custody, or welfare. The appropriate state or local law enforcement agency shall investigate that report if the agency determines an investigation should be conducted.

(d) The department may by rule assign priorities and prescribe investigative procedures for investigations based on the severity and immediacy of the alleged harm to the child. The primary purpose of the investigation shall be the protection of the child.

(e) As necessary to provide for the protection of the child, the department or designated agency shall determine:

(1) the nature, extent, and cause of the abuse or neglect;

(2) the identity of the person responsible for the abuse or neglect;

(3) the names and conditions of the other children in the home;

(4) an evaluation of the parents or persons responsible for the care of the child;

(5) the adequacy of the home environment;

(6) the relationship of the child to the persons responsible for the care, custody, or welfare of the child; and

(7) all other pertinent data.

(f) An investigation of a report to the department of serious physical or sexual abuse of a child shall be conducted jointly by an investigator from the appropriate local law enforcement agency and the department or agency responsible for conducting an investigation under Subchapter E.

(g) The inability or unwillingness of a local law enforcement agency to conduct a joint investigation under Subsection (f) does not constitute grounds to prevent or prohibit the department from performing its duties under this subtitle. The department shall document any instance in which a law enforcement agency is unable or unwilling to conduct a joint investigation under Subsection (f).

Added by Acts 1995, 74th Leg., ch. 20, § 1, eff. April 20, 1995. Amended by Acts 1995, 74th Leg., ch. 751, § 94, eff. Sept. 1, 1995; Acts 1995, 74th Leg., ch. 943, § 2, eff. Sept. 1, 1995; Acts 1997, 75th Leg., ch. 1022, § 70, eff. Sept. 1, 1997; Acts 1997, 75th Leg., ch. 1137, § 1, eff. Sept. 1, 1997.

[1] V.T.C.A., Family Code § 261.401 et seq.

Section 13(a) of Acts 1995, 74th Leg., ch. 943 provides:

"This Act takes effect September 1, 1995, and applies to a proceeding in which an investigation of the abuse of a child is pending on or after that date."

§ 261.3015. Flexible Response System

(a) In assigning priorities and prescribing investigative procedures based on the severity and immediacy of the alleged harm to a child under Section 261.301(d), the board by rule shall establish a flexible response system to allow the department to allocate resources by investigating serious cases of abuse and neglect and providing assessment and family preservation services in less serious cases.

(b) The classification under the flexible response system of a case may be changed as warranted by the circumstances.

(c) The department may implement the flexible response system by establishing a pilot program in a single department service region. The department shall study the results of the system in the region in determining the method by which to implement the system statewide.

Added by Acts 1997, 75th Leg., ch. 1022, § 71, eff. Sept. 1, 1997.

§ 261.3019. Pilot Programs for Investigations of Child Abuse

Text of section effective until September 1, 2001

(a) On or after September 1, 1997, but not later than March 1, 1998, the department shall enter into two agreements, one with a sheriff of a county with a population of not less than 500,000 and if necessary for jurisdictional purposes any other law enforcement agency, and one with a sheriff of a county with a population of 25,000 or less and if necessary for jurisdictional purposes any other law enforcement agency, under which the sheriff or law enforcement agency shall conduct investigations of reports of abuse. The commissioners court of a county that is eligible to establish a pilot program and that intends to do so shall inform the department of the county's interest.

(b) An agreement under this section shall:

(1) specify the respective roles of law enforcement and department staff in the investigative process;

(2) provide for the department to assist in the removal of a child under Chapter 262 as necessary for the protection of the child;

(3) provide for the use of any available children's advocacy center or multidisciplinary team under Subchapter E, Chapter 264;

(4) include provisions for the reimbursement by the department from available state and federal funds of the costs incurred by the sheriff or law enforcement agency in conducting an investigation of a report of abuse;

(5) develop a plan for the transfer of calls received by the state child abuse hotline to the local law enforcement agency;

(6) develop a plan to be submitted to the department that specifies the manner in which the county's law enforcement agency shall handle investigations, investigator training, and the processing of reports made to the local agency;

(7) permit an additional contract with other appropriate local law enforcement agencies, if necessary for jurisdictional purposes, to implement the pilot program; and

(8) contain provisions the department and the sheriff and law enforcement determine to be necessary and appropriate.

(c) The department may provide advice and technical assistance to the county to ensure that the county complies with state and federal law in implementing and operating the pilot program.

(d) Under each pilot program, the department shall provide to a participating county law enforcement agency:

(A) information regarding:

(i) the average number of child abuse cases that are typically investigated; and

(ii) staff and investigator training; and

(B) other assistance necessary to adequately implement and fund the pilot program.

(e) Under the pilot program, the commissioners court shall establish an independent local citizens review board composed of seven volunteers who represent the community, including members who have experience in matters relating to child abuse and including one member who is licensed as a psychologist, one member licensed as a medical or health professional, and one member who is a licensed or ordained priest, rabbi, or officer of a religious organization. A member of a review board may not be an employee of or contract with any participating law enforcement agency or the department. The citizens review board shall prepare and make available to the public on an annual basis a report containing a summary of the activities of the board.

(f) The commissioners court may apply for any grants and research other sources of funding for the county's participation in the pilot program.

(g) An agreement under Subsection (a) is not required to provide for:

(1) the investigation of abuse alleged to have occurred in a facility or home regulated by the department under Chapter 42, Human Resources Code; or

(2) an investigation conducted under Section 48.081, Human Resources Code, or Section 261.404.

(h) The state auditor shall perform an audit and evaluation of the pilot program under this section. In preparing the evaluation, the auditor shall consider any report prepared by a citizens review board established under Subsection (e). The auditor shall report, not later than March 1, 2001, the results of the audit and evaluation to the presiding officers of both houses of the 77th Legislature and to the governor. The report must include an evaluation of the strengths and weaknesses of the pilot program and a recommendation about the feasibility of expanding the pilot program statewide.

(i) The department shall adopt rules necessary to perform the department's duties under this section.

(j) This section expires September 1, 2001.

Added by Acts 1997, 75th Leg., ch. 1022, § 72, eff. Sept. 1, 1997.

§ 261.302. Conduct of Investigation

(a) The investigation may include:

(1) a visit to the child's home, unless the alleged abuse or neglect can be confirmed or clearly ruled out without a home visit; and

(2) an interview with and examination of the subject child, which may include a medical, psychological, or psychiatric examination.

(b) The interview with and examination of the child may:

(1) be conducted at any reasonable time and place, including the child's home or the child's school;

(2) include the presence of persons the department or designated agency determines are necessary; and

(3) include transporting the child for purposes relating to the interview or investigation.

(c) The investigation may include an interview with the child's parents and an interview with and medical, psychological, or psychiatric examination of any child in the home.

(d) If, before an investigation is completed, the investigating agency believes that the immediate removal of a child from the child's home is necessary to protect the child from further abuse or neglect, the investigating agency shall file a petition or take other action under Chapter 262 to provide for the temporary care and protection of the child.

(e) An interview with a child alleged to be a victim of physical abuse or sexual abuse shall be audiotaped or videotaped unless the investigating agency determines that good cause exists for not audiotaping or videotaping the interview in accordance with rules of the agency. Good cause may include, but is not limited to, such considerations as the age of the child and the nature and seriousness of the allegations under investigation. Nothing in this subsection shall be construed as prohibiting the investigating agency from audiotaping or videotaping an interview of a child on any case for which such audiotaping or videotaping is not required under this subsection. The fact that the investigating agency failed to audiotape or videotape an interview is admissible at the trial of the offense that is the subject of the interview.

Added by Acts 1995, 74th Leg., ch. 20, § 1, eff. April 20, 1995. Amended by Acts 1995, 74th Leg., ch. 751, § 95, eff. Sept. 1, 1995; Acts 1997, 75th Leg., ch. 575, §§ 13, 14, eff. Sept. 1, 1997; Acts 1997, 75th Leg., ch. 1022, § 73, eff. Sept. 1, 1997.

§ 261.303. Interference With Investigation; Court Order

(a) A person may not interfere with an investigation of a report of child abuse or neglect conducted by the department or designated agency.

(b) If admission to the home, school, or any place where the child may be cannot be obtained, then for good cause shown the court having family law jurisdiction shall order the parent, the person responsible for the care of the children, or the person in charge of any place where the child may be to allow entrance for the interview, examination, and investigation.

(c) If a parent or person responsible for the child's care does not consent to a medical, psychological, or psychiatric examination of the child that is requested by the department or designated agency, the court having family law jurisdiction shall, for good cause shown, order the examination to be made at the times and places designated by the court.

Added by Acts 1995, 74th Leg., ch. 20, § 1, eff. April 20, 1995. Amended by Acts 1995, 74th Leg., ch. 751, § 96, eff. Sept. 1, 1995.

§ 261.304. Investigation of Anonymous Report

(a) If the department receives an anonymous report of child abuse or neglect by a person responsible for a child's care, custody, or welfare, the department shall conduct a preliminary investigation to determine whether there is any evidence to corroborate the report.

(b) An investigation under this section may include a visit to the child's home and an interview with and examination of the child and an interview with the child's parents. In addition, the department may interview any other person the department believes may have relevant information.

(c) Unless the department determines that there is some evidence to corroborate the report of abuse, the department may not conduct the thorough investigation required by this chapter or take any action against the person accused of abuse.

Added by Acts 1995, 74th Leg., ch. 20, § 1, eff. April 20, 1995.

§ 261.305. Access to Mental Health Records

(a) An investigation may include an inquiry into the possibility that the child, a parent, or a person responsible for the care of the child has a history of medical or mental illness.

(b) If the parent or person responsible for the care of the child does not allow the department or designated agency to have access to medical or mental health records requested by the department or agency, the court having family law jurisdiction, for good cause shown, shall order that the department or agency be permitted to have access to the records under terms and conditions prescribed by the court.

(c) If the court determines that the parent or person responsible for the care of the child is indigent, the court shall appoint an attorney to represent the parent or person responsible for the child at the hearing to obtain medical or mental health records. The fees for the appointed attorney shall be paid by the department or designated agency.

(d) A parent or person responsible for the child's care is entitled to notice and a hearing when the department or designated agency seeks a court order to allow a medical, psychological, or psychiatric examination or access to medical or mental health records.

(e) This access does not constitute a waiver of confidentiality.

Added by Acts 1995, 74th Leg., ch. 20, § 1, eff. April 20, 1995. Amended by Acts 1997, 75th Leg., ch. 575, § 15, eff. Sept. 1, 1997.

§ 261.306. Removal of Child From State

(a) If the department or designated agency has reason to believe that a person responsible for the care, custody, or welfare of the child may remove the child from the state before the investigation is completed, the department or designated agency may file an application for a temporary restraining order in a district court without regard to continuing jurisdiction of the child as provided in Chapter 155.

(b) The court may render a temporary restraining order prohibiting the person from removing the child from the state pending completion of the investigation if the court:

(1) finds that the department or designated agency has probable cause to conduct the investigation; and

(2) has reason to believe that the person may remove the child from the state.

Added by Acts 1995, 74th Leg., ch. 20, § 1, eff. April 20, 1995.

§ 261.307. Information Relating to Investigation Procedure

As soon as possible after initiating an investigation of a parent or other person having legal custody of a child, the department shall provide to the person a brief and easily understood summary of:

(1) the department's procedures for conducting an investigation of alleged child abuse or neglect, including:

(A) a description of the circumstances under which the department would request to remove the child from the home through the judicial system; and

(B) an explanation that the law requires the department to refer all reports of alleged child abuse or neglect to a law enforcement agency for a separate determination of whether a criminal violation occurred;

(2) the person's right to file a complaint with the department or to request a review of the findings made by the department in the investigation;

(3) the person's right to review all records of the investigation unless the review would jeopardize an ongoing criminal investigation;

(4) the person's right to seek legal counsel;

(5) references to the statutory and regulatory provisions governing child abuse and neglect and how the person may obtain copies of those provisions; and

(6) the process the person may use to acquire access to the child if the child is removed from the home.

Added by Acts 1995, 74th Leg., ch. 20, § 1, eff. April 20, 1995.

§ 261.308. Submission of Investigation Report

(a) The department or designated agency shall make a complete written report of the investigation.

(b) If sufficient grounds for filing a suit exist, the department or designated agency shall submit the report, together with recommendations, to the court, the district attorney, and the appropriate law enforcement agency.

(c) On receipt of the report and recommendations, the court may direct the department or designated agency to file a petition requesting appropriate relief as provided in this title.

Added by Acts 1995, 74th Leg., ch. 20, § 1, eff. April 20, 1995. Amended by Acts 1995, 74th Leg., ch. 751, § 97, eff. Sept. 1, 1995.

§ 261.309. Review of Department Investigations

(a) The department shall by rule establish policies and procedures to resolve complaints relating to and conduct reviews of child abuse or neglect investigations conducted by the department.

(b) If a person under investigation for allegedly abusing or neglecting a child requests clarification of the status of the person's case or files a complaint relating to the conduct of the department's staff or to department policy, the department shall conduct an informal review to clarify the person's status or resolve the complaint. The immediate supervisor of the employee who conducted the child abuse or neglect investigation or against whom the complaint was filed shall conduct the informal review as soon as possible but not later than the 14th day after the date the request or complaint is received.

(c) If, after the department's investigation, the person who is alleged to have abused or neglected a child disputes the department's determination of whether child abuse or neglect occurred, the person may request an administrative review of the findings. A department employee in administration who was not involved in or did not directly supervise the investigation shall conduct the review. The review must sustain, alter, or reverse the department's original findings in the investigation.

(d) Unless a civil or criminal court proceeding or an ongoing criminal investigation relating to the alleged abuse or neglect investigated by the department is pending, the department employee shall conduct the review prescribed by Subsection (c) as soon as possible but not later than the 45th day after the date the department receives the request. If a civil or criminal court proceeding or an ongoing criminal investigation is pending, the department may postpone the review until the court proceeding is completed.

(e) A person is not required to exhaust the remedies provided by this section before pursuing a judicial remedy provided by law.

(f) This section does not provide for a review of an order rendered by a court.

Added by Acts 1995, 74th Leg., ch. 20, § 1, eff. April 20, 1995.

§ 261.310. Investigation Standards

(a) The department shall by rule develop and adopt voluntary standards for persons who investigate suspected child abuse or neglect at the state or local level. The standards shall encourage professionalism and consistency in the investigation of suspected child abuse or neglect.

(b) The standards must provide for a minimum number of hours of annual professional training for interviewers and investigators of suspected child abuse or neglect.

(c) The professional training curriculum developed under this section shall include information concerning:

(1) physical abuse and neglect, including distinguishing physical abuse from ordinary childhood injuries;

(2) psychological abuse and neglect;

(3) available treatment resources; and

(4) the incidence and types of reports of child abuse and neglect that are received by the investigating agencies, including information concerning false reports.

(d) The standards shall recommend:

(1) that videotaped and audiotaped interviews with a suspected victim be uninterrupted;

(2) a maximum number of interviews with and examinations of a suspected victim;

(3) procedures to preserve evidence, including the original notes, videotapes, and audiotapes; and

(4) that an investigator of suspected child abuse or neglect make a reasonable effort to locate and inform each parent of a child of any report of abuse or neglect relating to the child.

Added by Acts 1995, 74th Leg., ch. 20, § 1, eff. April 20, 1995.

§ 261.311. Notice of Report

(a) When during an investigation of a report of suspected child abuse or neglect a representative of the department or the designated agency conducts an interview with or an examination of a child, the department or designated agency shall make a reasonable effort before 24 hours after the time of the interview or examination to notify each parent of the child and the child's legal guardian, if one has been appointed, of the nature of the allegation and of the fact that the interview or examination was conducted.

(b) If a report of suspected child abuse or neglect is administratively closed by the department or designated agency as a result of a preliminary investigation that did not include an interview or examination of the child, the department or designated agency shall make a reasonable effort before the expiration of 24 hours after the time the investigation is closed to notify each parent and legal guardian of the child of the disposition of the investigation.

(c) The notice required by Subsection (a) or (b) is not required if the department or agency determines that the notice is likely to endanger the safety of the child who is the subject of the report, the person who made the report, or any other person who participates in the investigation of the report.

(d) The notice required by Subsection (a) or (b) may be delayed at the request of a law enforcement agency if notification during the required time would interfere with an ongoing criminal investigation.

Added by Acts 1995, 74th Leg., ch. 20, § 1, eff. April 20, 1995. Amended by Acts 1997, 75th Leg., ch. 1022, § 74, eff. Sept. 1, 1997.

§ 261.312. Review Teams; Offense

(a) The department shall establish review teams to evaluate department casework and decision-making related to investigations by the department of child abuse or neglect. The department may create one or more review teams for each region of the department for child protective services. A review team is a citizen review panel or a similar entity for the purposes of federal law relating to a state's child protection standards.

(b) A review team consists of five members who serve staggered two-year terms. Review team members are appointed by the director of the department and consist of community representatives and private citizens who live in the region for which the team is established. Each member must be a parent who has not been convicted of or indicted for an offense involving child abuse or neglect, has not been determined by the department to have engaged in child abuse or neglect, or is not under investigation by the department for child abuse or neglect. A member of a review team is a department volunteer for the purposes of Section 411.114, Government Code.

(c) A review team conducting a review of an investigation may conduct the review by examining the facts of the case as outlined by the department caseworker and law enforcement personnel. A review team member acting in the member's official capacity may receive information made confidential under Section 40.005, Human Resources Code, or Section 261.201.

(d) A review team shall report to the department the results of the team's review of an investigation. The review team's report may not include confidential information. The findings contained in a review team's report are subject to disclosure under Chapter 552, Government Code. This section does not require a law enforcement agency to divulge information to a review team that the agency believes would compromise an ongoing criminal case, investigation, or proceeding.

(e) A member of a review team commits an offense if the member discloses confidential information. An offense under this subsection is a Class C misdemeanor.

Added by Acts 1995, 74th Leg., ch. 943, § 3, eff. Sept. 1, 1995. Amended by Acts 1997, 75th Leg., ch. 575, § 16, eff. Sept. 1, 1997.

Section 13(a) of the 1995 Act provides:

"This Act takes effect September 1, 1995, and applies to a proceeding in which an investigation of the abuse of a child is pending on or after that date."

[Section 261.313 reserved for expansion]

§ 261.314. Testing

(a) The department shall provide testing as necessary for the welfare of a child who the department believes, after an investigation under this chapter, has been sexually abused, including human immunodeficiency virus (HIV) testing of a child who was abused in a manner by which HIV may be transmitted.

(b) Except as provided by Subsection (c), the results of a test under this section are confidential.

(c) If requested, the department shall report the results of a test under this section to:

(1) a court having jurisdiction of a proceeding involving the child or a proceeding involving a person suspected of abusing the child;

(2) a person responsible for the care and custody of the child as a foster parent; and

(3) a person seeking to adopt the child.

Added by Acts 1995, 74th Leg., ch. 943, § 7, eff. Sept. 1, 1995.

Section 13(a) of the 1995 Act provides:

"This Act takes effect September 1, 1995, and applies to a proceeding in which an investigation of the abuse of a child is pending on or after that date."

§ 261.315. Exemption From Fees for Medical Records

Text of section as added by Acts 1997, 75th Leg., ch. 575, § 17

The department is exempt from the payment of a fee otherwise required or authorized by law to obtain a medical record from a hospital or health care provider if the request for a record is made in the course of an investigation by the department.

Added by Acts 1997, 75th Leg., ch. 575, § 17, eff. Sept. 1, 1997.

For text of section as added by Acts 1997, 75th Leg., ch. 1022, § 75, see § 261.315, post.

§ 261.315. Removal of Certain Investigation Information From Records

Text of section as added by Acts 1997, 75th Leg., ch. 1022, § 75

(a) At the conclusion of an investigation in which the department determines that the person alleged to have abused or neglected a child did not commit abuse or neglect, the department shall notify the person of the person's right to request the department to remove information about the person's alleged role in the abuse or neglect report from the department's records.

(b) On request under Subsection (a) by a person whom the department has determined did not commit abuse or neglect, the department shall remove information from the department's records concerning the person's alleged role in the abuse or neglect report.

(c) The board shall adopt rules necessary to administer this section.

Added by Acts 1997, 75th Leg., ch. 1022, § 75, eff. Sept. 1, 1997.

For text of section as added by Acts 1997, 75th Leg., ch. 575, § 17, see § 261.315, ante.

[Sections 261.316 to 261.400 reserved for expansion]

SUBCHAPTER E. INVESTIGATIONS OF ABUSE OR NEGLECT IN CERTAIN FACILITIES

§ 261.401. Agency Investigation

(a) A state agency that operates, licenses, certifies, or registers a facility in which children are located shall make a prompt, thorough investigation of a report that a child has been or may be abused or neglected in the facility. The primary purpose of the investigation shall be the protection of the child.

(b) A state agency shall adopt rules relating to the investigation and resolution of reports received as provided by this subchapter. The Health and Human Services Commission shall review and approve the rules to ensure that all agencies implement appropriate standards for the conduct of investigations and that uniformity exists among agencies in the investigation and resolution of reports.

Added by Acts 1995, 74th Leg., ch. 20, § 1, eff. April 20, 1995. Amended by Acts 1995, 74th Leg., ch. 751, § 98, eff. Sept. 1, 1995.

§ 261.402. Investigative Reports

(a) A state agency shall prepare and keep on file a complete written report of each investigation conducted by the agency under this subchapter.

(b) A state agency shall immediately notify the appropriate state or local law enforcement agency of any report the agency receives, other than a report from a law enforcement agency, that concerns the suspected abuse or neglect of a child or the death of a child from abuse or neglect. If the state agency finds evidence indicating that a child may have been abused or neglected, the agency shall report the evidence to the appropriate law enforcement agency.

(d)[1] A state agency that licenses, certifies, or registers a facility in which children are located shall compile, maintain, and make available statistics on the incidence of child abuse and neglect in the facility.

(e) A state agency shall compile, maintain, and make available statistics on the incidence of child abuse and neglect in a facility operated by the state agency.

Added by Acts 1995, 74th Leg., ch. 20, § 1, eff. April 20, 1995. Amended by Acts 1995, 74th Leg., ch. 751, § 99, eff. Sept. 1, 1995.

[1] So as amended; there is no (c).

§ 261.403. Complaints

(a) If a state agency receives a complaint relating to an investigation conducted by the agency concerning a facility operated by that agency in which children are located, the agency shall refer the complaint to the agency's board.

(b) The board of a state agency that operates a facility in which children are located shall ensure that the procedure for investigating abuse and neglect allegations and inquiries in the agency's facility is periodically reviewed under the agency's internal audit program required by Chapter 2102, Government Code.

Added by Acts 1995, 74th Leg., ch. 20, § 1, eff. April 20, 1995.

§ 261.404. Investigations in Facilities Under Department of Mental Health and Mental Retardation

The department shall investigate a report of abuse or neglect in a facility operated by, regulated by, or providing services under a contract with the Texas Department of Mental Health and Mental Retardation under rules developed jointly between the department and the Texas Department of Mental Health and Mental Retardation.

Added by Acts 1995, 74th Leg., ch. 751, § 100, eff. Sept. 1, 1995.

§ 261.405. Investigations in Pre-Adjudication and Post-Adjudication Secure Juvenile Facilities

Text of section as amended by Acts 1997, 75th Leg., ch. 162, § 2

A report of alleged abuse or neglect in a public or private juvenile pre-adjudication secure detention facility, including hold-over facilities, or public or private juvenile post-adjudication secure correctional facility, except for a facility operated solely for children committed to the Texas Youth Commission, shall be made to a local law enforcement agency for investigation. The local law enforcement agency shall immediately notify the Texas Juvenile Probation Commission of any report the agency receives.

Added by Acts 1995, 74th Leg., ch. 751, § 100, eff. Sept. 1, 1995. Amended by Acts 1997, 75th Leg., ch. 162, § 2, eff. Sept. 1, 1997.

For text of section as amended by Acts 1997, 75th Leg., ch. 1374, § 8, see § 261.405, post.

§ 261.405. Investigations in County Detention Facilities Involving Children

Text of section as amended by Acts 1997, 75th Leg., ch. 1374, § 8

A report of alleged abuse or neglect in a county juvenile detention facility or other secure detention facility in which a child is placed shall be made to a local law enforcement agency for investigation.

Added by Acts 1995, 74th Leg., ch. 751, § 100, eff. Sept. 1, 1995. Amended by Acts 1997, 75th Leg., ch. 1374, § 8, eff. Sept. 1, 1997.

For text of section as amended by Acts 1997, 75th Leg., ch. 162, § 2, see § 261.405, ante.

Section 10 of Acts 1997, 75th Leg., ch. 1374 provides:

"The change in law made by this Act applies only to a child taken into custody on or after the effective date of this Act."

§ 261.406. Investigations in Schools

(a) On receipt of a report of alleged or suspected abuse or neglect of a child in a public or private school under the jurisdiction of the Texas Education Agency, the department shall perform an investigation as provided by this chapter.

(b) The department shall send a written report of the department's investigation to the Texas Education Agency, the agency responsible for teacher certification, the local school board or local governing body, and the school principal, unless the principal is alleged to have committed the abuse or neglect, for appropriate action. On request, the department shall provide a copy of the report of investigation to the parent, managing conservator, or legal guardian of a child who is the subject of the investigation and to the person alleged to have committed the abuse or neglect. The report of investigation shall be edited to protect the identity of the persons who made the report of abuse or neglect or provided information for the report of abuse or neglect. Section 261.201(b) applies to the release of confidential information relating to the investigation of a report of abuse or neglect under this section and to the identity of the person who made the report of abuse or neglect.

(c) Nothing in this section may prevent a law enforcement agency from conducting an investigation of a report made under this section.

(d) The Board of Protective and Regulatory Services shall adopt rules necessary to implement this section.

Added by Acts 1995, 74th Leg., ch. 751, § 100, eff. Sept. 1, 1995. Amended by Acts 1997, 75th Leg., ch. 575, § 18, eff. Sept. 1, 1997.

CHAPTER 262. EMERGENCY PROCEDURES IN SUIT BY GOVERNMENTAL ENTITY

SUBCHAPTER A. GENERAL PROVISIONS

SUBCHAPTER B. TAKING POSSESSION OF CHILD IN EMERGENCY

SUBCHAPTER C. ADVERSARY HEARING

SUBCHAPTER A. GENERAL PROVISIONS

§ 262.001. Authorized Actions by Governmental Entity

A governmental entity with an interest in the child may file a suit affecting the parent-child relationship requesting an emergency order or take possession of a child without a court order as provided by this chapter.

Added by Acts 1995, 74th Leg., ch. 20, § 1, eff. April 20, 1995.

§ 262.002. Jurisdiction for Emergency Procedures

A suit brought by a governmental entity requesting an emergency order under this chapter may be filed in a court with jurisdiction to hear the suit in the county in which the child is found.

Added by Acts 1995, 74th Leg., ch. 20, § 1, eff. April 20, 1995.

§ 262.003. Civil Liability

A person who takes possession of a child without a court order is immune from civil liability if, at the time possession is taken, there is reasonable cause to believe there is an immediate danger to the physical health or safety of the child.

Added by Acts 1995, 74th Leg., ch. 20, § 1, eff. April 20, 1995.

§ 262.004. Accepting Voluntary Delivery of Possession of Child

A law enforcement officer or a juvenile probation officer may take possession of a child without a court order on the voluntary delivery of the child by the parent, managing conservator, possessory conservator, guardian, caretaker, or custodian who is presently entitled to possession of the child.

Added by Acts 1995, 74th Leg., ch. 20, § 1, eff. April 20, 1995. Amended by Acts 1995, 74th Leg., ch. 751, § 101, eff. Sept. 1, 1995.

§ 262.005. Filing Petition After Accepting Voluntary Delivery of Possession of Child

When possession of the child has been acquired through voluntary delivery of the child to a law enforcement officer or juvenile probation officer, the law enforcement officer or juvenile probation officer taking the child into possession shall cause a suit to be filed not later than the 60th day after the date the child is taken into possession.

Added by Acts 1995, 74th Leg., ch. 20, § 1, eff. April 20, 1995. Amended by Acts 1995, 74th Leg., ch. 751, § 102, eff. Sept. 1, 1995.

§ 262.006. Living Child After Abortion

(a) An authorized representative of the Department of Protective and Regulatory Services may assume the care, control, and custody of a child born alive as the result of an abortion as defined by Chapter 161.

(b) The department shall file a suit and request an emergency order under this chapter.

(c) A child for whom possession is assumed under this section need not be delivered to the court except on the order of the court.

Added by Acts 1995, 74th Leg., ch. 20, § 1, eff. April 20, 1995.

§ 262.007. Possession and Delivery of Missing Child

(a) A law enforcement officer who, during a criminal investigation relating to a child's custody, discovers that a child is a missing child and believes that a person may flee with or conceal the child may take possession of the child and provide for the delivery of the child as provided by Subsection (b).

(b) An officer who takes possession of a child under Subsection (a) shall deliver or arrange for the delivery of the child to a person entitled to possession of the child.

(c) If a person entitled to possession of the child is not immediately available to take possession of the child, the law enforcement officer shall deliver the child to the Department of Protective and Regulatory Services. Until a person entitled to possession of the child takes possession of the child, the department may, without a court order, retain possession of the child not longer than 14 days after the date the child is delivered to the department. While the department retains possession of a child under this subsection, the department may place the child in foster home care. If a parent or other person entitled to possession of the child does not take possession of the child before the 15th day after the date the child is delivered to the department, the department shall proceed under this chapter as if the law enforcement officer took possession of the child under Section 262.104.

Added by Acts 1995, 74th Leg., ch. 776, § 1, eff. Sept. 1, 1995.

§ 262.008. Abandoned Children

(a) An authorized representative of the Department of Protective and Regulatory Services may assume the care, control, and custody of a child:

(1) who is abandoned without identification or a means for identifying the child; and

(2) whose identity cannot be ascertained by the exercise of reasonable diligence.

(b) The department shall immediately file a suit to terminate the parent-child relationship of a child under Subsection (a).

(c) A child for whom possession is assumed under this section need not be delivered to the court except on the order of the court.

Added by Acts 1997, 75th Leg., ch. 600, § 4, eff. Jan. 1, 1998.

For application provision of Acts 1997, 75th Leg., ch. 600, see notes following V.T.C.A., Family Code § 162.012.

[Sections 262.009 to 262.100 reserved for expansion]

SUBCHAPTER B. TAKING POSSESSION OF CHILD IN EMERGENCY

§ 262.101. Filing Petition Before Taking Possession of Child

A petition or affidavit filed by a governmental entity requesting permission to take possession of a child in an emergency shall be sworn to by a person with personal knowledge and shall state facts sufficient to satisfy a person of ordinary prudence and caution that:

(1) there is an immediate danger to the physical health or safety of the child or the child has been a victim of neglect or sexual abuse and that continuation in the home would be contrary to the child's welfare; and

(2) there is no time, consistent with the physical health or safety of the child, for an adversary hearing or to make reasonable efforts to prevent or eliminate the need for the removal of the child.

Added by Acts 1995, 74th Leg., ch. 20, § 1, eff. April 20, 1995. Amended by Acts 1995, 74th Leg., ch. 751, § 103, eff. Sept. 1, 1995; Acts 1997, 75th Leg., ch. 752, § 1, eff. June 17, 1997.

§ 262.1015. Removal of Alleged Perpetrator; Offense

(a) If the department determines after an investigation that child abuse has occurred and that the child would be protected in the child's home by the removal of the alleged perpetrator of the abuse, the department shall file a petition for the removal of the alleged perpetrator from the residence of the child rather than attempt to remove the child from the residence.

(b) A court may issue a temporary restraining order in a suit by the department for the removal of an alleged perpetrator under Subsection (a) if the department's petition states facts sufficient to satisfy the court that:

(1) there is an immediate danger to the physical health or safety of the child or the child has been a victim of sexual abuse;

(2) there is no time, consistent with the physical health or safety of the child, for an adversary hearing;

(3) the child is not in danger of abuse from a parent or other adult with whom the child will continue to reside in the residence of the child; and

(4) the issuance of the order is in the best interest of the child.

(c) The order shall be served on the alleged perpetrator and on the parent or other adult with whom the child will continue to reside.

(d) A temporary restraining order under this section expires not later than the 14th day after the date the order was rendered.

(e) A temporary restraining order under this section and any other order requiring the removal of an alleged perpetrator from the residence of a child shall require that the parent or other adult with whom the child will continue to reside in the child's home make a reasonable effort to monitor the residence and report to the department and the appropriate law enforcement agency any attempt by the alleged perpetrator to return to the residence.

(f) The court shall order the removal of an alleged perpetrator if the court finds that the child is not in danger of abuse from a parent or other adult with whom the child will continue to reside in the child's residence and that:

(1) the presence of the alleged perpetrator in the child's residence constitutes a continuing danger to the physical health or safety of the child; or

(2) the child has been the victim of sexual abuse and there is a substantial risk that the child will be the victim of sexual abuse in the future if the alleged perpetrator remains in the residence.

(g) A person commits an offense if the person is a parent or other person with whom a child resides, the person is served with an order containing the requirement specified by Subsection (e), and the person fails to make a reasonable effort to monitor the residence of the child or to report to the department and the appropriate law enforcement agency an attempt by the alleged perpetrator to return to the residence. An offense under this section is a Class A misdemeanor.

(h) A person commits an offense if, in violation of a court order under this section, the person returns to the residence of the child the person is alleged to have abused. An offense under this subsection is a Class A misdemeanor, except that the offense is a felony of the third degree if the person has previously been convicted under this subsection.

Added by Acts 1995, 74th Leg., ch. 943, § 4, eff. Sept. 1, 1995. Amended by Acts 1997, 75th Leg., ch. 575, § 19, eff. Sept. 1, 1997.

Section 13(a) of the 1995 Act provides:

"This Act takes effect September 1, 1995, and applies to a proceeding in which an investigation of the abuse of a child is pending on or after that date."

For application provisions of Acts 1997, 75th Leg., ch. 575, see note following V.T.C.A., Family Code § 102.003.

§ 262.102. Emergency Order Authorizing Possession of Child

(a) Before a court may issue a temporary restraining order or attachment of a child in a suit requesting an emergency order brought by a governmental entity, the court must find that:

(1) there is an immediate danger to the physical health or safety of the child or the child has been a victim of sexual abuse and that continuation in the home would be contrary to the child's welfare; and

(2) there is no time, consistent with the physical health or safety of the child and the nature of the emergency, to hold an adversary hearing or to make reasonable efforts to prevent or eliminate the need for removal of the child.

(b) In determining whether there is an immediate danger to the physical health or safety of a child, the court may consider whether the child's household includes a person who has:

(1) abused or neglected another child in a manner that caused serious injury to or the death of the other child; or

(2) sexually abused another child.

(c) If, based on the recommendation of or a request by the department, the court finds that child abuse or neglect has occurred and that the child requires protection from family violence by a member of the child's family or household, the court shall render a temporary order under Chapter 71 for the protection of the child. In this subsection, "family violence" has the meaning assigned by Section 71.01.

Added by Acts 1995, 74th Leg., ch. 20, § 1, eff. April 20, 1995. Amended by Acts 1995, 74th Leg., ch. 751, § 104, eff. Sept. 1, 1995; Acts 1997, 75th Leg., ch. 752, § 2, eff. June 17, 1997.

§ 262.103. Duration of Temporary Restraining Order and Attachment

A temporary restraining order or attachment of the child issued under this chapter expires not later than

14 days after the date it is issued unless it is extended as provided by the Texas Rules of Civil Procedure.

Added by Acts 1995, 74th Leg., ch. 20, § 1, eff. April 20, 1995.

§ 262.104. Taking Possession of a Child in Emergency Without a Court Order

If there is no time to obtain a temporary restraining order or attachment before taking possession of a child consistent with the health and safety of that child, an authorized representative of the Department of Protective and Regulatory Services, a law enforcement officer, or a juvenile probation officer may take possession of a child without a court order under the following conditions, only:

(1) on personal knowledge of facts that would lead a person of ordinary prudence and caution to believe that there is an immediate danger to the physical health or safety of the child;

(2) on information furnished by another that has been corroborated by personal knowledge of facts and all of which taken together would lead a person of ordinary prudence and caution to believe that there is an immediate danger to the physical health or safety of the child;

(3) on personal knowledge of facts that would lead a person of ordinary prudence and caution to believe that the child has been the victim of sexual abuse;

(4) on information furnished by another that has been corroborated by personal knowledge of facts and all of which taken together would lead a person of ordinary prudence and caution to believe that the child has been the victim of sexual abuse; or

(5) on information furnished by another that has been corroborated by personal knowledge of facts and all of which taken together would lead a person of ordinary prudence and caution to believe that the parent or person who has possession of the child is currently using a controlled substance as defined by Chapter 481, Health and Safety Code, and the use constitutes an immediate danger to the physical health or safety of the child.

Added by Acts 1995, 74th Leg., ch. 20, § 1, eff. April 20, 1995. Amended by Acts 1997, 75th Leg., ch. 575, § 20, eff. Sept. 1, 1997.

For application provisions of Acts 1997, 75th Leg., ch. 575, see note following V.T.C.A., Family Code § 102.003.

§ 262.105. Filing Petition After Taking Possession of Child in Emergency

When a child is taken into possession without a court order, the person taking the child into possession, without unnecessary delay, shall:

(1) file a suit affecting the parent-child relationship;

(2) request the court to appoint an attorney ad litem for the child; and

(3) request an initial hearing to be held by no later than the first working day after the date the child is taken into possession.

Added by Acts 1995, 74th Leg., ch. 20, § 1, eff. April 20, 1995.

§ 262.106. Initial Hearing After Taking Possession of Child in Emergency Without Court Order

(a) The court in which a suit has been filed after a child has been taken into possession without a court order by a governmental entity shall hold an initial hearing on or before the first working day after the date the child is taken into possession. The court shall render orders that are necessary to protect the physical health and safety of the child. If the court is unavailable for a hearing on the first working day, then, and only in that event, the hearing shall be held no later than the first working day after the court becomes available, provided that the hearing is held no later than the third working day after the child is taken into possession.

(b) The initial hearing may be ex parte and proof may be by sworn petition or affidavit if a full adversary hearing is not practicable.

(c) If the initial hearing is not held within the time required, the child shall be returned to the parent, managing conservator, possessory conservator, guardian, caretaker, or custodian who is presently entitled to possession of the child.

Added by Acts 1995, 74th Leg., ch. 20, § 1, eff. April 20, 1995.

§ 262.107. Standard for Decision at Initial Hearing After Taking Possession of Child Without a Court Order in Emergency

(a) The court shall order the return of the child at the initial hearing regarding a child taken in possession without a court order by a governmental entity unless the court is satisfied that:

(1) there is a continuing danger to the physical health or safety of the child if the child is returned to the parent, managing conservator, possessory conservator, guardian, caretaker, or custodian who is presently entitled to possession of the child or the evidence shows that the child has been the victim of sexual abuse on one or more occasions and that

there is a substantial risk that the child will be the victim of sexual abuse in the future; and

(2) the nature of the emergency and the continuing danger to the welfare of the child make efforts to allow the child to remain with or return to the person entitled to possession of the child impossible or unreasonable.

(b) In determining whether there is a continuing danger to the physical health or safety of a child, the court may consider whether the household to which the child would be returned includes a person who has:

(1) abused or neglected another child in a manner that caused serious injury to or the death of the other child; or

(2) sexually abused another child.

Added by Acts 1995, 74th Leg., ch. 20, § 1, eff. April 20, 1995. Amended by Acts 1995, 74th Leg., ch. 751, § 105, eff. Sept. 1, 1995.

Section 129 of Acts 1995, 74th Leg., ch. 751 provides:

"This Act takes effect September 1, 1995, and applies to a pending suit affecting the parent-child relationship without regard to whether the suit was commenced before, on, or after the effective date of this Act."

§ 262.108. Unacceptable Facilities for Housing Child

When a child is taken into possession under this chapter, that child may not be held in isolation or in a jail, juvenile detention facility, or other secure detention facility.

Added by Acts 1995, 74th Leg., ch. 20, § 1, eff. April 20, 1995. Amended by Acts 1997, 75th Leg., ch. 1374, § 9, eff. Sept. 1, 1997.

Section 10 of Acts 1997, 75th Leg., ch. 1374 provides:

"The change in law made by this Act applies only to a child taken into custody on or after the effective date of this Act."

§ 262.109. Notice to Parent, Conservator, or Guardian

(a) The department or other agency must give written notice as prescribed by this section to each parent of the child or to the child's conservator or legal guardian when a representative of the Department of Protective and Regulatory Services or other agency takes possession of a child under this chapter.

(b) The written notice must be given as soon as practicable, but in any event not later than the first working day after the date the child is taken into possession.

(c) The written notice must include:

(1) the reasons why the department or agency is taking possession of the child and the facts that led the department to believe that the child should be taken into custody;

(2) the name of the person at the department or agency that the parent, conservator, or other custodian may contact for information relating to the child or a legal proceeding relating to the child;

(3) a summary of legal rights of a parent, conservator, guardian, or other custodian under this chapter and an explanation of the probable legal procedures relating to the child; and

(4) a statement that the parent, conservator, or other custodian has the right to hire an attorney.

(d) The written notice may be waived by the court at the initial hearing on a showing that the parents, conservators, or other custodians of the child could not be located.

Added by Acts 1995, 74th Leg., ch. 20, § 1, eff. April 20, 1995. Amended by Acts 1997, 75th Leg., ch. 1022, § 76, eff. Jan. 1, 1998.

Section 108(a) and (b) of Acts 1997, 75th Leg., ch. 1022, provides:

"(a) The change in law made by Sections 76 and 77 and Sections 80 through 90 of this Act takes effect January 1, 1998.

"(b) Except as provided by Subsection (c) of this section, Sections 76 and 77 and Sections 80 through 90 of this Act apply to a pending suit affecting the parent-child relationship regardless of whether the suit was commenced before, on, or after the effective date of this Act."

§ 262.110. Taking Possession of Child in Emergency With Intent to Return Home

An authorized representative of the Department of Protective and Regulatory Services, a law enforcement officer, or a juvenile probation officer may take temporary possession of a child without a court order on discovery of a child in a situation of danger to the child's physical health or safety when the sole purpose is to deliver the child without unnecessary delay to the parent, managing conservator, possessory conservator, guardian, caretaker, or custodian who is presently entitled to possession of the child.

Added by Acts 1995, 74th Leg., ch. 20, § 1, eff. April 20, 1995.

§ 262.111. Finding That Child Cannot Remain in or be Returned to Home

In the absence of a specific finding to the contrary, the issuance of a temporary restraining order or attachment pending a full adversary hearing or the issuance of an order after a full adversary hearing constitutes a finding by the court that for the child to remain in the home is contrary to the child's welfare or safety and that the emergency made efforts to prevent or eliminate the need for the removal of the child impossible or unreasonable.

Added by Acts 1995, 74th Leg., ch. 751, § 106, eff. Sept. 1, 1995.

§ 262.112. Expedited Hearing and Appeal

(a) The Department of Protective and Regulatory Services is entitled to an expedited hearing under this chapter in any proceeding in which a hearing is required if the department determines that a child should be removed from the child's home because of an immediate danger to the physical health or safety of the child.

(b) In any proceeding in which an expedited hearing is held under Subsection (a), the department, parent, guardian, or other party to the proceeding is entitled to an expedited appeal on a ruling by a court that the child may not be removed from the child's home.

(c) If a child is returned to the child's home after a removal in which the department was entitled to an expedited hearing under this section and the child is the subject of a subsequent allegation of abuse or neglect, the department or any other interested party is entitled to an expedited hearing on the removal of the child from the child's home in the manner provided by Subsection (a) and to an expedited appeal in the manner provided by Subsection (b).

Added by Acts 1995, 74th Leg., ch. 943, § 1, eff. Sept. 1, 1995. Renumbered from V.T.C.A., Family Code § 262.111 by Acts 1997, 75th Leg., ch. 165, § 31.01(29), eff. Sept. 1, 1997.

Section 13(a) of Acts 1995, 74th Leg., ch. 943 provides:

"This Act takes effect September 1, 1995, and applies to a proceeding in which an investigation of the abuse of a child is pending on or after that date."

[Sections 262.113 to 262.200 reserved for expansion]

SUBCHAPTER C. ADVERSARY HEARING

§ 262.201. Full Adversary Hearing; Findings of the Court

(a) Unless the child has already been returned to the parent, managing conservator, possessory conservator, guardian, caretaker, or custodian entitled to possession and the temporary order, if any, has been dissolved, a full adversary hearing shall be held not later than the 14th day after the date the child was taken into possession by the governmental entity.

(b) At the conclusion of the full adversary hearing, the court shall order the return of the child to the parent, managing conservator, possessory conservator, guardian, caretaker, or custodian entitled to possession unless the court finds sufficient evidence to satisfy a person of ordinary prudence and caution that:

(1) there was a danger to the physical health or safety of the child which was caused by an act or failure to act of the person entitled to possession and for the child to remain in the home is contrary to the welfare of the child;

(2) the urgent need for protection required the immediate removal of the child and makes efforts to eliminate or prevent the child's removal impossible or unreasonable; and

(3) notwithstanding reasonable efforts to eliminate the need for the child's removal and enable the child to return home, there is a substantial risk of a continuing danger if the child is returned home.

Text of subsection (c) as amended by Acts 1997, 75th Leg., ch. 600, § 5; Acts 1997, 75th Leg., ch. 603, § 1; and Acts 1997, 75th Leg., ch. 1022, § 77

(c) If the court finds sufficient evidence to satisfy a person of ordinary prudence and caution that there is a continuing danger to the physical health or safety of the child and for the child to remain in the home is contrary to the welfare of the child, the court shall:

(1) issue an appropriate temporary order under Chapter 105; and

(2) inform each parent in open court that parental and custodial rights and duties may be subject to restriction or to termination unless the parent or parents are willing and able to provide the child with a safe environment.

Text of subsection (c) as amended by Acts 1997, 75th Leg., ch. 752, § 3

(c) If the court finds sufficient evidence to satisfy a person of ordinary prudence and caution that there is a continuing danger to the physical health or safety of the child and for the child to remain in the home is contrary to the welfare of the child, the court shall issue an appropriate temporary order under Chapter 105. If the court finds that the child requires protection from family violence by a member of the child's family or household, the court shall render a protective order under Chapter 71 for the child. In this subsection, "family violence" has the meaning assigned by Section 71.01.

(d) In determining whether there is a continuing danger to the physical health or safety of the child, the court may consider whether the household to which the child would be returned includes a person who:

(1) has abused or neglected another child in a manner that caused serious injury to or the death of the other child; or

(2) has sexually abused another child.

Text of subsection (e) as added by Acts 1997, 75th Leg., ch. 575, § 21

(e) When citation by publication is needed for a parent or alleged or probable father in an action brought under this chapter because the location of the parent, alleged father, or probable father is unknown, the court may render a temporary order without delay at any time after the filing of the action without regard to whether notice of the citation by publication has been published.

Text of subsection (e) as added by Acts 1997, 75th Leg., ch. 1022, § 78

(e) The court shall place a child removed from the child's custodial parent with the child's noncustodial parent or with a relative of the child if placement with the noncustodial parent is inappropriate, unless placement with the noncustodial parent or a relative is not in the best interest of the child.

Added by Acts 1995, 74th Leg., ch. 20, § 1, eff. April 20, 1995. Amended by Acts 1995, 74th Leg., ch. 751, § 107, eff. Sept. 1, 1995; Acts 1997, 75th Leg., ch. 575, § 21, eff. Sept. 1, 1997; Acts 1997, 75th Leg., ch. 600, § 5, eff. Jan, 1, 1998; Acts 1997, 75th Leg., ch. 603, § 1, eff. Jan. 1, 1998; Acts 1997, 75th Leg., ch. 752, § 3, eff. June 17, 1997; Acts 1997, 75th Leg., ch. 1022, § 77, eff. Jan. 1, 1998; Acts 1997, 75th Leg., ch. 1022, § 78, eff. Sept. 1, 1997.

For application provisions of Acts 1997, 75th Leg., ch. 575, see note following V.T.C.A., Family Code § 102.003.

For application provision of Acts 1997, 75th Leg., ch. 600, see notes following V.T.C.A., Family Code § 162.012.

Section 14 of Acts 1997, 75th Leg., ch. 603 provides:

"(a) The change in law made by this Act takes effect January 1, 1998.

"(b) Except as provided by Subsection (c) of this section, this Act applies to a pending suit affecting the parent-child relationship regardless of whether the suit was commenced before, on, or after the effective date of this Act.

"(c) If the Department of Protective and Regulatory Services has been appointed temporary managing conservator of a child before January 1, 1998, the court shall at the first hearing conducted on or after that date under Chapter 263, Family Code, establish a date for dismissal of the suit not later than the second anniversary of the date of the hearing, unless the court has rendered a final order before the dismissal date."

For application provision of Acts 1997, 75th Leg., ch. 1022, see notes following V.T.C.A., Family Code § 262.109.

§ 262.2015. Accelerated Trial on the Merits

The court may accelerate the trial schedule to result in a final order for a child under the care of the department at an earlier date than provided by Subchapter D, Chapter 263,[1] if the court:

(1) orders at the conclusion of the full adversary hearing that the child may not be placed in the child's home;

(2) finds that the child is a victim of serious bodily injury or sexual abuse; and

(3) finds that there is probable cause to believe that a party to the suit has engaged in conduct against the child that would constitute an offense under the following provisions of the Penal Code:

(A) Section 21.11 (indecency with a child);

(B) Section 22.011 (sexual assault);

(C) Section 22.02 (aggravated assault);

(D) Section 22.021 (aggravated sexual assault);

(E) Section 22.04 (injury to a child, elderly individual, or disabled individual);

(F) Section 22.041 (abandoning or endangering child);

(G) Section 25.02 (prohibited sexual conduct);

(H) Section 43.25 (sexual performance by a child); or

(I) Section 43.26 (possession or promotion of child pornography).

Added by Acts 1997, 75th Leg., ch. 1022, § 79, eff. Sept. 1, 1997.

[1] V.T.C.A., Family Code § 263.301 et seq.

§ 262.202. Identification of Court of Continuing, Exclusive Jurisdiction

If at the conclusion of the full adversary hearing the court renders a temporary order, the governmental entity shall request identification of a court of continuing, exclusive jurisdiction as provided by Chapter 155.

Added by Acts 1995, 74th Leg., ch. 20, § 1, eff. April 20, 1995.

§ 262.203. Transfer of Suit

(a) On the motion of a party or the court's own motion, if applicable, the court that rendered the temporary order shall transfer the suit in accordance with procedures provided by Chapter 155:

(1) to the court of continuing, exclusive jurisdiction, if any; or

(2) if there is no court of continuing jurisdiction, to the court having venue of the suit affecting the parent-child relationship under Chapter 103.

(b) Notwithstanding Section 155.204, a motion to transfer under this section is timely if made at any time after the date a suit was filed under this chapter.

Added by Acts 1995, 74th Leg., ch. 20, § 1, eff. April 20, 1995. Amended by Acts 1997, 75th Leg., ch. 575, § 22, eff. Sept. 1, 1997.

For application provisions of Acts 1997, 75th Leg., ch. 575, see note following V.T.C.A., Family Code § 102.003.

§ 262.204. Temporary Order in Effect Until Superseded

(a) A temporary order rendered under this chapter is valid and enforceable until properly superseded by a court with jurisdiction to do so.

(b) A court to which the suit has been transferred may enforce by contempt or otherwise a temporary order properly issued under this chapter.

Added by Acts 1995, 74th Leg., ch. 20, § 1, eff. April 20, 1995.

CHAPTER 263. REVIEW OF PLACEMENT OF CHILDREN UNDER CARE OF DEPARTMENT OF PROTECTIVE AND REGULATORY SERVICES

SUBCHAPTER A. GENERAL PROVISIONS

§ 263.001. Definitions

(a) In this chapter:

(1) "Department" means the Department of Protective and Regulatory Services.

(2) "Child's home" means the place of residence of at least one of the child's parents.

(3) "Household" means a unit composed of persons living together in the same dwelling, without regard to whether they are related to each other.

(4) "Substitute care" means the placement of a child who is in the conservatorship of the department or an authorized agency in care outside the child's home. The term includes foster care, institutional care, adoption, or placement with a relative of the child.

(b) In the preparation and review of a service plan under this chapter, a reference to the parents of the child includes both parents of the child unless the child has only one parent or unless, after due diligence by the department in attempting to locate a parent, only one parent is located, in which case the reference is to the remaining parent.

Added by Acts 1995, 74th Leg., ch. 20, § 1, eff. April 20, 1995. Amended by Acts 1995, 74th Leg., ch. 751, § 108, eff. Sept. 1, 1995.

§ 263.002. Review of Placements by Court

In a suit affecting the parent-child relationship in which the department or an authorized agency has been appointed by the court or designated in an affidavit of relinquishment of parental rights as the temporary or permanent managing conservator of a child, the court shall hold a hearing to review the conservatorship appointment and substitute care.

Added by Acts 1995, 74th Leg., ch. 20, § 1, eff. April 20, 1995. Amended by Acts 1995, 74th Leg., ch. 751, § 109, eff. Sept. 1, 1995.

§ 263.003. Voluntary Placements: Suit

(a) A parent, managing conservator, or guardian of a child and the department may voluntarily agree to the surrender of the custody, care, or control of a child.

(b) Not later than 60 days after taking possession of or exercising control of the child, the department shall file a suit affecting the parent-child relationship under Chapter 155 in the court of continuing jurisdiction, if any, or in the court with proper venue under Chapter 103.

(c) The department shall request a review of substitute care, and its petition shall state that the purpose of the suit is to initiate periodic review of the necessity and propriety of the child's placement under this chapter.

(d) A copy of the agreement between the department and the parent, managing conservator, or guardian of the child shall be filed with the petition.

Added by Acts 1995, 74th Leg., ch. 20, § 1, eff. April 20, 1995. Amended by Acts 1995, 74th Leg., ch. 751, § 110, eff. Sept. 1, 1995.

§ 263.004. When Child is at Home

(a) If the department or authorized agency returns a child to a parent for custody, care, or control, the department or authorized agency shall notify the court having continuing jurisdiction of the suit of the department's action and, so long as the child remains under the custody, care, or control of the parent, no review of that placement is required under this chapter.

(b) If a child has been returned to a parent and the department or authorized agency resumes the custody, care, or control of the child or designates a person other than a parent to have the custody, care, or control of the child, the department or authorized agency shall notify the court of its action.

(c) If the department or authorized agency resumes the custody, care, or control of a child or designates a person other than a parent to have the custody, care, or control of the child within three months after returning the child to a parent, the period that the child was under the custody, care, or control of his or her parent may not be considered in determining the date for the next placement review hearing.

Added by Acts 1995, 74th Leg., ch. 20, § 1, eff. April 20, 1995.

§ 263.005. Enforcement of Family Service Plan

The department shall designate existing department personnel to ensure that the parties to a family service plan comply with the plan.

Added by Acts 1995, 74th Leg., ch. 943, § 5, eff. Sept. 1, 1995.

Section 13(a) of the 1995 Act provides:

"This Act takes effect September 1, 1995, and applies to a proceeding in which an investigation of the abuse of a child is pending on or after that date."

§ 263.006. Warning to Parents

At the status hearing under Subchapter C [1] and at each permanency hearing under Subchapter D [2] held after the court has rendered a temporary order appointing the department as temporary managing conservator, the court shall inform each parent in open court that parental and custodial rights and duties may be subject to restriction or to termination unless the parent or parents are willing and able to provide the child with a safe environment.

Added by Acts 1997, 75th Leg., ch. 600, § 6, eff. Jan. 1, 1998; Acts 1997, 75th Leg., ch. 603, § 2, eff. Jan. 1, 1998; Acts 1997, 75th Leg., ch. 1022, § 80, eff. Jan. 1, 1998.

[1] V.T.C.A., Family Code § 263.201 et seq.

[2] V.T.C.A., Family Code § 263.301 et seq.

For application provision of Acts 1997, 75th Leg., ch. 600, see notes following V.T.C.A., Family Code § 162.012.

For application provisions of Acts 1997, 75th Leg., ch. 603, see note following V.T.C.A., Family Code § 262.201.

For application provisions of Acts 1997, 75th Leg., ch. 1022, see notes following V.T.C.A., Family Code § 262.109.

[Sections 263.007 to 263.100 reserved for expansion]

SUBCHAPTER B. SERVICE PLAN

§ 263.101. Department to File Service Plan

Not later than the 45th day after the date of the conclusion of a full adversary hearing under Chapter 262, the department or other agency appointed as the managing conservator of a child shall file a service plan.

Added by Acts 1995, 74th Leg., ch. 20, § 1, eff. April 20, 1995.

§ 263.1015. Service Plan Not Required

A service plan is not required under this subchapter in a suit brought by the department for the termination of the parent-child relationship for a child who has been abandoned without identification and whose identity cannot be determined.

Added by Acts 1997, 75th Leg., ch. 600, § 7, eff. Jan. 1, 1998.

For application provision of Acts 1997, 75th Leg., ch. 600, see notes following V.T.C.A., Family Code § 162.012.

§ 263.102. Service Plan; Contents

(a) The service plan must:

(1) be specific;

(2) be in writing;

(3) be prepared by the department or other agency in conference with the child's parents;

(4) state appropriate deadlines;

(5) state whether the goal of the plan is:

(A) return of the child to the child's parents;

(B) termination of parental rights and placement of the child for adoption; or

(C) because of the child's special needs or exceptional circumstances, continuation of the child's care out of the child's home;

(6) state steps that are necessary to:

(A) return the child to the child's home if the placement is in foster care;

(B) enable the child to remain in the child's home with the assistance of a service plan if the placement is in the home under the department's or other agency's supervision; or

(C) otherwise provide a permanent safe placement for the child;

(7) state the actions and responsibilities that are necessary for the child's parents to take to achieve the plan goal during the period of the service plan and the assistance to be provided to the parents by the department or other authorized agency toward meeting that goal;

(8) state the name of the person with the department or other agency whom the child's parents may contact for information relating to the child if other than the person preparing the plan; and

(9) prescribe any other term or condition that the department or other agency determines to be necessary to the service plan's success.

(b) The service plan shall include the following statement:

TO THE PARENT: THIS IS A VERY IMPORTANT DOCUMENT. ITS PURPOSE IS TO HELP YOU PROVIDE YOUR CHILD WITH A SAFE ENVIRONMENT WITHIN THE REASONABLE PERIOD SPECIFIED IN THE PLAN. IF YOU ARE UNWILLING OR UNABLE TO PROVIDE YOUR CHILD WITH A SAFE ENVIRONMENT, YOUR PARENTAL AND CUSTODIAL DUTIES AND RIGHTS MAY BE RESTRICTED OR TERMINATED OR YOUR CHILD MAY NOT BE RETURNED TO YOU. THERE WILL BE A COURT HEARING AT WHICH A JUDGE WILL REVIEW THIS SERVICE PLAN.

(c) If both parents are available but do not live in the same household and do not agree to cooperate with one another in the development of a service plan for the child, the department in preparing the service plan may provide for the care of the child in the home of either parent or the homes of both parents as the best interest of the child requires.

Added by Acts 1995, 74th Leg., ch. 20, § 1, eff. April 20, 1995.

§ 263.103. Service Plan: Signing and Taking Effect

(a) Before the service plan is signed, the child's parents and the representative of the department or other agency shall discuss each term and condition of the plan.

(b) The child's parents and the person preparing the service plan shall sign the plan, and the department shall give each parent a copy of the service plan.

(c) If the department or other authorized agency determines that the child's parents are unable or unwilling to sign the service plan, the department may file the plan without the parents' signatures.

(d) The plan takes effect when:

(1) the child's parents and the appropriate representative of the department or other authorized agency sign the plan; or

(2) the department or other authorized agency files the plan without the parents' signatures.

(e) The service plan is in effect until amended by the court.

Added by Acts 1995, 74th Leg., ch. 20, § 1, eff. April 20, 1995.

§ 263.104. Amended Service Plan

(a) The service plan may be amended at any time.

(b) The amended service plan supersedes the previously filed service plan and takes effect when:

(1) the child's parents and the appropriate representative of the department or other authorized agency sign the plan; or

(2) the department or other authorized agency determines that the child's parents are unable or unwilling to sign the amended plan and files it without the parents' signatures.

(c) The amended service plan remains in effect until amended by the court.

Added by Acts 1995, 74th Leg., ch. 20, § 1, eff. April 20, 1995.

§ 263.105. Review of Service Plan

(a) The service plan currently in effect shall be filed with the court along with the next required status report.

(b) The court shall review the plan at the next required hearing under this chapter after the plan is filed.

Added by Acts 1995, 74th Leg., ch. 20, § 1, eff. April 20, 1995.

§ 263.106. Court Implementation of Service Plan

The court may render appropriate orders to implement or require compliance with an original or amended service plan.

Added by Acts 1995, 74th Leg., ch. 20, § 1, eff. April 20, 1995.

[Sections 263.107 to 263.200 reserved for expansion]

SUBCHAPTER C. STATUS HEARING

§ 263.201. Status Hearing; Time

Not later than the 60th day after the date the court renders a temporary order appointing the department as temporary managing conservator of a child, the court shall hold a status hearing to review the child's status and the permanency plan developed for the child.

Added by Acts 1995, 74th Leg., ch. 20, § 1, eff. April 20, 1995. Amended by Acts 1997, 75th Leg., ch. 600, § 8, eff. Jan. 1, 1998; Acts 1997, 75th Leg., ch. 603, § 3, eff. Jan. 1, 1998; Acts 1997, 75th Leg., ch. 1022, § 81, eff. Jan. 1, 1998.

For application provision of Acts 1997, 75th Leg., ch. 600, see notes following V.T.C.A., Family Code § 162.012.

For application provisions of Acts 1997, 75th Leg., ch. 603, see note following V.T.C.A., Family Code § 262.201.

For application provision of Acts 1997, 75th Leg., ch. 1022, see notes following V.T.C.A., Family Code § 262.109.

§ 263.202. Status Hearing; Findings

(a) If all parties entitled to citation and notice under this chapter were not served, the court shall make findings as to whether:

(1) the department or other agency has exercised due diligence to locate all necessary persons; and

(2) if only one parent is before the court, that parent has furnished to the department all available information necessary to locate an absent parent through the parental locator service.

(b) A status hearing shall be limited to matters related to the contents and execution of the service plan filed with the court. The court shall review the service plan that the department or other agency filed under this chapter for reasonableness, accuracy, and compliance with requirements of court orders and make findings as to whether:

(1) a plan that has the goal of returning the child to the child's parents adequately ensures that reasonable efforts are made to enable the child's parents to provide a safe environment for the child; and

(2) the child's parents have reviewed and understand the service plan and have been advised that unless the parents are willing and able to provide the child with a safe environment, even with the assistance of a service plan, within the reasonable period of time specified in the plan, the parents' parental and custodial duties and rights may be subject to restriction or to termination under this code or the child may not be returned to the parents.

(c) The court shall advise the parties that progress under the service plan will be reviewed at all subsequent hearings.

Added by Acts 1995, 74th Leg., ch. 20, § 1, eff. April 20, 1995. Amended by Acts 1995, 74th Leg., ch. 751, § 111, eff. Sept. 1, 1995.

[Sections 263.203 to 263.300 reserved for expansion]

SUBCHAPTER D. PERMANENCY HEARINGS

Acts 1997, 75th Leg., ch. 600, § 9, Acts 1997 75th Leg., ch. 603, § 4, and Acts 1997 75th Leg., ch. 1022, § 82 all amended the Subchapter heading by substituting "Permanency" for "Review".

§ 263.301. Notice

(a) Notice of a permanency hearing shall be given as provided by Rule 21a, Texas Rules of Civil Procedure, to all persons entitled to notice of the hearing.

(b) The following persons are entitled to at least 10 days' notice of a permanency hearing and are entitled to present evidence and be heard at the hearing:

(1) the department;

(2) the foster parent or director of the group home or institution where the child is residing;

(3) each parent of the child;

(4) the managing conservator or guardian of the child;

(5) an attorney ad litem appointed for the child under Chapter 107;

(6) a volunteer advocate appointed for the child under Chapter 107; and

(7) any other person or agency named by the court to have an interest in the child's welfare.

(c) If a person entitled to notice under Chapter 102 or this section has not been served, the court shall review the department's or other agency's efforts at attempting to locate all necessary persons and requesting service of citation and the assistance of a parent in providing information necessary to locate an absent parent.

Added by Acts 1995, 74th Leg., ch. 20, § 1, eff. April 20, 1995. Amended by Acts 1997, 75th Leg., ch. 600, § 10, eff. Jan. 1, 1998; Acts 1997, 75th Leg., ch. 603, § 5, eff. Jan. 1, 1998; Acts 1997, 75th Leg., ch. 1022, § 83, eff. Jan. 1, 1998.

For application provision of Acts 1997, 75th Leg., ch. 600, see notes following V.T.C.A., Family Code § 162.012.

For application provisions of Acts 1997, 75th Leg., ch. 603, see note following V.T.C.A., Family Code § 262.201.

For application provision of Acts 1997, 75th Leg., ch. 1022, see notes following V.T.C.A., Family Code § 262.109.

Section 108(c) of Acts 1997, 75th Leg., ch. 1022 provides:

"If the Department of Protective and Regulatory Services has been appointed temporary managing conservator of a child before January 1, 1998, the court shall at the first hearing conducted on or after that date under Chapter 263, Family Code, establish a date for dismissal of the suit not later than the second anniversary of the date of the hearing, unless the court has rendered a final order before the dismissal date."

§ 263.302. Child's Attendance at Hearing

The child shall attend each permanency hearing unless the court specifically excuses the child's attendance. Failure by the child to attend a hearing does not affect the validity of an order rendered at the hearing.

Added by Acts 1995, 74th Leg., ch. 20, § 1, eff. April 20, 1995. Amended by Acts 1997, 75th Leg., ch. 600, § 11, eff. Jan. 1, 1998; Acts 1997, 75th Leg., ch. 603, § 6, eff. Jan. 1, 1998; Acts 1997, 75th Leg., ch. 1022, § 84, eff. Jan. 1, 1998.

For application provision of Acts 1997, 75th Leg., ch. 600, see notes following V.T.C.A., Family Code § 162.012.

For application provisions of Acts 1997, 75th Leg., ch. 603, see note following V.T.C.A., Family Code § 262.201.

For application provision of Acts 1997, 75th Leg., ch. 1022, see notes following V.T.C.A., Family Code § 262.109.

§ 263.3025. Permanency Plan

(a) The department shall prepare a permanency plan for a child for whom the department has been appointed temporary managing conservator. The department shall give a copy of the plan to each person entitled to notice under Section 263.301(b) not later than the 10th day before the date of the child's first permanency hearing.

(b) In addition to the requirements of the department rules governing permanency planning, the permanency plan must contain the information required to be included in a permanency progress report under Section 263.303.

(c) The department shall modify the permanency plan for a child as required by the circumstances and needs of the child.

Added by Acts 1997, 75th Leg., ch. 600, § 12, eff. Jan. 1, 1998; Acts 1997, 75th Leg., ch. 603, § 7, eff. Jan. 1, 1998; Acts 1997, 75th Leg., ch. 1022, § 85, eff. Jan. 1, 1998.

For application provision of Acts 1997, 75th Leg., ch. 600, see notes following V.T.C.A., Family Code § 162.012.

For application provisions of Acts 1997, 75th Leg., ch. 603, see note following V.T.C.A., Family Code § 262.201.

For application provision of Acts 1997, 75th Leg., ch. 1022, see notes following V.T.C.A., Family Code § 262.109.

§ 263.303. Permanency Progress Report

(a) Not later than the 10th day before the date set for each permanency hearing other than the first permanency hearing, the department or other authorized agency shall file with the court and provide to each party, the child's attorney ad litem, and the child's volunteer advocate a permanency progress report unless the court orders a different period for providing the report.

(b) The permanency progress report must:

(1) recommend that the suit be dismissed; or

(2) recommend that the suit continue, and:

(A) identify the date for dismissal of the suit under this chapter;

(B) provide:

(i) the name of any person entitled to notice under Chapter 102 who has not been served;

(ii) a description of the efforts by the department or another agency to locate and request service of citation; and

(iii) a description of each parent's assistance in providing information necessary to locate an unserved party;

(C) evaluate the parties' compliance with temporary orders and with the service plan;

(D) evaluate whether the child's placement in substitute care meets the child's needs and recommend other plans or services to meet the child's special needs or circumstances;

(E) describe the permanency plan for the child and recommend actions necessary to ensure that a final order consistent with that permanency plan is rendered before the date for dismissal of the suit under this chapter; and

(F) with respect to a child 16 years of age or older, identify the services needed to assist the child in the transition to adult life.

(c) A parent whose parental rights are the subject of a suit affecting the parent-child relationship, the attorney for that parent, or the child's attorney ad litem or guardian ad litem may file a response to the department's or other agency's report filed under Subsection (b). A response must be filed not later than the third day before the date of the hearing.

Added by Acts 1995, 74th Leg., ch. 20, § 1, eff. April 20, 1995. Amended by Acts 1995, 74th Leg., ch. 751, § 112, eff. Sept. 1, 1995; Acts 1997, 75th Leg., ch. 600, § 13, eff. Jan. 1, 1998; Acts 1997, 75th Leg., ch. 603, § 8, eff. Jan. 1, 1998; Acts 1997, 75th Leg., ch. 1022, § 86, eff. Jan. 1, 1998.

For application provisions of Acts 1997, 75th Leg., ch. 603, see note following V.T.C.A., Family Code § 262.201.

For application provision of Acts 1997, 75th Leg., ch. 1022, see notes following V.T.C.A., Family Code § 262.109.

§ 263.304. Initial Permanency Hearing; Time

Not later than the 180th day after the date the court renders a temporary order appointing the department as temporary managing conservator of a child, the court shall hold a permanency hearing to review the status of, and permanency plan for, the child to ensure that a final order consistent with that permanency plan is rendered before the date for dismissal of the suit under this chapter.

Added by Acts 1995, 74th Leg., ch. 20, § 1, eff. April 20, 1995. Amended by Acts 1995, 74th Leg., ch. 751, § 113, eff. Sept. 1, 1995; Acts 1997, 75th Leg., ch. 600, § 14, eff. Jan. 1, 1998; Acts 1997, 75th Leg., ch. 603, § 9, eff. Jan. 1, 1998; Acts 1997, 75th Leg., ch. 1022, § 87, eff. Jan. 1, 1998.

For application provision of Acts 1997, 75th Leg., ch. 600, see notes following V.T.C.A., Family Code § 162.012.

For application provisions of Acts 1997, 75th Leg., ch. 603, see note following V.T.C.A., Family Code § 262.201.

For application provision of Acts 1997, 75th Leg., ch. 1022, see notes following V.T.C.A., Family Code § 262.109.

§ 263.305. Subsequent Permanency Hearings

A subsequent permanency hearing before entry of a final order shall be held not later than the 120th day after the date of the last permanency hearing in the suit. For good cause shown or on the court's own motion, the court may order more frequent hearings.

Added by Acts 1995, 74th Leg., ch. 20, § 1, eff. April 20, 1995. Amended by Acts 1997, 75th Leg., ch. 600, § 15, eff. Jan. 1, 1998; Acts 1997, 75th Leg., ch. 603, § 10, eff. Jan. 1, 1998; Acts 1997, 75th Leg., ch. 1022, § 88, eff. Jan. 1, 1998.

For application provision of Acts 1997, 75th Leg., ch. 600, see notes following V.T.C.A., Family Code § 162.012.

For application provisions of Acts 1997, 75th Leg., ch. 603, see note following V.T.C.A., Family Code § 262.201.

For application provision of Acts 1997, 75th Leg., ch. 1022, see notes following V.T.C.A., Family Code § 262.109.

§ 263.306. Permanency Hearings: Procedure

At each permanency hearing the court shall :

(1) identify all persons or parties present at the hearing or those given notice but failing to appear;

(2) review the efforts of the department or another agency in:

(A) attempting to locate all necessary persons;

(B) requesting service of citation; and

(C) obtaining the assistance of a parent in providing information necessary to locate an absent parent;

(3) return the child to the parent or parents if the child's parent or parents are willing and able to provide the child with a safe environment and the return of the child is in the child's best interest;

(4) place the child with a person or entity, other than a parent, entitled to service under Chapter 102 if the person or entity is willing and able to provide the child with a safe environment and the return of the child is in the child's best interest;

(5) evaluate the department's efforts to identify relatives who could provide the child with a safe environment, if the child is not returned to a parent or another person or entity entitled to service under Chapter 102;

(6) evaluate the parties' compliance with temporary orders and the service plan;

(7) determine whether:

(A) the child continues to need substitute care;

(B) the child's current placement is appropriate for meeting the child's needs; and

(C) other plans or services are needed to meet the child's special needs or circumstances;

(8) if the child is placed in institutional care, determine whether efforts have been made to ensure placement of the child in the least restrictive environment consistent with the best interest and special needs of the child;

(9) if the child is 16 years of age or older, order services that are needed to assist the child in making the transition from substitute care to independent living if the services are available in the community;

(10) determine plans, services, and further temporary orders necessary to ensure that a final order is rendered before the date for dismissal of the suit under this chapter; and

(11) determine the date for dismissal of the suit under this chapter and give notice in open court to all parties of:

(A) the dismissal date;

(B) the date of the next permanency hearing; and

(C) the date the suit is set for trial.

Added by Acts 1995, 74th Leg., ch. 20, § 1, eff. April 20, 1995. Amended by Acts 1995, 74th Leg., ch. 751, § 114, eff. Sept. 1, 1995; Acts 1997, 75th Leg., ch. 600, § 16, eff. Jan. 1, 1998; Acts 1997, 75th Leg., ch. 603, § 11, eff. Jan. 1, 1998; Acts 1997, 75th Leg., ch. 1022, § 89, eff. Jan. 1, 1998.

For application provision of Acts 1997, 75th Leg., ch. 600, see notes following V.T.C.A., Family Code § 162.012.

For application provisions of Acts 1997, 75th Leg., ch. 603, see note following V.T.C.A., Family Code § 262.201.

For application provision of Acts 1997, 75th Leg., ch. 1022, see notes following V.T.C.A., Family Code § 262.109.

§ 263.307. Factors in Determining Best Interest of Child

(a) In considering the factors established by this section, the prompt and permanent placement of the child in a safe environment is presumed to be in the child's best interest.

(b) The following factors should be considered by the court, the department, and other authorized agencies in determining whether the child's parents are willing and able to provide the child with a safe environment:

(1) the child's age and physical and mental vulnerabilities;

(2) the frequency and nature of out-of-home placements;

(3) the magnitude, frequency, and circumstances of the harm to the child;

(4) whether the child has been the victim of repeated harm after the initial report and intervention by the department or other agency;

(5) whether the child is fearful of living in or returning to the child's home;

(6) the results of psychiatric, psychological, or developmental evaluations of the child, the child's parents, other family members, or others who have access to the child's home;

(7) whether there is a history of abusive or assaultive conduct by the child's family or others who have access to the child's home;

(8) whether there is a history of substance abuse by the child's family or others who have access to the child's home;

(9) whether the perpetrator of the harm to the child is identified;

(10) the willingness and ability of the child's family to seek out, accept, and complete counseling services and to cooperate with and facilitate an appropriate agency's close supervision;

(11) the willingness and ability of the child's family to effect positive environmental and personal changes within a reasonable period of time;

(12) whether the child's family demonstrates adequate parenting skills, including providing the child and other children under the family's care with:

(A) minimally adequate health and nutritional care;

(B) care, nurturance, and appropriate discipline consistent with the child's physical and psychological development;

(C) guidance and supervision consistent with the child's safety;

(D) a safe physical home environment;

(E) protection from repeated exposure to violence even though the violence may not be directed at the child; and

(F) an understanding of the child's needs and capabilities; and

(13) whether an adequate social support system consisting of an extended family and friends is available to the child.

(c) In the case of a child 16 years of age or older, the following guidelines should be considered by the court in determining whether to adopt the permanency plan submitted by the department:

(1) whether the permanency plan submitted to the court includes the services planned for the child to make the transition from foster care to independent living; and

(2) whether this transition is in the best interest of the child.

Added by Acts 1995, 74th Leg., ch. 20, § 1, eff. April 20, 1995.

§§ 263.308, 263.309. Repealed by Acts 1997, 75th Leg., ch. 603, § 13, eff. Jan. 1, 1998; Acts 1997, 75th Leg., ch. 1022, § 104(a), eff. Sept. 1, 1997.

SUBCHAPTER E. FINAL ORDER FOR CHILD UNDER DEPARTMENT CARE

§ 263.401. Dismissal After One Year; Extension

(a) Unless the court has rendered a final order or granted an extension under Subsection (b), on the first Monday after the first anniversary of the date the court rendered a temporary order appointing the department as temporary managing conservator, the court shall dismiss the suit affecting the parent-child relationship filed by the department that requests termination of the parent-child relationship or requests that the department be named conservator of the child.

(b) On or before the time described by Subsection (a) for the dismissal of the suit, the court may extend the court's jurisdiction of the suit for a period stated in the extension order, but not longer than 180 days after the time described by Subsection (a), if the court has continuing jurisdiction of the suit and the appointment of the department as temporary managing conservator is in the best interest of the child. If the court grants an extension, the extension order must also:

(1) schedule the new date for dismissal of the suit; and

(2) make further temporary orders for the safety and welfare of the child as necessary to avoid further delay in resolving the suit.

(c) If the court grants an extension, the court shall render a final order or dismiss the suit on or before the date specified in the extension order and may not grant an additional extension.

(d) For purposes of this section, a final order is an order that:

(1) requires that a child be returned to the child's parent;

(2) names a relative of the child or another person as the child's managing conservator;

(3) without terminating the parent-child relationship, appoints the department as the managing conservator of the child; or

(4) terminates the parent-child relationship and appoints a relative of the child, another suitable person, or the department as managing conservator of the child.

Added by Acts 1997, 75th Leg., ch. 600, § 17, eff. Sept. 1, 1997; Acts 1997, 75th Leg., ch. 603, § 12, eff. Jan. 1, 1998; Acts 1997, 75th Leg., ch. 1022, § 90, eff. Jan. 1, 1998.

For application provisions of Acts 1997, 75th Leg., ch. 603, see note following V.T.C.A., Family Code § 262.201.

For application provisions of Acts 1997, 75th Leg., ch. 1022, see note following V.T.C.A., Family Code § 262.109.

§ 263.402. Return of Child to Parent or Placement With Relative

(a) Notwithstanding Section 263.401, the court may retain jurisdiction and not dismiss the suit or render a final order as required by that section if the court renders a temporary order that:

(1) finds that retaining jurisdiction under this section is in the best interest of the child;

(2) orders the department to return the child to the child's parent or to place the child with a relative of the child;

(3) orders the department to continue to serve as temporary managing conservator of the child; and

(4) orders the department to monitor the child's placement to ensure that the child is in a safe environment.

(b) If the court renders an order under this section, the court shall:

(1) include in the order specific findings regarding the grounds for the order; and

(2) schedule a new date, not later than the 180th day after the date the temporary order is rendered, for dismissal of the suit.

(c) If a child placed with a parent or relative under this section must be moved from that home by the department before the dismissal of the suit or the rendering of a final order, the court shall, at the time of the move, schedule a new date for dismissal of the suit. The new dismissal date may not be later than the original dismissal date established under Section 263.401 or the 180th day after the date the child is moved under this subsection, whichever date is later.

(d) If the court renders an order under this section, the court must include in the order specific findings regarding the grounds for the order.

Added by Acts 1997, 75th Leg., ch. 600, § 17, eff. Sept. 1, 1997; Acts 1997, 75th Leg., ch. 603, § 12, eff. Jan. 1, 1997; Acts 1997, 75th Leg., ch. 1022, § 90, eff. Jan. 1, 1997.

For application provisions of Acts 1997, 75th Leg., ch. 603, see note following V.T.C.A., Family Code § 262.201.

For application provisions of Acts 1997, 75th Leg., ch. 1022, see note following V.T.C.A., Family Code § 262.109.

§ 263.403. Final Order Appointing Department as Managing Conservator Without Terminating Parental Rights

(a) The court may render a final order appointing the department as managing conservator of the child without terminating the rights of the parent of the child if the court finds that:

(1) appointment of a parent as managing conservator would not be in the best interest of the child because the appointment would significantly impair the child's physical health or emotional development; and

(2) it would not be in the best interest of the child to appoint a relative of the child or another person as managing conservator.

(b) In determining whether the department should be appointed as managing conservator of the child without terminating the rights of a parent of the child, the court shall take the following factors into consideration:

(1) that the child will reach 18 years of age in not less than three years;

(2) that the child is 12 years of age or older and has expressed a strong desire against termination or being adopted;

(3) that the child has special medical or behavioral needs that make adoption of the child unlikely; and

(4) the needs and desires of the child.

Added by Acts 1997, 75th Leg., ch. 600, § 17, eff. Sept. 1, 1997; Acts 1997, 75th Leg., ch. 603, § 12, eff. Jan. 1, 1998; Acts 1997, 75th Leg., ch. 1022, § 90, eff. Jan. 1, 1998.

Section 22(c) of Acts 1997, 75th Leg., ch. 600 provides:

"If the Department of Protective and Regulatory Services has been appointed temporary managing conservator of a child before January 1, 1998, the court shall at the first hearing conducted on or after that date under Chapter 263, Family Code, establish a date for dismissal of the suit not later than the second anniversary of the date of the hearing, unless the court has rendered a final order before the dismissal date."

For application provisions of Acts 1997, 75th Leg., ch. 603, see note following V.T.C.A., Family Code § 262.201.

For application provisions of Acts 1997, 75th Leg., ch. 1022, see note following V.T.C.A., Family Code § 262.109.

§ 263.404. Court Information System

The Office of Court Administration of the Texas Judicial System shall consult with the courts presiding over cases brought by the department for the protection of children to develop an information system to track compliance with the requirements of this subchapter for the timely disposition of those cases.

Added by Acts 1997, 75th Leg., ch. 600, § 17, eff. Sept. 1, 1997.

[Sections 263.405 to 263.500 reserved for expansion]

SUBCHAPTER F. PLACEMENT REVIEW HEARINGS

§ 263.501. Placement Review After Final Order

(a) If the department has been named as a child's managing conservator in a final order that does not include termination of parental rights, the court shall conduct a placement review hearing at least once every six months until the child becomes an adult.

(b) If the department has been named as a child's managing conservator in a final order that terminates a parent's parental rights, the court shall conduct a placement review hearing at least once every six months until the date the child is adopted or the child becomes an adult.

(c) Notice of a placement review hearing shall be given as provided by Rule 21a, Texas Rules of Civil Procedure, to each person entitled to notice of the hearing.

(d) The following are entitled to not less than 10 days' notice of a placement review hearing:

(1) the department;

(2) the foster parent or director of the group home or institution in which the child is residing;

(3) each parent of the child;

(4) each possessory conservator or guardian of the child;

(5) the child's attorney ad litem and volunteer advocate, if the appointments were not dismissed in the final order; and

(6) any other person or agency named by the court as having an interest in the child's welfare.

(e) The court may dispense with the requirement that the child attend a placement review hearing.

Added by Acts 1997, 75th Leg., ch. 600, § 17, eff. Sept. 1, 1997; Acts 1997, 75th Leg., ch. 603, § 12, eff. Jan. 1, 1998; Acts 1997, 75th Leg., ch. 1022, § 90, eff. Jan. 1, 1997.

For application provisions of Acts 1997, 75th Leg., ch. 603, see note following V.T.C.A., Family Code § 262.201.

For application provisions of Acts 1997, 75th Leg., ch. 1022, see note following V.T.C.A., Family Code § 262.109.

§ 263.502. Placement Review Report

(a) Not later than the 10th day before the date set for a placement review hearing, the department or other authorized agency shall file a placement review report with the court and provide a copy to each person entitled to notice under Section 263.501(d).

(b) For good cause shown, the court may order a different time for filing the placement review report or may order that a report is not required for a specific hearing.

(c) The placement review report must:

(1) evaluate whether the child's current placement is appropriate for meeting the child's needs;

(2) evaluate whether efforts have been made to ensure placement of the child in the least restrictive environment consistent with the best interest and special needs of the child if the child is placed in institutional care;

(3) identify the services that are needed to assist a child who is at least 16 years of age in making the transition from substitute care to independent living if the services are available in the community;

(4) identify other plans or services that are needed to meet the child's special needs or circumstances; and

(5) describe the efforts of the department or authorized agency to place the child for adoption if parental rights to the child have been terminated and the child is eligible for adoption.

Added by Acts 1997, 75th Leg., ch. 600, § 17, eff. Sept. 1, 1997; Acts 1997, 75th Leg., ch. 603, § 12, eff. Jan. 1, 1998; Acts 1997, 75th Leg., ch. 1022, § 90, eff. Jan. 1, 1998.

For application provisions of Acts 1997, 75th Leg., ch. 603, see note following V.T.C.A., Family Code § 262.201.

For application provisions of Acts 1997, 75th Leg., ch. 1022, see note following V.T.C.A., Family Code § 262.109.

§ 263.503. Placement Review Hearings; Procedure

At each placement review hearing, the court shall determine whether:

(1) the child's current placement is appropriate for meeting the child's needs;

(2) efforts have been made to ensure placement of the child in the least restrictive environment consistent with the best interest and special needs of the child if the child is placed in institutional care;

(3) the services that are needed to assist a child who is at least 16 years of age in making the transition from substitute care to independent living are available in the community;

(4) other plans or services are needed to meet the child's special needs or circumstances; and

(5) the department or authorized agency has exercised due diligence in attempting to place the child for adoption if parental rights to the child have been terminated and the child is eligible for adoption.

Added by Acts 1997, 75th Leg., ch. 600, § 17, eff. Sept. 1, 1997; Acts 1997, 75th Leg., ch. 603, § 12, eff. Jan. 1, 1998; Acts 1997, 75th Leg., ch. 1022, § 90, eff. Jan. 1, 1998.

For application provisions of Acts 1997, 75th Leg., ch. 603, see note following V.T.C.A., Family Code § 262.201.

For application provisions of Acts 1997, 75th Leg., ch. 1022, see notes following V.T.C.A., Family Code § 262.109

CHAPTER 264. CHILD WELFARE SERVICES

SUBCHAPTER A. GENERAL PROVISIONS

§ 264.001. Definition

In this chapter, "department" means the Department of Protective and Regulatory Services.

Added by Acts 1995, 74th Leg., ch. 20, § 1, eff. April 20, 1995.

§ 264.002. Duties of Department

(a) The department shall:

(1) promote the enforcement of all laws for the protection of abused and neglected children; and

(2) take the initiative in all matters involving the interests of children where adequate provision has not already been made.

(b) The department shall give special attention to the dissemination of information through bulletins and visits, where practical, to all agencies operating under a provision of law affecting the welfare of children.

(c) Through the county child welfare boards, the department shall work in conjunction with the commissioners courts, juvenile boards, and all other officers and agencies involved in the protection of children. The department may use and allot funds for the establishment and maintenance of homes, schools, and institutions for the care, protection, education, and training of children in conjunction with a juvenile board, a county or city board, or any other agency.

(d) The department shall visit and study the conditions in state-supported eleemosynary institutions for children and shall make actions for the management and operation of the institutions that ensure that the children receive the best possible training in contemplation of their earliest discharge from the institutions.

(e) The department may not spend state funds to accomplish the purposes of this chapter unless the funds have been specifically appropriated for those purposes.

Added by Acts 1995, 74th Leg., ch. 20, § 1, eff. April 20, 1995.

§ 264.003. Memorandum of Understanding on Services for Multiproblem Children and Youth

(a) The Department of Protective and Regulatory Services, the Texas Department of Mental Health and Mental Retardation, the Texas Department of Health, the Texas Youth Commission, the Texas Juvenile Probation Commission, the Texas Rehabilitation Commission, the Texas Commission for the Blind, and the Central Education Agency shall adopt a joint memorandum of understanding to implement a system of local level interagency staffing groups to coordinate services for multiproblem children and youth.

(b) The memorandum must:

(1) clarify the financial and statutory responsibilities of each agency in relation to multiproblem children and youth, including subcategories of funding for different services such as prevention, family preservation and strengthening, emergency shelter, diagnosis and evaluation, residential care, aftercare, information and referral, and investigation services;

(2) include a functional definition of "multiproblem children and youth";

(3) define procedures for interagency cost sharing;

(4) define procedures aimed at eliminating duplication of services relating to assessment and diagnosis, treatment, residential placement and care, and case management of multiproblem children and youth;

(5) define procedures for addressing disputes between the agencies that relate to the agencies' areas of service responsibilities;

(6) provide that each local level interagency staffing group will include a local representative of the department and each agency and not more than five representatives of local private sector youth agencies;

(7) provide that if an agency is not able to provide all the services a child requires, the agency may submit the child's case history to the local level interagency staffing group for consideration;

(8) provide that a local level interagency staffing group may be called together by a representative of any member agency;

(9) provide that an agency may be excused from attending a meeting if the staffing group determines that the age or needs of the children or youth to be considered are clearly not within the agency's service responsibilities;

(10) provide that records that are used or developed by the department and other agencies and that relate to a particular child are confidential and may not be released to any other person or agency except as provided in this section or by other law; and

(11) provide a procedure that permits the department and other agencies to share confidential information while preserving the confidential nature of the information.

(c) The agencies that participate in the formulation of the memorandum of understanding shall consult with and solicit input from advocacy and consumer groups.

(d) Not later than the last month of each state fiscal year, the department and the other agencies listed in this section shall review and update the memorandum.

(e) Each agency by rule shall adopt the memorandum of understanding and all revisions to the memorandum.

Added by Acts 1995, 74th Leg., ch. 20, § 1, eff. April 20, 1995.

§ 264.004. Allocation of State Funds

(a) The department shall establish a method of allocating state funds for children's protective services programs that encourages and rewards the contribution of funds or services from all persons, including local governmental entities.

(b) Except as provided by this subsection, if a contribution of funds or services is made to support a children's protective services program in a particular county, the department shall use the contribution to benefit that program. The department may use the contribution for another purpose only if the commissioners court of the county gives the department written permission.

(c) The department may use state and federal funds to provide benefits or services to children and families who are otherwise eligible for the benefits or services, including foster care, adoption assistance, medical assistance, family reunification services, and other child protective services and related benefits without regard to the immigration status of the child or the child's family.

Added by Acts 1995, 74th Leg., ch. 20, § 1, eff. April 20, 1995. Amended by Acts 1997, 75th Leg., ch. 575, § 23, eff. Sept. 1, 1997.

§ 264.005. County Child Welfare Boards

(a) The commissioners court of a county may appoint a child welfare board for the county. The commissioners court and the department shall determine the size of the board and the qualifications of its members. However, a board must have not less than seven and not more than 15 members, and the members must be residents of the county. The members shall serve at the pleasure of the commissioners court and may be removed by the court for just cause. The members serve without compensation.

(b) With the approval of the department, two or more counties may establish a joint child welfare board if that action is found to be more practical in accomplishing the purposes of this chapter. A board representing more than one county has the same powers as a board representing a single county and is subject to the same conditions and liabilities.

(c) The members of a county child welfare board shall select a presiding officer and shall perform the duties required by the commissioners court and the department to accomplish the purposes of this chapter.

(d) A county child welfare board is an entity of the department for purposes of providing coordinated state and local public welfare services for children and their families and for the coordinated use of federal, state, and local funds for these services. The child welfare board shall work with the commissioners court.

(e) A county child welfare board is a governmental unit for the purposes of Chapter 101, Civil Practice and Remedies Code.

(f) A county child protective services board member may receive information that is confidential under Section 40.005, Human Resources Code, or Section 261.201 when the board member is acting in the member's official capacity.

(g) A child welfare board may conduct a closed meeting under Section 551.101, Government Code, to discuss, consider, or act on a matter that is confidential under Section 40.005, Human Resources Code, or Section 261.201.

Added by Acts 1995, 74th Leg., ch. 20, § 1, eff. April 20, 1995. Amended by Acts 1997, 75th Leg., ch. 575, § 24, eff. Sept. 1, 1997.

§ 264.006. County Funds

The commissioners court of a county may appropriate funds from its general fund or any other fund for the administration of its county child welfare board. The court may provide for services to and support of children in need of protection and care without regard to the immigration status of the child or the child's family.

Added by Acts 1995, 74th Leg., ch. 20, § 1, eff. April 20, 1995. Amended by Acts 1997, 75th Leg., ch. 575, § 25, eff. Sept. 1, 1997.

§ 264.007. Cooperation With Department of Health and Human Services

The department is the state agency designated to cooperate with the United States Department of Health and Human Services in:

(1) establishing, extending, and strengthening public welfare services for the protection and care of abused or neglected children;

(2) developing state services for the encouragement and assistance of adequate methods of community child welfare organizations and paying part of the cost of district, county, or other local child welfare services in rural areas and in other areas of special need; and

(3) developing necessary plans to implement the services contemplated in this section and to comply with the rules of the United States Department of Health and Human Services under the federal Social Security Act (42 U.S.C. Section 651 et seq.).

Added by Acts 1995, 74th Leg., ch. 20, § 1, eff. April 20, 1995.

§ 264.008. Child Welfare Service Fund

The child welfare service fund is a special fund in the state treasury. The fund shall be used to administer the child welfare services provided by the department.

Added by Acts 1995, 74th Leg., ch. 20, § 1, eff. April 20, 1995.

§ 264.009. Legal Representation of Department

(a) Except as provided by Subsection (b), (c), or (f), in any action under this code, the department shall be represented in court by the county attorney of the county where the action is brought, unless the district attorney or criminal district attorney of the county elects to provide representation.

(b) If the county attorney, district attorney, or criminal district attorney is unable to represent the department in an action under this code because of a conflict of interest or because special circumstances exist, the attorney general shall represent the department in the action.

(c) If the attorney general is unable to represent the department in an action under this code, the attorney general shall deputize an attorney who has contracted with the department under Subsection (d) or an attorney employed by the department under Subsection (e) to represent the department in the action.

(d) Subject to the approval of the attorney general, the department may contract with a private attorney to represent the department in an action under this code.

(e) The department may employ attorneys to represent the department in an action under this code.

(f) In a county with a population of 2.8 million or more, in an action under this code, the department shall be represented in court by the attorney who represents the state in civil cases in the district or county court of the county where the action is brought. If such attorney is unable to represent the department in an action under this code because of a conflict of interest or because special circumstances exist, the attorney general shall represent the department in the action.

Added by Acts 1995, 74th Leg., ch. 20, § 1, eff. April 20, 1995. Amended by Acts 1995, 74th Leg., ch. 751, § 116, eff. Sept. 1, 1995; Acts 1997, 75th Leg., ch. 1022, § 91, eff. Sept. 1, 1997.

§ 264.010. Child Abuse Plan; Limitation on Expenditure of Funds

(a) Funds appropriated for protective services, child and family services, and the purchased service system for the department may only be spent on or after March 1, 1996, in a county that provides the department with a child abuse prevention and protection plan. If a plan is not submitted to the department under this section, the department shall document the county's failure to submit a plan and may spend appropriated funds in the county to carry out the department's duties under this subtitle.

(b) A child abuse prevention and protection plan may be submitted by the governing body of a county or of a regional council of governments in which the county is an active participant.

(c) The department may not require a child abuse prevention and protection plan to exceed five double-spaced letter-size pages. The county or council of governments may voluntarily provide a longer plan.

(d) A child abuse prevention and protection plan must:

(1) specify the manner of communication between entities who are parties to the plan, including the department, the Texas Department of Human Services, local law enforcement agencies, the county and district attorneys, members of the medical and social service community, foster parents, and child advocacy groups; and

(2) provide other information concerning the prevention and investigation of child abuse in the area for which the plan is adopted.

Added by Acts 1995, 74th Leg., ch. 943, § 6, eff. Sept. 1, 1995.

Section 13(a) of the 1995 Act provides:

"This Act takes effect September 1, 1995, and applies to a proceeding in which an investigation of the abuse of a child is pending on or after that date."

§ 264.011. Local Accounts

(a) The department may establish and maintain local bank or savings accounts for a child who is under the managing conservatorship of the department as necessary to administer funds received in trust for or on behalf of the child.

(b) Funds maintained in an account under this section may be used by the department to support the child, including for the payment of foster care expenses, or may be paid to a person providing care for the child.

Added by Acts 1997, 75th Leg., ch. 575, § 26, eff. Sept. 1, 1997.

§ 264.012. Funeral Expenses for Child in Foster Care

The department may spend funds appropriated for the child protective services program to pay reasonable and necessary funeral expenses for a child for whom the department has been appointed managing conservator and who dies in foster care.

Added by Acts 1997, 75th Leg., ch. 575, § 26, eff. Sept. 1, 1997.

[Sections 264.013 to 264.100 reserved for expansion]

SUBCHAPTER B. FOSTER CARE

§ 264.101. Foster Care Payments

(a) The department may pay the cost of foster care for a child:

(1) for whom the department has initiated a suit and has been named managing conservator under an order rendered under this title,

who is a resident of the state, and who has been placed by the department in a foster home or child-care institution, as defined by Chapter 42, Human Resources Code; or

(2) who is under the placement and care of a state agency or political subdivision with which the department has entered into an agreement to reimburse the cost of care and supervision of the child.

(b) The department may not pay the cost of protective foster care for a child for whom the department has been named managing conservator under an order rendered solely under Section 161.001(1)(J).

(c) The payment of foster care, including medical care, for a child as authorized under this subchapter shall be made without regard to the child's eligibility for federally funded care.

(d) The Board of Protective and Regulatory Services may adopt rules that establish criteria and guidelines for the payment of foster care, including medical care, for a child and for providing care for a child after the child becomes 18 years of age if the child is regularly attending high school, an institution of higher education, or a vocational or technical program.

(e) The department may accept and spend funds available from any source to pay for foster care, including medical care, for a child in the department's care.

(f) In this section, "child" means a person who:

(1) is under 22 years of age and for whom the department has been appointed managing conserva-

tor of the child before the date the child became 18 years of age; or

(2) is the responsibility of an agency with which the department has entered into an agreement to provide care and supervision of the child.

Added by Acts 1995, 74th Leg., ch. 20, § 1, eff. April 20, 1995. Amended by Acts 1997, 75th Leg., ch. 575, § 27, eff. Sept. 1, 1997.

§ 264.1015. Liability of Child's Estate for Foster Care

(a) The cost of foster care provided for a child, including medical care, is an obligation of the estate of the child and the estate is liable to the department for the cost of the care.

(b) The department may take action to recover from the estate of the child the cost of foster care for the child.

Added by Acts 1997, 75th Leg., ch. 575, § 28, eff. Sept. 1, 1997.

§ 264.102. County Contracts

(a) The department may contract with a county commissioners court to administer the funds authorized by this subchapter for eligible children in the county and may require county participation.

(b) The payments provided by this subchapter do not abrogate the responsibility of a county to provide child welfare services.

Added by Acts 1995, 74th Leg., ch. 20, § 1, eff. April 20, 1995.

§ 264.103. Direct Payments

The department may make direct payments for foster care to a foster parent residing in a county with which the department does not have a contract authorized by Section 264.102.

Added by Acts 1995, 74th Leg., ch. 20, § 1, eff. April 20, 1995.

§ 264.104. Parent or Guardian Liability

(a) The parent or guardian of a child is liable to the state or to the county for a payment made by the state or county for foster care of a child under this subchapter.

(b) The cost of foster care for a child, including medical care, is a legal obligation of the child's parents, and the estate of a parent of the child is liable to the department for payment of the costs.

(c) The funds collected by the state under this section shall be used by the department for child welfare services.

Added by Acts 1995, 74th Leg., ch. 20, § 1, eff. April 20, 1995. Amended by Acts 1997, 75th Leg., ch. 575, § 29, eff. Sept. 1, 1997.

§ 264.105. Medical Services Payments

The department shall attempt to maximize the use of federal funding to provide medical care payments authorized by Section 264.101(c) for children for whom the department has been named managing conservator.

Added by Acts 1995, 74th Leg., ch. 20, § 1, eff. April 20, 1995. Amended by Acts 1997, 75th Leg., ch. 575, § 30, eff. Sept. 1, 1997.

§ 264.106. Contracts for Substitute Care Services

(a) The department shall:

(1) assess the need for substitute care services throughout the state; and

(2) contract with substitute care providers only to the extent necessary to meet the need for those services.

(b) Before contracting with a substitute care provider, the department shall determine whether:

(1) community resources are available to support children placed under the provider's care; and

(2) the appropriate public school district has sufficient resources to support children placed under the provider's care if the children will attend public school.

(c) In addition to the requirements of Section 40.058(b), Human Resources Code, a contract with a substitute care provider must include provisions that:

(1) enable the department to monitor the effectiveness of the provider's services; and

(2) authorize the department to terminate the contract or impose sanctions for a violation of a provision of the contract that specifies performance criteria.

(d) In determining whether to contract with a substitute care provider, the department shall consider the provider's performance under any previous contract for substitute care services between the department and the provider.

(e) In this section, "substitute care provider" means a person who provides residential care for children for 24 hours a day, including:

(1) a child-care institution, as defined by Section 42.002, Human Resources Code;

(2) a child-placing agency, as defined by Section 42.002, Human Resources Code;

(3) a foster group home or foster family home, as defined by Section 42.002, Human Resources Code; and

(4) an agency group home or agency home, as defined by Section 42.002, Human Resources Code, other than an agency group home, agency home, or a foster home verified or certified by the department.

Added by Acts 1995, 74th Leg., ch. 20, § 1, eff. April 20, 1995. Amended by Acts 1997, 75th Leg., ch. 1022, § 92, eff. Sept. 1, 1997.

Section 103 of Acts 1997, 75th Leg., ch. 1022, provides:

"(a) Representatives from each state agency that purchases substitute care services for children under the state's care shall meet to:

"(1) assess the total need for substitute care services in this state; and

"(2) develop and implement a competitive bidding process to purchase substitute care services.

"(b) Except as provided by Subsection (c) of this section, each state agency must use the competitive bidding process created under Subsection (a) of this section to purchase substitute care services.

"(c) A state agency is not required to use the competitive bidding process to purchase:

"(1) foster family care services;

"(2) substitute care services in a geographic area of this state that has a shortage of service providers; or

"(3) specialized substitute care services if there is a shortage of providers of the specialized services.

"(d) The state agency representatives shall meet and develop the competitive bidding process for purchasing substitute care services as soon as possible after the effective date of this Act.

"(e) Not later than September 1, 1998, the Department of Protective and Regulatory Services shall develop and implement a pilot program under which the department purchases substitute care services through a competitive bidding process. The department must design the pilot program to produce a substitute care system that is outcome-based and that uses the department's outcome measures."

§ 264.1061. Foster Parent Performance

The department shall monitor the performance of a foster parent who has been verified by the department in the department's capacity as a child-placing agency. The method under which performance is monitored must include the use of objective criteria by which the foster parent's performance may be assessed. The department shall include references to the criteria in a written agreement between the department and the foster parent concerning the foster parent's services.

Added by Acts 1997, 75th Leg., ch. 1022, § 92, eff. Sept. 1, 1997.

§ 264.107. Placement of Children

(a) The department shall use a system for the placement of children in contract residential care, including foster care, that conforms to the levels of care adopted and maintained by the Health and Human Services Commission.

(b) The department shall use the standard application for the placement of children in contract residential care as adopted and maintained by the Health and Human Services Commission.

Added by Acts 1995, 74th Leg., ch. 20, § 1, eff. April 20, 1995.

§ 264.1075. Use of Assessment Services

Before placing a child in substitute care, the department shall use assessment services provided by a child-care facility or child-placing agency in accordance with Section 42.0425, Human Resources Code, to determine the appropriate substitute care for the child.

Added by Acts 1997, 75th Leg., ch. 1022, § 93, eff. Sept. 1, 1997.

§ 264.108. Race or Ethnicity

(a) The department may not make a foster care placement decision on the presumption that placing a child in a family of the same race or ethnicity as the race or ethnicity of the child is in the best interest of the child.

(b) Unless an independent psychological evaluation specific to a child indicates that placement or continued living with a family of a particular race or ethnicity would be detrimental to the child, the department may not:

(1) deny, delay, or prohibit placement of a child in foster care because the department is attempting to locate a family of a particular race or ethnicity; or

(2) remove a child from foster care with a family that is of a race or ethnicity different from that of the child.

(c) The department may not remove a child from foster care with a family that is of a race or ethnicity different from that of the child for the sole reason that continued foster care with that family may:

(1) strengthen the emotional ties between the child and the family; or

(2) increase the potential of the family's desire to adopt the child because of the amount of time the child and the family are together.

(d) This section does not prevent or limit the department's recruitment of minority families as foster care families, but the recruitment of minority families may not be a reason to delay placement of a child in foster care with an available family of a race or ethnicity different from that of the child.

(e) An employee who violates this section is subject to immediate dismissal.

(f) The department by rule shall define what constitutes a delay under Subsections (b) and (d).

(g) A district court, on the application for an injunction or the filing of a petition complaining of a violation of this section by any person residing in the county in which the court has jurisdiction, shall enforce this section by issuing appropriate orders. An action for an injunction is in addition to any other action, proceeding, or remedy authorized by law. An applicant or petitioner who is granted an injunction or given other appropriate relief under this section is entitled to the costs of the suit, including reasonable attorney's fees.

Added by Acts 1995, 74th Leg., ch. 20, § 1, eff. April 20, 1995. Amended by Acts 1995, 74th Leg., ch. 879, § 2, eff. June 16, 1995.

§ 264.109. Assignment of Support Rights in Substitute Care Cases

(a) The placement of a child in substitute care by the department constitutes an assignment to the state of any support rights attributable to the child as of the date the child is placed in substitute care.

(b) If a child placed by the department in substitute care is entitled under federal law to Title IV-D child support enforcement services without the requirement of an application for services, the department shall immediately refer the case to the Title IV-D agency. If an application for Title IV-D services is required and the department has been named managing conservator of the child, then an authorized representative of the department shall be the designated individual entitled to apply for services on behalf of the child and shall promptly apply for the services.

(c) The department and the Title IV-D agency shall execute a memorandum of understanding for the implementation of the provisions of this section and for the allocation between the department and the agency, consistent with federal laws and regulations, of any child support funds recovered by the Title IV-D agency in substitute care cases. All child support funds recovered under this section and retained by the department or the Title IV-D agency and any federal matching or incentive funds resulting from child support collection efforts in substitute care cases shall be in excess of amounts otherwise appropriated to either the department or the Title IV-D agency by the legislature.

Added by Acts 1995, 74th Leg., ch. 751, § 117, eff. Sept. 1, 1995.

§ 264.110. Adoptive Parent Registry

(a) The department shall establish a registry of persons who are willing to accept foster care placement of a child in the care of the department. The child may be placed temporarily with a person registered under this section pending termination of the parent-child relationship.

(b) A person registered under this section must satisfy requirements adopted by rule by the department.

(c) The department shall maintain a list of persons registered under this section and shall make a reasonable effort to place a child with the first available qualified person on the list if a qualified extended family member is not available for the child.

(d) Before a child may be placed with a person under this section, the person must sign a written statement in which the person agrees to the immediate removal of the child by the department under circumstances determined by the department.

(e) A person registered under this section is not entitled to compensation during the time the child is placed in the person's home but may receive support services provided for the child by the department.

(f) A person registered under this section has the right to be considered first for the adoption of a child placed in the person's home if the parent-child relationship is terminated with regard to the child.

(g) The department may refuse to place a child with a person registered under this section only for a reason permitted under criteria adopted by department rule.

(h) The department shall make the public aware of the existence and benefits of the adoptive parent registry through appropriate existing department communication methods.

Added by Acts 1995, 74th Leg., ch. 943, § 8, eff. Sept. 1, 1995. Renumbered from V.T.C.A., Family Code § 264.109 by Acts 1997, 75th Leg., ch. 165, § 31.01(30), eff. Sept. 1, 1997.

Section 13(a) of Acts 1995, 74th Leg., ch. 943 provides:

"This Act takes effect September 1, 1995, and applies to a proceeding in which an investigation of the abuse of a child is pending on or after that date."

§ 264.111. Adoption and Substitute Information

(a) The department shall maintain in the department's central database information concerning children placed in the department's custody, including:

(1) for each formal adoption of a child in this state:

(A) the length of time between the date of the permanency plan decision of adoption and the date of the actual placement of the child with an adoptive family;

(B) the length of time between the date of the placement of the child for adoption and the date a final order of adoption was rendered;

(C) if the child returned to the department's custody after the date a final order of adoption was rendered for the child, the time between the date the final adoption order was rendered and the date the child returned to the department's custody; and

(D) for the adoptive family of a child under Paragraph (C), whether the family used postadoption program services before the date the child returned to the department's custody; and

(2) for each placement of a child in substitute care:

(A) the level of care the child was determined to require;

(B) whether the child was placed in an appropriate setting based on the level of care determined for the child;

(C) the number of moves for the child in substitute care and the reasons for moving the child;

(D) the length of stay in substitute care for the child from the date of initial placement to the date of approval of a permanency plan for the child;

(E) the length of time between the date of approval of a permanency plan for the child and the date of achieving the plan;

(F) whether the child's permanency plan was long-term substitute care;

(G) whether the child's achieved permanency plan was placement with an appropriate relative or another person, other than a foster parent, having standing; and

(H) whether the child was adopted by the child's foster parents.

(b) In addition to the information required in Subsection (a), the department shall compile information on:

(1) the number of families that used postadoption program services to assist in maintaining adoptive placements;

(2) the number of children returned to the department's custody after placement with an adoptive family but before a final adoption order was rendered;

(3) the number of children returned to the department's custody after the date a final order of adoption was rendered for the child;

(4) the number of adoptive families who used postadoption program services before the date a child placed with the family returned to the department's custody;

(5) the percentage of children who were placed in an appropriate setting based on the level of care determined for the child;

(6) the percentage of children placed in a department foster home;

(7) the percentage of children placed in a private child-placing agency;

(8) the number of children whose permanency plan was long-term substitute care;

(9) the number of children whose achieved permanency plan was placement with an appropriate relative or another person, other than a foster parent, having standing;

(10) the number of children adopted by the child's foster parents; and

(11) the number of children whose achieved permanency plan was removal of the disabilities of minority.

(c) The department shall make the information maintained under this section, other than information that is required by law to be confidential, available to the public by computer.

Added by Acts 1997, 75th Leg., ch. 600, § 18, eff. Sept. 1, 1997.

§ 264.112. Report on Children in Substitute Care

(a) The department shall report the status for children in substitute care to the Board of Protective and Regulatory Services at least once every 12 months.

(b) The report shall analyze the length of time each child has been in substitute care and the barriers to placing the child for adoption or returning the child to the child's parent or parents.

Added by Acts 1997, 75th Leg., ch. 600, § 18, eff. Sept. 1, 1997.

[Sections 264.113 to 264.200 reserved for expansion]

SUBCHAPTER C. CHILD AND FAMILY SERVICES

§ 264.201. Services by Department

(a) When the department provides services directly or by contract to an abused or neglected child and the child's family, the services shall be designed to:

(1) prevent further abuse;

(2) alleviate the effects of the abuse suffered;

(3) prevent removal of the child from the home; and

(4) provide reunification services when appropriate for the return of the child to the home.

(b) The department shall emphasize ameliorative services for sexually abused children.

(c) The department shall provide or contract for necessary services to an abused or neglected child and the child's family without regard to whether the child remains in or is removed from the family home. If parental rights have been terminated, services may be provided only to the child.

(d) The services may include in-home programs, parenting skills training, youth coping skills, and individual and family counseling.

Added by Acts 1995, 74th Leg., ch. 20, § 1, eff. April 20, 1995.

§ 264.202. Standards and Effectiveness

(a) The department, with assistance from national organizations with expertise in child protective services, shall define a minimal baseline of in-home and foster care services for abused or neglected children that meets the professionally recognized standards for those services. The department shall attempt to provide services at a standard not lower than the minimal baseline standard.

(b) The department, with assistance from national organizations with expertise in child protective services, shall develop outcome measures to track and monitor the effectiveness of in-home and foster care services.

Added by Acts 1995, 74th Leg., ch. 20, § 1, eff. April 20, 1995.

§ 264.203. Required Participation

(a) Except as provided by Subsection (d), the court on request of the department may order the parent, managing conservator, guardian, or other member of the abused or neglected child's household to participate in the services the department provides or purchases for alleviating the effects of the abuse or neglect and to permit the child and any siblings of the child to receive the services.

(b) The department may request the court to order the parent, managing conservator, guardian, or other member of the child's household to participate in the services whether the child resides in the home or has been removed from the home.

(c) If the person ordered to participate in the services fails to follow the court's order, the court may impose community service as a sanction for contempt.

(d) If the court does not order the person to participate, the court in writing shall specify the reasons for not ordering participation.

Added by Acts 1995, 74th Leg., ch. 20, § 1, eff. April 20, 1995.

§ 264.204. Repealed by Acts 1995, 74th Leg., ch. 262, § 100(a), eff. Jan. 1, 1996

§ 264.205. Swift Adoption Teams

(a) The department shall develop swift adoption teams to expedite the process of placing a child under the jurisdiction of the department for adoption.

(b) A swift adoption team shall consist of department personnel who shall operate under policies adopted by rule by the department. The department shall set priorities for the allocation of department resources to enable a swift adoption team to operate successfully under the policies adopted under this subsection.

(c) The department shall, using a system of measurement developed by the department, report to the legislature on the success of swift adoption teams in expediting the administrative procedures and the length of time in placing children for adoption. The report shall include recommendations by the department concerning legislation that would enable the department to further improve adoption placements. The department shall report under this section on or before December 1 of each even-numbered year.

Added by Acts 1995, 74th Leg., ch. 943, § 9, eff. Sept. 1, 1995.

Section 13(a) of the 1995 Act provides:

"This Act takes effect September 1, 1995, and applies to a proceeding in which an investigation of the abuse of a child is pending on or after that date."

§ 264.206. Search for Adoptive Parents

(a) The department shall begin its efforts to locate qualified persons to adopt a child, including persons registered with the adoptive parent registry under Subchapter B, at the time the department's permanency plan for the child becomes the termination of the parent-child relationship and adoption of the child.

(b) The department shall report to the court in which the department petitions for termination of the parent-child relationship on the child's adoptability and the department's search for prospective adoptive parents for the child, including information relating to the department's efforts to work with licensed child-placing agencies.

Added by Acts 1997, 75th Leg., ch. 600, § 19, eff. Sept. 1, 1997; Acts 1997, 75th Leg., ch. 1022, § 94, eff. Sept. 1, 1997.

§ 264.207. Department Planning and Accountability

(a) The department shall adopt policies that provide for the improvement of the department's services for children and families, including policies that provide for conducting a home study within four months after the date an applicant is approved for an adoption and documenting the results of the home study within 30 days after the date the study is completed. The policies adopted under this section must:

(1) be designed to increase the accountability of the department to individuals who receive services and to the public; and

(2) assure consistency of services provided by the department in the different regions of the state.

(b) To accomplish the goals stated in Subsection (a), the department shall:

(1) establish time frames for the initial screening of families seeking to adopt children;

(2) provide for the evaluation of the effectiveness of the department's management-level employees in expeditiously making permanent placements for children;

(3) establish, as feasible, comprehensive assessment services in various locations in the state to determine the needs of children and families served by the department;

(4) emphasize and centralize the monitoring and promoting of the permanent placement of children receiving department services;

(5) establish goals and performance measures in the permanent placement of children;

(6) seek private licensed child-placing agencies to place a child in the department's managing conservatorship who has been available for permanent placement for more than 90 days;

(7) provide information to private licensed child-placing agencies concerning children under Subdivision (6);

(8) provide incentives for a private licensed child-placing agency that places a child, as defined by Section 162.301, under Subdivision (6);

(9) encourage foster parents to be approved by the department as both foster parents and adoptive parents;

(10) address failures by the department's service regions in making permanent placements for children in a reasonable time; and

(11) require the department's service regions to participate in the Texas Adoption Resources Exchange.

Added by Acts 1997, 75th Leg., ch. 600, § 19, eff. Sept. 1, 1997; Acts 1997, 75th Leg., ch. 1022, § 94, eff. Sept. 1, 1997.

[Sections 264.208 to 264.300 reserved for expansion]

SUBCHAPTER D. SERVICES TO AT-RISK YOUTH

§ 264.301. Services for At-Risk Youth

(a) The department shall operate a program to provide services for children in at-risk situations and for the families of those children.

(b) The services under this section may include:

(1) crisis family intervention;

(2) emergency short-term residential care;

(3) family counseling;

(4) parenting skills training;

(5) youth coping skills training;

(6) mentoring; and

(7) advocacy training.

Added by Acts 1995, 74th Leg., ch. 20, § 1, eff. April 20, 1995. Amended by Acts 1995, 74th Leg., ch. 262, § 58, eff. Jan. 1, 1996.

§ 264.302. Early Youth Intervention Services

(a) This section applies to a child who:

(1) is seven years of age or older and under 17 years of age; and

(2) has not had the disabilities of minority for general purposes removed under Chapter 31.

(b) The department shall operate a program under this section to provide services for children in at-risk situations and for the families of those children.

(c) The department may not provide services under this section to a child who has:

(1) at any time been referred to juvenile court for engaging in conduct that violates a penal law of this

state of the grade of felony other than a state jail felony; or

(2) been found to have engaged in delinquent conduct under Title 3.

(d) The department may provide services under this section to a child who engages in conduct for which the child may be found by a court to be an at-risk child, without regard to whether the conduct violates a penal law of this state of the grade of felony other than a state jail felony, if the child was younger than 10 years of age at the time the child engaged in the conduct.

(e) The department shall provide services for a child and the child's family if a contract to provide services under this section is available in the county and the child is referred to the department as an at-risk child by:

(1) a court under Section 264.304;

(2) a juvenile court or probation department as part of a progressive sanctions program under Chapter 59;

(3) a law enforcement officer or agency under Section 52.03; or

(4) a justice or municipal court under Section 54.022.

(f) The services under this section may include:

(1) crisis family intervention;

(2) emergency short-term residential care for children 10 years of age or older;

(3) family counseling;

(4) parenting skills training;

(5) youth coping skills training;

(6) advocacy training; and

(7) mentoring.

Added by Acts 1995, 74th Leg., ch. 262, § 58, eff. Jan. 1, 1996. Amended by Acts 1997, 75th Leg., ch. 575, § 31, eff. Sept. 1, 1997; Acts 1997, 75th Leg., ch. 1086, § 30, eff. Sept. 1, 1997.

§ 264.303. Commencement of Civil Action for Determination of At-Risk Children

(a) The department may file a civil action to request any district court or county court, other than a juvenile court, to determine that a child is an at-risk child. A person with whom the department contracts to provide services under Section 264.302 may file an action under this section if the department has approved the filing.

(b) Notice of the action must be provided to:

(1) the child;

(2) the parent, managing conservator, or guardian of the child; and

(3) any other member of the child's household who may be affected by an order of the court if the court finds that the child is an at-risk child.

(c) A person served with notice of the action may, but is not required, to file a written answer. Any answer must be filed before the hearing on the action begins.

Added by Acts 1995, 74th Leg., ch. 262, § 58, eff. Jan. 1, 1996.

§ 264.304. Hearing; Determination of At-Risk Child

(a) Unless a later date is requested by the department, the court shall set a date and time for the hearing not later than 30 days after the date the action is filed.

(b) The court is the trier of fact at the hearing.

(c) The court shall determine that the child is an at-risk child if the court finds that the child has engaged in the following conduct:

(1) conduct, other than a traffic offense and except as provided by Subsection (d), that violates:

(A) the penal laws of this state; or

(B) the penal ordinances of any political subdivision of this state;

(2) the unexcused voluntary absence of the child on 10 or more days or parts of days within a six-month period or three or more days or parts of days within a four-week period from school without the consent of the child's parent, managing conservator, or guardian;

(3) the voluntary absence of the child from the child's home without the consent of the child's parent, managing conservator, or guardian for a substantial length of time or without intent to return;

(4) conduct that violates the laws of this state prohibiting driving while intoxicated or under the influence of intoxicating liquor (first or second offense) or driving while under the influence of any narcotic drug or of any other drug to a degree that renders the child incapable of safely driving a vehicle (first or second offense); or

(5) conduct that evidences a clear and substantial intent to engage in any behavior described by Subdivisions (1)–(4).

(d) The court may not determine that a child is an at-risk child if the court finds that the child engaged in conduct violating the penal laws of this state of the grade of felony other than a state jail felony when the child was 10 years of age or older.

Added by Acts 1995, 74th Leg., ch. 262, § 58, eff. Jan. 1, 1996.

§ 264.305. Court Order for Services

(a) Except as provided by Subsection (b), if the court finds that the child is an at-risk child under Section 264.304, the court may order the child, the child's parent, managing conservator, or guardian or any other member of the child's household to participate in services provided by the department under Section 264.302 and contained in a plan approved by the court.

(b) The court may order an at-risk child to participate in services involving emergency short-term residential care only if the court finds that the child engaged in conduct described by Section 264.304(c)(1), (2), (3), or (4).

(c) An order rendered by a court under this section expires not later than six months after the date the order was rendered.

Added by Acts 1995, 74th Leg., ch. 262, § 58, eff. Jan. 1, 1996.

§ 264.306. Sanctions

(a) A child who violates a court order under Section 264.305 by failing to participate in services provided by the department engages in conduct indicating a need for supervision and the department shall refer the child to an appropriate juvenile authority for proceedings under Title 3 for that conduct.

(b) A parent, managing conservator, guardian, or other member of the child's household who violates a court order under Section 264.305 by failing to participate in services provided by the department is subject to contempt of court. The court may under its contempt powers impose a community service requirement.

Added by Acts 1995, 74th Leg., ch. 262, § 58, eff. Jan. 1, 1996.

[Sections 264.307 to 264.400 reserved for expansion]

SUBCHAPTER E. CHILDREN'S ADVOCACY CENTERS

§ 264.401. Definition

In this subchapter, "center" means a children's advocacy center.

Added by Acts 1995, 74th Leg., ch. 255, § 1, eff. Sept. 1, 1995.

§ 264.402. Establishment of Children's Advocacy Center

(a) On the execution of a memorandum of understanding under Section 264.403, a children's advocacy center may be established by the participating entities.

(b) A center may be established to serve two or more contiguous counties.

Added by Acts 1995, 74th Leg., ch. 255, § 1, eff. Sept. 1, 1995.

§ 264.403. Interagency Memorandum of Understanding

(a) Before a center may be established under Section 264.402, a memorandum of understanding regarding participation in operation of the center must be executed among:

(1) the division of the department responsible for child abuse investigations;

(2) representatives of county and municipal law enforcement agencies that investigate child abuse in the area to be served by the center;

(3) the county or district attorney who routinely prosecutes child abuse cases in the area to be served by the center; and

(4) a representative of any other governmental entity that participates in child abuse investigations or offers services to child abuse victims that desires to participate in the operation of the center.

(b) A memorandum of understanding executed under this section shall include the agreement of each participating entity to cooperate in:

(1) developing a cooperative, team approach to investigating child abuse;

(2) reducing, to the greatest extent possible, the number of interviews required of a victim of child abuse to minimize the negative impact of the investigation on the child; and

(3) developing, maintaining, and supporting, through the center, an environment that emphasizes the best interests of children and that provides investigatory and rehabilitative services.

(c) A memorandum of understanding executed under this section may include the agreement of one or more participating entities to provide office space and administrative services necessary for the center's operation.

Added by Acts 1995, 74th Leg., ch. 255, § 1, eff. Sept. 1, 1995.

§ 264.404. Board; Administration of Center

(a) The executive officer or board of each participating entity executing a memorandum of understanding that establishes a center under this subchapter shall appoint a member to serve on the governing board of the center.

(b) A governing board member serves at the pleasure of the appointing executive officer or board.

(c) Service on a center's board by a public officer or employee is an additional duty of the office or employment.

Added by Acts 1995, 74th Leg., ch. 255, § 1, eff. Sept. 1, 1995.

§ 264.405. Duties

A center shall:

(1) assess victims of child abuse and their families to determine their need for services relating to the investigation of child abuse;

(2) provide services determined to be needed under Subdivision (1);

(3) provide a facility at which a multidisciplinary team appointed under Section 264.406 can meet to facilitate the efficient and appropriate disposition of child abuse cases through the civil and criminal justice systems; and

(4) coordinate the activities of governmental entities relating to child abuse investigations and delivery of services to child abuse victims and their families.

Added by Acts 1995, 74th Leg., ch. 255, § 1, eff. Sept. 1, 1995.

§ 264.406. Multidisciplinary Team

(a) A center's board shall appoint a multidisciplinary team to work within the center to review new and pending child abuse cases for the purpose of coordinating the activities of entities involved in investigation, prosecution, and victim services.

(b) A multidisciplinary team may review a child abuse case in which the alleged perpetrator does not have custodial control or supervision of the child or is not responsible for the child's welfare or care.

(c) A multidisciplinary team shall consist of persons who are involved in the investigation or prosecution of child abuse cases or the delivery of services to child abuse victims and their families.

(d) A multidisciplinary team shall meet at the call of the board. The board shall call a meeting of the multidisciplinary team if:

(1) a new child abuse case is received; or

(2) a pending child abuse case requires attention.

(e) At each meeting, the multidisciplinary team shall discuss each active case and the actions of the entities involved in investigation, prosecution, and victim services.

(f) When acting in the member's official capacity, a multidisciplinary team member is authorized to receive information made confidential by Section 40.005, Human Resources Code, or Section 261.201 or 264.408.

Added by Acts 1995, 74th Leg., ch. 255, § 1, eff. Sept. 1, 1995. Amended by Acts 1997, 75th Leg., ch. 575, § 32, eff. Sept. 1, 1997.

§ 264.407. Liability

(a) A person is not liable for civil damages for a recommendation made or an opinion rendered in good faith while acting in the official scope of the person's duties as a member of a multidisciplinary team or as a board member, staff member, or volunteer of a center.

(b) The limitation on civil liability of Subsection (a) does not apply if a person's actions constitute gross negligence.

Added by Acts 1995, 74th Leg., ch. 255, § 1, eff. Sept. 1, 1995.

§ 264.408. Use of Information and Records; Confidentiality and Ownership

(a) The files, reports, records, communications, and working papers used or developed in providing services under this chapter are confidential and not subject to public release under Chapter 552, Government Code, and may only be disclosed for purposes consistent with this chapter. Disclosure may be to:

(1) the department, department employees, law enforcement agencies, prosecuting attorneys, medical professionals, and other state agencies that provide services to children and families; and

(2) the attorney for the child who is the subject of the records and a court-appointed volunteer advocate appointed for the child under Section 107.031.

(b) Information related to the investigation of a report of abuse or neglect under Chapter 261 and services provided as a result of the investigation is confidential as provided by Section 261.201.

(c) The department, a law enforcement agency, and a prosecuting attorney may share with a center information that is confidential under Section 261.201 as needed to provide services under this chapter. Confidential information shared with or provided to a center remains the property of the agency that shared or provided the information to the center.

(d) A videotaped interview of a child made at a center is the property of the prosecuting attorney involved in the criminal prosecution of the case involving the child. If no criminal prosecution occurs, the videotaped interview is the property of the attorney involved in representing the department in a civil action alleging child abuse or neglect. If the matter involving the child is not prosecuted, the videotape is the property of the department if the matter is an investigation by the department of abuse or neglect. If the department is not investigating or has not investigated the matter, the videotape is the property of the agency that referred the matter to the center. If the center employs a custodian of records for videotaped interviews of children, the center is responsible for the custody of the videotape. A videotaped interview may be shared with other agencies under a written agreement.

(e) The department shall be allowed access to a center's videotaped interviews of children.

Added by Acts 1997, 75th Leg., ch. 575, § 33, eff. Sept. 1, 1997.

§ 264.409. Administrative Contracts

The department may contract with a statewide organization of individuals or groups of individuals who have expertise in the establishment and operation of children's advocacy center programs. The statewide organization shall provide training, technical assistance, and evaluation services for local children's advocacy center programs.

Added by Acts 1997, 75th Leg., ch. 575, § 33, eff. Sept. 1, 1997.

§ 264.410. Contracts With Children's Advocacy Centers

(a) The statewide organization with which the department contracts under Section 264.409 shall contract for services with eligible centers to enhance the existing services of the programs.

(b) The contract under this section may not result in reducing the financial support a local center receives from another source.

Added by Acts 1997, 75th Leg., ch. 575, § 33, eff. Sept. 1, 1997.

§ 264.411. Eligibility for Contracts

(a) A public entity or nonprofit entity is eligible for a contract under Section 264.410 if the entity:

(1) has a signed memorandum of understanding as provided by Section 264.403;

(2) operates under the authority of a governing board as provided by Section 264.404;

(3) has a multidisciplinary team of persons involved in the investigation or prosecution of child abuse cases or the delivery of services as provided by Section 264.406;

(4) holds regularly scheduled case reviews as provided by Section 264.406;

(5) operates in a neutral and physically separate space from the day-to-day operations of any public agency partner;

(6) has developed a method of statistical information gathering on children receiving services through the center and shares such statistical information with the statewide organization and the department when requested;

(7) has an in-house volunteer program;

(8) employs an executive director who is answerable to the board of directors of the entity and who is not the exclusive salaried employee of any public agency partner; and

(9) operates under a working protocol that includes a statement of:

(A) the center's mission;

(B) each agency's role and commitment to the center;

(C) the type of cases to be handled by the center; and

(D) procedure for case reviews.

(b) The statewide organization may waive the requirements specified in Subsection (a) if it determines that the waiver will not adversely affect the center's ability to carry out its duties under Section 264.405. Any waiver that is granted must be identified in the written contract with the center. If a request for a waiver is denied, an appeal of the decision may be made to the department's executive director, who may reverse the decision. If the executive director approves a request for a waiver on appeal, the statewide organization shall contract with the center and shall include the waiver in the contract.

Added by Acts 1997, 75th Leg., ch. 575, § 33, eff. Sept. 1, 1997.

[Sections 264.412 to 264.500 reserved for expansion]

SUBCHAPTER F. CHILD FATALITY REVIEW AND INVESTIGATION

§ 264.501. Definitions

In this subchapter:

(1) "Autopsy" and "inquest" have the meanings assigned by Article [1] 49.01, Code of Criminal Procedure.

(2) "Bureau of vital statistics" means the bureau of vital statistics of the Texas Department of Health.

(3) "Child" means a person younger than 18 years of age.

(4) "Committee" means the child fatality review team committee.

(5) "Council" means the Children's Trust Fund of Texas Council.

(6) "Department" means the Department of Protective and Regulatory Services.

(7) "Health care provider" means any health care practitioner or facility that provides medical evaluation or treatment, including dental and mental health evaluation or treatment.

(8) "Meeting" means an in-person meeting or a meeting held by telephone or other electronic medium.

(9) "Preventable death" means a death that may have been prevented by reasonable medical, social, legal, psychological, or educational intervention. The term includes the death of a child from:

(A) intentional or unintentional injuries;

(B) medical neglect;

(C) lack of access to medical care;

(D) neglect and reckless conduct, including failure to supervise and failure to seek medical care; and

(E) premature birth associated with any factor described by Paragraphs (A) through [2] (D).

(10) "Review" means a reexamination of information regarding a deceased child from relevant agencies, professionals, and health care providers.

(11) "Review team" means a child fatality review team established under this subchapter.

(12) "Unexpected death" includes a death of a child that, before investigation:

(A) appears to have occurred without anticipation or forewarning; and

(B) was caused by trauma, suspicious or obscure circumstances, sudden infant death syndrome, abuse or neglect, or an unknown cause.

Added by Acts 1995, 74th Leg., ch. 255, § 2, eff. Sept. 1, 1995; Acts 1995, 74th Leg., ch. 878, § 1, eff. Sept. 1, 1995.

[1] Acts 1995, 74th Leg., ch. 252, § 2 here read "Section" in lieu of "Article".

[2] Acts 1995, 74th Leg., ch. 252, § 2 here read "—" in lieu of "through".

§ 264.502. Committee

(a) The child fatality review team committee is composed of:

(1) a person appointed by and representing the state registrar for the bureau of vital statistics;

(2) a person appointed by and representing the director of protective services for families and children of the department;

(3) a person appointed by and representing the director of the bureau of epidemiology of the Texas Department of Health;

(4) a person appointed by and representing the executive director of the council; and

(5) individuals selected under Subsection (b).

(b) The members of the committee who serve under Subsections (a)(1) through [1] (4) shall select the following additional committee members:

(1) a criminal prosecutor involved in prosecuting crimes against children;

(2) a sheriff;

(3) a justice of the peace;

(4) a medical examiner;

(5) a police chief;

(6) a pediatrician experienced in diagnosing and treating child abuse and neglect;

(7) a child educator;

(8) a child mental health provider;

(9) a public health professional;

(10) a child protective services specialist;

(11) a sudden infant death syndrome family service provider;

(12) a neonatologist;

(13) a child advocate; and

(14) a chief juvenile probation officer.

(c) Members of the committee selected under Subsection (b) serve two-year terms that expire on February 1 of each even-numbered year.

(d) Members selected under Subsection (b) must reflect the geographical, cultural, racial, and ethnic diversity of the state.

(e) An appointment to a vacancy on the committee shall be made in the same manner as the original appointment.

(f) Members of the committee shall select a presiding officer from the members of the committee.

(g) The presiding officer of the committee shall call the meetings of the committee, which shall be held at least quarterly.

(h) A member of the committee is not entitled to compensation for serving on the committee but is entitled to reimbursement for the member's travel expenses as provided in the General Appropriations Act. Reimbursement under this subsection for a person serving on the committee under Subsection (a)(1) or (3) shall be paid from funds appropriated to the Texas Department of Health. Reimbursement for other persons serving on the committee shall be paid equally from funds appropriated to the department and funds appropriated to the council.

Added by Acts 1995, 74th Leg., ch. 255, § 2, eff. Sept. 1, 1995; Acts 1995, 74th Leg., ch. 878, § 1, eff. Sept. 1, 1995.

[1] Acts 1995, 74th Leg., ch. 252, § 2 here read "—" in lieu of "through".

Section 6 of Acts 1995, 74th Leg., ch. 255, provides:

"(a) The executive directors of the Children's Trust Fund of Texas Council and the Department of Protective and Regulatory Services shall jointly call a meeting of the individuals to serve on the child fatality review team committee under Subdivisions (1) through (4), Subsection (a), Section 264.502, Family Code, as added by this Act, to be held not later than October 1, 1995. Those members of the committee shall select the members to serve under Subsection (b), Section 264.502, Family Code, as added by this Act, not later than December 1, 1995.

"(b) The initial members of the committee are appointed to serve terms expiring February 1, 1996.

"(c) The first meeting of the child fatality review team committee that includes members selected under Subsection (b), Section 264.502, Family Code, as added by this Act, shall be held not later than January 1, 1996."

Section 6 of Acts 1995, 74th Leg., ch. 878, provides:

"(a) The executive directors of the Children's Trust Fund of Texas Council and the Department of Protective and Regulatory Services shall jointly call a meeting of the individuals to serve on the child fatality review team committee under Subdivisions (1) through (4), Subsection (a), Section 264.502, Family Code, as added by this Act, to be held not later than October 1, 1995. Those members of the committee shall select the members to serve under Subsection (b), Section 264.502, Family Code, as added by this Act, not later than December 1, 1995.

"(b) The initial members of the committee are appointed to serve terms expiring February 1, 1996.

"(c) The first meeting of the child fatality review team committee that includes members selected under Subsection (b), Section 264.502, Family Code, shall be held not later than January 1, 1996."

§ 264.503. Purpose and Duties of Committee and Specified State Agencies

(a) The purpose of the committee is to:

(1) develop an understanding of the causes and incidence of child deaths in this state;

(2) identify procedures within the agencies represented on the committee to reduce the number of preventable child deaths; and

(3) promote public awareness and make recommendations to the governor and the legislature for changes in law, policy, and practice to reduce the number of preventable child deaths.

(b) To ensure that the committee achieves its purpose, the department, the council, and the Texas Department of Health shall perform the duties specified by this section.

(c) The department shall:

(1) recognize the creation and participation of review teams;

(2) promote and coordinate training to assist the review teams in carrying out their duties;

(3) assist the committee in developing model protocols for:

(A) the reporting and investigating of child fatalities for law enforcement agencies, child protective services, justices of the peace and medical examiners, and other professionals involved in the investigations of child deaths;

(B) the collection of data regarding child deaths; and

(C) the operation of the review teams; and

(4) develop and implement procedures necessary for the operation of the committee.

(d) The council shall promote education of the public regarding the incidence and causes of child deaths, the public role in preventing child deaths, and specific steps the public can undertake to prevent child deaths. The committee shall enlist the support and assistance of civic, philanthropic, and public service organizations in the performance of the duties imposed under this subsection.

(e) The Texas Department of Health shall:

(1) collect data under this subchapter and coordinate the collection of data under this subchapter with other data collection activities; and

(2) perform annual statistical studies of the incidence and causes of child fatalities using the data collected under this subchapter.

(f) The committee shall issue annual reports on the committee's activities, including findings and recommendations relating to each purpose and duty of the committee described by this section. Not later than December 1 of each even-numbered year, the committee shall publish the report and submit a copy of the report to the governor, lieutenant governor, and speaker of the house of representatives.

Added by Acts 1995, 74th Leg., ch. 255, § 2, eff. Sept. 1, 1995; Acts 1995, 74th Leg., ch. 878, § 1, eff. Sept. 1, 1995.

§ 264.504. Meetings of Committee

(a) Except as provided by Subsections (b), (c), and (d), meetings of the committee are subject to the open meetings law, Chapter 551, Government Code, as if the committee were a governmental body under that chapter.

(b) Any portion of a meeting of the committee during which the committee discusses an individual child's death is closed to the public and is not subject to the open meetings law, Chapter 551, Government Code.

(c) Information identifying a deceased child, a member of the child's family, a guardian or caretaker of the child, or an alleged or suspected perpetrator of abuse or neglect of the child may not be disclosed during a public meeting.

(d) Information regarding the involvement of a state or local agency with the deceased child or another person described by Subsection (c) may not be disclosed during a public meeting.

(e) The committee may conduct an open or closed meeting by telephone conference call or other electronic medium. A meeting held under this subsection is subject to the notice requirements applicable to other meetings. The notice of the meeting must specify as the location of the meeting the location where meetings of the committee are usually held. Each part of the meeting by telephone conference call that is required to be open to the public shall be audible to the public at the location specified in the notice of the meeting as the location of the meeting and shall be tape-recorded. The tape recording shall be made available to the public.

(f) This section does not prohibit the committee from requesting the attendance at a closed meeting of a person who is not a member of the committee and who has information regarding a deceased child.

Added by Acts 1995, 74th Leg., ch. 255, § 2, eff. Sept. 1, 1995; Acts 1995, 74th Leg., ch. 878, § 1, eff. Sept. 1, 1995.

§ 264.505. Establishment of Review Team

(a) A multidisciplinary and multiagency child fatality review team may be established for a county to review child deaths in that county. A review team for a county with a population of less than 50,000 may join with an adjacent county or counties to establish a combined review team.

(b) Any person who may be a member of a review team under Subsection (c) may initiate the establishment of a review team and call the first organizational meeting of the team.

(c) A review team may include:

(1) a criminal prosecutor involved in prosecuting crimes against children;

(2) a sheriff;

(3) a justice of the peace or medical examiner;

(4) a police chief;

(5) a pediatrician experienced in diagnosing and treating child abuse and neglect;

(6) a child educator;

(7) a child mental health provider;

(8) a public health professional;

(9) a child protective services specialist;

(10) a sudden infant death syndrome family service provider;

(11) a neonatologist;

(12) a child advocate; and

(13) a chief juvenile probation officer.

(d) Members of a review team may select additional team members according to community resources and needs.

(e) A review team shall select a presiding officer from its members.

Added by Acts 1995, 74th Leg., ch. 255, § 2, eff. Sept. 1, 1995; Acts 1995, 74th Leg., ch. 878, § 1, eff. Sept. 1, 1995.

§ 264.506. Purpose and Duties of Review Team

(a) The purpose of a review team is to decrease the incidence of preventable child deaths by:

(1) providing assistance, direction, and coordination to investigations of child deaths;

(2) promoting cooperation, communication, and coordination among agencies involved in responding to child fatalities;

(3) developing an understanding of the causes and incidence of child deaths in the county or counties in which the review team is located;

(4) recommending changes to agencies, through the agency's representative member, that will reduce the number of preventable child deaths; and

(5) advising the committee on changes to law, policy, or practice that will assist the team and the agencies represented on the team in fulfilling their duties.

(b) To achieve its purpose, a review team shall:

(1) adapt and implement, according to local needs and resources, the model protocols developed by the department and the committee;

(2) meet on a regular basis to review child fatality cases and recommend methods to improve coordination of services and investigations between agencies that are represented on the team;

(3) collect and maintain data as required by the committee; and

(4) submit to the bureau of vital statistics data reports on deaths reviewed as specified by the committee.

(c) A review team shall initiate prevention measures as indicated by the review team's findings.

Added by Acts 1995, 74th Leg., ch. 255, § 2, eff. Sept. 1, 1995; Acts 1995, 74th Leg., ch. 878, § 1, eff. Sept. 1, 1995.

§ 264.507. Duties of Presiding Officer

The presiding officer of a review team shall:

(1) send notices to the review team members of a meeting to review a child fatality;

(2) provide a list to the review team members of each child fatality to be reviewed at the meeting;

(3) submit data reports to the bureau of vital statistics not later than the 30th day after the date on which the review took place; and

(4) ensure that the review team operates according to the protocols developed by the department and the committee, as adapted by the review team.

Added by Acts 1995, 74th Leg., ch. 255, § 2, eff. Sept. 1, 1995; Acts 1995, 74th Leg., ch. 878, § 1, eff. Sept. 1, 1995.

§ 264.508. Review Procedure

(a) The review team of the county in which the injury, illness, or event that was the cause of the death of the child occurred, as stated on the child's death certificate, shall review the death.

(b) On receipt of the list of child fatalities under Section 264.507, each review team member shall review the member's records and the records of the member's agency for information regarding each listed child.

Added by Acts 1995, 74th Leg., ch. 255, § 2, eff. Sept. 1, 1995; Acts 1995, 74th Leg., ch. 878, § 1, eff. Sept. 1, 1995.

§ 264.509. Access to Information

(a) A review team may request information and records regarding a deceased child as necessary to carry out the review team's purpose and duties. Records and information that may be requested under this section include:

(1) medical, dental, and mental health care information; and

(2) information and records maintained by any state or local government agency, including:

(A) a birth certificate;

(B) law enforcement investigative data;

(C) medical examiner investigative data;

(D) juvenile court records;

(E) parole and probation information and records; and

(F) child protective services information and records.

(b) On request of the presiding officer of a review team, the custodian of the relevant information and records relating to a deceased child shall provide those records to the review team.

(c) This subsection does not authorize the release of the original or copies of the mental health or medical records of any member of the child's family or the guardian or caretaker of the child or an alleged or suspected perpetrator of abuse or neglect of the child which are in the possession of any state or local government agency as provided in Subsection (a)(2). Information relating to the mental health or medical condition of a member of of[1] the child's family or the guardian or caretaker of the child or the alleged or suspected perpetrator of abuse or neglect of the child acquired as part of an investigation by a state or local government agency as provided in Subsection (a)(2) may be provided to the review team.

Added by Acts 1995, 74th Leg., ch. 255, § 2, eff. Sept. 1, 1995; Acts 1995, 74th Leg., ch. 878, § 1, eff. Sept. 1, 1995.

[1] So in enrolled bill.

§ 264.510. Meeting of Review Team

(a) A meeting of a review team is closed to the public and not subject to the open meetings law, Chapter 551, Government Code.

(b) This section does not prohibit a review team from requesting the attendance at a closed meeting of a person who is not a member of the review team and who has information regarding a deceased child.

(c) Except as necessary to carry out a review team's purpose and duties, members of a review team and persons attending a review team meeting may not disclose what occurred at the meeting.

(d) A member of a review team participating in the review of a child death is immune from civil or criminal liability arising from information presented in or opinions formed as a result of a meeting.

Added by Acts 1995, 74th Leg., ch. 255, § 2, eff. Sept. 1, 1995; Acts 1995, 74th Leg., ch. 878, § 1, eff. Sept. 1, 1995.

§ 264.511. Use of Information and Records; Confidentiality

(a) Information and records acquired by the committee or by a review team in the exercise of its purpose and duties under this subchapter are confidential and exempt from disclosure under the open records law, Chapter 552, Government Code, and may only be disclosed as necessary to carry out the committee's or review team's purpose and duties.

(b) A report of the committee or of a review team or a statistical compilation of data reports is a public record subject to the open records law, Chapter 552, Government Code, as if the committee or review team were a governmental body under that chapter, if the report or statistical compilation does not contain any information that would permit the identification of an individual.

(c) A member of a review team may not disclose any information that is confidential under this section.

(d) Information, documents, and records of the committee or of a review team that are confidential under this section are not subject to subpoena or discovery and may not be introduced into evidence in any civil or criminal proceeding, except that information, documents, and records otherwise available from other sources are not immune from subpoena, discovery, or introduction into evidence solely because they were presented during proceedings of the committee or a review team or are maintained by the committee or a review team.

Added by Acts 1995, 74th Leg., ch. 255, § 2, eff. Sept. 1, 1995; Acts 1995, 74th Leg., ch. 878, § 1, eff. Sept. 1, 1995.

§ 264.512. Governmental Units

The committee and a review team are governmental units for purposes of Chapter 101, Civil Practice and Remedies Code. A review team is a unit of local government under that chapter.

Added by Acts 1995, 74th Leg., ch. 255, § 2, eff. Sept. 1, 1995; Acts 1995, 74th Leg., ch. 878, § 1, eff. Sept. 1, 1995.

§ 264.513. Report of Death of Child

(a) A person who knows of the death of a child younger than six years of age shall immediately report the death to the medical examiner of the county in which the death occurs or, if the death occurs in a county that does not have a medical examiner's office or that is not part of a medical examiner's district, to a justice of the peace in that county.

(b) The requirement of this section is in addition to any other reporting requirement imposed by law, including any requirement that a person report child abuse or neglect under this code.

(c) A person is not required to report a death under this section that is the result of a motor vehicle accident. This subsection does not affect a duty imposed by another law to report a death that is the result of a motor vehicle accident.

Added by Acts 1995, 74th Leg., ch. 255, § 2, eff. Sept. 1, 1995; Acts 1995, 74th Leg., ch. 878, § 1, eff. Sept. 1, 1995.

§ 264.514. Procedure in the Event of Reportable Death

(a) A medical examiner or justice of the peace notified of a death of a child under Section 264.513 shall hold an inquest under Chapter 49, Code of Criminal Procedure, to determine whether the death is unexpected or the result of abuse or neglect. An inquest is not required under this subchapter if the child's death is expected and is due to a congenital or neoplastic disease. A death caused by an infectious disease may be considered an expected death if:

(1) the disease was not acquired as a result of trauma or poisoning;

(2) the infectious organism is identified using standard medical procedures; and

(3) the death is not reportable to the Texas Department of Health under Chapter 81, Health and Safety Code.

(b) The medical examiner or justice of the peace shall immediately notify an appropriate local law enforcement agency if the medical examiner or justice of the peace determines that the death is unexpected, and that agency shall investigate the child's death.

(c) In this section, the terms "abuse" and "neglect" have the meaning assigned those terms by Section 261.001.

Added by Acts 1995, 74th Leg., ch. 255, § 2, eff. Sept. 1, 1995; Acts 1995, 74th Leg., ch. 878, § 1, eff. Sept. 1, 1995. Amended by Acts 1997, 75th Leg., ch. 1022, § 95, eff. Sept. 1, 1997; Acts 1997, 75th Leg., ch. 1031, § 2, eff. Sept. 1, 1997.

Section 110 of Acts 1997, 75th Leg., ch. 1022 provides:

"The changes in law made by this Act to Article 49.10, Code of Criminal Procedure, and Section 264.514, Family Code, take effect September 1, 1997, and apply only to a death of a child younger than six years of age that occurs on or after September 1, 1997. A death of a child that occurs before September 1, 1997, is governed by the law as it existed immediately before the effective date of this Act, and that law is continued in effect for that purpose."

Section 3 of Acts 1997, 75th Leg., ch. 1301 provides:

"This Act takes effect September 1, 1997, and applies only to a death of a child younger than six years of age that occurs on or after September 1, 1997. A death of a child that occurs before September 1, 1997, is governed by the law as it existed immediately before the effective date of this Act, and that law is continued in effect for that purpose."

§ 264.515. Investigation

(a) The investigation required by Section 264.514 must include:

(1) an autopsy, unless an autopsy was conducted as part of the inquest;

(2) an inquiry into the circumstances of the death, including an investigation of the scene of the death and interviews with the parents of the child, any guardian or caretaker of the child, and the person who reported the child's death; and

(3) a review of relevant information regarding the child from an agency, professional, or health care provider.

(b) The review required by Subsection (a)(3) must include a review of any applicable medical record, child protective services record, record maintained by an emergency medical services provider, and law enforcement report.

(c) The committee shall develop a protocol relating to investigation of an unexpected death of a child under this section. In developing the protocol, the committee shall consult with individuals and organizations that have knowledge and experience in the issues of child abuse and child deaths.

Added by Acts 1995, 74th Leg., ch. 255, § 2, eff. Sept. 1, 1995; Acts 1995, 74th Leg., ch. 878, § 1, eff. Sept. 1, 1995.

Section 7 of Acts 1995, 74th Leg., ch. 255 and section 5 of Acts 1995, 74th Leg., ch. 878 provide:

"The child fatality review team committee shall develop the protocol required by Subsection (c), Section 264.515, Family Code, as added by this Act, not later than September 1, 1996."

[Sections 264.516 to 264.600 reserved for expansion]

SUBCHAPTER G. COURT–APPOINTED VOLUNTEER ADVOCATE PROGRAMS

§ 264.601. Definitions

In this subchapter:

(1) "Abused or neglected child" means a child who is:

(A) the subject of a suit affecting the parent-child relationship filed by a governmental entity; and

(B) under the control or supervision of the department.

(2) "Volunteer advocate program" means a volunteer-based, nonprofit program that provides advocacy services to abused or neglected children with the goal of obtaining a permanent placement for a child that is in the child's best interest.

Added by Acts 1995, 74th Leg., ch. 20, § 1, eff. April 20, 1995.

§ 264.602. Contracts With Advocate Programs

(a) The statewide organization with which the attorney general contracts under Section 264.603 shall contract for services with eligible volunteer advocate programs to expand the existing services of the programs.

(b) The contract under this section may not result in reducing the financial support a volunteer advocate program receives from another source.

(c) The attorney general shall develop a scale of state financial support for volunteer advocate programs that declines over a six-year period beginning on the date each individual contract takes effect. After the end of the six-year period, the attorney general may not provide more than 50 percent of the volunteer advocate program's funding.

(d) The attorney general by rule shall adopt standards for a local volunteer advocate program. The statewide organization shall assist the attorney general in developing the standards.

Added by Acts 1995, 74th Leg., ch. 20, § 1, eff. April 20, 1995. Amended by Acts 1995, 74th Leg., ch. 751, § 118, eff. Sept. 1, 1995; Acts 1997, 75th Leg., ch. 1294, § 7, eff. Sept. 1, 1997.

For application provisions of Acts 1997, 75th Leg., ch. 1294, see note following V.T.C.A., Family Code § 107.001.

§ 264.603. Administrative Contracts

(a) The attorney general shall contract with one statewide organization of individuals or groups of individuals who have expertise in the dynamics of child abuse and neglect and experience in operating volunteer advocate programs to provide training, technical assistance, and evaluation services for the benefit of local volunteer advocate programs. The contract shall require measurable goals and objectives for expanding local volunteer child advocate programs to areas of the state in which those programs do not exist.

(b) The contract under this section shall provide that not more than 12 percent of the annual legislative appropriation to implement this subchapter may be spent for administrative purposes by the statewide organization with which the attorney general contracts under this section.

Added by Acts 1995, 74th Leg., ch. 20, § 1, eff. April 20, 1995. Amended by Acts 1995, 74th Leg., ch. 751, § 119, eff. Sept. 1, 1995; Acts 1997, 75th Leg., ch. 600, § 20, eff. Sept. 1, 1997.

§ 264.604. Eligibility for Contracts

(a) A person is eligible for a contract under Section 264.602 only if the person is a public or private nonprofit entity that operates a volunteer advocate program that:

(1) uses individuals appointed as volunteer advocates or guardians ad litem by the court to provide for the needs of abused or neglected children;

(2) has provided court-appointed advocacy services for at least two years;

(3) provides court-appointed advocacy services for at least 10 children each month; and

(4) has demonstrated that the program has local judicial support.

(b) The statewide organization with which the attorney general contracts under Section 264.603 may not contract with a person that is not eligible under this section. However, the statewide organization may waive the requirement in Subsection (a)(3) for an established program in a rural area or under other special circumstances.

Added by Acts 1995, 74th Leg., ch. 20, § 1, eff. April 20, 1995. Amended by Acts 1995, 74th Leg., ch. 751, § 120, eff. Sept. 1, 1995; Acts 1997, 75th Leg., ch. 1294, § 8, eff. Sept. 1, 1997.

For application provisions of Acts 1997, 75th Leg., ch. 1294, see note following V.T.C.A., Family Code § 107.001.

§ 264.605. Contract Form

A person shall apply for a contract under Section 264.602 on a form provided by the attorney general.

Added by Acts 1995, 74th Leg., ch. 20, § 1, eff. April 20, 1995.

§ 264.606. Criteria for Award of Contracts

The statewide organization with which the attorney general contracts under Section 264.603 shall consider the following in awarding a contract under Section 264.602:

(1) the volunteer advocate program's eligibility for and use of funds from local, state, or federal governmental sources, philanthropic organizations, and other sources;

(2) community support for the volunteer advocate program as indicated by financial contributions from civic organizations, individuals, and other community resources;

(3) whether the volunteer advocate program provides services that encourage the permanent placement of children through reunification with their families or timely placement with an adoptive family; and

(4) whether the volunteer advocate program has the endorsement and cooperation of the local juvenile court system.

Added by Acts 1995, 74th Leg., ch. 20, § 1, eff. April 20, 1995. Amended by Acts 1995, 74th Leg., ch. 751, § 121, eff. Sept. 1, 1995.

§ 264.607. Contract Requirements

(a) The attorney general shall require that a contract under Section 264.602 require the volunteer advocate program to:

(1) make quarterly and annual financial reports on a form provided by the attorney general;

(2) cooperate with inspections and audits that the attorney general makes to ensure service standards and fiscal responsibility; and

(3) provide as a minimum:

(A) independent and factual information in writing to the court and to counsel for the parties involved regarding the child;

(B) advocacy through the courts for permanent home placement and rehabilitation services for the child;

(C) monitoring of the child to ensure the safety of the child and to prevent unnecessary movement of the child to multiple temporary placements;

(D) reports in writing to the presiding judge and to counsel for the parties involved;

(E) community education relating to child abuse and neglect;

(F) referral services to existing community services;

(G) a volunteer recruitment and training program, including adequate screening procedures for volunteers;

(H) procedures to assure the confidentiality of records or information relating to the child; and

(I) compliance with the standards adopted under Section 264.602.

(b) The statewide organization with which the attorney general contracts under Section 264.603 may require that a contract under Section 264.602 require the volunteer advocate program to use forms provided by the attorney general.

(c) The attorney general shall develop forms in consultation with a statewide organization of individuals or groups of individuals who have expertise in the dynamics of child abuse and neglect and experience in operating volunteer advocate programs.

Added by Acts 1995, 74th Leg., ch. 20, § 1, eff. April 20, 1995. Amended by Acts 1995, 74th Leg., ch. 751, § 122, eff. Sept. 1, 1995; Acts 1997, 75th Leg., ch. 1294, § 9, eff. Sept. 1, 1997.

For application provisions of Acts 1997, 75th Leg., ch. 1294, see note following V.T.C.A., Family Code § 107.001.

§ 264.608. Report to the Legislature

(a) Before each regular session of the legislature, the attorney general shall publish a report that:

(1) summarizes reports from volunteer advocate programs under contract with the attorney general;

(2) analyzes the effectiveness of the contracts made by the attorney general under this chapter; and

(3) provides information on:

(A) the expenditure of funds under this chapter;

(B) services provided and the number of children for whom the services were provided; and

(C) any other information relating to the services provided by the volunteer advocate programs under this chapter.

(b) The attorney general shall submit copies of the report to the governor, lieutenant governor, speaker of the house of representatives, the Legislative Budget Board, and members of the legislature.

Added by Acts 1995, 74th Leg., ch. 20, § 1, eff. April 20, 1995.

§ 264.609. Rule–Making Authority

The attorney general may adopt rules necessary to implement this chapter.

Added by Acts 1995, 74th Leg., ch. 20, § 1, eff. April 20, 1995.

§ 264.610. Confidentiality

The attorney general may not disclose information gained through reports, collected case data, or inspections that would identify a person working at or receiving services from a volunteer advocate program.

Added by Acts 1995, 74th Leg., ch. 20, § 1, eff. April 20, 1995.

§ 264.611. Consultations

In implementing this chapter, the attorney general shall consult with individuals or groups of individuals who have expertise in the dynamics of child abuse and neglect and experience in operating volunteer advocate programs.

Added by Acts 1995, 74th Leg., ch. 20, § 1, eff. April 20, 1995.

§ 264.612. Funding

(a) The attorney general may solicit and receive grants or money from either private or public sources, including by appropriation by the legislature from the general revenue fund, to implement this chapter.

(b) The need for and importance of the implementation of this chapter by the attorney general requires priority and preferential consideration for appropriation.

(c) Repealed by Acts 1995, 74th Leg., ch. 751, § 128, eff. Sept. 1, 1995.

Added by Acts 1995, 74th Leg., ch. 20, § 1, eff. April 20, 1995. Amended by Acts 1995, 74th Leg., ch. 751, § 128, eff. Sept. 1, 1995.

SUBCHAPTER H. CHILD ABUSE PROGRAM EVALUATION

§ 264.701. Child Abuse Program Evaluation Committee

(a) The Child Abuse Program Evaluation Committee is established within the Department of Protective and Regulatory Services.

(b) The committee is appointed by the Board of Protective and Regulatory Services and is composed of the following 15 members:

(1) an officer or employee of the Texas Education Agency;

(2) an officer or employee of the Department of Protective and Regulatory Services;

(3) an officer or employee of the Texas Juvenile Probation Commission;

(4) an officer or employee of the Texas Department of Mental Health and Mental Retardation;

(5) an officer or employee of the Children's Trust Fund of Texas Council;

(6) an officer or employee of the Health and Human Services Commission;

(7) three members of the public who have knowledge of and experience in the area of delivery of services relating to child abuse and neglect;

(8) three members of the public who have knowledge of and experience in the area of evaluation of programs relating to the prevention and treatment of child abuse and neglect; and

(9) three members of the public who are or have been recipients of services relating to the prevention or treatment of child abuse or neglect.

(c) In appointing members to the committee under Subsection (b)(9), the board shall consider appointing:

(1) an adult who as a child was a recipient of services relating to the prevention or treatment of child abuse or neglect; and

(2) a custodial and a noncustodial parent of a child who is or was a recipient of services relating to the prevention or treatment of child abuse or neglect.

(d) A committee member appointed to represent a state agency or entity serves at the pleasure of the board or until termination of the person's employment or membership with the agency or entity. The public members serve staggered six-year terms, with the terms of three public members expiring on September 1 of each even-numbered year.

(e) A member of the committee serves without compensation. A public member is entitled to reimbursement for travel expenses and per diem as provided by the General Appropriations Act.

(f) The committee shall elect from its members a presiding officer and any other officers considered necessary.

(g) Appointments to the committee shall be made without regard to the race, color, handicap, sex, religion, age, or national origin of an appointee.

(h) The committee shall:

(1) develop and adopt policies and procedures governing the system each state agency uses to evaluate the effectiveness of programs to prevent or treat child abuse or neglect with which the agency contracts;

(2) develop and adopt standard definitions of "child abuse treatment" and "child abuse prevention" to be used in implementing and administering the evaluation system created under this subchapter;

(3) develop and adopt standard models and guidelines for prevention and treatment of child abuse to be used in implementing and administering the evaluation system created under this subchapter;

(4) develop and adopt, in cooperation with each affected state agency, a schedule for each agency's adoption and implementation of the committee's evaluation system that considers each agency's budget cycle;

(5) develop and adopt a standard report form and a reporting schedule for the affected agencies;

(6) develop and adopt objective criteria by which the performance of child abuse programs may be measured after reports under this subchapter are submitted and evaluated; and

(7) report annually to the Board of Protective and Regulatory Services, governor, lieutenant governor, and speaker of the house of representatives on the results of the committee's evaluation process.

(i) In adopting an evaluation system under this subchapter, the committee shall allow the affected agencies as much latitude as possible in:

(1) the methods used to collect the required data; and

(2) the timetable for full implementation of the system, allowing for gradual implementation of the system according to classes of program providers.

(j) Each agency that contracts with a public or private entity for services relating to a program for the prevention or treatment of child abuse or neglect shall adopt and implement the committee's evaluation system and shall report to the committee as required by this subchapter.

Added by Acts 1991, 72nd Leg., 1st C.S., ch. 14, § 5.02(a), eff. Nov. 12, 1991. Amended by Acts 1995, 74th Leg., ch. 76, § 8.128, eff. Sept. 1, 1995. Renumbered from V.T.C.A., Government Code § 772.007 and amended by Acts 1995, 74th Leg., ch. 943, § 12, eff. Sept. 1, 1995. Amended by Acts 1997, 75th Leg., ch. 165, § 6.10, eff. Sept. 1, 1997.

Section 13 of Acts 1995, 74th Leg., ch. 943 provides:

"(a) This Act takes effect September 1, 1995, and applies to a proceeding in which an investigation of the abuse of a child is pending on or after that date.

"(b) Not later than January 1, 1996, the Board of Protective and Regulatory Services shall make appointments to the Child Abuse Program Evaluation Committee that are necessary to accomplish the change in the committee's composition required by Subchapter H, Chapter 264, Family Code, as added by this Act. A public member of the committee serving on the effective date of this Act shall serve the remainder of the member's appointed term.

"(c) The term of a public member of the Child Abuse Program Evaluation Committee whose term before the enactment of this Act was to expire on February 1, 1997, shall expire on September 1, 1996.

"(d) The term of a public member of the Child Abuse Program Evaluation Committee whose term before the enactment of this Act was to expire on February 1, 1999, shall expire on September 1, 1998.

"(e) The term of a public member of the Child Abuse Program Evaluation Committee whose term before the enactment of this Act was to expire on February 1, 2001, shall expire on September 1, 2000."

PENAL CODE

TITLE 6. OFFENSES AGAINST THE FAMILY

CHAPTER 25. OFFENSES AGAINST THE FAMILY

§ 25.03. Interference With Child Custody

(a) A person commits an offense if he takes or retains a child younger than 18 years when he:

(1) knows that his taking or retention violates the express terms of a judgment or order of a court disposing of the child's custody; or

(2) has not been awarded custody of the child by a court of competent jurisdiction, knows that a suit for divorce or a civil suit or application for habeas corpus to dispose of the child's custody has been filed, and takes the child out of the geographic area of the counties composing the judicial district if the court is a district court or the county if the court is a statutory county court, without the permission of the court and with the intent to deprive the court of authority over the child.

(b) A noncustodial parent commits an offense if, with the intent to interfere with the lawful custody of a child younger than 18 years, he knowingly entices or persuades the child to leave the custody of the custodial parent, guardian, or person standing in the stead of the custodial parent or guardian of the child.

(c) It is a defense to prosecution under Subsection (a)(2) that the actor returned the child to the geographic area of the counties composing the judicial district if the court is a district court or the county if the court is a statutory county court, within three days after the date of the commission of the offense.

(d) An offense under this section is a state jail felony.

Acts 1973, 63rd Leg., p. 883, ch. 399, § 1, eff. Jan. 1, 1974. Amended by Acts 1979, 66th Leg., p. 1111, ch. 527, § 1, eff. Aug. 27, 1979; Acts 1987, 70th Leg., ch. 444, § 1, eff. Sept. 1, 1987; Acts 1989, 71st Leg., ch. 830, § 1, eff. Sept. 1, 1989; Acts 1993, 73rd Leg., ch. 900, § 1.01, eff. Sept. 1, 1994.

Section 4 of the 1987 amendatory act provides:

"(a) The change in law made by this Act applies only to an offense committed on or after the effective date of this Act. For purposes of this section, an offense is committed before the effective date of this Act if any element of the offense occurs before the effective date.

"(b) An offense committed before the effective date of this Act is covered by the law in effect when the offense was committed, and the former law is continued in effect for this purpose."

Section 2 of the 1989 amendatory act provides:

"(a) The change in law made by this Act applies only to an offense committed on or after the effective date of this Act. For purposes of this section, an offense is committed before the effective date of this Act if any element of the offense occurs before the effective date.

"(b) An offense committed before the effective date of this Act is covered by the law in effect when the offense was committed, and the former law is continued in effect for that purpose."

§ 25.031. Agreement to Abduct From Custody

(a) A person commits an offense if the person agrees, for remuneration or the promise of remuneration, to abduct a child younger than 18 years of age by force, threat of force, misrepresentation, stealth, or unlawful entry, knowing that the child is under the care and control of a person having custody or physical possession of the child under a court order or under the care and control of another person who is exercising care and control with the consent of a person having custody or physical possession under a court order.

(b) An offense under this section is a state jail felony.

Added by Acts 1987, 70th Leg., ch. 444, § 3, eff. Sept. 1, 1987. Amended by Acts 1993, 73rd Leg., ch. 900, § 1.01, eff. Sept. 1, 1994.

Section 4 of the 1987 Act provides:

"(a) The change in law made by this Act applies only to an offense committed on or after the effective date of this Act. For purposes of this section, an offense is committed before the effective date of this Act if any element of the offense occurs before the effective date.

"(b) An offense committed before the effective date of this Act is covered by the law in effect when the offense was committed, and the former law is continued in effect for this purpose."

§ 25.05. Criminal Nonsupport

(a) An individual commits an offense if he intentionally or knowingly fails to provide support for his child younger than 18 years of age, or for his child who is the subject of a court order requiring the individual to support the child.

(b) For purposes of this section, "child" includes a child born out of wedlock whose paternity has either been acknowledged by the actor or has been established in a civil suit under the Family Code or the law of another state.

(c) Under this section, a conviction may be had on the uncorroborated testimony of a party to the offense.

(d) It is an affirmative defense to prosecution under this section that the actor could not provide support for his child.

(e) The pendency of a prosecution under this section does not affect the power of a court to enter an order for child support under the Family Code.

(f) An offense under this section is a state jail felony.

Acts 1973, 63rd Leg., p. 883, ch. 399, § 1, eff. Jan. 1, 1974. Amended by Acts 1987, 70th Leg., 2nd C.S., ch. 73, § 13, eff. Nov. 1, 1987; Acts 1993, 73rd Leg., ch. 900, § 1.01, eff. Sept. 1, 1994.

Section 15 of the 1987 amendatory act provides:

"(a) This Act takes effect November 1, 1987.

"(b) This Act applies only to an offense of criminal nonsupport committed on or after the effective date of this Act. For purposes of this section, an offense of criminal nonsupport is committed before the effective date of this Act if any element of the offense occurs before that date.

"(c) An offense of criminal nonsupport committed before the effective date of this Act is covered by the law in effect when the offense was committed, and the former law is continued in effect for this purpose."

§ 25.07. Violation of Protective Order or Magistrate's Order

(a) A person commits an offense if, in violation of an order issued under Section 6.504 or Chapter 85, Family Code, under Article 17.292, Code of Criminal Procedure, or by another jurisdiction as provided by Chapter 88, Family Code, the person knowingly or intentionally:

(1) commits family violence or an act in furtherance of an offense under Section 42.072;

(2) communicates:

(A) directly with a protected individual or a member of the family or household in a threatening or harassing manner;

(B) a threat through any person to a protected individual or a member of the family or household; and

(C) in any manner with the protected individual or a member of the family or household except through the person's attorney or a person appointed by the court, if the order prohibits any communication with a protected individual or a member of the family or household; or

(3) goes to or near any of the following places as specifically described in the order:

(A) the residence or place of employment or business of a protected individual or a member of the family or household; or

(B) any child care facility, residence, or school where a child protected by the order normally resides or attends.

(b) For the purposes of this section, "family violence," "family," "household," and "member of a household" have the meanings assigned by Section 71.01, Family Code.

(c) If conduct constituting an offense under this section also constitutes an offense under another section of this code, the actor may be prosecuted under either section or under both sections.

(d) Reconciliatory actions or agreements made by persons affected by an order do not affect the validity of the order or the duty of a peace officer to enforce this section.

(e) A peace officer investigating conduct that may constitute an offense under this section for a violation of an order may not arrest a person protected by that order for a violation of that order.

(f) It is not a defense to prosecution under this section that certain information has been excluded, as provided by Section 71.111, Family Code, or Article 17.292, Code of Criminal Procedure, from an order to which this section applies.

(g) An offense under this section is a Class A misdemeanor unless it is shown on the trial of the offense that the defendant has previously been convicted under this section two or more times or has violated the protective order by committing an assault or the offense of stalking, in which event the offense is a third degree felony.

Added by Acts 1983, 68th Leg., p. 4049, ch. 631, § 3, eff. Sept. 1, 1983. Amended by Acts 1985, 69th Leg., ch. 583, § 3, eff. Sept. 1, 1985; Acts 1987, 70th Leg., ch. 170, § 1, eff. Sept. 1, 1987; Acts 1987, 70th Leg., ch. 677, § 8, eff. Sept. 1, 1987; Acts 1989, 71st Leg., ch. 614, §§ 23 to 26, eff. Sept. 1, 1989; Acts 1989, 71st Leg., ch. 739, §§ 4 to 7, eff. Sept. 1, 1989; Acts 1991, 72nd Leg., ch. 366, § 2, eff. Sept. 1, 1991. Renumbered from § 25.08 and amended by Acts 1993, 73rd Leg., ch. 900, § 1.01, eff. Sept. 1, 1994. Amended by Acts 1995, 74th Leg., ch. 658, §§ 2, 3, eff. June 14, 1995; Acts 1995, 74th Leg., ch. 660, §§ 1, 2, eff. Sept. 1, 1995; Acts 1995, 74th Leg., ch. 1024, § 23, eff. Sept. 1, 1995; Acts 1997, 75th Leg., ch. 1, § 2, eff. Jan. 28, 1997; Acts 1997, 75th Leg., ch. 1193, § 21, eff. Sept. 1, 1997.

Section 4 of the 1983 Act provides:

"Section 25.08, Penal Code, as added by this Act applies only to:

"(1) an order issued on or after the effective date of this Act; or

"(2) an order issued before the effective date of this Act and amended after the effective date of this Act to include the prohibitions required by Subsection (b), Section 71.11, Family Code."

Section 2 of Acts 1987, 70th Leg., ch. 170, provides:

"(a) The change in law made by this Act applies only to an offense committed on or after the effective date of this Act. For purposes of this section, an offense is committed before the effective date of this Act if any element of the offense occurs before the effective date.

"(b) An offense committed before the effective date of this Act is covered by the law in effect when the offense was committed, and the former law is continued in effect for this purpose."

Section 9 of Acts 1987, 70th Leg., ch. 677 provides:

"This Act applies to an action in which a protective order was filed on or after the effective date of this Act. An action in which a protective order was filed before the effective date of this Act is governed by the law in effect at the time the protective order was filed and that law is continued in effect for this purpose."

Acts 1989, 71st Leg., ch. 2, § 16.01(29) relettered subsec. (f), as added by Acts 1987, 70th Leg., ch. 677, § 8, as subsec. (g); however, Acts 1989, 71st Leg., ch. 614, § 26 relettered subsec. (f) as amended by Acts 1987, 70th Leg., ch. 170, § 1 as subsec. (g). The relettering by Acts 1989, 71st Leg., ch. 2, § 16.01(29) did not take effect according to Acts 1989, 71st Leg., ch. 2, § 16.03 which provided:

"If the number, letter, or designation assigned by this article conflicts with a number, letter, or designation made by another Act of the 71st Legislature, the other Act controls and the number, letter, or designation assigned by this article has no effect."

Sections 30 and 31 of Acts 1989, 71st Leg., ch. 614, provide:

"Sec. 30. This Act applies only to a court order made on or after the effective date of this Act. An order made before the effective date of this Act is governed by the law in effect at the time the order was made, and that law is continued in effect for that purpose.

"Sec. 31. (a) The change in law made by Sections 24 and 25 of this Act applies only to the prosecution of an offense committed on or after the effective date of this Act. For purposes of this section, an offense is committed before the effective date of this Act if any element of the offense occurs before the effective date.

"(b) An offense committed before the effective date of this Act is covered by the law in effect when the offense was committed, and that law is continued in effect for that purpose."

Sections 33 and 34 of Acts 1989, 71st Leg., ch. 739, provide:

"Sec. 33. This Act applies only to a court order made on or after the effective date of this Act. An order made before the effective date of this Act is governed by the law in effect at the time the order was made, and that law is continued in effect for this purpose.

"Sec. 34. (a) The change in law made by Sections 1 through 7 of this Act applies only to the prosecution of an offense committed on or after the effective date of this Act. For purposes of this section, an offense is committed before the effective date of this Act if any element of the offense occurs before the effective date.

"(b) An offense committed before the effective date of this Act is covered by the law in effect when the offense was committed, and that law is continued in effect for this purpose."

Section 2 of Acts 1995, 74th Leg., ch. 660 provides:

"(a) The change in law made by this Act applies only to an offense committed on or after the effective date of this Act. For purposes of this section, an offense is committed before the effective date of this Act if any element of the offense occurs before the effective date.

"(b) An offense committed before the effective date of this Act is covered by the law in effect when the offense was committed, and the former law is continued in effect for that purpose."

Section 26 of Acts 1997, 75th Leg., ch. 1193 provides:

"(a) The changes in law made by this Act to Subsections (a) and (g), Section 25.07, Penal Code, apply only to an offense committed on or after the effective date of this Act. For purposes of this section, an offense is committed before the effective date of this Act if any element of the offense occurs before that date.

"(b) An offense committed before the effective date of this Act is covered by the law in effect when the offense was committed, and the former law is continued in effect for that purpose."

CONSTITUTION OF THE STATE OF TEXAS 1876

ARTICLE XVI

GENERAL PROVISIONS

§ 15. Separate and community property of husband and wife

Sec. 15. All property, both real and personal, of a spouse owned or claimed before marriage, and that acquired afterward by gift, devise or descent, shall be the separate property of that spouse; and laws shall be passed more clearly defining the rights of the spouses, in relation to separate and community property; provided that persons about to marry and spouses, without the intention to defraud pre-existing creditors, may by written instrument from time to time partition between themselves all or part of their property, then existing or to be acquired, or exchange between themselves the community interest of one spouse or future spouse in any property for the community interest of the other spouse or future spouse in other community property then existing or to be acquired, whereupon the portion or interest set aside to each spouse shall be and constitute a part of the separate property and estate of such spouse or future spouse; spouses also may from time to time, by written instrument, agree between themselves that the income or property from all or part of the separate property then owned or which thereafter might be acquired by only one of them, shall be the separate property of that spouse; if one spouse makes a gift of property to the other that gift is presumed to include all the income or property which might arise from that gift of property; and spouses may agree in writing that all or part of their community property becomes the property of the surviving spouse on the death of a spouse.

Amended Nov. 2, 1948; Nov. 4, 1980; Nov. 3, 1987.

INDEX

Abbreviations

Const. Art. . . . . Constitution of Texas
Fam . . . . Family Code
Pen . . . . Penal Code

†